THE
PRESIDENT
IS DEAD!

Also by Louis L. Picone

Where the Presidents Were Born

THE PRESIDENT IS DEAD!

The Extraordinary Stories of the Presidential Deaths, Final Days, Burials, and Beyond

LOUIS L. PICONE

Skyhorse Publishing

First Edition

Skyhorse Publishing books may be purchased in bulk at special discounts for sales promotion, corporate gifts, fund-raising, or educational purposes. Special editions can also be created to specifications. For details, contact the Special Sales Department, Skyhorse Publishing, 307 West 36th Street, 11th Floor, New York, NY 10018 or info@skyhorsepublishing.com.

Skyhorse® and Skyhorse Publishing® are registered trademark of Skyhorse Publishing, Inc.®, a Delaware corporation.

Visit our website at www.skyhorsepublishing.com.
Visit the author's website at www.LouisPicone.com.

10 9 8 7 6 5 4 3 2 1

Library of Congress Cataloging-in-Publication Data

Names: Picone, Louis L., author.
Title: The president is dead!: the extraordinary stories of the presidential
   deaths, final days, burials, and beyond / Louis L. Picone.
Description: First edition. | New York, NY: Skyhorse Publishing, 2016. |
   Includes bibliographical references and index.
Identifiers: LCCN 2016013528 (print) | LCCN 2016014139 (ebook) |
ISBN 978-1-5107-0376-6 (hardcover: alk. paper) | ISBN 978-1-5107-0377-3
(ebook)
Subjects: LCSH: Presidents—United States—Death. | Presidents—United
   States—Biography.
Classification: LCC E176.1 .P4979 2016 (print) | LCC E176.1 (ebook) | DDC
   973.09/9—dc23
LC record available at http://lccn.loc.gov/2016013528

Cover design by Laura Klynstra
Cover photo credit: Library of Congress

Printed in China

To my Mom and Dad

Contents

Introduction

Coming after my first book, *Where the Presidents Were Born: The History and Preservation of the Presidential Birthplaces*, this one may seem like the natural follow-up, given its subject. In fact, I can't tell you how many people, upon learning that I had written a book about where the presidents were born, had the wiseacre response, "What's your next book gonna be about? Where they died?" (They all thought they were being original.) I hadn't originally planned to write a book on this subject, but the more I thought about it, the more intrigued I became.

The truth is, after years of researching and writing about the presidents, I wasn't quite ready to say goodbye to them yet. There is something enormously compelling about the presidents—the good, the bad, and the mediocre. They have each held the most powerful position in America, if not the world, and almost every aspect of their lives has been meticulously studied and written about—but that is not the case with their deaths. It is always frustrating to me to read a weighty presidential biography only to have their exit and aftermath summed up in a line or two. There is much to learn from their final days, when these once all-powerful men are at their most vulnerable, and perhaps, the most human. In their deaths we often can understand how they *wanted* to be remembered, but in their funerals and death-related monuments, we learn how the American public *chose* to remember them. While sometimes moving and poignant,

their deaths and the sites related to their demise are also teeming with fascinating stories.

For this book I vowed to dig deep and travel far to find the true stories of how the presidents' illustrious lives came to an end. Birth and death, while the bookends of life, were vastly different to research and write about. The place where a president was born only became "historic in the rearview mirror," as I like to say, after he achieved prominence and won the office many years later. Nobody knew he would grow up to be president, and his birth would have been a major event to relatively few people outside of the family. What scant details were recorded were often lost and replaced years later with embellishments and folklore. But that is not the case with death and burial, where often the minutest detail is documented and the most trivial artifact is preserved. While the difficulty of writing about birthplaces was finding sufficient credible sources, the challenge of writing this book was processing the abundance of information.

In writing *The President Is Dead!*, my guiding principle was "follow the body" as I explored the presidents' final journeys, from their last breath to the grave and everything in between—and, in fact, beyond, into the public afterlife that all presidents have. And as the title suggests, burial is sometimes not the end of the journey. More than a third of the presidents have been reinterred, and a handful more than once. Often the end of their lives is replete with fascinating and bizarre stories—mysterious circumstances of death, attempted grave robbings, and a corpse temporarily misplaced. Of course, I explore graves and funerals, but also hospitals, viewing sites, funeral homes, and all locations in between. Many people are interested in all sites presidential, no matter how obscure. But while George Washington Slept Here signs dot the landscape as well as a few scattered Millard Fillmore Studied Here and Harry S Truman Ate Here, rarely do you see a marker that Chester Arthur Was Embalmed Here or Benjamin Harrison's Funeral Was Here. This book includes such sites. It is for both the reader of history who wants to know what occurred after the presidents' deaths and the traveler who wants to visit those locations. Some are closer than you realize. In downtown Manhattan, for instance, there are many hipster fashion stores, but I bet only a handful of passersby could point out the one that sits at the location where James Monroe died. Sometimes you may be at a historic location and have no idea that a dead president once occupied the same space—in a train station, hospital, or government building. That is because death, while obviously not something to be celebrated, is rarely even *recognized*. In fact, of the many historic markers at death-site locations, most dance around the obvious and do not even mention it is there that the president expired.

You may notice something strange when you first open the book. Seeing the table of contents, you may have said to yourself, "John Adams was the *second* president—so why is his the *third* chapter?" But before you get excited and contact the publisher to report a mistake, understand that the chapters are presented in the order in which the presidents *died*, not in which they served. This is to enable a narrative as their deaths occurred and show how the histories of medical practices, funeral customs, and pageantry have evolved over time. How the death-related locations have pro-

gressed is also fascinating. Today, it is hard to believe that both Washington's Mount Vernon and Jefferson's Monticello were in ruins and almost lost forever, as were the graves of William Henry Harrison, Zachary Taylor, and James Buchanan, to name a few. You will read here about the evolution of their graves—from humble crypts and unmarked mounds to the grandiose monuments and memorials of the Victorian era to the current tradition of grave sites at presidential libraries. One thing I've learned—while we Americans are proud that our presidents are *of* the people and *from* the people, we have often have treated them in death more like Roman emperors or Egyptian pharaohs. And for some strange reason, the closest thing one can come to immortality in America is to be a president from Ohio (visit the graves of McKinley, Harding, Grant, and Garfield to see what I mean).

I am excited to include the fun and quirky "Almost Presidents" section, which features four men who have claims to serving as the president of American territory. While their claims may be tenuous and debatable, one thing that is indisputable is that their death stories are darned interesting! If nothing else, their stories may come in handy the next time you play Trivial Pursuit.

I tried to write this book with reverence and tact. And after two books about the minutiae of the presidents' births and deaths and many topics in between, the 43 men who held the most important job in the world feel like old friends. I've grown to admire and respect them. (I even got to meet Jimmy Carter and Bill Clinton in my travels.) For obvious reasons, I chose not to include chapters about our living presidents, and I hope an expanded edition is not required for a long, long while. In the meantime, I am confident you will enjoy the rich history, fascinating stories, and remarkable lives of our presidents *after* their deaths. I hope you feel inspired to take a road trip of your own to visit some of the notorious and obscure death-related sites!

THE
PRESIDENT
IS DEAD!

Bloodletting and Blistering

★★★★★★★★★★★★★★★★★★★★★★★★★★★★★★★★★★★★★

George Washington ★ *1789–1797*

CRITICAL DEATH INFORMATION:

Date of death:	December 14, 1799, between 10:20 and 11:00 p.m.
Cause of death:	Acute epiglottitis (a viral throat infection)
Age at death:	67 years, 295 days
Last words:	"'Tis well."
Place of death:	Mount Vernon, Virginia
Funeral:	Mount Vernon, Virginia
Final resting place:	Mount Vernon, Virginia
Reinterred:	Yes
Cost to visit grave:	$15.00
For more information:	www.Mount Vernon.org
Significance:	The first president was the first to die

Thursday, December 12, 1799, was a cold winter day in northern Virginia. Almost three years earlier, George Washington had left the presidency, and now he spent most of his days at his beloved estate, Mount Vernon. As he did nearly every day, Washington saddled his horse around 10:00 a.m. to inspect his farm. Almost immediately snow began to fall, until about three inches had gathered. Returning five hours later, he did not change out of his soaked clothing. The next day, Washington awoke with a severe sore throat, but the tough old general who had braved Morristown and Valley Forge would not be deterred from venturing back outside into the snow. That night his condition grew worse, but he was still strong at 67 and not one to complain, and he forewent medicine and treatment. His condition declined throughout the night. By 3:00 a.m. on Saturday, December 14, he struggled to breathe and speak. Finally, Washington conceded he needed medical attention, although had he known what he would endure at the hands of his doctors, he might have reconsidered.

The first call was not to his family doctor but to overseer George Rawlins, a skilled bleeder who also cared for Washington's slaves. Washington held out his arm and reassured him: "Don't be afraid." Rawlins cut, and blood began to trickle out. Washington looked at the incision and said weakly, "The orifice is not large enough." So Rawlins cut deeper and the blood flowed freely until 12 to 14 ounces had drained.[1] By 6:00 a.m., Washington was worse: his throat was raw, he struggled to breathe, and he had a fever. His next call was to his good friend and physician of 40 years, Dr. James Craik. Before Craik arrived from Alexandria, Washington's personal secretary, Tobias Lear, gave him a cocktail of butter, molasses, and vinegar to ease his pain, but instead, it nearly choked him.[2]

Craik arrived at 9:00 a.m. and found Washington in the upstairs master bedroom. He applied a "blister of cantharides" to his throat, an excruciating practice that was believed to "draw out the deadly humors." Craik then drew more blood, this time from Washington's neck and arm. At noon, he performed an enema and later had Washington gargle with sage tea and vinegar. With the president's condition, not surprisingly, worsening, Dr. Craik sent for two consulting physicians, Dr. Elisha Cullen Dick and Dr. Gustavus Richard Brown from Port Tobacco. Before they arrived, between 3:00 and 4:00 p.m., Dr. Craik

again bled the president. The three doctors surveyed the patient and apparently decided that if there was any blood left, it should be removed. Another 32 ounces was siphoned out of the weakened Washington. All told, a staggering 82 ounces of blood—almost 2.5 liters—was drained in a matter of hours! Finally, the doctors mercifully stopped, but the fact that Washington was still alive after 40 percent of his blood was drained showed how tough the old general was.

Those with him during those final hours admired how Washington faced the excruciating and humiliating treatment and prospect of death with the same dignity and courage he demonstrated in the rest of his life. But his primary concern was perhaps a fate worse than death: being buried alive. And this fear—taphephobia—was not unfounded. At the end of the 18th century, doctors could not always distinguish a comatose patient from a dead one, and in some instances, people were indeed buried before their time. This led to the invention of "safety coffins," which were equipped with a string inside attached to a bell located above ground. For several days after the burial, someone would stand guard and listen for a ring to alert them that the person in the coffin was still alive.

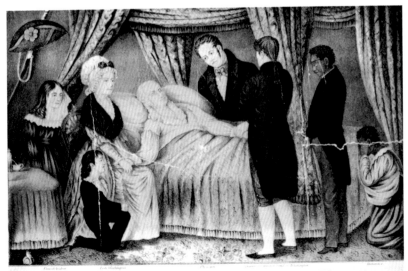

DEATH OF WASHINGTON, DEC. 14, A.D. 1799.

Currier & Ives lithograph, *Death of George Washington*. (Library of Congress)

In a barely audible voice, Washington pleaded with Tobias Lear: "I am just going. Have me decently buried, and do not let my body be put into the vault in less than three days after I am dead." A saddened Lear nodded, but Washington was so worried about being buried alive that he would not let a silent nod suffice. "Do you understand me?" he demanded, in as strong a voice as he could muster. Lear replied, "Yes, sir." Satisfied, Washington uttered what were to be his final words, "'Tis well."[3] At 10:20 p.m., Washington leaned back and placed his fingers on his wrist to feel his own weak pulse. Sometime before 11:00 p.m. on the evening on Saturday, December 14, Washington's fingers slipped off his wrist; he took his last breath, and died. With him were his wife, Martha; Dr. Craik; Lear; his valet, Christopher Sheels; and three of his slaves. Dr. Craik gently closed Washington's eyes.

In those final hours, Washington's step-granddaughter, Elizabeth Parke Custis Law, had summoned another doctor, William Thornton. Dr. Thornton believed a tracheotomy, a rare and risky procedure at the time, would save his life, but when he arrived at Mount Vernon, Washington was already dead. Thornton was not ready to concede. Convinced the cold weather would hold Washington in a state of suspended animation, Thornton proposed . . . well, what Thornton proposed is probably best told in his own words: "First to thaw him in cold water, then to lay him in blankets, and by degrees and by friction to give him warmth, and to put into activity the minute blood vessels, at the same time to open a passage to the lungs by the trachea, and to inflate them with air, to produce an artificial respiration, and to transfuse blood into him from a lamb."[4] Thankfully, Washington was spared this desecration when the other doctors wisely convinced him it would not work. Thornton later suggested that the president should rest for eternity not at Mount Vernon, as Washington himself wished, but in the capital city named in his honor. In addition to being a doctor, Thornton

was the architect who designed the United States Capitol. In it he planned a rotunda, and envisioned this would be where the president should rest in peace.

Since construction of the rotunda had not begun, for the time being Washington's own wishes would be carried out. Washington had made arrangements for his final resting place in his will (dated July 9, 1799), selecting a serene spot on Mount Vernon for a new, aboveground crypt large enough for family members who wished to join him in eternal rest.[5]

In addition, Washington's will included an astounding clause in which he arranged for the immediate freedom of his "mulatto man, William," and that the rest of his slaves were to be freed upon the death of his wife (Washington did not consider the unintended ramifications of his decision—Martha feared the slaves would kill her when she realized that her death was the only thing preventing the freedom of over 300 enslaved people). Washington's will also stipulated that his heirs would clothe and feed those unable to care for themselves. And for those young and without parents, he instructed they be taught to read and trained for work that was allowable by law.[6]

The body was placed in a mahogany casket made in Alexandria. Inscribed on the casket at the head was SURGE AD JUDICIUM (rise to judgment) and at the middle, GLORIA DEO (Glory to God). Attached to the coffin was a silver plate that read:

GEORGE WASHINGTON
BORN FEB 22, 1732
DIED DECEMBER 14, 1799[7]

Despite Washington's specific request in his will that his "Corpse may be Interred in a private manner, without parade, or funeral Oration," the Masonic Fraternity of Alexandria was permitted to honor their fellow Free Mason (Washington was a member of the Washington-Alexandria Lodge #22 at the time of his death). The funeral was held on Wednesday, December 18, and hundreds gathered at Mount Vernon. The pall-bearers were Washington's friends and business associates. Protestant Episcopal funeral services were read by Reverend Thomas Davis from the Christ Church in Alexandria.[8] It was scheduled to start at noon, but due to people arriving late, the procession did not start until 3:00 p.m. It was led by the clergymen and Washington's horse, who walked with an empty saddle draped with Washington's holster and pistols.

Colonel Thomas Blackburn, Washington's aide during the Revolutionary War and a relative through marriage, led the short procession to the redbrick vault. About a dozen mourners followed the Masonic pallbearers as an Alexandria band played a funeral dirge. At the tomb, Reverend Davis read the Episcopal Order of Burial, and Reverend James Muir (from the Alexandria Presbyterian Church) and Dr. Cullen Dick performed the ceremonial Masonic funeral rites. Also officiating was Reverend Walter Dulany Addison, the first deacon of the Protestant Episcopal Church. The shroud was pulled back for a final look at Wash-

ington before the coffin was sealed and placed in the tomb. A 21-gun artillery salute concluded the ceremony. Afterward, the Free Masons walked back to Washington's home to pay their respects to Martha before leaving. This first presidential funeral was now concluded. It contained military traditions that are still employed today, including the 21-gun salute and the riderless horse. The funeral cost was tallied at $99.25, which included $2.00 to rent the bier.

All throughout the nation, somber mock funeral parades were held and public eulogies were delivered. The most famous occurred on December 26, 1799, in Philadelphia, the nation's capital at the time. After a funeral procession that featured everything except the body of Washington, Virginia representative Henry Lee delivered the eulogy. Lee was a Revolutionary War officer, father of Robert E. Lee, and a close friend of Washington. His words of praise have been immortalized as possibly the greatest presidential tribute: "First in war, first in peace and first in the hearts of his countrymen." Lee continued, "He

The original tomb of George Washington and the site of the attempted theft of his skull.

was second to none in the humble and endearing scenes of private life. Pious, just, humane, temperate and sincere—uniform, dignified and commanding—his example was as edifying to all around him as were the effects of that example lasting. . . . Correct throughout, vice shuddered in his presence and virtue always felt his fostering hand. The purity of his private character gave effulgence to his public virtues. . . . Such was the man for whom our nation mourns."[9]

The family vault where George Washington was placed was located about 250 yards south of the mansion and was originally built in 1745 for George's brother, Lawrence Washington. It overlooked the Potomac River but was prone to flooding. Those in Congress considered the Mount Vernon burial place to be temporary. To formalize Thornton's suggestion, Congress passed a secret resolution on December 23, 1799, "That a marble monument be erected by the United States in the capital of the city of Washington, and that the family of General Washington be requested to permit his body to be deposited under it." President John Adams, the first president without any living predecessors, wrote Martha to ask her consent. She agreed, on the condition that she be allowed to rest beside her husband when she died. Adams agreed, and Martha gave her official permission on December 31 in a written reply to President Adams.

On May 22, 1802, Martha Washington passed away, just 11 days shy of her 71st birthday. Curiously, her coffin was engraved with a mistake in her age: MARTHA, CONSORT OF WASHINGTON; DIED MAY 22, 1802, AGED *71* YEARS.[10] With construction of the rotunda and crypt still on hold—"Due to a shortage of funds and materials [and] sporadic construction phases, and the fire set by the British in 1814"—she was placed in the Mount Vernon tomb with her husband.[11] In 1818, the rotunda was completed, and the tomb area was built two floors directly below. That same year, a young congressman, James Buchanan, led the effort to move Washington's remains to the

crypt when he pleaded, "[Washington] has been sleeping with his fathers for almost a quarter of a century, and his mortal remains have yet been unhonored by that people, who, with justice, call him the father of their country."[12] But despite overtures from national leaders, no progress was being made on moving the remains from Mount Vernon.

After Martha died, Washington's nephew Bushrod, an associate justice on the US Supreme Court, inherited Mount Vernon and was charged with building the new tomb. Bushrod died 30 years after Washington, on November 26, 1829, without starting construction. He too was placed in the crumbling, waterlogged tomb that he had been tasked with replacing. By this time, the tomb held about 20 family members and many of the wooden coffins were rotting away, exposing bones that spilled onto the damp floor. (The Washingtons were spared such desecration as their coffins were placed on a wooden table.)

After Bushrod died, Washington's nephew John Augustine Washington took over Mount Vernon. One of the first things he did was to fire one of the gardeners. However, this man did not go gently into the night. Instead, he sought revenge in a most gruesome manner. After getting liquored up, he returned to Mount Vernon, stumbled into the old family tomb, and stole what he believed was the skull of Washington! Luckily, with all of the dead bodies in the tomb, he actually made off with the skull of a member of the Blackburn family, the in-laws of one of Washington's nephews. The inebriated gardener did not get far and was captured the next day in Alexandria.[13]

Another bizarre incident occurred years later when a rumor surfaced that the skull of Washington had been stolen. In this tale, the perpetrator was not a drunk gardener but rather French sailors from a vessel anchored near Mount Vernon. According to Henry Lamb, who lived nearby, the skull was brought to France, where it was sold to phrenologists—pseudo-scientists who specialized in determining human characteristics by measuring the skull. If this is so, then whose skull is currently in the tomb? To his dying day, Lamb swore that the skull was replaced with that of a slave that belonged to Washington's friend, Colonel William Fairfax.[14]

The attempted theft by the disgruntled gardener did have a silver lining: it finally motivated Washington's nephew, Major Lawrence Lewis, and step-grandson, George Washington Parke Custis, to start construction on the new vault later that year. The structure, located 100 yards west of the old tomb, was made of brick and had a metal roof, 12-foot-high walls, and iron bars. Above the entrance, the words WASHINGTON FAMILY were inscribed. When Washington's body was moved there one year later, a new coffin was required. John Struthers of Philadelphia volunteered to build one for the venerated president, and Lewis accepted his "very liberal and polite offer."[15] It was determined that the coffin would not be hidden in the vault but rather placed where it could be seen. An antechamber was subsequently built in front.

The sarcophagus, completed in 1837, was cut from a single piece of Pennsylvania marble. On top was carved an eagle above a shield covered with the stripes of the flag, with the family name inscribed below it. Struthers may have offered his services for free, but he wanted to make sure people knew about his generosity. At the base he added another inscription, "By the permission of Lawrence Lewis, Esq. This Sarcophagus of Washington was presented by John Struthers, of Philadelphia, Marble Mason." He added a second inscription on the other side: "This Sarcoph-

agus containing the remains of George Washington, first President of the United States, was made and presented for the purpose by John Struthers of Philadelphia this day of A.D. 1837." He also created a coffin for Martha, correcting her age in the process.

On October 7, 1837, the door to the vault was opened for the first time since 1831. After moving several other coffins to get to Washington's, it was found that the wooden case that enclosed the lead coffin had rotted, causing it to sink. The coffin was opened and the body, nearly 38 years dead, was gently removed and placed in a new coffin along with the plate from the rotted coffin. It was then cemented shut and placed outside of the vault in the antechamber, where to this day it can be seen behind the locked gate.[16]

The tomb is reverently marked and inscribed. Above it is an engraving that reads:

I AM THE RESURRECTION AND THE LIFE, SAITH THE LORD. HE THAT BELIEVETH IN ME, THOUGH HE WERE DEAD YET SHALL HE LIVE, AND WHOSOEVER LIVETH AND BELIEVETH IN ME SHALL NEVER DIE
ST. JOHN, XI.25.26

Washington's tomb, 1980. (Library of Congress)

Above the arched entrance to the tomb is an engraving that reads:

WITHIN THIS ENCLOSURE REST THE REMAINS OF
GENL. GEORGE WASHINGTON

Also to the left of the tomb today sits a marker that reads:

TOMB OF WASHINGTON
ERECTED 1830–31
SITE & MATERIALS SPECIFIED IN
WASHINGTON'S WILL

Watching over the new tomb was Edmund Parker. He was a descendent of one of Washington's slaves and gatekeeper for the tomb for an astounding 57 years until his death on August 27, 1898.[17]

Around the same time that construction on the new tomb began in 1830, a House committee was formed to move Washington's body to the Capitol rotunda. A resolution was passed to reinter the remains on February 22, 1832, on what would have been Washington's 100th birthday. An initial request for consent was sent to George Washington Park Custis, who gave his permission on February 14, 1832: "I give my most hearty consent to the removal of the remains, after the manner requested, and congratulate the Government upon the approaching consummation of a great act of national gratitude."[18] However, the plan hit a major obstacle when a letter was received the next day from John Augustine Washington. Having recently completed the new tomb, albeit over 30 years late, he politely overruled: "When I recollect his will, in respect to the disposition of his remains, has been recently carried out in full effect and that they now repose in perfect tranquility, surrounded by those of other endeared members of the family. I hope Congress will do justice to the motives which seem to me to require that I should not consent to their separation."[19]

Had it not been for the attempted theft of Washington's skull that prompted the building of a new tomb, the outcome might have been different. But, supporting the wishes of the family, the General Assembly of Virginia passed a resolution on February 20, 1832, that "unanimously resolved that the proprietor be earnestly requested, in the name of the state, not to consent to the removal of his remains from Mount Vernon." With permission formally denied, Congress gave up their pursuit of the remains. The crypt built for Washington remained vacant but was opened to visitors. It was later closed to the general public and could be seen by special permission only, "on account of acts of vandalism perpetrated by souvenir hunters."[20]

The idea of moving Washington's body again resurfaced in 1897. After the completion of Ulysses S. Grant's tomb in Manhattan's Riverside Park, a movement started for a bigger, better memorial for our nation's first president at the same location. After almost a century, the prospect of moving Washington's remains from Mount Vernon sparked outrage. The *New York Times* called the suggestion "sacrilegious" and the idea fizzled as quickly as it started.[21]

A century ago, the tomb of George Washington was one of the most venerated sites in America. Visiting was the equivalent of a Holy Land tour, as an 1892 publication, *The American Nation*, described: "The Grave of Washington has so long been the Mecca of thousands of patriotic Americans."[22] For many years, the tomb was the central attraction at Mount Vernon, with the home being relegated as a side attraction. In 1895 a *New York Times* reporter asked, "Who can gaze upon the tomb of Washington and Martha his wife without a feeling of awe? A strange sensation comes over one as he realizes that in the marble sarcophagus before him reposes the dust of the founder of this Republic."[23]

Today at Mount Vernon, visitors can step on the same ground that many great men and women have walked before. Washington was frequently visited by other founding fathers, including John Adams, Thomas Jefferson, James Monroe, and first president under the Articles of Confederation, John Hanson. After he died, many esteemed leaders made the pilgrimage to Mount Vernon. Its proximity to Washington, DC, made it a quick and convenient trip.[24] In the fall of 1801, future President John Quincy Adams visited Mount Vernon for two days,[25] and in October 1860, James Buchanan escorted the Prince of Wales to the tomb, where they planted an oak tree.

On December 14, 1899, 100 years after Washington's death, the Free Masons held a ceremony at his tomb. It started at the old tomb, where a speech was made by the Grand Master of the Masons of Colorado, as his state conceived the event six years earlier. They then marched to the new tomb, where "beautiful and impressive Masonic services were conducted." The groups deposited several symbolic items on the sarcophagus, including a lambskin apron, a white glove, and "festoons of evergreens." Fellow Free Mason President William McKinley addressed the crowd. Later that same day, a second ceremony was conducted by the fraternal organization, the Improved Order of Red Men.[26]

Most dignitaries have chosen to visit on Washington's birthday to lay a memorial wreath at the tomb. On February 22, 1912, William Howard Taft "walked between hundreds of sightseers" to place a wreath of white roses and carnations.[27] In 1932, Herbert Hoover laid a wreath before speaking to several thousand members of the National Educational Association at Mount Vernon. It was heard on over 150 radio stations and was the first ever broadcast from Mount Vernon.[28]

Perhaps no president visited the tomb more than Franklin Roosevelt, stopping by at least five times during his 12 years in office. On February 22, 1934, Franklin and First Lady Eleanor braved a "downpour of rain." The presidential car drove to within 10 feet of the tomb and only a small group of people witnessed the event, proving it a sincere observance of respect and not a mere publicity stunt. Roosevelt approached the tomb and stood for a minute in silence.[29] Roosevelt visited again in 1935 and 1937 to lay a

wreath.[30] He also made pilgrimages with visiting dignitaries. On June 9, 1939, Roosevelt accompanied King George VI of England as he "paid homage to America's foremost shrine." The king placed a wreath of white lilies, iris, and carnations with a card that read "From George R. I. and Elizabeth R." before a handful of invited guests,

Franklin Roosevelt visits the Washington tomb on February 22, 1935. (Library of Congress)

including members of the Mount Vernon Ladies' Association.[31] Roosevelt visited again on January 8, 1942, along with Winston Churchill. The next year on February 22, 1943, Eleanor accompanied the Chinese first lady Madame Chiang Kai-shek to lay several wreaths at the grave.[32]

After the war, President Harry S Truman continued the birthday wreath tradition when he visited in 1947. Truman "motored over the snow covered roads" to place the floral arrangement of red carnations, and was greeted by a group of amputees from Walter Reed Hospital.[33] On July 11, 1961, John F. Kennedy held a state dinner at Mount Vernon for the president of Pakistan, Ayub Khan. On February 22, 1982, Ronald Reagan, along with First Lady Nancy, laid a wreath and spoke from the steps of Mount Vernon.[34]

Today, there are special wreath-laying ceremonies at the tomb each day at 10:00 a.m. and 3:00 p.m., April through October, and at noon from November through March.

THE GEORGE WASHINGTON DEATH SITES

One of the convenient things about visiting the Washington death site is that Mount Vernon is a "one-stop shopping" locale: you can see where he died, where his funeral took place, and the old and new tombs in one location. The land was first acquired by Washington's great-grandfather John in 1674, and the home was built by his father, Augustine Washington, in 1735. It was later owned by Washington's half-brother Lawrence, who named the estate Mount Vernon in honor of his former commander in the British navy, Admiral Edward "Old Grog" Vernon. When Lawrence died, he passed Mount Vernon on to George Washington in 1753.[35] The future president made extensive changes to the home: in 1758 he built another floor, and during the 1770s he added wings on either side. The exterior walls were made of wood, cut and painted to resemble stone. Washington played an active role during construction and was kept apprised of progress while serving as general of the Continental army in the Revolutionary War.[36]

The second-floor room where Washington died is referred to as "The Washingtons' Bedchamber." This large room—19 feet wide by 15 feet long, with seven-foot-nine-inch ceilings—was where George and Martha slept, wrote letters, and read their Bible. The six-and-a-half-foot-long bed they shared, where Washington died, was built in Philadelphia in the early 1790s, while he was serving his first term as president.

Mount Vernon remained in the Washington family through several different owners, but the home fell into disrepair. By the 1850s, it was "rotting away, and its floor seemed hardly secure enough to justify the visitor in trusting himself upon it."[37] One of the columns went missing from the portico and was replaced with a sailing mast, which simultaneously looked ridiculous and sad. What seems inevitable today—that this historic home and property should be preserved for the ages—would not have been the case if not for a group of women that pioneered the historic preservation movement.

When it comes to the Americans, Washington is a legend. Even when it comes to the presidents, men who are giants, Washington still towers over them, perhaps only rivaled by Lincoln. To Harry Lee's famous eulogy of him as "First in war, first in peace and first in the hearts of his countrymen," a few more firsts can be added: first in death, and his ancestral home was first in historic preservation. It began in 1853, when

Mount Vernon, where Washington died on December 14, 1799.

Ann Pamela Cunningham from Virginia visited Mount Vernon and was appalled by its horrible condition. Inspired by a sense of purpose, she organized like-minded women to save it. They met for the first time on June 12, 1854, and called themselves the "Mount Vernon Ladies' Association of the Union." John Augustine Washington owned the home at the time, and had been unsuccessfully trying to turn it over to the federal government. Fully aware the home needed to be preserved, he was not initially receptive to their offer: "He was filled with horror that *women* should do that which should so emphasize the degeneracy of men."[38] The women were persistent, and in 1856 the state of Virginia passed an act authorizing them to purchase the home.[39] They began a drive to raise the necessary funds, which included a $50 donation from President Martin Van Buren's family in Kinderhook, New York.[40] After reaching their goal for a down payment, John Augustine Washington put his sexism aside and sold Mount Vernon on April 8, 1858, for $200,000.[41] They officially took over management on February 22, 1860, what would have been Washington's 128th birthday, charging visitors a quarter to see the historic estate.[42]

Shortly afterward, the nation was plunged into Civil War. The first superintendent of Mount Vernon, Upton H. Herbert, stayed at his post, later boasting, "I never left Mount Vernon during the war." Revered by both Union and Confederate soldiers, the property was considered neutral territory. Despite their differences, one thing they could agree upon was their love for the first president and the estate "constituted the one spot upon which Union and Confederates could meet and fraternize."[43] One soldier—whether Union or Confederate is unknown—did not share that respect, and climbed over the iron railing, breaking off one of the eagle's talons. After the incident, a second, impregnable iron gate was installed that reached to the top of the arch. Reportedly, to ensure such vandalism never again occurred, the key was thrown into the depths of the Potomac River (presumably a duplicate key was made beforehand).

Throughout the years, the tomb has required constant restorations and maintenance, largely due to the dampness of the riverfront area. In 1891, a hole was cut into the back and an iron grate installed to vent moisture. In 1903, it was reported that the tomb was "fast crumbling away" and "with the finger one can scrape away layer after layer."[44] Repairs were done, but one of the bricks that contained the Masonic emblem was unsalvageable and a replica had to be created.

Even after more than two centuries, authentic and recreated relics from Washington's death still exist in abundance. A full-scale replica of the Mount Vernon home can be found across the country, on the outskirts of Olympic National Park in Port Angeles, Washington. The building—which is actually a hotel—is named the George Washington Inn and, according to its website (www.GeorgeWashingtonInn.com), "was inspired by Mount Vernon and built as a replica of George Washington's home, here on the west coast in honor of our first president's faith and legacy. As a luxury inn fit for a president, [one can] enjoy its waterfront panorama and breathtaking views of the Olympic Mountains, all in a rural setting similar to Mount Vernon."

Pieces of the rotted wood from the original coffin were saved and distributed as mementos—one shard is now on display at the Smithsonian Museum in Washington, DC.[45] A replica of the first coffin can be seen at the Education Center in Mount Vernon, and several medical instruments used to treat Washington in his final hours are on display at the George Washington Masonic National Memorial in Alexandria, Virginia. In a glass case at the National Museum of Funeral History in Houston, Texas, is the original funeral billing statement.

As Washington was the commanding general of America's first army, it was appropriate that I visited Mount Vernon on Veterans Day. It was crowded, and roaming the estate were many of our modern-day heroes from the armed forces. I was more than happy to wait in line for almost an hour behind America's finest for my turn to tour the home. On such a busy day, tourists are quickly ushered past the room where Washington died. I then visited the tomb, where a young woman was fielding questions from tourists. I could not resist asking her about the infamous drunken-gardener-skull-robbing episode. After a momentary pause, she recoiled in horror and blurted, "I never heard of that!"

After visiting the tomb, I crossed the Potomac River to take a tour of the Capitol building and to see the proposed crypt. While not part of the tour, I did have a guide nice enough to take me there after the tour officially ended. The empty crypt lies two floors beneath the rotunda, in a cramped space with an arched ceiling. It now houses a historic black catafalque. The structure was first built in 1865 to hold the remains of Abraham Lincoln as he lay in state two floors above. It has been used by 10 more presidents since. The floor between the crypt and rotunda is called the United States Capitol Crypt, so named because it was intended to be the entrance to the tomb below. On the floor is a "Compass Stone," beneath which the proposed tomb of the first president lies. At one time, a statue of Washington stood on this spot.

An interesting occurrence of a paranormal nature took place in the spring of 1806 when Massachusetts politician Josiah Quincy III visited Bushrod at Mount Vernon. It is notable as it appeared in a 19th century family history written by Josiah's son. The gracious host took his guest on a tour of the old tomb. Quincy was appalled when he saw Washington's final resting place in shambles, and later wrote that the "velvet cover of the coffin was hanging in tatters, it having been brought to this condition by the assaults of relic-hunters." At the end of the day, Bushrod escorted Quincy to Washington's bedchamber where he would sleep for the night.

The empty crypt built for Washington's remains beneath the United States Capitol building.

As he walked out, Bushrod offered an ominous warning: "An interview with Washington had been granted to some of its former occupants." Perhaps that statement coupled with the experience in the tomb induced a strange vision, because that night Josiah claimed to have been visited by the ghost of George Washington! His son recounted his experience years later: "And during the night he *did* see Washington, and this is all I have to say about it. If I gave the particulars, I should feel bound to give a full explanation of them by Dr. Hammond, or some other expert in cerebral illusions; and this would occupy too much space for an episode. It may be worthwhile to say that nothing my father saw, or thought he saw, was useful in confirming his faith in a spiritual world. His assurance in this matter was perfect. He believed that brain action (if that is the correct expression) was at times set up in us by friends no longer in the flesh, and that his own life had been guided by these mysterious influences."[46]

Mount Vernon is located at 3200 Mount Vernon Memorial Highway, Mount Vernon, Virginia, 22309. The site is open 365 days a year, and hours vary throughout the year. For the latest information, visit: www.MountVernon.org.

Thomas Jefferson ★ *1801–1809*

CRITICAL DEATH INFORMATION:

Date of death:	July 4, 1826, 12:50 p.m.
Cause of death:	Multiple ailments including intense diarrhea, kidney disease, and pneumonia
Age at death:	83 years, 82 days
Last words:	"No, doctor, nothing more." (last recorded words)
Place of death:	Monticello, Virginia
Funeral:	Monticello, Virginia
Final resting place:	Monticello, Virginia
Reinterred:	No
Cost to visit grave:	$22.00 (the most expensive presidential grave)
For more information:	www.Monticello.org
Significance:	Ended longest period when no presidential deaths occurred

After George Washington died, more than 26 years passed without a presidential death—a record that still stands to this day. That ended when Thomas Jefferson died on the 50th anniversary of the signing of the Declaration of Independence. It would then be less than six hours before the nation was again saddened by a presidential death.

After his presidency, Jefferson lived in Monticello, his beloved home in Virginia that he designed himself. He focused on his farming and his family, stayed politically active, and dedicated much time and energy to founding the University of Virginia. Jefferson had sporadic health issues, including severe diarrhea that plagued him in his later years. In the fall of 1819, premature rumors of Jefferson's death circulated following a severe case of blood poisoning, but by the end of the year he had recovered. In May 1825, Jefferson developed bladder problems, causing him pain when he urinated. He was cared for by Dr. Robley Dunglison, professor of anatomy and medicine at the University of Virginia. Dunglison prescribed opium, a drug that Jefferson had taken over the years to alleviate his aches and pains. His doses increased, and by the end of 1825, Jefferson considered taking the drug "to be [his] habitual state."[1] To prepare for the end, he made his will on March 16, 1826, leaving Monticello to his daughter Martha and a "gold-mounted walking staff" to his presidential successor James Madison.

In May 1826, his health further declined. At 83 years of age, Jefferson suffered from multiple ailments, including, besides intense diarrhea, boils on his backside, a kidney infection, kidney damage, and pneumonia. On June 24, he called for Dunglison, who two days later wrote that the health problems were "making a decided impact on his bodily powers." Jefferson was confined to his bed and had no illusions that he would live much longer. The family was on a death watch as the nation approached the 50th anniversary of the signing of the Declaration of Independence—and its author desperately hoped to survive for the historic milestone.

On July 3, Jefferson slept most of the day, heavily medicated on opiates and fading in and out of consciousness.[2] With him were his granddaughter's husband Nicholas Trist, Dr. Dunglison, and his grandson, Thomas Jefferson Randolph. Jefferson awoke in the early evening and asked, "This is the Fourth?" Jefferson then repeated himself, "This is the Fourth?" Trist opted to tell a white lie and nodded an affirmative. These would have been romantic and appropriate last words, but Jefferson was not done speaking. He responded, "Just as I had wished," and went back to sleep, satisfied that he had lived to see the historic date. A few hours later, Jefferson awoke again, at about 7:00 p.m., to find Dr. Dunglison by his bedside. He weakly said, "Ah! Doctor, are you still here?" He again asked, "Is it the Fourth?" Dunglison truthfully answered, "It soon will be."

Jefferson fell asleep and awoke around 9:00 p.m. Dr. Dunglison asked him if he wanted an opiate to make him more comfortable, but he was finished with the drug and responded, "No, doctor, nothing more." These were his last *recorded* words but not the last words he would speak. About 4:00 a.m. on July 4, Jefferson awoke. He called his servants in, but what exactly was said is unknown.

He next woke at 10:00 a.m., uncomfortable and unable to speak. Understanding what was wrong, his house slave Burwell Corbert adjusted his pillow. Jefferson dozed again and awoke at 11:00 a.m. He moved his lips to indicate he was thirsty, and his grandson placed a wet sponge to his mouth.[3] At 12:50 p.m., Thomas Jefferson's heart stopped beating—he was dead. His grandson closed Jefferson's eyes, and Trist clipped off a lock of hair that still had strands of the red from his youth.[4]

Jefferson was placed in a simple wooden coffin, probably built by his slave John Hemmings. A small funeral was held the next day, on July 5, without pomp or circumstance. As with many of his death preparations, Jefferson's wishes were explicit: invitations were not to be sent, but rather, all were welcome. Because he was buried so quickly, many people who might have liked to attend were unaware of the funeral and possibly even of his death.[5] One young man who did travel to Monticello that day was a 17-year-old student, Edgar Allan Poe. The funeral was held at 5:00 p.m. in the falling rain. The crowd stood around Jefferson's coffin, which lay on planks placed over the grave. The service was conducted by Reverend Frederick Hatch, rector of the Episcopal Church in Charlottesville, and Thomas Jefferson Randolph read from the Book of Common Prayer. At the conclusion of the ceremony, the coffin was lowered into a grave that had been dug by Jefferson's slave, Wormley Hughes.[6]

In 1771, Jefferson had written a detailed description about where he wanted to be buried: "Choose some unfrequented vale in the park, where is no sound to break the stillness, but a brook that bubbling winds among the woods—no mark of human shape that has been there, unless the skeleton of some poor wretch who sought that place out of despair to die in. Let it be among ancient and venerable oaks; intersperse some gloomy evergreens. Appropriate one half to the use of my family; the other to strangers, servants, etc." When his best friend and brother-in-law, Dabney Carr, died at the young age of 30 in 1773, Jefferson had to put his plan into effect prematurely. As children, Carr and Jefferson promised each other they would be buried together at their favorite spot in the shade of a great oak tree. Jefferson cleared an 80-square-foot section for the graveyard and later added trees, landscaping, and a path to the house. In September 1782, he buried his young wife, Martha Wayles Skelton Jefferson, there, and several family members and friends were later buried alongside her.[7] By the time Jefferson died, there were 12 graves in the cemetery.

Jefferson also specified his tombstone's shape, material, and what was (and was not) to be inscribed on it. He wrote: "Could the dead feel any interest in monuments or their incumberances, the following would be to my Manes and most gratifying: On my grave a plain die or cube of three feet, without any mouldings, surmounted by an Obelisk of six feet, each of a single stone. On the face of the Obelisk the following inscription, & not a word more: 'Here was buried Thomas Jefferson, Author of the Declaration of American Independence, of the Statute of Virginia for religious freedom & Father of the University of Virginia' because by these, as testimonials that I have lived, I wish most to be remembered. to be of the coarse stone of which my columns are made, that no one might be tempted hereafter to destroy it for the value of the materials . . . on the Die of the Obelisk might be engraved 'Born Apr. 2, 1743 O.S. Died_____'."

The *O.S.* indicates that his birth date was in the old style, which was in use until 1752, when we switched to the Gregorian calendar. This resulted in eleven days being added to historical dates, so Jefferson's birthday was April 2 under the old style, and April 13 in the new calendar. Significantly, there was no mention of the presidency, which was apparently not a position for which Jefferson "wish[ed] to be remembered."

The original tombstone was erected in 1833 and made of Vermont granite. The inscription was made on a marble slab affixed to the tombstone, not directly on the granite, as Jefferson had instructed. Regarding his request to use "coarse stone . . . that no one might be tempted hereafter to destroy if for the value of the materials," unfortunately what he did not anticipate was that the tombstone would be damaged not for its material value but rather by souvenir hunters for its historic value. It was later written, "The monument was beaten and battered into a ruin by relic-hunters; even the inscription was beaten off, except the part that tells his birth and death."[8] But the inscription was not "beaten off"—to ensure that the entire tombstone was not destroyed, years earlier, Randolph had moved the marble slab to his home in Edgehill for safekeeping.

In 1837, a nine-foot brick wall with an iron gate was built around the graveyard, to protect it from vandalism and to allow visitors to see the grave. Over the following decades the cemetery deteriorated—the south wall crumbled away, the iron gates rusted shut, and shrubs and weeds obscured the gravestones, many of which were defaced and broken. In 1878, Congress proposed to replace Jefferson's tombstone, but only under the condition that ownership of the graveyard would pass to the government. The family agreed but countered with their own stipulation that Jefferson's remains would never be removed and the grandchildren and their spouses could also be buried there.[9] The government did not accept these conditions. Four years later, in April 1882, a joint resolution of Congress provided $10,000 to create a new monument, this time without stipulations. Lieutenant Colonel Thomas L. Casey of the Corps of Engineers was placed in charge of the project. The eight-ton monument was built out of Virginia granite and had an inscription identical to the original.

Thomas Jefferson's original grave marker, now on display in the Francis Quadrangle on the campus of the University of Missouri.

On October 22, 1883, Casey announced to Congress that the monument was completed and had come in below budget, at $8,852.83. Later that year, 10 horses pulled the massive monument to the grave site and set it in place.[10]

Requests poured in for the original tombstone, despite its battered condition. One such inquiry came from the president of the University of Missouri, Samuel Spahr Laws, and Alexander F. Fleet, a professor there. They offered two arguments—first was the state's association with the Louisiana Purchase and Lewis and Clark's exploration, and second was Jefferson's passion for higher learning, as he founded Virginia State University. Laws presented his case to Jefferson's heir, Mary B. Randolph, who granted the request but was bewildered that anyone would want the damaged hunk of rock: She wrote: "As Dr. Laws has seen the monument and knows its dilapidated condition, and still desires to place it in the grounds of the University of Missouri, thereby doing honor to Mr. Jefferson's memory, we all agree it would be the best disposition to make of the old monument, and we will send the marble slab that has the inscription on it with the monument."[11]

Laws and Fleet were elated. They didn't consider the tombstone worthless, but saw the damage as "battle scars." Fleet wrote, "I feel that that old monument is as much more valuable than the new, as the bullet-pierced and torn and soiled battle flag that has passed through the way is expressibly more precious because of its memories, than the most costly and elegant new one that could be presented."[12] The stone was officially presented to the university on July 4, 1883. Not everyone was thrilled with the decision, including Virginia residents, who believed their state university would have been more appropriate. The issue became so contentious that Fleet had to remove the stone from Monticello at night, under the cover of darkness.

In October 1901, 250 members of the Jefferson Club of St. Louis, Missouri, visited

Monticello, bringing with them a memorial shaft made of red native granite that had the following inscription:

THOMAS JEFFERSON
CITIZEN STATESMAN PATRIOT
THE GREATEST ADVOCATE OF HUMAN LIBERTY, OPPOSING SPECIAL PRIVILEGES, HE LOVED AND TRUSTED THE PEOPLE.
TO COMMEMORATE HIS PURCHASE OF LOUISIANA ERECTED BY THE JEFFERSON CLUB OF ST. LOUIS, MO ON THEIR PILGRIMAGE OCT 12, 1901 TO EXPRESS THEIR DEVOTION TO HIS PRINCIPLES[13]

Presenting the statue, Missouri Congressman Macaenas E. Benton said, "The first stone erected to Jefferson's memory now stands on the campus of Missouri's great state university. The Jefferson Club, for itself and the Missouri Democracy, presents to Virginia another."[14]

Like Washington, Jefferson sits among the elite presidents in American history. Also like Washington, many envisioned Jefferson's grave somewhere more prominent and accessible than his family cemetery. The first to propose relocating Jefferson's remains was Virginia governor Henry Alexander Wise, who sought to create a Virginia "Presidents Cemetery" at Hollywood Cemetery in the 1850s, but was never able to fulfil his vision. In 1882, there was a proposal from the Glenwood Cemetery in Washington, DC. Jefferson's granddaughter Septimia Anne Meikleham agreed, but as she was not mentioned in Jefferson's will, her consent was "worth nothing."[15] In 1913, there began another effort to relocate his remains to Arlington National Cemetery. Fortifying the argument in favor of this was the neglected state of Monticello and the prospect that, at Arlington, Jefferson's remains would be under the "perpetual care of the Government."[16]

Jefferson's family maintained the cemetery and, to deter vandals, they planted thorn bushes at strategic locations where someone could squeeze through the gates. However, the maintenance responsibility became too onerous for the family, and in 1913, 13 Jefferson descendants met in Charlottesville to form the "Monticello Graveyard Association," drafting a constitution and choosing trustee members to care for the cemetery. This group still exists and is now known as the Monticello Association.

Over the years, several presidents have visited Jefferson's home and grave. On June 17, 1903, President Theodore Roosevelt was in the area for the University of Virginia commencement ceremony and visited Monticello for a private tour.[17] More than three decades later, on July 4, 1936, Franklin Delano Roosevelt followed in his footsteps. At 10:00 a.m., he spoke before 2,000 people. Immediately after his speech, Roosevelt visited the grave to lay a laurel wreath.[18] Eleven years later, on July 4, 1947, President Harry S Truman gave a speech from Monticello in which he denounced the Soviet Union for not cooper-

Photograph of Jefferson's grave, taken sometime between 1914 and 1918, when Jefferson Levy owned Monticello. (Library of Congress)

ating with the Marshall Plan. Afterward, he laid a wreath at the grave.[19] On July 5, 1976, Gerald Ford swore in 100 newly naturalized citizens from 23 countries at Monticello. After the ceremony, he also visited the grave.[20]

On March 24, 1984, President Ronald Reagan and the First Lady took a helicopter ride from Washington, DC, for an unannounced "spring jaunt" to the historic home. They joined a group of about 20 people and were led by guide Elizabeth Jones. On January 17, 1993, three days before his inauguration, president-elect William Jefferson Clinton made a symbolic journey to the nation's capital accompanied by vice president-elect Al Gore and their spouses, and he began at Monticello. Clinton, named in honor of Thomas Jefferson, wanted to follow in the footsteps of third president in his 1801 inauguration. After a tour of the home, they boarded a bus for the 121-mile trip to Washington, DC.[21]

On July 4, 2008, President George W. Bush spoke at a Monticello naturalization ceremony, welcoming 72 new American citizens before a crowd of 3,000.[22] On February 10, 2014, President Barack Obama visited Monticello with his French counterpart, François Hollande, making Obama the first sitting president to visit with a foreign head of state.[23]

THE THOMAS JEFFERSON DEATH SITES

As with Washington, the significant sites relating to the death, funeral, and burial of Jefferson are all located in one place. Monticello may be the most recognizable of any presidential home—you may even have a pocketful of Monticellos right now, all worth 5¢ each! You may also live in the vicinity of one of several replicas of Monticello. In Paducah, Kentucky, at 1333 Lone Oak Road, a spinal surgeon's office is located inside a facsimile of the famous home. In Monticello, Indiana, a replica is used as the main branch of the Lafayette Bank and Trust. In Colts Neck, New Jersey, a replica of Monticello serves as a private residence.[24]

Monticello as it looks today. (Library of Congress)

Construction on Monticello (Italian for "little mountain") began in 1768, and the unique 10,660-square-foot Roman neo-classical structure featured the first dome for any home in America. Jefferson moved in during a snowstorm on January 1, 1772, with his bride, Martha. Jefferson later wrote, "All my wishes end where I hope my days will end, at Monticello."[25]

During the Revolutionary War, on June 4, 1781, Jefferson narrowly escaped when British soldiers tried to capture him at home. He evaded his pursuers by running down the mountain, and the British eventually took command of Monticello. It was saved from looting when a British officer nobly "ordered all private rooms to be locked and forbade any damage."[26]

One can imagine the historic guests who visited Jefferson throughout his lifetime. One account places Jefferson at dinner with the two fellow Virginia natives who succeeded him, James Madison and James Monroe. He was also visited by our eighth president, Martin Van Buren. On November 4, 1824, an aging Marquis de Lafayette, suffering from gout and barely able to walk, paid a visit to Monticello. It was the first time he had seen Jefferson in 30 years, and afterward the old friends were joined by Madison.[27]

When Jefferson died, the home went to his daughter Martha and her husband, Thomas Mann Randolph Jr. The two had an unhappy marriage, and shortly afterward, Martha left her husband and took her children to Boston. While she was gone, the home remained unoccupied for much of the time and fell into ruin. Sightseers and tourists roamed freely, and souvenir hunters took what wasn't nailed down. It became so bad that a year after Jefferson's death, a visitor wrote that the home was "dark & much dilapidated with age & neglect."[28]

Martha was unable to pay the debts she had inherited from her father and was forced to place the home for sale, seeking between $15,000 and $20,000.[29] In 1831, the home and 273 acres of the property were purchased by James Turner Barclay of Staunton, Virginia, for only $4,700.[30] Not included in his purchase was the graveyard, which Martha retained and passed on to her son Jeff Randolph upon her death in 1836. Barclay was not interested in preserving Jefferson's home, and some accounts portray him as *hating* Jefferson. Barclay planned to use the estate to grow his silkworm business, and thus the home suffered greatly under his watch. But his business did not flourish and he grew irritated with the uninvited visitors. Five years later, he sold the estate to a Jewish navy officer, Uriah Phillips Levy, for only $2,500.[31]

Levy's family would later contend that his purchase was inspired by admiration for the third president. Other fabrications and tall tales abound as to his rationale. One puts Levy on a train where he met a man planning to purchase Monticello on behalf of a group from Philadelphia. After the nameless Philadelphian got drunk and sidetracked, Levy seized the opportunity to purchase Monticello for himself. Years later, an apocryphal story emerged: in a meeting with President Andrew Jackson, Levy was told, "I understand a fellow intends to purchase [Monticello] and exhibit the tomb of the great 'Apostle of Liberty' at a shilling a head. It is to be sold on Tuesday." Jackson ordered him, "Go down and buy it." Levy protested and explained that he was more suited for the deep waters than the land. But Jackson would have none of it and told him, "That matters not," before commanding, "Go and buy it."[32] Unfortunately, no proof exists of their ever meeting.

Levy did not live at Monticello year-round and left the daily oversight to Joel Wheeler, who moved into the home and opened it to anyone willing to pay him two bits. During the Civil War, the property had no protector like Mount Vernon, and Levy remained absent. The Confederate government seized Monticello as an alien property and camped in its vicinity. A reporter for *Frank Leslie's Illustrated Newspaper* lamented, "During this unhappy rebellion [Monticello] has been confiscated, with all its lands, negroes, cattle, farming utensils, furniture, paintings, wines, etc."[33] Soldiers regularly chipped pieces off the home and tombstone and scrawled their names on the walls. When the Union seized the area, General William Tecumseh Sherman assigned guards to ensure it would suffer no further damage.

By late 1864, the Confederate government was in desperate need of money and forced to sell Monticello. An auction was held on November 17, and Confederate Lieutenant Colonel Benjamin Franklin Ficklin placed the winning bid of $80,500 (in Confederate dollars).[34] The end of the Civil War brought confusion and debate as to the true owner of the home. Being on the losing side, Ficklin had no legal right to the property and it was confiscated. Levy had died in 1862, leaving the home to the federal government. Levy's will was complicated and included a peculiar stipulation: "I give, devise, and bequeath my farm and estate at Monticello, in Virginia, formerly belonging to President Thomas Jefferson . . . for the sole and only purpose of establishing and maintaining at said farm of Monticello, Virginia, an agricultural school, for the purpose of educating, as practical farmers, children of the warrant officers of the United States navy, whose fathers are dead."[35] His family disputed the will, and with the confusion left by the Civil War and the complexities of Levy's request, the government relinquished its rights and Monticello was transferred to Levy's heirs. But the estate they inherited was severely neglected and had been ransacked by vandals. In 1866, a *New York Times* reporter bemoaned the home "a deserted ruin, its occupants being a freedman and his family" and "everything about the place is rapidly going to decay."[36]

Monticello as it looked in 1906, when the home was owned by Jefferson Levy. (Library of Congress)

The Levy heirs put Monticello up for auction on March 20, 1879, and the winning bid of $10,050 was placed by the 27-year-old nephew of Uriah Phillips Levy, Jefferson Monroe Levy. Jefferson Levy put a stop to unwanted visitors traipsing through the home and allowed only those with a printed permit, and "a four-bit entrance fee" which went to local charities.[37] For the most part, visitors were welcomed by him, "if the person is not a vandal," but were requested to limit their stay to 20 minutes.[38] Upon their arrival, "an old Negro, descendent of some of the original retainers at Monticello" opened the gate and rang a loud bell to notify the Levy family that visitors had arrived.[39]

Levy made substantial improvements to restore the home to its original appearance, investing thousands of dollars in renovations. His purchase also paved the way for the federal government to place a more suitable memorial at the grave, along with a new iron fence. This time there was no condition that ownership would

transfer from the family. Concurrent to Levy's restoration efforts, the nation's attitudes about who should own historic properties—which some believed *sacred*—began to evolve.[40] In 1897, the *New York Sun* published a controversial editorial by Congressman Amos Cummings entitled "A National Humiliation," in which he attacked the current owner: "Monticello is now owned by a Levy, who charges patriotic Americans, Democrat and Republican, 25¢ admission to the grounds alone, and refuses admission to the house at any price during his absence."[41]

By 1912, the movement to turn the home over to the nation was led by New Yorker Maud Littleton, who had organized the Jefferson-Monticello Memorial Association. Three years earlier, she had visited Monticello. While her host was gracious, she was appalled that so little of Jefferson was represented in home and felt overwhelmed by the presence of the Levy family. She believed that Monticello should be preserved as a historic shrine to Jefferson. Levy, now an influential New York Congressman, did not want to sell. Littleton stated her case on Congressman Levy's home turf, the House of Representatives floor, arguing persuasively that Monticello belonged to the entire nation, not just one man. Levy held his ground, doubling down on his hardline position and defiantly stating, "Every stone and every brick in the house of Jefferson, every tree, every nook and corner, every foot of Monticello is dear and sacred to me and *never* will I listen to any suggestion for disposing of it, whether coming from a private or public source."[42] As it turned out, "never" was about two years, and in 1914, in response to a letter from William Jennings Bryan, he finally agreed to sell Monticello.

Levy's asking price was $500,000, which he considered a bargain as he had invested over $1,000,000 in repairs. His only stipulation was that Monticello be reserved as a home for the presidents to use as a retreat, similar to what Camp David would later become.[43] The government thought Monticello was worth only $50,000 and Littleton conceded $200,000 was appropriate. Despite the initial momentum to purchase the house, by 1916 the government had left the debate and the sale began to lose steam.

Several groups formed to negotiate the purchase, including the Thomas Jefferson Memorial Association, led by Ruth Read Cunningham. She was following in the footsteps of her ancestor Ann Pamela Cunningham, who had founded the Mount Vernon Ladies' Association and successfully acquired Washington's home in 1858. On April 13, 1923, a second organization was formed, the Thomas Jefferson Foundation, headed by Stuart Gibboney, a Virginia native and New York resident. Gibboney's group agreed to Levy's original price of $500,000 and focused on fund-raising. They took ownership of the land through a $100,000 down payment made on December 1, 1923.[44] The graveyard was not included in the sale and was formally deeded to Jefferson's descendants. The group continued to raise money for the remainder of the payment through national subscription. However, the mortgage would not be completely paid off until 1940. In 1953 and 1954, Monticello was closed while major renovations were undertaken.

Monticello is located at 931 Thomas Jefferson Parkway, Charlottesville, Virginia, 22902. It is open 365 days a year. The hours vary throughout the seasons, so for the latest information visit: www.Monticello.org.

The Original Tombstone

On July 20, 1883, the battered tombstone arrived at the University of Missouri and was placed in a temporary location. Two years later it was unveiled on July 4, 1885, on the university campus near the entrance to Academic Hall.

In 1932, a marker was placed in front of the slab. It was moved around the campus several times over the years, most recently in 1976. Today, the stone sits in the Thomas Jefferson Garden in the Francis Quadrangle, where the *St. Louis Dispatch* noted it is "878 miles from where you'd expect to find it." However, the tombstone is not complete. Upon its arrival in 1883, the 160 pound detached marble tablet was deemed too brittle to secure to the tombstone. It was broken in several spots, weathered, and the inscription faded and barely legible. The plaque was initially put on display in Academic Hall before it was packed away and later damaged in a building fire in 1892. Occasionally, it has been taken out for special events, but the last time was at the annual Tap Day sometime in the 1960s. It was again packed away in an attic where it remained for almost half a century. Recently, the Smithsonian has decided to restore the historic marble. As of this writing, their efforts are still in progress.[45]

John Adams ★ *1797–1801*

CRITICAL DEATH INFORMATION:

Date of death:	July 4, 1826, 6:20 p.m.
Cause of death:	Heart failure due to "debility at the age of ninety"
Age at death:	90 years, 247 days
Last words:	"Help me, child, help me."
Place of death:	Peacefield, Quincy, Massachusetts
Funeral:	First Congregational Church, Quincy, Massachusetts
Final resting place:	United First Parish Church, Quincy, Massachusetts
Reinterred:	Yes
Cost to visit grave:	Free (donation suggested)
For more information:	www.UFPC.org
Significance:	First president to be reinterred (1828, three years before George Washington), first buried outside of his home estate, and first funeral in a church

As with his old friend Thomas Jefferson, John Adams desperately battled to survive to July 4, 1826, the 50th anniversary of the signing of the Declaration of Independence. His presence was in high demand, but at 90 years old, age had taken its toll and a public appearance was not possible. Adams had spent the years since his presidency at his beloved farm estate, Peacefield, in Quincy, Massachusetts; and now his physical ailments confined him to this home. On June 30, he was visited by a local delegation hoping for a few words to pass along at a local celebration. Adams was happy to oblige and barked a simple, powerful proclamation: "Independence Forever!"

By the next day, Adams was barely able to

speak. He was treated at home by his doctor, Amos Holbrook, who remained with him until the end. Over the following days, Adams's health declined and breathing became more difficult. When he awoke on July 4 to the celebratory sound of fireworks and cannons, he proclaimed, "It's a great and glorious day!"[1]

Adams dozed as the day gave way to rain. In the afternoon he awoke and in a voice barely above a whisper, said "Thomas Jefferson survives." Adams was wrong—unbeknownst to him, his fellow Founding Father died earlier that day. Like Jefferson's "Is it the fourth?" many believe these to be his last words.[2] These words would seem fitting for the lives of Adams and Jefferson, the two minds behind the Declaration of Independence, but the truth is perhaps more poignant, because these larger than life figures were human, and they were suffering. Sometime later, John Adams weakly uttered to his granddaughter Susanna, "Help me, child, help me," and then fell silent. At 6:20 p.m., before sunset, John Adams died. His cause of death was listed as heart failure due to "debility at the age of 90"—in other words, old age. Exactly

where Adams took his last breath is not certain. The National Park Service, which manages the home, is unsure if he died in his study or in the guest bedroom. Family members would later recall with amazement that at the exact moment he died, "a clap of thunder shook the house," and then "a splendid rainbow arched immediately over the heavens."[3]

While over 26 years separated our first and second presidential deaths (Washington and Jefferson), a mere five and a half hours separated the second and third. The 1919 *Encyclopedia Americana* called the nearly simultaneous deaths of Jefferson and Adams "the most remarkable necrological coincidence in the history of our country!"[4] That extraordinary coincidence soon became so ingrained in the national consciousness that, in remarks made after the dual victories of Vicksburg and Gettysburg on July 4, 1863, Abraham Lincoln included it when he evoked other historic events that had occurred on the same glorious date.[5] Adams's death also had another distinction: at 90 years old, he lived longer than any other president, a record held for a staggering 178 years, only to be surpassed when Ronald Reagan died at the age of 93. (Reagan would be topped by Gerald Ford two years later.)

On July 7, family and friends gathered at Peacefield for Adams's funeral. Commencing at 4:00 p.m., the funeral procession was led by the citizens of Quincy, followed by the pallbearers flanking the hearse, including Harvard University president John T. Kirkland, Massachusetts governor Levi Lincoln Jr., and Lieutenant Governor Thomas L. Winthrop. According to the official order of procession printed in newspapers across the country,

Peacefield, the home where John Adams died, is now part of the Adams National Historical Park.

next came his male relatives, various local politicians, city officials, scholars, members of the clergy and military, and then, "strangers." Trailing behind were 12 mourning coaches, carrying female relatives.[6] During the half-mile procession, guns boomed in tribute from nearby Mount Wallaston.

At the First Congregational Church, the coffin was carried inside. Four thousand people were in attendance. However, one notable person was not there: Adams's son and the current president of the United States, John Quincy Adams—who was not yet even *aware* that his father had died! Several days later, still unaware that his father had died, John Quincy Adams departed Washington, DC, for Peacefield. When his carriage stopped in Baltimore on July 9, five days after his father's death, he was finally informed of the news.[7]

The officiating pastor was Reverend Peter Whitney, who read an appropriate verse from 1 Chronicles: "He died in good old age, full of days."[8] After the funeral, the coffin was carried across the street and placed in a tomb in Hancock Cemetery. As it was a temporary burial location, the tomb was not marked. Adams's permanent burial site was to be underneath the unbuilt United First Parish Church. Before his death, Adams was intimately involved in the project and had donated the land and granite to be used in the construction. He left money for the completion of the project in his will.

Shortly after Adams's death, his son purchased space within the church that was to be built across the street from Hancock Cemetery. The deed was for a "portion of soil in the cellar, situated under the porch and containing fourteen feet in length and fourteen feet in breadth."[9] On September 8, 1826, John Quincy Adams wrote the supervisors of the church with more specifics, in which he conveyed his father's request that "at my expense, a vault or tomb may be constructed under the temple, where may be deposited the mortal remains of the late John Adams and of Abigail, his beloved and only wife" and that it be a "plain and modest monument to his memory . . . divested of all ostentation."[10] Being entombed within a church was an honor that dated back to the earliest English settlements, a distinction reserved for priests, ministers, and the most influential congregants. For John Adams, our second president and a significant donor toward the church's construction, the honor was well deserved.[11]

Two years later, construction had progressed enough to move the bodies from the unmarked graves to the basement of the church. John and Abigail Adams were reinterred on April 1, 1828, into granite coffins cut from stone quarried from Quincy, Massachusetts.[12]

Eleven years before he died, Adams had written his own epitaph. He believed avoiding

The temporary tomb used by both John Adams and his son John Quincy Adams. In the background is the United First Parish Church, more commonly known as the "Church of the Presidents," where the remains of both men now reside in the basement crypt.

war with France was the crowning achievement of his presidency and wrote that his gravestone should read: HERE LIES JOHN ADAMS, WHO TOOK UPON HIMSELF THE RESPONSIBILITY OF THE PEACE WITH FRANCE IN THE YEAR 1800.[13] In the end, the inscription on his tomb was much more austere, reading JOHN ADAMS. Adams would later be joined by his son, John Quincy Adams, who died in 1848 and was interred in the crypt in 1852. In 1900, 89 members of the John Adams Chapter of the Daughters of the American Revolution placed a marble plaque at the entrance to the tomb.[14]

THE JOHN ADAMS DEATH SITES

While not quite as convenient as visiting Mount Vernon or Monticello, it is still easy to tour all of the significant sites related to John Adams's death in Quincy, Massachusetts. Differing from Washington and Jefferson, who were given funeral and burial rites on their home estates, Adams had more traditional final ceremonies: a funeral in a church and burial in a local cemetery.

Location of Death

The home where Adams died was first built in 1731 and was used as a summer home to West Indian sugar plantation owner Major Leonard Vassall. Just like Mount Vernon, Adams's home started out as a small structure of only seven rooms and eventually grew to 21. After Vassall died, the home went to his daughter, Anna. She moved to Cambridge, Massachusetts, in 1765 and leased the home to tenant farmers for the next decade. By the mid-1770s, Quincy, Massachusetts was at the heart of the brewing Revolutionary War. Anna, a loyalist, felt threatened by the patriots and left the colonies for England in 1775, leaving the home vacant. During this period, the National Park Service contends the home fell into "dubious legal status." To protect it from destruction, the governor of Massachusetts ordered the home confiscated. He stayed there for two weeks in 1775 and also used it to shelter refugees fleeing Boston. After the war, Anna returned to reclaim her estate and eventually gave it to her son, Leonard Vassall Borland.

In 1787, Adams was approaching the end of his time in Europe serving as ambassador to England and the Netherlands. Having accumulated furniture, books, and numerous other items during his sojourn, he was concerned that his current home, a small saltbox structure, was not large enough. To accommodate his new possessions and fulfill his dream of a simple farmer's lifestyle, he purchased the 76 acre estate for £600 on September 26, 1787.

When Adams returned to America the following year, he moved into his new home where he took pleasure in farming the land and walking the grounds. In a tribute to the peace that followed the Revolutionary War, he named the home "Peacefield." Adams was living there when he was elected the nation's first vice president and second president. After losing his reelection bid to Thomas Jefferson, he returned to Peacefield in 1801 to live the remainder of his years. He built a long room for entertaining guests, among them James Monroe, Ralph Waldo Emerson, and General Marquis de Lafayette in 1824.[15]

After Adams's death, the home went to John Quincy Adams. He did not live in the home year-round like his father but retained ownership until his own death on February 23, 1848. The home then went to his son, Charles Francis Adams, and his wife, Abigail, who transformed the property into a "gentleman's country estate."[16] They owned Peacefield for 41 years, until 1889. Through 1927, the home was owned by Charles's son Brooks and his wife Evelyn Adams, but as they aged they sold off parcels for development. The once-sprawling homestead was now more confined. To preserve and care for the historic property after his death, Brooks Adams established the Adams Memorial Society on March 28, 1927. The group took ownership of the home that same year and held it until 1946, when it was donated to the federal government and the Adams National Historic Site was established. As a result of the long lineage of Adams owners, the home contains many original pieces that belonged to the family.[17]

The home is located at 135 Adams Street, Quincy, Massachusetts, 02169. You can only visit by taking a tour, and tickets are available at the Adams National Historical Park visitor center in downtown Quincy. For more information, visit: www.nps.gov/adam.

Original Cemetery: Hancock Cemetery

John Adams was originally buried in Hancock Cemetery, located across the street from the United First Parish Church and next door to City Hall in downtown Quincy. Founded in the 1630s, this would serve as the main cemetery in Quincy for the next two centuries. The oldest surviving gravestone is from 1666, for Reverend William Thompson, and the first person to be placed in a burial crypt was Dr. Leonard Hoar in 1675. Until the early 19th century, horses and cattle freely cavorted throughout the cemetery, meandering among the headstones and grazing on the grass. Thankfully, that ended in 1809 when a group of citizens, including Adams, purchased the land and donated it to Quincy with the condition that "the town shall never hereafter allow the said burial ground to be used as a pasture or any horse or cattle to run at large therein."[18] The crypt used by John Adams abuts the front wall of the cemetery. Above the entrance is the inscription "J. Q. Adams," as the crypt was also used by his son two decades later. Behind it, the stone wall is crumbling with age and the entrance has been sealed with bricks. Several Adams family member remains are still inside, including John and Abigail's daughter, Nabby; and John Quincy's sons, George and John.

On January 28, 1982, the cemetery was placed on the National Register of Historic Places (#82004421). It is located at 1307 Hancock Street, Quincy, Massachusetts, 02169. For more information, visit: www.QuincyMA.gov/Government/PLANNING/HistoricHancockCemetery.cfm.

The Funeral

The First Congregational Church was built as a small wooden meeting house in 1732 and expanded in 1806 to accommodate the growing congregation. It served the community until its final service on October 12, 1828. Later that year, it was torn down and the congregation moved to the newly completed United First Parish Church.[19]

Church: The Entombment Site

The church where Adams is entombed was designed by Alexander Parrish and has been called "the finest example of a Greek revival church in New England."[20] The money for construction was donated by both Adams presidents and was built using land and granite donated by John Adams. The only portion of the church the Adamses did not fund was the front four massive columns. The cornerstone was laid on June 11, 1827, with Reverend Peter Whitney addressing the crowd in attendance. Construction took over a year and cost $30,488.56. To help fund the endeavor, pews were sold, and today's visitors can sit in Pew 54, purchased and used by John Quincy Adams for two decades. The church was dedicated on November 12, 1828, seven months after Adams was reinterred in the basement.[21] Over the years, the United First Parish Church has gone by various monikers, including "The Stone Church," "The Stone Temple," "The Church of the Presidents," and "The Adams Temple."

In the 19th century, while tourists flocked to Mount Vernon to see Washington's tomb and Monticello to see Jefferson's grave, the final resting place of Adams was poorly maintained and closed to the public. In 1881, it was written that the tombs were "dingy and dirty."[22] It was not until 1891, 63 years after John Adams's interment, that the tombs were opened to the

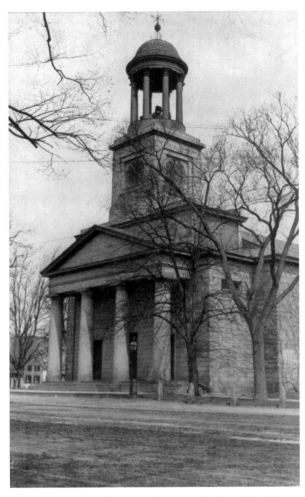

A 1908 photograph of the United First Parish Church in Quincy, Massachusetts. The Adamses' crypt is beneath the church. (Library of Congress)

public. However, the experience was not a gratifying one for the rare visitor. After opening a creaky granite door, one would be confronted by an iron gate blocking their entrance and limiting their view of the crypt. To make the tombs more visitor-friendly, Charles Francis Adams helped fund improvements in 1903.

Several presidents visited the church in the 20th century, notably all while they were still in office. The first to visit was President William Howard Taft in 1910, while in Quincy to see an air show at the dawn of the aviation age. On July 15, 1925, President Calvin Coolidge and First

Lady Grace entered the church basement and stood in silence for several minutes.[23] President Franklin Roosevelt stopped by the front of the church on October 21, 1936, but did not make it down to see the tomb. Just a week before the 1948 election, President Harry S Truman made a campaign speech on the church steps.[24]

The crypt was temporarily closed due to lack of funds in April 1999. After Massachusetts secretary of state William F. Galvin pledged $15,000 toward operating costs, the room reopened to visitors several weeks later.[25] The church was listed on the National Register of Historic Places (#70000734) on December 30, 1970. It is located at 1306 Hancock Street in Quincy, Massachusetts, 02169. For more information, visit: www.UFPC.org.

PERSONAL NOTE

In my research, I came across a fascinating article from the *Spokesman Review* (August 23, 1921) that revealed an amazing discovery made by Quincy mayor Joseph Whiton. At the end of his term, Whiton was cleaning out his desk when he found a 95-year-old letter written by John Quincy Adams, dated September 8, 1826. John Quincy Adams wrote the five supervisors of the soon-to-be-built United First Parish Church to express his father's request that a basement be built for his mortal remains. The find was a historical treasure, written by one president detailing the requests of another.[26] While finding the letter is amazing in its own right, an event that occurred 89 years later is what made this extraordinary. After being lost for almost a century, the letter was *again* misplaced. On April 21, 2010, CBS news reported in a nearly identically worded article that the current Quincy mayor, Thomas P. Koch, "discovered" the same letter while working in the City Hall basement, proving that history does indeed repeat itself![27] I wrote the mayor to let him know of my findings and received a gracious reply.

James Monroe ★ *1817–1825*

CRITICAL DEATH INFORMATION:

Date of death:	July 4, 1831, 3:30 p.m.
Cause of death:	Heart failure
Age at death:	73 years, 67 days
Last words:	"I regret that I should leave this world without again beholding him."
Place of death:	His daughter's home, New York City, New York
Funeral:	St. Paul's Chapel, New York City, New York
Final resting place:	Hollywood Cemetery, Richmond, Virginia
Reinterred:	Yes
Cost to visit grave:	Free
For more information:	www.Hollywood Cemetery.org
Significance:	First to die outside of birth state, first not to die in his own home, and first death home that no longer exists

After retiring from the presidency in 1825, James Monroe moved to his Oak Hill estate in Loudoun County, Virginia. Like George Washington, Thomas Jefferson, and John Adams before him, he wished to live out the rest of his days in his familial home. However, Monroe fell on hard financial times and, after his wife Elizabeth died on September 23, 1830, it was no longer possible for him to remain in his home. He left Oak Hill for New York City, to the three-story home of his daughter Maria and his son-in-law, New York postmaster Samuel L. Gouverneur. Gouverneur had served as Monroe's private secretary, and his marriage to Maria in March of 1820 was the first wedding to take place in the White House.[1]

In New York, Monroe attempted to lead a quiet existence, partaking in "common chores," such as grocery shopping at the Centre Market, "where all the stallmen knew and honored him."[2] For the most part, he was just another aged citizen of New York and kept out of public affairs. But as a former president, he had a difficult time roaming the streets incognito and, shortly after arriving, was cajoled into presiding over a ceremony celebrating the downfall of France's king, Charles X.[3] When Monroe turned 73, his health quickly worsened and he was attended by the Gouverneurs' family physician, Dr. Berger.[4] He was visited toward the end of his life by former president John Quincy Adams. Shortly before his death, Monroe spoke of his predecessor, James Madison, and lamented, "I regret that I should leave this world without again beholding him." Those were Monroe's last words. At 3:30 p.m. on July 4, 1831, James Monroe died of heart failure. His friend, General Winfield Scott, was by his side and gently closed Monroe's eyes.[5]

Amazingly, Monroe became the third consecutive president to die on Independence Day, following Adams's and Jefferson's near-simultaneous death five years earlier. Monroe's passing also represented a seismic shift in presidential death history, for he did not pass away in the comfort of his ancestral home, following the script of his predecessors. If luck had gone Monroe's way, he would have died in Oak Hill and been buried on the grounds. Had that happened, the story of his life *after* his death would not have been nearly as fascinating.

For several days after Monroe's death, the *Richmond Enquirer* reported, "many friends . . . called to look upon the remains of the good and great man."[6] The president was placed in a mahogany coffin with the simple inscription on a silver plate, JAMES MONROE OF VIRGINIA, DIED 4TH JULY 1831; AGED 74 YEARS. Years later, Gouverneur would explain that the "of Virginia" portion of the inscription indicated Monroe's wish was to be reinterred in his birth state at a later date.[7]

The funeral was held on Thursday, July 7. The coffin was placed in a hearse covered in black cloth with touches of gold, topped by four black feathers that waved gently in the breeze. The caisson was pulled by four black horses and escorted by a military honor guard along with pallbearers on either side. On the left were the Honorable Samuel L. Southard of New Jersey, Colonel Richard Varick, naval officer John Ferguson, and former member of the House of Representatives, John Watts. On the right were the famous artist Colonel John Trumbull, New Jersey governor Aaron Ogden, US Marshal Thomas Morris, and the Honorable David Brooks.

The procession left the home at approximately 3:00 p.m. and proceeded down Broadway to City Hall. The coffin was placed on a platform in front of the building, and at 4:00 p.m. the president of Columbia College, William Alexander Duer, addressed the crowd. The procession then continued to St. Paul's Trinity Church for the funeral ceremony, officiated by Bishop Benjamin T. Onderdonk and Dr. Jonathan Mayhew Wainwright. Afterward, the procession, led by General James Morton, marched to the cemetery. The parade stretched for a staggering three miles, and 100,000 people lined the route.

The procession included public and fraternal societies and marched up Broadway to Bleecker Street, where military lined each side to pay respects to the former commander in chief. It continued to Second Street to the Marble Cemetery, where a large crowd had gathered.[8] For a former president, the whole scene did not seem right. It was a small cemetery in a strange city and his remains were placed in a $500 shared crypt that Gouverneur had purchased some time ago. Monroe did not even receive a dedicated tombstone. Inscribed on the two-square-foot Tuckahoe marble slab was:

JAMES MONROE
ROBERT TILLOTSON
Vault No. 147

To conclude the ceremony, soldiers fired three volleys over the grave. Monroe was now the first president buried outside his birth state and the first buried in a different location from his wife, who was buried at Oak Hill.

It was later written that "His funeral was a very imposing one—the largest that at the time had ever been seen in New York."[9] However, after the magnificent send-off, the grave succumbed to the ravages of neglect as New Yorkers quickly forgot that a former president was buried in their proverbial, and literal, backyard. After 25 years, the *New York Times* brought this to the public's attention in 1856: "It is a curious neglect that leaves the precious dust of one of the purest patriots that our country has been blest with, to rest in such obscurity. Thousands pass every day by the spot admiring the well-kept grounds, pausing for the fragrance of the flowering shrubs, listening to the songs of the birds that find this oasis in the city's desert, but never dreaming that the author of the Monroe

Doctrine, the President of the United States, lies within a few feet of them. Monuments to men of half his intellectual stature, and a tithe of his industry and goodness of heart, are going up all over the land. Shall he who was reelected to the presidency by a vote unanimous with a single exception and who never disgraced his position have no more than this?"[10]

When news of the grave's condition reached Virginia, there began a movement to have the remains transported back to his native state. Around the same time in 1857, a group of Virginians living in New York sought a less complex tribute—to erect a monument over Monroe's vault. The effort was led by Dr. A. Jones, who had known Monroe personally and felt that his grave deserved a better memorial than a grass-covered slab. Jones wrote to Virginia governor Henry Alexander Wise to notify him that an appropriate monument would be placed over Monroe's remains in New York. The news caused an uproar, and Governor Wise acted quickly to push through a resolution to have the body returned to Virginia soil. It was passed on April 6, 1858, with an appropriation of $2,000 for the effort.[11]

New York's Marble Cemetery as it looks today.

Once the resolution was passed, there was little resistance. In New York, a committee was formed to take Monroe home with the proper ceremony, pomp, and spectacle, and the city allocated $2,500 toward the effort.[12] An announcement and call for volunteers for the "Removal of President James Monroe's Remains" was posted in the New York newspapers on June 1. Soon afterward, it was discovered that there were unpaid bills on the vault "of many years standing."[13] How the debts were settled is unknown, but perhaps a portion of the New York monetary allocation was used for that purpose. The first meeting of volunteers was held on June 3 at 8:00 p.m. at the Metropolitan Hotel. Despite the short notice, a large crowd of Virginia expatriates attended. A reinterment date of July 5, 1858, was set. With only a month to prepare, what the group was able to coordinate was truly impressive.

The committee also consulted Monroe's son-in-law Samuel L. Gouverneur, who made one request: that the removal of the body be done as discreetly as possible. After 27 years he knew that the task would not be pleasant due to the "long period during which the remains have moldered in the tomb [and] the season of the year."[14]

At 4:30 a.m. on July 2, a small group gathered at Marble Cemetery. People were aware that the removal of Monroe's remains was pending, but the time and date had been kept secret and even the press was left uninformed to avoid a crowd. Gouverneur, along with other surviving relatives—the former president's namesake nephew, former congressman James Monroe,

and grandson Samuel L. Gouverneur Jr. were in attendance. Shortly before 5:00 a.m., the vault doors were opened and the coffin was removed. It was found to be in "excellent preservation, the only decay visible being the wearing away of the bright polish of the mahogany."[15] It was placed on the grass for a few moments, and at 5:15 a.m. undertaker Henry Wilson arrived with the new coffin. The men pried open the 27-year-old coffin, and the body, which had been buried before the advent of embalming, was transferred, by all accounts, with respect, decorum, and reverence. The remains were discreetly carted down Broadway to the Church of the Annunciation located on West 14th Street.

A procession was scheduled to start at 4:00 p.m., but around noon people started gathering outside the church and along Broadway to secure a good spot. As the sidewalks filled, police arrived to maintain order. At 3:00 p.m., the church doors were opened. There was no service or sermon; instead, the time was used for citizens to view the coffin. In just over one hour, a staggering 10,000 people shuffled past. The colorful church sexton, Mr. Brown, kept the crowd moving. When some stopped too long, he chided, "Pass on, pass on, my friend, you can read it tomorrow." To the mourner wearing glasses, Brown bellowed, "Seventy-four years of age, my man, mind that; and who knows but you'll remember it all your life!" and then to his friend standing next to him, he confided, "I was told something like that when I was a boy, and I remember it yet."[16]

Shortly after 4:00 p.m., the coffin was loaded into a glass hearse; 45 minutes later, the funeral procession began. The massive group that marched

"Exhuming the Remains of President Monroe at the Second Street Cemetery," from *Harper's Weekly*, 1858. (Library of Congress)

down Broadway to City Hall was led by various military units, including several regiments from the New York State Militia. The soldiers were followed by the funeral car, adorned with black and white plumage and tassels and pulled by eight gray horses. Following the hearse were 10 carriages with dignitaries and an astounding 33 honorary pallbearers, one for each state of the union. Next were family members, followed by a contingent of military representatives, including 101 aged veterans from the War of 1812. Just like today, the placement in the parade is commensurate with the significance of the marchers, and toward the end were state and local politicians and dignitaries and, pulling up the rear, the "Masters of vessels in the Port of New York." The participants stretched on for two thirds of a mile, passing crowds on the streets, in the windows, and on rooftops. Flags were at half-mast, church bells rang, and minute guns were fired.

The procession arrived at City Hall at 6:00 p.m. and the remains were placed in the Governor's Room. After an official inspection, the doors were closed. The responsibility of honor guard was assigned to Company C of the Eighth Regiment under the command of Captain Burger, who delegated 10 soldiers to watch over the remains in two-hour shifts. The *New York Times* reported the "affair was admirably conducted."[17] Once the crowds dispersed and the soldiers were left alone, the admirable conduct ended and the party started! The soldiers broke out bottles and proceeded to have a drunken celebration, entertaining each other with mock speeches and eulogies for the former commander in chief. The next morning, they were found passed out amid a mess of broken furniture and empty bottles.[18] At 6:00 a.m., Company C was relieved by a sober Company F of the Eighth Regiment under Captain Buck. After the room was cleaned, people began to file in to pay their last respects until 11:00 a.m., when 500 members of the National Guard arrived for the ceremony in which New York City mayor Daniel Fawcett Tiemann was to officially transfer the remains to Congressman John Cochrane and thereby end the viewing period. There was one problem: Cochrane was nowhere to be found! That didn't stop the creative Mayor Tiemann. Pressed for time, he "concluded to deliver his address to an imaginary John Cochrane, and accordingly looking at the vacancy, spoke," according to the *New York Times*. Once the speech was completed, the National Guard presented arms, drums rolled, and the coffin was placed into a hearse. It rode down Broadway to Liberty Street to the North River, led by eight white horses and African American grooms.

An impressive 5,000 people waited at Pier 13 on the North River to see the coffin taken aboard the steamboat *Jamestown* to be brought to Richmond. Mayor Tiemann made another speech, and by this time, Congressman Cochrane had reappeared. If

Scene from the public viewing in New York City Hall, from *Harper's Weekly*, 1858. (Library of Congress)

he was to hear one of Tiemann's speeches, he chose the right one. Tiemann was eloquent and concluded with "Virginia, mother, it is thus that New York gives back to you your son."[19] This vignette of cooperation and respect between states north and south of the Mason-Dixon Line was one of the last gestures of national civility before the Civil War began in 1861.

At 3:30 p.m. the *Jamestown* set sail, while the Seventh Regiment, the official escorts, followed on a separate ship, the *Ericsson*, spending their time playing cards, "stag dancing," smoking cigars, and drinking brandy before retiring to straw mattresses strewn on the deck.[20] The next day, the *Jamestown* arrived at Norfolk, Virginia, and was greeted by flags at half-mast and salutary gunfire. The first speech was delivered by Norfolk mayor William Wilson Lamb. Afterward, the crew of the *Jamestown* accepted an invitation to imbibe "a good old fashioned Virginia mint-julep."[21]

At 8:30 a.m. on Monday, July 5, the *Jamestown* arrived at Richmond, where thousands of people crammed the docks to greet the ship.[22] Governor Wise and the mayor of Richmond, Joseph C. Mayo, boarded to formally accept the remains, and the Seventh Regiment was officially relieved by a platoon of Richmond Grays led by Captain Elliot. In preparation for this day, a Richmond committee met to determine how to commemorate the reinterment, but they scheduled no viewings or services. At 11:30 a.m., six white horses, each accompanied by a "colored groom," led a procession to Hollywood Cemetery. Bands played, drums rolled, guns fired, and flags flew at half-mast as the journey began up Main Street to Second to Cary Street before arriving at the cemetery at 1:00 p.m. At the cemetery, Governor Wise made a speech in which he praised Monroe and thanked his guests. In his long-winded address, he insinuated the initial burial was part of some master plan: "New York gave to him a 'hospitable grave.' Virginia respectfully allowed his ashes to lie long enough to consecrate her sister's soil, and now has duti-

fully taken them to be 'earth to her earth and ashes to her ashes,' at home in the land of his cradle."[23] A final prayer was delivered by Reverend Charles H. Read of the United Presbyterian Church before the coffin was lowered five feet into a brick and granite vault. Three salvos were fired to officially end the formalities.

That night there were parties aboard the *Jamestown* and the *Ericsson*. The two ships were latched together and connected by a plank. Unbeknownst to the rest of the passengers, a young soldier named Laurens Hamilton, Alexander Hamilton's grandson, fell overboard and drowned (perhaps crossing between ships after a few drinks). The ships set sail, and when he was later not found on board, it was assumed he was still in Richmond and would return by train. Later, his body was discovered and the tragedy became apparent.[24]

Above Monroe's grave was placed an eight-by-four foot block of polished Virginia marble plaque, upon which was inscribed:

JAMES MONROE
BORN IN WESTMORELAND COUNTY 28 APRIL, 1758.
DIED IN THE CITY OF NEW YORK 4 JULY, 1831.
BY ORDER OF THE GENERAL ASSEMBLY
HIS REMAINS WERE REMOVED TO THIS CEMETERY 5 JULY, 1858.
AS AN EVIDENCE OF THE AFFECTION OF VIRGINIA FOR HER GOOD AND HONORED SON

On the other side:

JAMES MONROE
GOVERNOR OF VIRGINIA 1799 TO 1802, 1811
PRESIDENT OF THE U.S., 1817 TO 1825

However, you will not see this one today—it was later stolen and never recovered.[25]

The next year, an ornate iron structure was erected above the tomb, designed by Albert Lybrock, who was inspired by the grave of Heloise and Abelard in the Père Lachaise cemetery in Paris.[26] The peculiar structure was cast by the Philadelphia company Wood and Perot for $1,682. It was designed to protect the grave from further vandalism, which was a concern after the rear plate was stolen, while still allowing the tomb to be viewed by the public.[27] Regardless of its noble influence, most feel it looks like a birdcage—and it is definitely one of the oddest presidential graves. The National Register of Historic Places calls it a "flamboyant Gothic Revival Style," which is a huge understatement.[28] Shortly after its construction, Monroe's tomb fell into disrepair. An 1881 article in the *Utah Journal* lamented, "The temple is painted [a] drab color and sanded. The iron is considerably rusted."[29]

On December 2, 1923, there was a grand ceremony at the grave site to mark the 100th anniversary of the Monroe Doctrine. The event was led by Virginia governor E. Lee Trinkle, William Jennings Bryan spoke, and soldiers from all branches of the military were in attendance.

The peculiar tomb of James Monroe in Hollywood Cemetery, located in Richmond, Virginia. (Library of Congress)

The grave was piled high with flowers, and more were dropped from low-flying planes, followed by a 21-gun salute by the Richmond Howitzers.[30] Almost a half century later, the tomb of James Monroe was given a unique honor when it was designated a National Historic Landmark (#71001044) on November 11, 1971. While other graves have been designated as national historic treasures, they are grand and imposing tombs that one can enter (such as Lincoln's and Garfield's), but Monroe's is the only traditional grave to be given this honor.

THE JAMES MONROE DEATH SITES
Location of Death

Before Monroe, the homes where the presidents died were ancestral estates—Mount Vernon, Peacefield, and Monticello. The history of the house where Monroe died is much more interesting because it was obscure and so few people cared what happened to it.

The home was located in New York, at 63 Prince Street, in what is now a bustling part of Manhattan. Originally a farm, it was owned by Nicholas Bayard, who passed it on to his son when he died in 1765, along with a mountain of debt. To help settle his father's bills, his son began to sell off parcels of land. In 1771, he sold 400 lots to Phillip Livingston, which included the plot that would become 63 Prince Street.[31] Fifty-one years later, the lot where Monroe would die was owned by Phillip Brasher. In 1822, Gouverneur, husband of the president's daughter, purchased a plot from Brasher for $2,159.[32] He built a three-story home the following year, which at the time was considered ostentatious for what was one of the most exclusive streets in Manhattan. After Monroe's death, the home was sold to Miles R. Burke for $10,750 on April 16, 1832. Burke sold it to John Ferguson three years later for $12,000. The Ferguson family owned the home for almost four decades, eventually selling to Charles H. Contolt, owner of Contolt's Gardens Resort, in 1873.[33] Posters and advertisements were plastered on the walls; the side was painted with "McCann's Celebrated Hats" and the front with "Billiard Table Factory."[34] Contolt died in 1897, and his estate continued to own the home for the next three years. In February 1900, it was sold it at auction to Daniel F. Mahoney, along with several other buildings for $116,500.[35]

For all of these years, the home stood unrecognized and unmemorialized as it slowly deteriorated. In a city saturated with history, probably not one in a thousand that walked past it knew of its significance. That would change on April 28, 1905, when the Women's Auxiliary to the American Scenic and Historic Preservation Society affixed a commemorative tablet to the home and staged a grand dedication. Prayers were read by Reverend W. Montague Geer of St. Paul's Church—where 74 years earlier James Monroe's funeral had been held—and a military band from Governor's Island entertained the crowd of thousands. The guest speaker was Ulysses S. Grant's son, Frederick, and after he spoke, Monroe's great-great-grandson unveiled the plaque.[36]

The marker read:

IN THIS HOUSE DIED JAMES MONROE FIFTH PRESIDENT OF THE UNITED STATES, WHO PROCLAIMED THE MONROE DOCTRINE. UPON WHICH DEPENDS THE FREEDOM OF THE AMERICAN REPUBLICS AND THE SAFETY OF THE UNITED STATES AGAINST FOREIGN AGGRESSION. BORN APRIL 28, 1758. DIED JULY 4, 1831 SOLDIER IN THE CONTINENTAL ARMY, MEMBER OF THE CONTINENTAL CONGRESS, AMERICAN ENVOY TO GREAT BRITAIN, FRANCE AND SPAIN, NEGOTIATOR OF THE LOUISIANA PURCHASE, SECRETARY OF STATE, SECRETARY OF WAR. TWICE GOVERNOR OF VIRGINIA, TWICE PRESIDENT OF THE UNITED STATES. THIS TABLET IS ERECTED BY THE WOMEN'S AUXILIARY TO THE AMERICAN SCENIC AND HISTORIC PRESERVATION SOCIETY. APRIL 28, 1905

The marker is unique in that it highlights the site as the place of his death. However, the high placement made it difficult to read. At this time, the home was being used by multiple businesses, including a Jewish restaurant owned by Samuel Greensching and a rag dealer, Vessa and Deddata.[37] The home was also used as a boarding house for a time.

In October 1919, it was announced that the home would be put up for auction; by now the room where Monroe had died was being used as a carpenter's shop. Concurrently, the site where Theodore Roosevelt was born, located just over a mile north, was being rebuilt, leading historic preservations societies to hope the same could be done for the Monroe home. Letters to the editor flooded in to city newspapers, including one to the *New York Times* from a local member of the American Legion, bemoaning that they lacked the funds to use part of the home as a clubhouse.[38] In an editorial, the prestigious newspaper appealed to New York pride and patriotism in making a plea to save the house: "Had Mr. Monroe been a French-man the house where he died would have been made a national monument."[39] In the end, capitalism trumped preservation. On November 12, 1919, the auction was held on Vesey Street, with the bids starting at $100,000. When the auctioneer called the bidding to an end, Joseph B. Cronin of the Charles N. Noyes Company owned the home for $138,000.[40]

Four years later, as the home hit its 100th year, it had again fallen on hard times and sat abandoned by its legitimate tenants. Instead, it was used by "a gang as a poker club," by "waste paper dealers," and by "junk men," but that may have been a euphemism for people dumping trash in the home.[41] It also became mysteriously prone to fires, which broke out on October 4, 1922, February 28, 1923, and again on May 4, 1923. Thankfully some people were not ready to give up on it yet. In December of 1922, a group led by civic-minded people—including as honorary president New York governor Al Smith and members Richard E. Enright, former police commissioner Henry E. Fruhauf, and former secretary of state Robert Lansing—incorporated the James Monroe Memorial Association and Foundation (known as the Monroe Home Association). Their goal was to purchase the home and restore it to how it looked when Monroe lived there, creating a "Pan-American shrine to stand through the centuries to come as a memorial to unselfish international amity and a fitting monument to the memory of the great good-will President of the United States." They set a goal to raise $200,000, of which a third would be used to purchase the home, a third to refurnish it, and the remainder to "establish a $100,000 annual lecture foundation for spreading through schools, colleges and communities the ideals of Pan-American friendship and accord."[42] The group added prestige to their roster when President Warren G. Harding was named an honorary officer. They set a goal of completing their vision within a year, to coincide with the 100th anniversary of the signing of the Monroe Doctrine.

Over the next year they were unable to raise sufficient funds, and by 1924, the home was a shell of its former self, with all of the fine interior woodwork either destroyed or pilfered. On May 7, 1925, the dilapidated home was sold not to preservationists but to developers, who planned to demolish the building to make way for a factory.[43] Nearly three months later, on July 29, 1925, a bale of newspapers in the home erupted into flames, the fifth fire in two years.[44]

Some good news came for the decrepit old home in September 1925, when the Monroe Home Association secured a deal to purchase it. There was a catch: they would need to move the house. The location they chose was around the corner, at 95 Crosby Street, where a one-story ocean-green restaurant had been purchased for $22,000. Another $4,000 was allocated to move the home.[45]

Any euphoria was short-lived. In the move,

the home was damaged when it was discovered too late that the slot at 95 Crosby Street was not wide enough. The attempt to force the old home in clipped off a fire escape. Part of the upper floor collapsed as bricks rained to the ground (they were later "carefully salvaged").[46] The roof and back wall were also destroyed. The home was eventually pushed into place, but despite the preservationists' best efforts, its fate was all but sealed. They were unable to raise additional funds for repair (which potential donors must have realized was now a lost cause), so the home stood roofless for two years, exposed to the elements and held together by cables and braces as vandals continued to chip

Photograph of the home being taken down from the *Brooklyn Daily Eagle* on November 26, 1927. The caption read: "One of New York City's famous landmarks was doomed when workers began demolishing the historic home at 95 Crosby Street, Manhattan, in which President James Monroe lived for many years and where he died."

away at it. By 1927, Theresa D. Browning, who held the deed for the Monroe Home Corporation, was no longer able to make payments toward the $15,770 still remaining on the mortgage. The Women's Auxiliary to the American Scenic and Historic Preservation Society, which had commemorated the home 22 years earlier, made a public appeal for money to continue to preserve it. Despite their efforts, the home was again put up for auction on September 13, 1927.[47] Assemblyman Frederick L. Hackenburg, who was placed in charge of the sale, lamented, "This could never happen abroad. I'd gladly give my fees and double them if someone one would raise funds to preserve the house."[48] When the auction ended, a familiar name won the bidding: the home was repurchased by Theresa D. Browning for $10,000. She had no illusions the home could be saved, but was hoping to resell the home to recoup some of her losses.

In late November 1927 the ramshackle structure was razed and lost forever to history (in place of the dangerously crumbling structure a garage was built).[49] While the James Monroe Memorial Association and Foundation had proclaimed a goal to create a museum that would "stand through the centuries," the home lasted only about five years after that. This tragic loss gives Monroe the sad distinction of becoming the first president whose death location is no longer in existence.

In November 1962 there was an office building located at the original home site and Felix J. Cuervo, a Veterans Administration officer, took matters into his own hands when he affixed a paper historic marker on the building that occupied 63 Prince Street. The watchman was not amused and barked, "Look mister, what am I gonna say when the super comes?" Cuervo responded in dramatic fashion, "Tell him that President Monroe used to live in a house that stood here and it's a shame . . . that we have no respect for the place where he lived and died." According to *New York Times* reporter Gay Talese, the unimpressed watchman "shrugged and walked off."[50] Cuervo would later graduate from taping handwritten markers to become president of the Native New Yorkers Historical Association. Two years after the lackluster response at Monroe's home, he would be instrumental in having a permanent marker placed at the home where Chester Arthur died.

63 Prince Street, where Monroe died in Manhattan. Today, the site is a youth fashion store called "G-Star Raw." At the location, there is no indication that Monroe lived or died there. (Courtesy of Francesca Leipzig Picone)

The Funeral

Founded in 1766 as a "chapel-of-ease" for Trinity Church, St. Paul's Chapel is a historic icon. Today it is considered the oldest public building in Manhattan still in use. After the spire was added in 1796, it was the tallest structure in New York, and it once sat in the shadow of the Twin Towers. Today, the Freedom Tower proudly looms overhead. However, when you visit, you will be hard-pressed to find information on the only presidential funeral to be held at St. Paul's Chapel. Historic pamphlets and placards have a lot of information about another of its presidential congregants, George Washington, but make no mention of Monroe's funeral services. On October 15, 1966, St. Paul's Chapel was added to the National Register of Historic Places (#66000551).

St. Paul's Chapel is located at Broadway and Fulton Street in Manhattan, New York, 10007. For more information, visit: www.TrinityWall Street.org/about/StPaulsChapel.

The Original Cemetery

The Marble Cemetery is located on Second Street, between Second and First Avenues. It was originally known as "Stillwell's Burial Ground" and was established shortly before Monroe's death.[51] It is a small, quiet cemetery that today seems oddly placed in the middle of a busy New York street. The scenic little oasis was added to the National Register of Historic Places on September 17, 1980 (#80002703). It next made the news 30 years later, on October 10, 2010, when the cemetery opened for Sunday tours and a volunteer "discovered a decaying garbage bag filled with 10 pounds of military-grade C-4 explosives!" A caretaker had apparently found the trash bag in the early summer of 2009, and instead of discarding it had moved it under a tree and forgotten about it.[52]

The cemetery is located at 60 East 2nd Street, New York, New York, 10003. For more information, visit: www.nycmc.org.

Public Viewing, 1858

New York City Hall was constructed from 1803–1812 and is today the oldest City Hall in America that has continuously been used for its intended government functions. It was designed in the Federal style by New Yorker John McComb Jr.,

and Joseph François Mangin, a Frenchman. In addition to the Monroe viewing, the remains of Abraham Lincoln and Ulysses S. Grant also laid in repose within the iconic structure. On October 15, 1966, the building was added to the National Register of Historic Places (#66000539). New York City Hall is located at City Hall Park, New York, New York 10007. For more information, including tour times, visit: www1.nyc.gov/site/designcommission/public-programs/tours/city-hall.page.

Hollywood Cemetery

See Chapter 11: John Tyler

Stonewall Cemetery

As if Monroe's postmortem existence were not fascinating enough, there is another interesting site of note. On October 24, 1817, Monroe received a strange gift—a plot of land about three miles west of Lancaster, Ohio.[53] The only stipulation was that this land be available to Monroe and all of his presidential successors to use as a burial ground. This peculiar gift was made by the farmer Nathaniel Wilson, one of the earliest settlers in Lancaster. He first purchased the land in 1798 and promptly built a log cabin for his family. He wanted his property to be used as a family burial ground after he died and devised the idea of bequeathing the land to the presidents to ensure it would never be disturbed.

The will was witnessed by his neighbor, and, after his death, his family obtained Monroe's formal acceptance. Monroe did not take him up on the offer, but ironically, his death in New York City would have made him a prime candidate to accept. A subsequent deed sent on April 12, 1838, to President Martin Van Buren read: "I give and devise to Martin Van Buren as president of the United States, and his successors in office forever that certain lot of land known as my locust grove to be by him and his successors in office forever held in trust for the purpose herein described. The grove shall remain

Stonewall Cemetery near Lancaster, Ohio, which was donated to Monroe for use as a president's cemetery.

forever unoccupied and the trees thereon be used for the sole purpose of repairing my family burying-ground and I hereby direct it and enjoin on my son and executors that they keep the said grove in good condition taking care to keep up the fences or enclosures and by removing the briars that may grow or accumulate thereon at least once during the month of August of each year."[54]

Each inauguration day, this practice has continued through its current owner, President Barack Obama. On the land, Wilson's son built a wonderful memorial in 1838. Today, you can still see the impressive 12-sided stone wall with an iron gate. It stands eight feet tall and four feet thick, and the *New York Times* praised it as "the finest example of dry masonry in Ohio."[55] In the center, a cedar of Lebanon was planted, which is claimed to have come from Palestine. Above the entrance is a center arch with the inscription:

THIS WALL WHICH ENCLOSES THE FAMILY BURYING GROUND OF NATHANIEL WILSON (ONE OF THE EARLY PIONEERS OF THE WEST) WHO EMIGRATED FROM CUMBERLAND COUNTY PA AND SETTLED NEAR THIS PLACE AD 1798, WHEN ALL AROUND WAS ONE CONTINUED AND UNINHABITED WILDERNESS, WAS COMMENCED BY HIM AD 1838 & FINISHED IN THE FOLLOWING YEAR BY HIS SON GUSTIN, THE FORMER HAVING SUDDENLY DIED ON MAY 12, 1839

While no presidents have taken Wilson up on his offer or even come to visit their inheritance for that matter, there are nine bodies buried at the site, all members of the Wilson family. Although in 1838 none of the presidents had been from Ohio, the next 70 years would turn out seven from the Buckeye State. The cemetery is located on Stonewall Cemetery Road off Route 22 in Lancaster, Ohio.

James Madison ★ *1809–1817*

CRITICAL DEATH INFORMATION:

Date of death:	June 28, 1836, in the morning
Cause of death:	Heart failure
Age at death:	85 years, 104 days
Last words:	"Nothing more than a change of mind, my dear."
Place of death:	Montpelier, Virginia
Funeral:	Montpelier, Virginia
Final resting place:	Montpelier, Virginia
Reinterred:	No
Cost to visit grave:	$16.00
For more information:	www.Montpelier.org
Significance:	First president buried in an unmarked grave

After James Monroe's unusual death story, James Madison's passing and burial at his familial home, Montpelier, represented a return to the dignified ending that was customary at the time. Madison's mind remained sharp into his mid-80s, but toward the end of 1835 his health began to fail. Bedridden and unable to walk, Madison moved from his upstairs bedroom to a room downstairs in the rear of the home. He was cared for by Robley Dunglison, the same doctor who treated Thomas Jefferson. By the end of June 1836, Madison was aware his days were few. Ten years earlier, both John Adams and Jefferson struggled to survive until the 50th anniversary of America's Independence Day, and Monroe died on the 55th anniversary.

Now, with the 60th anniversary in Madison's sights, Dunglison suggested drugs to attempt to prolong his life to reach the sexagennial celebration. A dignified Madison declined, choosing to let nature take its course.[1]

One evening, as he lay in his makeshift bedroom, Madison overheard his family eating dinner with his physician. In one of his last recorded utterances, he chided, "Doctor, are you pushing about the bottles? Do your duty, Doctor, or I must cashier you."[2] Perhaps the scene of his final moment is best set by a man who was there, his slave Paul Jennings. In 1865, Jennings wrote *A Colored Man's Reminiscences of James Madison.* Jennings greatly admired the fourth president, writing, "Mr. Madison, I think, was one of the best men that ever lived." Jennings described that fateful morning of June 28, 1836: "Sukey brought him his breakfast, as usual. He could not swallow. His niece, Mrs. Willis, said 'What is the matter, Uncle James?' [He replied] 'Nothing more than a change of mind, my dear.' His head instantly dropped and he ceased breathing as quietly as the snuff of a candle goes out."[3]

The funeral was held the next day, on June 29, 1836, in the 70–by–95-foot family cemetery on the grounds of Montpelier. The pallbearers included former governor of Virginia James Barbour, Supreme Court associate justice Philip Pendleton Barbour, neighboring farmers Charles P. Howard and Reuben Conway, and 100 of Madison's slaves. Governor Barbour later described the scene: "His slaves [were] decently attired in attendance, and their orderly deployment; the profound silence was now and then broken by their sobs."[4]

In Madison's last will and testament, dated April 19, 1835, he provided, "I give and bequeath my ownership in the negroes and people of colour held by me to my dear wife, but it is my desire that none of them should be sold without his or her consent or in case of their misbehaviour; except that infant children may be sold with their parent who consents for them to be

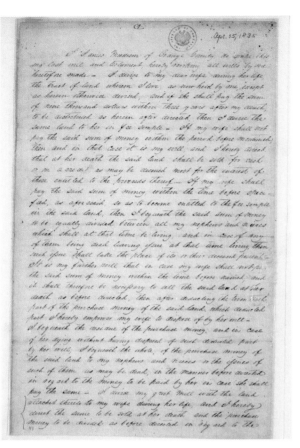

James Madison's last will and testament, dated April 15, 1835. (Library of Congress)

sold with him or her, and who consents to be sold." As to the gold-mounted walking staff that was bequeathed to him in Jefferson's will, Madison returned it to the Jefferson family, giving it to his grandson Thomas J. Randolph along with "the esteem I have for him as of the knowledge I have of the place he held in the affection of his grand-father."[5]

The fourth president's grave was not adorned with a headstone and remained unmarked for more than 21 years. In the late 1850s, local citizens banded together to properly memorialize Madison's grave site. To pay for a monument, the group raised $700 by subscriptions throughout Virginia.[6] By September 1857, they were ready to erect the monument. However, in an attempt to erect it over the grave, the workers encountered a problem—after 21 years, no one knew exactly where the former president was buried.[7] They dug until they discovered the coffin. When they lifted the rotted boards that covered the casket, they found the coffin lid had shifted out of place, allowing them to peer inside:[8] "The body was much decayed. The bones and breast, the ribs, the lower jaw, were returned to their original dust, the only portions of the skeleton remaining being the skull, portions of the cheek bones, the vertebra of the neck, spine, and large bones of the arms."[9] The workers then sealed the coffin and reburied it. Upon the spot a 16-ton, 25-foot-tall obelisk was placed, made of seven pieces of James River granite that bore the simple inscription:

MADISON

BORN MARCH 16, 1751

DIED JUNE 28, 1836

In 2000, the tombstone was discovered to be leaning toward the northeast, indicating the structure was unstable. The monument was dismantled and the foundation reset. Today, approximately 100 people are buried in the small cemetery, although only 31 graves are marked. Among the unmarked graves are Madison's parents.

THE JAMES MADISON DEATH SITES

The death sites of James Madison harken back to the first presidential death sites of his fellow Founding Fathers in that they are all consolidated on his family plantation of Montpelier. Originally called Mount Pleasant, the estate was settled in 1723 by Madison's grandfather, Ambrose Madison. Ambrose apparently did not have a good rapport with his slaves: several of his slaves poisoned him, killing him on August 17, 1732. This ominous death led Ambrose to become the first person buried in the Madison family cemetery. After his death, his widow managed the estate until her son, James Madison Sr., came of age in 1741. In 1755, Madison Sr. began construction on the home, which he named Montpelier. While the 10-room home built in the Georgian style was sizable, it was not yet the mansion it would become (it was later expanded in 1797 and 1809). After his father died in 1801, Madison inherited the home.

The upstairs library can be considered the most historical room of the house. It was there

Montpelier, the home where Madison died.

in 1786 that Madison put pen to paper to author the United States Constitution. Over the years, Madison had many important visitors to Montpelier, including Thomas Jefferson and James Monroe. After serving out the second term of his presidency in 1817, Madison returned to live and farm at Montpelier. However, crop failures and falling produce values put him deep into debt from which he never recovered. Just like Jefferson and Monroe, he was haunted by financial troubles in his later years. When he died, he passed his debt and the financial burden of the home on to his wife, Dolley. She kept Montpelier for as long as she could but was forced to sell it in 1844.[10]

After Dolley, there were five more owners of Montpelier throughout the remainder of the 19th century.[11] One of those was Frank Carson, who owned Montpelier from 1857 until his death in 1881. After Carson, the home was owned by a Boston fertilizer company until 1891.[12] During these years, the cemetery fell into disrepair and became overgrown with weeds. Visiting the grave was not only difficult but dangerous, prompting the New York Times to warn its readers in 1883 that the hallowed ground was "inhabited by snakes."[13]

In 1901, the home was purchased by William and Anne du Pont of the famous Delaware industrial family. They doubled the size of the house and remodeled many of the existing rooms. Unfortunately, but possibly unbeknownst to them, the room where Madison died was turned into a stairwell.[14] After William died in 1928, the home passed to his daughter, Marion du Pont, who continued to own the property for the next 55 years until her death in 1983. Marion appreciated the history of Montpelier and left the house to the National Trust for Historic Preservation. The trust completed renovations to return Montpelier to its appearance when Madison lived there, including removing the stairwell. In 1987, Montpelier was opened to the public.

On March 16, 2001, what would have been James Madison's 250th birthday, 2,500 schoolchildren visiting Montpelier formed a living American flag as the US Marine Corps played the National Anthem. Joining in the tribute were the descendants of Madison, along with impersonators of Thomas Jefferson, George Washington, and James Monroe.

Montpelier is located at 11350 Constitution Highway, Montpelier Station, Virginia, 22957. It is open seven days a week (except Thanksgiving, Christmas, and select weeks in January). The hours vary throughout the seasons. For the latest information, visit: www.Montpelier.org.

Madison's grave in 1908. The Montpelier estate was owned by the du Pont family at the time. (Library of Congress)

THE NINTH PRESIDENT
William Henry Harrison ★ *1841*

CRITICAL DEATH INFORMATION:

Date of death:	April 4, 1841, 12:30 a.m.
Cause of death:	Pneumonia
Age at death:	68 years, 54 days
Last words:	"Sir, I wish you to understand the true principles of the government. I wish them carried out. I ask nothing more."
Place of death:	The White House
Funeral:	The White House
Final resting place:	North Bend, Ohio
Reinterred:	Yes
Cost to visit grave:	Free
For more information:	www.OhioHistory.org/visit/museum-and-site-locator/william-henry-harrison-tomb
Significance:	First president to die in office

After overcoming concerns about his age to win the presidency, 68-year-old William Henry Harrison used his inauguration on March 4, 1841, to showcase his virility and prove to the nation that he was not too old for the job. He began the day by forgoing the customary carriage ride and instead rode to the inauguration on horseback. Stripping off his jacket and standing out in the blustery cold, Harrison delivered the longest inaugural address in history, clocking in at an impressive 104 minutes.

Harrison began to feel ill shortly afterward, but forged ahead and immersed himself in his new responsibilities. On March 26, day 22 in office, Harrison complained of anxiety and fatigue and was examined by Dr. Thomas Miller, the White

House physician who had served since Martin Van Buren. Miller made no diagnosis that day, and Harrison's condition was not debilitating enough to prevent him from working.[1] The next day, the president began his day with a morning walk through the market, where it was noted he had "an elastic step and bright eye of manhood."[2] However, later in the day he was struck with a dangerously high fever and severe chills. The next day, Dr. Miller diagnosed him with "pneumonia, with congestion of the liver and derangement of the stomach and bowels."[3] Due to Harrison's age, Miller decided to forgo the panacea of the era, bloodletting, and treated him with enemas and "cupping," or creating a blister by placing a hot cup on his skin to draw out the disease.[4] Miller also prescribed laudanum, castor oil, opium, and a cocktail of camphor, wine, and brandy. Not surprisingly, some medical historians have blamed Miller's treatment for Harrison's ultimate fate.

On Saturday, April 3 at 1:00 p.m., Harrison was visited by consulting physician Dr. Ashton Alexander from Baltimore. He announced that the president was recovering, sending a short-lived surge of optimism through the city. Two hours later, the president suffered a bout of diarrhea and took an "alarming" turn. An hour after that, his doctors began talking about the unspeakable: that Harrison might die. By 5:00 p.m., the president was delirious and incoherent as violent bouts of diarrhea sapped his remaining strength. His cabinet was summoned to his bedside an hour later, except for Vice President John Tyler, who was not in Washington, DC, at the time. The hour-by-hour progress report prepared the nation for the inevitable. The 6:00 p.m. report was grim, "The symptoms all worse. His physicians give him up."[5]

Under the care of Dr. N. W. Worthington, the next few hours were a downward spiral as Harrison's skin grew cold and clammy and his vital signs faded. At 8:45 p.m., Harrison spoke, in a surprisingly strong voice, "Sir, I wish you to understand the true principles of the government. I wish them carried out. I ask nothing more." These were his last words, but who he was directing them to is unknown—perhaps in his delirium, his statement was to the absent Tyler. By 10:00 p.m., Harrison's state was reported as "insensible, feeble indeed and no one now indulges in hope." Harrison was blessed with the sacrament of last rites by Reverend William Hawley from St. John's Episcopal Church. At 12:30 a.m., on Sunday, April 4, 1841, his 31st day in office, William Henry Harrison died in the second-floor bedroom of the White House without a struggle. Reverend Hawley gently closed his eyes.

Funeral directors dressed and shaved the corpse and placed it in a cedar-lined coffin, covered with black velvet and silver lace. John Quincy Adams came to the White House to pay his respects and was dismayed to find the coffin in a hall, unattended and unguarded.[6] Yet Harrison's

Currier & Ives lithograph, *Death of Harrison, April 4 A.D. 1841*. (Library of Congress)

The public vault in Congressional Cemetery, Washington, DC, where William Henry Harrison's body rested temporarily. Later, it would also house the remains of John Quincy Adams and Zachary Taylor.

funeral was a watershed event, with the theatrics and public display that set the precedent for modern-day state funerals, for Harrison was the first president to die in office and the first to die in Washington, DC.

At sunrise on April 7, several military outposts in the vicinity fired cannons to usher in the solemn day.[7] Crowds flocked into the city by rail and steamboat, businesses closed, and windows were draped in mourning, prompting Harrison's niece to write that every house was "festooned with black cloth, crepe or cambric."[8] The body had been removed from the original casket and now lay in a mahogany coffin covered in black velvet and gold lace on a catafalque in the center of the East Room. The scent of flowers hung in the air and Harrison's good friend, John Johnson, said he looked "calm and natural; his white hair lying close to his head and his features regular and peaceful."[9]

In attendance was the new president, John Tyler, as well as former president John Quincy Adams and future president Zachary Taylor. At 11:30 a.m., Reverend Hawley began the ser-

vice and directed attention to a Bible on a table besides the coffin, as he told mourners that Harrison had purchased it after he had arrived in Washington and began every day by reading it.[10] At noon, 30 pallbearers wearing white sashes and representing each state and territory brought the coffin outside and placed it in a funeral carriage that was pulled by six white horses (the same steeds were later used for John Quincy Adams's funeral in 1848). Harrison's beloved horse, Whitey, marched riderless in accordance with military tradition, the first time in a presidential funeral since George Washington's.[11] The procession was the largest ever witnessed in the city, with estimates ranging from 10,000 to 40,000 participants. It included military and patriotic organizations, among which the Potomac Dragoons, Eagle Artillerists, a group called "the Invincibles," the "very richly attired" Society of Odd Fellows, the Washington Catholic Temperance Association, and the Typographical Society.[12]

The procession marched down Pennsylvania Avenue toward the Capitol building, in a different Washington than the congested city we know today. After reaching Capitol Square, the procession continued to the Congressional Burying Ground. Cannon fire boomed 68 times, one for each year of Harrison's life. Reverend Hawley led an Episcopal service, and the remains were then placed in the public vault. After the ceremony, armed guards were posted at the entrance to the vault, which was to be a temporary resting place until Harrison's body could be moved to a permanent grave. For the first publicly funded presidential funeral, the cost came to $3,088.09. Of that sum, $35 was for the original casket, $75 for the mahogany coffin, and $20 for preparing the body, which before the days of embalming, consisted of cleaning, shaving, and dressing the corpse.[13]

Harrison died so soon after taking office that his wife, Anna, never had time to move to the capital, and she was not there to attend the Washington funeral. Instead, she began preparations for his burial in the family cemetery on the Harrison property in North Bend, Ohio. Harrison remained in the Congressional vault for nearly three months until the weather improved and the Ohio plans were finalized. On June 26, 1841, the remains were removed from Congressional Cemetery. There was a farewell ceremony attended by Harrison's son, John Scott Harrison (President Benjamin Harrison's father), President Tyler, a committee from both houses of Congress, and a crowd of citizens. An attachment of marines oversaw the return trip to North Bend by steamship, escorted by several barges draped in black.[14]

Eleven days later, on July 7, Harrison's remains were placed in a marble sarcophagus within a newly built vault in North Bend. The vault was situated on a 100-foot-high knoll called Mount Nebo that overlooked the Ohio River near Congress Green Cemetery. Years earlier, Harrison had come to the spot daily to review progress of work being done to his farm and he chose it for his final resting place.[15]

The vault was not an elaborate design but rather had the "the plainest construction conceivable."[16] It was 20 square feet, set 5 feet underground and 2 feet above, resembling a pillbox bunker more than a vault. Made of brick, it was covered with stucco and wooden shingles and sat atop a large flat stone. To enter, one had to descend wooden steps to an iron door, above which was a blank marble slab that may have been meant to display the name "Harrison," but was never inscribed. By all accounts, this was an unmarked grave. Over the years, additional family members made use of the vault including Harrison's wife, Anna, who died in 1864. Today,

there are 24 coffins within the vault, several of which remain unmarked.[17]

Over the years, the grave was largely forgotten and deteriorated due to neglect. The Illinois Central Railroad tracks were built only several yards away, making it not only unattractive, but loud.[18] In 1871, it was said to be "covered with turf and weeds," and the wood began to rot and sink into the ground.[19] The situation became dire later that decade, when, in nearby Congress Green Cemetery, grave robbers stole Harrison's father's body. Recognizing that the family was not doing his memory justice, and fearful a similar fate might befall the ninth president, Harrison's son offered the site to the state with the condition that the tomb be maintained. The offer would remain unaccepted until 48 years later, in 1919.[20]

The site continued to succumb to the elements and lack of attention until the 1880s, when Dr. John Warner of the Forestry Association began to care for it. In 1885, his contribution was recognized when the site was described as "an unfenced mound over a family vault, formerly neglected, but more recently carefully kept."[21] Three years later, in 1888, Harrison's grandson, Benjamin Harrison, was elected the nation's 23rd president, yet having his grandson in the White House did little to ameliorate the conditions of the grave. Visitors came to the site, but, as one newspaper noted, "Not less to see the tomb than to enjoy the magnificence and beauty of nature here unfolded."[22] To remind people that a former president's grave was on this scenic hilltop, an effort was made that same year to erect a suitable memorial, and the House and Senate approved $25,000 for the project. But the bill, padded with memorials for other "illustrious dead," did not pass. Throughout the remainder of Benjamin Harrison's presidency, there appeared to be no further efforts at restoration. On July 9, 1896, now out of office, Benjamin Harrison visited his grandfather's grave for an hour and was appalled and disappointed by its "ruinous condition." He still envisioned a suitable memorial consisting of a marble tomb, big enough for all of the Harrison clan.[23] Benjamin Harrison died on March 13, 1901, never to see his vision fulfilled.

In the early years of the 20th century, there were some notable events at the grave site. On November 11, 1901, a ceremony was held to mark the 90th anniversary of the Battle of Tippecanoe, where then-governor of Indiana Territory William Henry Harrison defeated a Native American confederation led by Tecumseh.[24] On Sunday, November 16, 1902, a ceremony was planned to dedicate a flag on a 57-foot pole over the tomb that would be visible for 12 miles in all directions. However, the Harrison family objected to having the ceremony on a Sunday and the event was canceled. Three days later, bunting was hung in the early morning without any ceremony.[25]

Despite the quaint events at the site, these were not good times for the tomb. In September 1912, it was suggested that the body be moved to Fort Meigs, the War of 1812 battlefield where Harrison fought General Henry Proctor and again confronted the Shawnee leader, Tecumseh.[26] But the grave remained in North Bend,

where a startling event occurred later that year. In December 1912, George Smedley, a 16-year-old boy, was playing by the tomb with his two friends when they found the door open. They all stepped inside, but the joke was on Smedley—his two buddies ran out, shut the iron door, and braced it with a heavy stick, locking Smedley in the tomb with the dead president! For four hours, he beat on the door and screamed for help until his cries were heard by Mrs. S. Gabriel, who was walking on a nearby road.[27] The next year, another horrendous event occurred on September 18, 1913, when vandals broke into the tomb and "daubed [it] with some unsightly substance."[28]

It would take another six years before the tide began to turn. On April 1, 1919, when Horace Bonser, a member of the General Assembly of Ohio, introduced a bill to allocate $10,000 for the effort "of placing the tomb and the ground upon which the tomb of William Henry Harrison is located, in a suitable and decent condition in order that the memory of Ohio's first President and gallant soldier, William Henry Harrison, may be fittingly commemorated." The bill was promptly signed into law by Governor James Middleton Cox. The 1871 land offer from the Harrison family was finally accepted.

The William Henry Harrison Memorial Commission was formed to study the area. Two years later, on January 4, 1921, they released a report that diplomatically stated the obvious: that the current tomb "is not a fitting last resting place of so great an American." Given the desperate state of the tomb, and the other presidential historic preservation efforts that were under way in the first decades of the 20th century, such as Monticello

Harrison's tomb, 1908. (Library of Congress)

and James Monroe's death home, the time had come to properly commemorate William Henry Harrison's burial place. On October 24, 1921, groundbreaking ceremonies were held, and by the following spring landscaping was completed. Over the next two years, a 60-foot-tall Bedford limestone shaft was erected in front of the existing tomb. To accommodate a new entrance by way of the shaft, the existing doorway was sealed and the steps buried. A vestibule and a second entrance with another iron door were added. The interior was also raised, and today you can still see the line a few inches above the Harrison coffin where the old roof used to be. The next year, on December 14, 1922, a marker rich with information was erected in the tomb.[29]

THE WILLIAM HENRY HARRISON DEATH SITES

The White House

The site for the White House (originally called the Executive Mansion but formally renamed the White House by Theodore Roosevelt) was selected by George Washington in 1791. A design competition was held the following year, and the best of the nine entries was submitted by Irish architect James Hoban. The cornerstone was laid on October 13, 1792, and construction took eight years. The first president to live there was John Adams, who moved in during the last year of his term. Over the years the exterior of the edifice was embellished, but the interior went through sporadic waves of neglect and attention. Many presidents complained of the deplorable conditions upon moving in, and by the time Harry S Truman took residence in 1945, the deterioration was undeniable. When his daughter Margaret's piano began to poke through the floor, puncturing the ceiling of the State Room, immediate action was imperative. In 1949, major renovations and reinforcements began. While the three-year project completely gutted the interior of the building, many Americans were unaware of the extent of the

renovations as Truman was adamant that the exterior remain untouched. The White House has had an illustrious history, including the death of two presidents and five more whose remains have rested within.[30]

Congressional Cemetery

The original plot of land overlooking the Anacostia River that became Congressional Cemetery was four and a half acres (known as Square 1115). It was purchased on April 4, 1807 (34 years to the day before Harrison died), for $200 as a private burial ground for members of Christ Church. Five years later, Henry Ingle deeded the tract to Christ Church, establishing the "The Washington Parish Burial Ground." The name was shortened on May 30, 1849, to "Washington Cemetery." Despite these names, it has been known as the Congressional Cemetery since 1807, when Senator Uriah Tracy of Connecticut was reinterred here from Rock Creek Cemetery on July 19 of that year.[31]

During the first half of the 1800s, before the use of railroads and embalming practices, it was not always possible to transport a deceased congressman to his hometown for burial, and thus Congressional Cemetery became a popular choice. In 1817, Christ Church set aside 100 plots to be used for congressmen, and in 1823 an additional 300 plots were donated. When Congress requested Benjamin Henry Latrobe to create markers, the designer of the US Capitol created square "cenotaphs," or monuments to commemorate someone buried elsewhere, of Aquia Creek sandstone. As time and technology changed, the cemetery's use by congressmen dwindled. The founding of Arlington National Cemetery after the Civil War was one blow, but perhaps the final one came when Senator George Frisbie Hoar of Massachusetts commented about Latrobe's cenotaphs that the thought of being buried under "one of these atrocities added a new terror to death." The practice of erecting the monuments in honor of congressmen buried elsewhere was officially ended by an Act of Congress on May 23, 1876.[32]

The public receiving vault was built in 1835 for $5,000, which was provided by the government. It was designed in the Early Republic style, constructed of marble, earth, and brick with an iron door with the words "Public Vault" punched out of it. Over the years more than 6,000 people have made a temporary use of the vault, including William Henry Harrison, John Quincy Adams, and Zachary Taylor. The remains of first ladies Louisa Adams and Dolley Madison also spent time there. In 2005 the historic vault underwent $35,000 of repairs.

No longer a burial location for congressmen or a purgatory for presidents, the cemetery waned in significance in the latter half of the 20th century. Despite being added to National Register of Historic Places (#69000292) on June 23, 1969, it had fallen into disrepair, and by the 1970s monuments and vaults were crumbling away. Christ Church could no longer afford to pay for the maintenance. The church tried to turn the property over to the National Park Service but after determining it would take $10 million to restore, the federal government declined. In 1976, a group of citizens banded together to form the Association for the Preservation of Historic Congressional Cemetery (HCC) and took over managing the property. Yet the cemetery was another victim of the times, becoming more popular with prostitutes and drug dealers than mourners visiting the departed. Graves were desecrated and urns and sculptures stolen; it was discovered that "self-styled satanic worshippers broke into burial vaults to steal remains!"[33] Yet HCC valiantly fought to preserve the historic grounds. By day its members would walk the grounds with dogs, cleaning up the hypodermic needles that littered the ground from the night's depraved activities. These civic-minded dog walkers grew in numbers, and their plight gained national attention in 1997, when the National Trust for Historic Preservation listed Congressional Cemetery on its annual list of "11 Most Endangered Historic Places." That summer, members of all forces of the military descended on the grounds with lawnmowers and sickles, and a group of patriotic Marines rescued 1,000 tombstones that had sunk into the ground. This started an annual tradition, and thanks to these efforts, the cemetery has returned to its former glory.

Today the site encompasses 35 acres and contains the remains of 67,000 people, including famous Americans like Civil War photographer Matthew Brady; Elbridge Thomas Gerry, James Monroe's vice president and a signer of the Declaration of Independence; Thomas P. "Tip" O'Neill; and J. Edgar Hoover.

Congressional Cemetery is located at 1801 E Street Southeast, Washington, DC, 20003. For more information, visit: www.Congressional Cemetery.org.

The Tomb

I visited the tomb in the summer of 2013 and was the only visitor, which is not unusual for a presidential grave. Walking down the entrance path, I met Bev Meyer, one of the founders of the Harrison-Symmes Memorial Foundation, who asked if I would like to see the inside of the tomb. For me, this was like hitting the lottery! Standing inside the claustrophobic tomb, I first could not take my mind off George Smedley and his experience. To the right of the entrance was the president's vault and to the left, a large American flag covered much of the crypt wall.

Care for the tomb was sporadic through much of the 20th century. The state began efforts to relinquish ownership in 1934, and management was eventually transferred to the Ohio Historical Society (OHS). The OHS quickly discovered that managing this site was a challenge when in early June of that year, Clifford Martin, a 30-year-old resident of North Bend,

Inside Harrison's tomb.

one ascends to the tomb. Atop each pillar is a bronze eagle, wings spread; the eagles' heads are turned toward each other. The left pillar is inscribed with text from the original 1922 marker: THAT THE MEMORY OF OHIO'S FIRST PRESIDENT AND GALLANT SOLDIER, WILLIAM HENRY HARRISON, MAY BE FITTINGLY COMMEMORATED. The inscription on the undated pillar concludes: THIS MEMORIAL IS ERECTED BY A GRATEFUL STATE. The pillar to the right lists Harrison's lifetime accomplishments.

Bev, along with eight other civic-minded people, formed the Harrison-Symmes Memorial Foundation in 1990. It took six years for the group to become a 501(c) organization and obtain funding, but during that time the members rolled up their sleeves and went to work. They got people to assist, including probationers who helped with landscaping and restoring the tomb (for every day of service they do, they get two days removed from their sentence). The foundation's "citizen lobbying" paid off when, in 1996, the general assembly of Ohio allocated $640,000 for the site.

broke into the tomb and stole tools.[34] Throughout the 1950s, a caretaker did the best he could to maintain the tomb. On November 10, 1970, the site was added to the National Register of Historic Places (#70000499). Throughout the years there have been ceremonies on Harrison's birthday, but for a little-known 31-day president born in the middle of winter, crowds are often sparse.[35] On February 9, 1976, 40 people were in attendance and President Ford sent a wreath. Sixteen years later, about 50 people gathered at the grave to dedicate a three-and-a-half-foot gray granite cylinder that had been donated by the Monument Builders of Ohio. The inscription contains a quote from his inaugural speech: AS LONG AS THE LOVE OF POWER IS A DOMINANT PASSION OF THE HUMAN BOSOM, AND AS LONG AS THE UNDERSTANDINGS OF MEN CAN BE WARPED AND THEIR AFFECTIONS CHANGED BY OPERATIONS UPON THEIR PASSIONS AND PREJUDICES, SO LONG WILL THE LIBERTIES OF A PEOPLE DEPEND ON THEIR OWN CONSTANT ATTENTION TO ITS PRESERVATION. In May 1997, a crowd of 100 people came out for a rededication ceremony at the tomb.[36]

Two identical pillars stand at the base of the steps, making an impressive entrance before

The grounds are open all year and starting each March, the dedicated members of the Harrison-Symmes Memorial Foundation stop by every morning to open the front door, which allows visitors to view the tomb through the iron gate. During peak time, about 20 visitors a day will stop by and sign the guest book. The most visitors come from (in order) Ohio, Indiana, Kentucky, California, and Texas, and the farthest a visitor has come is from Moscow. Every so often, someone claims to be a direct descendent of President Harrison, which is possible, as he had 10 children. The Harrison-Symmes Memorial Foundation members will

Harrison's tomb today.

close up the tomb for the season, when, as Bev told me, they have the first full week when no signatures appear on the guest register, usually in December.

The William Henry Harrison Tomb is located at 2 Cliff Road, North Bend, Ohio, 45052. For more information, visit: www.OhioHistory.org/visit/museum-and-site-locator/william-henry-harrison-tomb.

THE SEVENTH PRESIDENT
Andrew Jackson ★ *1829–1837*

CRITICAL DEATH INFORMATION:

Date of death:	June 8, 1845, 6:00 p.m.
Cause of death:	Originally believed to be heart failure, later proven to be kidney failure
Age at death:	78 years, 85 days
Last words:	"What is the matter with my dear children, have I alarmed you? Oh, do not cry—be good children and we will all meet in heaven."
Place of death:	The Hermitage, Nashville, Tennessee
Funeral:	The Hermitage, Nashville, Tennessee
Final resting place:	The Hermitage, Nashville, Tennessee
Reinterred:	No
Cost to visit grave:	$18.00
For more information:	www.TheHermitage.com
Significance:	Last president whose death, funeral, and burial all occurred on his family estate

After two terms as president, Andrew Jackson returned to his beloved Nashville estate, the Hermitage, in 1837. By the spring of 1845, Jackson was suffering from lung disease, dropsy (fluid in his chest and limbs), and diarrhea, but his primary affliction was plain old age.[1] As he approached his 78th birthday, the question of where Jackson would be buried became a topic of morbid curiosity. Jackson received an odd offer from Commodore Jesse D. Elliot to use a sarcophagus Elliot had brought to America six years earlier that was once the "repository of the roman emperor, Alexander Saverus, procured at Bayroot, in Syria." Jackson was flattered, but the flourish of pomp and royalty was not his style, and he politely responded in a letter dated March 27: "The whole proceedings call for my most grateful thanks, which are hereby tendered to you, and through you to the president and directors of the National Institute. But with warmest sensations that can inspire a grateful heart, I must decline accepting the honor intended to be bestowed. I cannot consent that my mortal body shall be laid in a repository prepared for an emperor or a king. My republican feelings and principles forbid it; the simplicity of our system of government forbids it."[2]

As it was difficult for him to climb stairs, Jackson was confined to the first floor of the Hermitage, where he spent most of his time in his bedroom to the right of the entrance. However, he was not yet ready to die, as the *St. Joseph Gazette* reported: "Several times of late, the flickering light of life seemed upon the point of going out, but by timely aid and skillful medical attendance it was temporarily revived."[3] On May 20, Jackson sat for a portrait for the last time with artist George P. A. Healy. Healy painted a sad, droopy-faced elder with a full shock of white hair, a far cry from the normal depiction of Jackson as a virile man often on horseback.

On June 2, doctors operated to drain fluid from his body. Each night, Jackson would bid farewell to his family members in anticipation that he might not wake. On June 5, he dictated instructions for his funeral, requesting no spectacle; despite the enormous pride he took in his title of general, he did not want a military funeral. He requested that Reverend John Todd Edgar, pastor of the First Presbyterian Church, officiate. For his burial, his will was explicit: "My desire is, that my body be buried by the side of my dear departed wife, in the garden at the Hermitage, in the vault prepared in the garden."[4]

The next night Jackson wrote his last letter, a long note to his fellow Nashville resident and protégé, President James K. Polk, on the subject of foreign relations with the Republic of Texas.[5] The following day, Jackson received a letter from Colonel Thomas Marshall from Kentucky inquiring about his health. Too weak to write, he dictated a response for his son, but signed the letter himself—his last signature.

On Sunday, June 8, family physician Dr. John N. Esselman was called to the home. He found Jackson in the downstairs front bedroom and recorded his final hours, which appeared in newspapers 11 days later under the title "The Last Moments of Gen. Jackson." Upon arriving, Esselman could see that death was mere hours away, but the feisty Jackson had one more surprise up his sleeve. As he sat in his armchair surrounded by his family and slaves, he suddenly went limp. It appeared that his suffering had finally come to an end and Esselman solemnly pronounced that Andrew Jackson was dead. Suddenly, to their amazement, Jackson opened his eyes! His time was soon, but he had only fainted and was not dead yet.[6] The stunned doctor moved Jackson to his bed. Surprisingly verbose and eloquent for the circumstances, Jackson reportedly told his death watchers, "My dear children, do not grieve me; it is true, I am going to leave you; I am well aware of my situation, I have suffered much bodily pain; but my sufferings are as nothing compared with that which our blessed Savior endured upon the cross, that we might all be saved who put their trust in him." He had no illusions that he would survive much longer, but had a strong faith in God that he was going to a better place.[7] As with many of his era, Jackson was a paradox: an unrepentant slaveholder (amassing approximately 150 by the time of his death) and, as president, responsible for the ruthless treatment of American Indians, culminating in the infamous Trail of Tears; but he was also a man of strong Christian faith, who often quoted Scripture and spoke of his belief that he would soon meet the Lord and be with his wife Rachel again in Heaven. In his final weeks, Jackson often spoke as if he welcomed death.[8]

After his revival, Jackson bid farewell to individual family members. First, he thanked his daughter-in-law Sarah for her kindness and care during his illness; then Marion Adams, his sister-in-law, for caring for him over the past months. Next, his adopted son Andrew, whom he instructed that, while in the future he might need to sell the Hermitage, his dying request was that his and his wife's graves remain on the grounds "until the final day of judgment, when our Lord and master will call for us."[9] Jackson's grandchildren next approached. Jackson kissed each of them and then listed several mandates to follow: be obedient, go to church each Sunday, and read the New Testament. With two grandsons at Sunday school, Jackson asked that they be sent for so he could bid them farewell. His son took his father's hand and tenderly asked, "How do you feel? Do you know me?" Jackson replied, "Know you, yes, I would know you all, if I could but see! Bring my spectacles." Jackson shook hands with his slaves and mustered the fortitude to "deliver one of the most impressive lectures on the subject of religion that Esselman ever heard." Jackson spoke for almost 30 minutes "with strength and indeed, with animation!"

He concluded with the words, "My dear children, and friends and servants, I hope and trust to meet you all in heaven, both white and black," before repeating, "Both white and black."[10] And in what must have seemed more like the grand finale of an amazing show rather than a death watch, Jackson spoke his last recorded words to his saddened and rapt audience: "What is the matter with my dear children, have I alarmed you? Oh, do not cry—be good children and we will all meet in heaven." He then fell asleep at about 4:00 p.m. The *St. Joseph Gazette* reported, "It became apparent that the skill of the physicians was exhausted, and the demands of the grim monster could no longer be resisted."[11] At 6:00 p.m. on June 8, 1845, death finally took Andrew Jackson.

Arriving at the Hermitage an hour too late was the two-time president of the Republic of Texas, Sam Houston, who had left his home in Huntsville, Texas, in May in an attempt to see his good friend and longtime supporter before he died. The next day, invitations were hastily sent out for Jackson's funeral at the Hermitage, to be held on Tuesday, June 10 at 11:00 a.m. Jackson's body lay in repose in the hall at the front entrance. A crowd of 3,000 citizens gathered that morning, but it was estimated that five times as many would have attended if it were held a day later. Due to the Tennessee summer heat, the body could not remain unburied any longer. His 70 or 80 slaves had "tears rolling down their dark faces"; perhaps some tears were shed from sadness, but most certainly many more were due to their anxiety over their now-uncertain future.[12] Businesses in Nashville closed, church bells tolled, and guns were fired.

The funeral service was held

Currier & Ives lithograph, *Death of Genl. Andrew Jackson: President of the United States from 1829 to 1837.* (Library of Congress)

on the front porch as the crowd stood on the lawn. All guests were respectful during the solemn ceremony—except one attendee who was eventually evicted. This guest was a parrot, one that Jackson had trained in the art of foul language. Before the service, the bird's cursing was politely ignored, but once it began, the shrieking and swearing could no longer be tolerated. Jackson was always amused by the parrot's colorful vocabulary and especially enjoyed when its cursing filled awkward silences while guests were visiting. As Reverend William Menefee Norment later recollected, Jackson's slaves did not see the humor as they "rolled their eyes fearfully and declared it was an ill omen." Finally, a slave expelled the bird, carrying him far from the home and out of earshot.[13] After the feathered miscreant was removed, Reverend Edgar continued the service. He read from Revelation 7:13–14. (Perhaps Revelation 18:2 would have been more appropriate, lamenting that Babylon has become "a prison of every unclean and hateful bird!")

After the service, pallbearers carried the coffin to the grave site. General W. G. Harding commanded the Nashville Blues, a volunteer militia group from Tennessee, to fire volleys over the grave as a final military salute to end the ceremony.[14]

The inscription on Jackson's tomb had been written by Jackson himself.[15] Despite being president for eight years, he authored a simple inscription that only identified himself as "General":

GENERAL ANDREW JACKSON
BORN MARCH 15, 1767
DIED JUNE 8, 1845

Not all were heartbroken. After hearing of Jackson's death, former political rival John Quincy Adams was asked for comment. His impromptu eulogy began respectfully enough: "Jackson was a hero," but Adams then took a sharp detour off the high road when he added that the deceased was also "a murderer, an adulterer [who] in his last days of his life belied and slandered me before the world and died."[16]

As early as 1860, there were discussions to move Jackson's remains to the grounds of the state capitol, plans that were against his explicit deathbed wishes. The state senate passed a bill for the relocations, but after Jackson Jr. appealed to the governor, the idea was abandoned. Yet, at the Hermitage, the memorial was not getting the care it deserved, and within a decade it was "neglected and slowly going to decay."[17]

In July 1894, the situation hit rock bottom when a grave robber attempted to steal Jackson's body. It was discovered that a three-foot-deep hole had been dug near Jackson's head, and the miscreant had tried to use a long plank to pry out the coffin. Armed with just a shovel and a plank, he probably would not have been able to penetrate the stone masonry even if he had worked for several more hours. According to the *Baltimore Herald*, "suspicion rests upon a well-dressed negro [who] went to the residence of a white man living half a mile from the Hermitage yesterday afternoon and borrowed a shovel, which he returned this morning."[18] Two years later, an Italian man, Carabonne Torriani, confessed to the dastardly deed on his deathbed, claiming to have worked at the behest of "a wealthy physician who had a mania for studying the skeletons of noted people." Perhaps his confession should be taken with a grain of salt as it was made while Torriani was a patient at New York's Bellevue Hospital.[19]

Throughout the years, several presidents have visited Jackson's grave. On October 22, 1907, Theodore Roosevelt visited the Hermitage after first stopping at the nearby grave of James K. Polk. Andrew Jackson's granddaughter, Rachel Jackson Lawrence, gave him a tour of the home. Sometime during his visit, Roosevelt was handed a cup of coffee brewed at a local Nashville hotel. The president emptied the mug and declared, "This is the kind of stuff I

President Theodore Roosevelt at the tomb of Andrew Jackson on October 22, 1907. (Library of Congress)

like to drink, by George, when I hunt bears!" While that statement was recorded in the local newspapers, it was another unverified declaration credited to Roosevelt that made history, when he also proclaimed that it was "Good to the last drop!" The hotel was Maxwell House, and Roosevelt's alleged endorsement became their motto that is still used to this day.[20] After his tour, Roosevelt walked to the tomb, where he spoke in favor of federal funding to preserve the estate: "I know the objection will be made that if we begin to take care of this house we shall be expected to take care of the houses of all the presidents. I draw a sharp distinction between Old Hickory and a great many Presidents. The Hermitage should be cared for by the nation in the same spirit that we now care for Mount Vernon. Of course Mount Vernon stands absolutely unique among all places, but The Hermitage represents the home of one of the three or four greatest presidents this nation has ever had; of one of the three or four greatest public men that any nation has developed in the same length of time."[21] Roosevelt was a man of his word, and the following year, $5,000 was allocated by Congress toward the upkeep of the home.

Twenty-seven years later, on November 17,

1934, President Franklin Roosevelt and his wife, Eleanor, paid their respects, also stopping at Polk's grave prior to their visit. Before becoming president, Harry S Truman visited the Hermitage in the 1930s when he was serving as a Jackson County judge. He had commissioned an equestrian statue of Andrew Jackson, his hero, and visited to get measurements to ensure the sculpture was historically accurate (today it is located in front of the Jackson County Courthouse in Independence, Missouri).[22]

President Lyndon Johnson visited on the 200th anniversary of Jackson's birth on March 15, 1967, and spoke warmly of the seventh president, saying he "triumphed in his time."[23] On March 15, 1982, Ronald Reagan visited the Hermitage for President Jackson's 215th birthday and laid a wreath at the grave.[24] Two weeks earlier, a team had been sent to the Hermitage to check out the grounds and ensure Reagan's safety. Arriving at night, they found the gates locked, leading a Secret Service agent and a member of the advance team to hop the fence, where they were promptly greeted by a guard with his gun drawn. Luckily, the confusion was cleared up before any shots were fired, but the duo was warned: "Down here in Tennessee they shoot first and ask questions later!"[25]

At the time of his death, given Jackson's advanced age and litany of ailments, heart failure was accepted as the cause. However, historians would later speculate about what truly ended his life. Some believed that Jackson had died a slow death from mercury and lead poisoning from two bullets that remained lodged in his body. Others believed he died from medicine that he had taken for his intestinal problems. In 1999, researchers analyzed two strands of Jackson's hair taken at different points of his life. While they did find that the mercury and lead levels in Jackson's body were higher than normal, the amounts were not fatal. From their analysis, they determined that Jackson actually died of kidney failure.[26]

THE ANDREW JACKSON DEATH SITES

Andrew Jackson is the last of the "one-stop-shopping" for death-site travelers: his death, funeral, and burial all occurred on the grounds of his Hermitage estate. The land was first owned by Nathaniel Hays, dating back to 1780. In 1800, Hays built a two-story log cabin home on the grounds. Jackson bought 425 acres on July 5, 1804, for $3,400 and, being no stranger to log cabins (he was the first president born in one), he moved into the home. He originally dubbed his new estate his "rural retreat" but later changed its moniker to "The Hermitage." Using money made during a three-year cotton boom, Jackson built a two-story Federal-style brick mansion in 1819.[27] It was finished in 1821 but little resembles what stands there today. In 1829, when Jackson became president, his adopted son, Andrew Jr., cared for the home. Two years later it was renovated, with the addition of a second-story colonnade, dining room, and library wing.[28] On October 13, 1834, tragedy stuck when an accidental fire engulfed the home. A Boston newspaper wrote, "The entire edifice, with the exception of a dining room was, in a few hours consumed. . . . The fire is supposed to have communicated to the roof by the falling of a spark from one of the chimnies [sic], and there being at the time a light breeze, the progress of the flames proportionably [sic] rapid."[29] The upstairs was destroyed and most of the first floor badly damaged, but the walls and frame remained intact. Jackson hired master builders Joseph Reiff and William Hume to rebuild, and they added the Greek revival columns that give the home its White House appearance. During the eight years Jackson was president, he visited the Hermitage only four times, as it was an 18-day journey there from Washington, DC. After leaving office, Jackson returned to live at the Hermitage. His famous visitors included James Monroe, Martin Van Buren (in 1842), James K. Polk, Franklin Pierce, and Aaron Burr.[30]

After his death in 1845, the home passed to his adopted son, Andrew Jr., who was a poor businessman and deep in debt. By the 1850s, he was forced to sell off parcels of the land. In 1856, he sold 500 acres, including the home and family tomb, for $48,000 to the state of Tennessee and departed for the Gulf Coast. The state attempted to put the home to public use, but plans did not materialize. By 1860, Andrew Jr. had again fallen on hard times. Back in Nashville, he was permitted to rent the home and live there as a tenant. During these years, several uses for the Hermitage were mooted, including turning it into the governor's mansion and a state-run military school. The idea of preserving it was also proposed by Governor Isham Harris in 1860, but the impending Civil War stalled the idea. During the war, the Hermitage was often visited by both Confederate and Union troops, who paid their respects at Jackson's grave. Even though Andrew Jr. supported the South, a Union commander made sure no harm would come to the home. Despite this protection, one of his troops noted in a letter to his family that, "through neglect, [the home has] pretty well run to weeds."[31]

After the war, the only action taken to halt the decay was in 1865, when Governor William G. Brownlow had repairs made to the tomb. That same year, Andrew Jr.'s life came to an abrupt end when he shot himself in a hunting accident on the grounds of the Hermitage. After his death, his wife, Sarah Yorke Jackson, and her sister, Marion Yorke Adams, remained in the old home.[32] However, the two women weren't able to care for it adequately, and the Hermitage suffered its worst period of decay and neglect, most notably in the upper floor and dining room. In 1871, a bill was introduced in the Tennessee legislature to sell the Hermitage, but a public outcry ensued, both for the preservation of the historic home and for the treatment of Jackson's daughter-in-law. Demands that the widow be left undisturbed were accompanied by cries that it would be abhorrent to "place the tomb of

Andrew Jackson . . . in the possession of strangers" and that "if the state needs money it does not need to take it to that extent; for no money could atone for such heartlessness."[33]

In the end, the state held on to the property and continued to dole out small amounts for maintenance, while noting it needed much more work. On March 8, 1883, the General Assembly appropriated $350 to repair the tomb and put an iron fence around it.[34]

After Sarah's death in 1888, the state proposed to convert the Hermitage into a hospital for Tennessee's Confederate veterans. Similar to those that saved Mount Vernon, wealthy Nashville women chartered the Ladies' Hermitage Association, led by Andrew Jackson's granddaughter-in-law, Rachel Jackson Lawrence, on February 19, 1889.[35] On April 5, 1889, the Tennessee State Legislature passed Bill No. 461, officially turning over control of the home and 25 surrounding acres to the association. Three months later the women opened the home to the public for the first time. On that first day a tour cost 50¢, and the home has remained open for tours ever since. Even before it was under the auspices

of the Ladies' Hermitage Association, people frequently stopped by to see the home. Since Jackson death, the unofficial tour guide was Alfred Jackson, a former slave of the seventh president. In 1886, when a reporter from the *Chicago Tribune* visited, Alfred gave him the tour and described the funeral. Quoted here verbatim, the vernacular and spelling were insulting at best and racist and demeaning at worst. However, the description vividly describes the scene and sentiment of that day: "It war a great funeral. All de military companies was yere from Nashville and de garden was full of people. De sojers fired dere guns, company after company, de people bowed dere heads, we colored chillum stood aroun' cryin', and it was a drefful moment. De Gin'l was lowered right down under dat slab. He had bricked up de grave long befo' he died, and he said dere must be no dirt throwed on him. De coffin had a think glass top and he left orders dat it must be put in the bricked-up grave and covered with a plank only, and then dat slab put on top."[36] The Ladies' Hermitage Association hired Alfred as the official tour guide. He was devoted to carrying on the memory of

The Hermitage, the home where Jackson died on June 8, 1845.

Jackson. After the grave robbery attempt, he even offered to sleep at the grave site to guard it from further intrusion.[37] He died 56 years after Jackson in 1901 and is buried in the family cemetery. His tombstone bears the simple inscription, "Uncle Alfred."

In the 1930s, in the midst of the Great Depression, the Works Progress Administration (WPA) allocated $70,000 to restore the Hermitage. The work included funding for an entrance road and additional buildings to be used as a gift shop and museum. In December 1966 it was listed as a National Historic Landmark (#6600072), and 11 years later it was added to the National Register of Historic Places. Today, much of the furniture is original from when the president lived there, including the bed he died on. These pieces were obtained from Andrew Jackson III, who charged the Ladies' Hermitage Association a hefty sum for them.

The Hermitage is located at 4580 Rachel's Lane, Nashville, Tennessee, 37067. It is open from mid-October to mid-March (except Thanksgiving and Christmas) from 9:00 a.m. to 4:00 p.m., and from mid-March to mid-October 8:30 a.m. to 5:00 p.m. For more information, visit: www.TheHermitage.com.

The Tomb

Rachel Jackson died on December 22, 1828, the year Andrew Jackson won the presidency. That election was a particularly nasty one and included a rumor that Jackson had married Rachel before she had finalized her divorce from her first husband, Lewis Robards. The scandal took its toll on Rachel, and Jackson believed that it contributed to her death. After she died, she was placed in a simple tomb, which cost the president $55. He covered it with a stark wooden temporary shelter that was completed on January 17, 1829. In 1831, Jackson paid Nashville architect David Morrison $1,000 to build a "temple & monument" for Rachel, and eventually for Jackson too.[38] Jackson's inspiration for the memorial came from a scene depicted from Homer's *Odyssey* from, of all places, their wallpaper. Today, this original wallpaper (which Jackson had ordered from Paris) still hangs in the downstairs hall at the Hermitage, and the scene can be seen between the staircase and the entrance to the right wing of the home. To carry out Jackson's vision, Morrison paid $400 to stonemason Thomas Harrison, who used Tennessee limestone to construct the memorial.[39] It is 18 feet across, the domed copper roof is supported by eight fluted Greek Doric columns, and in the center is a pyramid. Jackson was eager for the tomb to be finished, and while he was in Washington, DC, he placed his son, Andrew Jr., in charge. On May 13, 1832, he urged him to do his best to have the project completed, writing "I pray you hasten the completion of the monument over my wifes [sic] Grave."[40] The tomb was completed later that same year. Jackson also wrote the epitaph inscribed on her grave, which

Jackson's tomb, modeled after an image on his wallpaper.

expresses his heartfelt adoration for her. When he was at the Hermitage, he visited her grave every night.

Maintenance has been done over the years, starting in 1862 with minor structural repairs through 1998 when a fence was repaired after being damaged in a tornado. In the bicentennial year 1976, major renovations and repairs were undertaken.

A marker that cited Jackson's Revolutionary War service was erected by the Old Glory Chapter of the Daughters of the American Revolution on a bitter cold March 15, 1916. At the tender age of 14, Jackson was captured by British soldiers in the Battle of Hanging Rock near his Waxhaws birthplace in the North Carolina–South Carolina border area. When he was ordered to clean a British officer's boots, Jackson defiantly refused. The officer responded by striking the cocksure boy in the head with his sword, leaving a gash that remained with him the rest of his life.

John Quincy Adams ★ *1825–1829*

CRITICAL DEATH INFORMATION:

Date of death: February 23, 1848, 7:20 p.m.

Cause of death: Stroke

Age at death: 80 years, 277 days

Last words: "This is the end of Earth. I am composed."

Place of death: Speaker's room at the Capitol building, Washington, DC

Funeral: Capitol building, Washington, DC

Final resting place: United First Parish Church, Quincy, Massachusetts

Reinterred: Twice

Cost to visit grave: Free (donation suggested)

For more information: www.ufpc.org

Significance: First president's remains to be carried by funeral train

When John Quincy Adams took the oath of office on March 4, 1825, there were four living former presidents—the first time that occurred in American history. After serving out his single term, Adams became the first chief executive to get back into the political fray as a member of the House of Representatives. He served from 1831 for nine terms, during which he transformed from an unpopular former president to an elder statesman. In his later years, Adams generally enjoyed good health, but this abruptly changed on November 20, 1846. While walking with his friend Dr. George Parkman to visit the new Harvard Medical College, he suddenly was unable to take another step. Adams had suffered a stroke, perhaps his second but certainly his most severe. It left him partially paralyzed and bedridden for several weeks, but he recovered more quickly than expected. Returning to Washington, DC, he was greeted on the House floor with a standing ovation. Following his stroke, he stopped writing in his journal after having chronicled his life regularly for more than half a century. When he resumed writing four months later, he began with gallows humor, labeling the entry his "Posthumous Memoir," because "from that hour [of the stroke], I date my decease and consider myself, for every useful purpose to myself and fellow creatures, dead."[1]

While Adams was premature in predicting his own demise, his participation in House debates did noticeably drop off, and as 1847 drew to a close, the 80-year-old's health was in rapid decline. On Monday, February 21, 1848, he rose early in good spirits, wrote a few stanzas of poetry, a lifelong passion, and later signed two autographs. As he arrived at work that morning, his attendants noted the "cheerful step with which he ascended the steps of the capitol."[2] In the afternoon, a vote was called to commend seven generals for their service in the Mexican War. Adams, an outspoken opponent of the conflict who called it "a most unrighteous war," bellowed an emphatic "No!" when it was his turn. That declaration was his last official word spoken on the floor. Several minutes later, at approximately 1:30 p.m., he stood to address the speaker, but became flushed and collapsed, falling into the arms of Ohio representative David Fisher. Adams had suffered yet another stroke. This one was to be his last.

Someone shouted, "Mr. Adams is dying!" and in the ensuing confusion, House members pushed toward where he had collapsed. Massachusetts representative Joseph Grinnell cooled Adams's face with ice water. Several members then lifted Adams's limp body and placed him on the floor before the clerk's table in the front of the room, as Speaker Robert Charles Winthrop officially adjourned the session. A sofa was brought in, and Adams was gently placed onto it and carried to the hall of the rotunda. The sofa was placed near a window, but it was cold and drafty and Adams was moved again, this time into the speaker's office, where the doors "were closed to all but professional gentlemen."[3]

Fifteen minutes after his stroke, a report went out over the telegraph wires that Adams "is sinking." In the speaker's room, he briefly regained consciousness and a 2:00 p.m. update offered a glimmer of hope, saying "he shows signs of life." He was attended to by fellow House members and the physicians William A. Newell, George Fries, Thomas O. Edwards, John W. Jones, and Frederick W. Lord. Two more doctors were also summoned. Almost 50 years after the death of our first president, there had been little advancement beyond the primitive medical practices

Currier & Ives lithograph, *Death of John Quincy Adams at the U.S. Capitol Feby. 23d 1848.* (Library of Congress)

of George Washington's day. The doctors tried bleeding Adams in addition to leeching, cupping, and applying mustard plasters. In a moment of lucidity, he called for his wife, Louisa, who had arrived earlier with his niece and nephew. Adams tried to thank the representatives for their care before uttering his final serene words of resignation, "This is the end of Earth. I am composed."

The House did not go back into session until the next day, when they briefly reconvened and ceremoniously adjourned the session out of respect for Adams. With no work to do, congressmen gathered in groups, some occasionally popping into the speaker's room for an update. Many said that this was the way Adams would have wanted to go, dying on the House floor, and I believe their sentiment was accurate. Adams lay unconscious all day Monday and Tuesday, February 22. A reporter hedged his bets when he mused, "He may survive the night; but, on the other hand, may expire at any moment with little previous warning."[4] Finally, at 7:15 p.m. on Wednesday, February 23, 1848, John Quincy Adams died.

Much of the nation learned of Adams's death almost immediately when messages were sent over telegraph wires, making him the first president whose death was announced through the new medium. Speaker Winthrop praised Adams, saying, "After a life of 80 years, devoted from its earliest maturity to the public service, he has at length gone to his rest. He has been privileged to die at his post; to fall while in the discharge of his duties; to expire beneath the roof of the capitol." He continued, "To have his last scene associated forever, in history, with the birthday of that illustrious patriot, whose just discernment brought him first into the service of his country,"[5] noting the correlation of his death with George Washington's birthday.

A committee was formed to plan the funeral, comprised of 30 members, one person for each state and territory, including "Mr. Lincoln of Illinois." Adams's remains were placed in a coffin made by Mr. Lee and Mr. Espy. It was covered with black velvet with silver lace ornamentation, and the silver breastplate, written by Daniel Webster and manufactured by Mr. S. Masi, read:

JOHN QUINCY ADAMS
BORN AN INHABITANT OF MASSACHUSETTS,
JULY 11, 1767
DIED A CITIZEN OF THE UNITED STATES,
IN THE CAPITOL OF WASHINGTON,
FEBRUARY 23, 1848
HAVING SERVED HIS COUNTRY FOR
HALF A CENTURY,
AND ENJOYED ITS HIGHEST HONORS

For two days Adams lay in repose in the Capitol while thousands shuffled past to pay their last respects. On Saturday, February 26, funeral services were held in the House chamber at noon. The room was draped in black, including Adams's empty chair. With all members of the House and Senate, justices of the Supreme Court, and President James K. Polk present, the scene resembled a modern-day State of the Union address. The chaplain of the House, Reverend Ralph Randolph Gurley, read from the Book of Job and was noted to have "conducted [the service] with great decorum and dignity."[6]

Chief Marshal Joseph H. Bradley led a mile-long funeral procession of about 15,000 people. In the front was the military band, followed by the chaplains of the House and Senate, the physicians who attended Adams, and members of the committee of arrangements. They were followed by the funeral hearse, built and driven by J. F. Harvey. The coffin lay beneath a black velvet canopy covered by an eagle with its wings spread, and was pulled by white horses (seven years earlier, the same steeds had also pulled the hearse of William Henry Harrison).[7] Flanking the elaborate hearse were 12 pallbearers, all wearing white scarves, including John C. Calhoun, vice president to both Adams and Andrew Jackson. Next were members of Adams's family, representatives from the House and Senate, and President Polk, followed by various organizations, some widely known such as the Free Masons and the Odd Fellows and others more obscure, like the Columbian Typographical Society. The hearse arrived at Congressional Cemetery, and the coffin was placed in the public receiving vault, the same structure that had held Harrison's remains almost seven years earlier.

As with Harrison, this was a temporary stop, and the House of Representatives appointed a second 30-member committee to return President Adams to Quincy, Massachusetts, for a proper burial. On March 5, a small delegation of family and colleagues attended a ceremony at the vault. The remains were then carried to the Washington train station to be transported by steam train in the first presidential funeral train in history.[8] This would have delighted Adams, who was amazed by the speed at which a train could carry him back home from Washington, DC. The train was covered in black for the 500 mile journey to Massachusetts and along the way, citizens demonstrated their respect and reverence in ways that would be repeated over many decades. In locations along the way, through Baltimore, Philadelphia, New York City, and beyond, businesses closed when the train passed, flags were flown at half-mast, bells tolled, and guns fired. Crowds gathered along the route to hold civil and military demonstrations.

After five days, the train arrived at the Worchester depot on March 10. Despite a heavy rain that kept family members at home, a large crowd of military and civilians welcomed the train. The body was removed and placed on a newly built funeral caisson pulled by six black horses and adorned with plumes. It passed large crowds as it rode down Lincoln Street to Summer, Washington, Boylston, Tremont, Park, and Beacon, back to Tremont, to Court, State, Commercial, and South Market Street. At Faneuil Hall, the body was received by the Committee of Massachu-

setts Legislature, as bands played a solemn dirge. The coffin was placed on the speaker's platform in the black-draped room. Chairman Joseph T. Buckingham made a speech to officially transfer the remains to Boston mayor Josiah Quincy Jr.: "We place these sacred remains in your possession, to be conveyed to their appointed home to sleep in the sepulchre and with the dust of his fathers."[9] Quincy Jr. then spoke before the public viewing began.

The next day, the remains were carried to the Boston Old Colony Railroad depot and a train slowly rode to the Quincy station as a salvo was fired from President's Hill. The remains were brought to the Peacefield mansion where his father John Adams had died 22 years earlier. There a procession escorted the remains to the United First Parish Church, with John L. Dimmock serving as chief marshal. Leading the march was a military escort followed by citizens and clergymen. Next came the hearse, where the coffin rested behind velvet curtains, flanked by pallbearers on either side and trailed by family, state politicians, and a member of Congress from each of the 30 states who had accompanied the remains from Washington, DC. At the United First Parish Church, the funeral ceremony was delivered by Reverend William P. Lunt.[10] After the service, at 5:00 p.m., the remains were carried across the street to Hancock Cemetery, enclosed in an airtight case, and placed in the family vault.

This was intended to be John Quincy Adams's final resting place, and his name was carved on the crypt entrance. However, Quincy's son later decided that his father should rest beside his grandfather, John Adams, in the basement of the United First Parish Church. To prepare for a reinterment, the crypt under the church was expanded and a sarcophagus was built. On the morning of December 16, 1852, the coffin was removed from the vault and carried to the basement of the church.[11] While attempting to move it into the crypt, an awkward discovery

The tomb of John Quincy Adams (with the flag on it) in the basement crypt of the United First Parish Church. Beside him lies his wife, Louisa Catherine.

was made—it was too big and would not fit! Stonemasons were quickly called in to widen the entrance. While they chiseled away, those moving the coffin could not resist a peek at the remains of the sixth president. Adam's grandson, Charles Francis Adams, was among those who noted "the sunken face of a very old man, on which a short stubbly beard had grown in death."[12]

His hearse was preserved in the church basement and enclosed in glass to "prevent relic hunters from dismantling it." This was necessary after someone cut off some of the draperies.[13] On November 17, 1927, the Abigail Phillips Quincy Chapter of the Daughters of the American Revolution placed a marble plaque at the entrance to the tomb. It was presented by the regent of the chapter, Mrs. James L. Kerr, to the Reverend Fred Albau Well, pastor of the United First Parish Church.[14]

THE JOHN QUINCY ADAMS DEATH SITES
Room Where He Collapsed
The room where Adams collapsed is not the room currently used by the House of Representatives for its sessions. In 1848, they convened in what is today the National Statuary Hall. At one point, the room was used as a farmer's market. In 1864, President Abraham Lincoln authorized

the creation of Statuary Hall, when he "invite[d] each and all of the States to provide and furnish statues, in marble or bronze, not exceeding two in number for each State, of deceased persons who have been citizens thereof, and illustrious for their historic renown or for distinguished civic or military services." Initial enthusiasm was tepid, and statues slowly trickled in; by the 1880s there were only about a dozen.[15] Today, the room resembles a clothing store warehouse for mannequins with figures scattered all about.

On the floor where he collapsed is a marker that reads,

JOHN QUINCY ADAMS
REPRESENTATIVE FROM MASSACHUSETTS
1831–1848 DESK LOCATION

The Room Where He Died
After his death, a plaque was placed at the spot where he died.[16] Today, the room is off limits on the Capitol tour, and while I managed to wrangle my way to the Washington Crypt, I did not have the clout to gain entrance into the John Quincy Adams death room. However, I was told that the couch on which he died is still in that room.

Funeral Site at Peacefield
See Chapter 3: John Adams

Original Tomb: Congressional Cemetery
See Chapter 6: William Henry Harrison

Second Tomb: Hancock Cemetery
See Chapter 3: John Adams

United First Parish Church—Crypt Where Buried
See Chapter 3: John Adams

Memorial Service
Faneuil Hall dates back to 1742 when a very successful Boston merchant, Peter Faneuil, built a central market. It served a dual purpose: merchants sold their wares downstairs, while the upstairs was used as a government

The House of Representatives room where Adams collapsed at his desk. The site is marked with a plaque (foreground). In the rear is the door to the speaker's room, where Adams died.

a location for heated political debate. In June 1843, President John Tyler attended a dinner at Faneuil Hall to honor the 68th anniversary of the battle of Bunker Hill (much to the dismay of John Quincy Adams, who did not care for Tyler). In 1846, John Quincy Adams made his last public appearance in Boston, when he presided over a meeting at Faneuil Hall to discuss the matter of a free black who had recently been kidnapped by a Boston merchant and sold into slavery.[17] Prior to the Civil War, on October 12, 1858, soon-to-be Confederate president Jefferson Davis spoke at the hall.[18] On September 10, 1878, General James A. Garfield addressed the Massachusetts Young Republicans organization at Faneuil Hall.[19] And on November 7, 1960, the night before the election, presidential and vice presidential candidates John F. Kennedy and Lyndon Johnson spoke there. More recently on October 30, 2013, President Barack Obama spoke there to discuss his signature health-care law. In total, 14 presidents have visited the storied hall. Today, the historic building is part of the Boston National Historical Park, adroitly managed by the National Park Service, and has recently been named one of "America's 25 Most Visited Tourist Sites" by *Forbes Traveler* magazine.

meeting space. It was here that much of the early sentiments of revolution were voiced and argued over. After America gained its independence, Faneuil Hall continued to serve as

James Knox Polk ★ *1845–1849*

CRITICAL DEATH INFORMATION:

Date of death:	June 15, 1849, 4:42 p.m.
Cause of death:	Cholera
Age at death:	53 years, 225 days
Last words:	"I love you Sarah, for all eternity, I love you."
Place of death:	Polk Place, Nashville, Tennessee
Funeral:	McKendree Methodist Church, Nashville, Tennessee
Final resting place:	Tennessee State Capitol, Nashville, Tennessee
Reinterred:	Twice
Cost to visit grave:	Free
For more information:	www.Capitol.tn.gov
Significance:	Youngest president to die of natural causes and died 103 days after leaving office—the shortest time elapsed between presidency and death

At the conclusion of his presidency, James K. Polk departed Washington, DC, at 3:00 a.m. on March 6, 1849, for a roundabout trip to Nashville, called his "triumphal tour." He visited several Southern states, which included areas like New Orleans, where cholera was rampant. Shortly after visiting the Crescent City, he began to suffer diarrhea. However, by early April, as Polk approached Nashville, he was on the mend. On April 2, he wrote in his diary, "I was much better this morning, but was quite feeble from the effects of medicine and my indisposition."[1] By early June he was again sick and was treated by Dr. Felix Robertson (who was the first white child born in Nashville).[2] As his disease progressed, Polk realized death was imminent. Polk retained consciousness through most of the ordeal, and by all accounts, accepted his fate with stoicism and dignity. On his deathbed, he was baptized into the Methodist church by Reverend John B. McFerrin. His final words were a touching declaration to his wife: "I love you Sarah, for all eternity, I love you." James K. Polk died quietly, "without a murmur or a struggle" on Friday, June 15, 1849, at 4:42 p.m.[3]

At 53 years old, Polk became the youngest president to pass away and, only 103 days out of the presidency, he died sooner after leaving office than any other president before or since. President Zachary Taylor, who issued a proclamation for the suspension of all public business in Washington, DC, on Polk's death, became the second president to serve without a living predecessor. The 1840s were a deadly decade, when we lost four presidents, the most at that point in history. Nashville leaders, denied the honor, prestige, and influence of a former president living in their midst, "passed resolutions deploring the visitation of Providence which had deprived them of the society and services of their distinguished townsman, tendering to his afflicted family their condolence for the heavy misfortune that had befallen them, and

requesting the citizens of the town to close all houses of business or recreation on the day of his funeral as a mark of respect to the deceased."[4]

Members of the Free Masons placed Polk's remains in a walnut coffin and delivered their ritualistic funeral ceremony at his home. Cholera victims needed to be buried quickly to prevent the spread of the disease, and the day after the president died, a public funeral was held at the McKendree Methodist Church. While the hearse passed through the streets, businesses were closed and homes were draped in black as townsfolk paid their respects. The 3:00 p.m. service was delivered by Reverend McFerrin, who read from 1 Peter 1:3–5 and praised Polk as someone who "seemed almost a man of destiny. His success in life was remarkable." He continued, "Against his moral character, no charge was ever brought. No man in the United States, filling the highest offices that he has occupied, ever maintained a purer character for sound morality. His Christian principles were genuine; his belief in God and the inspiration of the Holy Scriptures was firm, unshaken."[5]

A procession, made up of Free Masons, local politicians, "and a long train of mourning citizens," escorted the remains to the Nashville City Cemetery.[6] At the receiving vault, the Free Masons placed a sprig of acacia on the coffin to symbolize the immortality of the soul. Next, a brief address was made by the Masonic Provincial Grand Master Wilkins Tannehill, and a benediction by Reverend McFerrin ended the ceremony. Polk's interment record was filed under volume 4-1849, number 416 at the Nashville City Cemetery, but this was to be a temporary location.[7] In his will,

Polk Place, the home where James K. Polk died, was his second burial site. Today, there is a historic marker is at this location.

Polk expressed his wish to be buried beside his wife at his home, "Polk Place," emulating several of the presidents who died before him—George Washington, Thomas Jefferson, James Madison, and his mentor, Andrew Jackson. Polk did not want the home to go to strangers and willed the property to the state after his wife's death with the stipulation that a Polk family member must always be assigned as caretaker. The will even mandated that the caretaker have the last name of Polk, and only if no Polks could be found would a non-Polk blood relative suffice.[8]

Shortly after Polk's death, work began at Polk Place on the tomb, which was designed by Colonel William Strickland, the same architect who had designed Washington's tomb. The tomb, which took 10 months to complete, was a 12-square-foot limestone monument, with a roof supported by Grecian Doric columns beneath which a square stone rose five feet from the ground.[9] It sat in the front of the home, a few feet from the gate of the old mansion, and was approached by a white shell path. The inscription on the eastern side read:

JAMES KNOX POLK
ELEVENTH PRESIDENT OF THE UNITED STATES
BORN NOVEMBER 2, 1795
DIED JUNE 15, 1849

It continued on the front and other sides:
THE MORTAL REMAINS OF
JAMES K. POLK
ARE RESTING IN THE VAULT BENEATH.
HE WAS BORN IN MECKLENBURG COUNTY, NORTH CAROLINA,
AND EMIGRATED WITH HIS FATHER,
SAMUEL POLK,
TO TENNESSEE, IN 1806.
THE BEAUTY OF VIRTUE WAS ILLUSTRATED IN HIS LIFE; THE EXCELLENCE OF
CHRISTIANITY WAS EXEMPLIFIED IN HIS DEATH.
BY HIS PUBLIC POLICY HE DEFINED, ESTABLISHED AND EXTENDED
THE BOUNDARIES OF HIS COUNTRY.

HE PLANTED THE LAWS OF THE AMERICAN UNION ON THE SHORES OF THE PACIFIC.
HIS INFLUENCE AND HIS COUNSELS TENDED TO ORGANIZE
THE NATIONAL TREASURY ON THE PRINCIPLES OF THE CONSTITUTION,
AND TO APPLY THE RULE OF FREEDOM TO NAVIGATION, TRADE AND INDUSTRY.
HIS LIFE WAS DEVOTED TO THE PUBLIC SERVICE.
HE WAS ELEVATED SUCCESSIVELY TO THE FIRST PLACES OF THE STATE
AND FEDERAL GOVERNMENTS;
A MEMBER OF THE GENERAL ASSEMBLY;
A MEMBER OF CONGRESS;
CHAIRMAN OF THE MOST IMPORTANT CONGRESSIONAL COMMITTEES;
SPEAKER OF THE HOUSE OF REPRESENTATIVES;
GOVERNOR OF TENNESSEE, AND PRESIDENT OF THE UNITED STATES.

Polk's reinterment was held on Wednesday, May 22, 1850. At 7:00 a.m., a group gathered at Nashville City Cemetery to retrieve the remains. Led by architect Colonel Strickland and undertaker James McCombs, they found the coffin had not deteriorated; only the sprig of acacia had withered. The coffin was put in a new shiny black walnut shell and placed in a hearse. At 10:00 a.m., the boom of minute guns from College Hill announced the beginning of the procession led by four members of the escort committee and trailed by Knights Templar on horseback in full regalia. They were followed by the hearse, drawn by four gray horses. Behind it followed Colonel Strickland and McCombs, the remaining four members of the Committee of Escort, and the citizens of Nashville, both on foot and in carriages.[10] The procession marched down Cherry Street to Broad Street, where it converged with a second Masonic parade, at which point Strickland ceremoniously transferred possession of the coffin to the Masonic Grand Marshals.

The combined processions marched to Summer Street and Church Street before arriving at Polk Place on Vine Street. The coffin was carried to the memorial, where a prayer was read by Reverend McFerrin, who also officiated at the first funeral a year earlier. After an original hymn with music by Otto Ruppius, a sermon by Bishop James Hervey Otey followed. A friend of Polk for over 30 years, he said of him, "In the private relations of life: with his friends, in his deportment toward his fellow-citizens, in the transactions of business, in punctuality to meet his engagements, in the civilities due to strangers, to station and to age, Mr. Polk was all that could be reasonably expected or desired. He was a dutiful son, an affectionate brother, a faithful friend, a kind husband and easy and merciful master, a good neighbor and last of all, but not least, he was a humble believer in Christ."

In his lengthy speech, Otey focused on Polk's deathbed decision to be baptized, of which he said had righted "a grievous defect, a defect which he himself acknowledged and deplored, which he atoned for, to the best of his ability, and opportunity, on the bed of his last sickness." He continued, "I saw him on that bed of pain, and within a few hours of the closing scene, and his language then was, 'If any man in the world has reason to acknowledge his debt and gratitude to God for his mercies, and to deplore his forgetfulness of Him, I am the man. For twenty years past, I have been sensible of my duty to God, and intending to do it, but the cares of life and incessant occupation with public business, have interfered to prevent me.'"[11] The tomb was then closed and the ceremony ended.

Polk's wife, Sarah, died on August 14, 1891, and was buried beside her husband. After her death, the provision that the home be turned over to the state went into effect, but problems arose when Polk's heirs contended that the state had no authority to execute the president's instructions. They did not want the home for themselves nor sought to preserve it, but instead wanted to sell it. In court, Polk's children successfully argued that since the grave was moved, the other stipulations that the home be turned over to the state should no longer be executed.[12] Fortunately, during this period of contention the tomb was "beautified by flowers and kept with loving care."[13] In 1898, Polk's children sold it to Jacob McGavock Dickinson, who would later become the secretary of war in 1909 under William Howard Taft.

Dickinson was not thrilled with the fact that he had two graves on his property, even if one was a president. Disregarding Polk's last wishes, the General Assembly passed a resolution to move the tomb around the block to the State Capitol grounds and allocated $1,500 for the reinterment and memorial relocation to a "gentle well-shaded knoll in the northern section of the grounds."[14] Despite many unhappy citizens who thought the move was disrespectful, the reinterment was scheduled for September 19, 1893, before which the memorial was disassembled. At 5:00 a.m. on the day of the reinterment, immediate family members gathered at the tomb and both coffins were carried inside Polk Place. After 43 years, Polk's casket was in perfect condition. Both coffins were placed in cedar caskets and displayed by the mantel, beneath oil paintings of Washington and Polk. Family members, friends, and pallbearers gathered to pay their last respects. Upon each coffin Polk's grand-niece and great-grand-niece placed "a wreath of Mermot roses tied with a satin ribbon."[15]

At 11:00 a.m., the coffins were placed in a hearse and the procession to the capitol grounds began when the Washington Light Artillery fired a 21-gun salute. The *Nashville Daily Gazette* reported that around 1,000 people gathered at the capitol. Reverend S. A. Steel, pastor from McKendree Methodist Church, delivered a prayer and was followed by Reverend J. H. McNeilly, who closed with a benediction.[16] The memorial tomb was relocated at a later date.

In later years, Polk's grave was visited by both Roosevelt presidents, each stopping by before continuing on to visit Andrew Jackson's former home, the Hermitage. Theodore Roosevelt paid his respects on October 22, 1907. Twenty-seven years later, Franklin Delano Roosevelt visited on November 17, 1934, but unfortunately, his polio prevented him from getting too close and waited in the presidential motorcade while Eleanor laid a wreath at the tomb.

THE JAMES K. POLK DEATH SITES
Funeral
Polk's funeral was held at McKendree Methodist Church, but the house of worship there today is not the same one. The current building is actually the fourth on this site. The first was built in 1833 and hosted Polk's funeral in 1849. The following year, in 1850, the Convention of Southern Secession was held at the church. The original building was then replaced with another church in 1876, which burned down shortly afterward. In 1882, yet another church was built, but it met the same fate as building number two and was destroyed by fire in 1905. The building on the site today is over 100 years old and was dedicated October 1912.

McKendree Methodist Church is located at 523 Church Street in Nashville, Tennessee, 37219. For more information, visit: www.MckendreeToday.com.

Nashville City Cemetery
The picturesque Nashville City Cemetery has the distinction of being the oldest continuously operated cemetery in Nashville. The land was originally owned by Richard Cross, who sold four acres to the city on March 9, 1820. Some of the first burials here were relocations from Nashville's other cemeteries. When it was opened for new interments on January 1, 1822, it quickly became a popular burial ground. In 1836, additional acres were added, and by 1850, over 11,000 people were buried on the premises. Six years later, that number had nearly doubled. It was a nonpartisan cemetery, and during the Civil War both Confederate and Union soldiers were buried there. Most were later reinterred elsewhere, but Confederate generals remain there. In 1878, the cemetery was closed to new interments and the grounds suffered a period of neglect during the 20th century. By the 1950s, the cemetery was being called "a disgrace to the city."[17] There were several efforts at preservation, but they were largely unsuccessful. In 1972, the site received positive attention when it was added to the National Register of Historic Places (#72001235).[18] By the turn of the last century, the cemetery was dilapidated, in disrepair, and had been defaced by vandals. The most recent efforts to preserve the historic grounds began in 2006, when Mayor Bill Purcell

The plot at Nashville City Cemetery where Polk was buried the day after his death.

allocated $3 million for improvements, thanks to which the cemetery regained much of its former glory.

The plot where Polk was buried is located within an iron fence among graves from the Grundy and Winder families ranging from 1828 to 1891. There is no historic marker, nor mention in the cemetery brochure to let people know that President Polk was once buried here.

Nashville City Cemetery is located at 1001 4th Avenue S, Nashville, Tennessee, 37203. For more information, visit: www.TheNashvilleCity Cemetery.org.

Polk Place: The Home Where He Died and the Location of His Second Grave

The home where Polk died was built in 1815 by his friend and mentor, Felix Grundy. The brick house, built in the Federal style, was located on Vine and Union Street in the heart of Nashville. Polk purchased the home in 1847, while president, with the intention of using it after leaving office. At the time, the home had been known as "Grundy Place," but thereafter became known as "Polk Place." Polk favored the Greek revival style over the Federal style and hired James

M. Hughes to redesign the home. The new look was short-lived—soon after completion, a powder magazine across the street exploded and destroyed much of the home. Hughes then shifted from a redesigner to a rebuilder.[19]

During the Civil War, the Union army occupied Nashville and, by all accounts, was respectful and ensured no harm came to the president's widow and her home. The home was purchased in 1898 by Jacob McGavock Dickinson, but its story came to an end after he sold it to J. Craig McLanahan of Philadelphia, who tore it down to make room for an apartment complex he called "Polk Flats." Fortunately, much of the furniture was saved by Polk's great-niece and today can be seen at the Polk Ancestral Home in Columbia, Tennessee.

The Tennessee Historical Commission placed a historic marker at the site between the "David G. Stone" building on 211 7th Avenue North and the recently closed Hunt Brothers Pizza.

Tennessee State Capitol

The third and final burial site for Polk is located on the grounds of the Tennessee State Capitol on Charlotte Avenue in Nashville, Tennessee. Today, it is located on the right toward the back on the building, where it is overshadowed by a massive statue of Andrew Jackson on horseback. When the grave was first erected, the entrance to the state house was on the side and the carriage path up the hill took visitors right past Polk's grave.

The Tennessee State Capitol is located at 600 Charlotte Ave, Nashville, Tennessee, 37243. Since the grave is located outdoors, it can be visited anytime. For more information about the State Capitol, visit: www. Capitol.tn.gov.

Polk's third and final grave, on the grounds of the Tennessee State Capitol.

Zachary Taylor ★ 1849–1850

CRITICAL DEATH INFORMATION:

Date of death:	July 9, 1850, 10:30 p.m.
Cause of death:	Cholera morbus
Age at death:	65 years, 227 days
Last words:	"I am not afraid to die. I have done my duty. My only regret is leaving those who are dear to me."
Place of death:	The White House
Funeral:	The East Room of the White House
Final resting place:	Zachary Taylor National Cemetery, Louisville, Kentucky
Reinterred:	Yes, at least twice
Cost to visit grave:	Free
For more information:	www.cem.va.gov/cems/nchp/ZacharyTaylor.asp
Significance:	The last president to be treated with bloodletting

On July 4, 1850, President Zachary Taylor was the guest of honor at a dedication ceremony to commemorate placing a stone in the still incomplete Washington Monument. The stone was carved "The City of Washington to Its Founder" and was created with cement mixed with dirt from Krakow, Poland, hometown of freedom-loving patriot, Tadeusz Kościuszko. It was a blistering hot summer day. By this time, an astounding seven of nine presidents had died in either June or July, and unfortunately, Taylor would soon become number eight. After returning to the White House, Taylor ate a bowl of unwashed cherries and washed it down with a glass of iced milk. Normally, this would not be a recipe for disaster, but Washington, DC, was in the midst of an Asiatic cholera epidemic and the public had been warned to avoid unsanitary foods. Taylor must have realized his mistake when he started to feel sick almost immediately. After an uncomfortable night, he awoke the next day feeling better, but by the next day he was again ill. Army surgeon Dr. Alexander S. Wotherspoon examined Taylor and diagnosed him with cholera morbus, a bacterial infection in his small intestine. He prescribed calomel and opium, which temporarily abated his symptoms, but Taylor was in bad shape the next day and two more doctors were called in. James C. Hall and assistant surgeon Richard H. Coolidge tried the medical practices of the time, including blistering his skin and bleeding his body.[1] This was the last time a president would be treated in his final days with the barbaric practice of bloodletting, or phlebotomy. The treatment that dated back to ancient Egypt was already being criticized by some as ineffective, and by the end of the century it was practically eliminated from a physician's toolkit.[2]

The next day, on July 8, Taylor was coming to grips with the drastic turn of fate that had befallen him and predicted, "In two days I shall be a dead man." This prophecy turned out to be eerily accurate. Later that day, a statement was released to prepare the nation for the worst: "The President is laboring under a bilious remittent fever, following an attack of severe cholera morbus, and is considered by his physicians seriously ill."[3] The next day, at about 10:00 a.m., Taylor called his wife, Margaret, to his bedside in the second-floor guest room. He tried to comfort her when he spoke his final words, saying "I am not afraid to die. I have done my duty. My only regret is leaving those who are dear to me."[4] Shortly afterward, he lost consciousness, and at 10:30 a.m. on July 9, 1850, surrounded by his family, Zachary Taylor died.

The sudden turn of events was too much for his wife to handle. She did not allow a death mask to be made or for the body to be embalmed, which was a practice still in its infancy, but she did permit an artist to sketch Taylor in his deathbed. The body was then placed in a bed of ice to slow the inevitable deterioration in the summer heat.[5]

The next day, the new president, Millard Fillmore, released a statement in which he lamented "I have to perform the melancholy duty of announcing to you that it has pleased Almighty God to remove from this life Zachary Taylor, late President of the United States. He deceased last evening at the hour of half-past 10 o'clock, in the midst of his family and surrounded by affectionate friends, calmly and in the full possession of all his faculties. Among his last words were these: 'I have always done my duty. I am ready to die. My only regret is for the friends I leave behind me.'"

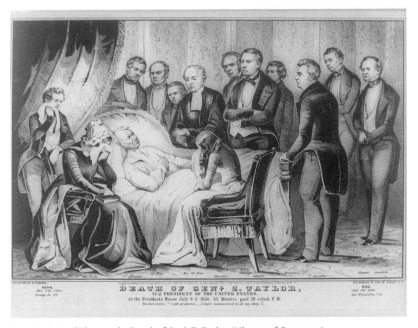

Currier & Ives lithograph, *Death of Genl. Z. Taylor.* (Library of Congress)

On Friday, July 12, Taylor's remains lay in state in the center of the East Room in a black walnut coffin lined with white velvet. Taylor was wrapped in a white satin burial shroud and a white cravat was placed around his neck. His remains lay beneath a black and silver canopy and covered in flowers. The newspapers painted the scene of the public viewing: "The countenance there exposed was one not to be passed over with a slight or transient gaze. It fixed every eye. It had three things impressively written upon it: uprightness, benevolence, and peace. The face looked just as in life: frank, manly, simple, kind, with almost a smile about the mouth."[6] Many mourners placed a small token on the casket, a flower or leaf, before quickly snatching it back to keep forever as a memento. Some that did not bring their own took one of the flowers that had been placed at the coffin.[7]

The next day, sunrise artillery salutes were heard throughout the city. People began to descend upon Washington, DC, from all states of the Union to witness the solemn spectacle. In the morning, final services were performed in the East Room, attended by military representatives, foreign dignitaries, members of the clergy, and members from all branches of government. Sitting at the foot of the bier was President Fillmore. In Victorian tradition, the distraught widow mourned in her room, consoled by Varina Davis, while her husband, Mississippi senator Jefferson Davis, attended the funeral. Episcopal ceremonies were led by the rector of St. John's Episcopal Church, Reverend Smith Pyne, and the chaplain of the Senate, Reverend C. B. Butler.[8]

Shortly after 1:00 p.m., a band played the funeral march as marines carried the body to a hearse constructed by Mr. Haslup and Mr. Weeden at their Washington, DC, coach factory. They built an impressive caisson: 11 feet long and six and a half feet wide, covered in black and white silk and topped by a bald eagle. Eight white horses, each led by an attendant dressed in Arabic garb replete with a white turban and frock, slowly pulled the hearse. Following was Old Whitey, General Taylor's beloved horse. Reporters of the day took pity on the steed: "Poor fellow! He stepped proudly; but how would his pride have been quelled, could he have known that he now accompanied his beloved master for the last time!"[9]

The procession included clergymen, congressional leaders, and military organizations such as the Patapsco Riflemen, German Yagers, German Washington Guards, First Baltimore Sharpshooters, the Independent Greys of Baltimore, and the National Greys of Washington. One company of the US Artillery was led by the man credited with inventing baseball, 31-year-old Lieutenant Abner Doubleday. Twenty pallbearers followed, including Henry Clay, Missouri senator Thomas Hart Benton, Daniel Webster, and George Washington's step-grandson, George Washington Parke Custis, followed by carriages in which rode family and President Fillmore.

The outpouring of public mourning was staggering as 100,000 people lined the streets to watch more than 100 carriages, draped in black, ride two miles to Congressional Cemetery. At the public receiving vault, a crowd was gathered. Those that had arrived early had secured a spot in the shade while the latecomers stood in the hot summer sun. The Reverend Pyne read an Episcopal liturgy and the door to the vault was closed.

As Taylor lay in the temporary tomb that William Henry Harrison and John Quincy Adams had occupied before him, attention turned to where he would be permanently buried. The city council of Frankfort, Kentucky, made a request to the widow for the body. She wanted him to rest in the Taylor family cemetery, located about five miles from Louisville on the Brownsboro Turnpike. In October 1850, the Senate allocated $8,146.73 to cover the funeral expenses and added $4,000 to transport his remains to

Kentucky.[10] That same month, the president's brother, General Joseph P. Taylor, arrived in Washington, DC, to retrieve the remains. The coffin was placed on a train bound for Pittsburgh, Pennsylvania. It arrived on Monday, October 28, and the casket was then transferred to the steamboat *Navigator*, bound for Louisville. The boat sailed slowly, stopping along the route for local ceremonies. On November 1, it arrived in Louisville and the remains were carried to the family cemetery where they were received by the Louisville Legion.[11] Taylor was placed in a limestone vault built into the side of a hill, with the back wall embedded into the earth. There was no monument at the site, and over the door was a simple inscription that read:

Z. TAYLOR

Born Nov. 24, 1784

Died July 9, 1850

The door was locked and the key given to his nephew, General Richard Taylor. He kept the key but did little else, and over the following decades the tomb deteriorated. The *New York Times* made several pleas to draw attention to its sorry state, including an August 15, 1873, article lamenting "it is mortifying to relate that it is in a sadly neglected condition, underbrush, weeds and ailanthus trees rendering it very difficult to access . . . the place does indeed appear forgotten. A stone wall encloses the little graveyard and a

The tomb of Zachary Taylor from November 1, 1850 to May 6, 1926.

rusty and unused iron gate frowns upon the visitor. It evidently had not been opened for years."[12]

A grassroots movement began to call for the remains to be relocated to a more suitable location, and at some point this sentiment morphed into a mistaken belief that Taylor actually *did* get moved. In June 1878, the *New York World* wrote of the horrendous condition of the tomb and went on to drop a bombshell: "The old family burial-ground had, in years of neglect, gone to complete ruin, the rotten palings had crumbled away or been laid prostrate by storms or breachy cattle; and weeds and rank grass were matted over the sunken mounds when Taylor's nephew, Richard Taylor, removed the bones of his distinguished relative to Cave Hill, where their present resting-place is indicated by a small and plain slab of white marble. In the course of the summer they will be taken to Frankfort, where over them the State will erect an appropriate monument."[13]

The only problem was that Taylor's remains had not been moved to Cave Hill or any other cemetery for that matter. This was the first case of confusion over the actual location of a president's body. This story was parroted in several newspapers over the following years, which definitively stated that Taylor's remains had been removed. However, nowhere in the Cave Hill National Register of Historic Places documentation is this mentioned.[14] In his lifetime, Taylor did in fact purchase a tomb there, which may have contributed to the confusion. In 1889, the plot was offered for Jefferson Davis's remains, but his widow declined.[15]

Deplorable presidential tomb conditions were a sad but familiar story, but losing track of a president's body was uncharted territory! In the same year these rumors took root, the state finally made an effort to improve the cemetery conditions. Instead of improving the crypt, Kentucky governor James B. McCreary proposed a resolution in 1878 asking Congress to erect a monument in the vicinity of the tomb. Soon afterward, the state of Kentucky allocated $5,000 for the construction of a memorial shaft.[16]

The monument was built of Maine gray granite and white Italian Carrara marble and completed on July 4, 1883. The impressive structure has the following inscription:

MAJ. GEN. ZACHARY TAYLOR
TWELFTH PRESIDENT OF THE UNITED STATES
BORN NOVEMBER 24, 1784
DIED JULY 9, 1850

Other carvings on the structure dedicated to Taylor's military heroics include a listing of the battles in which he fought. The list included a typographical error, as "Buena" was incorrectly spelled *Beuna,* which *you* can still see today. The full list reads:

PALO ALTO
RESACA DE LA PALMA
MONTERREY
BEUNA VISTA
FORT HARRISON
BLACK HAWK
OKEECHOBEE

Taylor's final words to his wife are also inscribed on the tomb. The monument was unveiled on September 20, 1883, before several hundred spectators, including 40 veterans from the Mexican War. Bishop Kavanaugh and Dr. E. T. Perkins performed religious exercises and were followed by the principal speaker, General Thomas L. Crittenden.

Amazingly, throughout the five years it took to conceive, design, and complete the memorial shaft, the confusion persisted over where exactly Zachary Taylor's body was. Finally, his nephew, who still held the key to the vault, made a statement more than three months *after* the monument was dedicated, on New Year's Eve, 1883. Setting the record straight, he declared that, "General Zachary Taylor has never been buried, notwithstanding the many stories to the contrary. He died in 1850, and his remains were immediately brought to Kentucky by his brother, Commissary General Joseph P. Taylor, and placed in

a vault in the Taylor cemetery, on his father's old farm, five miles from Louisville, on the Jefferson and Brownsboro turnpike road. A few months later, his wife died at Washington city, and was brought and placed in the vault, and I have had the key of the vault and cemetery ever since."[17]

Though this finally confirmed that Taylor's body never left the grounds of the cemetery, false statements continued to be published for another decade, based on the earlier accounts. An August 24, 1892 article in the *Paterson Daily Press* detailed the location of all deceased presidents. Regarding Taylor, the article started with accurate statements: "His remains were removed several times. First they were placed in a cemetery at Washington, then in a lot on the Taylor homestead, near Louisville." However, it then went astray, parroting earlier falsities: "then to Cave Hill cemetery, and they are now in a cemetery in Frankfort, KY."[18]

By the end of the century, the deplorable condition of the tomb had again become a frequent topic in newspapers. Efforts to have Taylor moved to Baton Rouge, where he had once lived, did not materialize.[19] In 1903, an Iowa newspaper, the *Clinton Morning Age,* chided, "For over half a century [the tomb] has lacked the care of a kindly hand and is fast falling into decay. Apparently nobody cares. . . . Visitors are rare. It is doubtful if half a dozen tourists visit the tomb in twelve months. . . . Not one in ten thousand knows the place of this sepulchre."[20] While the federal government sympathized, it did not help, for the property was owned by the state. With the cemetery in limbo, the condition of the tomb continued to deteriorate. In January 1905, J. J. Taylor, a relative from Chicago, visited the grave to see what repairs were required.[21] Six years later, in 1911, it was written that the grave was "sadly neglected."[22]

Finally, with the state and family unable or unwilling to improve the tomb, the federal government intervened and took ownership on February 19, 1925, when President Calvin

Coolidge created the "Zachary Taylor National Cemetery," authorizing $10,000 for the creation of a new mausoleum. It was made of Indiana limestone with a granite base. Taylor's remains were moved into it on May 6, 1926.

After all of these years, it was believed that Zachary Taylor's remains could finally rest in peace, but alas, that was not to be. In June 1991, while researching a biography about Taylor, college professor Clara Rising was convinced that he did not die of natural causes but instead, was *murdered* for his opposition to slavery! Rising presumed the murder weapon was arsenic poisoning, and she convinced the descendants of Zachary Taylor to exhume his body to prove her suspicions. About 200 people were on hand for the bizarre ceremony to see the flag-draped coffin removed from the mausoleum. The coffin was then taken to the Jefferson County coroner's office where hair, bone, and nail samples were removed for testing (his burial shroud and a glove were also analyzed). Several hours later, President Taylor was returned to the cemetery, and five members of the Kentucky National Guard held a brief reinterment ceremony. The samples were sent to the Oak Ridge National Laboratory where they were subjected to neutron activation analysis. The exhumation cost $1,200, which was paid for by Rising, and in the end, her theory was disproved when tests concluded that he did not die from arsenic poisoning.[23]

THE ZACHARY TAYLOR DEATH SITES
Location of Death: The White House
See Chapter 6: William Henry Harrison

Original tomb: Congressional Cemetery
See Chapter 6: William Henry Harrison

Grave
The 1850 burial site is now within the boundaries of the Zachary Taylor National Cemetery. A bronze marker above the doorway reads:

THE FIRST BURIAL SITE
OF THE 12TH PRESIDENT OF THE U.S.
ZACHARY TAYLOR
PRESENTED BY COLONEL GEORGE READE
CHAPTER
COLONIAL DAMES XVII CENTURY
OCTOBER 2, 1976

By 1980, the tomb was in a disgraceful condition. It resembled a shack, desecrated with graffiti and a peace sign sloppily spray-painted in the upper left corner.[24] Since then, the tomb has been cleaned and restored. The cemetery register lists Taylor in Grave #1 in section "ZT." It was placed on the National Register of Historic Places (#83003733) on November 3, 1983, and there is a historic marker at the entrance to the cemetery.

The Zachary Taylor National Cemetery is located at 4701 Brownsboro Road, Louisville, Kentucky, 40207. It is open every day sunrise to sunset. For more information, visit: www.cem.va.gov/cems/nchp/ZacharyTaylor.asp.

Taylor's current tomb.

THE DEADLIEST DECADE

★★★★★★★★★★★★★★★★★★★★★★★★★★★★★★★★★★★★★★★

THE TENTH PRESIDENT
John Tyler ★ *1841–1845*

CRITICAL DEATH INFORMATION:

Date of death:	January 18, 1862, 12:15 a.m.
Cause of death:	Bilious fever
Age at death:	71 years, 295 days
Last words:	"Perhaps it is best."
Place of death:	Exchange Hotel, Richmond, Virginia
Funeral:	St. Paul's Church, Richmond, Virginia
Final resting place:	Hollywood Cemetery, Richmond, Virginia
Reinterred:	No
Cost to visit grave:	Free
For more information:	www.Hollywood Cemetery.org
Significance:	Only presidential death unrecognized by the sitting president

As former president, John Tyler was the highest-level official to support secession in the Civil War. Vilified in the North but beloved in the South, Tyler was a member of the provisional Confederate Congress before being elected to the Confederate House of Representatives in November 1861. Tyler was one of five living former presidents when Abraham Lincoln took office, a first in American history.

Following his election, Tyler moved into the Exchange Hotel in the Confederate capital of Richmond, Virginia, and became ill almost immediately after his arrival. On Sunday, January 12, he awoke feeling dizzy and vomited. But he was dismissive of the symptoms and went downstairs for his morning tea in the hotel dining room. While sipping his tea, Tyler was struck by "sudden faintness" and fell to the floor.[1] Dr. Miller was the first to come to his aid (and was later joined by three more physicians, Doctors Crockett, Brown, and Fairfax).[2] Dr. Miller led Tyler to the ladies' parlor to rest, but Tyler had suffered vertigo in the past and was not overly concerned. Dr. Miller then helped Tyler to his room to examine him more thoroughly. The doctor's diagnosis was bilious fever, which was not considered life-threatening at the time. They administered morphine and left Tyler in his bed to recover. Over the next few days, his health began to improve and Tyler made plans to return to his home, Sherwood Forest, in Charles City, Virginia. On Friday, January 17, the night before he was to depart, his condition took a turn for the worse when he awoke in the late evening with extreme difficulty breathing. Dr. Brown gave him some brandy and tried to apply mustard plasters to his chest, but Tyler resisted the treatment. When Dr. William Peachy arrived after midnight, Tyler lamented, "I am dying, doctor." Another physician appealed to Tyler,

"Mr. President, let me give you some stimulant." But Tyler bluntly declined, saying, "I will not have it." He was resigned to his fate when he said his last words, "Perhaps it is best."[3]

At 12:15 a.m. on Saturday morning, January 18, John Tyler died in his hotel room. With him at his final moment were Doctors Brown, Peachy, and Miller; a neighbor from Charles City, Josiah C. Wilson; the proprietors of the hotel, Mr. and Mrs. John P. Ballard; and Tyler's wife Julia and infant daughter Pearl. It had been over 11 years since the last presidential death, of Zachary Taylor, the longest stretch since the 26 years between George Washington and Thomas Jefferson. Tyler's death was the first of the 1860s and ushered in the deadliest decade for presidents in history.

In Richmond, flags were lowered to half-mast, bells tolled, and state offices were closed in deference. In the Confederate Congress, members lined up to pay tribute and be recorded in the official record. In the North, it was another story. Tyler's death was ignored at best; at worst, Tyler was vilified as a traitor. Lincoln made no official proclamation to observe his predecessor's death, a first in American history.[4] The *New York Times* obituary was blunt and bitter, but also a few years premature in reporting the fall of the South: "JOHN TYLER, of Virginia, the only Ex-President resident in the seceded States, is dead . . . He ended his life suddenly, last Friday [actually Saturday], in Richmond—going down to death amid the ruins of his native State. He himself was one of the architects of its ruin; and beneath that melancholy wreck his name will be buried, instead of being inscribed on the Capitol's monumental

EXCHANGE HOTEL & BALLARD HOUSE,
RICHMOND. Vª

The Exchange Hotel (right), where John Tyler died shortly after midnight on January 18, 1862. (The Miriam and Ira D. Wallach Division of Art, Prints and Photographs: Print Collection, The New York Public Library)

marble, as a year ago he so much desired."[5] The reporter continued, labeling Tyler "the most unpopular public man," who "devoted himself to the cultivation of his estate, the increase of his negroes and the accumulation of money."[6]

Tyler's wish to be buried in Sherwood Forest was explicitly stated in his will dated October 10, 1859: "I empower my dear wife to make out of my estate suitable provision for my burial, which I wish to be accompanied with no unnecessary expense. Let the people of this county, whose fathers helped me on in my battles of life with a zeal and constancy rarely ever equaled and never surpassed, be invited to attend my funeral obsequies; and let my body be consigned to the tomb in the earth of the county wherein I was born, there to repose until the day of resurrection. My wife will select the spot on 'Sherwood Forest,' and mark it by an uncostly monument of granite or marble."[7] But, despite his instructions, on the day he died, a resolution was passed in the General Assembly to bury Tyler in the Confederate capital: "With the consent of his family, his remains be deposited in Hollywood Cemetery, in the city of Richmond, near the remains of James Monroe, and that the Governor of this State be authorized to cause a suitable monument to be erected to his memory."[8] Perhaps satisfied that her husband would be buried in his native state and flattered by the Confederate Congress's offer, Julia Gardiner Tyler dutifully accepted. Four years earlier, Virginia governor Henry Alexander Wise had declared his intent for Hollywood Cemetery to become the burial location for all native Virginia presidents. Tyler would be the last of the United States presidents buried there.

The day after Tyler's death, at 3:00 p.m. on Sunday, January 19, the Public Guard escorted his remains to the Virginia state capitol building. The coffin was draped in the Confederate flag and lay in repose for the public for two days. Mourners solemnly walked past the coffin to view, beneath a glass plate, the "placid and calm" face of Tyler.[9] On January 21, a rainy Tuesday morning, a service was held and several people spoke eulogies, including Confederate Secretary of State Robert M. T. Hunter and Virginia delegate William C. Rives.

At noon the coffin was placed in a hearse and pulled by four white horses, each with a "colored groom." One hundred and fifty carriages pulled Southern dignitaries, including President Davis and Vice President Alexander Hamilton Stephens, as well as members of the Confederate cabinet, Congress, and Senate.[10] The cortege arrived at St. Paul's Church, where the *Richmond Enquirer* reported: "The church was filled to its utmost capacity with citizens from all parts of the Confederacy."[11] Sixteen pallbearers carried the coffin inside. The Armory Band played solemn music and Reverend Bishop Johns, who was a long-time friend of Tyler, read Romans 13:7. After the funeral, the procession marched to Hollywood Cemetery, where a small crowd witnessed the burial ceremony. However, according to the *Richmond Whig*, "had the weather been more propitious, the attendance at the funeral would have been much larger."[12]

The grave was unmarked at the time of the burial, with plans to place a marker at a later date. Virginia passed a resolution to erect a suitable monument, but the state was never "in funds."[13] It remained unmarked, with the only landmark of distinction being a small nearby magnolia tree, leading the few visitors to ask the superintendent for directions.[14] He would obligingly point them to "President's Hill," where Tyler was buried near James Monroe, then instruct them to locate the grave of Tyler's daughter and look for the nearby mound. The contrast between the two graves was striking: Monroe's prominent memorial, while peculiar in appearance (often called "the birdcage"), was appropriate for a former president; Tyler's grave was an unmarked mound of dirt. The concern was not just aesthetic—had the cemetery records been destroyed, the exact location of his grave would have been lost.[15]

Thirty-seven years later, in 1899, the United States Congress felt the time had come to mark the grave with a suitable monument and attempted to allocate $10,000 to build one. However, not all were ready to memorialize the secessionist president, and the proposal failed. The Hollywood Cemetery Company decided to act, and, in October of that same year, they erected a modest marker of local granite.[16] It was small and simple and the date of his death, listed as *January 17*, was incorrect. It bore the following inscription:

JOHN TYLER
PRESIDENT OF THE UNITED STATES
FROM 1841–1845
BORN IN CHARLES CITY COUNTY, VA
MARCH 29, 1790
DIED AT RICHMOND, VA
JAN. 17, 1862

Tyler's grave, 1908. The tombstone, with the date of death listed incorrectly as January 17 instead of January 18, was erected by Hollywood Cemetery in October 1899. (Library of Congress)

A decade later, Virginia senator Thomas S. Martin introduced another bill in 1909 to erect a memorial. The bill was passed in both the Senate and the House on March 4, 1911, and Congress allocated $10,000 for the effort on August 24, 1912.[17] The next year, Secretary of War Lindley Miller Garrison was tasked to complete the monument and ensure that "suitable ceremonies will attend the unveiling."[18]

On December 16, 1913, Garrison held a design competition. After reviewing 25 submissions, the contract was awarded to T. F. McGann & Sons Company of Boston, who designed a monolithic 17-foot-tall granite shaft topped by a bronze sculpture of a Greek urn supported by two eagles. Each side featured a bas-relief, one representing Tyler's service to Virginia and his country, the other signifying "memory." The massive shaft stood on a granite base upon a concrete foundation. In the front was a bronze bust of Tyler, and on the shaft was following inscription:

JOHN TYLER
PRESIDENT OF THE UNITED STATES
1841–1845
BORN IN CHARLES CITY COUNTY, VA
MARCH 29, 1790
DIED IN THE CITY OF RICHMOND
JANUARY 18, 1862

On Saturday, June 9, 1915, the monument was placed over Tyler's grave without ceremony.[19] Four months later, on October 12, Virginia governor Henry Carter Stuart presided over a dedication. Reverend Robert A. Gibson began with an invocation, followed by Virginia representative John Lamb, who had helped push through the bill to fund the memorial. The Coast Artillery Band from Fort Monroe played music, and an address was made by poet Armistead Churchill Gordon, who delivered a long-winded speech, more like a dissertation than dedication. In it, he recounted every detail of Tyler's life, starting with the birth of his great-great-grandfather—it

Tyler's grave today. (Courtesy of Joseph F. Picone)

was not until the 15th paragraph that he got to John Tyler's birth![20]

After the marathon oration, Tyler's only surviving daughter, Mrs. Pearl Tyler Ellis, who was with her father when he died, unveiled the monument. A salvo was fired by the Richmond Howitzers, and a benediction by Reverend Collins Denny concluded the event.

THE JOHN TYLER DEATH SITES
Location of Death
Construction began on the Exchange Hotel in 1840, and it was completed the next year. Located at the southeast corner of Franklin and Fourteenth Streets, it was designed by Isaiah Rogers in the Classical style and cost $125,000 to build. The *Richmond Dispatch* described the Exchange as "One of the most comfortable and elegant in the Confederate States, having about 140 rooms, embracing saloons, drawing-rooms, dining halls, offices,

bed rooms, kitchens, gas, water, and every other arrangement adapted to promote the convenience of guests."[21] During the Civil War the hotel became a hot spot of intriguing activity, including several accidental shootings, thefts, and one sighting of a "Yankee Spy" in the hotel parlor.[22]

By the end of 1862, owner John P. Ballard was looking to sell the Exchange. Several years earlier, he had built another hotel called the Ballard House and connected it to the Exchange with a second-story bridge. Ballard wanted to focus solely on his namesake hotel, and on November 24, the Exchange was sold at auction for $137,500 to R. A. Lancaster.[23] Two years later, in the waning months of the Civil War, half of the hotel was repurposed for use by Confederate soldiers from Louisiana. The *Richmond Sentinel* reported that it would now be "Where the weary may find rest and comfort and entertainment, among the soldiers of his own State."[24] Two days after the fall of Richmond, on April 4, 1865, Abraham Lincoln visited the decimated Confederate capital with his son Tad, and his walk took him right past the Exchange Hotel.[25] By 1896, the hotel was closed, and it was demolished four years later. Today, a parking garage can be found at this location.

Public Viewing: State Capitol/Hall of Congress
The Virginia state capitol building was designed by our third president, Thomas Jefferson, and its bold Monumental Classical style was the first such building in America. The cornerstone was laid in 1785 and construction was completed in 1788. It still serves as the seat of government and is recognized as "the oldest legislature continuously operating in the Western Hemisphere."[26] In 1893, after being reinterred from New Orleans, Confederate president Jefferson Davis's public viewing was also held in the building. The state capitol was added to the National Register of Historic Places on October 15, 1966 (#66000911).

The Capitol is located at 1000 Bank Street, Richmond, Virginia, 23219. The building is open to visitors on Monday through Saturday from 8:00 a.m. to 5:00 p.m. On Sundays it is open from 1:00 p.m. to 5:00 p.m. For more information, visit: www.VirginiaCapitol.gov.

Funeral: St. Paul's Church

This Greek Revival–style church, consecrated in 1845, was modeled after the Church of St. Luke and the Epiphany in Philadelphia. The congregation even hired the same architect, Thomas S. Stewart, to design it. During the Civil War, St. Paul's was the preferred house of worship for Confederate leaders. The house of worship was listed on the National Register of Historic Places (#69000357) on June 4, 1969.

St. Paul's Church is located at 815 E. Grace Street in Richmond, Virginia, 23219. For more information, including visitors' hours and service schedule, visit: www.StPauls-Episcopal.org.

Hollywood Cemetery

The land was first owned by William Byrd III, who in 1758 built a country house called "Belvidere" on the property. When he found himself in financial straits, he sold off the land in parcels of 100 acres. One was purchased by the Harvie family in 1769 and thus became known as "Harvie's Woods." The land was purchased to be used as a cemetery in 1847 by William Haxall and Joshua Fry and 40 prominent Richmond citizens of the Hollywood Cemetery Company. The cemetery was designed by John Notman of Philadelphia to differ from the "grid-like monotony" of the other cemeteries that dotted Richmond at the time. For his services he charged $300, and it was Notman that first suggested the name "Holly-Wood," due to the large number of holly trees on the property. In 1849, the first grave site was purchased.

Eleven years after the cemetery's creation, James Monroe was reinterred there from New York City. Virginia governor Wise, who was instrumental in retrieving Monroe's remains, revealed his ultimate goal when he declared, "Now we must have *all* the Native presidents of Virginia buried in this inclosure." An alderman from New York put his hand on Wise's shoulder and offered some encouragement, "Go ahead, Governor, you'll fotch 'em."[27] Unfortunately for Wise, he never did "fotch 'em." While Southern loyalist John Tyler was buried there in 1862, Wise was never able to relocate Virginia's big fish,

St. Paul's Church in Richmond, Virginia, in 1865, three years after Tyler's funeral was held there. (Library of Congress)

like Washington, Jefferson, and James Madison. He still believed Hollywood was the final resting place of choice and chose to be buried there himself (he died on September 12, 1876).

Thirty-one years after Tyler's death, the only president of the Confederate States of America, Jefferson Davis, was reinterred from New Orleans in Hollywood Cemetery. Monroe's and Davis's relocations were not without sequel, for, over the years, many people from less bucolic cemeteries were reinterred at Hollywood, including 7,000 soldiers killed at Gettysburg.[28]

When I visited Hollywood Cemetery, my first stop was "The Presidents Circle" to see the graves of Tyler and Monroe. Tyler's grave is still largely ignored. Presidential graves are typically adorned with flags and floral arrangements, but not so for John Tyler. I found the same situation only a few feet away at the grave of James Monroe and was equally surprised. Perhaps in a state that gave us Washington, Jefferson, Madison, and Woodrow Wilson, these two native Virginians suffer by comparison. I walked back to my car with a little less spring in my step, unable to recall any other presidents' graves that were similarly disregarded. As I approached the grave of Jefferson Davis, I was astounded! While Tyler and Monroe are ignored, Davis is adorned and decorated. Stone pavers lead to the grave, and several Confederate Stars and Bars were planted, waving in the light wind on that crisp autumn morning, including one on a pole located directly behind a towering sculpture of Davis. Several red, white, and blue floral arrangements covered the grave.

Hollywood Cemetery was listed on the National Register of Historic Places (#69000350) on November 12, 1969. It is located on 412 South Cherry Street in Richmond, Virginia, 23220. It is open from 8:00 a.m. to 5:00 or 6:00 p.m. depending on the time of year. For more information, visit: www.HollywoodCemetery.org.

Martin Van Buren ★ *1837–1841*

CRITICAL DEATH INFORMATION:

Date of death:	July 24, 1862, 2:00 a.m.
Cause of death:	Bronchial asthma
Age at death:	79 years, 231 days
Last words:	"There is but one reliance, and that is upon Christ, the free Mediator of us all."
Place of death:	Lindenwald, Kinderhook, New York
Funeral:	Kinderhook Reformed Church, Kinderhook, New York
Final resting place:	Kinderhook Reformed Cemetery, Kinderhook, New York
Reinterred:	No
Cost to visit grave:	Free
For more information:	www.nps.gov/mava
Significance:	Lived through a record eight presidents *after* he left office

After his presidency ended in 1841, Martin Van Buren retired to a quiet life in the town of Kinderhook, New York, where he was born. He enjoyed good heath until 1861 when he contracted pneumonia, after which he was confined to his bed in the southern end of his Lindenwald mansion. In July 1862, Van Buren suffered a severe attack of bronchial asthma and his health rapidly began to decline. His last recorded words were to his clergyman, "There is but one reliance, and that is upon Christ, the free Mediator of us all."[1] Martin Van Buren died on July 24, 1862, at 2:00 a.m.; however, the nation's newspapers, engrossed in the Civil War, barely noticed. His *New York Times* obituary included sparse details of his death, summing

The room where Martin Van Buren died at 2:00 a.m. on July 24, 1862.

up his illness and passing in a mere four sentences.[2] But Van Buren's hometown took the news hard, as the *Times* reported: "In the village of Kinderhook the emblems of mourning were of a more heartfelt character, and betokened a deeper sorrow at the loss of an old neighbor, a kind friend, and an esteemed citizen."[3]

Van Buren, the eighth president, died during the administration of the sixteenth president, Abraham Lincoln. No other president before or since has survived to see eight successors, a fact that reflects the mediocrity of the presidents who succeeded him—who each served only a single term, with two dying in office. The presidency had become a revolving door as nine men served during the 20 years from 1841 to 1861.

Van Buren's body was placed in a rosewood coffin with silver trimming, and on the lid was a silver plate that read:

MARTIN VAN BUREN

DIED JULY 24, 1862

AGED

79 YEARS, 7 MONTHS, 19 DAYS

For three days his body lay in repose in the

large dining room at Lindenwald.[4] Mourners passed the open casket and the *New York Times* reported, "Those who have been in the habit of seeing the Ex-President in his later years said that the corpse bore a very natural appearance."[5] The funeral was held on July 28, and New York City mayor George Opdyke called for all flags to be at half-mast. At noon, Reverend J. Romeyn Berry conducted a service in Van Buren's home. In attendance were his brother, three sons, New York governor Edwin D. Morgan, future governor Samuel J. Tilden, and the Committee of the Sachems of Tammany Hall. A hearse carried the remains to Kinderhook Reformed Church, and Kinderhook locals served as pallbearers: Nathan Wild, Henry Snyder, William H. Tobey, David Van Schaack, Cornelius Wiltsie, Hugh Van Alstyne, Abraham A. Van Alen, Albert Hoes, Ephraim Best, C. H. Wendover, John Frisbee, Chester Jarvis, William R. Mesick, and Charles Whiting. There were hundreds in attendance, and only the Van Buren pew was empty. Those that could not fit gathered in solidarity outside. At 1:30 p.m. the service began, officiated by Reverend Berry, Bishop Alonzo Potter, and former pastor Reverend Van Zandt. The choir sang Psalm 19 and Reverend Berry spoke for almost a full hour, in which he "forebore to eulogize, rather teaching the grave lessons of patriotism and religious truth."[6] Reverend Van Zandt then spoke a closing prayer.

A large procession led by Fire Company No. 2 and 81 carriages escorted the hearse to the cemetery, congesting the small town roads. Bishop Potter delivered the final burial rites, and the coffin was lowered into a plot beside his wife in the northeastern corner of the cemetery. Later

Van Buren's grave in Kinderhook Reformed Cemetery, in Kinderhook, New York.

on, a small sparse marker was placed there with his initials, "M. V. B."

A 15-foot granite shaft was later erected with the inscription, which is today worn and barely legible:

MARTIN VAN BUREN
VIIITH PRESIDENT
OF THE UNITED STATES
BORN DEC. 5, 1782.
DIED JULY 24, 1862

HANNAH VAN BUREN
HIS WIFE
BORN MARCH 8, 1783.
DIED AT ALBANY, N.Y.
FEB. 6, 1819

As the graves of the greatest presidents succumbed to the ravages of neglect and disrepair, it is not surprising that Van Buren's did not fare any better. In 1908, the *Youngstown Vindicator*

lamented: "The grave of President Van Buren has had less attention than any other President of the United States. The cemetery lot is not even fenced off from hundreds of surrounding graves. His monument is less prominent and less attractive and his cemetery lot is less extensive than many others in the same little village burying ground. It is almost pathetic to recall that the Martin Van Buren, whose name is carved on the side of the simple granite shaft, was once the first citizen of the republic. . . . His tomb is not in harmony with his prominence with which he figured in early American history."[7] While no record exists of a visit by a president or anyone else of prominence, on December 6, 1932 (the 150th anniversary of his birth), President Herbert Hoover sent a wreath. The floral arrangement was placed upon the grave by Brigadier General Charles D. Roberts of Fort Ontario.[8] Since the Lyndon Johnson administration, a wreath has been sent by the White House every year on his birthday.

Van Buren even takes second fiddle in his own hometown, surpassed by the fictional character Ichabod Crane (who was based on a real-life schoolteacher from Kinderhook). By 1982, the eighth president's stature in his hometown hit rock bottom when it was written: "For years, weeds grew around the neglected granite monument on his grave. Junk accumulated in the hallways and rooms of the Van Buren mansion, mixing with the historic artifacts."[9] In 1988, his legacy was further sullied when Garry Trudeau's comic strip *Doonesbury* featured a disturbing storyline, in which Van Buren's grave is robbed by the infamous Yale Skull and Bones Society. Officials at Lindenwald were not amused, and acting superintendent Carol Kohan offered a stern reprimand: "I think it's in extremely poor taste—that's our official position—and grotesque." Kohan also feared it would encourage vandalism.[10] Oddly enough, this story was not pulled from thin air. Rumors, or perhaps urban legends, do abound that in addition to Geronimo's and Che Guevara's, the (not so) secret Yale society does indeed possess Van Buren's cranium.[11]

THE MARTIN VAN BUREN DEATH SITES
Lindenwald

The first owners of the estate located on Old Post Road were the Powell family, dating back to 1664. In 1671, it was purchased by the Van Alstyne family, who lived in a small home on the property. It remained in their family until 1780, when Lambert Thomas Van Alstyne sold it to Peter Van Ness, a Revolutionary War commander, who built a larger home in 1797 (the knocker on the front door bears this date to this day) and called it "Kleinrood." When Peter passed away, the home was inherited by his son and Van Buren's good friend, William Peter Van Ness. Due to financial problems, William lost the home to creditors in 1824. Former New York City mayor William Paulding Jr. purchased the home at public auction for $8,500. Paulding was an absentee owner, and over the next 15 years, the neglected home fell into disrepair. In 1839, in the midst of his presidency, Van Buren purchased the estate from Paulding for a hefty $14,000. In 1849, he hired architect Richard Upjon to expand the home to its current 36 rooms. Inspired by other presidential mansions such as Monticello and the Hermitage, Van Buren decorated it extravagantly with furniture and wallpaper from Europe, painted the home its unique yellow color, and named the mansion "Lindenwald."[12]

After his term, Van Buren returned to live in Kinderhook in 1841. To help fill its many rooms, he invited his sons to live with him. During those years, Van Buren turned the estate into a working farm and relished his new profession so much that he listed his occupation as "farmer" in the 1850 census. While there are no known visits by other presidents to Lindenwald, Van Buren entertained numerous famous Americans, including writers John L. Stephens and Washington Irving; senators Thomas Hart Benton, Henry Clay, and Charles Sumner; General Winfield Scott; the Earl of Carlisle; and New York governor Samuel J. Tilden.

On Van Buren's death in 1862, Lindenwald passed to his three sons, who kept it for two years. The next owner was Leonard Walter Jerome and, while his name may not resonate, that of his grandson, Winston Churchill, will live on for many generations. It was rumored that Jerome won the home in game of cards.[13] In total, there were eight owners over the years after Van Buren's death, during which time it was used as a tea house, an antiques store, a nursing home, and a private residence.[14]

Starting at the turn of the century, efforts began to save the mansion. From 1907 to 1914, there were at least four attempts by the state to acquire the home. A 1937 bill had high expectations but failed to pass.[15] Lindenwald was finally purchased by the National Park Service in 1973 for $102,000, a miniscule sum

Lindenwald, the home where Van Buren died.

compared to the whopping $2,700,000 that was appropriated for renovations to the home and grounds.[16] On October 26, 1974, the site was officially established as the Martin Van Buren National Historic Site by Gerald Ford. In October 1982, the home was first opened to the public when 1,000 people marched through the town and toured the mansion.

Lindenwald is located at 1013 Old Post Road, Kinderhook, New York, 12106. Tours of the home run on the hour every day from 9:00 a.m. to 4:00 p.m. For more information, visit: www.nps.gov/mava.

Funeral site

There have been four Reformed Churches in Kinderhook. The first was built in 1677 and the second 40 years later. The third, where Van Buren's funeral was held, was built in 1814. It was badly damaged by a fire in 1867 and rebuilt two years later. This last incarnation stands today. While some of it may have been in place at the time of Van Buren's funeral, much is the reconstruction.[17] To the right of the entrance is a marker commemorating Van Buren that resembles a gravestone inscribed with his birth and death dates.

The Kinderhook Reformed Church is located at 21 Broad Street, Kinderhook, New York, 12106. For more information, visit: www.Kinder hookReformedChurch.com.

Cemetery

On March 31, 1817, a group of Kinderhook citizens convened to discuss a cemetery, to be managed by the Reformed Protestant Dutch Church. The piece of land chosen was near a store owned by brothers Henry and Aaron Van Vleck, and a portion was also already being used as a small burial ground. The group created a petition on behalf of the "Minister, Elders and Deacons of the Reformed Protestant Dutch Church of Kinderhook" and delegated Van Buren, then a state senator, to present it to the Court of Chancery.

The petition was approved with the condition that within 40 days the buyers had to remove the "relics of those who have been interred in the old burying ground." It cost $400 for two acres to be used as the cemetery. As for the current deceased residents, "The ground was ploughed over and then scraped to the depth of three feet, after which spades were used. If relatives of the dead objected to the scraper, spades only were employed." Shortly after the bodies were removed, "the Highway Commissioners laid out a road four rods wide through the abandoned burial ground, thus obliterating all traces of its locality."[18] The Kinderhook Cemetery was expanded in 1845 for $330, and again 13 years later with the $100 purchase of additional land to the south.

The cemetery is located on Hudson Street about two miles north of Route 9. There is no fence, but a sign states it is open sunrise to sunset.

Abraham Lincoln ★ *1861–1865*

CRITICAL DEATH INFORMATION:

Date of death:	April 15, 1865, 7:22:10 a.m.
Cause of death:	Assassination
Age at death:	56 years, 62 days
Last words:	"She won't think anything about it."
Place of death:	Petersen house, Washington, DC
Funeral:	The White House
Final resting place:	Oak Ridge Cemetery, Springfield, Illinois
Reinterred:	Yes, six times
Cost to visit grave:	Free
For more information:	www.OakRidge Cemetery.org
Significance:	First president to be assassinated

After shepherding the nation through the bloodiest war in our history, President Abraham Lincoln had reason to be in high spirits. On April 14, 1865, Lincoln awoke in a good mood, and those who saw him remembered him to be more cheerful and jubilant than he had been in a long time. At 7:00 a.m., he ate breakfast while chatting with his son Robert, who had served with Ulysses S. Grant and witnessed the surrender of General Robert E. Lee at Appomattox Court House. His wife, Mary, told him she would like to go Ford's Theatre that evening to see *Our American Cousin*. Lincoln enjoyed the theater, and he agreed with her suggestion, even if it was Good Friday.

Lincoln met with his cabinet at 11:00 a.m. and

discussed the peaceful restoration of the Confederacy to the United States and his commitment to his pledge of "malice towards none and charity for all."[1] Afterward, Lincoln ate lunch with his wife and later toured the USS *Montauk* at the Washington Navy Yard. After returning to the White House, Lincoln met with several visitors before excusing himself to prepare for the theater.

Lincoln arrived at the theater at 8:30 p.m. and slipped into his seat during the first act. The Lincolns were accompanied by Major Henry Reed Rathbone and his fiancée, Clara Harris (daughter of New York senator Ira Harris). As Lincoln entered, actress Laura Keene stopped in mid-performance to acknowledge the president, and the 1,700 people in attendance gave him a standing ovation as the orchestra struck up "Hail to the Chief."[2]

When the ovation died down, Lincoln slipped into a red horsehair rocking chair. His personal bodyguard, John Parker, stood at the entrance to the balcony, but soon decided to head next door to Taltavul's Star Saloon for a drink, leaving the president unguarded. Mary sat to Lincoln's right and held his hand. Approaching 10:00 p.m., Mary hugged him but self-consciously whispered, "What will Miss Harris think of my hanging on to you so?" Lincoln put her at ease and replied gently, "She won't think anything about it." These would be his final words.

Fifteen minutes later, John Wilkes Booth entered the balcony during the third act and bolted the door behind him. Onstage, characters bickered and the audience erupted in laughter. Just as Booth had planned, the raucous noise gave him the cover he needed. He yelled "Freedom!" and pulled the trigger of a small single-shot .44 caliber Derringer pistol only inches away from Lincoln's head.

As Booth leapt from the balcony onto the stage, his boot got tangled in an American flag, breaking his leg in the fall. Brandishing a dagger, he yelled, "The South is avenged!" and *"Sic sem-per tyrannis!"* Latin for "Thus always to tyrants." Amid the confusion, Booth amazingly escaped the crowded theater.[3] Immediately, someone shouted, "Is there a doctor in the house?" and the first physician to respond was Charles Augustus Leale. Since Booth had bolted the entrance to the balcony, Dr. Leale was lifted into the box. A 23-year-old assistant surgeon of the United States Volunteers and recent graduate of Bellevue Hospital Medical College, he had come to the play to catch a glimpse of Lincoln but instead found himself as the physician in charge of the president until his death. He immediately took over, demanding that people fetch him brandy and water. While Mary held her husband, Leale gently lowered him to the floor. First, he felt for a pulse but found none. Having seen Booth with the dagger, he assumed the president had been stabbed, but could not find a wound. He opened Lincoln's eyes and could see there was brain trauma, so he felt through his blood-matted hair until he found the open wound where "some of his brain was oozing out."[4] He removed a blood clot, but Leale knew the president would die. Nobody had ever survived such a wound.

While Leale made his initial examination, two more doctors arrived, army surgeons Dr. Charles Sabin Taft and Dr. Albert Freeman Africanus King. In a desperate attempt to restore Lincoln's vital signs, Leale pressed his diaphragm as Taft and King pumped his arms. After several moments, Lincoln's heart again started to beat and his lungs took in air. Leale administered artificial respiration to strengthen his breathing, but he knew he had only delayed the inevitable. He ominously pronounced, "The wound is mortal; it is impossible for him to recover."

Dr. Leale poured brandy and water into Lincoln's mouth and he reflexively swallowed. This would be the only "medication" administered to Lincoln that night. Suddenly, Keene appeared in the box and audaciously asked Leale if she could cradle the president's head. Leale allowed her to do so while he spoke with Taft and King.

They decided that further medical care on a balcony floor was neither wise nor dignified. But they had no illusions—they understood it was not a question of *whether* President Lincoln would die but rather *when* and *where* he would die. Leale did not think Lincoln could survive the trip to the White House. The doctors carried the president down the steps and, once in the lobby, found a wooden partition and used it as a stretcher. They took him outside, trailing blood along the way and stopping several times for Leale to clear clots from the wound.[5]

The doctors considered taking Lincoln to Taltavul's Star Saloon, but before they could choose such an undignified location, a man on a doorstep directly across from the theater beckoned them. The man was Henry S. Safford, and the home belonged to a German tailor, William Petersen and his wife, Anna. Safford led the doctors to a room in the back that was being

The Petersen home where Abraham Lincoln died, now part of the Ford's Theater National Historic Site.

rented by Private William T. Clarke, a Union soldier from the Massachusetts Infantry who was out celebrating the end of the war.

The room was miniscule—a claustrophobic 15 by 9 feet—and so was the bed, requiring the six-foot-four-inch Lincoln to be laid in it diagonally. People crowded in until Leale ordered them out so he could examine Lincoln. The doctors checked for additional wounds and placed hot water bottles and blankets on his legs, which had already turned cold. Leale sent for Lincoln's pastor, Reverend Phineas Densmore Gurley, from the New York Avenue Presbyterian Church, as well as additional doctors: Dr. Willard Bliss, Surgeon General Joseph Barnes, Assistant Surgeon General Charles H. Crane, and Lincoln's personal physician, Dr. Robert E. Stone. They took turns probing the president's wound to locate the bullet using their unsanitary fingers and a Nelaton probe, a device that resembled a stick used for roasting marshmallows.[6] More physicians arrived, including Dr. Ezra W. Abbott and Dr. Hall. However, Leale was in charge and set the ground rules. He permitted the others to take a pulse, so they could one day boast that they had treated Lincoln in his final hours, but forbade them from touching the head wound.[7] Throughout the night, more than 90 people came to see the president.

During the initial hours of the crisis, Secretary of War Edwin McMasters Stanton took control of the government. He held meetings with all members of Lincoln's cabinet with the exception of Secretary of Treasury Hugh McCulloch and Secretary of State William Henry Seward, who had also been attacked that night. The men understood they were witnessing history and wanted to ensure that the night's dialogue was transcribed for posterity. At midnight, General Christopher C. Augur stepped outside to find someone who knew shorthand. He found 21-year-old James Tanner, a Civil War veteran who had lost both legs. He was in the right place at the right time with the right skill to become a witness to one of the most tragic events in American history.[8]

At 2:00 a.m., Vice President Andrew Johnson arrived. Later that evening, Robert Lincoln arrived with senators Charles Sumner, John Conness, and William Stewart. Throughout the night, Dr. Abbott dutifully recorded Lincoln's vital signs. His pulse seesawed from a weakened 42 at 11:15 p.m., before racing to 95 at 1:30 a.m. At 12:40 a.m., it was noted: "right eye much swollen, and echmoses [sic]," and 15 minutes later: "struggling motion of arms."[9] Leale held Lincoln's hand, in the hope that he would know he was not alone. He knew Lincoln could not see but thought he might be able to hear, and sent for Robert and Mary Todd.

It was raining at dawn, and, as the city awoke to the tragic news, a crowd gathered outside the house while guards stood at the door and on the roof. At the end of Lincoln's life, Dr. Taft noted the precise seconds, information not recorded for any other president: Abraham Lincoln took his last breath at 7:21:55, and fifteen seconds later his heart stopped beating. At 7:22:10 on April 15, 1865, Abraham Lincoln died. Besides the physicians, Senator Charles Sumner, Major John Hay, General Henry Halleck, General Montgomery C. Meigs, Reverend Gurley, Secretary of War Stanton, stenographer James Tanner, and Lincoln's son, Robert, were in the room when he died.

A silence hung over the room and was broken by Stanton, who uttered the brief and poignant statement, "Now he belongs to the ages." Leale gently placed two nickels over Lincoln's eye (they would later be replaced with half dollars). The custom of placing coins over the eyes of the dead originated in ancient Greece, and it was believed that the money would pay for safe passage across the river of death.[10] Leale crossed the president's arms, smoothed his hair, and covered his head with the white sheet. Reverend Gurley said a prayer and stepped outside to console Mary Todd. One by one they left the room until Stanton stood alone. He pulled back the white sheet and snipped a lock of Lincoln's hair and placed it in an envelope for Mary Jane Welles, wife of the secretary of the navy.

Lincoln's deathbed scene is the most iconic of all of the presidents. Days later, Currier and Ives began to produce commemorative lithographs titled, "The Death-Bed of the Martyr President, Abraham Lincoln." The sanitized, bloodless images were filled with inaccuracies, including the presence of Lincoln's other son, Tad.

Shortly after the president's death, Mary Todd walked outside. Looking across the street at Ford's Theatre, she murmured, "Oh that dreadful house, that dreadful house," before entering a carriage to take her to the White House.[11] At 9:00 a.m., members of the Veterans Reserve Corps wrapped Lincoln's body in an American flag and placed him in a simple pine box. They placed it in a hearse, removed their hats, and silently walked beside it to the White House.

Incredibly, nobody thought to clean up the room or preserve the artifacts for posterity. Moments after the body was removed, another tenant at the home, Julius Ulke, took a photograph of the room, capturing the bloodied pillow. When Private William T. Clarke returned to discover his room had been used in the president's

The historically inaccurate lithograph, *The Death-Bed of the Martyr President, Abraham Lincoln,* was mass-produced by Currier & Ives. Little Tad was never at the Petersen home on the night his father was slain. (Library of Congress)

dying hours, he found the bloodied tokens. He kept some as souvenirs, including, as he wrote his sister days later, "a piece of linen with a portion of his brain."[12]

At 11:00 a.m., six members of the Quartermaster's Department carried the coffin inside the White House. The body was placed in the same second-floor guest room where Zachary Taylor had died fifteen years earlier, and an autopsy was performed by Doctors Joseph Janvier Woodward and Edward Curtis. They were assisted by Surgeon General Barnes (who was also present at the John Wilkes Booth autopsy), Doctors Stone, Taft, and H. M. Notson, and Assistant Surgeon General Crane. Seven doctors were not required, as there was no mystery to the cause of death, but this was a gruesome event that none wanted to miss (except for Dr. Leale, who declined to attend). Andrew Johnson, now the seventeenth president, stood as a witness. Lincoln's skull was cut open and the brain carefully removed.[13] As they gingerly removed the gray matter, the tense silence was broken by the sound of a metallic "plink" as the bullet fell out of the brain and landed in a tray. The small piece of metal that forever changed history was sent to the Army Medical Museum (today the National Museum of Health and Medicine). The official autopsy report written by Dr. Woodward read, "There was a gunshot wound of the head around which the scalp was greatly thickened by hemorrhage into its tissues. The ball entered through the occipital bone about one inch to the left of the median line and just above the left lateral sinus, which it opened. It then penetrated the dura mater, passed through the left posterior lobe of the cerebrum, entered the left lateral ventricle and lodged in the white matter of the cerebrum just above the anterior portion of the left corpus striatum, where it was found."[14]

The body was moved to the second-floor bedroom for preparation by the undertakers, Charles Brown and Joseph B. Alexander. During the Civil War, the two men advanced the prac-

tice of embalming with a new patented technique that would make the skin "marble-like in character."[15] Lincoln would be the first president ever embalmed. For a task of this magnitude, they called upon Henry P. Cattell, "master embalmer" (three years earlier, Cattell had also embalmed Lincoln's son, William Wallace).[16] The firm later charged the federal government $100 for the embalming, as well as an additional $160 for Brown and Alexander to accompany the funeral train and perform necessary touch-up work along the route. The preparation of the body, especially the head, was difficult, as the skull had been sawed open during the autopsy. Cattell arched Lincoln's eyebrows, shaped his mouth into a smile, and snipped off several more locks of his hair for posterity.[17] A more gruesome relic, the blood drained from his jugular, was poured into jars and "sacredly preserved."[18] Cattell was satisfied with the embalming, except for a purple bruising around Lincoln's right eye he could not disguise. Stanton chose the suit in which Lincoln would be buried, the same one that he had worn to his inauguration barely a month earlier. After he was dressed, the body of the president was placed on the undertaker's table, where it remained for the next two days.[19]

For the first time in American history, a president had been assassinated. As Lincoln was no ordinary president, Americans could not hold a regular funeral. The size and scope would be unrivaled in the history of the country and became the gold standard of presidential funerals, one that many subsequent funerals would be compared to and modeled after. The task of planning the Washington portion of his funeral was assigned to Assistant Secretary of the Treasury George Harrington. Subsequent plans depended on where the body would be buried, and that was Mary Todd's decision.

Many thought that Lincoln should rest at Mount Vernon, beside George Washington, the only other man who came close to him in a "Greatest President" competition.[20] Congress suggested he be buried in the Capitol crypt that had been built for Washington. Mary Todd was adamant that he be buried in Chicago, but Robert and Lincoln's good friend and advisor, Supreme Court associate justice David Davis, persuaded her to choose Springfield, where the Lincolns had lived and planned to return after the presidency. Springfield leaders also tried to influence her decision. The National Lincoln Monument Association was hastily formed to ensure an appropriate memorial tomb and $20,000 was allocated for the construction. Mary Todd's one condition was that her son William be reinterred with his father. She knew that a spectacle could not be avoided for her husband, but Mary Todd wanted "no display made of her son's remains."[21]

Focus turned to how to get the president's body across the country to Illinois. In 1861, the incumbent president had taken an extended train route from Springfield to Washington. Now his corpse would traverse the same route in reverse, and, along the way, it would be put on public display to a degree never seen in America before or since. Two days after the assassination, a 10-person congressional committee was formed to make arrangements. Senators Charles Sumner, Ira Harris, Reverdy Johnson, Alexander Ramsey, and John Conness, and Representatives William B. Washburn, Green C. Smith, Robert C. Schenck, Frederick A. Pike, and Alexander Hamilton Coffroth were present at the first meeting. They selected pallbearers from among their peers and a congressman from each state and territory to accompany the body on the journey back to Springfield.

On April 18, the viewing at the White House started at 10:00 a.m., but crowds started to gather by 8:30 that morning. By the time the doors opened, the line was five people wide and stretched for a half mile. The throng entered the White House at the main entrance and walked to the East Room, where they shuffled past Lincoln's body in a solid walnut coffin lined with lead and adorned with silver handles. The cas-

ket, which had been purchased from Harvey & Sands Undertakers for $1,500, was small and narrow by today's standards—six and a half feet long and only 18 inches at shoulder—barely larger than the president's frame.[22] On it was a silver plate that read,

ABRAHAM LINCOLN,
SIXTEENTH PRESIDENT OF THE
UNITED STATES,
BORN FEBRUARY 12, 1809,
DIED APRIL 15, 1865

That day, 25,000 people saw Lincoln's "sweet, placid, natural expression, and the discoloration caused by the wound was so slight as not to amount to a disfigurement."[23]

For Lincoln, this scene in the East Room would have been eerily familiar, as he had envisioned it in a dream. In his dream, he wandered through an empty White House, working his way to the East Room, where a crowd was gathered around a coffin atop a catafalque. Lincoln asked a soldier whose body was in the coffin and was given a haunting reply—it was *the president* who had been killed by an assassin. Lincoln was so troubled by this dream that he later told his wife and a few friends. Several times he told friends that he felt he would not survive to see the end of the war. Lincoln had received numerous death threats, filing them away in a folder he labeled "Assassinations."[24]

The next day, Wednesday, April 19, 600 guests with tickets crammed into the East Room, sitting on bleachers that had been built for the occasion. President Johnson, Lincoln's first-term vice president Hannibal Hamlin, and an emotional Ulysses S. Grant were all in attendance. Representing the family were Robert and Tad. Mary was still in a fragile state of deep despair, leaving her unable to attend any of the funeral ceremonies.[25]

At 10 past noon, Reverend Charles H. Hall, rector of the Epiphany, read John 11:25–26, "I am the resurrection and the life, saith the Lord;

he that believeth in me, though he were dead, yet shall be live, and whosoever liveth and believeth in me shall never die." He was followed by Bishop Matthew Simpson of the Methodist Episcopal Church and Reverend Gurley. The crowd bowed their heads as Reverend Edwin H. Gray, chaplain of the Senate and pastor of the E Street Baptist Church, said a prayer to close the two-hour funeral.

The coffin was carried to a 15-foot-tall black hearse, placed on a bed of evergreens, and covered with white flowers. Six white horses slowly pulled the glass-sided hearse to the Capitol, followed by the president's physicians. President Johnson's carriage was guarded by cavalry on either side with sabers drawn, as the federal government was taking no more chances. Dozens of military units also marched, and midway through, the Twenty-Second US Colored Infantry found themselves leading. This place of honor by African Americans was utterly appropriate and entirely unplanned.[26] There were a staggering 50,000 marchers, and it took them two hours to pass. Thirty bands played simultaneous funeral dirges, which, accompanied by salutary gunfire and tolling bells, created an uncoordinated, un-harmonic cacophony of noise.

At the Capitol, the coffin was removed by 12 sergeants, each from a different company of the Veteran Reserve Corps, and gently placed on a black catafalque beneath the rotunda (today this catafalque, which was later used for other presidents, resides in the Washington crypt beneath the Capitol and is occasionally removed to be placed on display). A brief service was held by Reverend Gurley, and at 4:00 p.m., Stanton ordered the rotunda cleared, ending a day that the *New York Times* described as "the greatest pageant ever tendered to the honored dead on this continent . . . the spectacle has been the most impressive ever witnessed in the national capital."[27]

Overnight, the remains were guarded by members of the Twenty-Fourth Regiment Veteran Reserves, and at 6:00 a.m. on April 20, the doors were again opened to an awaiting crowd. It was raining, but 30,000 people walked past the remains with many more still outside at day's end. The statues in the room were all covered in black, except for that of George Washington, which was adorned with a black sash. At 9:30 p.m., the doors closed and Brigadier General James A. Hall arrived to take guard of the remains.

On April 21, six days after Lincoln's death, the Washington, DC, viewing finally came to a close. This was longer than any previous president had remained unburied, besting the four days for Washington and Martin Van Buren. For Lincoln, his time above ground was just getting started. At 6:00 a.m. dignitaries, cabinet members, and pallbearers arrived at the rotunda, and Reverend Gurley said a brief prayer. At 6:40 a.m., members of the Quartermaster General's Volunteers gently carried the coffin outside in the rain and placed it in the hearse. The procession was not intended to have the pomp and circumstance of the march to the Capitol building, but despite the bad weather and early hour, massive crowds gathered in silence to see it pass on its way to the Baltimore and Ohio Railroad Company depot on New Jersey Avenue. Earlier in the morning, the military had arrived at the station to clear the way for the hearse, allowing only those who were part of the demonstration or were taking a train that morning near the station. At 7:30 a.m., the coffin was placed on board (Willie's coffin had already been discreetly placed in the train). Once again, Reverend Gurley said a brief prayer before the train departed at precisely 8:00 a.m.

The train was commanded by Brigadier General Edward Davis Townsend and on board were about 150 people, including members of Congress from every state, a large judicial and military delegation from Illinois, several governors, dozens of active military and veterans, reporters, Supreme Court associate justice Davis, and an honor guard of high-ranking military officials. The only immediate family member on board was Robert, but he did not stay on all the way to Illinois and instead departed early to return to Washington, DC. Throughout the journey, several men had the honor of piloting the train (the first was Hanover, Pennsylvania native Carrolus A. Miller).

While neither the first nor last funeral train, this train was larger than life. Reporters called it "The Lincoln Funeral Train," and it has become a part of Lincoln history and folklore as much as any part of his death. The nine-car train was pulled by a steam engine called the Old Nashville and over the large cowcatcher hung a portrait of Lincoln. The last car was the 16-wheeled President's Car, where the president's coffin was placed on one end and his son's on the other.

After 2 hours and 38 miles, the train arrived in Baltimore at 10:00 a.m. Maryland governor Augustus Williamson Bradford, his staff, officers from the army and navy, and a crowd of "people of all ages and both sexes, white and black," were there to receive the remains. Sergeants from the Invalid Corps carried the coffin and placed it in a glass coach described as "the most beautiful car ever seen in this city," which was slowly pulled by four black horses.[28] The funeral procession consisted of government dignitaries and soldiers, including the United States Marines and the Eleventh Indiana Volunteers stationed at nearby Fort McHenry. It was almost 1:00 p.m. when the procession arrived at the Merchant's Exchange Building. The coffin was placed on a catafalque beneath a 14-foot all-black canopy embroidered with a large black velvet star, studded with 36 smaller stars. The ceremony in Baltimore was not well organized—the Merchants Exchange was opened to the public for only 90 minutes following the three hours it took to get the coffin there, frustrating thousands. After the coffin's return, the train then switched to the Northern Central Railway Company line and, shortly after 3:00 p.m., began the 58-mile trip to

Harrisburg, Pennsylvania. Crowds throughout Maryland gathered along the route and near the state line, Pennsylvania governor Andrew Gregg Curtin boarded the train.

At 6:53 p.m. the train stopped briefly at York Station in Pennsylvania, where seven women were permitted to board.[29] The train arrived at the Pennsylvania Railroad Station in Harrisburg at 8:20 p.m. and 1,500 people escorted the remains to the state capitol to lie in state beneath the rotunda. Despite the torrential rain, a massive crowd was ushered in for the late night viewing. At midnight, the doors were shut and the long day finally came to a close. The next day, the doors opened at 7:00 a.m. to an awaiting throng of people. At 10:00 a.m., the Carlisle Barracks Band led the procession back to the station. Sixteen pallbearers walked beside the hearse and were followed by Governor Curtin, military bands, veterans units, and fraternal organizations, including the Sons of Malta, Odd Fellows, and Free Masons. The train slowly pulled out of the station at 11:15 a.m. for the 106-mile trip to Philadelphia.

After passing through crowds gathered at Middletown, Elizabethtown, Mount Joy, Landisville, and Dillerville, there was a brief stop in Lancaster, where James Buchanan, Lincoln's predecessor, and Congressman Thaddeus Stevens, Lincoln's political adversary, boarded to pay their respects. The train continued through crowds in Penningtonville, Parkesburg, Coatesville, Gallagherville, Downingtown, Oakland, and West Chester before arriving in Philadelphia.[30]

Cannon fire announced the arrival of the train at Broad and Prime Street, and the coffin was gingerly placed in a magnificent custom-built hearse under the direction of Philadelphia's Committee of Reception. Drawn by eight black horses decorated with silver harnesses, the hearse left the station at 5:15 p.m. with a full military escort. The march, which lasted almost three hours, was later called "one of the largest and most imposing . . . in any city on the route between Washington and Springfield."[31] Estimates place the crowd at half a million people and the procession was seven miles long. A few minutes before 8:00 p.m., the hearse arrived at Independence Square, and the remains were received by the Union League Association. The area was "brilliantly illuminated with calcium lights, about 60 in number, composed of red, white, and blue colors, which gave a peculiar and striking effect to the melancholy spectacle."[32] The coffin was placed on a black platform, next to the Liberty Bell and beneath a statue of George Washington, in the same room where the Declaration of Independence had been signed 89 years earlier. A flag was removed from the coffin and the lid raised, exposing the seven-day-dead Lincoln's head and chest. The doors opened at 10:00 p.m. and over the next two hours, people streamed in as a band looped a somber dirge. When the doors closed at midnight, only a fraction of those waiting had been able to see Lincoln. Hundreds camped out overnight to ensure they would not miss out the following day.

At 6:00 a.m. on Sunday, April 23, the doors opened for the longest period of viewing thus far. The crowds became dangerous, as the *Philadelphia Inquirer* conveyed: "Never before in the history of our city was such a dense mass of humanity huddled together. Hundreds of persons were seriously injured from being pressed in the mob, and many fainting females were extricated by the police and military and conveyed to places of security. Many women lost their bonnets, while others had nearly every particle of clothing torn from their persons."[33] Finally, at 2:00 a.m. on Monday, April 24, after a mind-boggling 300,000 people had viewed the casket in 20 hours, the doors were closed. The bands played a dirge as the military escorted the hearse to Kensington Station, a different depot from which it had arrived. Shortly before 4:00 a.m., the train slowly began its journey north for the 86-mile trip to New York.

At 5:30 a.m., the funeral train crossed the Delaware River into New Jersey and stopped briefly to pick up Governor Joel Parker and his staff to officially escort the body through his state. The bells tolled as the train chugged into Trenton, where it stopped at 5:45 a.m. and was met by the Reserved Veteran and Invalid Corps, the Trenton Band, and Mayor Franklin S. Mills, who spoke briefly.

The train pushed north through Princeton and stopped briefly in New Brunswick, then rolled on through Rahway and Elizabeth, passing signs of support and solemnly decorated homes. It continued to the Broad Street Station in Newark and at 10:03 a.m. came to a halt in the Camden and Amboy Railway Depot in Jersey City. A German group from nearby Hoboken sang a sad dirge, and the clock at the station stood at 7:22, the moment Lincoln died. Here the body was removed from the train for its first boat ride, on the ferry *Jersey City*. Soldiers with swords drawn guarded the coffin as the procession entered the shipyard gates. The crowd stood silent, and the only sound was the booming minute guns. New York mayor Charles Godfrey Gunther boarded the ship to escort the coffin across the Hudson.

At 10:50 a.m., *Jersey City* arrived at Desbrosses Street in Manhattan, where it was met by thousands on the streets and rooftops. The mahogany coffin was placed in an elaborate glass hearse to allow spectators to view it as it passed. The "elegant piece of workmanship" was 14 feet long and towered 15 feet high.[34] Six gray horses covered in black cloth slowly led the hearse, which was flanked by the Seventh Regiment of the National Guard and followed by sergeants of the Invalid Corps. Trailing the mile-long march were the German singers and the city police. The procession marched to Canal Street and then to Broadway, where 20,000 people were waiting for the coffin's arrival at City Hall at 11:30 a.m. The coffin was placed on a catafalque in the black-draped Governor's Room, which was also used for James Monroe.

The undertaker raised the lid, and guards assumed their position to prepare for viewing. Before the doors were opened, New York photographer Jeremiah Gurney captured the scene.[35] At 1:00 p.m., the doors were opened to a line that stretched three quarters of a mile. Mourners ascended a staircase on one side and viewed Lincoln's corpse for a brief second before descending on the other side. The crowd was remorseful and respectful, and several women even had to be restrained from planting a kiss on Lincoln's cold lips. By midnight, an estimated 60,000 people had walked past, but the tired crowds continued to pour in.

Around 2:00 a.m., French sketch artist Pierre Morand entered to pay his respects. Morand paused long enough to pull out his pencil and make a quick sketch. Morand later made additional copies of his death sketch, which today are prized artifacts (one was valued in 2014 at a hefty $175,000).[36] Of those who did get a brief glimpse of Lincoln, many left with a feeling of unease. After 10 days, the specter of death could not be hidden by even the best of embalmers. It was written that, "To the public, the exhibition of the discolored face of the President was not desirable. . . . The features were so very unnatural, the color so thoroughly turned, and the general appearance so unpleasant, that none could regard the remains with even a melancholy pleasure."[37] At 5:00 a.m., Brown tried to improve the appearance as dust brought in from the crowds had discolored Lincoln's face and his mouth had slacked open. The final guard took their positions at 10:00 a.m., and included in this watch was Brigadier General Daniel Butterfield, commander of the Third New York Brigade, who three years earlier wrote the simple Taps melody that would become a mainstay at future presidential funerals.

Captain Parker Snow, who had commanded expeditions to both the Arctic and Antarctic, was among the mourners and presented "relics of Sir John Franklin's ill-fated expedition [that] consisted of a tattered leaf of a Prayer Book, on which the first word legible was the word 'Martyr,' and a piece of fringe and some portions of uniform."[38] Later, a careless mourner tossed a lit cigar onto the floor and the embers ignited the catafalque drapery! Fortunately, the fire was put out before much damage could be done, and a disaster was averted. Additional damage occurred earlier in the night when a bust of George Washington was broken, but the crowds cleaned up the mess themselves by carting away shards as souvenirs. Finally, after almost 23 hours during which 150,000 people passed by the remains, the doors closed. Along with the scores of disgruntled New Yorkers who were unable to get in were "highly decorated representatives of Great Britain, Russia and France," who arrived a moment too late.[39]

Before closing the lid and screwing it shut, the undertaker dusted off Lincoln's face. At 12:50 p.m., the coffin was carried back to the hearse. The return procession was billed as the "grandest, most imposing ever organized in the United States."[40] Approximately 60,000 people, a quarter of whom were soldiers, marched in the procession that stretched for five miles and was watched by a half million people. The hearse was drawn by 16 gray horses, each led by an African American groom. Following were carriages carrying dignitaries, including New York governor Fenton, New York City mayor Gunther, and Illinois governor Richard J. Oglesby, as well as dozens of judges, senators, and city officials. The parade also included the Mechanic's Association, New York Caulkers Association, and "coloured delegates from Benevolent Societies."[41] African Americans were originally banned, but, "aided by strong hints from the War Department," city officials relented. Several of the 200 black citizens were flanked by police to ensure their safety and held a banner that read "Abraham Lincoln, our Emancipator! Two Millions of Bondemen he Liberty Gave."

When the hearse passed the home of Cornelius Roosevelt, an eerily spectacular meeting of past and future presidential titans was captured in a photograph. In it, the hearse can be seen along with two little boys in a second-story window—Elliot Roosevelt and his seven-year-old brother, Theodore. Moments later, the hearse paused in Union Square for a brief ceremony hosted by the notorious William Magear "Boss" Tweed.[42] The parade was an unprecedented spectacle, prompting the *New York Herald* to write: "The city never saw a greater throng, nor a more orderly one."[43]

At 2:10 p.m., the head of the procession reached the Hudson River Railroad Depot, but it would be another hour before the hearse arrived. Shortly after 3:00 p.m., the sergeants of the Invalid Corps carried the coffin onto the train, which was being guarded by 12 policemen to keep the crowd and souvenir hunters at bay. There were two engines in the station: the pilot engine *Constitution* left 10 minutes ahead and the more elaborately decorated *Union* led the funeral train. Engineer William Raymond and Assistant Superintendent J. M. Toucey were granted the honor of piloting the train for the next leg of the journey. An hour and fifteen minutes later, Toucey yelled, "All aboard!" and the train began its 141-mile trip to Albany.[44]

The train chugged north through Fort Washington, Mount St. Vincent, Yonkers, Hastings, Dobbs Ferry, Irvington, Tarrytown, Ossining, Montrose, and Peekskill.[45] When it stopped briefly at West Point at 6:20 p.m., cadets passed quickly through the funeral car and guns were fired in salute while a band played a funeral dirge. Thirty miles north, the train paused briefly in Poughkeepsie to pick up a delegation. It continued along the Hudson corridor, passing several trackside memorials, including one that featured 100 schoolgirls dressed in white. Almost seven hours after leaving New York City, the train pulled into East Albany at 11:00 p.m.[46] A delegation met the train, and four horses

pulled a hearse onto a ferry to cross the Hudson River, where the docks were lit by the torches of a dozen fire companies. At the Albany capitol building, the coffin was placed on a simple platform draped in black velvet in the Assembly Chamber. At 1:00 a.m. on Wednesday, April 26, crowds began to file in two at a time and continued unabated over the next 13 hours. While mourners passed, 400 miles to the south on a farm owned by Richard Garrett in Port Royal, Virginia, Lincoln's assassin, John Wilkes Booth, was finally captured and killed. At 2:00 p.m., the doors were closed, followed by a procession to the Central Railway Depot. The hearse rode down Broadway to State Street and onto Lumbar Street and was seen by 60,000 people. At 4:00 p.m., the train, now led by conductor Homer P. Williams and General Superintendent H. W. Chillinden, left the station for the 298-mile trip to Buffalo.

Traversing the state from east to the west, the train was greeted by weeping crowds in Schenectady, Amsterdam, Little Falls, Palatine Bridge, Fort Plain, St. Johnsville, Herkimer, Utica, and Oriskany. At 11:15 p.m., there was a brief stop in Syracuse, where 35,000 people had gathered. The train then continued through Warners, Memphis, Jordan, Weedsport, Port Byron, Savannah, Clyde, and Lyons. At a brief stop in Rochester at 3:20 a.m., it was met by the Fifty-Fourth New York Regiment. On the train's arrival in Batavia at 5:18 a.m., former president and Buffalo resident Millard Fillmore boarded and president number thirteen escorted number sixteen the remaining 40 miles. It was 7:00 a.m. when the train pulled into Buffalo's Exchange Street Station, where it was greeted by the firing of cannons and tolling of church bells. The coffin was placed in an elaborate hearse that was draped in black and pulled by six white horses. At 8:00 a.m. the procession started up Exchange Street to Main Street to Niagara to Delaware to Tupper, back to Main Street and then to Eagle Street, where the coffin was placed in an elaborately decorated room in St. James Hall and the viewing began at 9:35 a.m. Approximately 100,000 people walked past the remains, including Fillmore and future president Grover Cleveland. Many Canadians crossed the border to pay tribute to the American martyr, and several women passed out from the commotion. The doors closed at 8:15 p.m., and an escort returned the remains to the station. At 10:00 p.m. the train departed for the 183-mile trip to Cleveland, Ohio.

At 1:00 a.m., there was a brief stop in Westfield, New York, for five tearful women to place a wreath and cross beside the coffin. (In 1860, an eleven-year-old Westfield resident, Grace Bedell, wrote a clean-shaven president-elect Lincoln and suggested that he "grow whiskers" to appeal to his female constituents. The president liked the idea, replied to young Grace, and immediately grew his trademark beard.) A few miles farther along, the train stopped to allow the New York contingent to depart and the Pennsylvania delegation to board. The train then crossed into Wickcliffe, Ohio, where General Joseph Hooker boarded along with several Ohio dignitaries to accompany the remains to Cleveland.

On Friday, April 28, artillery shots announced the train's impending arrival. Crowds had flooded into Cleveland for the funeral, filling every hotel in the city. At 7:00 a.m., when the train pulled into Euclid Street Station, eight members of the Veterans Reserve Corps placed the coffin on a hearse that was pulled by six white horses, each attended by an African American groom. The procession also featured the Knights Templar, decked out in full regalia, along with the Order of Free and Accepted Masons. Following the fraternal organizations were the Order of the Odd Fellows, the Father Matthew Temperance Society, the Fenian Brotherhood, the Ancient Order of Good Fellows, the Ohio City Lodge of Good Fellows, the Hungarian Association, the German Benevolent Mutual Society, the 1188 Grand United Order of Odd Fellows, and

the Eureka Lodge No. 14 of Colored Masons. Dozens of organizations marched, totaling over 6,000 people in the parade.

The procession arrived at the Public Square in downtown Cleveland, where the city had built a new structure for the funeral. The building resembled a Chinese pagoda with a second smaller room atop the first. It sat upon a 36-by-24-foot base, adorned with golden eagles, and the "floor of the building was covered thickly with matting, so as to deaden every sound."[47] The Veterans Reserves placed the coffin on the dais, and a band played a dirge as a delegate of local women placed floral arrangements beside it. The undertaker opened the coffin lid and did a quick inspection to confirm the body was presentable, both in sight and smell, before the ceremony began. The bishop of the Diocese of Ohio, Reverend Charles Pettit McIlvaine, spoke of Lincoln's truncated life and enjoined President Johnson to follow in the footsteps of his predecessor. The first to walk past the coffin were wounded soldiers, where "many a bronzed veteran's eyes were wet as he gazed upon him who had laid down his life for his country."[48]

Throughout the day there was a steady rain, but mourners streamed in unabated as bands played their solemn tunes from hotel balconies. At 10:10 p.m., after 100,000 to 150,000 people had walked past the coffin two at a time, the viewing in Cleveland came to an end. An hour afterward, the hearse and its military escort rode down Superior Street to Vineyard Street to the train station.

Conductor Charles Gale headed south for the 135-mile trip to Columbus, Ohio, through the torrential rain. At 7:30 a.m. on Saturday, April 29, the train pulled in to Union Depot, where it was met by a large crowd and solemn music. The hearse had been especially built for the occasion. It was a 17-square-foot structure shaped like a Chinese pagoda. It was ornately decorated, draped in silk flags and black cloth, and on each side was the name LINCOLN in large silver letters. Six decorated white horses pulled the hearse accompanied by a prominent military escort. Throughout the journey, host cities saw sights that were unrivaled by anything in their history, and Columbus was no exception. It was written that this procession "was the most imposing and the most impressive which ever marched through the streets of Columbus. The slow, measured tread of the troops, the muffled drum, and the dead march, told their own tale of the fearfully solemn occasion on which they were passing in review before the assembled thousands who had congregated as witnesses."[49]

At 9:00 a.m., the hearse arrived at the west entrance to the Capitol Square, and the coffin was placed in the rotunda of the State Capitol building. The lid was opened to reveal the head and upper torso of Lincoln, and at 9:30 a.m. the crowds began to pass two at a time. Ohio Congressman Job E. Stevenson of Chillicothe spoke to the crowds outside at 4:00 p.m.; they listened in respectful silence as he mourned the tragic loss, but when he demanded that justice be done to the assassins, the crowd seethed in vengeful agreement.

At 6:00 p.m., the doors were closed after an estimated 60,000 people had walked past. The coffin was returned to the Great Central Railway depot, and at 8:00 p.m., the train began the 187-mile trip to Indianapolis. As the train rolled across the countryside, bonfires lit up the night, warming hundreds of people who came out to witness history. Its first stop was in Woodstock, Ohio, for a group of women to place flowers on the coffin. After 15 miles, it stopped again in Urbana at 10:45 p.m., where 3,000 people had crowded the depot. Large crowds gathered to watch the train in towns such as Piqua, Gettysburg, and Greeneville. In New Paris, it passed beneath a 25-foot evergreen arch that had been built for the occasion.[50]

The train stopped at 3:10 a.m. in Richmond, where it was met by 15,000 people as church bells rang to announce its arrival. A large arch had been constructed, beneath which was a platform 18 feet off the ground, where a young woman representing the "Genius of Liberty" wept over a coffin flanked by two boys acting as soldiers in a bizarre Kabuki theater.[51] Wreaths were presented, including one for Willie—one of the first of the journey, as by this time the secret passenger had been revealed. Indiana Governor Oliver P. Morton boarded, and the funeral train continued, slowing to a crawl in the towns of Centreville, Cambridge City, Dublin, Lewisville, Coffin's Station, Ogden, Raysville, Knightstown, and Charlottesville, where it was noted that a large group of black citizens viewed it as it passed. Despite the nocturnal hour, crowds still gathered, bands played, and soldiers ceremoniously guarded its passage.

Proceeding through Greenfield and Cumberland, it arrived at Union Depot in Indianapolis, Indiana, at 7:00 a.m. on Sunday, April 30. Here, too, the coffin was solemnly carried from the train while a band played before a hushed crowd. In this location, the band played an original song written for the occasion by Cincinnati resident Charles Hess, called "Lincoln's Funeral March"; it was later published by A. C. Peters and Brothers. Due to the pouring rain, Major General Alvin P. Hovey, who was placed in charge of the day's events, decided to forgo the elaborate funeral procession and allow more time for viewing. The coffin was placed on a black velvet catafalque in the center of the great hall beneath the rotunda. In Indianapolis, lots of attention was given to the military honors of guarding the coffin: shifts were broken into nine watches to allow many soldiers to stand in the coveted position of honor. At 9:00 a.m., the doors were opened, and citizens poured in to get their brief glimpse of Lincoln.

One hundred thousand paid their respects in Indianapolis, and at 10:00 p.m., the viewing came to an end. After a brief closing ceremony, the coffin was escorted by a military guard back to the Union Depot through streets lit by bonfires and torches. At midnight, the train departed for the 210-mile journey to Chicago. Passing small towns in the early hours of Monday, May 1, the train was greeted with bonfires, tolling bells, and funeral music. It traveled onward through Augusta, Zionsville, Lebanon, Colfax, Stockwell, Battle Ground, Brookston, Chalmers, Bradford, Medaryville, Westville, and LaCroix.

At 8:25 a.m., the train arrived at Michigan City, Indiana, stopping beneath an elaborate 35-foot-high Gothic arch topped by a flag flying at half-mast, one of 27 memorial arches erected for the funeral train. Sixteen women dressed in white and black serenaded the train, singing the lyrics of "Praise God, from Whom All Blessings Flow" to the hymn "Old Hundredth," accompanied by 36 women, all holding small flags. The 16 singers then entered the train to place flowers on the coffin. Illinois senator Lyman Trumbull also boarded for the remaining leg of the journey to Chicago. The train made its final state border crossing into Illinois at Lake Calumet at 11:00 a.m., announced by ceremonial gunfire.

At last, the gloomy weather that had persisted for much of the ride abated, and the sun welcomed the train to Chicago. It stopped about a mile from the Chicago station, at a temporary depot by Park Row. Citizens packed the streets and rooftops to catch a glimpse of Lincoln's funeral train. At the temporary station stood the largest arch of the journey, a triple-peaked Gothic structure that had been designed and constructed by W. W. Boyington. It was adorned with flags, and beneath it was a platform where the coffin was placed. The Great Western Light Guard Band played "The Lincoln Requiem," an original

piece written for the occasion. Thirty-six high school girls placed flowers on the coffin, which had been carried in on a custom-built hearse, designed and constructed by Coan and Ten Broecke. The massive, elaborate structure was 18 feet long, 15 feet high, and featured state-of-the-art shock absorbing springs to steady the body in transit. The procession was massive, bested only by the one in New York City.

Leading the way were Chicago police officers and the hearse, pulled by 10 black horses, followed next by a military escort and the past and present mayors of Chicago. All told, there were approximately 37,000 people in the march. For four long hours, 150,000 bystanders respectfully watched the procession snake its way through the streets of Chicago, from Park Row to Michigan Avenue to Lake Street to Clark Street and then into the east gate of the Court House Square. According to the *Chicago Tribune*, "The procession was a solemn tribute to his memory, and evinced the devotion with which all classes looked up to Mr. Lincoln. Its composition was

The impressive triple-peaked Gothic funeral arch erected in Chicago at a temporary depot to welcome the Lincoln funeral train. (Library of Congress)

varied, and embraced all nationalities, all creeds, and all sects [and] bronzed, war-worn and gray-bearded heroes of the army and navy; veteran soldiers, incapacitated for active service by honorable wounds." At 12:45 p.m., the hearse arrived at the courthouse. After General Joseph Hooker surveyed the area, the coffin was brought in through the south door and placed on a catafalque in the middle of the rotunda, beneath a solemn and patriotic canopy supported by iron columns. Cut into the canopy were 36 stars with mirrors strategically placed to reflect them onto the body. The effect was called "new and solemn" at the time.

Before mourners entered at 5:00 p.m. (through a door beneath the inscription "Illinois clasps to her bosom her slain but glorified son"), the embalmer did some touch-up work. The decaying and discolored features of the slain president disturbed many of the people.[52] After 16 days, it was becoming increasingly difficult to cover the aroma of death emanating from the decaying corpse. To help mask the scent of embalmed death, flowers were strewn about and placed at each corner of the coffin.

Wooden sidewalks and fences buckled under the weight of the enormous crowd. People hustled past the closed coffin at an astounding clip of 7,000 people per hour, but at times the crowds became so bottlenecked they stood still for an hour. At 9:00 p.m. it started raining again, but the crowds did not slow. Songs were sung throughout the evening, including another original piece, "Farewell, Father, Friend and Guardian," written by L. M. Dawn and George F. Root, and at midnight, several hundred German citizens chanted a funeral song. People continued to stream in throughout the night and into the next day. At 8:00 p.m., on May 2, the 27-hour marathon viewing came to a close after 125,000 people had filed past the body. Sergeants of the Veteran Reserve Corps carried the coffin to the awaiting hearse, and a torchlit procession meandered to the St. Louis and Alton Railway Station. A 300-member German choir sang a final solemn farewell.

At 9:30 p.m., the train departed for its final 184 miles to Springfield, Lincoln's hometown. For the last leg, the train overflowed with dignitaries, including Illinois governor Richard J. Oglesby and Kentucky governor Thomas Elliott Bramlette. The rain did not deter crowds gathered around bonfires in Summit, Joyes, and Lennox, and at 11:33 p.m. it passed a one-minute gun salute in Lockport. As it slowly rolled beneath a memorial arch in the city of Joliet, a meteor shot across the sky, stunning the 12,000 mourners that had gathered. The train continued into the morning of Tuesday, May 3, through Elwood and Hampton and was viewed by 5,000 people in Wilmington at 1:00 a.m. It passed through Gardner, Dwight, Odell, Cayuga, and Lexington, where bells tolled upon its arrival. At 4:30 a.m., it passed Towanda; at 5:00 a.m., it was greeted by a crowd of 5,000 in Bloomington; and at 7:00 a.m., it passed under another arch in Lincoln's namesake town (the first in the country named in his honor), where 2,500 had gathered.

After almost nonstop rain and cloudy weather, it was sunny in Springfield when the Lincoln funeral train made its final stop. The arrival was announced with cannon fire from the Battery K, Second Missouri Light Artillery. For the last time, the pallbearers, this time old friends of the president, entered the train to remove the coffin. The coffin was placed upon an ornate gold, silver, and crystal funeral carriage. Springfield did not have its own lavish caisson, and the hearse, valued at $6,000, was provided by the mayor of St. Louis and pulled by its owner, Jesse Arnot (the historic carriage was later destroyed in a fire at Arnot's stable on February 9, 1887).[53] The procession included the customary dignitaries, governors, clergy, and military, but in a sad irony, in Lincoln's hometown "colored citizens" were relegated to the end of the parade, right after "citizens generally."[54]

The hearse was pulled down Jefferson Street to Fifth Street to Monroe and then east to Sixth Street before its arrival at the Springfield State House (today known as the "Old Capitol"). Veterans carried the coffin into the House of Representatives hall and placed it on an elaborately decorated catafalque, adorned with 36 silver stars and perched upon a dais in the middle of the room beneath the dome. Above the coffin hung a portrait of George Washington, and on the wall were the prophetic words that Lincoln had spoken at Independence Hall in Philadelphia on February 22, 1861: "Sooner than surrender these principles, I would be assassinated on the spot" (a life-size representation of this scene can be seen today at the nearby Abraham Lincoln Presidential Library and Museum).

Brown, assisted by a local undertaker, Thomas Lynch, made preparations for the final viewing. By this time, Lincoln's face had become so discolored that they had to purchase rouge chalk to lighten up his features. The doors were opened at 10:00 a.m., and the awaiting crowd was ushered in. Over the next 24 hours, 75,000 people viewed the remains, more than six times the population of Springfield at the time. After the viewing ended on Thursday, May 4, the coffin was closed for the final time, and the lid was soldered shut. After 19 days, Lincoln's body would finally be entombed.

Prior to the train's arrival, a Committee of Arrangements had been established in Springfield under the direction of General Hooker and several other military leaders, funded by $16,000 from city coffers. On the morning of the funeral, trains arrived and swelled the already overcrowded streets of Springfield, until 150,000 people had crammed into the city. At 11:30 a.m., the procession began as the band struck up "Lincoln's Funeral March." The parade was divided into eight divisions, three before the hearse and five trailing. An extensive military escort led the parade, followed by the Surgeons and Physicians of the Deceased.[55] The hearse, flanked by the pallbearers, came next, followed by the president's horse, Old Bob, led by Reverend Henry Brown, an African American minister who had worked for Lincoln as a handyman. Following Old Bob was a carriage with Lincoln's family members: Robert and Tad, cousin John Hanks, and Mary's cousin Elizabeth Todd Grimsley. The remaining divisions consisted of various military, religious, civic, and political leaders and fraternal organizations.

The processions passed his former home on 8th and Jackson Street, still owned by the Lincoln family. At the time of his death, it was being rented by Lucien Tilton, and she had decorated the home with evergreens and the color of mourning in anticipation of the attention it would receive. (Today this home is preserved as the Lincoln Home National Historic Site.) The procession continued to 4th Street, and at 1:00 p.m., it arrived at Oak Ridge Cemetery. The cortege continued to the public receiving vault, located on the south side of the cemetery. The tomb had only recently been restored after it was confirmed the body would rest in Springfield.

The Veteran Reserve Guard stood by the hearse as Robert, Tad, and other family members and friends removed the coffin and carried it inside the stone walls of a temporary public vault that had been covered in black velvet. After Willie had been placed inside, the funeral ceremony began with a prayer by Reverend Albert Hale of the Second Presbyterian Church, followed by the hymn "Farewell, Father, Friend and Guardian." Reverend N. W. Miner quoted Scripture from Saints John and Paul, and Reverend A. C. Hubbard read Lincoln's final inauguration address, concluding the service with, "With malice toward none, with charity for all, with firmness in the right as God gives us to see the right, let us strive on to finish the work we are in, to bind up the nation's wounds, to care for him who shall have borne the battle and for his widow and his orphan, to do all which may achieve and cherish a just and lasting peace among ourselves and with all nations."

Bishop Simpson then delivered a lengthy sermon, recounting the accomplishments of Lincoln's abbreviated life, the magnitude of his character, and the profoundness of the nation's loss. This was followed by another original funeral song, "Over the Valley the Angels Smile," a closing prayer by Reverend Simeon W. Harkey, and final words from Reverend Gurley. The heavy iron doors of the tomb were closed, and at long last, the ceremony had ended. The key to the padlock was handed to Robert Lincoln, who passed it along to his mother's cousin, John Todd Stuart. The *Cincinnati Commercial* summed up the longest presidential funeral in history, when it wrote, "Thus has the nation buried Abraham Lincoln with a burial more illustrious than that of kings."

The long journey was finally over: 1,700 miles, and 1.5 million people had viewed the remains of the martyred president, and 7 million more watched the train or the hearse pass. Amazingly, the 20-day pageant—a hastily arranged logistical behemoth, which cost the government $28,985.31—was completed with nary a hitch. If anyone deserved to rest in peace, it was Lincoln, but it was not to be.

The vault where Lincoln's remains were placed was only temporary. Shortly after Lincoln's death, 13 prominent Springfield citizens formed the National Lincoln Monument Association to create a permanent memorial. They chose a spot in the heart of the city accessible to tourists, purchased the block (known as the Mather Block), and even erected a vault, all without first getting Mary Todd's consent. When she decided that she preferred the public cemetery on the outskirts of the city, the group was left with no other choice than to accede to her wishes, so the National Lincoln Monument Association redirected plans for a monument a stone's throw from the temporary vault.[56] Immediately, donations came in from all over the country: $50,000 from the state of Illinois, $10,000 from New York, $28,000 donated by "old soldiers and sailors"; "colored" regiments chipped in $8,000.

The public receiving vault where Abraham Lincoln's body was placed on May 4, 1865, 19 days after his death. On the hill behind it was the second temporary tomb, which is no longer in existence.

An additional $110,000 was donated by various individuals and organizations.[57]

Once funding was secured, a contest was held to choose a design. The winner, selected in September 1868, was Larkin G. Meade, a sculptor from Brattleboro, Vermont. Prior to Lincoln, presidential tombs were simple, humble structures. Even Washington's tomb was not elaborate. Lincoln was not only a great president, he was our first to be assassinated, so Meade's design was bigger and bolder than anything seen before in America and more closely resembled the final resting place of an emperor or pharaoh than a president. Ground was broken the same year, and over the next three years, the massive monument was constructed. The towering structure built of Quincy gray granite, marble, and bronze featured an 85-foot-tall obelisk perched on top of a terrace and in each corner was a 25-foot circular pedestal. Its footprint was 119 by 72 feet, and within the base was a memorial room and catacomb.[58] The final cost for the monument was $206,550, although some quotes run as high as $270,000.

On December 21, 1865, Lincoln was moved to a family receiving vault when the temporary one was needed for another deceased. This second location was between the public receiving vault and the location of the final monument, and he remained there for six years. On September 19, 1871, with the memorial nearing completion, he was moved to a crypt inside the tomb. Three years later, on October 15, 1874, the coffin was moved again to the catacomb in a marble sarcophagus placed on a platform in an airtight lead case. Later that day, President Grant, accompanied by members of his cabinet, dedicated the monument.

With the monument completed and dedicated and the body now in its fourth and presumed final location, the tale of Lincoln's traveling remains should have ended. At the time, John Carroll Power was the custodian of the tomb, but there was no groundskeeper or night watchman. The only thing protecting the sarcophagus was the chamber door and a padlock. Perhaps nobody thought further security was needed, but an Irish gang from Chicago saw this as an opportunity to hatch a nefarious plot.[59]

In early 1876, a small-time gang led by Big Jim Kennally had fallen on hard times when their ace counterfeiter, Benjamin Boyd, was arrested and held in the Illinois State Penitentiary in Joliet for a ten-year sentence. Somehow, Kennally came up with the bizarre plot to liberate Boyd by stealing Lincoln's body! Kennally planned to bury the body in the sand dunes of Indiana, where the wind would blow away all traces of their deed. In return for the remains, he would demand the release of Boyd and $200,000 to boot. This plan was not as unusual as it sounds today, as grave robbing for medical research and profit was a booming business in the late 1800s. Nor was this a ridiculous Keystone Cops caper—given the minimal security, they had a very good chance of pulling it off. Kennally, literally not wanting to get his hands dirty, recruited saloonkeeper Terence Mullen, who worked at the Hub, a tavern that Kennally co-owned, to do the deed. The Hub was a plain Irish bar located at 294 West Madison Street in Chicago. It was far from fancy, but one adornment on display there was a bust of Lincoln. Kennally also recruited another counterfeiter, Jack Hughes, along with Billy Brown to be the getaway driver. But while the three knew counterfeiting, they had no expertise in grave robbing, so they found someone more experienced in the field—Lewis Swegles. Swegles turned out to be a $5-a-day paid informant for the new Secret Service agency, founded to combat counterfeiting.[60] Not only was Swegles an informant, but so was Billy Brown. Of five criminals, two were moonlighting for the Secret Service.

The gang planned the crime for election night, November 7, 1876. With attention on the race between Samuel J. Tilden and Rutherford B. Hayes, they believed they had the cover they needed. That night, they surreptitiously entered the cemetery and sawed the lock off the door. They easily lifted the lid off of the sarcophagus but then discovered it was much more difficult to remove the 500-pound lead-lined coffin than they had anticipated. So they sawed off the side of the marble sarcophagus and managed to pull the coffin out about 15 inches. Thanks to Swegles and Brown, the Secret Service was waiting nearby in the memorial room for the ideal moment to make the arrest. However, a detective accidentally fired his pistol, and the criminals escaped into the night. With Swegles's help, they were easily tracked down three days later and arrested. Charged for attempting to steal the $75 casket (!), they were sentenced to a year in Illinois State Penitentiary in Joliet. Big Jim Kennally was never charged with the scheme but was jailed for another crime a few years later.[61]

Shortly after the incident, John Todd Stuart visited the custodian. He was paranoid after the attempted grave robbery, and together they devised a plan to secretly relocate the coffin while the public still believed it was inside the sarcophagus. On November 13, in the dead of night, the two men, along with Adam Johnson (a marble dealer), Colonel John Williams (Lincoln's close political ally), and Jacob Bunn (a bank clerk), secretly moved the coffin to a corner of the monument basement. There was no ventilation in the damp, foul-smelling room, and the task was hard for the men, the youngest being 56 years old. Over the next few days Power dug the grave, but he stopped when water seeped into the hole. Instead of digging another plot, they left the coffin where it was and covered it beneath a pile of plywood. Few people went in the basement, so their secret was safe for a while. But in the summer of 1877, when two bronze sculptures were placed by the entrance of the tomb, construction workers needed access to the basement. Power was forced to bring the superintendent of the crew into his plan. Within two days, Springfield was buzzing about the rumor. Power dismissed it as outlandish (which it was), but since he was unable to devise an alternative plan, the coffin sat there for another year. Finally, after it had sat two years under a stack of moldy wood, Power recruited a much younger group of confidantes to assist him in a reburial. They were not famous or connected but rather ordinary men with ordinary vocations—a bank clerk, a railroad ticket agent, and hotel owners. On the evening of November 18, 1878, the team dug a shallow grave in another corner of the basement, where the water table was not an issue. The expanded team dubbed themselves the "Lincoln Guard of Honor," and the nine men held their first official meeting at the monument on February 12, 1880, on what would have been Lincoln's 71st birthday. The group was not secret, but the mission to protect the coffin was.

On July 15, 1882, after a tormented life, Mary Todd passed away. Robert was concerned her body would also be a target for grave robbers. At her funeral, she was placed in a prepared crypt, but the cover was not cemented on. That night, the Lincoln Guard of Honor removed her coffin and buried it in a shallow grave next to her husband, where, amazingly, the two stayed side by side for another five years. In 1887, a six-foot-deep vault was dug in the catacomb chamber of the memorial tomb. It was lined with 18 inches of cement and was large enough for both Lincoln and his wife. On April 14 of that year, the Lincoln Guard of Honor and the Lincoln Monument Association supervised stone masons as they excavated the hidden coffins.[62] The public was meant to be kept unaware, but word had leaked out. Eleven years after the attempted grave robbing, they finally learned the truth about the whereabouts of the Lincoln coffin.

With all of the coffin's movements, the morbidly curious group wanted to confirm that the body was indeed inside. They opened the lid and discovered "the body was found to be in a remarkable state of preservation and easily recognizable." After their inspection, both caskets were lowered into the vault and covered with cement, and a military guard watched over it until the cement hardened. As this tomb was deemed impenetrable, they were confident that never again would anyone view Lincoln's remains. However, as seen already, one can never say never when referring to Lincoln's body.

For the next seven years, John Carroll Power remained vigilant at his post as custodian of Oak Ridge Cemetery, ensuring a theft would never be attempted again. He died on January 11, 1894, and was also buried in Oak Ridge Cemetery.

In 1894, after the last member of the National Lincoln Monument Association died, the state acquired the tomb and still administers it to this day. However, time, neglect, and water had taken their toll and the tomb was deteriorating. It was alarming that the monument was slowly sinking, but it had been built on clay and not solid bedrock. Fixing this oversight was a massive project, and the state of Illinois appropriated $100,000. In 1899, the monument was completely dismantled and the foundation rebuilt. As a precaution, the public was not allowed anywhere near the work site. One of the hardest parts proved to be the removal of the coffins, which required construction workers to dig through the concrete lining of the tomb. For one week they chipped away until they finally freed them. On March 10, 1900, there was a small, "wholly informal" ceremony attended by local officials, members from the Lincoln Guard of Honor, and members of the Grand Army of the Republic to move the coffins to a "nearby subterranean vault."[63] After the coffins were lowered into the 12-square-foot brick vault, it was sealed with four stone slabs, each weighing two tons. Finally, the entire vault was buried beneath 30 feet of earth. Thirty-six years had passed since Lincoln's assassination and apparently curiosity had started to wane, for only 50 people showed up for the reinterment. However, the paranoia had not diminished, and armed guards were stationed at that tomb day and night.

During the reconstruction, the obelisk was raised 15 feet to augment its majestic appearance. On April 24, 1901, the rebuilt monument was ready. About 200 people showed up to view the proceedings, but this was not a formal event. In fact, it was so nonchalant that the contractors served as pallbearers. Incredibly, the coffin was placed in the same sarcophagus that had been vandalized by Kennally's gang a quarter century earlier! Planners felt that the additional security measure of a more imposing iron gate to keep out the ne'er-do-wells was sufficient. When Robert Lincoln found out about this lax arrangement, he contacted Illinois governor Richard Yates and demanded his father's remains be better secured. A new plan was devised to protect the coffin permanently. It would be buried 10 feet beneath the tomb within a steel cage, the reinterment would be completed without ceremony, and, as Robert demanded, the coffin would not be reopened. So for one last time (to date), the remains would be moved.

The reinterment was held on September 26, 1901, and 20 people gathered in the tomb at 11:30 a.m., including the last four members of the Lincoln Guard of Honor. There was no ceremony, as Robert had requested, and again the work crew doubled as pallbearers. In defiance of Robert's demand, the small group could not resist the temptation to open the coffin and take one last look at the 16th president. Before they did so, they covered the windows with newspapers to stop anyone from seeing them. One of the last remaining guardsman, Joseph P. Lindley, pulled his 13-year-old son, Fleetwood, out of school to view the body. The group hushed as two plumbers, Leon P. Hopkins and his nephew, Charles L. Willey, cut the lead-lined coffin.[64] As they opened the lid a fetid odor filled the room and then slowly dissipated. The corpse still looked remarkably like the president, but his skin was a striking marble-white color. Back in 1887, Lincoln's skin was a dark bronze. The following day the *Illinois State Journal* wrote,

"Fourteen years ago when the remains were opened the face was very dark, almost black, and the change to an immaculate white is not understood unless the suggestion that a mold has overspread the features is correct."[65]

After 23 people had viewed Lincoln's corpse, the coffin was closed. Pallbearers used leather straps to lower it into a steel cage within the 10-foot-deep vault in the catacomb chamber and then buried it in Portland cement. The tomb was rededicated on October 15, 1901.

Thirty years later, another reconstruction project gave visitors access to the burial chamber. Now that it was much more secure than in the days of Kennally, there was no concern of the body being stolen in the night. During construction, the original sarcophagus was left outside, with plans to preserve the relic. Those plans were short-lived when a truck backed over it, smashing it to pieces. Even a smashed sarcophagus is still worth preserving when it once contained the body of Abraham Lincoln. The shards were placed back in the tomb, sealed over, and their location became lost over time, only to be rediscovered in February 1979.[66] Today, a piece of the original tomb is on display inside the memorial. On June 17, 1931, there was a rededication ceremony with Herbert Hoover in attendance. He became the eighth president to visit the tomb, but the first to view the interior. There he saw the new sarcophagus built of Red Ozark marble, which rose nine feet above the spot where the body was buried. Also in attendance were a few members of the Grand Army of the Republic, 66 years after the Civil War.[67]

The list of presidential visits since the rededication is long and illustrious, many while campaigning for office. Franklin D. Roosevelt visited while campaigning for his first term on October 21, 1932. On August 19, 1954, President Dwight Eisenhower laid a wreath at the tomb, and on October 24, 1959, candidate John F. Kennedy visited the tomb (he also visited on October 19, 1962, while in town to speak at the Illinois State Fairgrounds to endorse fellow Democrat, Representative Sidney Yates).[68] On August 19, 1968, Richard Nixon visited while campaigning in Illinois (he also visited as vice president on January 14, 1956), and Ronald Reagan visited on October 18, 1980.[69]

Almost 91 years to the day of Lincoln's assassination, Samuel J. Seymour passed away on April 12, 1956. As a five-year-old boy, Seymour was in Ford's Theatre the night Lincoln was shot, making him the last living person to witness the event. In the few years before his death, Seymour had attained a small celebrity status when his account of that day's events was published in the newspaper. In the interview, he said he sometimes relives the horror of that night when he is "dozing in [his] rocker, as an old codger like [him] is bound to do."[70] Two years later, Seymour—hard of hearing but still sharp as a

Lincoln's tomb in Oak Ridge Cemetery in Springfield, Illinois.

tack—appeared on the TV game show *I've Got a Secret*. Actress Jayne Meadows (who later guest-starred in episodes of *The Love Boat* and *Fantasy Island*) won the challenge by guessing the tragic event he had witnessed as a youth. Seymour died two months later at the age of 95. Young Fleetwood Lindley later went on to become the president of the Oak Ridge Cemetery. He died on February 1, 1963, and was buried in Oak Ridge Cemetery. He was the last person to lay eyes on the face of Abraham Lincoln.

THE ABRAHAM LINCOLN DEATH SITES
Assassination Site

In 1861, John T. Ford, a successful theater owner from Baltimore, was searching for a venue to stage shows in Washington, DC, when he found the First Baptist Church on 10th Street. The church, built in 1833–1834 by Reverend Obadiah B. Brown, was no longer used as a house of worship after merging with a nearby church in 1859. It sat vacant, occasionally rented for events, and Ford chose to stage his first show there, an opera featuring Miss Carlotta Patti on November 19, 1861. Happy with its success, he signed a five-year lease on December 7. He later bought it and converted it into a music hall. He named it Ford's Athenaeum, and the first show, "Christy Minstrels," opened just three days later. Following its two-month run, Ford invested $10,000 to remodel the theater, and three months later, on May 28, 1862, Lincoln attended his first show there.

At 5:00 p.m. on December 30, 1862, a defective gas meter led to a fire that engulfed the entire theater. It was bitter cold, and when it was finally put out the next morning the inside was gutted and charred. Ford's loss was estimated at $20,000, but undeterred, he hired architect James J. Gifford and invested $75,000 to rebuild. He tore down two adjoining buildings to make way for a much larger theater. After the cornerstone was laid on February 28, 1863, problems with the foundation soon arose, including

underlying quicksand that delayed construction. It was expected to take about two and a half months to build but dragged on for more than double that and was still not completed when the first performance of the romantic drama, "The Naiad Queen," was staged on August 27, 1863. The lengthy construction process proved to be worthwhile when the *Washington Sunday Chronicle* praised the theater as "an ornament to the city" and added that its "elegance has few superiors."[71] In addition to the spacious three-tiered seating that accommodated 2,500 patrons, it featured four boxes, two on either side of the stage. The two boxes on stage left were separated by a partition. When it was removed, as it was on the night Lincoln was shot, it was called the Presidential Box.

Over the next 20 months, the theater staged 495 productions featuring popular actors of the time. During this period, Lincoln was a frequent patron, attending about a dozen shows, including "The Marble Heart" starring the young actor John Wilkes Booth. The history of the theater changed dramatically after Lincoln was shot. With it now considered a crime scene, Stanton ordered Ford's seized, placed under 24-hour guard, and all upcoming performances canceled except for one: in a desperate search for clues, Stanton ordered a reenactment of the play Lincoln had been watching just for himself and his aides.[72]

Three days after Lincoln's death, Stanton had Ford, who was in Baltimore at the time of the murder, arrested on suspicion of conspiracy in the assassination. Ford spent 39 days in the Old Capitol prison before being released. Despite his strong desire to prevent Ford's Theatre from ever again being used for entertainment, Stanton eventually relented, and the theater reopened on July 7, 1865. Ford advertised a grand reopening for three days later, but the public was outraged. Ford received threats that the building would be burned if it reopened. Stanton determined the best way to avoid bloodshed was to seize the theater once again, and theatergoers were greeted with the sign, CLOSED BY ORDER OF THE SECRETARY OF WAR.[73] Ford protested, and in August 1865, a settlement was reached whereby the War Department leased the building from Ford for $1,500 per month with an option to buy for $100,000. The next year, the War Department exercised their option and purchased the building and converted the theater to office space.

On the outside, the theater retained its original appearance, but the inside was gutted and completely repurposed. Most of the relics from the building, including the balcony and furnishings, were either destroyed or lost. When renovations were completed on November 27, 1865, the beautiful theater had become a sterile, three-story office building occupied by the Record and Pension Bureau. Over the years, several other government agencies shared the office space, including the Army Medical Museum, which occupied the third floor from 1867 through 1887.[74]

On June 9, 1893, tragedy again struck the building, when, stressed under the weight of all of the records, a 40-foot section of the east façade on the third floor collapsed all the way through to the basement. Twenty-two people were killed, and another 68 were injured. The building was repaired and continued to serve as a government office for another 40 years. In 1928, however, ownership was transferred to the Office of Public Buildings and Public Parks of the National Capital, which converted the first floor into a Lincoln museum, displaying many pieces owned by Osborn H. I. Oldroyd, a prolific collector of Lincoln memorabilia. The museum opened on February 12, 1932, which would have been Lincoln's 124th birthday, and the next year it was placed under the control of the National Park Service.

The first congressional effort to restore the theater to its 1865 appearance began on February 6, 1946, when North Dakota senator Milton Ruben Young introduced Resolution 139 to estimate the cost of reconstruction. His persistence was rewarded eight years later when, on May 28, 1954, President Eisenhower signed the resolution into law. In 1960, Congress allocated $200,000 for the restoration and an additional $2 million in 1964. The building closed on November 29, 1964, for a three-year restoration period. The interior was gutted and with the aid of historic artifacts, including photographs taken by Civil War photographer Matthew Brady, the theater and furnishings, including the Presidential Box, were reconstructed to look as they did a century earlier. The only original artifacts on display were two pieces of furniture and the portrait of Washington that had hung on the wall that fateful evening. (The original rocking chair in which Lincoln sat now resides at the Henry Ford Museum in Dearborn, Michigan, after the automobile magnate purchased it at an auction in the 1920s.[75] There also exists a flag that is claimed not only to have hung in the theater but also to have been used to cushion Lincoln's bloodied head. The so-called "blood relic" eventually found its way to Milford, Pennsylvania and can be seen under temperature-controlled plate glass at the Columns Museum.[76])

In the midst of the renovations, on October 15,

The rebuilt interior of Ford's Theater. The balcony has been recreated to look as it did the day Lincoln was shot.

1966, the theater was added to the National Register of Historic Places (#66000034). A rededication ceremony was held on January 21, 1968, and in attendance was Senator Milton Ruben Young, who 22 years earlier first proposed the restoration. The first grand reopening performance was held nine days later in a nationally televised show that featured Harry Belafonte, Andy Williams, Henry Fonda, and Helen Hayes and was dedicated to "President Lincoln's love for the performing arts." On February 13, the theater was reopened to the public, and after 103 years, the first play staged at Ford's Theater was appropriately *John Brown's Body*. So soon after the assassination of JFK, curators of the Lincoln museum, which had been moved to the basement, focused more on his life and virtually ignored his murder. However, the public's curiosity to learn more about the historic events that had occurred in the very building in which they were standing led the National Park Service to close the museum in 1988 and reopen it two years later with a new focus on the assassination.[77] Today, there are two ways to visit the theater: going to see a show or as part of the National Park Service tour.

Ford's Theatre National Historic Site is open for tours from 9:00 am to 5:00 pm. It is located at 511 Tenth Street NW, Washington, DC, 20004. For more information, visit: www.nps.gov/foth or www.FordsTheatre.org.

Petersen House

The home where Abraham Lincoln died was owned by William and Anna Petersen, who purchased the lot on February 9, 1849, for $850. Shortly afterward, they built the plain three-story redbrick home. At the time of the assassination, the Petersens lived in the basement with their six children and rented the upstairs rooms (incredibly, one of the men who occasionally rented the room where Lincoln died was John Wilkes Booth). After the assassination, their lives changed dramatically. The notoriety of owning the home brought unwanted attention; souvenir hunters picked the room apart, and visitors constantly gathered outside. The boarders also became frustrated and chose to find rooms elsewhere, causing financial hardship for the Petersen couple. Six years later, William died of an accidental overdose of laudanum (a narcotic containing alcohol and opium) on June 18, 1871, and Anna died four months later. The home then passed to the Petersen children, but its contents—including many historical artifacts from Lincoln's death—were sold at auction, including the deathbed, which fetched $80, far exceeding its $7 valuation.[78]

In 1878, the heirs sold the home and its remaining furnishings to Louis Schade and his wife for $4,500. Schade was a lawyer and published the German-American newspaper, the *Washington Sentinel*, from the basement of the home. As the years went by, uninvited and unwelcome visitors eventually drove the Schades to move out. They retained ownership but rented the home to the Memorial Association of the District of Columbia, who in 1883 asked Oldroyd to live in the house as a caretaker. That same year, the home was recognized with a historic marble tablet that had been authorized by Congress. Oldroyd also hung a sign over the door, reading THE LINCOLN MUSEUM. HOME OF THE O. H. OLDROYD COLLECTION, and opened the home to tourists.

In April 1894, Thomas A. Jones visited the Lincoln Museum and told Oldroyd a fascinating story about how, almost 30 years earlier, he had aided Booth. He fed the assassin while he hid in the Maryland woods for several days after the shooting, before helping him cross the Potomac River into Virginia. Now, an unrepentant Jones was standing in the room where Lincoln died, the culmination of Booth's deed.[79]

In 1896, the federal government bought the home from the Schade family for $30,000, the first time a home had been purchased by the federal government for the sole purpose of using it as a museum. They placed ownership under the US Army Corps of Engineers and retained Oldroyd as caretaker. In 1924, a bronze marker replaced the 41-year-old marble tablet. Two years later, Illinois senator Henry Rathbone[80] introduced a bill to purchase Oldroyd's 3,000-piece Lincoln memorabilia collection for $50,000. In 1933, the Petersen Home, along with Ford's Theatre, was placed under the auspices of the National Park Service. When the building was later restored, it was discovered that the bedroom where Lincoln died had water damage, and the home was closed from 1979–1980 for a complete restoration. Today, none of the furnishings are original; however, based on the Julius Ulke photograph, the bedroom has been faithfully recreated to resemble how it looked the night Lincoln died.

The Petersen House is part of the Ford's Theatre National Historic Site and is open daily from 9:30 a.m. to 5:30 p.m. At the time of Lincoln's death the address was 453 Tenth Street; however, today it is 516 Tenth Street.

Funeral Train

The morning after Lincoln was entombed, the funeral train left Springfield to return to Washington, DC. Taking the direct route, the 900 miles were covered in 48 hours, and the train arrived Sunday morning, May 7, without incident or fanfare.[81] The car that held the body of Lincoln and his son Willie had been constructed the year before at the Car Shops of the Military Railroad System in Alexandria, Virginia, and was originally called the United States. The maroon funeral car had twelve windows on each side and interior paneling of a "deep chocolate color." It was originally designed by B. P. Lamarson specifically for President Lincoln and was used for trips to New York. It had been recently modified, and ironically Lincoln had planned to take a test ride on the day he died.

After the funeral, it was purchased by the Union Pacific Railroad for $6,850 and was used to carry some of the first passengers on the Transcontinental Railroad. It was later sold to entrepreneur Franklyn Snow for $2,000. Its last owner was Twin City Rapid Transit Company President Thomas Lowrey, who bought it in 1905. He had it restored and planned to put it on display, but before he could do so he died in 1909. His estate donated it to the Minnesota Federation of Women's Clubs who stored the car in Columbia Heights on 37th Avenue between Quincy and Jackson streets in northeast Minneapolis.[82] On March 18, 1911, a nearby prairie fire broke out and destroyed the historic train car. All that was left was "a mass of charred wood and iron,"[83] but a window frame was salvaged from the rubble. It was passed down through several generations and is currently in the possession of an anonymous owner in Minnesota.[84]

Funeral Train Sites

The funeral train provides an abundance of Lincoln death sites, and there's a good chance you may live close to one of these locations. The first stop was in Baltimore, Maryland, at the Camden Station of the Baltimore and Ohio Railroad on Camden and Howard Street. It was built in 1856 and still exists and can be seen adjacent to Camden Yards, home of the Baltimore Orioles. The first public viewing of Lincoln's body was at the Merchants Exchange Building at the southwest corner of Gay and Water Streets. The Greco-Roman building was designed by Benjamin Latrobe and Maximilien Godefroy and built between 1815–1820. It served many purposes, including as a stock exchange, bank, and hotel. The building was demolished during 1901 and 1902.[85]

The next stop in York, Pennsylvania, was a small stop for the Lincoln funeral train but a giant moment in York history. On April 21, 2010, 145 years after the original event, this dramatic scene was reenacted. The original station is long gone, replaced with the current one in the 1890s.[86] The station is located on North Street, between Duke and North Queen Streets, and today sits in the shadow of the Sovereign Bank

Stadium, home of the York Revolution, a minor league team in the Atlantic Baseball League.

The train proceeded to the Pennsylvania Railroad Station in Harrisburg. Today, the Harrisburg Transportation Center is at the same location at 4th and Chestnut Street, but it is not the 1865 station. The current station was first built in 1887 and redesigned in 1905 after a fire the previous year.

The Philadelphia train station was built by the Philadelphia, Wilmington & Baltimore Railroad in 1852 and located on Broad Street and Prime (today known as Washington Avenue). In later years, the station became obsolete after the creation of the Broad Street Station, and it was closed in January 1882. Today, the former location of the depot is a graffiti-ridden empty lot. A 2014 article on a Philadelphia news website lamented, "The vacant lot . . . has been an eyesore for decades."[87]

The Philadelphia viewing was held at one of the most significant buildings in American history, Independence Hall. The building was first constructed in 1732 and designed in the Georgian architectural style by Andrew Hamilton and Edmund Wooley. The building served as the Pennsylvania State House for the next 24 years. Prior to the American Revolution, the Pennsylvania legislature made a momentous decision and agreed to lend the assembly room to the Second Continental Congress. The heated discussions held in that room by delegates from all 13 colonies, including Washington, Adams, and Jefferson, culminated with the signing of the Declaration of Independence on July 4, 1776. Five years later, the Articles of Confederation were also adopted within its walls.[88] It is located at 520 Chestnut Street, Philadelphia, Pennsylvania, 19106 and is part of Independence National Historical Park. For more information, visit: www.nps.gov/inde.

The station where the funeral train departed Philadelphia was the Kensington Station at Front and Montgomery Streets. It was part of the Philadelphia and Trenton Railroad that linked the two cities, and was used by Lincoln in 1848, 1860, 1861, and 1862 in life, before his final time in 1865 in death.[89]

The train passed through Broad Street Station in Newark, New Jersey. Today, the station is still in the same location; however, it has changed much over the years. I took a historic tour of Newark in 2013 and my guide described the funeral train as the saddest day in its history.

In New York City, the funeral train departed the city from the Hudson River Railroad Depot, which is no longer there. Today, the site is occupied by the massive US Post Office Morgan General Mail Facility, which takes up the entire block of West 29th Street between 9th and 10th Avenues, including a structure covering the road. While there is no historic marker on the site, at both intersections on West 29th Street are signs directing traffic to, you guessed it, the Lincoln Tunnel.

In Buffalo, the train stopped at the Exchange Street Station at 75 Exchange Street. Today, there is a historic placard inside the station citing this occasion, but the current building is not the original. The original station that was there was built in 1855, replacing the first one built seven years earlier. The small station there today was built in the early 1950s and is currently used by Amtrak. The Buffalo viewing was held at St. James Hall, today the site of the M&T Bank Plaza. The public viewing was not Abraham Lincoln's first time in the public hall. Four years earlier, when he visited Buffalo en route to Washington, DC, for his first inauguration, he attended a lecture in St. James Hall about the plight of the Native Americans.[90]

In Cleveland, the public viewing was held in the Public Square where, 16 years later, James Garfield's body would lie in state in this same location. Thirteen years after that, the "Soldier's and Sailor's Monument" was built there and is now in the shadow of the Cleveland Horseshoe Casino. It was designed by Cleveland architect Levi Scofield and within its walls are bas-reliefs, two of which depict Abraham Lincoln (but none of Garfield). The approximate location of where Lincoln's body was situated is near a Route 6 sign. In 2015, to commemorate the 150th anniversary of Lincoln's death, a marker was erected by the Cleveland Lodge No. 781 Free & Accepted Masons, the Forest City Commandery No. 40 Knight's Temple, and the Ohio History Connection.

In Columbus, Ohio, the body lay in the State Capitol building, which was completed in 1861 after 22 years of construction. At the time, it was considered one of "America's finest examples of Greek Revival architecture."[91]

The Indianapolis State House is no longer in existence, but a new State House was erected on the same site and first used in 1887. On the south lawn, a historical marker to commemorate the funeral train was erected in 2009 by the Indiana Historical Bureau and Indiana Abraham Lincoln Bicentennial Commission.

The Chicago and Alton Depot on Jefferson Street, where the Lincoln funeral train made its final stop in Springfield, is no longer in existence. Today there is an Amtrak Station at the same site, on 3rd Street and Jefferson. The site was regularly sought out by tourists, but unrecognized for years. That changed on February 9, 2010, when a five-foot-tall monument was unveiled. The $8,000 marker is made of black polished granite and sits on the west-side platform.[92]

The Springfield State House, where the final viewing was held, is today known as the Old Capitol. The cornerstone for the sandstone building was laid on July 4, 1837, and it was first used as the State Capitol in 1839. The Lincoln-Herndon law office is located right across the street, and Lincoln spent many hours working in the Capitol building. The building also served as his informal headquarters for his 1860 presidential campaign. It was decommissioned in 1876 and later served as the Sagamon County courthouse. The site was purchased by the state in 1961, and on October 15, 1966, it was added to the National Register of Historic Places (#66000331). A three-year project, completed in 1969, restored the building to its former appearance when it served as the state house. Nearby is a plethora of historic markers, many Lincoln-related. One of the more intriguing markers was erected in 1957 and reads, LINCOLN SQUARE MARKS THE DEPARTURE POINT OF THE DONNER PARTY ON APRIL 15, 1846 FOR THEIR ILL-FATED TRIP TO CALIFORNIA.

The Cemetery

The initial concept for the Oak Ridge Cemetery came about in 1855 when government funding was requested to purchase 17 acres two miles north of Springfield, due to an ordinance that forbade the establishment of any additional cemeteries inside Springfield. It was founded the following year, and at the dedication ceremony Springfield's former mayor, James C. Conkling, made an address, with Lincoln and Mary Todd in attendance. Today, it is the largest cemetery in Illinois, with more than 400,000 visitors annually, second only to Arlington National Cemetery.

On December 19, 1960, the Lincoln tomb was designated as a National Historic Landmark and on October 15, 1966 it was placed on the National Register of Historic Places (#66000330), the same day that Ford's Theatre and the Springfield State House were also added to the register.

Special events are held at the grave today. On or around Lincoln's birthday is the American Legion Lincoln's Birthday Pilgrimage and the Veterans of Foreign Wars Annual Pilgrimage. Every year on April 15, the Sons of Union Veterans of the Civil War hold Lincoln's Death Anniversary Services.

The original tomb where Lincoln was placed was constructed in 1860 of Joliet limestone and stands 12 feet tall. You can still see it on the grounds of the Oak Ridge Cemetery, behind the memorial tomb at the base of the hill. After Lincoln was removed, it was used at least another dozen times over the next eight years, but by 1873 it no longer housed remains. In 1946, responsibility for the tomb was transferred to the state, and today it is part of the Lincoln Tomb State Historic Site. An informative marker is located near the tomb, and to the left of the entrance is a weather-beaten bronze plaque that reads THIS VAULT HELD THE REMAINS OF ABRAHAM LINCOLN FROM MAY 4, 1865 TO DECEMBER 21, 1865.

After Lincoln's body was removed from the vault, the slab upon which his body laid was preserved and the following text was carved into it:

IN MEMORY OF ABRAHAM LINCOLN
16TH PRESIDENT OF THE UNITED STATES
BORN FEB. 12, 1809, DIED APRIL 15, 1865.
THIS RELIC IS PRESERVED
IT BEING THE TABLET UPON
WHICH WERE FIRST PLACED
THE REMAINS OF OUR
ILLUSTRIOUS DEAD IN THE RECEIVING TOMB OF
OAK RIDGE CEMETERY MAY 4, 1865

In 1900, during the tomb restoration, a bell tower was erected a few hundred feet north of the public receiving vault and rung during funeral processions. The historic slab upon which Lincoln's body lay was affixed to the exterior wall of the bell tower.

The second family receiving vault, where his body lay for six years, was located on the hill between the public receiving vault and eventual location of the memorial tomb. The structure featured a peaked roof above the entrance and on both sides the walls curved toward columns. Shortly after the remains were removed in September 1871, the tomb was demolished. Today, there is a granite marker at the location.

The third tomb, used during the 1901 reconstruction, was located behind the memorial tomb, near the other two temporary tombs. After its use the tomb was destroyed and buried. Today the site is unmarked.

Oak Ridge Cemetery is located at 1441 Monument Avenue, Springfield, Illinois, 62702. The gates are open from 7:00 a.m. to 5:00 p.m. November through March and 7:00 a.m. to 8:00 p.m. April through October. For more information, visit: www.OakRidgeCemetery.org.

James Buchanan ★ *1857–1861*

CRITICAL DEATH INFORMATION:

Date of death:	June 1, 1868, 8:30 a.m.
Cause of death:	Originally attributed to "rheumatic gout" but is now generally accepted as pneumonia
Age at death:	77 years, 39 days
Last words:	"Oh Lord, God Almighty, as Thou wilt."
Place of death:	Wheatland, Lancaster, Pennsylvania
Funeral:	Wheatland, Lancaster, Pennsylvania
Final resting place:	Woodward Hill Cemetery, Lancaster, Pennsylvania
Reinterred:	No
Cost to visit grave:	Free
For more information:	www.Woodward HillCemetery.com
Significance:	Lived longer than any president during 100-year period from 1863 to 1963

After his presidency ended in March 1861, James Buchanan returned to his home, Wheatland, in Lancaster, Pennsylvania. While he enjoyed good health, history had not been kind to the 15th president. His position on slavery—inaction at best and tacit support at worst—caused further division in the country, culminating in the secession of the Southern states after Abraham Lincoln's election.[1]

In 1864, he suffered from rheumatism, gout, and dysentery, and in the fall a sprained ankle further weakened his condition. Buchanan was a patient of Dr. Henry Carpenter, who made a staggering 430 visits to Wheatland over the following years. In 1867, exhaustion, shortness of breath, and a weak heart were added to his list of ailments.[2] Buchanan spent many hours contemplating his own death, and according to his niece, Annie, he "spoke as if he expected it constantly."[3] Toward the end of May 1868, the 77-year-old former president contracted pneumonia. Buchanan was cared for by his faithful housekeeper of 34 years, Esther "Miss Hetty" Parker, who was joined by family members, including his brother Reverend Edward Young Buchanan, his nieces Henrietta Buchanan and Harriet Lane Johnston, and Harriet's husband.[4]

In the spring of 1868, Buchanan prepared for the inevitable. The previous winter, he had purchased a double plot in Woodward Hill Cemetery with a view of his beloved Lancaster and the Conestoga River, and now he requested that it be marked with a simple oblong tomb ("marble or granite would do"). Two days before he died, he gave instructions for his funeral: he wanted "no pomp and parade" but permitted Free Masons to participate, and he instructed that invitations be sent to his predecessors, Franklin Pierce and Millard Fillmore, and to the current president, Andrew Johnson (none chose to attend).[5] The only bachelor to ever serve as president, Buchanan had written a letter earlier in life to explain why he had never married and instructed his loved ones to open it after he had died. Now, on the brink of death, he had a change of heart and had the letter burned. While some suspect that this letter may have included an admission of homosexuality, its contents, and his sexual orientation, now forever remain a mystery.

On June 1 at 6:00 a.m., as he lay in the second-floor bedroom, he was given the sacrament of last rites. Parched, he asked his medical attendant to fetch a glass of water from the spring. He took a long drink and dramatically declared, "Doctor, if disembodied spirits ever come back, I believe that mine will be found about that spring." Shortly after, with his nieces at his side, he uttered his final words, "Oh Lord, God Almighty, as Thou wilt."[6]

At 8:30 a.m. on Monday, June 1, 1868, James Buchanan passed away. The cause of death was attributed to "rheumatic gout" but is now generally accepted as pneumonia. Over 100 years later, American novelist John Updike fictionalized these final moments in a laborious three-act play, *Buchanan Dying*.

His loved ones prepared for his funeral and diligently recorded the costs. For his medical care, Dr. Carpenter charged $3,200. Joseph Lebar, a local African American barber, cut Buchanan's hair, shaved him, and applied makeup for a fee of $33, which included his tab for previous haircuts.[7] The body was dressed in "a satin shroud, with white necktie and high collar," a look with which Buchanan had become so oft associated.[8] His remains were placed in a metal coffin with silver mountings and trimmings, purchased for $520 from Christian Widmyer, a local cabinetmaker and undertaker. It had a white

The room where James Buchanan died, decorated for the "December Yule Tide" tour.

satin interior and on the lid was a silver plate that read: JAMES BUCHANAN BORN APRIL 23, 1791 DIED JUNE 1, 1868. It was placed on two pedestals in the main hall of Wheatland that had been tastefully decorated with black mourning and $20 worth of immortelles strewn about. It is unknown if the president was embalmed.

The next day Wheatland was opened, and crowds filed past the casket on both sides. One reporter noted Buchanan's appearance: "The expression on the face was exceedingly natural and tranquil. We have seldom if ever seen a more natural expression on the face of the dead."[9] For three days, mourners paid their respects. The funeral was scheduled for June 4 at 4:00 p.m. A delegation from Congress, members of New York's Tammany Hall, and the Democratic Association of Philadelphia were in attendance. Local businesses and schools were closed, and students were required to attend the funeral.

The brief service was conducted by Buchanan's good friend, Reverend John Williamson Nevin, president of Franklin and Marshall College, who read the Litany of the German Reformed Church followed by Psalm 9, and delivered a sermon based on Thessalonians 4:13–14. After the brief ceremony was complete, the doors were opened to allow several hundred more mourners in. At 4:55 p.m., the pallbearers, all members from Lancaster Lodge 43 of the Order of Ancient York Rite Masonry, of which Buchanan had been a member, carried the coffin to a plain hearse (which cost $25 to rent from John Swartz). Twenty-two friends and associates also served as honorary pallbearers. Bells tolled as the cortege rode two and a half miles to the cemetery on the unpaved dirt roads from Marietta Turnpike to West King Street, Centre Square, and South Queen Street, passing 20,000 onlookers along the way. Lancaster police and fire departments led the procession, followed by the mayor, local politicians, physicians, educators, fraternal and religious organizations, and finally "Distinguished Strangers,

Citizens in Carriages, [and] Citizens on Horse." All told, there were 125 carriages (which cost $450) and the City Cornet Band played a solemn funeral march. Despite Buchanan's instructions, the procession was the antithesis of "no pomp and parade."

The procession entered the Woodward Hill Cemetery at 6:00 p.m., and the pallbearers placed the coffin over the open grave. Reverend Nevin read the Collect of the German Reformed Church followed by a prayer. The Free Masons, all dressed in identical black suits and tall silk hats, circled the grave, and Worshipful Master S. H. Reynolds performed the Masonic funeral rites. The coffin was then lowered into the ground, and each Free Mason dropped a sprig of boxwood onto it.[10] Mourners slowly left the cemetery and at 6:45 p.m. gravediggers began to fill in the grave.

An Italian marble tomb was designed by Major Charles M. Howell of Lancaster. It was adorned with limestone flags, placed on a 7,000-pound base of New Hampshire granite, and inscribed with words that Buchanan wrote himself. While some of the earlier leaders opted not to list "president" among their accomplishments, Buchanan included nothing else:

HERE REST THE REMAINS OF
JAMES BUCHANAN
FIFTEENTH PRESIDENT OF THE UNITED STATES
BORN IN FRANKLIN COUNTY, PA, APRIL 22, 1791
DIED AT WHEATLAND, JUNE 1, 1868

A 30-by-12-foot iron gate was erected around the plot (it has since been removed). For the grave marker and fence, Howell charged $2,500.

THE JAMES BUCHANAN DEATH SITES
Location of Death
The home was built in 1828 for William Jenkins, a wealthy Lancaster lawyer and president of the Farmer's Bank, who named it "The Wheatlands" after the fields of wheat that surrounded it. The 17-room, three-story Federal

style brick home featured a square central portion and wings on both sides. Jenkins sold it in 1841 to his son-in-law, Thomas F. Potter, for $9,000. On May 8, 1845, it was purchased by a member of the Select Council of Philadelphia, William Morris Meredith (he later became United States secretary of the treasury in 1849) for $6,750, to be used as a summer home. Three years later, Meredith put the home on the market to purchase another summer home. Buchanan, who was then secretary of state and living elsewhere in Lancaster, contacted him in June 1848 to make an offer, but when the deal to purchase the other home fell through, Meredith put Buchanan's deal on hold. The two carried on a polite correspondence until finally, on December 2, Buchanan bought the home and 22 acres for the exact $6,750 that Meredith had paid. Buchanan moved in the following spring, along with his niece and several servants. Buchanan resided in the home full-time, except from 1853 to 1856, his years as ambassador to England, and from 1857 to 1861, his time as president.[11]

During his lifetime, several historic events occurred in the home. Buchanan was at Wheatland when he was notified that he had received the Democratic presidential nomination. It was there that he delivered his first campaign speech and his victory address when he won the 1856 election. There were celebrations at Wheatland when he left for Washington, DC, and upon his return four years later. The home became so popular that it inspired several songs, such as "Wheatland Schottische," "Wheatland Polka," and "Wheatland March."

After Buchanan's death, the home passed to his niece and torch holder of his legacy, Harriet Lane. She used it as a summer residence and tended to her uncle's grave. On June 16, 1884, shortly after her husband's death, she sold the home to Lancaster businessman George B. Willson for approximately $20,000.[12] Willson sold 13 acres in 1893, but continued to live in the home until his death in 1929. The home then passed on to his cousin, Mary Willson Rettew.[13] One newspaper expressed concern over what would become of the estate: "The future of 'Wheatland' is problematical. Keen interest has been aroused in the disposition of the historic home and influential persons in Washington are understood to be interested in obtaining possession."[14] Rettew had a small family, and the 13,000-square-foot mansion was too big for her to maintain, but "the influential persons in Washington" did not reveal themselves.[15] Later, a committee was formed to try to purchase it to use as a museum but could not come to an agreement with Rettew, and in January 1931, the idea was abandoned.[16]

Rettew died in 1934, and the home and property, now pared to just shy of six acres, remained under the control

The home where Buchanan died was built in 1828 and named "The Wheatlands," after the fields of wheat that surrounded it.

of her estate and sat vacant while a buyer was sought. Concerned that Wheatland risked remaining under private ownership, several civic-minded women banded together to save it. On August 11, 1935, Mrs. William Shand, Mrs. J. W. B. Bausman, Mrs. John L. Atlee Jr., and Mrs. Henry A. Rohrer (identified only by their husband's names), all of the Junior League of Lancaster, incorporated the "James Buchanan Foundation for the Preservation of Wheatland." They raised $40,000, and on February 27, 1936, purchased Wheatland to preserve as a historic site.[17] They updated the electrical system and found original furnishings and artifacts for the home. On May 5, 1936, Wheatland opened to visitors. It quickly became a popular site for tourists, and 25,000 people visited before the home was dedicated on October 14, 1937. A crowd of 600 attended the event, which was presided over by Lancaster mayor James H. Ross. After an invocation by Reverend Henry B. Strock, the principal address was given by Pennsylvania governor George Howard Earle.[18]

Humble honors ensued over the following years. In 1956, Wheatland was featured on a stamp to commemorate the 100th anniversary of Buchanan's election.[19] The historic home was designated a National Historic Landmark in 1961 and, five years later, was added to the National Register of Historic Places (#66000669). Over the years the home has not undergone any major alterations, so it remains very similar to its original appearance.[20]

Today, the home and surrounding four acres and are still run by the James Buchanan Foundation for the Preservation of Wheatland. It is located at 230 North President Avenue, Lancaster, Pennsylvania, 17603. For more information, visit: www.LancasterHistory.org.

Grave

Woodward Hill Cemetery was founded in 1850 by the Trinity Lutheran Church. Almost three decades earlier, a movement had begun in the United States to create picturesque and serene "rural" cemeteries, and Woodward was designed in that spirit.[21] By the 1950s, the elements had taken their toll on Buchanan's marble tomb, which had deteriorated and cracked. The Pilot Club of Lancaster took up the challenge to construct a new tomb. They collected $10,000, with half coming from "pennies contributed by thousands of Pennsylvania schoolchildren."[22] In 1960, a tomb made of Barre granite was completed and the surrounding grounds were improved. A dedication ceremony was held on May 22 of that year.

Thirty years later, the grave had once again fallen into disrepair—although the issues were not due to the construction. The surrounding neighborhood had devolved into a high-crime area, and the cemetery had become a gathering spot for criminals and malcontents. Tombs were stained with graffiti and the grounds were littered with "beer bottles, crack vials, condoms and other trash."[23] In an unprecedented sign of depravity, the charred remains of a corpse were discovered only a few yards from Buchanan's tomb![24]

The situation hit bottom on September 1, 1994, when hoodlums spray-painted profanity on the former president's tomb.[25] Three days after the ugly incident, Eric Berman, owner of Berman Construction, generously donated his services to remove the offensive paint. Asked why he would spend his time and resources, Berman humbly replied, "I was real upset that this was done. Good God, this was a President of the United States."[26] A movement began to remove the grave from Woodward Hill Cemetery. The Buchanan Society of America sought public funds to relocate it to Wheatland, but none were available. A local editorial described the dire situation before adding a grim prognosis: "There appears to be little chance that things will get better."[27] Thankfully, the new millennium brought dramatic improvements and in 2005, the cemetery was added to the National Register of Historic Places (#05000098). When

Buchanan's grave in Woodward Hill Cemetery in Lancaster, Pennsylvania.

I visited a decade later, I found the grounds well maintained and gravestones that had been previously toppled over now respectfully placed in their original locations. Gone were the graffiti and R-rated garbage. Today, there are approximately 13,750 graves there.

The cemetery is located at 501 South Queen Street, Lancaster, Pennsylvania, 17604. There are several small signs that direct visitors to "Buchanan Tomb," where the American flag flies over the grave site. For more information, visit: www.WoodwardHillCemetery.com.

Franklin Pierce ★ 1853–1857

CRITICAL DEATH INFORMATION:

Date of death:	October 8, 1869, 4:40 a.m.
Cause of death:	Abdominal dropsy
Age at death:	64 years, 319 days
Last words:	Unknown
Place of death:	52 South Main Street, Concord, New Hampshire
Funeral:	St. Paul's Episcopal Church, Concord, New Hampshire
Final resting place:	Minot Enclosure of Old North Cemetery, Concord, New Hampshire
Reinterred:	No
Cost to visit grave:	Free
For more information:	www.ConcordNH.gov/Facilities/Facility/Details/45
Significance:	Died closest to his upcoming birthday than any other president (45 days away)

The fifth presidential death of the decade occurred when Franklin Pierce passed away in the finals months of the 1860s, on October 8, 1869. This somber milestone gave the 1860s the distinction as the "deadliest decade," surpassing the four presidential deaths of the 1840s—an ominous record that still stands.

Pierce left the presidency in 1857 and returned to live in his native New Hampshire. As a life-long resident of the Granite State, Pierce may have been a Northerner by residency, but for tacitly supporting the Confederacy during the Civil War, he was seen by many as a Southerner at heart. This conflicted loyalty left him unpopular in much of the country. Yet he remained well-liked in his hometown of Concord. Pierce had endured a lot of sadness in his life, including the deaths of three of his sons and his beloved wife, Jane Appleton Pierce, in 1863. To combat his depression, Pierce drank heavily, and in November 1865 his alcohol abuse led to an attack of "bilious fever," a now-obsolete medical term that described symptoms of nausea, diarrhea, and fever. Pierce's condition was grave, but the brush with death led to a spiritual awakening. He was baptized on December 3 at St. Paul's Episcopal, a church that appealed to Pierce due to its opposition of the abolitionist movement. Pierce also purchased a summer cottage at Little Boar's Head in North Hampton, New Hampshire, where he sought recreation and refuge.

Pierce still followed politics. He corresponded with his friend Jefferson Davis, who was imprisoned at Fort Monroe, and lobbied for the former Confederate president's better treatment and release. In August 1867, his alcohol abuse again led to serious illness. He recovered, but in July 1869, while at Little Boar's Head, he suffered from a swollen abdomen and was diagnosed with dropsy, a term for swollen tissues due to the accumulation of excess water. Pierce was now confined to his bed. His weight dropped below 100 pounds, but despite his failing health, he continued to drink. In late September, he developed a bad case of hiccups, a result of his alcoholism. At the end of the month, Pierce returned to his home in Concord. He confided in his doctors, "I am convinced I shall not recover."[1]

Mrs. Seth Hopkins moved in to care for Pierce, and reporters gathered outside on death watch, telegraphing frequent updates to their newspapers. On Thursday, October 7, Pierce was in agony as he lay in the southeast front bedroom of his home. He was able to talk until about 3:00 p.m., but six hours later, he could no longer recognize those at his bedside. He was surrounded by the family of his friend Willard Williams, and his physicians, including Dr. Charles P. Gage, but no family members were present. Despite the number of people in attendance, his final words were unrecorded and remain lost to history.[2]

Pierce opened his eyes one last time at 4:35 a.m. The *Boston Journal* newspaper described the scene: "He looked around the room for the last time, his eyes resting for a moment upon those in attendance with him, and then, as calmly and sweetly as a child would sink to its rest, he closed his eyes in his last sleep and passed away."[3] Franklin Pierce died at 4:40 a.m. on Friday, October 8, 1869.

Later that day, President Ulysses S. Grant issued an official announcement: "The painful duty devolves upon the President of announcing to the people of the United States the death of one of his honored predecessors, Franklin Pierce, which occurred at Concord early this morning. Eminent in the public councils and universally beloved in private life, his death will be mourned with a sorrow befitting the loss which this country sustains by his decease."[4] For three days Pierce lay in repose in his home, in a coffin covered with black cloth and silver trimmings. The funeral was held on Monday, October 11. Grant ordered all government buildings to be shut down and at noon, navy yards around the country fired a salute. In Concord, the mayor suspended all business from 11:00 a.m. to 2:00 p.m.

After a short ceremony in the bedroom where Pierce died, the coffin was removed from the home. At 10:00 a.m., a procession of twelve carriages brought the coffin to the statehouse, where it was placed in Doric Hall beneath a floral cross. At 11:00 a.m., the public was allowed in. Among those to see him during the brief, 90-minute lie in state were schoolchildren, townsfolk from Concord, and visitors from nearby communities. Many were deeply affected and "wept upon his well-remembered features."[5] Twelve pallbearers, all lawyers, carried the coffin across Park Street to St. Paul's Episcopal Church for the 1:00 p.m. funeral. Reverend Eames, rector at St. Paul's, and Dr.

Colt officiated and included the hymn, "While There I Seek, Protecting Power."

The service ended by 2:00 p.m. and the procession escorted the remains to the northwest corner of the Old North Cemetery, an area known as the "Minot Enclosure." A sizable crowd was gathered, larger than the number at the funeral. After a seven-minute ceremony, the body was lowered into the ground next to family members who had predeceased him—to his left, his wife, and to the right, two of his children. The day's events had moved along amazingly swiftly, and it took just over four hours from the time the remains were removed from the house until they were placed in the ground.

Pierce had left behind an estate of $72,386.01, mostly in stocks and properties. His fortune was split between 34 people. While the majority went to his nephew Frank, he also left several hundred dollars to the children of his good friends, including the author Nathaniel Hawthorne.[6]

THE FRANKLIN PIERCE DEATH SITES
Location of Death

The home on 52 South Main Street was built in 1852, by Pierce's friend Willard Williams, a foreman at the Abbot Downing Coach Company. After his term, Pierce moved into the squared Italianate-style home in 1857.[7] Several important events occurred at the residence: his wife, Jane, died in the house on December 2, 1863; Nathaniel Hawthorne visited in 1864; and after the assassination of Abraham Lincoln, Pierce addressed a crowd from his front steps (as a vocal opponent of Lincoln, he felt compelled to reassure the crowd of his patriotism).[8]

In the late 1880s, the home was redesigned in the French Second Empire style. It remained in private hands for some time and in 1910 was owned by Joseph Wentworth.[9] Years later, the home was used as a Swedish Baptist Church; to accommodate their services, the circular steps and a 40-foot section of wall were removed. The

The original grave of Franklin Pierce, 1908. (Library of Congress)

The home where Pierce died was destroyed in a fire September 17, 1981. (Library of Congress)

congregation eventually vacated the building after finding it too expensive to heat. In the following decades, the home fell into disrepair.

By 1941, the house was under bank ownership and destined for oblivion. Concerned that an important piece of history might be lost, New Hampshire history buff John B. Gravelle and his wife, Muriel, purchased the home. They renovated it, restored the section of wall that had been removed, and located the man who had removed the circular staircase, who was able to build a replica. The couple updated the utilities and decorated the home with period pieces and actual furnishings owned by the Pierce family, including the bed in which Pierce died. They named the historic attraction "The Franklin Pierce House" and erected a prominent sign.

On October 15, 1979, the home was listed on the National Register of Historic Places (#79000318) as "The Franklin Pierce House." On September 17, 1981, this good fortune came to an end when a fire erupted in the home and it was completely destroyed.[10] This devastating turn of events was made all the worse when the blaze was discovered to have been the result of arson.

Today all that is left is a cast-iron railing that runs the length of the property and two sets of granite steps. Located to the right of the more elaborate set of stairs is a historic marker. Appropriately, it looks like a gravestone and reads, "Site of home of President Franklin Pierce 1856 to Date of Death 1869." The area where the home once stood is now a parking lot beside the Waters Funeral Home. The site is located at 52 South Main Street and Wentworth Avenue, Concord, New Hampshire, 03301.

Lying in State

The viewing was held in the New Hampshire State House, a granite structure designed by Stuart J. Park that today is the oldest statehouse in the country in which the original chambers are still in use. Construction started in 1816, was completed three years later, and the building expanded in 1864. Doric Hall dates back to 1819 and was named for the eight central wooden Greek columns, in the same style used in the Parthenon. Today, this entrance is better known as the "Hall of Flags"—its 103 historic flags include many from New Hampshire military units from the Civil War, World War I, World War II, and Vietnam. A lunar rock from the Apollo 11 moon landing, courtesy of Alan B. Shepard of Derry, New Hampshire, is also in the hall.

The statehouse is located at 107 North Main Street, Concord, New Hampshire 03301. It is open weekdays from 8:00 a.m. to 4:30 p.m. For more information, including information on tours, visit: www.gencourt.state.nh.us/NH_Visitorcenter/default.htm.

The New Hampshire State House, where Pierce's public viewing was held. It is the oldest statehouse in the country in which the original chambers are still in use.

Funeral

The funeral was held at St. Paul's Episcopal Church, located on Park Street, across from the State House. Three years after Pierce's death home burned down, another suspicious fire occurred at the church on April 11, 1984, at 12:45 a.m. Firemen worked for three hours to get the inferno under control, but despite their valiant efforts, what remained was just a shell of the former edifice. The wooden interior was gutted, leaving only a skeletal brick structure, bell tower, and half the roof. Miraculously, the Bible on the lectern was not damaged and no one was injured. In the blaze, flaming embers blew across the street onto the statehouse but were doused before they could do any damage.

The church is located at 21 Centre Street, Concord, New Hampshire, 03301. While much of the original was destroyed in the fire, you can see the location of the pew where Pierce worshipped. For more information, visit: www. StPaulsConcord.org.

Grave

The Old North Cemetery, the oldest in Concord, is located in the northern part of Concord and is accessible from either North State Street or Bradley Street. It was established in 1730, and the first person buried there was four-year-old Sarah Walker, daughter of a minister, in 1736. During the 1850s, citizens seeking to separate themselves from the common folk of Concord purchased land within the cemetery. This plot was gated off and reserved for "wealthy and prominent Concord citizens desirous of a more elegant setting for themselves and their departed loved ones."[11] The

area became known as the Minot Enclosure (or Inclosure) after Pierce's law partner, Joseph Minot. By 1880, the enclosure was annexed to the Old North Cemetery and placed under its care.[12] Pierce originally purchased a plot in the main area, but after the Minot Enclosure was opened, he sold his original plot and bought Enclosure Lot #8 in 1855, while he was still president.[13] The two sons who had preceded him in death, Franky in 1843 and Benny in 1853, were later relocated to the Minot Enclosure.

Today, the Old North Cemetery is owned by the city of Concord and encompasses 5.85 acres. It contains approximately 2,300 graves, 62 of those within the Minot Enclosure. On November 9, 2008, the Old North Cemetery was added to the National Register for Historic Places (#08001031).

Pierce's grave was originally marked with a 12-foot-tall Italian marble shaft atop a three-foot granite base. On the panel was an inscription that read FRANCIS PIERCE BORN NOVEMBER 23, 1804 DIED OCTOBER 8, 1869. Why the stone was inscribed with Francis and not Franklin is

The rebuilt grave of Pierce, which was dedicated in 1946.

a mystery, but the lack of mention of his presidency was neither unusual nor unprecedented. In 1892, it was written: "The Pierce lot is one of the most ample and beautiful in the cemetery."[14]

Over the years, the grave and cemetery fell into decay. The *Windsor Daily Star* reported that the grave was "neglected for 85 years in a forgotten weed-grown corner of old North Cemetery" and "its location was unknown to most people except the cemetery attendants." This neglect led Grace Anderson, a Concord historian, to push for the cemetery to be cleaned up and to have a more appropriate marker erected. In 1945, her efforts were rewarded when the New Hampshire legislature appropriated $5,300 for "a suitable monument."[15] The monument was created by Joseph Comolli and built of gray Concord granite, with engravings for Jane Appleton to the left and their children to the right. Atop the monument is a draped cross, and the shaft was inscribed FRANKLIN PIERCE, BORN NOV 23, 1804, DIED OCT 8, 1869: FOURTEENTH PRESIDENT OF THE UNITED STATES, 1853–1857. The original monument was crushed and used for the new foundation.

The new monument was set in place on October 15, 1946, and a dedication ceremony was held a week later. Speaking at the event were New Hampshire governor Charles M. Dale and Concord mayor Charles C. Davie. Schoolchildren who had helped maintain the original gravestone were invited to attend, along with members of the Pierce family.[16] Pierce is honored each year on his birthday when the White House sends a wreath, which is laid in a ceremony by the Pierce Brigade and New Hampshire National Guard.

Old North Cemetery is located at North State Street, Concord, New Hampshire, 03301. At the North State Street entrance is a historic marker. For more information, visit: www.ConcordNH.gov/Facilities/Facility/Details/45.

THROUGH THE END
OF THE VICTORIAN ERA

★★★★★★★★★★★★★★★★★★★★★★★★★★★★★★★★★★★★★★

Millard Fillmore ★ *1850–1853*

CRITICAL DEATH INFORMATION:

Date of death:	March 8, 1874, 11:10 p.m.
Cause of death:	Stroke
Age at death:	74 years, 60 days
Last words:	"The nourishment is palatable."
Place of death:	Home in Buffalo, New York
Funeral:	St. Paul's Cathedral, Buffalo, New York
Final resting place:	Forest Lawn Cemetery, Buffalo, New York
Reinterred:	No
Cost to visit grave:	Free
For more information:	www.Forest-Lawn.com
Significance:	First presidential grave monument that was erected before the president's death

Millard Fillmore enjoyed good health for much of his life, and that continued in the years after his presidency ended in 1853. He attributed his wellness to his aversion to vice: "I never smoked or chewed tobacco . . . I never knew intoxication." He added, "I never allowed my usual hours of sleep to be interrupted."[1] This came to an abrupt end on February 13, 1874. While shaving that morning, Fillmore had a stroke and lost all sensation in the left side of his body. A few weeks later, as he was slowly recuperating, he suffered a second debilitating stroke that affected his throat, making it nearly impossible for him to swallow. After this second blow, his health declined quickly. Shortly before his death, after managing to take some food, he flatly told his doctors his last words, "The nourishment is palatable." On March 8, 1874, Millard Fillmore slipped out of consciousness and died that night at 11:10 p.m. in his home in Buffalo, New York.

Fillmore's remains were placed in a rosewood coffin, which was draped with white silk and adorned with eight silver handles. Affixed to the coffin was a silver plate that simply read: MILLARD FILLMORE. BORN JAN. 7TH 1800. DIED MARCH 8TH 1874. The coffin was moved to the west front room and several of the numerous floral arrangements that arrived at the home were placed nearby.[2]

Four days later, March 12, businesses were closed and flags hung at half-mast for Fillmore's funeral. At 8:00 a.m., family members began to gather at the home, and an hour later, Baptist reverend Velona Roundy Hotchkiss and Presbyterian reverend John C. Lord delivered the funeral service. After it was completed, the coffin was carried in a hearse drawn by two white horses. The procession was led by eight guards from Buffalo Company D and marched down Niagara to Pearl Street. At St. Paul's Cathedral, the coffin was carried through the East Street doors into the vestibule and placed on a catafalque covered in black velvet, where soldiers from Company D took up positions as an honor guard. At 10:00 a.m., people entered in single file to see the 13th president for the final time. The *New York Times* tactfully reported: "Although much emaciated, Mr. Fillmore's face bore the courtly appearance so characteristic of him in life."[3]

For the next three and a half hours, between 20,000 and 25,000 people paid their respects. At 1:45 p.m., a private viewing began. President Ulysses S. Grant and selected members of Congress, including Abraham Lincoln's former vice president, Hannibal Hamlin, were in attendance. A telegram arrived from former president Andrew Johnson offering his condolences and regrets that he could not attend. After the private ceremony, the body was moved to the cathedral for a 2:45 p.m. service. The funeral was led by Reverend William Shelton, a lifelong friend of Fillmore and the original rector at St. Paul's. Six military sergeants then carried the coffin to the hearse while the choir sang "Nearer, My God, to Thee."

The funeral procession comprised various military units followed by state and city representatives. The pallbearers were "eight of the oldest and most influential citizens [of Buffalo]," including the mayor.[4] The procession made its way down Delaware Avenue, then to Forest Lawn Cemetery for burial in a spot chosen by Fillmore beside his first wife, Abigail Powers Fillmore, who had died March 30, 1853.

A simple marker was placed over the grave, bearing only his initials "M. F." Another marker, an impressive 22-foot obelisk, also sits atop the Fillmore plot by the president's head. It was constructed of Scotch red granite atop a base of Lockport stone.[5] The inscription read:

MILLARD FILLMORE
BORN JANUARY 7, 1800
DIED MARCH 8, 1874

The grave of Millard Fillmore, in Buffalo, New York.

When this monument was erected is difficult to discern. The earliest reference to the monument is found in an article in the *St. Joseph Gazette* dated September 29, 1881.[6] An inquiry to the Forest Lawn Cemetery yielded a surprising reply—they really don't know! A clue can be found in *Forest Lawn Cemetery Illustrated*: this book includes a lithograph of the monument that towers over Fillmore's grave but it was published in 1855, almost two decades *before* the president's death![7] Prior to the book's publication, Fillmore's wife and daughter both passed away. Both women were buried in the Fillmore plot at Forest Lawn Cemetery and one can surmise that the impressive monument was placed over their grave in anticipation that in the future the president would lie by their side. This is unique in presidential grave history—never before had a prominent marker been erected upon a presidential grave *before* the president's death.

Unlike many of his peers, Fillmore's final resting place did not go through a period of neglect, to the credit of the citizens of Buffalo. In 1892, it was written that "the mounds are in beautifully kept, grassy plats, and bear evidence of care and attention."[8] On Memorial Day, May 30, 1932, a marker near the grave was erected by Millard Fillmore Republican Woman's Club. Fifty years later, a flagpole was erected at the site by the Abigail Fillmore Chapter NSDAR (National Society Daughters of the American Revolution).

Despite his low presidential ranking, there are frequent and quaint gatherings at the grave, especially on his birthday, January 7. In 1973, Dr. McAllister H. Hull Jr., dean of the Graduate School at the State University of Buffalo, was the principal speaker in a ceremony. Fillmore was the first chancellor of the University of Buffalo, and Hull reflected upon his support of education.[9] When President Jimmy Carter honored the tradition of sending a wreath to his grave in 1981, newspapers applauded the diehards in attendance, reporting "a handful of people gathered in 20-degree temperature to pay homage to the nation's 13th president."[10] In 1986, about 20 people showed up in 15-degree cold and President Reagan sent a wreath to commemorate what would have been his 186th birthday.

THE MILLARD FILLMORE DEATH SITES
Location of Death

The home where Fillmore died, located at 107 Delaware Avenue, has a long and interesting history. Years before there was any structure on the property, the land was owned by Albert H. Tracey, a New York congressman and state senator who had moved to the area to become a Unitarian parson. In 1831, the property was purchased by John Hollister, who built a home on the site in 1852. Hollister fell on hard times, and in 1858 he sold the home to former president Fillmore. For the next 16 years, Fillmore enjoyed his retirement while remaining active in Buffalo civic events. He welcomed several noteworthy visitors to the home, including John

Statler Towers today sits at the site where Fillmore died in downtown Buffalo.

Quincy Adams. His most famous houseguest, Abraham Lincoln, arrived for lunch on Sunday, February 17, 1861, when he was in Buffalo as part of a roundabout journey from Springfield to Washington, DC, for his first inauguration.[11]

After Fillmore died, his sons combined the home structure with an adjacent home formerly owned by M. S. Hawley to create the Hotel Fillmore in 1881. Twenty years later, in 1901, it was expanded and renamed Castle Inn to take advantage of the popularity of the Pan-American Exposition that opened that same year.[12] The Exposition was the incredibly popular World's Fair held in Buffalo, which at the time was the eighth most populous city in America. An advertisement in the *Buffalo Courier* read "A hundred rooms have been added to the Tudor Gothic mansion, once the palatial home of President Millard Fillmore, and the castellated character of the addition makes the name of Castle Inn singularly appropriate."[13]

In 1919, the Castle Inn, along with the last remnants of the original Fillmore home, was demolished to make way for the Statler Hotel. Construction began in May 1921, at a cost of $8 million. With 1,100 rooms, the hotel had more accommodations that all other Buffalo hotels *combined*! The grand opening for the new hotel was on May 19, 1923. The next year, the Buffalo Historical Society placed a plaque on the building facing Niagara Square that read:

IN HIS HOUSE ON THIS SITE MILLARD FILLMORE, THIRTEENTH PRESIDENT OF THE UNITED STATES RESIDED FROM 1858 UNTIL HIS DEATH HERE, MARCH 8, 1874. THIS TABLET ERECTED 1924 BY THE BUFFALO HISTORICAL SOCIETY OF WHICH HE WAS A FOUNDER AND THE FIRST PRESIDENT 1862–67

Funeral Site

In 1848, St. Paul's Cathedral was designed by Richard Upjohn, president of the American Institute of Architects, in the American Gothic Revival style. Perhaps in a symbolic move, the site they chose on Shelton Square had been the location of the last of Buffalo's burlesque houses, The Palace. Construction started on St. Paul's in the spring of 1850, using local Medina sandstone shipped along the Erie Canal from a quarry near Hulberton, about 50 miles away, and set in an ashlar, or random, pattern. It was completed and consecrated in October 1851 and the spire that towers 270 feet in the air was added in 1870. When it was completed, Buffalo proudly had its first architectural landmark.[14] In 1886, the church was chosen as the Episcopal Cathedral for the Diocese of Western New York, but in May 1888, a gas explosion destroyed much of the inside of the building. As with the church where Franklin Pierce's funeral was held, only the stone walls remained intact. Undeterred, the community rebuilt the church, this time designed by an Englishman, Robert W. Gibson. It reopened two years later, more ornate than before the fire.

On December 23, 1987, it was designated as a National Historic Landmark (#8702600), but Fillmore's funeral is not once mentioned in the National Historic Landmark nomination form.

St. Paul's Cathedral is located at 125 Pearl Street at the corner of Church and Pearl Streets in downtown Buffalo, New York, 14202. For more information, visit: www.StPaulsCathedral.org.

Photograph of St. Paul's Cathedral in 1890, where Fillmore's funeral was held. (Library of Congress)

Grave

The Forest Lawn Cemetery was established in 1849 when a local lawyer, Charles E. Clarke, purchased 80 acres to set aside for a public cemetery. A prominent community member, John Lay Jr., was the first person buried in the cemetery on July 12, 1850. On May 10, 1990, the cemetery was added to the National Register of Historic Places (#90000688).[15] Fillmore is appropriately located in plot F; a 30-by-40-foot area surrounded by an iron gate. Other notable graves at the site are Reverend Shelton and my personal favorite, funk music icon Rick "Super-freak" James! The cemetery has an unusual motto at its entrance: "The future is our past."

The cemetery is located at 1411 Delaware Ave, Buffalo, New York, 14209. There are two gates to enter the cemetery. Both open at 8:00 a.m., but hours vary by season. For more information, visit: www.Forest-Lawn.com.

Andrew Johnson ★ *1865–1869*

CRITICAL DEATH INFORMATION:

Date of death:	July 31, 1875, 2:30 a.m.
Cause of death:	Paralytic stroke
Age at death:	66 years, 214 days
Last words:	Unknown
Place of death:	His daughter's home near Elizabethton, Tennessee
Funeral:	Greeneville Court House, Greeneville, Tennessee
Final resting place:	Andrew Johnson National Cemetery, Greeneville, Tennessee
Reinterred:	No
Cost to visit grave:	Free
For more information:	www.nps.gov/anjo
Significance:	First president to have a national cemetery designated in his honor

After his presidency ended in 1869, Andrew Johnson returned home to Greeneville, Tennessee. He later chose to reenter public service and was elected to the Senate in 1875, representing his home state of Tennessee, and became the only former president to serve as a senator after leaving the White House. Two years prior to his senatorial election, in 1873, a severe case of cholera permanently damaged his lower limbs. He never fully regained use of his legs from the knees down, often stumbling when he walked. In the summer of 1875, Johnson began to suffer from exhaustion. In Greeneville he met with Dr. Marion Maloney and confided in him that "he was completely worn out," and "did not think he could hold out more than a year or two longer."[1] On Monday, July 26, 1875, Johnson met with his family physician, who also expressed concern with the former president's health. Johnson planned to visit his daughter, Mary Brown, at her farm 45 miles away in Elizabethton to recuperate. For the previous six weeks, his wife Eliza had been staying there, and Johnson was looking forward to reuniting with her. His son Andrew pleaded that "he was in too delicate a state of heath to attempt the journey," but Johnson was insistent.[2]

On Wednesday, July 28, Johnson boarded a 5:57 a.m. train to Elizabethton. He arrived at Carter's Station in good spirits and was greeted by one of his daughter's servants, who took him by carriage to Mary's house. It was a hot day, and after seven jostling miles, he arrived exhausted. After a "hearty dinner," he walked upstairs to rest in a bedroom.[3] Johnson gazed out the window at the grazing cattle as he talked with his granddaughter Lillie when suddenly he fell from his chair. He had suffered a stroke and could not speak or move the right side of his body. His family rushed to help, lifting him off the floor and placing him on the bed. They wanted to call a doctor, but Johnson waved them off, refusing medical assistance. Confident he would recover, he slowly regained his speech, and the next day partial movement on his right side was restored. But by Thursday, July 29, he conceded to call Dr. Abraham Jobe, a good friend and physician who lived two miles away. Jobe arrived at 5:00 p.m. along with Dr. Cameron. By the next day, although still in great pain, Johnson was able to talk with his physicians and family about such subjects as, of course, politics.

However, Jobe knew Johnson's condition was perilous and summoned his son Andrew and daughter Martha Patterson to the home. They arrived from Greeneville Friday night, along with Dr. Taylor and another physician, Dr. James F. Broyles. However, Johnson had suffered a second stroke and was again unable to speak.[4] At 7:00 p.m. that night, he slipped into a coma. Andrew Johnson died at 2:30 a.m. on Saturday, July 31, 1875. With him were Dr. Taylor, Dr. Broyles, his wife and three children, Andrew, Martha, and Mary, and Mary's two daughters and son. The only family members not present were his grandchildren, Andrew and Mary Belle.[5]

Church bells in Elizabethton tolled, and President Ulysses S. Grant, now the third president without any living predecessors, made a sterile and unemotional statement for the unpopular Johnson: "The Executive Mansion and the several departments of the government at Washington be draped in mourning until the close of the day designated for his funeral and that all public business be suspended on that day."[6] Newspapers were not kind to the first president ever impeached. The *Deseret News* reported, "He was acknowledgedly an honest

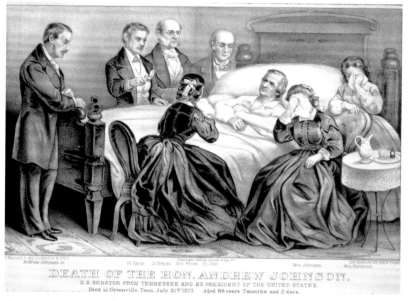

Currier & Ives lithograph, *Death of the Hon. Andrew Johnson: U.S. Senator from Tennessee and Ex-President of the United States.* (Library of Congress)

man, of decided convictions, but he had not the pleasantest nor the mildest manner of expressing them."[7]

One group that still held the former president in high regard was his loyal fellow Free Masons. They arrived at the home, wrapped the body in blankets, and placed it in a pine box packed with ice. Johnson had earlier chosen his burial location at the top of a 100-foot-high hill on a parcel of property he owned near his home in Greeneville. The family had also received offers from Knoxville and Nashville for the grave site. However, they chose to honor the president's wishes.

Early Saturday morning, August 1, the coffin was placed in a wagon and taken to Carter's Station for a train bound for Greeneville. Along the route, people gathered along the tracks to pay homage. The train stopped briefly to pick up Johnson's grandchildren Andrew and Mary Belle Patterson. It arrived later that day and was received by members of Mason Lodge Number 119, of which Andrew Johnson had been a member. After Masonic rituals, the coffin was placed on an ornately decorated hearse and taken to the Johnson homestead to prepare for burial. The remains were transferred to a silver-mounted casket adorned with Masonic symbols, upon which was a simple plaque that rounded up his age: ANDREW JOHNSON, AGED 67 YEARS.[8] One additional and most unique request made by Andrew Johnson was then fulfilled. In accordance with his wishes, his body was "wrapped in an American flag with his head resting on a copy of the Constitution."

The coffin was moved to the parlor and Masonic guards were stationed. It was opened for public viewing until noon on Monday, August 2. It was then carried down the street to the Greeneville Court House and placed in the middle of the room surrounded by flowers for another viewing. All throughout the room, portraits of the president were hung, prompting the *New York Times* to report, "The taste and industry of the ladies and the energy of the gentlemen of Green[e]ville had united to make the dingy old court-room beautiful."[9]

The funeral was held the next day, Tuesday, August 3. The morning was gloomy, and a mist hung over the town as the crowds arrived on the 7:00 and 10:00 a.m. trains, but as the day progressed the clouds dissipated and the sun came out. At noon the family arrived at the courthouse, and Free Masons carried the remains to the hearse. The hearse was escorted by 18 pallbearers, and the procession was led by the Johnson Guards, followed by the Patrons of Husbandry, Odd Fellows, a German band, the Dickinson Light Guards of Knoxville, and several Masonic lodges. Serving as honor guards, with swords drawn, were the Knights Templar, followed by Tennessee governor James D. Porter, family members (his wife had been too ill to make the trip), and then citizens on foot and horseback. The procession marched a half mile to the grave site.[10]

By this time the weather had turned, and a torrential

Johnson's casket and funeral bier. (Andrew Johnson National Historic Site)

rain was falling. A soaked crowd of 5,000 people gathered around the grave for the ceremony led by Commander Woodward with music by the Knoxville Glee Club. D. G. M. Connor of the Free Masons then spoke to close the funeral, and at 3:00 p.m., the coffin was lowered into a zinc-lined box within cement walls. Given the severe weather and pressing train schedule, most people departed immediately. Those from the east rushed to the station to catch the 4:00 p.m. while those heading west waited for the 7:00 p.m.

To appropriately mark the burial location, a tailors' association requested to honor the only member of their trade to ever to serve in the White House by erecting a monument over his grave. The family accepted; however, when two years had passed and no monument had been erected, his children took charge and hired Van Grunden, Young, and Drumm from Philadelphia to build a permanent memorial, which cost approximately $17,000. The firm designed a 27-foot-tall marble monument on a granite base. Atop the monument, a bug-eyed eagle is perched over a draped American flag.[11] At the base is a carving of an open Bible and the Constitution. Inscribed upon the stone are the words (the last line suggested by Brooklyn judge Thomas Kinsella):

ANDREW JOHNSON
SEVENTEENTH PRESIDENT U.S.A.

Johnson's grave in Greenville, Tennessee.

BORN DECEMBER 29, 1808. DIED JULY 31, 1875.
HIS FAITH IN THE PEOPLE NEVER WAVERED

On June 5, 1878, about 3,000 turned out for the unveiling ceremony and heard Johnson's friend George W. Jones speak.[12]

THE ANDREW JOHNSON DEATH SITES
Location of Death

The home where Andrew Johnson died was built in the 1800s sometime prior to the Civil War. It was a large two-story farmhouse, located on the north side of the Watauga River at the foot of Lynn Mountain. Its connection to the Johnson family dated back to Mary Johnson's marriage to Colonel Daniel Stover on April 17, 1852. Stover, a Union Soldier, died in the Civil War. Mary continued to live in the home and remarried William Ramsey Brown in 1869. Years later, the

The house where Johnson died, photographed in the 1930s. (Used by permission from Michelle Ganz Archivist, Special Collections Librarian from the Abraham Lincoln Library)

home became known as the Isaac Lincoln Plantation.

A portion of the home was subsequently razed, leaving a small two-room structure. In 1925 it was purchased by Dr. W. D. Ensor of Alva, Oklahoma, a physician born in Carter County who envisioned the home as a historic shrine. He soon became discouraged when he realized that no civic or historic groups shared his vision. In 1959 local businessman Clyde Campbell purchased the home from Dr. Ensor's widow. Campbell moved the building to Fuddtown in Rio Vista, carefully breaking down and reassembling it piece by piece. There it remained for over four decades until August 2004, when it was put up for auction.[13] The winning bid came from audiologist Dr. Daniel R. Schumaier, who moved the home to Brooks Farm at 1548 Blue Springs Road, where annual Civil War reenactments are held.[14] He placed it behind the circa-1820 farmhouse (which itself is on the National Register of Historic Places), and it is visible from the road.

Near the original home site is a historic marker on Stoney Creek Highway (Tennessee Highway 91) and Rufus Taylor Road at the north side of the Reverend Henry E. Colvard Memorial Bridge that reads, "About .1 mile S.W. at the home of the daughter, Mary Johnson Stover, Andrew Johnson died in 1875. He had been a senator from Tennessee: governor of Tennessee; military governor under Federal occupation, vice president of the United States and 17th President succeeding Abraham Lincoln."

Viewing

The viewing in Greeneville was held in the parlor of Andrew Johnson's homestead. Johnson purchased the two-story brick Greek Revival house in 1851 when he was a member of the House of Representatives from Tennessee's first district. During the Civil War, the home was confiscated by the Confederacy and turned into a hospital and later occupied by Union troops. Both sides did extensive damage to the home, but Johnson had it repaired before he returned to live there after his presidency ended in 1869. He continued to own it until his death, and it remained in the Johnson family for three generations. In 1942 the home was added to the newly established Andrew Johnson National Monument (now the Andrew Johnson National Historic Site). Today most of the furnishings are original pieces that were donated by his descendants.

The Johnson homestead is located at 209 South Main Street, Greeneville, Tennessee, 37743. It is open every day for tours except Thanksgiving, Christmas, and New Year's Day.

Grave

The burial location was originally purchased in 1852 by Andrew Johnson, who liked to climb the 100-foot hill to relax

The home where Johnson died as it looks today, in its new location on Brooks Farm.
(Thanks to Dr. Daniel R. Schumaier for permitting me onto his property to photograph it.)

on its bucolic summit and planted a willow tree to mark the spot where he wanted to be buried. During the Civil War, it was known as "Signal Hill" because soldiers climbed its heights to alert their comrades, but after the monument was built, it became known as "Monument Hill." The cemetery remained under ownership of the family for the next four decades after Johnson's death. In 1906 it was transferred to the War Department and transformed into a national cemetery.

In February 1907, the House of Representatives debated a $12,000 funding bill for the national cemetery. The bill had overwhelming support, but one member was not thrilled with the proposal. Michigan Representative Washington Gardner objected to the appropriation and argued that with only four Union soldiers buried in the cemetery, the funding was merely a backdoor way of having the federal government take care of Andrew Johnson's grave. His objection was met with a chorus of "Nos" and the appropriation passed.[15]

On May 31, 1909, the first Memorial Day celebration at the cemetery, the grave was patriotically decorated and an address was made by Martha W. Littleton from East Tennessee.[16] In 1942 it was placed under the auspices of the National Park Service, where it remains to this day. In August 1985, the National Park State-ment of Management determined that the monument was in need of repairs, and architectural conservator Benjamin Nestal-Miret warned that it was in "an advanced state of sugaring of the monument surfaces"[17] He also found stains and cracks that were partially the result of a cleaning in 1974 using hydrochloric acid. Two years later, funding was allocated to restore the monuments.

On December 29, 1998, President Bill Clinton sent a wreath to be placed over the grave. This is usually a routine annual event that does not garner much media attention, but this year was different. Earlier in the year Bill Clinton joined Andrew Johnson as the only president to be impeached by the House of Representatives. There were only about a dozen people participating in the graveside ceremony, but they were greeted by many reporters eager to point out the irony. To address the new reality of Andrew Johnson's place in history, the National Park Service hurriedly altered a display by the visitor center. The original text read "On February 24, 1868, Andrew Johnson became the first *and only* president to be impeached by the House of Representatives." A piece of tape was strategically placed to cover "*and only*."[18] For more information on the homestead and grave, visit: www.nps.gov/anjo.

THE TWENTIETH PRESIDENT

James Abram Garfield ★ *1881*

CRITICAL DEATH INFORMATION:

Date of death:	September 19, 1881, 10:35 p.m.
Cause of death:	Assassination (including subsequent medical treatment)
Age at death:	49 years, 304 days
Last words:	"Oh my! Swaim, what a pain I have right here!"
Place of death:	Francklyn Cottage, Elberon, New Jersey
Funeral:	United States Capitol, Washington, DC
Final resting place:	Lake View Cemetery, Cleveland, Ohio
Reinterred:	Yes
Cost to visit grave:	Free
For more information:	www.LakeView Cemetery.com
Significance:	Survived longer after being shot than any assassinated president

On July 2, 1881, President James Garfield entered the Baltimore and Potomac Railroad station in Washington, DC. Garfield was in good spirits, looking forward to visiting his alma mater, Williams College, in Williamstown, Massachusetts for his 26th reunion. He had no security as he walked to his train with his good friend, Secretary of State James Blaine, and his children, Jim and Harry. Suddenly, Charles J. Guiteau, who had snuck up behind Garfield, pulled out a .44 caliber British Bull Dog pistol and fired twice.[1] The first bullet grazed the president's arm and bore clear through a tool box carried by a stunned worker. The second bullet ripped Garfield's chest, broke a rib, and pierced his first lumbar vertebrae but missed his spinal column and all major organs. A shocked Garfield cried out, "My God, my God, what is this?"

Blaine shouted at the assailant, "In God's name, man, what did you shoot the president for?" Guiteau, a frustrated, delusional lawyer, who believed that Garfield owed him a patronage job as ambassador to Spain, coolly replied, "I am a Stalwart, and want Arthur for president." As a crowd rushed toward the fallen president, his son Harry tried to keep them away to give his father some air. Garfield weakly asked the ladies' room attendant for water, but after taking a drink, he began to vomit. Five minutes after the shooting, Dr. Smith Townsend, health officer from the District of Columbia, arrived. He checked Garfield's pulse and, finding it had dropped to 53 beats per minute, administered brandy and "aromatic spirits of ammonia" to prevent Garfield from fainting. The doctor poked his finger directly into the wound in Garfield's back to find the bullet. This was done on the filthy station floor, and Townsend hadn't washed his hands. It was in this moment that Garfield's slow death began. More doctors streamed toward the president until there were 10 hovering over him, poking and probing his body in a similar unsanitary fashion.[2] Townsend wanted to move Garfield away from the crowd to a private area where he could be better examined. The president was placed on a horsehair and hay mattress and carried upstairs to an empty room. Thirty-nine-year-old African American Charles Purvis, surgeon in chief at Freedman's Hospital, arrived and recommended that Garfield be kept warm with hot water bottles and blankets. In this brief examination, Purvis made history as the first African American doctor to ever treat a president.

Garfield lay on the mattress in a dire state, vomiting and drifting in and out of consciousness. His cabinet members arrived, including Secretary of War Robert Todd Lincoln, who sent for Dr. Doctor Willard Bliss (that's not a typo; his first name was *actually* Doctor, though he mostly went by Willard in his practice), who

had helped treat his father, Abraham Lincoln, on the night he was shot. Garfield had first met Bliss in Ohio almost four decades earlier, and Secretary Lincoln believed Garfield would be comfortable under his care.[3] As soon as Bliss arrived, he took control and inserted an unsterilized probe into Garfield's body to find the bullet, poking and prodding in flesh that had already become a well-traveled channel. Garfield, the battle-hardened Civil War veteran, withstood the immense pain without the benefit of anesthesia. Bliss then tried using his finger, sticking it inside Garfield's body far enough to feel bone. Unable to find the bullet, Bliss abandoned the search for the time being.[4]

Eventually, Garfield could not tolerate it any longer and asked to be taken to the White House. A half hour after he'd been shot, the president was carried down the steps and placed in an ambulance. False reports made their way to the public that he was already dead. To counter such rumors, Bliss released an extraordinarily optimistic official bulletin from the White House at 11:30 a.m.: "The president has returned to his normal condition. Will make another examination soon. His pulse is now 63." An hour later came another update: "The reaction from the shot injury has been very gradual. He is suffering some pain, but it is thought best not to disturb him by making an exploration for the ball until after the consultation at three o'clock in the afternoon."[5] The president's condition, if it ever was as rosy as Bliss reported, began to deteriorate almost immediately after the 12:35 p.m. bulletin. By 1:20 p.m., the report was grim: "Pulse 112. Some nausea and vomiting have occurred. Considerable hemorrhage has taken place from the wound." At 2:30 p.m., "The President's symptoms continue to grow more unfavorable." Finally, at 2:40 p.m., "President Garfield has but few chances of recovery, and . . . he may not live twelve hours." Those who saw the president confirmed the prognosis for the countless reporters who had gathered at the White House. Judge Samuel Shellabarger lamented, "There seems to be absolutely no hope of his rallying. His symptoms are growing more alarming and his death is thought to be very near."[6]

By 7:00 p. m., Garfield's pulse was at a feverish pace of 140. He was administered morphine to ease the pain, but few expected he would survive the first night. He asked about his chances, prompting a brutally honest physician to bluntly answer: "One chance in a hundred." He replied, "Then we will take that chance!"[7] Throughout the night, Garfield's sleep was interrupted almost every half hour by "regurgitation of the stomach."[8] Despite the long odds, Garfield survived the night and by the morning, his prognosis had improved.

The day after the shooting, Bliss summoned two surgeons to the White House, Dr. Davis Hayes Agnew, chief of surgery from the University of Pennsylvania, and Dr. Frank Hamilton from Bellevue Medical College in New York, while Garfield's wife, Lucretia, called upon the services of two more, Garfield's cousin, Dr. Silas Boynton, and Dr. Susan Ann Edson, one of the first female doctors in America and Lucretia's personal physician. Garfield rested in an upstairs White House bedroom, cordoned off by screens rendering him virtually invisible to most staff. Bliss strictly limited visitors' access and few were permitted to see the president. Bliss continually administered what now seems more like a recipe for a wild frat party—rum, wine, and morphine—but Garfield still experienced excruciating pain in his lower extremities, which he described as like being lacerated by "tiger's claws." By all accounts, he faced the situation with courage, grace, gratitude, and a sense of humor.

Bliss prescribed a rich diet of heavy meats and potatoes, washed down with a dose of brandy, which Garfield could not always keep down. His digestive system was further strained by daily doses of quinine to ward off malaria. In Washington's summer swelter, the heat and humidity were oppressive. To comfort the patient, navy engineers designed a complex system to pipe air into Garfield's room, cooled by three tons of ice each day (at a cost of $5 per ton). This revolutionary appliance, the country's first air conditioner, was first tried on July 11, and the air was found to be "cool, dry and ample in supply."[9]

Bliss began to feel optimistic after Garfield survived the first precarious days and told a *New York Times* reporter, "It was a happy wound after all. I think it's almost certain that we shall pull him through." On July 21, Lucretia told a friend that the president was "out of danger."[10] But the next morning, his health began to reverse course when the wound expelled a large amount of pus, cloth, and bone. On July 23, his temperature spiked to a dangerous 104 degrees, and he vomited bile three times. Bliss again sent for Hamilton and Agnew. Without anesthesia, they opened up his back to drain additional pus. Two days later, they operated to remove bone fragments, muscle, and tissue. While they did not find the bullet, they undoubtedly introduced copious amounts of germs into the wound.

The doctors still had not given up their quest for the elusive bullet. To aid in the search, Alexander Graham Bell offered his latest invention, a primitive metal detector. It was tried in secrecy for the first time in late July, with Bell making last-minute alterations to the machine up until he arrived at the White House. He was greeted by the president, who asked the young inventor to explain how the contraption worked. Bell found the president's appearance startling, having an "ashen gray colour, which makes one feel for a moment that you are not looking upon a living man." Bell was unable to locate the slug, and when Garfield tired, he called it off. His experiment a failure, Bell returned home to discover that the problem was a hasty last-minute adjustment he had made incorrectly. On August 1, at Bliss's request, Bell made another attempt. Bliss was convinced the bullet was near Garfield's liver on his right side and had the experiment focus on that area. The detector did signal it had located metal, and Bliss declared success, while Bell remained hesitant. It is now widely believed that the false positive was caused by metal coils beneath the horse-hair mattress.

On August 8, an operation was performed to drain more pus, which the stoic Garfield again endured without anesthesia. But it was futile—large pockets of toxic pus and bile had already ravaged his insides. One abscess in his salivary gland had become so enlarged that it burst, draining into his ear canal and mouth, and nearly drowning him. An oblivious Bliss still felt that the wound was not life-threatening, telling a reporter that "the wound is in a state that causes us no apprehension whatsoever." Even Bliss acknowledged concern over the president's shocking weight loss. When he was shot, Garfield weighed a robust 230 pounds, but now he regurgitated almost anything he tried to swallow. The only nourishment he could keep down was koumiss (fermented horse milk), which was not sufficient to prevent drastic weight loss. By the end of August, Garfield had dropped 80 pounds. Bliss resorted to rectally feeding him a meal called enemata, a nutrition-rich cocktail consisting of beef bouillon, egg yolks, milk, and opium.[11] As he monitored its effectiveness, he adjusted the formula, sometimes adding whiskey and replacing milk with charcoal. By this humiliating method, the president of the United States was fed every four hours, for eight consecutive days. In addition to speeding up his weight loss, it also caused severe dehydration.

The wounded Garfield wanted to leave Washington for more comfortable surroundings. His first inclination was to return to his home in Mentor, Ohio, but hoping the sea air would prove therapeutic, he opted for the ocean. Lucretia was against the idea, fearing the trip would be too arduous, and wanted to have him moved to the Soldier's Home in Washington, DC. Despite his weakened condition, Garfield

overruled his wife. New York financier and railroad magnate Charles G. Francklyn offered the use of his twenty-room cottage on the seashore in Elberon, New Jersey, a part of Long Branch frequented by the rich and famous of the era, and accustomed to hosting presidents such as Grant and Hayes (later presidents to stay in the seaside town included Arthur, Benjamin Harrison, McKinley, and Wilson). On the morning of September 6, Garfield was carried from the White House in a stretcher and placed in a carriage. At 6:10 a.m., the carriage was greeted at the station by a small, curious crowd that had gathered to see him off. A sheet covered his frail body to his neck, and his head was wrapped in bandages in an almost cartoonish fashion. What could be seen of the president horrified those in the crowd: "The skin was of a livid color, the cheeks were hollow and the nose was pinched." An exhausted Garfield could muster none of his good humor to provide a reassuring acknowledgement to the onlookers.

He was placed in car #33, and every effort was made render the journey comfortable and safe.[12] To reduce smoke and soot, heavy drapes were hung and clean-burning anthracite coal was used. Private residences along the route were secured as a precaution. At 6:20 a.m., General Train Master Charles Watts slowly pulled out of the station but almost immediately had to stop for another train's passage. Silent crowds gathered along the tracks, and men removed their hats in respect. Newspapers followed the president's journey meticulously; in addition to station and time, their reports frequently included his pulse. The train passed through Baltimore at 8:04 a.m. and Havre de Grace at 9:10 a.m., where it was reported that Garfield "appeared to be really enjoying the trip."[13]

In Delaware, the train stopped at a coaling station, and Bliss used the opportunity to give the president a sponge bath. Garfield was eager to arrive in Elberon—when asked if he would like to stop again, he replied, "Let us reach the end of our journey first. That is most important."[14] Garfield asked to have the engineer increase the speed. Hundreds of workers at the train yards in Philadelphia were instructed to lay down their tools so as not to disturb the president as he went by at 11:00 a. m. Shortly before noon, the train crossed into New Jersey, rolling by silent crowds on the bridge and in the Trenton depot. It rode through Princeton a minute before noon and Monmouth Junction at 12:07 p.m. Seven minutes later, the train switched onto the Freehold and Jamesburg Agricultural line for the final leg of its journey. It arrived in Elberon at 1:35 p.m., as Garfield's pulse hit 110. The *Omaha Daily Bee* made the obvious comparison, describing the spectacle as a "weird funeral-like trip."[15]

The night before Garfield's arrival, 2,000 workers had laid new track right up to the cottage. But now, with the home in sight, the train stalled at the bottom of a hill. In an inspiring scene, 200 men approached the train and pushed it the remaining distance so Garfield could be transferred directly into the home. Approximately 15,000 people had gathered in the small town to greet the president, but upon laying eyes

on his deathly appearance, many broke down in tears. After Garfield had settled into Francklyn Cottage, it seemed at first that the sea air was indeed therapeutic, and he appeared to be recuperating. Bliss, so often oblivious to the reality of the situation, declared, "The trouble has now passed its crisis, and is going away." Unfortunately, the crisis had not passed, and Garfield was in his final days on earth.[16]

On September 15, his pulse and temperature rose, and from then on, his health began to plummet. On September 19, Dr. Bliss was hopeful, and a 5:30 p.m. bulletin noted that Garfield's pulse ranged between 102 and 106 beats per minute. That night, Bliss asked Garfield if he was uncomfortable, and he replied "Not at all." Given Dr. Boynton's view that death was possible but not probable, the reporters departed to file their stories.[17]

At approximately 10:00 p.m., Garfield's friend David Gaskill Swaim sat alone with him as he slept. Suddenly, Garfield gasped. Swaim rushed to his bedside, and the two locked eyes. "Well, Swaim," the president said before grasping his heart and crying out his last words, "Oh my! Swaim, what a pain I have right here!" As word got out the end was imminent, people hurried to Garfield's room: Lucretia, his daughter Mollie, Garfield's secretary Joseph Stanley Brown, Colonel A. F. Rockwell and his wife, Dr. Bliss, Dr. Agnew, Dr. Boynton, his brother-in-law Camden A. Rockwell, and his African American servant Daniel Spriggs. They watched in silence as Dr. Bliss tried in vain to prevent the unpreventable. Finally at 10:35 p.m., on September 19, 1881, President James Garfield succumbed to his wounds and subsequent

Events related to the assassination of President James Garfield, including citizens pushing the train the final stretch to the cottage entrance in Elberon, New Jersey, from *Frank Leslie's Illustrated*. (Library of Congress)

medical treatment and died. At just 49, Garfield supplanted James K. Polk as the youngest president to die. Slowly, the crowd left the room, and Lucretia sat with the president for over an hour in solitude.

Given the optimistic reports earlier in the day, reporters were shocked at Garfield's death. A telegram was sent to Chester Arthur, who was at a summer hotel on Long Island, notifying him that he was now the president of the United States. He was sworn in the next day at his home in New York City, becoming the first president to take the oath of office outside of Washington, DC, since George Washington.

At approximately 4:00 p.m., an autopsy was performed by acting Assistant Surgeon General D. S. Lamb of the Army Medical Museum of Washington, DC, who was aided by six of Garfield's physicians, including Bliss, Hamilton, and Agnew. An Elberon physician, Dr. Andrew H. Smith, was also present to comply with New Jersey state law. Four hours later, Lamb had determined that after fracturing the right eleventh rib, the bullet had become lodged two and a half inches from the spine, but no major organs were hit. The bullet did not kill Garfield, but

Lamb discovered what had. Copious amounts of pus and infection had ravaged Garfield's body, notably in the cavities caused by the doctors' digging for the bullet. A fist-sized hemorrhage of blood was found in his abdominal cavity, and Lamb documented Garfield's official cause of death as "Secondary Hemorrhage from one of the Mesenteric Arteries adjoining the track of the ball."

Gruesome souvenirs were saved for posterity. Today, a flap of skin from Garfield's back is on display at the Mutter Museum in Philadelphia, and in 2006 his vertebrae were featured in an exhibit at National Museum of Health and Medicine on the campus of the Walter Reed Army Medical Center.

One of the goals of the autopsy was to allay the public's concern that the medical care had been botched and the death was preventable. While the doctors were diligent in reporting that death was inevitable, some knew immediately that better treatment would have saved the president. As lead physician, Dr. Bliss found himself in the crosshairs.[18] Most damning to Garfield's fate was Bliss's disregard of sterilization practices. The gunshot wounds themselves should not have been fatal, and in the end it was the infection caused by unsanitary medical practices that did Garfield in. Many American doctors at the time did not see the need to wash their hands or sterilize their instruments, though some European doctors had already begun sterilization practices. In 2006, medical historian Dr. Ira Rutkow, author and professor of surgery at the University of Medicine and Dentistry of New Jersey, claimed, "Garfield had such a nonlethal wound. In today's world, he would have gone home in

Currier & Ives lithograph, *Death of General James A. Garfield: Twentieth President of the United States.* (Library of Congress)

a matter or two or three days."[19] Some medical historians believe that, had doctors done *nothing*, Garfield could have survived, as the body's natural defenses would have rendered the bullet harmless.

Later that night, a plaster cast was made of Garfield's shriveled face and right hand, and the oil from the plaster severely discolored his skin. In the casket, the right hand was hidden from view, but nothing could be done to hide his face.[20] Once the cast was complete, the body was prepared for the funeral. Garfield was dressed in the same black suit and black satin tie he had worn at his inauguration, but outside of his dress, he bore no resemblance to the robust and vigorous man he was only six months earlier. He was placed in the coffin upon a bier in the center of a ground-floor room of the cottage. Despite his emaciated appearance and the plaster cast gone awry, the casket was opened. As with Lincoln, the nation felt a need to see their assassinated president one last time.

Despite the fact that no formal public viewing had been announced, the next morning 2,000 people, many of them reporters, congregated outside of the cottage on the chance they might see the deceased president. At 8:45 a.m., the crowd was rewarded and was permitted to view Garfield's remains. In each corner, a solider stood as honor guard, watching as people passed before exiting by the ocean. At 9:30 a.m., the coffin was closed, and Reverend Charles J. Young from the First Reformed Church of Long Branch read from Revelations 14:13. The service lasted only 10 minutes. Several minutes later, six undertakers exited the cottage and carried the coffin onto a funeral car that had been draped in black crepe and American flags. All of the seats were removed to allow the large bier to be placed in the middle, surrounded by funeral flowers. At 10:00 a.m., the train slowly pulled away from the cottage as the small Church of the Presidents tolled its bells. After about 300 yards, it pulled onto the main track, where it stopped briefly to connect to engine #658, the same engine that had brought the president to Long Branch.[21] Boarding at this juncture were former president Grant, President Arthur, and the members of his cabinet. A great crowd had gathered to see the historic meeting of three presidents, albeit one deceased. Reporters were not permitted to ride on the funeral train. At 10:12 a.m., the conductor yelled "All right!" and the train began its journey back to the capital.

Along the route, people gathered at the tracks, men removed their hats, and flags flew at half-mast. At 4:30 p.m. the train arrived in Washington at the Baltimore and Potomac Railroad Station, which was draped in black. Waiting on the platform were 200 army and navy officers under the command of General William Tecumseh Sherman. The first to exit was the president's widow, followed by Grant and President Arthur. Eight United States artillerymen carried the coffin as a band played "Nearer, My God, To Thee." With tears flowing, the artillerymen placed the coffin into a hearse as the song ended.

The procession, led by mounted police, members of the military, Free Masons, and Knights Templar, went directly to the Capitol building. It bypassed a ceremony at the White House, a first in Washington presidential funeral history. Along the three-quarter-mile route down Pennsylvania Avenue, a large, solemn crowd had gathered. At the Capitol, congressmen formed a line to receive Garfield's remains as the same eight artillerymen carried the coffin inside, followed by Arthur and Grant. The coffin was placed in the center of the room and beneath the rotunda, on the same catafalque used for Lincoln's viewing 16 years earlier. It was adorned with flowers and stuffed doves and draped in black with silver lining, but in accordance with Mrs. Garfield's wishes, there were "no ornaments or fringe upon it."[22] Capitol and Metropolitan police guarded the coffin, and honorary roles were given to soldiers from the Army of the Cumberland.

The public remained gruesomely fascinated with how different Garfield looked in death. At times, the line stretched a quarter mile long, and when it was over, approximately 100,000 citizens had paid their respects. At 1:45 p.m., the Knights Templar Beauzaunt Commandary from Baltimore filed past the coffin in full regalia. Invitations to the service were sent to about 800 people, but as soon as the doors opened, a mass of uninvited people broke down the barricades and flooded in. By the time order was restored, scores of funeral-crashers had already snagged seats, forcing many invited guests to stand in the aisles. Former presidents Hayes and Grant and President Arthur entered and took a moment to view the emaciated remains before taking their seats. At 3:00 p.m., Reverend F. D. Powers from the Vermont Avenue Church, where Garfield had attended, read the hymn, "Asleep in Jesus, Blessed Sleep." Reverend James J. Rankin read from Psalms, Reverend Isaac Everett offered a prayer, and Reverend Powers delivered a moving sermon. The service concluded at 4:00 p.m.[23]

A crowd of 40,000 people had gathered outside the Capitol to see the coffin carried to the funeral hearse. A procession escorted it to the Baltimore and Potomac Railroad station, passing thousands in the streets. At the station, the coffin was borne upon the shoulders of six soldiers from the Second Artillery and placed onto the funeral car. It was 5:15 p.m. when the funeral train finally pulled out and headed northwest toward Cleveland. Lucretia returned to a private car, Garfield's cabinet occupied the second car, and army and navy members sat in the third car. The fourth car transported the coffin and honor guard, including Major John H. Clapp, who had served with Garfield in the Ohio Volunteers, Lieutenant E. W. Weaver, Sergeant Major Salter, and eleven more officers. The fifth car carried a delegation from Congress. Former president Hayes was also on board, returning to his native Ohio. Flowers were scattered along the train

tracks, and thousands gathered at the station to see it off. Following the funeral train at about 30 minutes' distance was a second train comprised of additional congressional members.

Ninety minutes later, the train passed through Baltimore's Charles Street Station as people tossed flowers at the funeral car. At 8:20 p.m., the train passed a crowd of miners in York, Pennsylvania. At 9:39 p.m. the train stopped in Marysville, Pennsylvania, across the Susquehanna River from Harrisburg. There it switched to engine #91, under the command of Superintendent H. Carter, who led it over the Blue Ridge Mountains. Guards were placed along the track every half mile as it continued through the Keystone State and onward through Altoona. It continued through Johnstown, Derry, and to Union Station in Pittsburgh at 5:30 a.m. where 5,000 people had gathered. The train stopped for 14 minutes to switch to the Cleveland and Pittsburgh railroad track before departing. At Allegheny City, a car carrying a committee from Cleveland was attached to the train before it pulled out at 6:20 a.m.

The train arrived in Rochester, Pennsylvania, at 7:43 a.m., where it was greeted by aged members of the Grand Army of the Republic. Fifteen minutes later, it reached East Liverpool, Ohio, and passed beneath a custom-built arch as a band played a funeral dirge. A thousand people had gathered, including veterans from the Grand Army of the Republic (the arch is long gone, and today this town is best known as the home of the Largest Teapot in America).

The train stopped for water in Wellesville Junction, where a banner had been placed on a nearby building that read WE MOURN OUR DEAD PRESIDENT. Railroad employees and their wives gathered along the tracks to see the train, and former president Hayes reached out his window to shake hands with his fellow Ohioans. At 10:00 a.m., another engine was added to pull the train up a steep grade. Throughout Ohio, large crowds gathered at the stations as the train passed by. Finally, at 1:30 p.m., the train arrived at Euclid Avenue Station in Cleveland.

The coffin was placed in a hearse pulled by eight black horses, guarded by Knights Templar, and flanked by 10 members of the First City Troop on horseback. The procession was led by the Silver Grays Band, followed by the First City Troop, Reception Committee, Holyrood and the Oriental Commanderies of Knights Templar, the Escort Committee, and the Cleveland Grays, while veterans from Garfield's old regiment, the Forty-Second Ohio Volunteers, followed behind. Next were members of the cabinet, General Sherman, army and navy guard of honor, and United States congressmen. When the procession arrived in Public Square (the same location where Lincoln's body was on display 16 years earlier), the coffin was placed on a catafalque called the "finest temporary structure of the kind ever erected in America."[24] The custom five-foot-high structure sat on a huge platform beneath a canopy towering 72 feet in the air. It was 40 square feet at the base, with 36-foot-tall arches at all four sides, and on top of the canopy was a 24-foot angel with spread arms and wings perched atop a five-foot globe. The tips of the wings hovered an astonishing 96 feet in the air!

The detachments of the Cleveland Grays and Knights Templar took their place as honor guard. However, in Cleveland, there would be no open casket. Disturbed by her husband's ghastly appearance in the previous viewings, Lucretia directed that the coffin should now be closed.[25] Instead, a portrait of the president from better days was placed upon it for mourners to remember him by. At 11:00 a.m., the public viewing began and continued all day— at times, the line stretched for half a mile. At 5:00 p.m., the heat was broken by a brief rainstorm that lasted about half an hour and was followed by a "magnificent and bright rainbow," interpreted by many as a good omen.[26] When it became dark, "electric lights shone down upon the bared heads of these sorrowing friends and

the sleeping soldiers stretched upon the grass."[27] Two years earlier, Cleveland inventor Charles F. Brush had created the first arc lamp. He had placed his invention throughout the city, including Public Square, making Cleveland the first city in the country with electric street lighting.

When the sun rose on Monday, September 26, the viewing was still in process. At 9:10 a.m., after 22 hours and 100,000 people had passed the casket, it came to an end. A half hour later, dignitaries, including President Hayes, Ohio state senator Benjamin Harrison, and General Sherman, walked past the coffin. Garfield's good friend, the Honorable J. P. Robison, presided over the funeral service. At 10:40 a.m., the Cleveland Vocal Society played Beethoven's funeral hymn, and Bishop G. T. Bendell of the Protestant Episcopal Church followed, reading from the Scriptures (appropriately including the Book of Job), and Methodist reverend Ross M. Houghton offered a lengthy prayer. Reverend Isaac Errett, chosen by Lucretia, emphasized Garfield's strong Christian faith in his eulogy, which clocked in at 41 minutes. Reverend Jabez Hall of the Christian Church on Euclid Avenue then read the "Reaper Song," one of Garfield's favorites. By this point, the crowd had been sitting in the intense heat for almost two hours. The last scheduled speaker was Presbyterian reverend Charles S. Pomeroy. Just as he was about to step to the dais, Robison made an appeal, "Mr. Pomeroy, the ladies are fainting. You will please occupy the least possible time." Pomeroy obliged by reading a brief benediction to conclude the service.[28]

The honorary pallbearers were selected by the president's widow, but the actual pallbearers, or body bearers, were able-bodied artillerymen who lifted the casket as the marine band played "Nearer, My God, to Thee" and placed it in an elaborate hearse. It was designed in an Egyptian style and was 16 feet long, 8 feet wide, covered with silver fringe, and stood at 20 feet high. The casket sat beneath a canopy supported by four columns. The enormous structure was pulled by 12 sturdy black horses, each adorned with a black gold-fringed robe. The steeds were led by "six colored grooms," who 16 years earlier had performed the same solemn task when Lincoln's hearse rode in a processional in Cleveland.

The funeral procession was huge. It was five miles long and included 25,000 people.[29] The solemn parade went from Superior Street to Erie and on to Euclid Avenue, where it continued to Lake View Cemetery while dark clouds gathered overhead. The head of the column arrived just before 2:00 p.m., but the rest of the procession would take another two hours to file in.

Flowers were strewn all about. Some arrangements had arrived from across the world, while $250 worth of flowers had been placed there by local schoolteachers. At about 2:15 p.m., a heavy rain began to fall. A canopy was hastily erected, and when it began to sag under the pools of water, an industrious soldier poked holes in the tarp with his bayonet, spilling water to the ground like an open faucet. At 3:30 p.m., the hearse arrived, and the artillerymen carried the coffin into the public receiving vault. A marine band again played "Nearer, My God, to Thee," and Reverend J. H. Jones, chaplain of Garfield's old Forty-Second Regiment, delivered his sermon and asked the unanswerable: "When we sent General Garfield to the Capitol at Washington he weighed 210 pounds. He had a soul that loved his race; a splendid intellect that almost bent the largest form to bear it. You bring him back to us a mere handful of some 80 pounds, mostly of bones, in that casket. Now I ask, why is this?"[30]

A German choir sang Garfield's favorite funeral hymn, "The Nineteenth Ode of Horace," and Professor B. A. Hinsdale gave the benediction to conclude the service. The wrought-iron gate of the public receiving vault was closed, but the casket was still visible, and behind it hung an American flag. Family and friends soon departed, many stooping to pick up a flower

from the ground as a memento. Soon only a 12-man military guard was left.

Soldiers remained at the vault day and night until at least 1884, initially to honor the president but also out of legitimate fears that the remains might be stolen, since only five years earlier an attempt was made to rob Lincoln's grave. Few visitors were allowed in during the first weeks, and the remains were later moved to the nearby Schofield vault, described as a "beautiful gothic structure of gray sandstone built into the slope on an undulating hill and facing the stream that runs through the grounds."[31] The remains were later moved back to the public receiving vault. There is some mystery surrounding the exact whereabouts of Garfield's remains during these years, as the precise time when they were moved between the two vaults is unknown.

Shortly after Garfield's death, a group of his friends convened to plan a permanent monument. Only a decade since the completion of the Lincoln tomb, many Americans felt the second martyred president deserved to be honored in a similar fashion. This was a group with the influence and power to make it happen: Governor Charles Foster, Honorable Jeptha H. Wade, Senator H. B. Payne, Joseph Perkins, T. P. Handy, Dan P. Eells, W. S. Streator, J. H. Devereaux, Selah Chamberlain, John D. Rockefeller, H. B. Perkins, Honorable John Hay, J. H. Rhodes, and most importantly, Garfield's predecessor and good friend, Rutherford B. Hayes. What started with this small group would culminate nine years later with the "costliest and most imposing" monument erected at that time.[32]

In June 1882, the group was incorporated as the Garfield National Monument Association, and Hayes was named president. The Lake View Cemetery Association donated two and a half acres on the highest ground in the cemetery for the memorial. The lot was valued at $100,000, but the deed only listed the value as a dollar. Another $75,000 was donated by Garfield's friends, including John D. Rockefeller, and additional donations were made in small amounts from people throughout the country.

On October 11, 1883, the association held a contest to select the design: first prize was $1,000, second $750, and $500 for third. Over 50 people responded and included entries from England, Germany, Italy, and France. To ensure there was no favoritism, the association selected two architects, Henry Van Brunt of Boston and Calvert Vaux of New York City, to judge the entrants. Both experts agreed on the design submitted by George H. Keller of Hartford, Connecticut, which combined architectural styles from the Romanesque, Gothic, and Byzantine eras, and it was formally accepted on July 21, 1883. Keller toured Europe to seek inspiration to complete his concept. Upon his return, he awarded the stone masonry contract to Thomas Simmons on October 5, 1885, and the next day ground was broken.[33]

A wooden model was first constructed at the original size of 225 feet tall and later reduced to 180 feet. The savings on the masonry was used to make the interior more elaborate, but even with the reduction this was a monument that was unparalleled. The massive tomb was constructed of red sandstone quarried from Berea, Ohio. During construction, Keller was assisted by John S. Chapple of London, and the design evolved to include a round tower with a pagoda top. On the exterior are five terra-cotta panels sculpted by Casper Buberl that included over 110 life-size figures from Garfield's life.[34] One panel depicts Garfield's inauguration: behind him sits his predecessor, Hayes, and before him, his successor, Arthur. On the last of these panels is Garfield's body, lying in state beneath the Capitol rotunda as his open casket is approached by mourners. Within the interior circular Memorial Hall, where Garfield's body would reside, a marble mosaic frieze depicting the funeral procession encircles the walls. There are 14 memorial windows representing the original states plus one for Ohio, which includes a depiction of his log cabin birthplace, Garfield being the last president born in such a humble abode. In the center of the room is a large statue of him in white Carrara marble. Designed by Alexander Doyle of Steubenville, it stands 12 feet tall and cost $10,000.[35]

Inscribed over the door are the words ERECTED BY A GRATEFUL COUNTRY IN MEMORY OF JAMES ABRAM GARFIELD, 20TH PRESIDENT OF THE UNITED STATES. SCHOLAR, SOLDIER, STATESMAN, PATRIOT. BORN 19TH NOV., 1831 DIED 19TH SEP., 1881. A tomb this massive and elaborate had not been seen before in this country. It surpassed Lincoln's tomb in height. It was written that "the structure is believed to be universally regarded as truly imposing, both in magnitude and loftiness of situation, and a marvel of elaborate artistic external and internal decoration. It has been said to be the first real Mausoleum ever erected to the honor and memory of an American statesman, and the fourth of like structures known in history."[36]

Garfield Memorial at Lake View Cemetery in Cleveland, Ohio.

The final cost was approximately $150,000, and a detailed ledger was kept, totaling $134,755.76, with much of the remaining cost coming from interest paid at local banks where the deposits were held. Of this amount, $133,546.60 came from the United States, and international donations accounted for the rest—including $1,149.15 from France, $40 from Belgium, $12 from Australia, $5 from England and a whopping $3 from our neighbors to the north, Canada![37]

In 1889, eight years after Garfield's death, the monument was completed. A dedication ceremony was planned for the same year but was postponed because the statue was not ready.

May 20, 1890, was a rainy day and there were few visitors at the cemetery; the gloomy weather provided the perfect cover since what needed to be done that day required secrecy. The public receiving vault was unlocked, and the Lake View undertaker and superintendent entered. They unlocked the metal casket and peered inside at the dead body of the 20th president. After a quick glance, noting Garfield's "features were still plainly recognizable,"[38] the superintendent closed the casket and summoned eight workers, who hoisted the 700-pound casket and placed it in a hearse. There was no grand procession, and only members of the Garfield Memorial Association and Lake View Cemetery Association walked behind the hearse to the monument. At 10:00 a.m., the coffin was lowered into the basement crypt and placed on top of an elaborate bier. Even today, Garfield lies in the only exposed casket of any president. All others are buried or in a sarcophagus.

Ten days later, on Memorial Day, May 30, a grand dedication was held. A flag was draped over the entrance of the tomb, flowers were strewn about, a podium was set up for the litany of speakers, and a banner was hung that read WELCOME COMRADES. Shortly after 9:00 a.m., the cadence of a drum announced the arrival of the honored guests escorted by a procession of 5,000 men, led by 115 veterans from Garfield's

Forty-Second Regiment of Ohio Volunteer Infantry under the command of Captain C. E. Henry. Riding in the parade was a historic past, present, and future presidential group: Rutherford B. Hayes, Benjamin Harrison, and William McKinley. At 3:00 p.m., the distinguished guests approached the platform one at a time.

Rutherford B. Hayes, the day's master of ceremonies, gave a brief introduction, followed by a rendition of "America" by the Cleveland Grays Band. Hayes again took to the stand to tell the crowd they had gathered to dedicate "this impressive and enduring monument," that was built "to perpetuate to future generations his name and fame and memory."[39] Led by the Bishop of Ohio, Reverend William A. Leonard, the crowd bowed their heads in a prayer. Former governor of Ohio Jacob D. Cox spoke, making it clear that this was a celebration of Garfield's life and "not the mournful one which filled the streets of our cities with funeral pageants nine years ago."[40] He then recounted at length Garfield's life and strong character.[41] After Cox's marathon oration, President Benjamin Harrison promptly set expectations with his opening line when he thanked the crowd for their welcome and promised, "I shall not be betrayed by it into a lengthy speech." He compared the grandiose structure to the man when he said, "This monument, so imposing and tasteful, fittingly typifies the grand and symmetrical character of him in whose honor it has been builded [sic]."[42] His brief speech of 13 sentences was punctuated eight times with applause.

After several more speakers, architect George Keller was introduced to the crowd. Despite his prominent role, the New Englander was an outsider in this fraternity of Ohioans and Civil War veterans and was not even asked to speak. After still more speakers, the crowd grew impatient, and it was written, "It was impossible any longer to disregard the demands for Major McKinley. They had been vociferous and emphatic from the beginning, and the Major's quiet gestures, appealing for silence, had only served to augment the enthusiasm. The shouts that now ascended for 'McKinley' were simply irresistible!"[43] After a momentary demurral, he approached the podium. Each sentence was punctuated with applause, perhaps none more so than when he proclaimed "No president since the days of Washington and Lincoln and Grant has been closer to the hearts of the American people than was James A. Garfield."[44] Following McKinley the band played "O, Weep for the Brave," closing out the first portion of the dedication.

The event was then turned over to 1,000 Grand Commandary Knights Templar. The crowd turned their faces skyward to see the Knights, dressed in full regalia and swords drawn, strategically gathered on the balcony. The "Grand Prelate" L. F. Van Cleve delivered an invocation in which he declared, "As Abraham consecrated Machpelah and Jacob his Bethel—as Sinai became a witness and Joshua reared his Gilgal, so we meet, on this occasion, to consecrate this monument, that it may express the appreciation of a grateful people for Thy gift to them in the person of their knightly brother and honored ruler, James Abram Garfield."[45] After his speech, the Knights sang their "Doxology," which was followed by a benediction by Reverend Powers and then finally a 21-gun salute.

THE JAMES GARFIELD DEATH SITES
Assassination Site
The Baltimore and Potomac Railroad station was an imposing Victorian Gothic structure located at Sixth and B Streets. During its existence, many found the three-story red brick station to be an eyesore. Those who were not offended by its

appearance were most certainly annoyed by the smoke that spewed onto the National Mall. Garfield was no exception and called the station a "nuisance which ought long since to have been abated."[46] Two months after Garfield died, a marble tablet was placed inside the train station on the wall near the shooting location. The large tablet featured an American eagle with wings spread, beneath which was the simple inscription, JAMES ABRAM GARFIELD PRESIDENT OF THE UNITED STATES JULY 2, 1881. A brass star was placed on the floor at the exact location where the tragedy occurred. Many saw the memorials as sad reminders and complained they were inappropriate, but the railroad initially refused to remove them. But when there was a small fire at the train station on March 4, 1897, the marble was damaged and removed and the railroad never put it back up. Instead, an innocuous-looking piece of red tile was left to mark the spot, so inconspicuous that most were unaware of its significance.[47]

After Union Station opened in 1907, the Baltimore and Potomac Railroad station was torn down. In 1936, district city engineers set out to determine the spot where Garfield was shot.

The author standing at the approximate location where Garfield was shot, near the center of Constitution Avenue NW in Washington, DC.

Their best estimates placed the shooting at the center of Constitution Avenue NW, approximately 30–40 feet west of the Sixth Street corner. There is no marker at the location today, making the site the only presidential assassination site that is completely unrecognized.

Location of Death

The home where Garfield died was constructed in 1876 as part of the Elberon Hotel and designed by Charles F. McKim for the original owner, Conner T. Jones.[48] The ocean-front, 20-room cottage was later owned by New York financier Charles G. Francklyn. The Francklyn Cottage became one of the most popular vacation rentals in the era when Long Branch was a playground for the rich and powerful. Harrison, Hayes, McKinley, Garfield, Grant, and Woodrow Wilson all vacationed in Long Branch, and Arthur owned property there. After Garfield's death, the home became better known as "Garfield Cottage" or "Garfield Cabin."

On May 13, 1889, the home was purchased by lawyer W. D. Guthrie on behalf of Francklyn's cousin, Mary McEvers Gosling of England, who paid $50,000 for the cottage and $25,000 more for the furnishings.[49] Guthrie used the home as a rental and two years later put it on the auction block, but had no buyers.[50] The summer renters were so prestigious that each year their names and social events were chronicled in the *New York Times*. While many cottages raised their prices over the years, the Garfield Cottage resisted the trend—the price charged the year after Garfield died remained the same through 1900.[51] By 1920, the heyday of Long Beach was coming to an end, and the home had come into the possession of the Fidelity Trust Company of Newark, New Jersey. On June 15, 1920, while the home was being painted, a fire broke out, and, by the time it was extinguished, much of the roof and interior were destroyed.[52] What was left of the structure was razed shortly afterward, leaving nothing to let visitors know of the historic events that occurred at that location.

Sporadic efforts to mark the site had begun at the turn of the century. In 1901, the cottage residents proposed to mark the site for the 20th anniversary of Garfield's death. Two residents each committed to a $1,000 donation for the project, but the idea fizzled.[53] Another grassroots effort

"President Garfield's cottage, Long Branch, New Jersey." Stereograph produced by the Keystone View Company. (Library of Congress)

The roadside marker at the site where Garfield died in Long Branch, New Jersey.

began in 1906 for the 25th anniversary, when a goal was set for 500 citizens to donate a dollar each, but despite the best intentions, the idea never materialized.[54] In 1924, there was a proposal by the Monmouth County Historical Association to erect a historic marker. With the home now demolished, a marker to perpetuate the memory of the death site became even more significant. In 1930, Monmouth County Historical Association president Gilbert Van Mater set a goal to place one at the site by the 50th anniversary of Garfield's death on September 19, 1931.[55] The best the association could pull off was a 14-inch temporary wooden marker, which remained in the general location for about 30 years. As the neighborhood developed, a garage was built at the site by property owner Joseph Fisher, and the marker was moved to his garage window.

What rich renters, citizens, and the historical society failed to achieve, a young boy made happen. In 1957, Bruce Frankel, the son of an Asbury Park insurance broker, learned of Garfield's death so near his house while he was home sick watching television. Even at the age of seven, he knew a permanent marker was needed and decided to donate his weekly allow-ance to erect one. Quoted in the *New York Times*, the wise youngster stated that his goal was to raise hundreds of dollars and then turn it over to the historical society "to put up a real stone like other presidents have."[56] After four years, he had accrued only $60 in the bank, but hearing of his plight, the West Long Branch Ardolino Monument Company decided to help out. On September 19, 1961, 80 years after Garfield's death, a ceremony was held and Bruce unveiled the 36-square-inch permanent marker.[57]

Today it still stands at 12 Garfield Terrace, off Ocean Avenue, and reads:

JAMES A. GARFIELD
TWENTIETH PRESIDENT OF
THE UNITED STATES
BORN NOV 19, 1831 AT ORANGE, OHIO
DIED ON THIS SITE, SEPT. 19, 1881

The seaside location is still home to many well-to-do, although not quite of the caliber that resided there at the end of the 19th century. Only a few hundred feet away is the Church of the Presidents, where Harrison, Hayes, McKinley, Garfield, Wilson, Grant, and Arthur worshipped. Located on the grounds is the Garfield Tea House, a structure built from the temporary train tracks that were laid during the president's convalescence and disassembled after his death. It was built by an actor named Oliver Byron and relocated several times before it was acquired by the Long Branch Historical Museum Association and moved to the church grounds.

Lying in Repose Location
The Public Square in downtown Cleveland was first laid out in 1796, and today comprises nine

and a half acres. In 1860, at the dawn of the Civil War, the city chose to erect a monument to remember the last significant American military engagement and honor Admiral Oliver Hazard Perry, the War of 1812 naval hero. The monument remained in the location for 32 years, including during both the Lincoln and Garfield public viewings. In 1892, it was removed to make way for a new monument erected to honor the Civil War veterans of Cuyahoga County.[58] The Soldiers' and Sailors' Monument, which still dominates Public Square today, was dedicated on July 4, 1894. That day, the opening address was made by McKinley, two years before he was elected president. The monument includes a 125-foot-tall granite shaft topped by a 15-foot-tall statue representing liberty. It sits atop a 100-square-foot sandstone base and features bas-reliefs depicting important events in history. While there are several nods to Lincoln, there is no mention of Garfield. The monument was designed by Levi T. Scofield, who also designed the vault that temporarily housed Garfield's remains.[59]

Public Receiving Vault

The public receiving vault where Garfield's remains were originally placed had decayed over the years. After the nearby Wade Chapel was built in 1901, the vault was torn down.[60]

Schofield Vault

Years before he designed the Soldiers' and Sailors' Monument in Cleveland Public Square, architect Levi Scofield (using his preferred German spelling above the entrance) designed an impressive gothic vault in Lake View Cemetery to be used by his family. The vault is 15 square feet and is supported by four granite pil-

lars. After Garfield's remains were moved there, it became a popular tourist attraction. Nearby, the Garfield funeral car was placed on display in a small white building with glass walls.[61] While the funeral hearse is long gone, the Schofield Vault remains one of the most picturesque vaults in Lake View, or any other cemetery.

Tomb

In 1923, 50 years after its formation, the Garfield National Monument Association turned the monument over to the Lake View Cemetery Association, which still cares for it today. Each year about 28,000 people visit during the season that lasts from April 1 to the president's birthday, November 19. The truth is that it is not in a great area of Cleveland; the cemetery is in the vicinity of several run-down and abandoned buildings, but the cemetery is well cared for.

The day I visited it was raining, just like the day Garfield was first interred over 130 years earlier. Inside is something unique to Garfield's tomb—a gift shop! (One is located outside of Grant's tomb in a visitor center and there is none inside Lincoln's tomb.) When I mentioned this

The picturesque Schofield Vault, where Garfield's remains temporarily rested at Lake View Cemetery in Cleveland, Ohio.

and another unusual feature, the picnic tables outside, the guide explained that, intentional or not, they were reminiscent of the Victorian era tradition in which a picnic in the cemetery often followed church on Sunday. The cemetery is beautiful, and driving through, I came upon many large and impressive monuments, but none could prepare you for the immensity of Garfield's memorial. The monument was listed on the National Register of Historic Places (#73001411) on April 11, 1973.

The cemetery is located at 12316 Euclid Avenue, Cleveland, Ohio, 44106. Gates are open daily from 7:30 a.m. to 5:30 p.m., but the tomb is seasonal and open from April 1 to November 19 from 9:00 a.m. to 4:00 p.m. For more information, visit: www.LakeViewCemetery.com.

Ulysses Simpson Grant ★ *1869–1877*

CRITICAL DEATH INFORMATION:

Date of death:	July 23, 1885, 8:06 a.m.
Cause of death:	Tongue and throat cancer
Age at death:	63 years, 87 days
Last words:	"Water."
Place of death:	Home of Joseph W. Drexel in Mount McGregor, New York
Funeral:	City Hall, New York City, New York
Final resting place:	General Grant National Memorial, New York City, New York
Reinterred:	Yes
Cost to visit grave:	Free
For more information:	www.nps.gov/gegr
Significance:	Grant's Tomb is the largest mausoleum in North America

In 1881, Civil War hero and 18th president Ulysses S. Grant settled into a New York City brownstone at 3 East 66th Street that had been purchased for him by several wealthy friends. He was generally in good health, but had a bad leg that had been injured in the Battle of Vicksburg during the Civil War. He smoked about 20 cigars a day and it must have come as little surprise when he began suffering sore throats. On June 2, 1884, while at his vacation home in Elberon, New Jersey, Grant experienced a sharp pain when he bit into a peach. The juicy fruit hurt enough to make the tough veteran cry out in pain. A neighboring internist, Dr. Jacob M. Da Costa, checked Grant's throat and found a lesion. He advised Grant to schedule an appointment with his regular physician Dr. Fordyce Barker in New York for a more thorough examination, but Grant did not do so immediately. Two months later, while still in Elberon, he drew up his will, with his friend and neighbor, George W. Childs, and his guest, Reverend Dr. Morton, as witnesses.[1]

In October the pain returned, and Grant finally met with Dr. Barker. After finding an inflammation in his throat, Barker referred Grant to the foremost throat specialist on the East Coast, Dr. John Hancock Douglas. Grant had first met Douglas during the Civil War in 1862. Upon examination, Douglas found three small growths and a swollen gland in Grant's mouth. A scaly, inflamed growth at the base of Grant's tongue concerned Douglas the most. He made a sobering prognosis: Grant had advanced tongue and throat cancer. In 1884, cancer was a veritable death sentence. Douglas administered liquid cocaine for the pain and iodoform, a medication similar to chloroform, to treat the infection.[2] The treatment would, at least for a while, reduce the pain so Grant could eat and sleep.[3] Douglas called upon Dr. Barker and two additional specialists, Dr. Henry Sands and Dr. T. M. Markoe, to review his prognosis. Douglas also sent a biopsy to a noted microbiologist, Dr. George Frederick Shrady. The patient's identity was not revealed, allowing Shrady to make an impartial examination. Shrady's confirmation was disheartening: "This patient has a lingual epithelioma—cancer of the tongue." After he was told that the specimen had come from Grant, Shrady responded, "Then General Grant is doomed."[4]

To add to his misery, only a month before biting into the peach, Grant discovered he had been the victim of what would later be known as a Ponzi scheme when the investment firm Grant & Ward was exposed as a fraud (his son, Ulysses Jr., was a partner in name only; Ferdinand Ward was the mastermind behind the swindle).[5] While he was battling cancer, Grant was also bank-rupt. Knowing his time was limited, he focused on regaining financial security for his family. He had received offers to write a memoir many times and had declined, but now he reconsidered. With the help of his friend Mark Twain, he secured a publishing deal with Webster & Co. to provide for his family after he was gone. In his final months, Grant was in a race against time to complete his memoirs before his death.[6] As he prepared for the end, Grant had one final wish: he asked President Chester Arthur to strip him of his title of president and restore him to general. While he was beloved and revered, Grant's presidency was less than stellar—it had been rife with scandal, and he was considered to have been one of our nation's worst. "General" was the title he cherished most and it was as a general he wanted to die.[7] However this request was not just sentimental. As a general, he would also receive a pension, which his wife could live upon until royalties from the book began to arrive. President Arthur made this bill one of his top priorities. And as his last official act as president, he ordered Grant be notified by telegram of his reinstatement.[8]

The cancer metastasized rapidly, and by April 1885 it had spread throughout his throat and neck, leaving him unable to speak or swallow without pain. Grant's weight plummeted and he lost a staggering 75 pounds. As spring turned to summer, the city heat became unbearable, and Grant's doctors advised that a change of climate might prove beneficial to his health. Grant's good friend Joseph W. Drexel, a banker and staunch Republican, offered him his small cottage in Mount McGregor, a remote location 30 miles north of Saratoga Springs in upstate New York. Grant so desperately needed the fresh air and solitude that he accepted. On June 16, he boarded a 9:30 a.m. train. At Mount McGregor station, Grant was greeted by a small crowd. He tried to walk to the cottage, but it proved too strenuous, and he had to be carried. That first day, he sat outside for about an hour enjoying the view before retiring inside for a rest. S.

W. Willett, a veteran who had been hired to ensure unwanted visitors did not bother Grant, set up a small white tent near the home. Despite his desire for solitude, many reporters who had been on his death watch in the city had followed him to Mount McGregor.[9]

As it had for Garfield when he sought a more salubrious climate, the change of scenery initially improved Grant's condition. Grant worked on his book and enjoyed taking in the mountain air while sitting on the porch. Despite the pain and narcotic medication, his mind was sharp and his memory thorough. During his six weeks at the cabin, many soldiers made a pilgrimage to Mount McGregor. They would slowly walk past in the hope of seeing their former commander on the porch and being rewarded with a silent nod. Expressions of sympathy and admiration came in from across the country, and Grant was visited by many people, including Mark Twain, who stopped by to assist the novice author. Grant would speak in a low hushed voice until he could no longer talk, and then he would converse through notes.

However, the initial boost from the mountain air ended, and Grant's health began to decline. His weight fell to around 100 pounds. He tried several times to discuss plans for his burial with his family, but his wife, Julia, was too distraught at the thought of life without Ulysses and would not have the discussion. Unbeknownst to Grant, his family had inquired about a burial in Washington, DC, at the Soldiers' Home. Finally, on June 24, 1885, Grant wrote a note to his son that methodically detailed three options for his grave site and his rationale for each:

Ulysses S. Grant on the porch of the home where he died, at Mount McGregor, New York. (Library of Congress)

"West Point. —I would prefer this above others but for the fact that my wife could not be placed beside me there.

Galena, or some other place in Illinois. —Because from that State I received my first General's commission.

New-York. —Because the people of that city befriended me in my need."

His thoughts documented, he now left the final decision to his wife. By July 8, the bulk of the 400,000-word manuscript was written, and only final revisions remained. By July 20, the final edits were complete. The book was done, and with his last battle won, Grant could now die in peace. That day he wrote a note to Dr. Douglas in which he stated, "There is nothing more I should do to [the book] now, and therefore I am not likely to be more ready to go than at this moment."[10] In the end, the memoir was wildly successful and received with great acclaim. More importantly to Grant, it netted $420,000 for his wife.

Reverend John P. Newman, Grant's pastor from Washington, DC, arrived on the afternoon of July 20. Grant had never been baptized, and when Newman offered to do so, he politely declined. However, Newman was persistent and covertly baptized Grant as he slept.[11] On Wednesday, July 22, Grant attempted to muster his family's morale and told them "I don't want anybody to feel distressed on my account." This was his last verbal statement of significance. By 7:00 p.m., he drifted in and out of consciousness, and his doctors, Douglas, George Frederick Shrady, and Henry Sands, expected he would pass that evening. At around 10:00 p.m., Grant told those gathered around him to go to sleep, implying he was not ready to die yet. He was right, as he survived the night. In his final hours, doctors opened his throat to allow him to breathe easier, leaving it exposed and full of mucus. Through the late evening and into the early morning of July 23, he could only reply to questions in a hushed, single word whisper. At about 3:00 a.m., the nurse, Henry McSweeny, saw he needed something, so he bent down close and heard him whisper his final word, "Water."

An hour later, as mucus accumulated in his lungs, Dr. Shrady applied hot cloths and injected him with brandy through a hypodermic needle. They had no illusions that the treatment could restore the president—they only sought to provide him some comfort. At 5:00 a.m., Dr. Douglas issued a statement: "He is conscious, that is, he has not lost his power of recognition. He breathed; his heart lives; his lungs live; his brain lives," and added hopelessly, "and that is about all."[12]

Believing the end was imminent, Dr. Shrady sent for the family around 8:00 a.m. One of Grant's final wishes was to die painlessly, and by all accounts, this was mercifully granted. His wife grasped her husband's hand as he opened his eyes one last time. He looked around at those crowding the room: his wife and four children encircled the bed, his three daughter-in-laws at his feet, his three physicians and Nurse McSweeny in a corner, and his valet, Harrison Tyrrell, by the doorway. At 8:06 a.m., Thursday, July 23, 1885, Ulysses S. Grant closed his eyes and died. Dr. Shrady was the first to speak, whispering, "At last." His son Fred then stopped the clock, ensuring it would forever stay at the time Grant died.[13]

Soldiers encamped near the home in a nonstop vigil fired salutes as reporters raced to the nearest telegraph office to spread the news to the world. Shortly thereafter, President Grover Cleveland released a heartfelt statement: "The President of the United States has just received the sad tidings of the death of that illustrious citizen and ex-President of the United States, General Ulysses S. Grant, at Mount McGregor, in the State of New York, to which place he had lately been removed in the endeavor to prolong his life. In making this announcement to the people

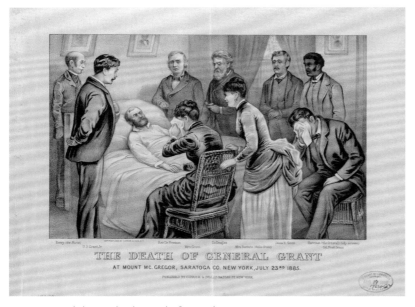

Currier & Ives lithograph, *The Death of General Grant: At Mount Mc.Gregor, Saratoga Co. New York, July 23rd 1885.* (Library of Congress)

of the United States the President is impressed with the magnitude of the public loss of a great military leader, who was in the hour of victory magnanimous, amid disaster serene and self-sustained; who in every station, whether as a soldier or as a Chief Magistrate, twice called to power by his fellow-countrymen, trod unswervingly the pathway of duty, undeterred by doubts, single-minded and straightforward. The entire country has witnessed with deep emotion his prolonged and patient struggle with painful disease, and has watched by his couch of suffering with tearful sympathy. The destined end has come at last, and his spirit has returned to the Creator who sent it forth. The great heart of the nation that followed him when living with love and pride bows now in sorrow above him dead, tenderly mindful of his virtues, his great patriotic services, and of the loss occasioned by his death."

Twenty minutes after Grant died, Karl Gerhardt, a sculptor from Hartford, Connecticut, made a molding of Grant's face to use to create a death mask. The grim scene of Grant's deathbed was later memorialized in a Currier and Ives lithograph. These deathbed lithographs, popular during the Victorian era, are much creepier than the depictions of sleigh rides over snow covered glades usually associated with Currier and Ives. Stoic figures surrounding the bed on three sides are presented in various shades and hues while the dying president is so white he is almost translucent, as if already a ghost. The earliest president memorialized by the famed printers was George Washington, decades after his death, and the honor was primarily reserved for the most revered of presidents (with the exception of Andrew Johnson). The depiction of Grant would be their last.

Doctors asked for permission to perform an autopsy, but the family declined. There was no mystery to the cause of death, and loved ones saw no need to further desecrate Grant's cancer-ravaged body.[14] The Stephen Merritt Burial & Cremation Company dressed Grant in a black Prince Albert suit and placed his remains in a temporary casket while a new one was being built 40 miles away in Troy, New York.[15] The widow found a letter in the president's pocket addressed to her. Its contents are unknown, but in response she wrote, "Farewell till we meet again in a better world," and placed the note in his suit pocket as he lay in the coffin. She also placed a ring on his finger that Grant had given to her when it no longer fit him. In his withered state, she could slip it back on with ease.[16]

For 11 long days, Grant's body remained at Mount McGregor, lying in state—and in wait—on a catafalque in the parlor. President Cleveland assigned General Winfield Scott to assist with the arrangements. Scott placed a guard of honor at the home under the command of Colonel Roger Jones. Soldiers paid their respects daily by bringing fresh flowers to his coffin. The delay was not unexpected: Grant wished to be embalmed at Mount McGregor, and that his body remain there until the summer heat subsided and his family could return in comfort. But the most pressing reason for the delay was that his burial location was still undetermined. Having avoided the subject during the illness, his family was now forced to wrestle with the decision. Upon learning that New York City had made Grant's short list, Mayor William Grace telegraphed the family to further promote his city. Grant's son, Fred, traveled to Manhattan in order to scout locations. The first spot he visited was Watch Hill in Central Park, located at 110th Street and 8th Avenue. When they climbed the hill, they could see a cancer hospital located four blocks away, and the awkward view eliminated Watch Hill from consideration.[17] Next they visited Riverside Park on 122nd Street, a scenic West Side location designed by Frederick Law Olmsted in 1873. In a letter to Julia written the day Grant died, Mayor Grace had noted its prominent height and location on the banks of the Hudson and was confident that it would make "an appropriate site for a great national monument."[18]

On July 28, Fred Grant sent Mayor Grace a terse telegraph of acceptance: "W. A. Grace. New York: Mother takes Riverside. The temporary tomb had better be in the same place. F. D. Grant."[19] Immediately, many from the public voiced their opposition, including people from Philadelphia, Baltimore, and Washington, DC, who did not feel Riverside Park had the proper solemnity and national identity inappropriate for a hero's grave site.[20] The family continued to wrestle with the permanent grave site decision, and after several months, both Fred and Julia agreed with Mayor Grace.[21]

With a location chosen, arrangements were made for the removal of Grant's body from Mount McGregor. On the evening of Monday, August 3, 1885, Reverend Newman conducted a funeral service for the family in the Mount McGregor home. Later that day, General Hancock arrived with 800 members of the National Guard, relieving General Scott. Hancock had been assigned the solemn task of transporting the body back to New York City and organizing the funeral events.[22] The next morning, Hancock was greeted at the home by Fred, and they entered to view Grant's remains. Half an hour later, the doors were opened and the public was permitted to pay their respects. At 10:00 a.m., a second service was held at the home before a crowd of 1,000 people. It included a reading of Psalm 90, a prayer by Bishop W. L. Harris, the hymn "My Faith Looks Up to Thee," and a heartfelt sermon by Reverend Newman in which he quoted the Apostle Matthew: "Well done, thou good and faithful servant, enter thou into the joy of thy Lord." Members of the Brooklyn Grant Post then carried the coffin to the train station, passing men with hats in hand. Julia remained at Mount McGregor, too distraught to leave the site of her husband's death.[23]

At 1:00 p.m., the seven-car mountain train departed as guns fired in salute. Crowds stood along the route as the train slowly passed. Thirty minutes later, it pulled into Saratoga Springs.

An honor guard carried the coffin in silence to a New York Central Railroad train and placed it on a catafalque in a special funeral car, the Woodlawn. The car was directly behind the engine and draped in mourning and an American flag. Behind the funeral car were seven more cars filled with dignitaries, including New York governor David Bennett Hill. Shortly after 2:00 p.m., conductor Thorton started the journey. It rode through Ballston and Cohoes, where crowds gathered by the tracks. The train reached West Troy at 3:28 p.m., and 12 minutes later arrived in Albany for a public viewing. The coffin was placed on a caisson drawn by six black horses, each led by honorary member from G.A.R. Posts 5 and 21. The procession included a military escort from the Fifth Artillery and the Company E Infantry. Four thousand people marched, including police and local military units and 900 veterans of the Grand Army of the Republic. The parade went down Spencer Street to North Pearl Street and then to State Street, onward to Eagle Street, Washington Street, Knox Street, and then back on State Street until it reached the Capitol building, where the remains were placed in the Senate chamber on a great catafalque.

At 5:00 p.m., the doors were opened, and crowds surged in to see Grant, but many were repulsed by what they saw. The *Ithaca Democrat* wrote, "The appearance of the remains was not natural. The skin of the face has the appearance of having been enameled in a bungling manner. The skin is a ghastly hue and has a scaly appearance."[24]

In the first hour alone, 7,400 people walked past the coffin. The viewing continued well into the night. At 1:00 a.m., the line finally slowed, and by 4:00 a.m., just a few stragglers passed by. Two hours later, as the sun rose over a bright, clear day, the crowd again began to thicken. The steady flow continued until the doors closed at 10:30 a.m. The final tally in over 19 hours was an impressive 77,200 people. When only the honor guard remained, the undertaker Stephen J. Merritt and his assistants transferred the body to the new coffin that had arrived from Troy that morning. It was made of Bessemer steel and adorned with silver handles, lined with purple velvet, and affixed with a gold plate that simply read "U. S. GRANT." The caretakers also prepared or, perhaps better stated, *repaired* the body for an open coffin viewing in New York City later that day.

At 11:30 a.m., 13 members of the honor guard removed the coffin from the Capitol. Trumpeters played a solemn dirge while they descended the steps and placed the coffin onto a black dais in the funeral carriage. The military procession fell into place as the six black horses pulled the hearse. Guns boomed, and thick crowds watched as the parade marched down State Street to Broadway to Steuben Street until it arrived at the Albany Central Depot. Thousands crowded the station and nearby rooftops to catch a glimpse of the coffin before it was placed onto the funeral train. The Jackson Corps played a solemn dirge as the train departed. The train passed through Poughkeepsie at 2:45 p.m., where employees of New York Central Railroad, who were already gathered at the station for payday, lined the track and removed their hats. Through Newburgh and then Fishkill at 3:11 p.m., people placed coins on the tracks for a flattened memento. Guns boomed in five-second intervals at Grant's alma mater, West Point. Cadets lined up and presented arms, and officers stood, hats in hand, to salute one of their own.[25]

The train passed through Harlem at 4:48 p.m. and pulled into Grand Central Station precisely at 5:00 p.m. The coffin was placed in a hearse beneath a plume-topped canopy. At 5:30 p.m., General Hancock gave the order, and the procession began its slow march. A small military escort that included the national guard, marines, and members of the Fifth Artillery Company A and Twelfth Infantry Company E led the hearse to 43rd Street and Fifth Avenue. There it met

up with a larger procession to escort the hearse downtown to City Hall. Along the route, flags hung at half-mast and stores were draped in black. Crowds packed the streets, and children climbed lamp and telegraph posts for a better view. Despite the throngs of people, the predominant sounds were of boots on cobblestone and the solemn dirges.

When the cortege arrived at 7:00 p.m., night had fallen. Thousands of people formed a dense throng at City Hall to watch the arrival, and many more descended upon the location, turning the scene into one of danger and confusion. Women and children were crushed and "screamed aloud in pain or fright." The casket was removed from the catafalque, and the 13 Brooklyn Grant Post honor guardsmen carried it inside. With the hearse relieved of its load, the driver began to depart. When a plume became entangled in an overhead electric wire and fell to the ground, the rambunctious crowd pounced on the treasure as though it was made of gold. The first prize of the "relic hunters" was won.

Inside the great hall, the coffin was placed in the corridor on the same catafalque that was used in Mount McGregor, which had arrived earlier that day. The room was shrouded in black, and heavy drapes hung over the catafalque. Atop the coffin was a plain wreath of oak leaves that Grant's daughter, Julia, had made at Mount McGregor. A massive guard of honor, including 50 policemen, protected the remains. There to formally receive the casket was Mayor Grace, who at that time was still in the process of lobbying for the permanent burial site. After the official transfer was completed, the coffin was removed to the Board of Aldermen. There the undertaker, Merritt, found the face to be "very hard and very pale, but in an excellent state of preservation, only a slight discoloration being noticeable around the eyes." Merritt applied marble powder to cover up the discolorations, and only after he was satisfied with his work did he consent to an open casket viewing. The casket was returned to the vestibule, where it was adorned with elaborate floral arrangements. Grant was now the third and last president to rest in the iconic New York City Hall, preceded by James Monroe in 1858 and Abraham Lincoln in 1865.[26]

At 9:00 p.m., New York superintendent Murray bellowed out, "Let them come in!" Among the crowd were "special mourners" sent by the Army of the Potomac, who included Abner Doubleday, a fellow West Point graduate who is credited with inventing baseball and had marched in the funeral procession of Zachary Taylor 35 years earlier.[27] At midnight, the flow of the crowd was temporarily interrupted for an electric light to be fixed. The doors closed an hour later, after 40,000 people had viewed the remains.

The crowds continued unabated for two more days. On Thursday, August 6, the doors opened at 6:00 a.m., and another 150,000 people viewed the remains. The next day, yet another 100,000 paid their respects. For the solemn funeral and entombment events planned for Saturday, August 8, General Hancock asked Robert E. Lee's nephew, Virginia governor and former Confederate general Fitzhugh Lee, to serve as his aide, prompting Lee to respond, "I accept the position, because by doing so, I can testify my respect for the memory of a great soldier and thus return, as far as I can, the generous feelings he has expressed toward the soldiers of the South."[28] Echoing Hancock's gesture of reconciliation, Grant's son had also suggested that "one or two ex-Confederate Generals serve as Pallbearers." Simon Bolivar Buckner and Joseph Johnston accepted the offer and, along with Union generals William Tecumseh Sherman, Philip Sheridan, and eight others, carried the coffin to the hearse. The casket sat upon a large catafalque and beneath a black canopy, which allowed the crowd to see it. Flanking the hearse was the Brooklyn Grant Post, which served as honor guard since the body left Mount McGre-

gor. However, this was no ordinary funeral hearse—almost seven decades after the funeral, Merritt revealed that they actually used an Ehret's Brewery truck covered in black crepe. To make for an impressive spectacle, it was pulled by 24 black brewery horses, each led by a groom dressed in black. With so many horses they needed to weigh down the carriage with 10 tons of pig iron, so the steeds would not run away with the president's body.[29]

At 9:30 a.m., General Hancock bellowed "Forward march!" and church bells tolled to commence the procession. The parade was enormous, including 18,000 Grand Army of the Republic veterans and 8,000 city workers led by Mayor Grace. One to one and a half million people saw the seven-mile procession, which took five hours to pass. The parade marched up Broadway to 14th Street to 5th Avenue. It continued to 57th Street, back to Broadway and onto 72nd Street to Riverside Drive, where it traveled north for 50 blocks. Sharing a carriage were former presidents Hayes and Arthur, while President Cleveland rode in his own carriage drawn by six horses.[30] There were a staggering 500 carriages, rented from the Stephen Merritt Burial & Cremation Company for $10 each. On top of the $150 they charged to carry the body from Mount McGregor to New York City, they also charged $30 to transport the floral arrangements to the burial site, $243 for 27 pallbearer scarves, and $500 for horse ornamentations. The final bill came to $14,163.75, paid by the United States government in two installments.[31]

When the hearse rode by, the crowds were respectfully silent, but the decibel level rose when President Cleveland passed. He was gracious and dignified enough to respond with stoic silence and refused to acknowledge the cheers. At 2:30 p.m., the procession arrived at the temporary vault in Riverside Park, built immediately after the family made their decision for the temporary burial location. It was designed by J. Wrey Mold and constructed of red and black brick and inner walls of white porcelain and marble.[32] The entranceway had two interior iron gates and two exterior oak doors, above which was a squared cross. The tomb area was reached by descending three stone steps.

The ceremony was brief. Reverend Newman said a benediction and the coffin was carried inside. After the ceremony, 56 steel bolts were driven into the front of the tomb and "welded while white hot." Inside the tomb, the coffin was placed within a steel casing and another 165 bolts used to secure it. The tomb was considered "air, water and burglar proof," but just in case, guards were stationed nearby.[33] Later, the round-the-clock guard detail became known as Camp Grant. Their primary mission was to keep the peace and protect against souvenir hunters. Not since Lincoln had any scrap related to a president's death become so sought after. Even while it was still in use, an offer of $5,000 was made by an unidentified person for the catafalque (the United States government refused). Unable to secure a souvenir, one inventive soul offered a guard a silver dollar not as a bribe, but to place on the tomb and hand back to him. The guard refused, but often the soldiers obliged the tourists' thirst for mementos. They would regularly dole out withered and rotten flowers no longer fit for the tomb.[34] On August 12, a gilded lock was placed upon the oak door, and a crowd of 50 people had gathered for an impromptu ceremony. An armed guard stood nearby, and when some asked for the oak slivers to take as a souvenir, the soldiers obliged. Starting on August 8, the War Department began a rotation of batteries from the Fifth Artillery to stand guard.[35]

During that time, hundreds of thousands visited the tomb, making it one of the most popular tourist destinations in the city along with the Statue of Liberty, which had been assembled during this same time frame. Park benches were set up near the tomb, and it became fashionable for ladies to take early morning carriage rides past the spot before the day's onslaught of tourists arrived. Many wanted to leave flowers at the grave, including one woman who wished to plant ivy that had been taken from Napoleon's tomb (this would not be the first correlation made between the two generals who rose to lead their countries). Seventeen canvas tents were hastily erected for the detachment of 30 men who were to stand guard. A kitchen was also constructed, but it lacked a roof. One soldier lamented that the mess hall did not have anything to "prevent a lot of ignorant people from staring at us while we eat."[36] Responding to these complaints, a proper kitchen was built on August 12. Construction began on more permanent 60-by-25-foot wooden structures, which were completed on November 9.[37]

Construction on the tomb also progressed. Built in a hurry, the temporary tomb was resurfaced with blue stone,

Guards at Grant's temporary tomb in Riverside Park, New York. (Library of Congress)

and the tar paper roof was covered in brick. A sentry building was erected outside the tomb to protect the guards from the elements. The soldiers remained in place for almost a full year, until June 30, 1886, when the War Department officially closed Camp Grant.[38]

Almost immediately after Grant's death, a committee that included former president Arthur and current president Cleveland was formed to create a permanent memorial (sadly, Arthur died the following year and would not live to see its completion). They set up the Grant Monument Fund to raise money, led by trustee Richard T. Greener, the first African American graduate of Harvard University. Within a week of Grant's funeral, they had raised $757.40, with $105 of that coming from employees of Liechtenstein Brothers and Company. A meticulous ledger was kept for all donations, regardless of how small; 20¢ from "Two Yankee women," 15¢ from "A German who gives up his beer," and a nickel from "A poor woman with ten children."[39] By September 1, 1885, the fund was up to $60,000. Scammers also began to fraudulently collect money in the name of the Grant Memorial Fund. On September 4, the *Miamisburg Bulletin* published a warning: "All persons that use the name of the [Grant] association for fraudulent purpose will be punished to the full extent of the law."[40]

On February 3, 1886, the group was incorporated as the Grant Monument Association. However, things moved slowly. A design competition for the memorial was not held until 1889. Shortly after Grant's death, one writer called for "An American Pantheon," a description consistent with what several architects submitted. The winner was John Hemmingway Duncan, who leveraged a classical design to create "a monumental tomb, no matter from what point of view it may be seen."[41] In the end, Duncan's vision was fulfilled, and today Grant's Tomb in New York City is still the largest mausoleum in North America.

While the design process was slow to start,

donations began to taper off. After five years, only about $150,000 had been collected, and the public and the federal government were losing patience. In December 1890, Kansas senator Preston Bierce Plumb proposed a bill that would pull the plug on the New York tomb and have Grant's remains moved to Arlington National Cemetery. The proposal was met with wide resistance. One voice of opposition cried out, "The resolution shocks our sense of decency, as it reminds us of the line 'Rattle his bones over the stones.' It is a revolting precedent!" Another senator likened the motion to body snatching and stated that, "You cannot break into a graveyard with a joint resolution of Congress."[42] The proposal was defeated, but it succeeded in spurring donations from wealthy Americans—the memorial fund again began to gain momentum, which may have been Plumb's goal all along. Association president Horace Porter published an open letter in the *New York Times* to urge the public to continue to send donations to meet the $350,000 goal and rectify the "humiliating spectacle of the remains of the most illustrious solider of his age . . . lying in a temporary vault in an open city park."[43] The public responded and eventually 90,000 people combined to donate $600,000 toward the memorial.

Progress, however slow, was also being made on the construction of the permanent memorial tomb just a few dozen feet from the temporary tomb. The association chose Grant's birthday to recognize the milestones. On April 27, 1891, what would have been his 69th birthday, there was a small groundbreaking ceremony as "Nearer, My God, to Thee" was sung to the crowd.[44] On April 27, 1892, 70 years after his birth, the cornerstone of the tomb was laid. There was a grand ceremony before a large crowd that numbered in the tens of thousands, and the David's Island Band entertained the masses. Grant's widow and sons were in attendance, as were President Benjamin Harrison and Vice President Levi P. Morton.[45] The first speaker that day was association president Porter, who spoke of the state of fund-raising and listed the contents of a copper box that was placed within the 12-ton cornerstone: the Bible, copies of the Constitution and the Declaration of Independence, a new silk American flag, the day's newspapers, an assortment of Grant's letters, a copy of his memoirs, and commemorative medals and coins from the US Mint.[46] President Harrison spread mortar on the stone using a ceremonial trowel that had been specially designed for the occasion. He then spoke, lowering expectations for his speech by saying, "No orator, however gifted, can overpraise General Grant," but raising them for the completion of the tomb, by saying, "I am glad to see here what seems to me to be positive assurance that this work, so nobly started upon, will be speedily consummated."[47] Despite Harrison's high hopes, the permanent monument would take another five years to complete.

The tomb was constructed of 8,000 tons of granite, with a 90-foot base, and towered 72 feet high. The interior was built of Carrara and Lee marble, and the walls were adorned with murals of the Civil War, including an image of Grant's respected rival, Robert E. Lee. Above the entrance, Grant's name, birth, and death dates were carved in Roman fashion: Vlysses S. Grant Born April XXVII MDCCCXXII Died Jvly XXIII MDCCCLXXXV. The eight-and-a-half-foot-long sarcophagus was constructed in Montello, Wisconsin, using two tons of local red porphyry. This feature is not unique, and in his initial design submission Duncan conceded that it "recalls the tomb of Napoleon, so far as the depressed crypt is concerned."[48] In the middle of March 1897 the sarcophagus arrived in New York and was placed in a subterranean crypt upon a foundation of Quincy granite. At the same time, an identical sarcophagus was being constructed for Grant's widow.[49]

With the sarcophagus in place, the body could now be transferred from the temporary vault to the permanent tomb. On April 10, laborers began to remove the 165 bolts from the steel casing that covered the coffin and completed the arduous job three days later, at 5:00 p.m. on April 13. The steel bolts were turned over to John Hemmingway Duncan, who ceremoniously distributed to them to members of the Grant Monument Committee.[50] The exact date for the reinterment was not made public, and citizens eager to witness the spectacle looked each day for an indication that the event was about to occur. When a dispatch of 130 police gathered at the tomb on the morning of April 17, they had their signal. People began to arrive with picnic lunches and blankets to get a good seat, and by the time the proceedings began, the onlookers numbered in the thousands. At about 2:30 p.m., a carriage pulled up and out stepped Fred and his son, Ulysses S. Grant III. The architect, James Hemmingway Duncan, was also present. A roofless enclosure was erected by the entrance

Grant's tomb today, in Riverside Park, New York.

to limit the public's view. The iron gate was unlocked by undertaker, James F. Quinn from J. Edward Winterbottom & Co., and the group walked inside. The lid of the steel casing was lifted off and the copper casket, still looking new, was removed. The wreath of oak leaves that had been made by Grant's granddaughter at Mount McGregor 12 years earlier sat atop the coffin and was carefully wrapped. At 3:30 p.m., an honor guard made of members of the US Grant Post 327 G.A.R. formed two lines, and 20 minutes later, six of Quinn's assistants emerged carrying the casket through the honor cordon to the memorial building. The coffin was placed in the sarcophagus, and Fred unwrapped the wreath and placed it back on top. The lead casing was soldered shut, and the sarcophagus closed. Eight policemen were left to guard the tomb.[51]

The dedication ceremony was held 10 days later, on April 27, on what would have been Grant's 75th birthday, and was almost as big as the funeral held 12 years earlier. In attendance were former president Cleveland, President William McKinley, dignitaries from 26 countries, and 15 state governors.[52] One million citizens viewed the ceremony and a staggering 53,000 military veterans, including Union and Confederate soldiers, paraded to the tomb, prompting Grant's famous words "Let Us Have Peace" to become the catch phrase of the day, appearing on banners all over the city. American battleships and ships from foreign countries filled the harbor, and a French spectator, who had also witnessed the reinterment of Napoleon, shouted out, "Great are Grant and Napoleon! Honored only among all men in such a way!"[53] This was more of a celebration of Grant's life than a mourning of his passing. The ceremony began with a prayer by Bishop John P. Newman, followed by an address from President McKinley, who said, "With Washington and Lincoln, Grant has an exalted place in the history and affections of the people." Lastly,

General Horace Porter from the Grant Monument Association spoke. The tomb was officially donated to the city of New York and accepted by Mayor William Lafayette Strong. The day's events were completed "with pomp and pageantry, ceremony and solemnity."[54] After the ceremony, dark skies appeared and a strong wind rose. Spectators who had been sitting in wooden stands, many erected by organizations that charged from $1 to $5 a seat, ran for the shelter of the tomb pillars.[55] Only the family of Grant was permitted to enter to be alone with their husband and father for 10 minutes before departing. Five years later, Julia was entombed next to her husband after her death on December 14, 1902.

THE ULYSSES S. GRANT DEATH SITES
Location of Death

Joseph W. Drexel's decision to offer his home to Grant in his dying days was never purely altruistic—he also owned the nearby Balmoral Hotel and believed that both while alive and in death Grant would draw throngs to the area.[56] After Grant passed away, Drexel acted quickly to preserve the structure as a historic site. The furnishings were left intact and he created the Mount McGregor Memorial Association to assume ownership and handle operations.[57] Today, you can see Grant's leather chair, where he slept in his final days, along with the personal notes he used to communicate with his family when he was unable to speak. One unusual remnant from Grant's brief stay is his "cocaine water"—while the water is long evaporated, sediment from the now-illegal narcotic remains.[58] In the early years, funding was provided by the Grand Army of the Republic, and the home was first opened to the public on September 15, 1890. The first caretakers were Civil War veteran Captain Oliver Clarke, who had been imprisoned at Andersonville, and his wife, Josephine.[59]

On August 20, 1891, President Harrison visited Mount McGregor. Harrison spoke fondly of his predecessor when he declared, "We are gathered here in a spot which is historic. This mountain has been fixed in the affectionate and reverent memory of all our people and has been glorified by the death on its summit of General Ulysses S. Grant."[60] After Captain Clarke died in 1917, his wife, and adopted Japanese daughter Suye Narita, took over the home. Care for the home remained in the Clarke family and after Josephine's death, Narita and her husband, Anthony Gambino, took over as caretakers. During World War II, she was declared an enemy alien, her radio was confiscated, and she was restricted to the mountain.[61] After Narita's death, her husband continued to oversee the home.

Management passed through several different state and local agencies. In 1924, the home was transferred to the New York Department of Education, although it was still owned by the Mount McGregor Memorial Association. In 1957, the deed was transferred to the New York Office of Parks, Recreation, and Historic Preservation. Thirty years later, it was jointly operated by the state and the Saratoga County Historical Society. For many years annual events were held at the home on or near the president's birthday.

In 1981, the home gained a new and unwelcome neighbor when the Mount McGregor Correctional Facility was built upon the hill. This ushered in tightened security, as visitors now had to deal with a checkpoint gate, armed guards, and razor-wire strung along the mountainside landscape. Some of the inmates lived outside the razor-wired enclosure, as close as 50 yards from the home's porch. Instead of the birds chirping in the Adirondacks, visitors would now hear "arguments on the prison ball field and rock music blaring from the recreation hall." Visitation plummeted. In later years, director John Simon called the home "a hidden treasure" but added it was "kind of a jewel, threatened by a monster!"[62]

The 1980s were a difficult time for Grant's death site. In the first years the home was open, 10,000 people visited each season, but by 1983 only 300 visitors braved the security gates annually. With attendance down, the museum was forced to shut its doors in 1985 and take the exhibit on the road to help drum up support. They even offered the building to prison officials to use as office space. Luckily, the idea was abandoned. Local politicians quickly decried the closure and, despite its challenges, lent their support. The attention piqued local interest and in the end the museum kept its doors open.[63] In 2014, the correctional facility ceased operations.

On February 18, 1971, the cottage was added to the National Register of Historic Places (#71000557). The cottage is located at 28 Mt. McGre-

The home where Grant died. Note the barbed wire and security tower of the nearby Mount McGregor Correctional Facility to the right.

gor Road, Gansevoort, New York, 12831. For more information, visit: www.GrantCottage.org.

Lying in State: Albany
Construction on the New York State Capitol building started in 1867, and the Romanesque Revival building took 32 years and $25,000,000 to complete. This hefty price tag in 19th-century dollars makes it one of the costliest public projects undertaken.[64] Along with the cottage, the state capital was also listed on the National Register of Historic Places (#71000519) on February 18, 1971. The New York State Capitol building is located at State Street and Washington Avenue, Albany, New York, 12224. For more information, including tour times, visit: http://www.ogs.ny.gov/esp/ct/tours/Capitol.asp.

Lying in Repose: New York City
See Chapter 4: James Monroe

Original Tomb
On August 30, 1896, several months before the permanent memorial was completed, Chinese prime minister Li Hung-Chang visited the tomb of "his old friend." A crowd of 20,000 gathered to welcome the foreign dignitary, who arrived in a carriage, stepped into his "chair of state," and was carried to the tomb by four very unhappy Irish policemen.[65] Li stepped out, approached the tomb, and bowed his head in reverence for several moments. He also gave two gifts: a garland of bay leaves and a $500 donation. Afterward, Li spoke and said visiting the tomb was one of the primary things he'd wished to do on his journey to America.[66]

Shortly after the completion of the permanent tomb, the temporary one was taken down. The bricks were saved and dispersed among dignitaries and donors as souvenirs. The National Park Service has three of these bricks in their collection. The original tomb is directly behind the permanent tomb and is surrounded by an iron fence. Within the area are two more gifts from Li Hung-Chang: a tree that was planted beside the tomb and, obscured by bushes, a plaque erected in May 1897 that reads in both English and Chinese:

THIS TREE IS PLANTED AT THE SIDE OF THE TOMB OF GENERAL U.S. GRANT, EX-PRESIDENT OF THE UNITED STATES OF AMERICA, FOR THE PURPOSE OF COMMEMORATING HIS GREATNESS BY LI HUNG-CHANG, GUARDIAN OF THE PRINCE, GRAND SECRETARY OF STATE EARL OF THE FIRST ORDER, YANG YU ENVOY EXTRAORDINARY AND MINISTER PLENIPOTENTIARY OF CHINA, VICE PRESIDENT OF THE BOARD OF CENSORS' KWANG HSU 23RD YEAR, 4TH MOON, MAY 1897.

Grant's Tomb
When Fred Grant chose the location for his father's tomb on a hill in Riverside Park, there was already a home there known as the Claremont House. It dated back to around 1765 and had been owned by the St. Claire family until it was purchased by the state and transformed into a snack stand run by the Parks Department. To make way for the tomb, the snack stand was demolished.[67] After the tomb's completion, it became one of the most popular tourist attractions in New York City. The New York Board of Park Commissioners and the Grant Monument Association handled the administration and the maintenance, which kept them busy.

Amid concerns of vandalism in 1909, veterans from the Grand Army of the Republic approached the New York police commissioner, who placed three guards at the tomb at all times.[68] While there were few actual reports of vandalism in these early years, the more prevalent danger was from traffic accidents. In the early years of the automobile, the unlit area around the tomb was termed "a veritable death trap."[69]

After its completion, funds were required for the continued upkeep, as there was no admission charge to the site. Souvenirs were sold inside the tomb, prompting one outraged visitor to write the *New York Times* to voice his disdain for the "venerable peddler shouting his wares in a raucous tone" (it has since been tactfully relocated to the nearby visitor center).[70] In 1939, flags were erected on either side of the entrance, dedicated to key members of the Grant Monument Association. The flag to the right honors Horace Porter, who served as president from 1891–1919, and the flag on the left honors Fred, eldest son of Grant and association member from 1908–1912.

In January 1956, the state, eager to rid itself of the $11,635 annual maintenance bill, authorized the transfer of the tomb to the federal government. The president of the Grant Monument Association, retired major General Edward J. McGrew, believed transferring ownership would ensure they "would not run the risk of the structure ever getting into a state of disrepair."[71] On August 14, 1958, President Eisenhower signed House Resolution 6274, transferring ownership to the National Park Service. The move was completed on May 1, 1959 and the tomb became known as the General Grant National Memorial. There was no ceremony for the transfer.[72]

In the 1960s, the tomb reentered the national consciousness when Groucho Marx first uttered the now-famous question on his quiz show, *You Bet Your Life*: "Who's buried in Grant's Tomb?" Not everybody found the joke amusing. Columnist E. V. Durling of the *Milwaukee Sentinel* wrote that the joke was in bad taste in an article titled, "Better Groucho Should Bury Grant's Tomb Gag."[73] Around this time, crime was on the rise, and the Grant Memorial, located near Harlem, was in the epicenter of one of the roughest areas in America. It suffered more than any other presidential tomb, becoming the poster child for urban decay. Earlier in the century it had been the most visited site in the city, but by the turbulent 1960s had become one of the least visited, and perhaps most dangerous, attractions. Since the tomb opened in 1897, approximately

300,000 people had visited each year. In 1966, a steady drop-off began, until attendance hit rock bottom in 1979, when only 35,117 visited.[74]

Things did not get any better in the next decade. In 1983, a visitor reported that the "graffiti and abandoned wrecked-out cars surrounding the tomb . . . are deplorable."[75] The pitiful conditions continued into the early 1990s, when homeless people, gang members, prostitutes, and drug addicts continued to make the graffiti-riddled tomb their home. Drug paraphernalia, empty booze bottles, human feces, and even remains of animal sacrifice littered the memorial. It had become a bad joke, but the truth was that the National Park Service and the city of New York were not living up their responsibilities. Disgusted into action, Illinois state senator Judy Baar Topinka introduced a resolution to move the remains to her home state, where Grant had once briefly lived in Galena. Supporting her claim was that Illinois was listed by Grant himself as one of the three places he wished to be buried. Ohio, Grant's birthplace, also joined the debate, claiming that if he were to be moved, it should be to his birth state.[76] Even the Grant family chimed in, when great-great-grandson Ulysses Grant Dietz complained, "It's a presidential tomb, and it's being treated as a subway station."[77]

In 1994, former astronaut and Ohio Senator John Glenn pledged federal support for repairs and increased security. With the pledged funding, the National Park Service drew up plans to restore the tomb to its former glory and published them on April 27, what would have been Grant's 172nd birthday.[78] Unconvinced by these promises, the Grant family sued the federal government five days after the announcement to force it to repair the monument.[79]

In the later years of the decade, the city made an incredible comeback, as did much of the country. Areas that were formerly too dangerous to visit became tourist friendly, and eventually, the same happened at the Grant Memorial. After

24 consecutive years of fewer than 100,000 visitors, in 1995, 115,800 people visited the tomb. While it would never reach its former glory as a top tourist destination, better times were ahead. By the year 2000, the addicts, vagrants, and gangs had been driven out of the area. In 2003, the most controversial event to take place at the site was a risqué song-and-dance performance on the steps of the memorial by Beyoncé, who sang her hit "Baby Boy" at a televised Fourth of July event. Frank Scaturro, president of the Grant Monument Association, called the performance "patently inappropriate" and continued: "At that location, a certain decorum should have been observed from which popular entertainers are not exempt."[80]

General Grant National Memorial is in Riverside Park in Manhattan. The entrance is near the intersection of Riverside Drive and West 122nd Street, New York, New York, 10027. It is open to visitors Wednesday through Sunday from 9:00 a.m. to 5:00 p.m. For more information, visit: www.nps.gov/gegr.

Chester Alan Arthur ★ *1881-1885*

CRITICAL DEATH INFORMATION:

Date of death:	November 18, 1886, 5:10 a.m.
Cause of death:	Cerebral apoplexy (stroke)
Age at death:	57 years, 44 days
Last words:	Unknown
Place of death:	Home at 123 Lexington Avenue, New York City, New York
Funeral:	Church of the Heavenly Rest, New York City, New York
Final resting place:	Albany Rural Cemetery, Albany, New York
Reinterred:	No
Cost to visit grave:	Free
For more information:	www.Albany RuralCemetery.org
Significance:	Only presidential death site that is now a grocery store and restaurant

Only a year after Chester Arthur became president following the assassination of James Garfield, he was diagnosed with Bright's disease, a kidney condition that he knew would eventually prove fatal. Historians believe that it was largely due to his illness that he decided not to run for the presidency in 1884. After leaving the White House, he returned to his New York brownstone at 123 Lexington Avenue, located about two miles from Ulysses S. Grant's residence. Arthur resumed his law practice, but his illness kept him largely secluded, and in the teeming city the former president soon became a forgotten man. So forgotten that, when he died, an obituary published by the *Corning Journal* lamented, "The ex-president finished his career in declining health and obscurity, at his home. Until his illness called attention to him again his name had scarcely been mentioned since he left Washington."[1]

Almost immediately after leaving office, he began to show signs of his disease. Within about a year, he was confined to his bed. He drank milk with pepsin to help his digestion, and his formerly-large girth had almost disappeared. Arthur began to prepare for the end when he wrote his will, leaving his property to his two children. His sisters, Regina and Mary, moved in to care for him, and by the summer of 1886, he showed signs of improvement. He left the city for his cottage in New London, Connecticut. When he returned to New York on September 27, friends noted his thin and pallid appearance, but Arthur felt he was on the mend. In the ensuing days, he even accepted an offer to be president of the Arcade Railway Company and took several carriage rides in the city.[2] Several days later he again felt ill. At first, he blamed the jostling rides in Central Park, but he soon realized his condition was more serious. He confined himself to his bedroom for a month, where he read books and newspapers and kept abreast of the upcoming municipal elections. Friends visited often and noted his improved appearance, and by November, he felt better than he had in months.

At 9:00 p.m. on Tuesday, November 16, the 57-year-old Arthur was examined in his home by his family physician and good friend, Dr. George A. Peters. They chatted about a fishing trip they planned to take the following summer in Canada on the Restigouche River, and Peters gave Arthur a clean bill of health before he left for the evening. Unfortunately, what the doctor was unable to detect was an imminent stroke. That day, essentially his last of vibrant life, an unaware Arthur ate a big bowl of clams and did some paperwork. Reminiscent of James Buchanan, Arthur also made the peculiar request that his friend Jimmy Smith destroy many of his personal

and presidential papers, denying this important historical documentation to future scholars.

The next morning at 8:00 a.m., the housemaid entered the upstairs bedroom to rouse Arthur, but found him unresponsive. Alarmed, she called for Arthur's son, who immediately called Dr. Peters. The doctor rushed to the home and found that Arthur had suffered a stroke and his right side was paralyzed. He grimly declared that the former "President's case was hopeless."[3]

William A. Valentine, a second doctor, arrived, as did several of Arthur's former law partners, including Judge Surrogate Rollins. Unable to speak and barely able to move, Arthur was still aware of his surroundings and could gently squeeze his doctor's hand and stick out his tongue when asked. His breathing fluctuated from once a second to long pauses with none taken, but he hung on that day and night, into November 18. In the early morning hours, Arthur blinked several times and turned his head on his pillow. Those were his last earthly movements, and at 4:30 a.m. he fell still. For Chester Arthur, the end mercifully came at 5:10 a.m. on November 18, 1886. By his bedside when he died were his son Alan, his two sisters, Surrogate Rollins, and Dr. Valentine.[4]

Dr. Peters released a statement in which he said he "had never known a more heroic patient." He went on to describe Arthur's final days: "The attack that ended his life was not anticipated by him. I had considered it as among the possibilities, for such an attack is one of the ways in which the disease he had terminates. When the attack came, however, I believe he realized that it was fatal, and if I can judge from the expression of his face I think he was gratified that he was to die so painlessly. He did not at any time suffer much actual pain. He could feel and see himself wasting—that was all."[5]

The family asked Clayton McMichael, who was appointed by Arthur as marshal of the District of Columbia, to handle the funeral arrangements. Their desire was for Arthur to be buried as a common citizen—or at least to have as ordinary a funeral as a president could have. Honoring the wishes of Arthur himself, they did not want a funeral full of excessive pomp and pageantry. While Arthur did serve in the New York State Militia during the Civil War, he did not see active combat and the family did not want a military parade. While several offers for a military presence were made, the appreciative family accepted only an escort for the short trip from the church to Grand Central Station, from where the funeral cortege would continue on to Albany for burial. The funeral was originally planned for the day after the former president passed away, Friday, November 19, but was moved to the following Monday to allow sufficient time for members of Arthur's cabinet to attend.

The day Arthur died, an undertaker, Mr. Davidson, prepared the remains, but he did not embalm the former president. He dressed him in a black suit and frock coat and placed him in a cloth-covered oak casket with silver handles upon which a silver plate read:

CHESTER A. ARTHUR
BORN OCT 5, 1830
DIED NOV. 18, 1886

The open casket was placed in the parlor, where it remained for four days, but the family requested there be no services at the house. The only decoration they wanted on the coffin was a wreath, but when President Grover Cleveland sent a floral cross and pillow inscribed "Requiescat in pace" (Latin for "Rest in peace"), they chose to display it by the casket. Due partially to the stroke and most to his being four days deceased without have been embalmed, the *Daily Argus News* reported that his "face was pallid and wasted."[6]

On Monday, November 22, policemen arrived at the home for the funeral. Flags flew at half-mast throughout the city. Only 17 months after the funeral of Ulysses S. Grant, which millions had attended, the city was prepared for throngs of people in the streets. However, Arthur was no Grant, and it was reported that "the number of would-be sight-seers was infinitesimal when compared with that which attended the last Presidential Funeral."[7] Still, enough people were milling near the home to require the police to line the route to keep the road clear. Friends and family began to arrive at 7:30 a.m., including his secretary of war, Robert Todd Lincoln. Shortly afterward, the coffin was closed for the last time. Just before 8:00 a.m., President Cleveland arrived in time to pay his respects, but too late for a final look at the remains of his predecessor. Twenty minutes later, the undertaker's four assistants carried the casket down to the hearse, a "plumeless vehicle drawn by two black horses."[8]

Next to exit the building were the honorary pallbearers, filing by two at a time and all wearing white sashes: Judge Walter Q. Gresham (former secretary of the treasury), Robert Todd Lincoln (former secretary of war), William E. Chandler (former secretary of the navy), Frank Hatton (former postmaster general), Benjamin H. Brewster (former attorney general), General Philip Sheridan, physician Cornelius Rea Agnew, Cornelius Newton Bliss (who would later serve as secretary of the interior under William McKinley), Robert G. Dun, George H. Sharpe, Charles Lewis Tiffany, and Cornelius Vanderbilt. Twenty-three carriages made up the modest funeral caravan. In the first rode his son, Chester Jr., daughter Nellie, and Arthur's three sisters. They were followed by President Cleveland and members of his cabinet.[9] Despite the prominent political figures, it was such an inconspicuous event that the *Daily Argus News* reported, "Excepting the crowds that blocked the streets in the vicinity of the family residence and along the route to the church, there was little to indicate that the man who had been ruler of the nation was being laid away."[10] The truth is that more people witnessed Arthur's funeral procession by accident than intentionally. Out of office for just over 20 months, the 21st president was all but forgotten.

At 8:30 a.m., the procession began its short journey up Lexington Avenue to 34th Street. It turned onto Madison Avenue, proceeded to 46th Street, and turned onto 5th Avenue to the Church of the Heavenly Rest. As it approached, soldiers and sailors lined up to create an imposing welcome. The church had been decorated in black cloth, and a large American flag hung in the portico. Arthur was not a member of the Church of the Heavenly Rest, but his wife Ellen, who had died six years earlier, had been. The night before, Clayton McMichael and Arthur's private secretary, James C. Reed, visited the church to check the capacity. It could accommodate only 840 people, and they decided to restrict admittance to invited attendees only, which included members of the Senate and House, representatives from the Lincoln Club, Coffee Exchange, Produce Exchange, Consolidated Stock, Petroleum Exchange, and Mercantile Exchange.[11] Members of the Ancient and Honorable Artillery Company of Massachusetts, of which Arthur was a member, were also in attendance, along with Reverend Henry Ward Beecher, General William Tecumseh Sherman, Mexican Minister Matías Romero, William Waldorf Astor, John Jacob Astor, and New York Governor David B. Hill.[12] Several people without an invitation were turned away at the door.

Six pallbearers carried the coffin to the steps and paused while Harry E. Reeves led the 35-member church choir in singing "Asleep to Jesus." The casket was carried inside and placed on a low catafalque in front of the altar. The crowd stirred when former president Rutherford B. Hayes entered, walking side by side with President Cleveland. At 9:00 a.m., the brief ceremony began and was led by Reverend D. Parker Morgan, rector of the Church of the Heavenly Rest. Assisting him were Reverend E. W. Babcock, also of the Church of the Heavenly

Rest; Reverend W. A. Leonard from St. John's in Washington, DC; and Reverend George Rainsford of St. George's Church. The simple service began with a reading from the First Epistle of St. Paul to the Corinthians and ended with the processional hymn "Abide By Me." The original schedule included a eulogy by Reverend Leonard, but the train would not wait beyond 10:15 a.m., even for the funeral of a president! With the eulogy nixed for time reasons, it was not surprising when the service was later described as "perhaps the most free form display that have characterized the funeral of any President of the United States."[13] The pallbearers carried the coffin outside to the hearse, while the band played a funeral dirge. Marines and the military band led the procession down 5th Avenue to 45th Street. Along the way, citizens—some lined the route for the occasion, but many more just happened to be walking by—removed their hats. The *Corning Journal* wrote that the "Crowd of spectators waited patiently on the sidewalk to witness the un-ostentatious display."[14]

The small procession arrived at Grand Central Station at 9:55 a.m., and authority for the remains was transferred to General Henry A. Barnum. The coffin was placed in the New York and Harlem Railroad funeral car, Woodlawn, where it was surrounded by floral arrangements; however, the funeral train was not draped in mourning. The previous year, this same train carriage had been used to transport Grant's remains, with much more fanfare. Cornelius Vanderbilt's palace car and the drawing room cars Aroostok and New York and car #543 were also a part of the funeral train. Presidents Hayes and Cleveland stood on the platform "arm in arm, engaged in earnest conversation," to see the train off. Many of the funeral attendees boarded to escort the remains to Albany. At 10:09 a.m., the train, engineered by Mr. Depew and Superintendent J. M. Toucey (who also engineered the Lincoln funeral train) departed. The funeral had been a quick event—only an hour and 40 minutes had passed since the procession left the Arthur home.[15]

Sadly, but not surprisingly, there were no crowds along the 141-mile trip—no prayer vigils, bonfires, no groups of schoolchildren. The only stop was in Poughkeepsie for water. When the train arrived in Albany at 1:22 p.m., only a small gathering greeted it. There would have been more people, but a mistake was made when announcing the train's arrival time and led several groups to expect it later in the day. The stop in Albany lasted only six minutes for the train to switch from the New York Central tracks to the Delaware and Hudson Railroad line. At 1:28 p.m., the train departed for Albany Rural Cemetery, where it arrived seven minutes later. It stopped by the entrance, and the coffin was removed. There were no ceremonial pallbearers; instead the undertaker's assistants carried the coffin to a hearse.

An honor guard flanked the hearse, which included four Blue Jackets, a lieutenant from the battleship *Vermont*, and five members of the Fifth United States Infantry from Governor's Island. They were followed by policemen and a carriage, in which rode the Bishop of Albany, Reverend William Croswell Duane. The delegation that came from New York City entered additional carriages. The procession arrived at

the grave at 2:10 p.m. and was met by the 200 people gathered for the burial. After the coffin was placed in the grave, Reverend Doane held an Episcopal funeral service. The mourners each threw a handful of dirt onto the coffin to bid farewell to our 21st president.[16]

After the burial, an iron "Grand Army of the Republic" plaque was placed at the grave, but friends of the president came together to erect an appropriate memorial. They commissioned Ephraim Keyser from New York to create the monument for a cost of approximately $25,000. He designed an Egyptian sarcophagus carved from highly polished brown Quincy granite that stands about five and a half feet tall. On Thursday, May 21, 1889, two and a half years after Arthur's passing, an eight-foot-tall bronzed, winged angel was placed a few feet from the grave.[17] The figure, now green with age, represents sorrow and holds a palm leaf in her left hand that stretches out over the coffin. The memorial is reached by climbing five granite steps.

On the base is inscribed simply:

ARTHUR

A plaque on the grave reads:

CHESTER ALAN ARTHUR
TWENTY-FIRST PRESIDENT OF THE UNITED
STATES
BORN OCTOBER 5TH, 1830
DIED NOVEMBER 18TH, 1886

The grave of Chester Alan Arthur at Albany Rural Cemetery in Albany, New York.

Notably, the birth date is incorrect both on his grave and the plaque that was placed on his coffin. Arthur was actually born in 1829, but this is not a simple typo. Like President Obama almost 130 years later, Arthur's birthplace was hotly disputed when he was the vice presidential candidate on the ticket with Garfield. Arthur claimed his birthplace was Fairfield, Vermont. However, the Democratic National Committee believed he was born outside of the United States and hired New York attorney Arthur P. Hinman to prove it. Hinman's research led him to believe that Arthur was born in Canada in 1829. Arthur had a younger brother who was born in Fairfield in 1830 and died shortly after birth. Hinman's theory was that Arthur had deviously appropriated his deceased younger brother's birth records so he could run for higher office. Arthur also added fuel to the fire when he lied about his birth year, often claiming he was born in 1830, instead of 1829. To conspiracy theorists, the incorrect date on the grave may be another clue that Arthur may have actually been constitutionally unqualified to serve as president of the United States![18]

THE CHESTER ARTHUR DEATH SITES
Location of Death

Arthur purchased a five-story brownstone at 123 Lexington Avenue around 1864.[19] The most significant event to take place in the home occurred the morning after James Garfield's death at 2:15 a.m. on September 20, 1881, when Arthur took the oath of office administered by Judge John R. Brady of the New York Supreme Court. He lived in the home for just 20 months after his presidency ended in 1885, during which time, when healthy, he focused on his law practice.

Shortly after Arthur's death, the home was purchased by L. J. Weil, who lived there with his family for about 15 years. Weil remodeled the home and removed an exterior staircase to the second floor. In 1900, the home was purchased by newspaper magnate William Randolph Hearst.[20] For the rich publisher, the residence was akin to slumming—he called it "The Shanty" and joked it was an "unfashionable address."[21] When he did stay there, he slept in the second-floor bedroom where Arthur died. In June 1910, Hearst filed plans to convert the home into "bachelor apartments" and change the ground floor to store space. He hired James C. Green as the architect for the project, which would cost $5,000.[22] In 1912 Hearst sold it to Samuel M. Schwab. In 1944, the bottom floor was converted to Kalustyan's, a grocery store

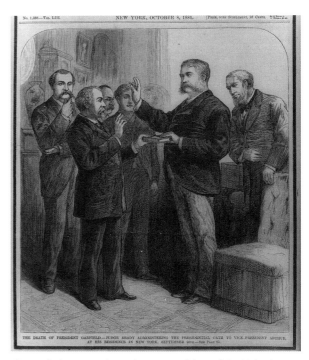

Chester being sworn in as the 21st president of the United States in his home at 123 Lexington Avenue, New York City, after James Garfield's death. Arthur was the first president to take the oath of office outside of Washington, DC, with the exception of George Washington, who was sworn in at Federal Hall in New York City. (Library of Congress)

that specialized in spices and food from India and the Middle East.[23] In 1955, the building was sold to Dr. Leo Lindenbaum. By this time, the floors above the store had been divided into six apartments.[24]

In the 1960s, the home received several recognitions. On January 16, 1964, the Native New Yorkers Historical Association and the New York Life Insurance Company placed a marker out front, but not surprisingly, there is no mention that Arthur died in the home. The building was added to the National Register of Historic Places (#66000534) on October 15, 1966, as the "Chester A. Arthur Home," but the documentation noted that "the entire house has undergone so many alterations since Arthur's death that the integrity is questionable," before adding, "the entire house is in poor condition."[25]

As early as 1965 and as late as 2004, a beauty salon occupied the second floor, but since then Kalustyan's has expanded and currently takes up the first and second stories and today has the distinction of being New York's oldest Indian grocery store. On September 26, 2013, I stopped by for lunch. After eating, I picked up some presidential souvenirs—a bag of Indian spices for myself and Kalustyan's cinnamon for my brother Joseph, who has a less exotic palate. I intended to visit anonymously, but when the clerk asked me if I enjoyed my meal, I couldn't resist responding, "The sandwich was delicious, but the reason I stopped by was to see where Chester Arthur lived!" The proprietor replied, "That's true, this *is* where he lived." I quickly

added, "And died!" This was news to him. He thought a moment before replying, "I didn't know that! Really, he died here?" and he looked around as if now seeing the building for the first time.[26]

Kalustyan's is located at 123 Lexington Avenue, New York, New York, 10016. It is open Monday through Saturday from 10:00 a.m. to 8:00 p.m. and 11:00 a.m. to 7:00 p.m. on Sundays. For more information, visit: www. Kalustyans.com.

Funeral

The Church of the Heavenly Rest was located on 551 Fifth Avenue between 45th and 46th Streets. It was founded by Civil War veterans in 1868 with the help of Reverend Robert Shaw Howland. In 1925, the church acquired its present location at 90th Street and Fifth Avenue. The original church was later demolished and today the Fred F. French building sits at its former location. The current building is also an architectural treasure, having been designated a New York City Landmark in 1986 and added to the National Register of Historic Places (#3001514) on January 28, 2004.

Grave Site

Plans for the Albany Rural Cemetery began on April 2, 1841, when an association was formed to locate land for new burial grounds. Three years later, on April 20, 1844, the group purchased a scenic 100-acre plot about three miles north of Albany from Thomas Hillhouse. The picturesque, undulating parcel featured ponds, streams, rocky cliffs, and a forest. On October 7 of that same year, the land was consecrated in a formal ceremony led by Daniel D. Brainard and included poetry by Alfred B. Street. The following May, the cemetery hosted its first burial.[27]

Arthur's grave site is located on one of the highest knolls in the western end of the cemetery. He is buried beside his wife, son, and

The building where Arthur died; now Kalustyan's, an Indian spice and specialty food store since 1944.

parents, and nearby is a memorial for his father-in-law, Captain Herndon, who was lost at sea in 1857 on the steamboat *Central America*. To the left of Arthur's grave is a flagpole, and outside of the cemetery gate is a marker erected in 1982 by the Cemetery Association and Historic Society.

Albany Rural Cemetery is located on Cemetery Avenue, Menands, New York, 12204. It is open every day starting at 7:30 a.m. to 4:30 p.m. (it remains open until 7:30 p.m. during daylight savings time). For more information, visit: www.AlbanyRuralCemetery.org.

Rutherford Birchard Hayes ★ *1887–1881*

CRITICAL DEATH INFORMATION:

Date of death:	January 17, 1893, 11:00 p.m.
Cause of death:	Heart attack
Age at death:	70 years, 105 days
Last words:	"I know that I am going where Lucy is."
Place of death:	Home at Spiegel Grove, Fremont, Ohio
Funeral:	Home at Spiegel Grove, Fremont, Ohio
Final resting place:	Spiegel Grove, Fremont, Ohio
Reinterred:	Yes
Cost to visit grave:	$7.50
For more information:	www.RBHayes.org
Significance:	Death site is now the Rutherford B. Hayes Presidential Center, considered to be the first Presidential Library.

After his presidency ended in 1881, Rutherford B. Hayes moved to Spiegel Grove, his family estate in Fremont, Ohio. He led a quiet life and dedicated much of his time to charitable organizations.[1] On a chilly night in January 1893, Hayes attended an out-of-town university trust meeting. When waiting at the train station to return to Spiegel Grove, Hayes suffered a heart attack. The hardened Civil War general decided a stiff brandy would be enough to get him home to rest and recover. Back at Spiegel Grove, his doctor placed him on bed rest, and there appeared to be an improvement before Hayes's health took a turn for the worse. By January 17, he was in critical condition. He found solace in his faith that he would soon see his

Spiegel Grove, the home where Rutherford B. Hayes died.

immediately went to New York's Grand Central Station upon hearing the news to travel to Ohio for the funeral.[3] Also in attendance was Ohio governor (and future president) William McKinley. Sitting president Benjamin Harrison sent a wreath of English ivy.

Members of the Loyal Legion from Massachusetts stood as honor guard when the service began at 2:00 p.m. Reverend L. J. Albritton of the Methodist Episcopal Church in Fremont read the 23rd Psalm, followed by a prayer from Reverend J. W. Bashford, who had married the Hayeses 43 years earlier.[4] As the weather was frigid, the planned Grand Army graveside services were instead held in the home. A benediction was made by Chaplain Webster of the Eugene Rawson Post to close the funeral. The pallbearers, all members of the 23rd Ohio Regiment, carried the coffin to the hearse.

The procession was led by the Cleveland City Troop and the Sixteenth Regiment of Battery D of Toledo and commanded by Colonel H. S. Bunker. It marched down Birchard Avenue, to Buckland Avenue, and on to the Oakwood Cemetery. Hayes was buried next to Lucy under a tombstone that Hayes had designed himself. It was made of granite quarried from his father's farm in Dummerstown, Vermont.

Twenty-two years later, on April 3, 1915, the bodies of Hayes and Lucy were reinterred to the grounds of the Spiegel Grove estate, in a 12-by-12-foot granite block located on the top of a knoll to the left of the home. The tombstone was also moved to the new location, and an iron fence surrounded the grave.[5] For years after Hayes's death, the dwindling survivors from his 23rd Regiment sent a wreath and continued the tradition at the new location. Nearby the grave

beloved wife, who had died four years earlier, when he uttered his last words: "I know I am going where Lucy is." That night, at 11:00 p.m. on January 17, 1893, as he lay in the arms of his son, Webb, Rutherford B. Hayes died.[2]

The remains were dressed and adorned with medals from past service. On his chest was the Decoration of Commander in Chief of the Loyal Legion, and on his left lapel was pinned a Decoration of the Army of West Virginia. His body was covered in black cloth and placed in a cedar coffin, upon which a silver plate was inscribed simply RUTHERFORD B. HAYES, JANUARY 17, 1893 and placed in the dining room for the viewing.

The funeral was held on January 20, three days after his death. That day, the temperature plummeted to a frigid -5 degrees, but thousands still braved the cold. At 9:00 a.m., schoolchildren marched through the mansion carrying an American flag, and at 11:35 a.m. Grover Cleveland arrived. The day after Hayes died, the president-elect was in Lakewood, New Jersey. The two had been friends, and Hayes had planned to attend Cleveland's upcoming inauguration. While Cleveland was not formally invited, he

Hayes's grave at his home, Spiegel Grove, in Freemont, Ohio.

is the final resting place of Hayes's beloved war horse, Old Whitey. The steed that carried Hayes into many a Civil War battle died on March 20, 1879, while Hayes was in the middle of his presidential term.

THE RUTHERFORD B. HAYES DEATH SITES
Home/Grave

Hayes's maternal uncle, Sardis Birchard, purchased property in Fremont, Ohio, on November 5, 1846. He named the estate Spiegel Grove due to the large puddles that accumulated on the property (*Spiegel* being German for "mirror"). Hayes's father died before he was born, and Sardis became a paternal figure and his legal guardian. Sardis enlisted his nephew to help design the home in 1859, along with Fremont architect Joseph Rumbaugh. Hayes preferred simplicity and told his uncle, "One thing you know I do not want any of the sort of cottage architecture ornamentation which is so common." Local contractor Daniel June began construction on August 22, 1859, but with materials scarce during the Civil War, the 4,000-square-foot, eight-bedroom home was not completed until 1864.[6]

After serving two terms as governor of Ohio,

Hayes moved into the home in 1873 and inherited Spiegel Grove when Sardis died in January 1874. Hayes hired Foster & Company to expand the house at the end of his presidency, in 1880. They nearly doubled its size, and when Hayes returned from Washington, DC, it was to a much larger structure. Further additions were made to the back in 1889, and currently there are 31 rooms, 18 of which are bedrooms. The room to the right of the front door is where Hayes's viewing was held, which was a part of the 1880 expansion. Off the porch is a casket window that opens to the floor to allow a coffin to be passed though. To the left is the parlor and behind it is the bedroom where Hayes died. After his death, the home passed to his children. In 1910, Rutherford's son, Webb, donated it to the state to be run by the Ohio State Archeological and Historical Society.

The Hayes Presidential Center beside the home was opened with a grand dedication ceremony at 10:30 a.m. on Memorial Day, May 30, 1916. Senator Warren G. Harding and President Woodrow Wilson were unable to attend, but the president sent his secretary of war, Newton D. Baker. Among those in attendance were 2,000 schoolchildren and veterans from the 23rd Ohio Regiment. Ohio governor Frank B. Willis started the service by recognizing the veterans "who valiantly marched forth to battle for liberty and union and the perpetuation of our Republic, the boys in blue of '61 to '65." Other seniors in the audience included members of the Eugene Rawson Post, an association of Grand Army of the Republic veterans that welcomed Hayes into its ranks in 1881, and members of the Croghan Lodge of Odd Fellows, which Hayes joined when he first moved to Fremont in 1849. Willis then spoke of Hayes's place in history, albeit overstated: "we shall go on unfolding the glorious destiny of the land of Washington, Lincoln and Rutherford B. Hayes."[7]

Opened almost a century ago, this museum is considered to be the first presidential library. After it opened, the family continued to live in the home. In total, four generations of Hayes family members resided at Spiegel Grove after his death. They donated the home in 1965 and it was opened for daily tours the next year.[8] An amazing 90 percent of the pieces in the home are original, as the family was meticulous about saving papers and items for posterity. An 1890s phone directory lists the resident as "General Hayes," using his preferred title. I found one of the most interesting items in the home to be a portrait of the president's son, Webb Hayes—I'll be darned if he doesn't look exactly like Teddy Roosevelt!

The home has had many famous visitors before and after Hayes's death: William McKinley attended his daughter's wedding there, presidents Grant and Cleveland also visited, and on October 4, 1920, then-Senator Warren G.

Harding attended the dedication of the Hayes Memorial Library. In his dedication speech, Harding spoke to a group of World War I veterans, praising Hayes and calling his service to America after the Civil War "more healing than heroic."[9]

The Rutherford B. Hayes Presidential Center is located at Spiegel Grove, 1337 Hayes Avenue, Fremont, Ohio, 43420. It is open from 9:00 to 5:00 except for Sundays, when it opens at noon. The museum is closed on Mondays. For more information, visit: www.RBHayes.org.

Original Cemetery

Oakwood Cemetery is a public cemetery. After President Hayes was reinterred, a new marker was erected at Oakwood that closely resembles the original tombstone but is slightly smaller and bears the simple inscription HAYES. The monument is surrounded by the graves of many of Hayes's family members, most with an indication of their familial association to the president (such as "Rutherford P. Hayes, son of Rutherford B. Hayes"). Burials of Hayes's relatives and descendants still continue to this day.

Oakwood Cemetery is located on the banks of the Sandusky River at 1225 Oakwood Street, Ballville, Ohio, 43420.

Oakwood Cemetery in Ballville, Ohio, where Hayes was buried until 1915, when he was reinterred at Spiegel Grove. The replacement marker resembles the original tombstone.

THE TWENTY-THIRD PRESIDENT

Benjamin Harrison ★ *1889–1893*

CRITICAL DEATH INFORMATION:

Date of death:	March 13, 1901, 4:45 p.m.
Cause of death:	Pneumonia
Age at death:	67 years, 205 days
Last words:	"Are the doctors here?"
Place of death:	Home in Indianapolis, Indiana
Funeral:	First Presbyterian Church, Indianapolis, Indiana
Final resting place:	Crown Hill Cemetery, Indianapolis, Indiana
Reinterred:	No
Cost to visit grave:	Free
For more information:	www.CrownHill.org
Significance:	First president to die in the 20th century

At the age of 67 and eight years out of office, Benjamin Harrison was in good health and looked forward to many more years as a private citizen. But in early March 1901, Harrison fell ill, and a single illness begat a quick downfall. He had only recently recovered from a minor cold when, on Thursday, March 7, after breakfast, Harrison cried out sharply for his wife. She rushed to him and found him in distress. He had experienced a severe chill and, struck by how suddenly the illness came on, said, "This could not have been more sudden if someone had hit me over the head with a hammer." A doctor was called to the house. The next day, Harrison suffered from severe neuralgia (nerve pain) and was diagnosed with pneumonia.[1] Letters arrived from across the country with unsolicited medical advice. Philo S. Armstrong of Milford, Ohio, sent a recipe for a potion that began with instructions to "Take 6 to 10 onions." Another, from a man who called himself "Black Bear X," was written on the back of a drawing of a tipi and "Offered to send a collar free of charge that will cure all throat disease, cough, bronchial sore throat." The *New York Times* reported that the family and physicians were annoyed by the "large number of offers and solicitations from all sorts of quacks and cranks."[2]

On March 12, Harrison lay in the master bedroom on the second floor of his home in a massive hand-carved bed, drifting in and out of consciousness. His four-year-old daughter, Elizabeth, made him a small apple pie, but Harrison could only muster a smile in response. In his delirium, most of his words he uttered were unintelligible but those present were able to make out "my lungs" and "doctor." He last spoke when he asked his wife, "Are the doctors here?" Afterward, he slipped into unconsciousness. The next day, doctors administered oxygen until about 4:00 p.m., at which time, according to the *Indianapolis Journal*, "came the unmistakable signs that the air cells could no longer receive the fluid and the cap was withdrawn from the mouth."[3] Doctors summoned Harrison's friends and family to his bedside. His wife, Mary, took his right hand as his physician, Dr. Henry Jameson, held his left and monitored his pulse. Also there were Attorney General William Henry Harrison Miller of Indianapolis, and his son Samuel Miller; Harrison's good friend and pastor of the First Presbyterian Church Reverend M. L. Haines; Frank Tibbott; Dr. F. O. Dorsey, Sergeant at Arms of the United States Senate Daniel M. Ransdell; Clifford Arrick; two nurses, Miss Ella Keene and Miss Suzanne Paris; his aunt; and his two sisters, Elizabeth Eaton and Anna Symmes Morris. Sadly, none of his children were with him at his final moment (his two older children were on their way to Indianapolis

and young Elizabeth had been taken from the room as death approached). At 4:45 p.m. on March 13, 1901, Dr. Jameson could no longer feel a pulse—Benjamin Harrison was dead. The *Baltimore Morning Herald* reported his death was "marked by a single gasp for breath as life departed from the body of the great statesman."[4] A silence fell over the room, broken only when Reverend Haines said a prayer.

President William McKinley issued a proclamation for flags on public buildings to fly at half-mast for 30 days, including at army posts in Cuba, Puerto Rico, Hawaii, and the Philippines. He also sent a letter to Harrison's widow with his condolences: "In the death of General Harrison, the country has lost a distinguished statesman, a devoted patriot and an exemplary citizen. The people of the Nation mourn with you. You have the heartfelt sympathy of Mrs. McKinley and myself in this hour of overwhelming sorrow in your home."[5] Former president Grover Cleveland, who had the odd distinction of both defeating and being defeated by Harrison, gave a sincere and heartfelt tribute: "I am exceedingly moved by the sad intelligence of Mr. Harrison's death, for, notwithstanding the late discouraging reports of his condition, I hoped his life might yet be spared. Not one of our countrymen should for a moment fail to realize the services which have been performed in their behalf by the distinguished dead. In public office he was guided by patriotism and devotion to duty—often at the sacrifice of temporary popularity—and in private station his influence and example were always in the direction of decency and good citizenship. Such a career and the incidents related to it should leave a deep and useful impression upon every section of our National life."[6] Indianapolis public school superintendent C. N. Kendall recommended that part of the school day on Friday be dedicated to lessons about President Harrison.

The night Harrison died, the Kregelo Brothers funeral directors embalmed the body at 6:00

p.m. in his bedroom. The next day, sculptor John Mahoney made a plaster death mask before the body was placed in a copper-lined red cedar coffin, which was inscribed simply with BENJAMIN HARRISON 1833–1901. Over the next three days, the body remained in the parlor on the south side of the home, a formal room where Harrison met with important guests. On Saturday, March 16, members of the Indiana National Guard and veterans from the Grand Army of the Republic, including several aged members of Harrison's 70th Indiana Volunteers, escorted the remains to the Indiana State Capitol. Four black horses pulled the hearse.[7] The coffin was placed beneath the rotunda, where it was surrounded by floral arrangements (the day before, Kregelo Brothers employees moved a staggering 14 carriages of flowers from the home to the state capital). At 1:10 p.m. the doors were opened to the public and remained opened until 10:00 p.m. It was written that, "with the exception that his pallor became more pronounced, there was no change in his appearance."[8] After 50,000 people

had paid their respects, the coffin was returned to the home.

On Sunday, March 17, about 150 people were at the home and at 1:00 p.m., President McKinley arrived, along with Indiana governor Winfield Taylor Durbin. A short service began as Reverend Haines read from the Scripture and spoke briefly about the life of the deceased. Reverend Samuel J. Niccolls from St. Louis, a good friend of Harrison's who spent several summers with him in the Adirondacks, then said a prayer. Mary, too distraught to attend, stayed upstairs. However when it was time to depart for the church, she entered the parlor for a final farewell.

Outside of the home, thousands had gathered. The first people to exit were the honorary pallbearers. Next followed the body bearers, carrying the coffin. They were then followed by the family, President McKinley, and Governor Durbin. The initial plans were for the procession to begin at 1:30 p.m., but it started about a half hour late.

Pallbearers remove the casket from Benjamin Harrison's home on Sunday, March 17, 1901. (Used by permission from Jennifer E. Capps, VP of Curatorship & Exhibition of the Benjamin Harrison Presidential Site)

The procession arrived at the First Presbyterian Church on Pennsylvania Street at 2:30 p.m. The *New York Times* wrote that "by the time the funeral procession arrived there was a solid mass of humanity stretching a block away on every sidewalk."[9] The railroads had reduced rates to Indianapolis, allowing many people to travel to the city, although only those with a ticket were allowed inside the church. Patrolling the streets were the police and Company C of the Second Infantry under Captain Porter.

The body bearers carried the coffin inside the church where Harrison worshipped for almost 50 years. The interior was decorated in black and white silk ribbons with flowers from the state house. There were, in fact, so many baskets of roses that there was not enough room to fit them all. Mrs. Harrison followed the body bearers up the aisle, leaning on the arm of her brother, Lieutenant Commander John F. Parker. President McKinley followed and sat in the front pew. Along with the Indiana governor, also in attendance were Illinois governor Richard Yates Jr. and Ohio governor George Kilbon Nash. Former president Cleveland could not attend.

Reverend Haines began the service by reading comforting words from the Book of John: "I am the resurrection, and the life: he that believeth in me, though he were dead, yet shall he live." Reverend Niccolls read from First Corinthians, and the choir sang "Rock of Ages" (humorously remembered as the only song Harrison would attempt to sing when he attended services). After additional Scripture readings by Reverend Haines and Reverend Niccolls, the service closed with a solo rendition of "Hark, Hark, My Soul." It was a somber service, but not all were entirely overcome with grief. During a particularly lengthy portion of the sermon, one of the pallbearers, James Whitcomb Riley, whispered a joke to the others: "He's explaining to God all about Ben so God will know how to get along with him—now he's got a program laid out to keep God busy for the next couple o' years." The men used their handkerchiefs to stifle their giggles![10]

The crowd departed for Crown Hill Cemetery, where 15,000 people had gathered for the graveside service on the brisk evening. Despite the large crowd, the *New York Times* wrote that the "stillness of the evening had come, [and] there was hardly a sound in the air."[11] The crowd, kept at a 50-yard distance behind a rope barricade, was watched over by police to ensure they remained in the designated area. Dignitaries, family, and friends were allowed within the ropes, including President McKinley, who stood with hat in hand. The *St. John Daily Sun* complimented that "all was well ordered and well performed."[12]

At 5:00 p.m., a simple and brief graveside service was performed by Reverend Niccolls and Reverend Haines, concluding with a prayer. Attendants slowly lowered the coffin into the ground of the Harrison family plot. The tomb was constructed of Vermont granite, five feet deep with four-inch granite walls, and the interior was decorated with ferns.[13] When the coffin was secured inside, the 1,200-pound granite cover was set in place, enclosing the remains forever. Immediately, the chilled spectators began to disperse as cannons boomed in a final salute. The *Toledo Blade* summed up the day perfectly when they called the ceremony "severe, almost fastidious in its simplicity and lack of ostentation."[14] This was exactly how Harrison had requested his final send-off.

The 10-foot-tall granite tombstone was already in place, selected by Harrison himself after the death of his first wife, Caroline Scott, in 1892.[15] At the time of the president's death, it only bore the name "Harrison" and was later inscribed with:

BENJAMIN HARRISON.
AUGUST 20, 1833.
MARCH 13, 1901.

LAWYER AND PUBLICIST.

COL. 70TH REG. IND. VOL. WAR 1861–1865.
BREVETTED BRIGADIER GENERAL, 1865.
U. S. SENATOR, 1881–1887.
PRESIDENT, 1889–1893.

STATESMAN, YET FRIEND TO TRUTH,
OF SOUL SINCERE;
IN ACTION FAITHFUL, AND IN
HONOUR CLEAR.

While not as large and imposing as other presidential graves, especially for those presidents

Harrison's grave, 1904. (Library of Congress)

The palatial, 10,000-square-foot home where Benjamin Harrison died on March 13, 1901.

born in Ohio, the *Sunday Vindicator* praised the memorial when it wrote, "The very simplicity of the monument and the epitaph are the strongest possible tributes to the sterling character of the man who the grave marks."[16]

Two days after the burial, the family had gathered in the parlor of the home, and Attorney General Miller read Harrison's last will and testament, written three years earlier. Shortly after the burial, the family received disturbing news when police notified them of a shocking plot to steal the body. In 1901, this was still a genuine concern, as 25 years earlier criminals had plotted to take Abraham Lincoln's body. More recently, the corpse of Harrison's own father, John Scott Harrison, was stolen only 24 hours after it was buried in Congress Green Cemetery in 1878. Luckily, in this case, the ghoulish thief never carried out his plan. Rufus Cantrell was arrested the following year and confessed to a scheme to steal the body, temporarily place it in a doctor's office, and pretend to locate it and claim the riches after the inevitable award was offered.[17]

THE BENJAMIN HARRISON DEATH SITES
Location of Death

In 1868, Harrison purchased a double lot on North Delaware Street, on the outskirts of Indianapolis (known today as the Old Northside neighborhood). In the early 1870s, he had an enormous 10,000-square-foot, two-and-a-half story brick home in the "Italianate spirit" built.[18] As a successful attorney, he was able to afford the $29,000 cost of construction. When it was completed in 1875, it had 16 rooms, a full basement, oak floors, and fine butternut woodwork. Several historic events happened at the home during Harrison's lifetime, for it was there he hosted Rutherford B. Hayes, he accepted the presidential nomination from his party in 1888, and he began his successful Ohio-style "front porch campaign." After his presidency ended in 1893, he returned there to live.

After his death, the home was owned by his widow, Mary, who was 25 years his junior. Starting in 1910, she used it as a rooming house until 1936. The next year, she sold the home and most of the furnishings, including the bed where Harrison died, to the Arthur Jordan Foundation. One stipulation of the sale was that the front three rooms would remain undisturbed as a tribute to Harrison, and thanks in part to that, today approximately 80 percent of the furnishings are original. For the next 15 years, it was used as a women's dormitory for the Jordan Music Conservatory. (The foundation later purchased neighboring lots and had the adjacent structures torn down.) In 1951, the home was acquired by Butler University, and the following year, the President

Benjamin Harrison Foundation (associated with the Arthur Jordan Foundation) restored the second floor. It was first opened to the public later that same year. On October 15, 1966, the home was designated a National Historic Landmark (#66000010). In the early 1970s, the home underwent extensive restorations using funds from a Lilly Endowment and was rededicated on October 6, 1974. The home is still owned by the Arthur Jordan Foundation and they receive no state or federal funding. Today, approximately 28,000 people visit each year, half of whom are schoolchildren.

The home is located at 1230 North Delaware Street, Indianapolis, Indiana, 46202. It is open Monday through Saturday from 10:00 a.m. to 3:30 p.m. The home is also open on Sundays during June and July from noon to 3:30 p.m. For more information, visit: www.President BenjaminHarrison.org.

Funeral Church

Harrison was designated a "church elder" at First Presbyterian Church at the tender age of 28. Located on the southwest corner of Pennsylvania and New York streets, it was actually the second church used by the congregation. Construction began in 1864, and the first service was held on December 29, 1867. The first pastor was Reverend J. Howard Nixon, who had already served the congregation for six years. Reverend M. L. Haines, who officiated at the Harrison's funeral, became pastor in 1885. A year before the funeral, the church location was designated for a new federal building, and shortly after the funeral, it was vacated and demolished.[19] The federal building was completed in 1905 and is today known as the Birch Bayh Federal Building and United States Courthouse. Directly across New York Street is an impressive sculpture of the 23rd president on the Indiana World War Memorial Plaza.

Crown Hill Cemetery

On September 25, 1863, Crown Hill Cemetery was incorporated. On October 16 of that same year, 236 acres were purchased from three local farmers for $51,000 (an additional 20 acres were added on June 1, 1869). The cemetery was dedicated on June 1, 1864, and the next day, it hosted its first burial for Lucy Ann Seaton. Some of the earliest burials were reinterments of Union soldiers who had died in local hospitals and been buried in the City Cemetery.[20] On Memorial Day, 1907, Theodore Roosevelt visited the grave to lay a wreath. Normally, these events were done with splendor and ceremony, but Roosevelt preferred to honor his predecessor in private, accompanied by members of Secret Service, Vice President Charles Fairbanks, Indiana governor Frank Hanly, and his personal secretary, William Loeb. Their carriage arrived at the cemetery at 5:25 p.m., and

Harrison's grave, today.

Roosevelt walked alone to the grave, paused a moment, and placed a wreath of lilies and ferns. The next day, the city newspaper said of the gesture, "The act had been simple—Rooseveltian—as simple as sincere."[21] Mary Harrison, who was in England at the time, was moved to personally write the president to thank him. Roosevelt quickly responded with a typed letter, "Your very kind and considerate letter has just reached me. Why, of course on Memorial Day I visited your husband's grave and put a wreath upon it. He was my old chief." Beneath the type, he appended a hand written note, "for whom I had a very profound respect and regard."[22]

The grave is located in section 13, lot 57, near the highest point of the cemetery. Unlike most presidential graves in public cemeteries, it was not easy to find. After driving around the sprawling cemetery (Crown Hill is the third largest in the country) for several minutes in search for a "President Harrison is buried this way" sign, I finally gave up and walked to the front office for a map. The grave is within a small, well-manicured plot, thanks to the Indianapolis Garden Club, who did a wonderful job landscaping the area in August 2013.

Not only does the cemetery have a former president buried there, but it also has three vice presidents: Thomas Marshall, section 72, lot 1 (1854–1925, vice president under Woodrow Wilson), Thomas A. Hendricks, section 29, lot 2 (1819–1885, vice president under Grover Cleveland), and Charles Fairbanks, section 24, lot 3 (1852–1918, vice president under Theodore Roosevelt).[23] The one burial that was more controversial than any politician was that of Public Enemy #1, John Dillinger, the notorious Prohibition-era gangster and serial bank robber. Born in Indianapolis, he was gunned down in Chicago on June 22, 1934. Three days later, his bullet-riddled corpse was laid to rest in Crown Hill Cemetery.

The cemetery is at 700 West 38th Street, Indianapolis, Indiana, 46208, but the main entrance is on Clarendon Road. From October 15 to March 31 the grounds are open from 8:00 a.m. to 6:00 p.m. and the remainder of the year the grounds remain open until 8:00 p.m. For more information, visit: www.CrownHill.org.

EVOLUTION OF THE MEGA FUNERAL

★★

THE TWENTY-FIFTH PRESIDENT
William McKinley ★ *1897–1901*

CRITICAL DEATH INFORMATION:

Date of death: September 14, 1901, 2:16 a.m.

Cause of death: Assassination (including subsequent medical treatment)

Age at death: 58 years, 228 days

Last words: "Good-bye, all, good-bye. It is God's way. His will be done."

Place of death: Home of John G. Milburn, 1168 Delaware Avenue, Buffalo, New York

Funeral: First Methodist Church, Canton, Ohio

Final resting place: The McKinley Monument, Canton, Ohio

Reinterred: Yes

Cost to visit grave: Free

For more information: www.mckinley museum.org

Significance: Oldest president to be assassinated

In June 1901, President William McKinley planned a visit to Buffalo, New York, for the Pan-American Exposition. When his wife, Ida, became ill, the trip was postponed. Two months later, McKinley was ready to make the journey. On the evening of Wednesday, September 4, McKinley arrived in Buffalo and was welcomed by throngs of people at the train station. Intermingled with the crowd of well-wishers and sightseers was Leon Frank Czolgosz, a deranged anarchist. He fancied himself a disciple of the most notorious anarchist of the day, Emma Goldman, and professed that no one man should have as much power as the president. Czolgosz believed that killing President McKinley would lead to the end of capitalism and return power to the masses. The day before McKinley's arrival, Czolgosz had visited Walbridge Hardware on Main Street and purchased a silver-plated .32 caliber Iver Johnson revolver for $4.50. The evening McKinley arrived, he did not get close enough to use it, but he was not easily deterred.

That night, McKinley slept at the home of Exposition president John G. Milburn. The next day was "President's Day" at the Exposition, and McKinley gave a speech—the last of his life and one that many consider his greatest. In it, he said words that would later be memorialized within his tomb: "Let us ever remember that our interest is in concord, not in conflict; and that our real eminence rests in the victories of peace, not those of war." Again, Czolgosz lurked in the audience and for the second time, the opportunity to shoot McKinley did not present itself.

McKinley started the next day, September 6, with an invigorating 20-minute walk along Delaware Avenue. At 9:00 a.m., he boarded a northbound train to take a tour of one of the country's most popular attractions, Niagara Falls. Czolgosz followed him, but the stalker again decided this was not the time or place and returned to Buffalo. McKinley enjoyed his visit, taking in a pleasant lunch and cigar before the return trip. Back in Buffalo, he went directly to the Exposition, arriving around 3:30 p.m. at the massive, ornately decorated Temple of Music concert building. McKinley positioned himself at the end of the room, and at 4:00 p.m., he began one of his favorite activities—a meet and greet with citizens. People lined up between columns of soldiers, who were there to protect the president. As the organist played a Bach sonata, Czolgosz approached McKinley. His hand was wrapped in a handkerchief to conceal his gun.[1]

The man in front of Czolgosz approached the president and grasped his hand. When he did not release McKinley's hand when expected, the guards quickly intervened to move him along. Distracted, they did not notice Czolgosz next in line with his handkerchief-wrapped hand. Czolgosz fired two shots at close range. The first shot was superficial and ricocheted off McKinley's breast plate, but the second lead bullet pierced his stomach, about five and a half inches below his left nipple.[2] The music came to a sudden halt, the president slumped, and Czolgosz's handkerchief was in flames. It was 4:07 p.m.

James Parker, a six-foot-four-inch African American man in line behind Czolgosz, sprang into action. He hit Czolgosz in the neck with one hand and grabbed the gun with the other, stopping him from getting off a third shot. A newspaper in Utica proclaimed that Parker "pounced upon the criminal with the fury of an enraged tiger!"[3] His heroic response provided the opening the guards needed to step in and take control. They attacked Czolgosz and beat him to a pulp. Panic erupted in the hall as people rushed toward the exit, but McKinley's first reaction was confusion. He kept his composure, but when he saw a blood stain on

William and Ida McKinley leaving the Millburn home on the day he was shot. He would die in that same house eight days later. (Library of Congress)

his shirt spreading quickly he began to comprehend what had happened. He asked his guards, "Am I shot?" Unsure himself, a guard unbuttoned the president's shirt and confirmed his worst suspicions: "I'm afraid that you are, Mr. President."

As the president lay on the ground, he commanded his men, who were still pummeling Czolgosz, in a soft voice, "Go easy on him, boys." Struggling into a chair, he continued compassionately, "Let no one hurt him." His next concern was his fragile wife, Ida. He told his personal secretary, George Bruce Cortelyou, "My wife, be careful, Cortelyou, how you tell her—oh be careful!"[4]

McKinley was carried to an ambulance and taken to the hospital on the Exposition grounds, arriving 18 minutes after the shots were fired. However, the hospital was ill-prepared. The only staff on hand were interns and nurses on a one-month assignment, more accustomed to treating the occasional heatstroke or stomachache rather than a gunshot wound. Twenty minutes later, surgeon Herman Mynter arrived. McKinley had met him the day before, but now, under dramatically different circumstances, he looked at Mynter and said, "Doctor, when I met you yesterday, I did not imagine that today I should have asked a favor of you."

McKinley was given an injection of morphine and strychnine, and Mynter determined an immediate operation was required. Several minutes later, Dr. Matthew D. Mann arrived, who, despite being a gynecologist and an obstetrician, was still deemed the most qualified to perform the surgery (the best surgeon in the area to perform a gunshot operation was Roswell Park, but he was in Niagara Falls performing another operation). At 5:20 p.m., McKinley was administered ether to render him unconscious. As the drug took effect, McKinley recited the Lord's Prayer and drifted into a deep sleep. Mann began the operation despite lack of proper surgical equipment and adequate lighting while

McKinley's personal physician, Presley Rixey, positioned a mirror to reflect sunlight onto the operating table to allow Mann to see what he was doing. However, "the greatest difficulty was the great size of President McKinley's abdomen and the amount of fat present."[5]

Mann poked around McKinley's wounds for the bullet. He did not find it, but did discover a hole in the president's stomach, which he sewed up with black silk stitches. More damaging than the bullet that remained in his body was Mann's decision not to drain the wound. This would later lead to the gangrene that eventually killed the president. Just as Mann was completing the operation, Park arrived, but his expertise proved too late.

After the surgery, an unconscious McKinley was taken back to the Milburn house at approximately 6:30 p.m. Silent onlookers lined the route as the carriage passed. The home was instantly transformed into both a hospital and the presidential headquarters. The surrounding blocks were roped off, and the Fourteenth US Army Regiment stood guard. The first floor became the makeshift reception area, while McKinley convalesced in a quiet back room on the second floor with a large marble fireplace. There, beneath a picture of George Washington, he could peacefully gaze out the side windows. Some visitors and well-wishers were permitted to see the president, and thousands of telegrams flooded the home. Doctors provided reports of the president's condition from the front porch to reporters who had set up camp in white tents staked in the front yard. The reporters published updates of the president's temperature, sleep, and eating habits nearly every hour. Over the next week, McKinley drifted in and out of consciousness as morphine eased his pain. With each passing day, Americans became more convinced that their burly president would survive the ordeal. To help locate the bullet, Thomas Edison sent a primitive X-ray machine to the home. It arrived September 9, but proved as useless as the metal detector used on James Garfield 20 years earlier.[6]

Doctors had McKinley on a liquid diet, but by September 12, he felt good enough for solid food and had a breakfast of chicken broth, toast, and coffee. The doctors were pleased with his progress but declined his request for a cigar. Soon after his meal, McKinley felt sick, but his doctors were not alarmed and attributed it to indigestion. Even after his pulse jumped to 128, the doctors reasoned that McKinley would be back on track once the food passed through his system. That night, after a much-anticipated bowel movement, McKinley's pulse dropped to 120 and the doctors were almost ready to declare the spell had passed. Their elation was short-lived when his pulse did not decrease any further and his temperature rose to 100.2.[7] By the next morning, the 8:30 a.m. report was again optimistic: "The president responded to medical treatment and is better. The doctors administered calomel and oil, and they proved effective. He is resting nicely now, and the feeling is better."[8] But the president was not feeling better. McKinley's stomach was infected with gangrene and the solid meal would be fatal. On Friday, September 13, he drifted in and out of consciousness. In the morning, he stirred and gazed out the window. It was an overcast day and McKinley weakly commented, "It is not so bright as it was yesterday." Looking at the leaves on the trees, he added, "It is pleasant to see them."[9]

By the evening, he only could open his eyes sporadically. Doctors administered "powerful heart stimulants, including oxygen" to pull him back to consciousness.[10] He weakly whispered to Dr. Rixey for his wife. Kneeling by his side, Ida clasped her husband's hands while he repeated the hymn, "Nearer, My God, to Thee." Fully aware his fate was now in God's hands, McKinley whispered his final words, "Good-bye, all, good-bye. It is God's way. His will be done." Dr. Mann hurriedly wrote the words down to keep for the ages.

McKinley lost consciousness for the last time at 7:50 p.m. Doctors desperately administered oxygen until 8:30 p.m. and then permitted nature to run its course. Within 90 minutes, his skin was cold and pulse barely perceptible. The press was told death was imminent, but McKinley lingered on. Early the next morning, Dr. Rixey felt for a pulse, but could find none. At 2:16 a.m. on September 14, 1901, William McKinley was pronounced dead. With him were his family: his wife Ida, brother Abner, sisters Helen and Sarah, nieces Mary and Sara, cousin F. M. Osborne, and nephews James, William, and John, along with Cortelyou, Comptroller of the Currency Charles G. Dawes, Rutherford B. Hayes's son, Colonel Webb C. Hayes, Colonel William C. Brown, several nurses, and marine hospital attendants.[11]

An autopsy was performed. The cause of death, as documented on his death certificate, was, "gangrene of both walls of the stomach and pancreas following gunshot wounds." After a four-hour search, the coroner could still not locate the bullet. The autopsy also exonerated the physicians in a debatable addendum, "Death was unavoidable by any surgical or medical treatment and was the direct result of the bullet wound."[12]

McKinley's cabinet immediately began to plan his funeral to include services in Buffalo, Washington, DC, and a September 19 burial in Canton, Ohio. Theodore Roosevelt, now thrust into the presidency, issued his first official proclamation, in which he declared, "I, Theodore Roosevelt, President of the United States of America, do appoint Thursday next, September 19, the day in which the body of the dead President will be laid in its last earthly resting place, as a day of mourning and prayer throughout the United States. I earnestly recommend all the people to assemble on that day in their respective places of divine worship, there to bow down in submission to the will of Almighty God, and to pay out of full hearts the homage of love and reverence to the memory of the great and good President, whose death has so sorely smitten the nation."

McKinley's body was placed in an open casket in the drawing room. It was draped in black and at the foot was a new silk American flag. A silver plate bore the simple inscription:

WILLIAM MCKINLEY
BORN JANUARY 29, 1843
DIED SEPTEMBER 14, 1901

The next day at 11:00 a.m., a service was held at the Milburn house for family and invited friends, including President Roosevelt, who had visited the home the day before to console Ida. Soldiers guarded each entrance to ensure no uninvited people entered. Reverend Charles Edward Locke from the Methodist Episcopal Church on Delaware Avenue read from 1 Corinthians Chapter 15, and a four-person choir from Buffalo's First Presbyterian Church performed "Lead, Kindly Light." The *New York Tribune* described the funeral as having "no pomp, no harsh stiffness of painful ceremony."[13] It was too much for McKinley's widow to bear. Ida, following the precedent set by several other first ladies, did not attend; instead, distraught and sedated, she listened from the top of the stairs.

Four servicemen lifted the coffin while the choir sang the president's favorite hymn that he had repeated in his final hours, "Nearer, My God, to Thee." Four black horses pulled the hearse down Delaware Avenue to the iconic Buffalo City Hall. The Milburn home, for the first time since McKinley's arrival, was quiet. The *Buffalo Evening News* reported that the house "was left to the curious ones and to the police," stationed outside to keep away souvenir hunters who tried to chip off pieces of the now-historic home.

The procession arrived at City Hall as a light rain began to fall. The soldiers carried the coffin inside and placed it on a catafalque beneath the rotunda. The viewing lasted from 1:20 p.m. to 10:35 p.m., and an estimated 100,000 to 200,000 people braved the rain to see the remains. They noted the president's appearance "was not greatly emaciated. The most noticeable difference was that his usual pallor had been succeeded by sallowness."[14] Five minutes later, the coffin was closed, and it remained in the great hall throughout the evening, guarded by soldiers from the battleship *Indiana*. At 7:51 a.m. on Monday, September 16, eight soldiers—four marines and four veterans from the Grand Army of the Republic—gingerly raised the coffin. A military band again played "Nearer, My God, to Thee" as they slowly walked down the hall, stepped outside, and placed it in a funeral hearse. The procession to the train station was led by the Buffalo police department, followed by several military regiments, including gray-haired veterans of the Grand Army of the Republic. They marched slowly from Church Street to Main Street, passing crowds who removed their hats and bowed their heads, silent save for the sounds of weeping. It was a short but solemn journey, and at 8:10 a.m. the procession arrived at the Central Depot on Exchange Street. Thirty-six years earlier, Abraham Lincoln's funeral train stopped at the same station.[15]

McKinley's body was placed in the last train car, Olympia, on a bier set high enough to be visible through the windows. The entire car was draped in black, the only color provided by the American flag that covered the casket. At 8:20 a.m., President Roosevelt arrived and boarded the car Hungary. Also in the funeral train were the cars Naples (in which rode John G. Milburn), Waldorf (the dining car), Pacific, and Raleigh pulled by engine #34 under the command of J. P. Heindell.[16]

At 8:37 a.m., the funeral train slowly began its trip to Washington, DC, and a few moments later, Ida asked to be alone with her husband's remains. The lid was raised and the honor guards left for 40 minutes. At 11:55 a.m., the engines and crew changed in Renova, Pennsylvania. The train passed through Williamsport, Pennsylvania, at 2:30 p.m., where 8,000 schoolchildren had gathered and church bells tolled. Throughout the 420-mile journey there were many tearful demonstrations beside the tracks: bands played, choirs sang, soldiers saluted, and ordinary citizens gathered on bridges and fences. Even mechanics on the job laid down their tools and removed their hats. It was estimated that half a million people saw the train along the 12-hour ride.

The train arrived on a cloudy Monday night at Washington's Pennsylvania Railroad Station. The station was crowded with soldiers and sailors in bright uniforms, and President Roosevelt stood confident and erect. If he was nervous at the enormity of his responsibility, he did not show it. Eight body bearers—four soldiers from Fort McHenry and four sailors—carried the coffin outside to Sixth Street and placed it into an "exquisitely carved" hearse as a bugler played Taps. Just as they were performing their duty, a photographer captured the scene. In 1901, the bright flash and pop of the bulb made quite a commotion, disturbing the solemn display and rendering President Roosevelt "momentarily disconcerted."[17] Six black horses, each led by an African American groom dressed in black, pulled the hearse down Pennsylvania Avenue. Leading the procession was a platoon of mounted police followed by soldiers from the Grand Army of the Republic and from the recent Spanish-American War (who walked along with cavalrymen on horseback). The hearse was followed by carriages, one of which carried the new president. Displays of mourning lined the route, and thousands of citizens witnessed the procession behind a rope barricade. The hearse arrived at the White House at 9:30 p.m., and the coffin was placed in the East Room on a black-draped bier. Dignitaries passed by the coffin, including President Roosevelt, but no ceremonies were held that evening. Eight honor guards, including two Civil War veterans, watched the remains overnight.

At 9:30 a.m. on Tuesday, September 17, a procession brought McKinley's remains to the Capitol building in a light drizzle. Earlier that morning, cleaning crews had worked double-time to clear scaffolding and heavy machinery, as the building was in the midst of renovations. President Roosevelt and the only living former president, Grover Cleveland, were both in the procession. Congressmen marched in unison in black suits and top hats, and the hearse was pulled by six midnight-black horses. It arrived at 10:12 a.m. and eight body bearers placed the remains beneath the rotunda on the same catafalque used years earlier for the funeral services of the only other two assassinated presidents, Abraham Lincoln and James Garfield.

The coffin was opened, and the crowd of 800 took their seats. The Methodist service began with "Lead, Kindly Light," followed by an invocation by Reverend Henry R. Naylor from the Washington District M. E. Church, and the choir sang "Some Time We'll Understand." Next was a sermon by McKinley's good friend, Bishop Edward G. Andrews from Ohio's Methodist Episcopal Church. He spoke eloquently of McKinley's moral character, noting that even his political opponents respected and admired him. He concluded by placing McKinley in the pantheon of the presidential elite, proclaiming that his "name shall be counted among the illustrious of the earth . . . Washington lives in the hearts of his countrymen. Lincoln, with his infinite sorrow, lives to teach us and lead us on. And McKinley shall summon all statesmen and his countrymen to purer living, nobler aims, sweeter faith and immortal blessedness." To conclude, Reverend W. H. Chapman, acting pastor of the Methodist Church, offered the benediction.[18]

The hall was opened to the public at approximately noon. Though the state funeral was originally planned for Wednesday, Ida had demanded that it be held on Tuesday, which led to a lower attendance than expected, particularly for those west of Chicago.[19] Still, 65,000 people paid their respects, and when the doors closed at 7:30 p.m., many were still waiting in line. Before the coffin was closed, the guards scurried over to gaze upon the deceased before the Eleventh Cavalry escorted the remains to the train station. This was a silent procession, without music or drum cadence, and those that lined the streets stood quietly. The coffin was placed in the funeral car, toward the back of the 20 cars that made up the elongated train. At 8:10 p.m., the train departed west for the final journey to Canton, Ohio.

Throughout the night, the funeral train traversed Pennsylvania, traveling through Harrisburg, Altoona, Pittsburgh, and over the Allegheny Mountains. Thousands of people lined the tracks, and coal miners exited their workplaces to catch a glimpse of the funeral car illuminated by electric lights. Crossing into Ohio, the train slowed down to allow citizens to get a better view in the morning light. Church bells tolled when it arrived in Canton at 11:08 a.m. on Wednesday, September 18.

Almost immediately after the announcement of the president's death, a funeral planning committee had been established in Canton, led by Mayor James Robertson. Canton swelled for the event, as 100,000 people flooded into the city of 30,000, along with the 6,000–7,000 Ohio National Guardsmen brought in to keep order. The eight honorary pallbearers escorted the coffin to a hearse provided by the Canton Home Furnishing Company, owned by local merchants Hugh Daniel McCrea and J. L. Arnold.[20] Four black horses slowly pulled the hearse to the Court House, where years earlier McKinley had argued cases as a Stark County prosecutor. Lining the route were 50,000 people, and the Grand Army of the Republic band once again played "Nearer, My God, to Thee," which had become the unofficial theme song for the McKinley funeral proceedings. The casket was placed on a bier and the lid opened. Only two lights were illuminated, strategically concealing the discolored features of McKinley, now four days deceased.

At 1:15 p.m., people entered to pass the coffin at a rate of approximately 10,000 per hour. At 6:00 p.m., with thousands more still in line, the doors were closed. The coffin was taken to the home that McKinley had shared with his wife at 723 Market Avenue North and placed in the library. On Thursday, September 19, Ida sat alone with the remains for one last time.[21]

At 1:14 p.m., the final procession began. The hearse was flanked by soldiers on both sides and followed by national and Ohio military regiments. Hundreds of civic and fraternal organizations marched in the two-mile parade, including Knights Templars from Canton, Louisville, and Pittsburgh; Knights of Pythias; Free Masons; and Odd Fellows. Playing a somber dirge was the Grand Army of the Republic Band and Thayer's Military Band. Soldiers stood with bayonets in hand to make way for the flower-covered casket as it was carried into the First Methodist Church at 120 Cleveland Avenue. With the organist playing Beethoven's funeral march, the casket was placed on the catafalque. Sitting up front was President Roosevelt, and behind him were 40 senators, 120 members of the House of Representatives, and many more government officials. The remaining members of McKinley's old regiment, the Twenty-Third Ohio, were also in attendance, carrying their tattered flags. McKinley's pew was vacant and draped in black. Not in the church that afternoon, still unable to deal with the sudden and shocking turn of events, was Ida.[22]

The church was decorated with black crepe, and at the foot of the bier was a portrait of McKinley framed within a wreath of brightly colored flowers. More flowers adorned the churches, including arrangements provided by the Knights and Free Masons. The ceremony started at approximately 2:00 p.m. and was officiated by religious leaders from many different churches. The Reverend O. B. Milligan, pastor of the First Presbyterian Church, began with the invocation, Dr. John B. Hall of Trinity

Lutheran Church read the 19th Psalm, Reverend E. P. Herbruck read from 1 Corinthians, Dr. C. E. Manchester delivered a 24-page sermon, and Bishop I. W. Joyce from Minneapolis said a brief prayer. Concluding the ceremony was yet another rendition of "Nearer, My God, to Thee" and a benediction by the chaplain of the Twenty-Ninth Infantry, Father Valtman, from Chicago.[23]

Cities around the country held memorial services to coincide with the funeral in Canton. One tribute made to McKinley was a first in presidential history. At 2:30 p.m., virtually all telegraph lines throughout the United States were silenced for five minutes. The Postal Telegraph Company was so adamant about ceasing messages during these moments that the "dynamos were disconnected at the ends, literally draining the circuits of electricity, so that everywhere all the wires were technically and literally 'dead.'"[24]

The service in Canton, long by presidential funeral standards, ended at 3:30 p.m. As Chopin's "Funeral March" played, the coffin was removed. A procession a mile and a half long then escorted the remains to the West Lawn Cemetery, marching from Tuscarwas Street to Lincoln Avenue to West Third Street. Soldiers and spectators lined the route and filled the windows and rooftops. The cortege arrived at 4:04 p.m. and proceeded to Werts Receiving Vault for a brief 20-minute ceremony read by Bishop Joyce. The services closed with Taps, hymns by Thayer's Military Band and the Knights Templar male chorus, and a final artillery salute by Cleveland's Battery A. People quickly filed out, but federal army sentries remained. They guarded the tomb from all angles; one stood in front of the vault, another on a grassy hill behind it, and another at the foot of the casket. The sentries remained at their post every day for the next six years. Less than two weeks after the burial, a sentry was stabbed by two prowlers, who escaped into the night.[25]

Ida, who did not attend the burial, visited in privacy the day after and would continue to do so every day for the next three years. After her death on May 26, 1907, her remains were placed alongside McKinley's in the receiving vault.

On the day of the interment, several of the president's closest advisors, including his former secretary of state, William R. Day, and Ohio senator Marcus Hanna, convened to discuss a permanent memorial. Shortly after his death, it was published that "in due time the body will be taken from the vault and committed to the little plot of ground further on. This is the McKinley lot. When that time comes a stately shaft of granite will rise above the grave, telling of the civic virtues, the pure life and the martyr death of William McKinley."[26] The two advisors chose a site often visited by McKinley. He had liked it so much that he had suggested

Werts Receiving Vault in Canton's West Lawn Cemetery, where McKinley's remains rested for six years.

that a monument to commemorate the soldiers and sailors from Stark County be built there.

On September 26, 1901, the McKinley National Memorial Association was formed "for the purpose of erecting and maintaining at Canton, Ohio, a suitable memorial to William McKinley and for the raising of necessary funds."[27] The Board of Trustees was appointed by President Roosevelt based on Ida's recommendations, with William R. Day and Marcus Hanna named president and vice president respectively. They met for the first time in Cleveland on November 6, after appealing to the public for $600,000 a month earlier. In a show of support, Ohio governor George K. Nash proclaimed January 29, 1902, which would have been McKinley's 58th birthday, a day for Ohio schoolchildren to donate their coins to the memorial fund. Small steel banks were placed throughout local communities, and by June 1903, they had raised enough to purchase 26 acres from the West Lawn Cemetery. In the end, more than one million people donated a total of approximately $600,000, an average of less than 60¢ per donor. With the land and funds secured, the association now focused on what to build there. On June 22, 1903, they announced a design competition, with a first prize of $1,500. Over 60 entries were submitted by the January 1, 1904, deadline. Architect Harold Van Buren Magonigle of New York was the winner.

Magonigle was born in New Jersey in 1867 and had once been employed by McKim, Mead and White, the firm that in 1915 designed the Romanesque National McKinley Birthplace Memorial in Niles, Ohio, and in 1949 directed renovations of the White House.[28] Magonigle's design was a massive structure resembling, from above, a combina-

tion cross and sword. The blade of the sword was created by using reflecting pools that stretched out 575 feet in front of the monument in five levels and were known as "The Long Water." On May 31, 1905, the Harrison Granite Company of New York was contracted to build the monument for $257,600 and the approaches for $109,462. Gotham Manufacturing of New York and Rhode Island was hired to do the bronze work for $10,670, and Ed Lander of Canton was hired to build the reflecting pools. When the final bills were tallied up, the cost of the tomb was $558,452.91.[29]

Construction officially began on June 6, 1905, when Magonigle ceremoniously dug the first shovelful of dirt. Excavation for the foundation began during the following month on July 20. On November 16, the cornerstone was laid at a ceremony attended by Ida and other family members. William R. Day was the Master of Ceremonies, and a time capsule filled with McKinley memorabilia was placed inside the cornerstone. Over the next two years, work continued on the memorial tomb. It incorporated material from nine states: Ohio supplied the concrete and brick, exterior granite came from Massachusetts, Tennessee provided the marble walls, pedestal, and part of the marble floor, and other materials came from New York, Pennsylvania, Vermont, Wisconsin, Illinois, and Rhode

The McKinley Monument in Canton, Ohio.

Island. The labor force was just as diverse as the materials, with many African Americans traveling from the South to work on the tomb, partially motivated by their admiration for the 25th president.

There are 108 steps to the memorial entrance and midway is a statue of the president sculpted by Ohio native Charles Henry Niehaus, depicting McKinley giving his last speech the day before he was shot. The entrance to the memorial is made of two great bronze doors, which were the world's largest when they were first built. Inside the memorial room is an interior dome 75 feet high and 50 feet in diameter. The original plans called for an elaborate red, white, and blue skylight with 45 stars, one for each state at the time of McKinley's death. A clear skylight was installed instead, possibly because at the time of the completion in September 1907, Oklahoma was on the verge of becoming state number 46.

With the monument completed, soldiers were placed on guard. On September 18, the two coffins in Werts Receiving Vault were pried open and the bodies were carefully removed and placed into new copper caskets purchased from the Arnold Funeral Home. The *Lewiston Morning Tribune* reported that the state of preservation of McKinley's body was "remarkably good."[30] The dedication ceremony, one of the biggest events in Canton history, took over one year to plan and was held on Monday, September 30, 1907. Day reprised his role as the master of ceremonies, and the president's sister, Helen McKinley, unveiled the statue in the middle of the staircase.[31] President Roosevelt, accompanied by Vice President Charles Warren Fairbanks, was also in attendance. In Roosevelt's address he said, "We have gathered together to pay our meed of respect and affection to the memory of William McKinley, who as president won a place in the hearts of the American people such as but three or four of all of the presidents of this century have ever won."[32] One detail the public

was not aware of was that the body of McKinley was not yet inside the new memorial. Whether this was an overt lie or a falsehood by omission is unknown. Ten days later, on October 10, the caskets were placed in the raised, green granite sarcophagi inside the monument. McKinley's daughters Katie and Ida, who had died as children, were also reinterred in the north wall of the memorial.

THE WILLIAM MCKINLEY DEATH SITES
Assassination Site

The site where William McKinley was shot is commemorated by a historic marker located on the median of suburban Fordham Drive between Elmwood Avenue and Lincoln Parkway. The bronze plaque on a granite boulder reads: IN THE PAN-AMERICAN TEMPLE OF MUSIC WHICH COVERED THIS SPOT PRESIDENT MCKINLEY WAS FATALLY SHOT SEPT. 4, 1901. THIS MARKER PLACED BY THE BUFFALO HISTORICAL SOCIETY.

The marker was unveiled on June 28, 1921, by the Buffalo Historical Society. A small crowd gathered for the ceremony, including representatives from the Historical Society and members of the Grand Army posts. The marker was not placed in the exact shooting location, for reasons explained in a 1921 Buffalo Historical Society publication: "We have not attempted to fix the exact point in the Temple of Music where the

The marker on Fordham Drive in Buffalo, New York, near the site where McKinley was shot at the Temple of Music.

president stood when shot. The marker has been set here because, in this strip of parking, it is readily seen without obstructing the street, without infringing on any private property, and because it is well within the area formerly covered by the Temple of Music."[33] When visiting, drive slowly and keep your eyes open, because despite the claim that it is "readily seen," it is quite easy to miss.

Location of Death

The home where the president died, located at 1168 Delaware Avenue, was built in 1861 for George C. Vaughan. Over the next 27 years, it changed hands frequently, having five more owners through 1888.[34] In 1888, the home was purchased by a prominent lawyer, John G. Milburn. After being chosen as president of the Pan-American Exposition Company, Milburn remodeled his home in anticipation of hosting dignitaries. When he learned of McKinley's visit, he extended an offer for the president and his wife to stay with him. They slept upstairs in a spacious 18-by-20-foot bedroom on the north side of the home.

The site of the Milburn home where McKinley died. The home was demolished in 1957 to make way for a parking lot.

After the president's death, tourists and locals alike would flock to see the historic home. Some would pick up a leaf, a twig, or blades of grass as a souvenir, while other relic hunters knocked off chips from their steps. The Milburns sold the home in 1904 to Phillip M. Shannon. On January 10, 1907, a fire broke out in the home. While the building was not completely lost, the room where McKinley died was heavily damaged. In November 1919, locals lamented that the "McKinley Death Chamber will soon disappear," after Shannon converted the historic home into apartments.[35] Shannon hired George W. Butler to do the construction and was committed to preserving the wood from the historic room. He also warned that once completed, the death chamber would be unrecognizable. In 1928, the apartment building was purchased by Conrad Wettlaufer, who expanded its capacity to eight units. In 1948, the Jesuit community of Canisius High School purchased the building, transformed it into a cloister, and moved into the apartments.

In 1957, the story of the Milburn home came to an end. The historic home was torn down for a parking lot. Today, the site where the home once stood is dubbed "Parking Lot 4." At the location is an undated roadside marker that reads: SITE OF THE MILBURN HOUSE HERE DIED WILLIAM MCKINLEY SEPTEMBER 14, 1901 BUFFALO HISTORICAL SOCIETY.

Lying in Repose: Canton Court House

The Stark County Court House is located at 115 Central Plaza North. The current courthouse is the third at that location, the first dating back to as early as 1818. The original was torn down and replaced with an Italianate structure that was constructed from 1868–1870. It was during these years that McKinley was elected prosecuting attorney of Stark County. Within 20 years, the county had outgrown the courthouse, and Cleveland architect George Hammond was commissioned to expand and redesign it. His design was in the Beaux Arts Classicism style, and he added the imposing clock tower crowned by the "Trumpeters of Justice." It was completed in 1895, six years before hosting the solemn McKinley viewing. On April 3, 1975, the building was added to the National Register of Historic Places (#75001534). In the 1990s, it underwent major renovations to return it to its original appearance.

Canton Home

The home that the McKinleys owned and where the remains were taken before McKinley's burial was located at 723 Market Avenue North. It is most noted as the home where he ran his "front porch campaign" for president in 1896, when approximately 750,000 people stood on his front lawn to hear him speak. After his death, Ida continued to live there and, except for almost daily visits to McKinley's tomb, she rarely left the house. The traumatized widow confided to friends that she dared not go out because she was waiting for her husband's ghost to contact her. For many years she was deeply depressed and told friends she wanted to join her husband in death. Later on, her desire to see the completion of the memorial became her inspiration to survive.[36] Sadly, she did not make it. Four months prior to its completion, Ida passed away in the home on May 26, 1907. Her deathbed was a familiar scene. With her at the end were her husband's personal secretary, Cortelyou, and his personal physician, Rixey, both of whom were also with McKinley when he died in Buffalo. Three days after Ida's death, a small funeral was held in the library, the same room where McKinley's body rested overnight on Septem-

ber 18, 1901. President Theodore Roosevelt traveled to Canton to attend the funeral services for Ida.[37] The home is no longer in existence and in its place is now the Stark County Library. In 2003, a historic marker was erected at the site by the Ohio Historical Society.

Canton Funeral

The First Methodist Church is located in downtown Canton at 120 Cleveland Avenue (known as the "Hall of Fame Corridor") and Tuscarawas (known as "The Lincoln Highway"). At the corner are the stairs where McKinley's body was carried in. It was added to the National Register of Historic Places (#79001948) on April 16, 1979.

Receiving Vault

The Werts Receiving Vault is in Canton's West Lawn Cemetery (adjacent to the McKinley National Memorial) to the left of the entrance. It was erected in 1893, after the Board of the Canton Cemetery Association voted to build a temporary receiving vault to use during winter months when freezing temperatures made the ground too difficult to dig. The cost for construction was covered by Mrs. Frank M. Werts in exchange for a plaque on the vault for her late husband (it can be seen atop the iron gate). Today, there is an undated informative display in front of the vault.

The Tomb

After its completion, the McKinley National Memorial Association continued to maintain the site, but over time it became a financial burden. They tried unsuccessfully to turn it over to the National Park Service in 1939. Failing, they continued to look for a suitor until finally, on October 23, 1943, the site was transferred to the Ohio State Archaeological and Historical Society (today known as the Ohio Historical Society).[38]

The tiered reflecting pools have not stood the

test of time, as the water that was intended to flow instead turned stagnant and fetid. In September 1920, Magonigle was the first to propose filling them in. Thirty years later, in 1951, this was finally done, and today there is a grassy divider between the entrance and exit roads.[39]

Several significant events happened over the following decades. On September 16, 1951, a rededication ceremony was held. In 1973, management of the site was transferred to the Stark County Historical Society (who also manages the adjacent William McKinley Presidential Library & Museum). Two years later, on May 15, 1975, it was recognized as a National Historical Landmark (#70000516). The following year, the original skylight design was installed.

On September 26, 1992, another rededication ceremony was held, featuring a Theodore Roosevelt impersonator, to recognize the partnership undertaken by the federal government, local foundations, and private citizens to honor the memory of McKinley.

Today, while the monument is second to the Football Hall of Fame for most Canton tourists, it is still visited by 200,000 people each year and is popular with joggers.

The tomb is located at 800 McKinley Monument Drive NW, Canton, Ohio, 44708. It is open from April 1 through November 1 from 9:00 a.m. to 4:00 p.m. Monday–Saturday and from noon to 4:00 p.m. on Sunday For more information, visit: www.McKinleyMuseum.org.

Grover Cleveland ★ *1885–1889 and 1893–1897*

CRITICAL DEATH INFORMATION:

Date of death:	June 24, 1908, 8:40 p.m.
Cause of death:	Heart failure complicated with pulmonary thrombosis and edema
Age at death:	71 years, 98 days
Last words:	"I have tried so hard to do right."
Place of death:	Home at 15 Hodge Road, Princeton, New Jersey
Funeral:	Home at 15 Hodge Road, Princeton, New Jersey
Final resting place:	The Princeton Cemetery, Princeton, New Jersey
Reinterred:	No
Cost to visit grave:	Free
For more information:	www.PrincetonOL.com/groups/cemetery
Significance:	Cleveland's life spanned a record-tying nineteen presidents: He was born during the Martin Van Buren administration and died during Theodore Roosevelt's (tied with Herbert Hoover).

During the last two years of his life, Grover Cleveland suffered from multiple medical ailments, including gastrointestinal, heart, and kidney disease. The former president was a private man and chose to deal with his health issues as such. In March 1908, Cleveland, who had been living in Princeton for more than a decade, went to recuperate at the Lakewood Hotel in southern New Jersey. But even under constant medical care, his condition continued to deteriorate. He longed for his home in Princeton and returned in late May.[1] By mid-June, with Cleveland's health improved, his children left for the family summer home in Tamworth, New Hampshire.

Things took a tragic turn when, at 2:00 p.m.

on June 23, he went into heart failure. His long-time friend and physician, Dr. Joseph D. Bryant, came from New York along with lung specialist George R. Lockwood. They arrived at the home at 4:24 p.m., where they joined Cleveland's family physician, Dr. John M. Carnochan. Unfortunately, there was little they could do. That night, Cleveland lay in his second-floor front bedroom and drifted in and out of consciousness. Much of what he mumbled was inaudible, but his final recorded words were, "I have tried so hard to do right." As a two-time president with a reputation as one of the most honest men to hold office, indeed he had. At about 6:30 a.m., he fell unconscious for the last time. Grover Cleveland died two hours later at 8:40 a.m. on Wednesday, June 24, 1908. Along with his three doctors, his wife Frances was also at his bedside at the final moment.[2]

His doctors released a statement: "Heart failure complicated with pulmonary thrombosis and edema were the immediate cause of death."[3] Later that night, a death mask was made by sculptor Edward Wilson. The mask startled those that had not seen Cleveland in a while. It showed how frail and withered the once robust president had become, as he had lost almost 100 pounds in the later years of his life. The *Toledo News* lamented, "It shows Cleveland had failed greatly since the last published photos of him were taken." The newspaper continued, "Wasting at the temples and just below the cheek bones betray the falling away that resulted from Mr. Cleveland's disease."[4]

President Theodore Roosevelt, now with no living predecessors, was about to leave for New London, Connecticut, when he learned of Cleveland's death. He immediately canceled his plans and made arrangements to travel to Princeton. He also issued a proclamation in which he called for 30 days of mourning and praised Cleveland's post-presidency years: "Since his retirement from the presidency he has continued to serve his countrymen by the simplicity, dignity and uprightness of his private life."[5]

Presidential candidate William Howard Taft was in New Haven, Connecticut, visiting his alma mater. That evening, he spoke at a Yale alumni dinner and devoted part of his speech to a touching and heartfelt tribute to Cleveland:

"He was a great man and a great president. He had the highest civic ideals, a rugged honesty, a high courage. These things will now make him happy in death. As he leaves the world he is revered, loved and respected by his countrymen."[6]

Cleveland's widow directed the funeral arrangements. Since her husband was so private in life, she wanted his funeral ceremonies to be as discreet as presidential decorum permitted. The funeral she planned was perhaps the most simple of all of the presidents'. The *Toledo News* summed it up,

The home where Grover Cleveland died, as it looked in 1903. (Library of Congress)

saying, "With none of the pomp and ceremony, which former President Grover Cleveland shunned, to mark the services, the body of the 'sage of Princeton' will be laid to rest."[7] Like Chester Arthur's widow, Frances did not want any military formalities, but when it was confirmed that Roosevelt would attend, she conceded to their presence to protect the president.

The day after his death, Cleveland's body was embalmed and placed in an oak casket with silver handles in the second-floor bedroom where he died.[8] Upon the casket was a silver plate with the plain inscription:

GROVER CLEVELAND
MARCH 18, 1837–JUNE 24, 1908

On Friday, June 26, simple services were held in the Cleveland home. Visitors began to arrive in Princeton around 2:00 p.m. on trains specially arranged for the occasion. Close friends and family made their way there, and, as the *New York Times* reported, the most intimate "Slipped upstairs for a last look at the face of their departed friend, white and composed in death."[9] Those not as close with the former president went to the Princeton Inn to wait for the funeral to start at 5:00 p.m. Before all of the guests had arrived, the lid was closed and the coffin was carried downstairs to a reception room and adorned with floral arrangements.

President Roosevelt and the First Lady arrived from Oyster Bay, New York, and were met at the station by New Jersey governor John Franklin Fort. Arriving after the casket had been sealed, Roosevelt was denied a final look upon his predecessor. He offered his condolences to Frances (who would turn 44 the next month) and promptly took his seat. There were about 100 people in attendance, filling the reception room and spilling into the adjoining library. Chief Justice Melville Weston Fuller, New York governor Charles Evans Hughes, Georgia governor Hoke Smith, and Secretary of the Treasury George Cortelyou, who had been with President William McKinley both when he was shot and when he died eight days later, were among the mourners.

At 5:00 p.m., the widow entered wearing a black veil and dress. Reverend Sylvester W. Beach of the First Presbyterian Church of Princeton, where the Clevelands worshipped, read the committal service. Cleveland's former pastor, Reverend Maitland V. Bartlett of the West Farms Presbyterian Church of New York, followed him with the president's favorite Scripture readings from the Books of John and Thessalonians. Reverend Henry Van Dyke, president of the Princeton Theological Seminary, then spoke: "According to the request of one whose slightest wish at this moment we all respect, there will be no address or sermon, but there was a poem written more than 100 years ago by William Wordsworth, which is expressive of his character," and he read "Character of the Happy Warrior"

The funeral procession for Grover Cleveland. (Library of Congress)

to conclude the service.[10] It lasted only 30 minutes, featured no singing, and, as Cleveland's widow wished, was "simple and unostentatious and conducted with extreme privacy."[11]

The pallbearers carried the coffin to the hearse and walked beside it to the cemetery.[12] Five minutes after the service ended, the 26-carriage procession was already in motion. In the seventh carriage rode President Roosevelt, followed by four Secret Service men. It passed flags at half-mast and homes and businesses decorated in mourning, the latter ordered closed by the mayor and town council. All was silent, save for the tolling bells from Nassau Hall. No military bands were playing. Nearly the entire Princeton population of 5,000 was scattered behind ropes along the route, heads bowed and hats in hand.[13] A much larger crowd had been expected. Out of concern that they might not be able to handle the masses, the small Princeton police force had been augmented by National Guardsmen from all over the state. Their task, as the *New York Times* reported, was to "handle the great crowd that was expected." However, as the *Times* continued, they "did not come."[14]

For three-quarters of a mile the procession wound its way through Princeton from Bayard Lane to Nassau Street to Vandeventer Avenue and then to Wiggins Street, until it reached the entrance of the Princeton Cemetery. When it arrived, shortly before 6:00 p.m., a small crowd of 200 people were gathered at the grave for the sunset burial. New York mayor George B. McClellan Jr., son of the Civil War general, led the way, followed by the pallbearers.

Reverend William M. Richards from Brick Presbyterian Church of New York read the graveside service. The brief service lasted only five minutes and, incredibly, the funeral, procession, and burial had taken barely an hour. Even before all of the carriages had arrived, the coffin was lowered into the open grave beside the Clevelands' daughter, Ruth, who had died four years earlier. Friends lined up to drop a shovelful of dirt into the grave. Roosevelt offered Frances his condolences before stepping into his carriage to return to the station.

Several days later, a headstone was placed on the grave with a simple inscription: GROVER CLEVELAND BORN CALDWELL, NJ MARCH 18TH, 1837 DIED PRINCETON, NJ JUNE 24TH, 1908. In later years there was a discussion about erecting a "handsome memorial" that never did come to fruition.[15]

While the remains of President Cleveland are now six feet beneath Princeton soil, one small piece of him can still be seen today. During his presidency, Cleveland had a secret operation on July 1, 1893, aboard a boat in the Long Island Sound to remove a tumor from his upper left jaw. This tumor is now on display at the Mutter Museum in Philadelphia. The cheek retractor and laryngeal mirror that had been used by Dr. Joseph Bryant, who cared for Cleveland on his deathbed, are also on display.[16]

THE GROVER CLEVELAND DEATH SITES
The Lakewood Hotel

The Lakewood Hotel, where Cleveland went to recuperate before his death, was constructed in 1891 by a group led by Nathan Strauss. It was built on 14 acres from Clifton Avenue to Lexington Avenue in Lakewood, New Jersey. Despite its proximity to the beach, the hotel's high season occurred during the winter, when it served as headquarters for the New York political machine, Tammany Hall. Cleveland arrived at the tail end of the season, but the hotel graciously stayed open to accommodate the former president. In later years, it was used as a rest and rehabilitation center for wounded World War I soldiers.[17]

Location of Death

The two-and-a-half story Colonial-style home where Cleveland died is located at 15 Hodge

Road, Princeton, New Jersey. In 1896, the Clevelands visited Princeton for the historic college's 150th anniversary and were enthralled with the small town and their warm reception. With the recommendation and encouragement of friend Andrew West, the Clevelands retired to Princeton after his term in 1897. The modest home was painted white and surrounded by pine trees, and, in honor of his friend, he named the home Westland. Cleveland was well received in the town. Students marched to his home to celebrate football victories and gathered at Westland to serenade him on his birthday.[18] For years he remained active and delivered an occasional lecture at the university. He was also awarded an honorary degree from the prestigious college.

After his death, several other families owned the home, and it remains a private residence. There have been a number of changes to the home, both interior and exterior. The home was recently owned by the Sipprelle family, who hung a portrait of Cleveland in their billiard room. In 2010, the owner told a reporter for the local *US-1* newspaper, "I sleep in the room that Grover Cleveland died in. I've become fascinated with his life story."[19] If you visit, please keep in mind it is a private residence and not open to visitors.

Cemetery

The Princeton Cemetery on the corner of Wiggins and Witherspoon Streets was established in 1757 on a single acre of land purchased by Princeton University (then known as the College of New Jersey) from Judge Thomas Leonard. Additional acreage was added in 1801 when Dr. Thomas Wiggins donated his farm situated adjacent to the cemetery. Additional donations brought the cemetery to its current 19 acres. With the large number of dignitaries buried on the grounds, it earned the moniker "The Westminster Abbey of the United States." The oldest grave in the cemetery is that of Aaron Burr Sr., father of Vice President Aaron Burr, who was also buried in the cemetery in 1757.

The area designated as the "President's Plot" is for the former presidents of Princeton University (all but four are buried here) and *not* where Cleveland is buried. Cleveland's grave (marked #11 on the cemetery map) is near Witherspoon Street, between Quarry and Green Streets. Like the man, it is not ostentatious and does not stand out in the cemetery. It can be easily spotted, as it is usually covered in coins and Hawaiian shell necklaces. The former can be found on many presidents' graves for the same reason people used to place coins on the deceased's eyes (see Lincoln chapter). The latter are offered because Cleveland is universally admired by natives of the Aloha State for having opposed the annexation of Hawaii and following a policy of nonintervention during both of his administrations.

Nearby are his good friend

The home where Cleveland died, as it looks today.

and pallbearer, John H. Finley, and George H. Gallup, founder of the American Institute of Public Opinion, today best known for his namesake polls. Another notable resident is Richard Stockton Jr., one of the signers of the Declaration of Independence. The cemetery is open from dawn to dusk every day.[20] The current superintendent is Douglas Sutphen, and his family has been running the cemetery for more than a century. When asked about the people who come to visit, Sutphen replied, "Oh yeah, they all want to see the same graves, Aaron Burr and Grover Cleveland. There are people who travel all over just seeing the presidents."[21]

On March 18, 2015, I visited Princeton for the annual birthday wreath-laying ceremony. After reading about so many of these tributes in old newspapers, I was eager to see one in person. I arrived early and parked on Hodge Road by the Cleveland home. I walked to the cemetery, following the same route of the funeral procession over a century earlier. At the end of Hodge, I turned south onto Bayard Lane. Today, this road is better known as Route 206. After two blocks, I turned left on to Nassau Street. This is the main

business area, and it is along this stretch that most of the 5,000 spectators would have been thinly dispersed. To the right is Princeton University where, during Cleveland's time, Woodrow Wilson was president of the college. The procession went the length of the business district before it turned left onto Vandeventer Avenue, which today is the site of the Princeton movie theater. At my leisurely pace, the walk took only 16 minutes, just a few minutes less than the 26-carriage procession took in 1908. I arrived at Princeton Cemetery about an hour before the ceremony was to begin and saw several military personnel. Some were setting up, and some milling about, trying to keep warm as a small crowd trickled in.

After reading about such ceremonies for the lesser-known presidents, I wasn't surprised that the organizers and participants far outnumbered the spectators. The small attendance made it more poignant that our nation was committed to this annual ceremony, ensuring that even the most obscure of the presidents shall never be forgotten. As the military band struck up "Hail to the Chief," I knew I was in for a memorable experience. After an invocation by Chaplain Lieutenant Colonel William Steen, the band played Taps. The master of ceremonies for the event, Brigadier General Mikey Kloster, then spoke. She had hosted several other wreath-laying ceremonies for Cleveland and spoke about the meaning of his first name, Grover, as in a grove of trees. She skillfully spun an analogy of how his defeat and the resurrection of his political career resembled the rebirth each season of a grove of trees. Several more distinguished guests spoke, each covering a different portion of the life and legacy of Cleveland, all managing

Wreath-laying ceremony at Cleveland's grave on March 18, 2015, on what would have been the president's 178th birthday.

to weave his last words, "I have tried so hard to do right," into their speeches. The final speaker, a New Jersey assemblywoman, mentioned the current owners of Cleveland's home, commending them for maintaining its historic integrity. She also read from William Wordsworth's "Character of the Happy Warrior" just as Reverend Van Dyke did 107 years earlier.

With military precision, the red, white, and blue wreath, created by Princeton's Monday Morning Flower Shop, adhering to White House instructions, was placed at the tombstone by two honor guards. After the ceremony concluded, I approached the tombstone and a small swath of blue in the green grass caught my eye—a petal from one of the flowers had fallen off the wreath. Without thinking, I reached down and picked it up, slipping it in my pocket.

Theodore Roosevelt ★ *1901–1909*

CRITICAL DEATH INFORMATION:

Date of death:	January 6, 1919, between 4:00 and 4:15 a.m.
Cause of death:	Blood clot in his lung
Age at death:	60 years, 71 days
Last words:	"Please put out that light, James."
Place of death:	Home at Sagamore Hill, Oyster Bay, New York
Funeral:	Christ Church, Oyster Bay, New York
Final resting place:	Youngs Memorial Cemetery, Oyster Bay, New York
Reinterred:	No
Cost to visit grave:	Free
For more information:	www.TRGravesite.org
Significance:	Last president to die in a home that he had built for himself First president to receive a tribute by airplane First president to have his remains carried in an automobile hearse

After leaving the presidency in 1909, Theodore Roosevelt led an adventurous life including a hunting trip in Africa, another run at the presidency in 1912, and a 1914 expedition in Brazil that nearly killed him. However, eventually time began to catch up with him and in the autumn of 1918, Roosevelt suffered from inflammatory rheumatism (arthritis) that had often left him bedridden. It was speculated that his condition was the result of an infected tooth from 20 years earlier or a remnant of his trip to Brazil. On that adventure, Roosevelt journeyed deep inside the Amazon jungle as part of the first group ever to sail the mysterious "River of Doubt" (renamed "Rio Roosevelt" midway through the expedition). A leg injury had quickly become infected and, suffering a high fever, Roosevelt became incapacitated and decided to take a lethal dose of morphine he had packed for such a desperate situation. Better to be left behind than risk the rest of the expedition, he reasoned in his weakened state. Thankfully, his son Kermit convinced him otherwise, and Roosevelt was able to complete his last, and perhaps greatest, adventure.[1]

On November 11, 1918, the former president was admitted to Roosevelt Hospital, but was not worried; rather his mind was focused on considering a reentry into the political fray and running in the 1920 presidential race. By the end of December, doctors told Roosevelt that he might be wheelchair-bound for the rest of his life. Roosevelt took this news as one more challenge after he had already faced and overcome so many. After a staggering 44 days, he finally returned to his home in Sagamore Hill, on Christmas day. He quickly settled in to a routine and even went for drives on December 29 and 30. When asked about his heath, Roosevelt would respond with his trademark "Bully!" His doctor, George W. Faller, visited twice a week and found Roosevelt's health to be improving. Despite the optimism, his health was in decline, and on New Year's Eve he suffered severe back, hand, and leg pains.

On Saturday, January 4, 1919, Roosevelt did a full day's work, including penning articles for the *Kansas City Star* and the *Metropolitan Magazine*. He saw several visitors, including his barber, John Gerardi. Earlier, Gerardi had sent the president information to solicit his help with a local festival. Roosevelt rose and shook his hand warmly and said, "You don't have to send any of your circulars to me when you want something for the feast of Saint Rocco. Come yourself, John."[2]

He spent the next day quietly resting, saw no visitors, and did little work besides dictating a few letters. In the evening he sat and gazed out the window and told his wife, "I wonder if you will ever know how I love Sagamore Hill." Romanticists prefer to believe these were Roosevelt's last words, but that is not accurate. Around 11:00 p.m., he experienced difficulty breathing and heart pain. After helping him sit up, his wife, Edith, sent for Dr. Faller, who gave him a dose of morphine to make him more comfortable. Roosevelt felt better, and Faller left unconcerned.[3]

Around midnight, servant James Amos helped Roosevelt settle in for the night. Amos had a long history with Roosevelt and had worked for him in the White House. As he lay in bed, Roosevelt asked his old friend, "Please put out that light, James." Those were his last words. At 2:00 a.m., Edith looked in on him, found her husband sleeping, and went to bed herself, asking James to sleep in the next room to keep watch over her husband. Two hours later, James checked on Roosevelt and was startled to find his breathing very shallow. He called the nurse, but by the time she arrived, Roosevelt had stopped breathing. The nurse rushed to wake Edith, who ran to her husband's side, but was too late. Theodore Roosevelt died sometime between 4:00 and 4:15 a.m. on Monday, January 6, 1919.

It was determined that his death was caused by a blood clot that had entered his lungs. It was unrelated to the rheumatism, tooth injury, or his Brazilian adventures.[4] Regardless of what finally did him in, Roosevelt had lived a hard life. While in the White House, he was injured in a boxing match that resulted in the loss of vision in one eye. He also died with a bullet lodged in his chest from a 1912 assassination attempt by John Flammang Schrank while on the campaign trail. That day, he notoriously refused to capitulate and delivered his speech still wearing the bloodied shirt. For the rest of his life the slug remained buried in his chest.

Later that morning, Roosevelt's son Archie cabled his brothers in Germany to break the news. Theodore Jr.'s reply is now legendary: "The old lion is dead."[5] That afternoon, a unique homage was paid to the first president to die in the age of aviation: a tribute came from above when, under the command of Lieutenant M. S. Harmon, airplanes flew over Sagamore Hill in a "V" formation, barely clearing the trees and dropped laurel wreaths upon the estate. Airplanes continued to fly over the home to "keep watch" for several days.

The funeral was held on Wednesday, January 8, 1919. It was a snowy winter morning, but soon the skies cleared to reveal brilliant sunshine. Troops had offered to travel to Oyster Bay to honor the hero of San Juan Hill, but the family politely declined the gesture. Like Chester Arthur and Grover Cleveland, Roosevelt had requested a simple funeral. Roosevelt's body had been placed in an oak coffin, upon which were draped an American flag and two Rough Rider regimental banners. His good friend and pastor from Christ Church, Reverend George E. Talmage, led a short service in the North Room at Sagamore Hill for about 60 family members. There was no music or eulogy, but instead, Reverend Talmage read Roosevelt's favorite hymn, "How Firm a Foundation." One of Roosevelt's last wishes was that the funeral be private. This larger-than-life man did not want a larger-than-life funeral. Talmage commented, "We knew Colonel Roosevelt as just a plain, ordinary, unassuming man and his funeral is in keeping with his life."[6]

A procession carried the remains to Christ Church for the public funeral. It was led by New York City policemen on horseback. In another first for presidential funerals, an automobile replaced the horse-drawn caisson. The church, still decorated with Christmas flowers, seated only 350 peo-ple, but almost 500 were invited. While the pews overflowed inside, outside the church 3,000 to 4,000 more people had gathered.

President Woodrow Wilson was in Paris at the time of Roosevelt's death, but from overseas he issued the customary proclamation ordering flags at half-mast for 30 days.[7] He asked Vice President Thomas Marshall to attend on his behalf. Marshall perhaps summed up the old warrior's passing best: "Death had to take him sleeping, for if Roosevelt had been awake there would have been a fight."

Congressmen (including Ohio senator Warren G. Harding) and army, navy, and State Department representatives were also in attendance; however, no cabinet members were, in keeping with Roosevelt's wish that the funeral be kept small. Other organizations attended to honor the outdoor enthusiast president, including the Camp Fire Club, Harvard Club, and Boone and Crockett Club.[8] Arriving late was former president William Howard Taft, who slipped in the back and sat with Roosevelt's servants. In their younger days, the two had been good friends and politically simpatico, but when Taft strayed from

Theodore Roosevelt's funeral procession. (Library of Congress).

Roosevelt's policies, they had a falling out. Later in life, they had reconciled. Archie approached Taft and implored, "You're a dear personal friend and you must come up further."[9]

Reverend Talmage started the simple service at 12:53 p.m., and after it was completed, six pallbearers escorted the remains to the snow-covered Youngs Memorial Cemetery. Lining the route was a crowd estimated at 5,000 people.[10] Inside the cemetery, a few hundred were gathered, including many schoolchildren. The ceremony was brief. After the Lord's Prayer, the body was lowered into the ground at 2:59 p.m.

Soon after Roosevelt's death, his last will and testament was read, and his estate was valued at $810,607.82 including Sagamore Hill, worth $180,500. Other exotic items included $3,000 in elephant tusks and a $100 mounted onyx head.[11] Almost immediately, Roosevelt's grave became a pilgrimage destination for people from all over the world, but perhaps no group embraced it more than the Boy Scouts of America. The organization was incorporated in 1910, during Roosevelt's first years out of office, and "Roosevelt was one of the stanchest [sic] supporters of the Boy Scout movement during its early days."[12] He was so revered by the organization that he was given the honorary title of "Chief Scout Citizen." Roosevelt would occasionally go on hikes with local Troop 39.[13]

Traveling to the grave site on Roosevelt's birthday became an annual tradition for the Boy Scouts. For the first birthday after his death, some scouts carried a flag all the way from Buffalo to his grave, an impressive 400 miles! The flag began its trip with thirteen stripes, but no stars, and along the way, stars were sewn on until a total of 48 emblazoned it. Each mile, the flag was handed off to another scout, and throughout the journey, patriotic ceremonies were held by other groups, including the Daughters of the American Revolution.[14] The following year, 1,500 Boy Scouts from New York City visited on November 26, 1920. At the cemetery, they

Roosevelt's grave in Youngs Memorial Cemetery, Oyster Bay, New York.

took a pledge to uphold "100% Americanism" by honoring the man they called "the greatest of present-day Americans." The president's son, Lieutenant Colonel Theodore Roosevelt Jr., stood nearby as each Boy Scout dropped a chrysanthemum on the grave.[15]

The crowds increased at the ceremony as the years went by. On October 27, 1928, another 1,000 Boy Scouts visited on what would have been the Old Lion's 70th birthday.[16] On October 20, 1934, another 5,000 Boy Scouts from New York, Pennsylvania, Connecticut, and New Jersey stopped by. This was the largest scout group ever to visit the small cemetery, and the 15th consecutive year the Boy Scouts made the pilgrimage.[17] They were topped three years later when 6,000 Boy Scouts from as far away as Rhode Island and Massachusetts made the trip on October 16, 1937. That day, Roosevelt Jr. again greeted the young patriots.[18] After the end of World War II, on October 21, 1945, another 2,500 Boy Scouts visited, which was called "the largest turnout since the rationing of gasoline." Sadly, Roosevelt Jr., who attended so many events, had died the previous year. After surviving the D-Day landing at Normandy, the brigadier general died a month later of a heart attack in France on July 12, 1944. His wife, Eleanor Butler Alexander Roosevelt, attended and carried on his tradition.[19]

Two thousand Boy Scouts attended a year later on October 20, 1946. After a benediction by Reverend John N. Warren from Christ Church, author Hermann Hagedorn was the principal speaker.[20] On October 16, 1948, another 3,500 Boy Scouts came out to pay tribute to both Roosevelt and his wife Edith, who had died two weeks earlier on September 30 and was buried beside her husband. Reverend Warren returned to give the invocation.[21]

Memorial Day also became a popular day for people to pay tribute to the 26th president. On May 28, 1922, 1,000 people visited the grave, including a modest group of 75 Boy Scouts from Brooklyn, who laid a wreath. The next day, 5,000 people paraded past the grave, including Roosevelt's two sons, Kermit and Archie.[22] In 1923, a parade started at the courthouse and featured 500 Grand Army of the Republic, Spanish-American, and World War I veterans, who marched alongside bagpipers to the cemetery. Roosevelt's old hiking buddies, Boy Scout Troop 39, which had renamed itself "Theodore Roosevelt Boy Scout Troop #39," laid a wreath with a note, "In Memory of Our Departed Scout."[23] Another wreath arrived from Cuba. The tradition continued during World War II, when, on Memorial Day in 1943, a brief ceremony at the grave was attended by 400 Legionnaires and British veterans. An invocation was made by Reverend Thomas Helfrich from St. Dominic's Roman Catholic Church and afterward, four soldiers fired a volley.[24]

The year after his death, the "Roosevelt Pilgrimage Society" was formed to "keep alive the doctrines of Colonel Roosevelt."[25] This formidable group was composed of former members of Roosevelt's cabinet, including Secretary of the Interior James R. Garfield. They chose to make their pilgrimage on the anniversary of his death and visited for the first time on January 6, 1921. In 1930, the small group attracted hundreds of spectators and followed the graveside ceremony with a visit to Sagamore Hill.[26] For years they were greeted by Roosevelt's wife, who attended every meeting up until 1933. After lunch, they held their annual meeting in the trophy room, often reading from Roosevelt's speeches. The numbers dwindled to 30 members in 1938 and 28 in 1940.[27] By the end of the 1940s, the group disbanded after most of its original members had passed away.

In addition to the Boy Scouts, Memorial Day travelers, and the Roosevelt Pilgrimage Society, many others came to pay their respects and offer unique tributes to this legendary individual. On April 6, 1919, three months after his death, hundreds of returning soldiers from World War I visited the grave. One soldier who had met Roosevelt at Sagamore Hill the previous summer was quoted in the *New York Times*: "We were in the trenches and when we heard of his death it was like losing a father, for he seemed like that when we were with him. No man was more loved by the soldier boys than he."[28]

On October 20, 1919, during what the *New York Times* called "Roosevelt Week," pilots flew airplanes over the grave and dropped wreaths from the Roosevelt Rough Riders, American Legion, Spanish-American War veterans, and Friendly Sons of St. Patrick.[29] The following year, a slab of limestone inscribed, TO THEODORE ROOSEVELT, FROM THE CANAL ZONE CHILDREN, DECEMBER 8, 1920, was carried 2,300 miles from the Panama Canal, one of Roosevelt's greatest presidential accomplishments, and placed by the grave at a small ceremony attended by Roosevelt's widow.[30] On October 27, 1929, on what would have been Roosevelt's 71st birthday, nine airplanes, led by Colonel Clarence D. Chamberlin, flew over his birthplace in Manhattan and proceeded to Oyster Bay, where they dropped flowers over Youngs Cemetery.[31] On January 9, 1948, 400 members of the Brooklyn-Long Island District of National League of Masonic Clubs visited Roosevelt's final resting place. Hosting the event was Roosevelt's former lodge, Matinecock No 806.[32]

Foreign dignitaries have also flocked to the small town to pay tribute to Roosevelt. On October 20, 1921, Italian general Armando Diaz visited the grave, bearing a wreath of asters and chrysanthemums with a ribbon that read: "To Theodore Roosevelt in the name of the people of Italy—General Diaz." Escorting him were three World War I veterans who had won the Congressional Medal of Honor (the next day Diaz also visited Grant's Tomb in New York City).[33] On July 9, 1922, several thousand people visited, including a 30-member delegation from the Rotary Club from London, England.[34] On November 19, 1922, Georges Clemenceau, the French prime minister during World War I, visited the grave "of America's wielder of the big stick." After a few silent moments at the graveside, he visited Sagamore Hill and was greeted by Roosevelt's son Archie, now a World War I veteran who had served in France.[35] On November 13, 1932, Dr. H. H. Kung, Chinese minister of industry and commerce and 76th descendent of Confucius, laid a wreath "to express the gratitude of the Chinese nation got the aid and friendship which Theodore Roosevelt gave to the country at a trying time in its history."[36] On October 27, 1957, what would have been Roosevelt's 99th birthday,

hundreds of people gathered at the grave. President Dwight Eisenhower sent a wreath for the occasion, and Vice President Richard Nixon sent a letter that was read aloud at the ceremony.[37] Even today, tens of thousands of people still visit the site every year.

THE THEODORE ROOSEVELT DEATH SITES
Location of Death

Roosevelt purchased 155 acres in Oyster Bay from Thomas Youngs in 1880 for $30,000, putting $10,000 down and financing the rest with a 20-year mortgage. In 1883, he hired the architectural firm Lamb & Rich to design a spacious home for him and his first wife, Alice Hathaway Lee. Roosevelt's life took a tragic turn when his mother and wife both died on February 14, 1884, only two days after his first child, Alice, was born. Two weeks later, on March 1, he used his mother's inheritance to contract John A. Wood & Son for $16,975 to build a suitable home for his infant daughter. Roosevelt had originally planned to call it "Leeholm" after Alice but changed it to "Sagamore Hill," the Algonquin word for "Chieftain," in tribute to Chief Sagamore Mohannis who had signed

Sagamore Hill, where Roosevelt died on January 6, 1919.

away his tribe's rights to the land many years earlier.[38]

After his tragic loss, Roosevelt sought refuge in North Dakota and left his newborn daughter under the care of his sister, Anna. He was still away when the home was completed in 1884, but his sister and daughter moved in. He returned to Sagamore Hill two years later with his new bride, Edith. Over the years, he added to the home until it was a three-story, 23-room Victorian mansion. During his presidency, the home was his retreat and summer residence, earning it the name "The Summer White House."

After Roosevelt died, Edith lived in the home until her death in 1948. After her passing, the house was unoccupied. Wanting to turn it in a national shrine, the Theodore Roosevelt Memorial Association, headed by Frank R. McCoy, worked with the heirs and real estate agent William M. Cruikshank of Guaranty Trust Company. They announced an arrangement on February 8, 1950, wherein the Theodore Roosevelt Memorial Association paid $104,000 for the home and $40,000 for the furnishings, including the trophies. However, the villagers were not happy about this plan. Cove Neck was, and still is, a quiet, sleepy village, and residents were concerned about potential traffic. To allay their concerns, on January 28, a new road was proposed, and it was agreed that only after it was completed could the house be opened to the public. This delay was not an issue, since the "rambling old house" needed a lot of work, and initial estimates were that it would take a year and cost between $500,000 and $750,000.[39] In the end, the restorations took three years but were under budget, costing only $250,000.

On Sunday, June 14, 1953, President Eisenhower visited Sagamore Hill to dedicate the home after a brief stop at Roosevelt's grave. Reverend John N. Warren from Christ Church gave an opening prayer. At 5:00 p.m. former president Herbert Hoover introduced Eisenhower, who delivered a brief five-minute speech from the home's front porch.[40] Two days later, at 10:00 a.m. the home was opened to the public for the first time. The cost was 50¢ for adults and children under 12 were free, and the most popular attraction was the trophy room.

In 1963, the Theodore Roosevelt Memorial Association donated the home to the American people. The estate is now known as the Sagamore Hill National Historic Site and is managed by the National Park Service. On October 15, 1966 it was also added to the National Register of Historic Places (#66000096). It is located at 20 Sagamore Hill Road, Oyster Bay, New York, 11771. Tours of the home are run on Wednesday through Sunday during the hours of 10:00 a.m. to 4:00 p.m. For more information, visit: www.nps.gov/sahi.

Funeral

Christ Church was originally founded in 1704, and the building where Roosevelt's funeral was

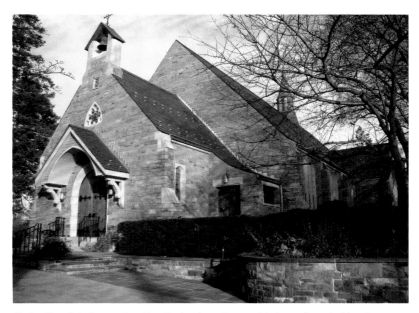

Christ Church in Oyster Bay, New York, where Roosevelt's funeral was held on January 8, 1919.

held was built in 1878 in the Carpenter Gothic style. The family pew, #36, was close to the entrance, since Roosevelt had the habit of being first to leave the service.[41]

Grave

Youngs Cemetery dates back to 1640, when Reverend John Youngs arrived in Long Island, and his son Thomas first began to use a hill near his home as a family burial plot in 1658. Over the years, as more Youngs family members were buried there, it became known as "Youngs Cemetery." In 1901, family descendent Thomas Youngs, an attorney and private secretary to Roosevelt, wanted to ensure that the land would be perpetually cared for; he established the graveyard as a not-for-profit corporation and opened it to local residents.

The plot where Roosevelt was buried was selected by Roosevelt himself, eight years prior to his death. After Edith had been thrown from a horse in 1911 and knocked unconscious for several days, the couple was forced to focus on such grim matters. Four years after Roosevelt was buried at the cemetery, his cousin, Emlen Roosevelt, purchased an adjoining 12 acres to ensure the surrounding area would not be developed and the natural surroundings preserved. Part of the land was used for additional burials, while the remainder was donated to the National Audubon Society. Given Roosevelt's love for nature, it is fitting that this donation became the first Audubon Songbird Sanctuary in the United States.

The cemetery is still active, but new burials are few and far between, averaging only two per year. There is a small parking area available at the foot of the hill and a symbolic 26 steps lead to the grave since Roosevelt was our 26th president.

Youngs Cemetery is located at the intersection of Cove Road and Cove Neck Road in Oyster Bay, New York, 11771. The cemetery is open to visitors all year from about 9:00 a.m. to dusk. For more information, visit: www.TRGravesite.org.

THE TWENTY-NINTH PRESIDENT
Warren Gamaliel Harding ★ 1921–1923

CRITICAL DEATH INFORMATION:

Date of death:	August 2, 1923, 7:32 p.m.
Cause of death:	Originally believed to be a stroke, but now presumed a heart attack
Age at death:	57 years, 273 days
Last words:	"That's good, go on; read some more."
Place of death:	Palace Hotel (room 8064), San Francisco, California
Funeral:	United States Capitol building
Final resting place:	Harding Memorial, Marion, Ohio
Reinterred:	Yes
Cost to visit grave:	Free
For more information:	www.OhioHistory.org/museums-and-historic-sites/museum-historic-sites-by-name/harding-memorial
Significance:	Only president to die in August and longest presidential funeral train in history in distance traveled

On June 20, 1923, Warren G. Harding embarked on a "Voyage of Understanding" to visit areas of the country never before seen by an American president. Harding was gearing up for his reelection campaign, and this was a way to get his message directly to the people, including a push for a World Court, a tough sell when America had so recently rejected Woodrow Wilson's League of Nations. He boarded his Presidential Special train in Washington, DC, settling into his personal car, the Superb. Accompanying Harding were his secretary of commerce, Herbert Hoover, and his doctor, Charles Sawyer. Harding had brought Sawyer from his hometown of Marion, Ohio, to Washington, DC. The president trusted him implicitly, and in the end, his blind faith in "Doc" Sawyer may have led to his undoing.

The president was not in good health, and the heat and busy schedule began to take its toll. In Kansas, he suffered bad sunburn while riding on a reaper in a wheat field, causing his lips to swell. His mental state was strained, as Harding had an inkling of the scandal within his administration that would soon be made public. His speeches were often greeted by sparse crowds and lukewarm enthusiasm, which did nothing to improve his outlook.[1] On July 4, he departed Tacoma, Washington, for Alaska, to visit remote villages never before seen by a president. This excursion gave him no respite from the hot temperatures, as Alaska was in the middle a heat wave, with temperatures in the 90s. Exhausted, Harding bowed out of several appearances. After reaching Fairbanks, he headed back southward and boarded a ship for Vancouver. On his final night at sea, the restless president was unable to sleep and decided to have a late night snack of crab legs and butter. The next day when the ship arrived, Harding felt well enough to speak at a welcoming party, but reporters noted his exhaustion. He slurred his words and even inadvertently called Alaska *Nebraska*. Shortly afterward, he complained of severe cramps and indigestion. Dr. Sawyer, not overly concerned, blamed the midnight crabs. Harding's next few days of appearances in Oregon were canceled, allowing him to recover as the train rode straight through to San Francisco. Another doctor, Joel T. Boone, examined Harding and found he had a dangerously enlarged heart. After having been informed of the doctor's assessment, Hoover arranged to have additional medical staff meet them on their arrival in San Francisco. Dr. Sawyer maintained that Harding's condition was not serious. Indeed, pulling into the San Francisco ferry station on Sunday, July 29, Harding was feeling much better, despite reporters noting that he looked "old and worn."[2] As Hoover had arranged, they were met by heart specialist Dr. Charles Minor Cooper and the president of Stanford University and member of the American Medical Association, Dr. Ray Lyman Wilbur.

Harding checked into the Palace Hotel and settled into room 8064 on the eighth floor, with a view of Market Street, while his wife, Florence, was in a separate room across the hall. His condition worsened the next day when his temperature spiked to 102 degrees and his pulse raced to 120. Harding was struggling to breathe, and Dr. Wilbur diagnosed him with bronchial pneumonia. The next day brought another turn as Harding's condition improved and it appeared the worst was behind him. Dr. Sawyer concurred, noting that his lungs were clearing up. By Wednesday, August 1, Harding was able to sit up in bed, eat solid foods, and read the newspapers. The next day, Thursday,

The Palace Hotel in San Francisco, where Warren G. Harding died on August 2, 1923. (Courtesy of Joseph F. Picone)

August 2, his improvement continued, and his doctors were confident a full recovery was imminent.

That evening, Harding was resting in his hotel room with his wife while the others were at dinner. What happened in the next half hour is one of the most mysterious episodes in presidential death history—accounts vary regarding who was where and when, and the discrepancies that surfaced have remained unresolved to this day.[3]

In the hotel suite, Florence was reading Harding the newspapers as he lay in bed resting. Suddenly, the president stiffened, appearing to suffer a bout of vertigo, and was instantly soaked with sweat. Dr. Sawyer rushed to take his pulse, but almost as soon as the episode came on, Harding felt better. "I don't know what happened to me," he said, "It was a very strange experience. Came on unbeknownst to me. Now I feel perfectly comfortable as though I never had such an experience."[4] After his nurse, Ruth Powderly, helped him change out of his sweat-soaked pajamas into a dry pair, he asked Florence to resume reading. She picked up where she left off, in a *Saturday Evening Post* article written by Samuel Blythe titled, "A Calm View of a Calm Man." In it, Blythe was impressed that Harding was able to stay focused in the face of mounting criticism. Harding liked what he heard and prodded his wife, "That's good, go on, read some more."[5] These were his last words. Having had a turbulent presidency that would become more mired in scandals after his death, his last words were positive, in appreciation of a supportive journalist.

Florence finished and retired to her own room, leaving the two nurses, Ruth Powderly and Sue S. Dauser, with the president. A few moments later, at approximately 7:10 p.m., the president had another, more violent episode. He shuddered and collapsed, his body slumping forward. Florence raced back to the room to see what had happened and then quickly ran out, urgently calling for Dr. Boone, "Come quick!"[6] Dr. Boone was at dinner, but Dr. Sawyer heard the anguished cries and rushed into the suite. He found the president still alive but fading fast. A moment later, he declared the shocking news, "The president is dead!" But Florence would not accept his assessment and pleaded, "Do something for him, give him something!" Sawyer, who had been giving Harding medication that he called "purgatives" throughout his illness, pulled out a hypodermic needle and injected "a stimulating liquid." But it was to no avail, as the president was gone. Just like so many other details of the final moments of Harding's life, the exact time of death is also muddled and confused. Reported times vary by 15 minutes, from 7:20 to 7:35, and the official death certificate listed the time of death at 7:20 p.m. Though the shock of his death was immense, Florence, who had tolerated her husband's philandering for years, was stoic. She turned to those in the room and told them, "I am not going to break down."[7]

Harding became the third president born in Ohio to die in office, preceded by Garfield and McKinley. After Woodrow Wilson was incapacitated by a stroke at the end of his term, and now with Harding's premature demise, *Time* magazine raised the prospect that, "the duties of the presidency be divided so that they should not fall with full heaviness upon one man."[8] As to his cause of death, there was disagreement among his doctors just as there was while he was ill. Dr. Sawyer was convinced that the cause was a cerebral hemorrhage or a stroke. Doctors Boone, Sawyer, Wilbur, Cooper, and Hubert Work, who was both postmaster general and a physician, jointly wrote a statement that explained the death, while simultaneously exonerating themselves: "Death was apparently due to some brain evolvement, probably an apoplexy. During the day he had been free from discomfort and there was every justification for anticipating a prompt recovery."[9] Whatever the doctors believed would never be confirmed, because Florence did not permit an autopsy. Neither would she allow a death mask.

The most common theory on the true cause of death was a heart attack resulting from medical incompetence. Due to the quick death, a heart attack is more likely than a stroke, which might have been prevented if not for inept medical care and Harding's misguided loyalty to Dr. Sawyer. Either Sawyer misdiagnosed Harding's heart condition or, perhaps worse, it was brought on by the mysterious "purgatives" that Sawyer administered throughout Harding's illness.[10] It is also possible that a lethal dose of the fluid was administered immediately preceding the fatal attack. The possibility that Sawyer could have accidentally killed the president may have led those in the room to conspire to concoct events so as to not implicate the doctor, thus creating the 15-minute discrepancy in time of death. A little over a year later, conspiracy theorists were given additional fodder when Dr. Sawyer suddenly died. The unexpected death prompted his son to say it "resembled that of President Harding in its 'suddenness.'"[11]

Another, more sinister theory pointed to murder, and to a perpetrator who was none other than Florence Harding! Her resistance to determine the true cause of her husband's death coupled with her cold demeanor helped feed a persistent conspiracy theory that she poisoned him. The speculation of her motive has ranged from his illicit affairs to an attempt to prevent an inevitable humiliating impeachment once the scandals became public.[12] And these were not the only theories. Playing "whodunit" became a national pastime, with culprits ranging from the KKK to several lone wolves whom Harding had encountered during his trip. Even today the cause of death remains a mystery. While most have debunked mariticide, experts doubt stroke as the cause of death.

In addition to not allowing an autopsy or death mask, Florence insisted her husband be embalmed immediately. The turn of events was head-spinning—less than two hours after she was reading to her husband, two undertakers and an embalmer from N. Gray and Company arrived. They found Harding lying on the bed where he died beneath a white sheet that the nurses had placed over him. They worked for six hours in the same room, into Friday, August 3, and then placed him back on the bed. Later that day, they dressed him in a cutaway jacket, black trousers, and a tie that Florence had selected. He was placed in a silk-lined, gray bronze casket located in the drawing room of the hotel suite and floral arrangements were strewn about to resemble a makeshift funeral parlor. The lid was opened, but a glass plate covered the body, forever sealing any evidence as to the true cause of death.[13]

Baptist minister James S. West made his way to the Palace Hotel to console the widow and offer his spiritual services. She accepted, but under the condition that a service was "not to exceed fifteen minutes." At 5:00 p.m., he performed a brief funeral ceremony for the members of the presidential party. Florence thanked the minister with, "It has been a great comfort to me," before restating what she had previously said only moments after her husband's death, "I won't break down; my thoughts will go just as fast as the train."[14]

The casket was closed and covered with an American flag. At 6:30 p.m., a delegation of soldiers, sailors, and marines carried the casket out of the presidential suite, through the hotel lobby, and out the front door. The exterior of the hotel had been decorated in black crepe and the flag lowered to half-mast. While nearby church bells tolled and a navy band played "The Star Spangled Banner" and "Lead, Kindly Light," they carefully placed the coffin in the funeral parlor's Pierce-Arrow hearse. The car drove slowly to Third and Townsend Streets, followed by honorary pallbearers Hoover, Hubert Work, Attorney General Harry Daugherty, Secretary of Agriculture Henry Cantwell Wallace, General John "Black Jack" Pershing, Speaker of the House Frederick Huntington Gillett, San Francisco mayor James Rolph, and governor of California Friend William Richardson. They were followed by detachments from the military, and the marine band played Chopin's "Funeral March."

The procession arrived at the Southern Pacific Depot, and the coffin was placed on a bier in the Superb, the same train Harding had used just days earlier, but now it was draped with black crepe. Florence stayed in the same train car for the journey along with four honor guards, two soldiers, a sailor, and a marine with rifle in hand. The presidential funeral train departed at 7:15 p.m. for Washington, DC. As it pulled out, the crowd began to sing "Lead, Kindly Light," while overhead airplanes dropped flowers in tribute.

Along the return trip, which newspapers called "the saddest transcontinental journey in history," people lined the tracks to pay their respects.[15] There were no planned ceremonial stops, but where the train stopped to switch engines, large crowds gathered, including Free Masons, Boy Scouts, youthful soldiers from World War I, and aged Civil War veterans. The crowds grew in size as the train rode east into denser, more populated areas. In Auburn, California, 300 people, a quarter of the entire town's population, came out in the early morning hours of August 4. Seventeen miles along, it passed through Colfax, California, at 1:35 a.m., witnessed by almost everyone from the town.[16] Into Nevada, it rode through the barren terrain of Sparks at 6:00 a.m. and Hazen 85 minutes later. The travelers endured extreme weather, including dust clouds in Cheyenne, Wyoming, that engulfed the train and vicious thunder and lightning in Chappell, Nebraska, followed by huge hailstones and ferocious winds. When this freak weather was replaced with a beautiful rainbow, the crowd interpreted it as providence.[17] On August 6, 40,000 people braved another thunderstorm in Omaha, Nebraska, to see the train pass at 2:56 a.m., and another 50,000 gathered in the Clinton, Iowa, train yards at 12:44 p.m., the largest crowd the small town had ever seen.

Crossing the Mississippi River into Illinois, the train passed a crowd of 12,000 people in Sterling. Thirteen miles east, it paused for three minutes in Dixon at 1:51 p.m., where it hurriedly picked up a delegation from Harding's hometown of Marion, Ohio.[18] In Chicago, a massive crowd of 300,000 people watched the train pass, and the Illinois National Guard 122nd and 124th Field Artillery fired a 21-gun salute. In Ohio, the train slowed to allow Harding's fellow Ohioans to get a good look, and Florence told the engineer to stop whenever he saw a crowd. In Pennsylvania, hardened and soiled steel workers stood, hard hats in hand, as the train rode through Pittsburgh. All along the route, young kids placed pennies on the tracks to keep the flattened copper orbs as souvenirs.

Four days after departing San Francisco, the train arrived in Washington, DC, on the sweltering evening of August 7 and was met by soldiers at the station. It was scheduled to get to the nation's capital by one in the afternoon but did not arrive until 10:22 p.m. The band played "Nearer, My God, to Thee" as the casket was removed through a special door in the funeral car. The soldiers who had accompanied the train ride hoisted the weight, while others flanked them with arms presented. Walking behind the coffin was Hoover. The new president, Calvin Coolidge, saluted, and the pallbearers placed the casket on a black-draped caisson and strapped it into place. Just before 11:00 p.m., "Six Bay horses and two khaki-clad outriders" pulled the burden, as the guards of honor walked beside. Riding behind the casket in separate automobiles sat President Coolidge and former president William Howard Taft. Tens of thousands lined the route for the procession.[19]

The procession arrived at the White House at 11:40 p.m. and the coffin was placed upon a bier in the East Room, the same room where the remains of William Henry Harrison, Zachary Taylor, Abraham Lincoln, and William McKinley had preceded him. Florence retired to get some rest but returned at 1:30 a.m. and sat for over an hour speaking to Harding. Witnesses in earshot recalled her comforting words to her deceased husband, "The trip has not hurt you one bit," and "No one can hurt you now, Warren."[20]

The next morning, there was a brief private service in the East Room, after which the military pallbearers carried the coffin to a black funeral caisson located beneath the portico. The bugler gave the signal at a few minutes past 10:00, and six brown horses slowly began to pull the hearse. Limousines followed the carriage. In one rode the new and former presidents Coolidge and Taft, and former president Wilson rode behind them in his Pierce-Arrow. Coolidge wanted Wilson to play a prominent role in the funeral ceremony, but he was frail, sickly, and unable to do so (six months later, Wilson too would be dead). On horseback was General Pershing, and many more members of the armed forces marched. The procession moved slowly down Pennsylvania Avenue, which, the *Winthrop News* reported, "ten thousand school children [had] carpeted with flowers."[21] It was

Harding's funeral cortege leaves the White House. (Library of Congress)

a blazing hot day, and several marines fainted from the heat.

At the Capitol building, while the marine band played "Lead, Kindly Light," military pallbearers carried the coffin inside and placed it on a catafalque beneath the rotunda (the same one built for Lincoln and used for Garfield and McKinley). Ten truckloads of flowers, including wreaths laid at the foot of the casket by Coolidge and Taft, had turned the sweltering rotunda into an aromatic space.

Reverend J. Freeman Anderson of the Calvary Baptist Church, where Harding was a congregant, officiated and was assisted by Reverend Jesse Swank of the Epworth Methodist Episcopal Church. After Anderson's initial words of consolation, the Calvary Baptist Church male choir sang Harding's favorite hymn, "Lead, Kindly Light." Reverend Anderson lamented, "We mourn most sincerely the departure of one of America's noblest sons; a devoted servant of God, a loyal and ardent patriot, a valiant leader, a princely gentleman, a gracious and inspiring friend."[22] The "Prayer for the President" was read by House of Representatives chaplain Reverend James Shera Montgomery before Reverend Anderson concluded with a benediction at 11:57 a.m. For the next five hours, crowds solemnly walked past to see Harding beneath the plate glass. At 5:00 p.m., the doors were closed to the general public, and President Coolidge and the honorary pallbearers paid their respects. The coffin was carried to Union Station, where it was placed back in the Superb for its final journey back home to Marion, Ohio. Along the way, through Baltimore, Maryland, and York and Harrisburg, Pennsylvania, people gathered at the tracks and sang hymns. The train crossed into Ohio at 4:35 a.m. on August 9. Florence once again ordered the train to stop frequently when crowds were encountered, leaving it behind schedule.

The town of Marion had been busy preparing for the arrival, hurriedly repairing sidewalks and erecting a huge pillared entrance to the ceme-

Harding's funeral procession at the United States Capitol. (Library of Congress)

tery.[23] The train had been scheduled to arrive at 10:00 in the morning, but as expected, it was late and did not reach Marion until 12:38 p.m. The ride of the Harding funeral train had finally come to an end. From San Francisco to Washington, DC, and back to Ohio, Harding's was the longest funeral train trip in history. At a staggering 3,500 miles, it was twice as long as Lincoln's final journey. To mark the arrival, church bells throughout Marion began to ring. Military pallbearers gently carried the flag-draped coffin to a funeral carriage, which, flanked by soldiers, slowly made its way to his father Dr. George T. Harding's home at 308 East Center Street. Buildings were draped in black, photographs of Harding were displayed in windows, bells tolled every 30 seconds, and large crowds gathered along the route. Many in the crowd were not locals. The town of 30,000 people was flooded with 60,000 to 75,000 visitors, tripling its population.[24] Those who could not find lodging set up tents and camped out in town. An additional 3,500 National Guardsman were deployed to Marion to keep order.

The procession arrived at 1:12 p.m., and the pallbearers carried the casket into a small parlor that had been cleared of its furniture. The lid was raised, and the family had a brief moment alone before the public viewing began at 2:00 p.m. The original plans were to close the doors at 10:00 p.m., but when the crowds did not abate, Florence again interceded and kept the doors open until everyone in line had paid their respects.[25] At 11:00 p.m., Thomas Edison and automobile magnates Henry Ford and Harvey Firestone arrived. The paparazzi went wild, surrounding Edison and snapping photographs. The inventor and the president had been good friends and had camped together two years earlier. While Edison was there to mourn, he may have also come to do scientific—or metaphysical—research. Edison had studied the afterlife and was convinced that "the soul does exist after death."[26] However, as to whether he could speak to Harding now that he was no longer among the living, he vacillated: "I cannot say that men, including the beloved President Harding, live after death."[27]

As in any presidential funeral, the flowers piled up, but one arrangement stood out among the others. Placed on the front lawn was a four-foot-tall cross made of brilliant red flowers, with white flowers arranged to form three identical letters—"K.K.K," a gift from the Marion Chapter of the Ku Klux Klan. There were 5,000 people still in line at midnight, but as the crowds thinned by 2:00 a.m., the doors were closed. After a few hours, people again began to gather for the next day. In general, they were orderly and respectful, although a minor incident of "some confusion and loud talk" was reported at 4:00 a.m. By 9:00 a.m., when the doors were reopened, the line stretched half mile long.[28]

When the doors were finally closed at 1:00 p.m., 35,000 to 40,000 people had viewed the deceased and an astounding 20,000 people were *still* in line. The body was prepared for the burial, and a small ceremony was held in the home at 4:00 p.m., with Coolidge and Taft in attendance. Businesses were closed in deference except for essential ones, such as the delivery of ice and milk.[29]

Six servicemen carried the flag-draped coffin down the steps to a gray funeral hearse followed by family, friends, and the widow, with her face concealed beneath a black veil. The procession was led by a flag carrier, and included all of the employees of the *Marion Star*, the newspaper once owned by Harding, which had closed its doors to allow workers to participate. It was a silent procession, as there were no bands for this final march.[30] After all of the pageantry of the past days, Florence had wanted a simple graveside service with no military display. Her one concession was to permit guns to fire in salute as the procession approached Marion Cemetery.[31] The cortege stopped at the cemetery entrance and the pallbearers carried the coffin through a cordon of senators and friends. They placed it on a brown catafalque at the entrance to the temporary resting place—an ivy-covered Victorian Gothic brownstone receiving vault shaded by two elm trees, set into the hillside and close to the graves of his mother and sister. The *New York Times* called it "A quiet and restful spot.

This God's acre of Warren G. Harding's home town, sweet-smelling from myriads of flowers piled thickly around his temporary tomb; a spot suggestive of all that God's acre should be."[32]

The remains were formally received by Reverend George M. Landis of the Trinity Baptist Church, Reverend Jesse Swank, and Bishop William F. Anderson of the Cincinnati Methodist Church. At the cemetery, there were only family members, Taft, Coolidge, and close friends including Edison, Ford, and Firestone (reporters were barred from this final farewell). The brief service began when the Trinity Baptist Girls' Choir sang "Lead, Kindly Light." Reverend Landis then read from Scripture, Reverend Swank said a prayer, and Bishop Anderson gave the benediction. The choir sang the final hymn, "Nearer, My God, to Thee," and the military honor guard slowly raised the casket and carried it into the receiving vault as a bugler played Taps. A 21-gun salute ended the ceremony. Florence walked into the receiving vault and remained alone for several minutes. After she exited, the iron gates were locked.[33]

After the funeral, people began to file into the cemetery to see the flag-draped coffin through the gate. The crowds continued all day, and the next day, there were still hundreds of cars parked nearby.[34] To prevent souvenir hunters from defacing the tomb, an army guard was placed on either side of the entrance with fixed bayonets. They remained at their posts, rotating every 30 minutes for the next six months. In October, Harding's coffin was placed in a 2,600 pound sarcophagus.

On September 5, Harding's will was read, in which he humbly requested a "simple marker at my grave."[35] But since he died in office and was

Harding's temporary tomb, where his remains stayed while the permanent memorial was constructed nearby. (Courtesy of Tim Bash)

from Ohio—just like Garfield and McKinley—a simple marker could never suffice. Despite his wishes, a movement began to create an appropriately Ohio-style memorial to last through the ages.[36] In October 1923, the Harding Memorial Association was founded with two powerhouse members: Calvin Coolidge and Herbert Hoover. They established the Harding Memorial Fund, and on October 11, kicked off fund-raising efforts. They were wildly successful, with over one million people donating $977,821.76, including pennies collected from 200,000 schoolchildren.[37]

The next task was to choose a design. One of the early ideas was to bury Harding in a sacred Indian mound. These ancient structures are plentiful in Ohio, but this plan was abandoned.[38] The association chose a tomb design created by Henry F. Hornbostel, an architect of New York's Hell's Gate Bridge and a graduate of École des Beaux in France. Hornbostel's design was inspired by the tombs along the Appian Way, one of the earliest roads in Ancient Rome. It included a combined 48 interior Ionic columns and exterior Tuscan columns, one for each state of the Union. The final cost for the mammoth structure was $783,103.

Just over a year after Harding passed away, Florence died on November 21, 1924. In her will she left all of Warren's documents to the Harding Memorial Association to "forever be preserved to the public, for the benefit of posterity."[39] Construction on the monument officially kicked off with a groundbreaking ceremony on Memorial Day, May 30, 1926. There was an impressive crowd of 50,000 people in attendance to see Vice President Charles Gates Dawes lay the cornerstone. Reverend Swank, who performed Harding's funeral three years earlier, also participated in the ceremony.[40] In December 1927, Harding and his wife were reinterred in the new monument.

A dedication ceremony was first planned for July 4, 1927, but did not materialize. When it was again planned in 1928, President Coolidge declined to attend, claiming it would not be appropriate in an election year. The truth was that since Harding's death, the former president had quickly fallen from hero to anathema. Mired in the scandals that had come to light, like Teapot Dome, his legacy was in tatters. But while Republicans wanted to distance themselves from the disgraced former president as much as possible, Marion residents felt his tomb deserved a proper dedication. Ohio politicians wrote impassioned editorials bashing Coolidge, and when Hoover won the election in 1928, Marion set its sights on him. Hoover was invited to another dedication scheduled for October 2, 1930, and with seven years gone since Harding's death and his own legacy in ruins, he decided the time was right to honor his former boss.[41] He accepted, but the dedication was again postponed.[42] Finally, on June 16, 1931, the ceremony was held, and both President Hoover and former president Coolidge traveled to Marion to attend. Despite the almost universal judgment that Harding's presidency had been a failure, an impressive crowd of 100,000 attended that day.[43]

The ceremony began with an invocation by Reverend William J. Spickerman of St. Mary's Catholic Church in Marion. Former senator Joseph Sherman Frelinghuysen Sr. made an address; it was on his estate that Harding had signed the Knox-Porter Resolution on July 2, 1921, officially ending American involvement in World War I. After a performance by the Republican Glee Club from Columbus, Ohio, Coolidge stepped to the microphone.[44] The crowd and the press listened attentively to see how the presidents would honor Harding's memory while also addressing the numerous scandals that tarnished his legacy. As vice president and secretary of commerce, Coolidge and Hoover were in the thick of the administration. While they did mention the controversy, both were tactful and flattering of their former boss, without whom they might never have become presidents themselves. Coolidge went a little over the top when he stated, "It would be difficult to find any peace time period of a little over two years when so much that was beneficial was accomplished as during his administration"—but almost two years into the Great Depression, even a Harding presidency may have seemed like the good old days!

After Coolidge, Ohio governor George White spoke and was followed by the Glee Club, before President Hoover stepped up to the dais. Addressing the scandals that engulfed the Harding legacy, he said that Harding had "a dim realization that he had been betrayed by a few of the men he trusted."[45] After a third performance by the Glee Club, Reverend Swank concluded with a benediction. By all accounts, it was a pleasant afternoon, marred only by three low-flying planes that buzzed the crowds while going back and forth to take photographs. Hoover, incensed by the loud interruptions and for what he saw as a safety hazard, called for the pilots to be punished. The next day, Hoover was off to Springfield, Illinois to rededicate the Lincoln tomb.[46]

THE WARREN G. HARDING DEATH SITES
Location of Death

In 1868, San Francisco banker William Ralston purchased land south of Market Street and seven years later erected the largest hotel in America, the Palace Hotel. It stood seven stories tall, had an amazing 800 rooms, and cost $5 million to build. The jewel of the city, designed by architect John P. Gaynor, first opened its doors on October 2, 1875. Though no expense had been spared to protect the building, it was severely damaged in the 1906 earthquake. It withstood the earthquake, but "the largest and perhaps most elegant hotel in the country was doomed to destruction, because every fire emergency had been considered except the possibility of an entire city burning around it."[47]

The hotel closed for three years. It was rebuilt by the New York firm Trowbridge & Livingston and reopened on December 15, 1909. Over the years, the Palace has hosted many of the nation's presidents: Ulysses S. Grant, Benjamin Harrison, William McKinley, Theodore Roosevelt, William Howard Taft, Franklin Delano Roosevelt (who wrote his 1932 inaugural speech there), and Bill Clinton all stayed there. It was at the Palace that Wilson proclaimed his support for the Versailles Treaty, and six days before the 1960 election, candidate John F. Kennedy was the star attraction at a $100-a-plate fund-raiser at the grand hotel. The Palace Hotel offers the rare opportunity to spend the night where a president died, but the death room, since renumbered to Room 888, costs about $2,900 a night.[48]

The Palace Hotel is located at 2 New Montgomery Street, San Francisco, California, 94105, and is managed by Starwood Hotels. For more information, visit: www.SFPalace.com.

Funeral Train Station

Today, the train station in Marion where Harding's funeral

The Harding Memorial tomb in Marion, Ohio.

train arrived houses the Marion Union Station Museum. It is located at 532 West Center Street, Marion, Ohio, 43302. For more information, visit: www.facebook.com/MarionUnionStation Association.

Lying in Repose: Home of Dr. George T. Harding

Dr. George T. Harding's home has been torn down and is now a parking lot and a nail salon. Downtown is a few blocks away, with plenty of Harding sites, like the *Marion Star* building and Hotel Harding. The main street resembles an old movie stage set.

Original Burial Location

The brownstone receiving vault is located in the middle of the Marion Cemetery, across the street from the Harding Tomb at 620 Delaware Avenue in Marion, Ohio 43302. The "Merchant Ball," an unusual tombstone topped with a gigantic granite orb that has moved over time, propelled by some unknown force, is also located in the cemetery and has been featured in *Ripley's Believe It or Not!*

Grave

The Harding Tomb is located at Vernon Heights Boulevard in Marion, Ohio, 43302. The memorial is managed by the Marion Technical College and is open year-round.

THE TWENTY-EIGHTH PRESIDENT
Woodrow Wilson ★ *1913–1921*

CRITICAL DEATH INFORMATION:

Date of death:	February 3, 1924, 11:15 a.m.
Cause of death:	Exhaustion following a digestive disturbance
Age at death:	67 years, 37 days
Last words:	"Edith."
Place of death:	Home at 2340 S Street, NW, Washington, DC
Funeral:	Washington National Cathedral
Final resting place:	Washington National Cathedral
Reinterred:	Yes
Cost to visit grave:	$10.00
For more information:	www.National Cathedral.org
Significance:	First presidential funeral broadcast over the radio

Throughout his life, Woodrow Wilson was prone to strokes. He suffered his first in 1896 at the age of 29, another in 1904, and a third in 1906 that left him blind in one eye.[1] He also overcame several other health problems, including high blood pressure and stomach ailments, to become our 28th president. During his second term, on October 2, 1919, Wilson suffered his most serious and debilitating stroke, which left him paralyzed on one side of his body and unable to speak clearly. Wilson went into seclusion and severely limited his interaction with outsiders. For the remainder of his presidency, the country was largely unaware of his frail condition. His wife, Edith Bolling Galt Wilson, served as a conduit between the public and her husband, relaying his presidential decisions. Many suspect her influence was much more substantial and, only partially in jest, refer to her as our first woman president.

For three years after his presidency, Wilson lived in Washington, DC, at 2340 S Street. The Woodrow Wilson Trust, a group of friends who had financed much of his post-presidency years, gave him a Rolls-Royce on his last birthday, December 28, 1923.[2] Undeterred by his frail condition, Wilson was considering another run for president and even began to draft a Democratic nomination acceptance speech. Despite his delusions, Wilson's already frail health was in decline.

On Sunday, January 26, 1924, his physician, Cary Grayson, left for a fishing trip in South Carolina. This choice for respite was not surprising. Grayson, a longtime friend and physician of Wilson, was a firm believer in the therapeutic benefit of leisure activities, and his most common prescription for Wilson's ailments throughout the years included golfing and horseback riding.[3] Wilson was uneasy about Grayson's departure and confided to his wife, "It won't be very much longer and I had hoped he would not desert me." Only a few days after Grayson departed, Wilson's condition worsened. On Wednesday, January 30, Edith sent a telegram asking Grayson to return immediately. The next day, Grayson examined Wilson and reassured the press that the former president had only suffered "one of his old indigestion attacks."[4] Edith was unconvinced and requested a second opinion from her internist, Dr. Sterling Ruffin, who told her that Wilson was gravely ill and suggested Grayson stay the night.

The activity at the home alerted reporters of Wilson's dire health. They gathered outside to receive hourly updates. Wilson could digest only a few sips of broth, and doctors gave him morphine to make him comfortable. On Friday, February 1, Wilson lay in his bed on the second floor of his home. During one of his moments of clarity, Grayson confided to him that the end was near. Wilson was unfazed: "I am a broken piece of machinery. When the machine is broken . . ." Unable to complete his thought, he simply whispered, "I am ready." These are often considered his last words. But he still had more to say. To comfort Dr. Grayson, Wilson put his hand on his arm and told him, "You have been good to me. You have done everything you could." Wilson soon lost consciousness. The next day, Thursday, February 2, Wilson awoke briefly and called for his wife one last time: "Edith." This was his last word.[5]

On Friday, February 3, Grayson released a statement that Wilson was unconscious but had survived the night. Surrounded by his wife and daughter, Margaret, Wilson suddenly opened his eyes. Edith spoke, but he did not respond. Ten minutes later, Woodrow Wilson closed his eyes for the last time. The end came at 11:15 a.m. on February 3, 1924. By his bedside were his wife, daughter Margaret, and brother Joseph.[6]

The bed where Woodrow Wilson died on February 3, 1924.

Five minutes later, Grayson fought back tears to make a statement on the front steps: "The heart muscle was so fatigued that it refused to act any longer. The end came peacefully." He died from "exhaustion following a digestive disturbance."[7] Later that day, a death mask was made, and Wilson's remains were placed in a closed black coffin.

President Calvin Coolidge was worshipping at First Congregational Church when he heard the news and immediately departed for Wilson's home. He offered the grieving widow whatever presidential or military services she wished for the funeral, but Edith declined. She wanted her husband's funeral to be personal and intimate, similar to those of Grover Cleveland and Theodore Roosevelt. Nor did she want a service in the White House or a viewing in the Capitol building. Coolidge issued a proclamation in which he called for flags in the capital to fly at half-mast for 30 days and praised Wilson as the man that "led the nation through the terrific struggle of the World War with a lofty idealism which never failed him."[8]

Former president William Howard Taft also came to the home the day Wilson died. Upon leaving the house, a reporter asked him about the funeral arrangements and Taft offered his opinion, "There should be a state funeral by all means, with Mr. Wilson's body lying in state, just as was done at the time of Mr. Harding's death. The world would not understand any other arrangement."[9] The final decision would ultimately be made by the family, but not until Wilson's daughter Eleanor arrived from Los Angeles.[10]

Questions about where Wilson would be buried were immediately raised, appearing as a column in the next day's edition of the *New York Times* titled "Arlington Burial Urged for Wilson." The assumption was one of two locations. The first was Princeton, New Jersey, where he had served as president of Princeton University and governor of the state and where he had lived for 30 years. The second and more popular choice was Arlington National Cemetery. At this time, no other commander in chief had been buried at the military cemetery. Representatives from other locations stated their respective cases: Staunton, Virginia, appealed as town of his birth; Richmond, Virginia, had not given up transforming Hollywood Cemetery into a President's Cemetery; and a request came from Columbia, South Carolina, where Wilson's parents and only sister were buried.[11] Unable to decide on a permanent location, the family chose the yet unfinished Washington National Cathedral on the Mount Saint Albans hilltop as a temporary location.

Wednesday, February 6, was a cold day. A small funeral was held in Wilson's home, with all of the attendees personally invited by Edith. She remained as protective of her husband in death

Pallbearers remove Wilson's remains from his home. (Library of Congress)

as she was in life. She invited President Coolidge, but after learning that Wilson's political adversary Henry Cabot Lodge was being delegated to attend in his place, she brazenly told him *not* to do so (he publicly explained his absence was due to a respiratory condition).[12] Taft was unable to attend, as he suffered an attack of indigestion on the day of the funeral. He was also slated to be an honorary pallbearer, so Supreme Court Justice Louis Dembitz Brandeis stood in as his replacement.[13] Edith was too grief-stricken to attend the service, instead listening from the top of the stairs as Ida McKinley had done 23 years earlier.

On the day of the funeral, gestures of respect were observed across the country. In New York, the Stock Exchange closed at noon and the Cotton, Coffee, and Sugar Exchanges shut their doors at 1:00 p.m. When the funeral began at 3:00 p.m., trains paused on the tracks.[14] In the Wilson home, Reverend James H. Taylor from the Central Presbyterian Church read Psalm 23, and Reverend Sylvester W. Beach, Wilson's pastor from Princeton, led the group in prayer. The service concluded with a reading from Wilson's own Bible by Bishop James E. Freeman.

The coffin was placed in a hearse and led by military escort to the National Cathedral. The procession included people from his graduating class at Princeton, members of his cabinet, and representatives from the House of Representatives and Senate. Crowds lined the streets, and a small cadre of soldiers accompanied the coffin. A second Episcopal service was held in the Bethlehem Chapel for 400 people, including President Coolidge and members of the Supreme Court.[15] It was broadcast over the radio on New York station WEAF (today WNBC), a first in presidential funeral history.

After Reverend Beach's sermon, the coffin was lowered into a crypt as Taps was played. On the floor over the casket was placed the words:

WOODROW WILSON
BORN DECEMBER 28, 1856
DIED FEBRUARY 3, 1924

The funeral cost $1,568, and an original copy of the bill can be seen on display at the National Museum of Funeral History in Houston, Texas. Though the bill was settled, Wilson's final resting place was not. There was still speculation that Wilson might be reinterred to another location. Any lingering doubt was extinguished in early 1925, when Edith requested that the Cathedral architects design a sarcophagus to be built in the nave of the church.[16] Over the next several weeks, Wilson's permanent resting place—an aboveground Mankato cream stone sarcophagus bearing the Crusader's Cross—was constructed in pieces and finally completed on January 29.[17]

THE WOODROW WILSON DEATH SITES
Location of Death
The home where Wilson died

Wilson's sarcophagus inside the Washington National Cathedral.

is now billed as "Washington D.C.'s only Presidential Museum." It was designed by Waddy Butler Wood and built in 1915 for $75,000. The sturdy 28-room structure has 12-inch-thick walls, steel beams, and reinforced concrete. In 1921, Wilson purchased it for a whopping $150,000. Presidents did not receive a pension at the time, so he paid for it using $50,000 awarded to him with his Nobel Peace Prize and donations from friends. His wife, in selecting the home, was quoted as saying, "I found an unpretentious, comfortable, dignified house, fitted to the needs of a gentlemen's home."[18]

Wilson's last act of his presidency was to attend Harding's inauguration, and afterward he went directly to his new home. To help the debilitated Wilson get around, a side door was installed, and an Otis elevator was added in 1921. This also helped the dignified former president avoid being seen struggling with the front steps. During his three years in the home, he was visited several times by his assistant secretary of the navy and future president, Franklin Roosevelt.

The house where Wilson died, located at 2340 S Street NW, Washington, DC.

After Wilson died, Edith stayed in the home for another three decades. The desperate widow was convinced she could communicate with her deceased husband and held séances there.[19] In 1954, she donated the home and its furnishings to the National Trust for Historic Preservation but continued to live there until her death in 1961. Her last guest was First Lady Jacqueline Kennedy. The home became a museum that year and 85 percent of the furnishings are the originals from Wilson's lifetime.

I visited on Veterans Day, since it was Woodrow Wilson who, in 1919, decreed that November 11 would be set aside as Armistice Day to commemorate those who perished in the World War I. He declared, "To us in America, the reflections of Armistice Day will be filled with solemn pride in the heroism of those who died in the country's service and with gratitude for the victory, both because of the thing from which it has freed us and because of the opportunity it has given America to show her sympathy with peace and justice in the councils of the nations."

The home is located in the Embassy District at 2340 S Street NW, Washington, DC, 20008. For more information, visit: www.Woodrow WilsonHouse.org.

Final Resting Place:

The cornerstone for Washington's National Cathedral was laid on September 29, 1907. That day, President Theodore Roosevelt spoke to a crowd of 10,000 people. This was no ordinary stone, as it traveled thousands of miles from a city near Bethlehem. Five years later, the church opened for services, but construction continued for a whopping 83 years and was not declared finished until 1990, when the West Towers were complete. Wilson's original resting place, Bethlehem Chapel, was the first part of the church to be opened and is located in the lower crypt level beside the original foundation stone. Facing the altar, the sarcophagus sat to the right of the seats before Wilson's remains

Bethlehem Chapel, on the lower level of Washington National Cathedral, where Wilson's remains resided for a year.

Washington National Cathedral, where Wilson's remains are interred.

were relocated upstairs to the nave of the church, where he rests today.

The Cathedral has always been a church of presidents: Wilson attended Thanksgiving Mass in 1918, Harding and Coolidge visited in 1921 and 1928 respectively, and the funerals of Lyndon Johnson, Ronald Reagan, and Gerald Ford were later held there.[20] The church was designed in the 14th-century Gothic style, and one of its most popular features is the gargoyles that adorn its exterior. In the 1980s, a contest was held to design a new gargoyle. Christopher Rader's entry was a drawing of one of the most infamous fic-

tional villains, Darth Vader. The bust of Lord Vader was sculpted by Jay Hall Carpenter and carved by Patrick J. Plunkett. Today it can be seen on the northwest tower of the Cathedral. However, if you are planning on visiting to see the Star Wars villain, heed the warning on the National Cathedral website and "bring binoculars!"

The Washington National Cathedral is located at 3101 Wisconsin Avenue NW, Washington, DC 20016. There used to be no charge for entrance; however, an admission fee was instituted in 2014. For more information, visit: www.National Cathedral.org.

William Howard Taft ★ *1909–1913*

CRITICAL DEATH INFORMATION:

Date of death:	March 8, 1930, 5:15 p.m.
Cause of death:	Cerebro-arterioscle-rosis (heart disease)
Age at death:	72 years, 174 days
Last words:	Unknown
Place of death:	Home at 2215 Wyoming Avenue, Washington, DC
Funeral:	All Souls Church, Washington, DC
Final resting place:	Arlington National Cemetery, Arlington, Virginia
Reinterred:	No
Cost to visit grave:	Free
For more information:	www.Arlington Cemetery.mil
Significance:	First presidential death site to be owned by a foreign government

After retiring from the presidency—a position he never really wanted—William Howard Taft was able to secure the job he had always dreamed of: Chief Justice of the Supreme Court. Perhaps best known as the president who got stuck in the White House bathtub, the rotund Taft battled weight problems throughout his life. He tried to stay in shape by walking three to four miles each day, but eventually his girth caught up with him and he developed myocarditis, a heart condition caused by a hardening of the arteries.[1] On January 6, 1930, on the advice of his physician and personal friend, Dr. Francis R. Hagner, Taft took a leave of absence from the Supreme Court. He checked into Garfield Hospital in

Washington, DC, where he stayed for eight days. On January 14, Taft was released and went south to Asheville, North Carolina, to recuperate. At first, a recovery seemed promising, when "it was disclosed that he was taking brisk walks as well as long rides in the country about Asheville."[2] However, after the temporary recovery, his health began to decline. On February 3, Taft came to the painful realization that he could no longer fulfill his judicial duties and officially retired from the Supreme Court. The next day he returned to his home in Washington, DC. Those who picked him up at the station were saddened by his frail and weakened appearance. At his home, photographers captured the pathetic sight of the once-robust Taft being carried by men on either side. The blinds were shut and policemen were stationed out front to allow Taft to rest peacefully and dissuade the morbidly curious. Undeterred, newsmen camped out a few doors down in a death watch. It was not a question of *if* his death was imminent but *when*.[3]

In Taft's home, Dr. Hagner monitored his health, and after a few days found he was improving. On February 9, it was reported that Taft was able to maintain a normal conversation and recognized people around him.[4] He had difficulty eating anything except broth, and the lack of solid food weakened his condition. During the following weeks he received few visitors, but made an exception to see President Hoover on February 5 and March 1. Toward the end of February, he appeared to make a slight recovery, but on February 26, he took a turn for the worse.[5] Fortunately, he was not in pain and appeared serene when conscious. On March 8 at 4:45 p.m., as Taft lay in his bedroom, he slipped into a coma. What he said before he lost consciousness was not recorded, leaving his last words lost to history. William Howard Taft died half an hour later, at 5:15 p.m. on March 8, 1930. With Taft when he died were his wife, Helen, a nurse, and Dr. H. G. Fuller (Dr. Hagner arrived a moment after his passing). In an uncanny coincidence, five hours earlier, another of the nine Supreme Court associate justices had also died—Edward Terry Sanford.

For the second time in six years, a former president had died in his home in Washington, DC, permitting the current president to be one of the first to visit the family. When President Hoover heard the news, he summoned a car to take him and his wife to console Taft's widow, Helen. He offered his condolences, as well as the East Room of the White House for the funeral. However, like Edith Wilson, Helen declined the gesture. Taft himself had said he wanted the funeral at All Souls Unitarian Church, and she intended to carry out his wishes. Still, Hoover wanted to help in any way possible and assigned

The horse-drawn procession for William Howard Taft outside the United States Capitol. (Library of Congress)

his aide, Colonel Campbell B. Hodges, to assist with the funeral arrangements. Hoover placed the Commanding General of the 16th Brigade from Fort Hunt, Virginia, in charge of a state funeral to be held in the rotunda.

The body was prepared and dressed in Taft's judicial robes. The day after his death, the family visited Arlington National Cemetery to choose a burial location and were accompanied by Colonel Hodges and Colonel Charles G. Mortimer, the officer in charge at Arlington. They chose a sparsely-used area on a wooded slope near the Fort Myer gate.[6]

On March 11, at 9:00 a.m., the coffin was carried from the house and placed in a horse-drawn caisson. A detachment of four army, two navy servicemen, and two marines were the body bearers while members of the Supreme Court were honorary pallbearers. A procession led by metropolitan policemen, including a squadron of cavalry, rode past the White House to the Capitol building. The coffin was placed beneath the rotunda, upon the catafalque that had previously held the weight of Abraham Lincoln, James A. Garfield, William McKinley, and Warren G. Harding. This was the first time a president who had not died in office was given the honor of resting on this catafalque. The viewing began around 10:30 a.m. and lasted just 90 minutes. Originally planned for three hours, the period was halved due to delays caused by what had become a torrential rainstorm.[7] During that brief time, 7,000 people somberly walked past the casket.

The coffin was placed back into the caisson and drawn by six horses. The procession included two service bands, battalions of infantry, field artillery, marines, and a company of Blue Jackets. They marched to All Souls Unitarian Church on Sixteenth Street, but the short trip took almost two hours in the driving rain. Throughout the journey, the army band continuously looped Chopin's "Funeral March" for the many saddened spectators who braved the

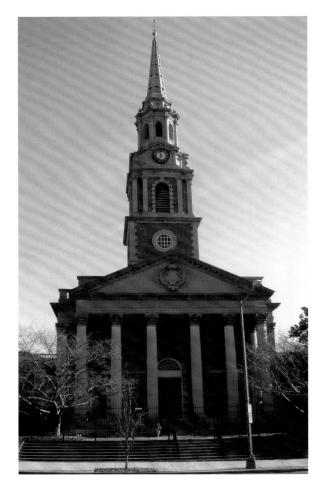

All Souls Church in Washington, DC, where Taft's funeral was held.

weather for the well-liked and respected leader. Church bells tolled as the flag-draped coffin was carried inside by the military body bearers, whose numbers increased to ten (four army, three navy, and three marines).[8]

The funeral was held at 2:00 p.m., but crowds had started to gather 90 minutes earlier. Taft's family sat behind his flower-covered pew, and President Hoover sat behind them. In the crowd of 900 friends and family were Vice President Charles Curtis, Chief Justice Charles Evan Hughes, and Associate Justice Oliver Wendell Holmes. One notable absence was former president Calvin Coolidge, who remained at his home in Northampton, Massachusetts. When a reporter had the temerity to ask him if he would be traveling to Washington, DC, for the funeral, he received an obstinate reply: "It is hard for Mrs. Coolidge and me to travel . . . most of all I should like to be left alone for a while."[9]

During the brief 35-minute ceremony, the choir sang two of Taft's favorite hymns, "Abide with Me" and "Lead, Kindly Light." The sermon included passages from Alfred Tennyson's "Ode on the Death of the Duke of Wellington" and William Wordsworth's "Character of the Happy Warrior" (also read at Grover Cleveland's funeral). The service was broadcast throughout the country over CBS radio stations using a microphone cleverly concealed within a floral arrangement.

For the procession to Arlington National Cemetery, the horse-drawn carriage was replaced with an automobile hearse. There was no military escort, and the 100-car procession was led by police on motorcycles. By the time it reached the gate 30 minutes later and paused for a 21-gun salute, the rain had stopped. A squadron of cavalry and the 3rd Cavalry Mounted Band escorted the hearse to the grave site, where a service band, a cavalry regiment, a battalion of engineers, and a company of marines, totaling 1,000 people, were waiting. Pastor Ulysses Grant Baker Pierce said a brief service followed by another 21-gun salute, and Taps concluded the ceremony. The funeral cost $1,649; an original copy of the bill is on display at the National Museum of Funeral History in Houston, Texas.

A month later, a temporary marker was placed at the grave, and military guards were posted to deter souvenir hunters and vandals.[10] Taft's widow commissioned sculptor James Earl Frazer to create a permanent memorial. He used Stoney Creek granite to create an impressive 14.5-foot-tall shaft, which was erected in 1932. It included a simple inscription:

WILLIAM HOWARD TAFT
1857–1930
PRESIDENT OF THE UNITED STATES
CHIEF JUSTICE OF THE UNITED STATES

As with Benjamin Harrison's gravestone, many found the marker's subdued strength and dignity mirrored the man. A reporter for the *Southeast Missourian* wrote, "Simplicity is to be the dominant characteristic of the marker, with an inscription telling in unaccented language of the greatness of the one who lies beneath."[11]

THE WILLIAM HOWARD TAFT DEATH SITES
Location of Death

The three-story, white-brick home where Taft died was built in 1904 in the Georgian Revival style. By 1955, it was being used as the Syrian embassy, making Taft's death site the first ever owned by a foreign entity.[12] Due to the war in Syria, the State Department closed the embassy

The home where Taft died. The building was later used as the Syrian embassy before it was closed in 2014.

on March 18, 2014, and ordered all Syrian diplomats to leave the United States.

The home is located at 2215 Wyoming Avenue, Washington, DC, 20008 in what is known as the "Kalorama" neighborhood, which is Greek for "fine view."

Funeral

The cornerstone for the redbrick All Souls Church was laid by Taft himself in 1913. Construction was completed and the church was dedicated 11 years later in 1924.[13] An informative marker in front of the church indicates it is part of the "Columbia Heights Heritage Trail." It is located at 1500 Harvard Street NW (at the corner of 16th Street and Harvard Street), Washington, DC, 20009. For more information, visit: www.All-Souls.org.

Grave

Arlington National Cemetery began as undeveloped forest across the Potomac River. In the early 1800s, the land was purchased by George Washington's adopted grandson, George Washington Parke Custis, whose daughter later married Robert E. Lee and lived in a home on top of a hill. After Virginia seceded from the Union in the Civil War, Robert E. Lee became commanding general for the Confederate Army of Northern Virginia. During the war, the federal government confiscated the land from Lee and used it to bury Union soldiers and freed slaves.[14] On our nation's first official Memorial Day, May 30, 1868, Civil War veteran and Ohio representative James A. Garfield dedicated the cemetery. In his speech, he proclaimed "Hither our children's children shall come to pay their tribute of grateful homage."[15]

Taft's grave is located in Section 30, Lot S-14. He was the first president to be buried in one our nation's most storied cemetery, but he is not the only one. Thirty-three years after Taft, John F. Kennedy joined him in the hallowed grounds. Kennedy's grave is the most visited site in the

Taft's grave in Arlington National Cemetery.

cemetery while, sadly, the tour bus does not even pause at Taft's grave.

Arlington National Cemetery is located in Arlington, Virginia, 22211. It is open every day, from 8:00 a.m. to 7:00 p.m. from April through September and 8:00 a.m. to 5:00 p.m. from October through March. For more information, visit: www.ArlingtonCemetery.mil.

THE THIRTIETH PRESIDENT
Calvin Coolidge ★ *1923–1929*

CRITICAL DEATH INFORMATION:

Date of death: January 5, 1933, 12:10 p.m.

Cause of death: Heart attack

Age at death: 60 years, 185 days

Last words: "How de do, Robert."

Place of death: Home at 16 Hampton Terrace, Northampton, Massachusetts

Funeral: Jonathan Edwards Congregational Church, Northampton, Massachusetts

Final resting place: Plymouth Cemetery, Plymouth Notch, Vermont

Reinterred: No

Cost to visit grave: Free

For more information: historicsites.vermont.gov/directory/coolidge/tour_site

Significance: Buried further north than any other president (latitude 43.5310° North)

In 1895, Calvin Coolidge first moved to Northampton, Massachusetts, into a modest house. Following his presidency and after publishing his life story, *The Autobiography of Calvin Coolidge*, in 1929, he was able to afford a larger home. The next year he purchased a mansion on Hampton Terrace, called "The Beeches," which afforded him the privacy that he greatly desired.[1]

On January 5, 1933, Coolidge awoke at 7:00 a.m. to a pleasant morning. At the age of 60, the former president generally enjoyed good health. He had complained of indigestion for the past three weeks, but it was not considered serious. In retrospect, he may have been experiencing heart pain. After breakfast, he went to his office around

8:30 a.m., where he met his personal secretary, Harry Ross. Shortly afterward, Coolidge felt ill and told Ross, "Well, I guess we'll go up to the house." They arrived a few minutes past 10:00 a.m., and Coolidge spoke briefly with his wife, Grace, before she went shopping.[2] "Don't you want the car?" he asked, but, since it was such a nice day, she declined and walked instead. Those were the last words he would speak to her.

Coolidge worked on a jigsaw puzzle of George Washington and spoke with Ross about his beloved birthplace in Plymouth Notch, Vermont. He reminisced about his ancestors, and the two spoke of a partridge hunting trip they had recently taken. Coolidge walked into the kitchen for a glass of water and at 11:30 a.m., Ross helped him upstairs to his bedroom for his daily nap. The president removed his jacket and vest and lay down, but about 20 minutes later felt a chill and went to the basement to stoke the furnace. There he saw the caretaker, Robert S. Smith, and greeted him in his usual casual manner, "How de do, Robert." These were his last words.[3] Coolidge returned to his bedroom to resume his nap. Grace returned at 12:25 p.m., and after Ross told her that her husband was not feeling well, she went upstairs to check on him. She found him, not in his bed, but sprawled on his back on the adjoining bathroom floor "with his arms out stretched and a calm look on his face."[4] Tragically, he was dead. Being found dead on a bathroom floor was not considered dignified for a former president and led some newspapers to report that Grace had found him on the bed.[5]

Coolidge's family physician, Dr. Edward W. Brown, estimated he had died 15 minutes before Grace found him and released a statement: "There is no doubt that Mr. Coolidge died as the result of a sudden heart attack. The technical name for his fatal attack as it will appear upon the death certificate is coronary thrombosis—the bursting of the large artery entering the heart."[6] With Coolidge's passing, there was no living former president. Herbert Hoover had lost the 1932 reelection campaign to Franklin Roosevelt, but at the time he was still president.

Coolidge's body was placed on his bed, where it remained for the night. He was dressed in striped trousers, wing collar shirt, and white-striped tie and was placed in a gray bronze casket with white satin lining and a plate that simply read CALVIN COOLIDGE 1872–1933. The next day the coffin was set in the living room by the fireplace.

There would be no elaborate state funeral. Grace knew her husband would have preferred a simple ceremony, free of pomp and ostentation. At 8:10 a.m. on January 7, six Northampton policemen carried the casket to a hearse. Honorary pallbearers included Coolidge's secretary of commerce, William F. Whiting; Superior Court Judge Thomas J. Hammond; Massachusetts state senator William M. Butler; Northampton mayor Homer C. Bliss; former Connecticut governor John H. Trumbull; the less notable Northampton book dealer and deacon at the Jonathan Edwards Congregational Church Clifford H. Lyman; Boston merchant and early presidential supporter Frank Stearns; manufacturer and neighbor Reuben B. Hills; attorney Walter L. Stevens; former law partner R. W. Hemenway; and Amherst College treasurer Charles E. Andrews.[7] Mayor Bliss had contemplated an order to close local businesses but decided that with all of the people coming in for the funeral, local merchants would miss out on a lot of sales. Bliss said, perhaps with tongue in cheek, "It is as Mr. Coolidge would wish it, I'm sure."[8]

There was no great procession; instead, the hearse followed a single policeman on a motorcycle. The coffin was carried inside the Jonathan Edwards Congregation Church and opened to reveal the president beneath plate glass. A reporter from Nashua, New Hampshire, reported his "expression was untroubled, serene."[9] Members of the National Guard served as the honor guard. The public viewing started at 8:30 a.m. and lasted a single hour. As the *Pittsburgh Post-Gazette* poetically described, the mourners included "the butcher, the barber, the baker, the friend and the neighbor," who walked with "the congressmen, the senator, the cabinet maker and the governor past the bier."[10] Reporters and photographers, permitted by the widow to enter the church only for a brief period, introduced their readers to some of these hometown locals. There was "the aged cobbler" James Lucey and Coolidge's good friend and barber, George Dragon.[11] For the only time in presidential history, public mourners were measured by the hundreds instead of thousands.

At 10:30 a.m., the service began when the organist played the prelude to Dvorak's "New World Symphony." A small delegation of 25 senators and Secretary of State Henry Lewis Stimson attended. President Hoover, along with his wife and the wife and son of president-elect Franklin Roosevelt, also traveled from Washington, DC.[12] Roosevelt had released a personal statement: "I am inexpressibly shocked at the news of Mr. Coolidge's death. The nation suffers a great loss. I shall never forget his generous and friendly telegram to me in 1920 when he defeated me for vice president."[13]

Traditionally, presidential funerals are hosted by multiple pastors, but the sole responsibility of officiating Coolidge's service fell to the 30-year-old reverend Albert J. Penner. The service would be notable for its simplicity: no sermon, only three songs (chosen by Grace), and lasting half an hour. In the church, the 1,000 people attending were silent, save for an occasional cough or crying baby heard from outside. Penner began with an invocation, followed by the oft-heard hymn, "Lead, Kindly Light." He read from various selections of Scripture: Psalm 46 and Psalm 121, Romans, Second Corinthians, and John. He then delivered a prayer, which the *Telegraph* described as "long, sonorous."[14] The four-person choir sang "O Love That Will Not Let Me Go," followed by the benediction to conclude the services at 11:05 a.m.[15]

Six Northampton policemen carried the coffin to the automobile hearse. The car drove 100 miles, through Greenfield, Brattleboro, Bellows Falls, and Ludlow to the Plymouth Cemetery, near Coolidge's birthplace in Plymouth Notch, Vermont (earlier that day, the grave had been dug by the cemetery sexton, Azro Johnson).[16] At 3:00 p.m., Reverend Penner led the five-minute ceremony in the light rain. Consistent with his funeral, Coolidge's tombstone is the most stark and simple of all of the presidents. The stone states (even though his actual first name was John):

CALVIN COOLIDGE
JULY 4, 1872
JANUARY 5, 1933

A crowd of mourners outside of the Jonathan Edwards Congregational Church for President Calvin Coolidge's funeral on January 7, 1933. The photograph was taken by Nelson Benjamin. (Historic Northampton, Northampton, Massachusetts)

Coolidge's simple grave in Plymouth Cemetery in Plymouth Notch, Vermont.

THE CALVIN COOLIDGE DEATH SITES
Location of Death

Coolidge's home was constructed in 1914 and designed in the English Revival style by Richard Henry Dana and Henry K. Murphy. The 16-bedroom, 4-bathroom house featured a gabled roof, shingled siding, and two granite gateposts at the entrance. It became known as "The Beeches" for the 80 beech trees on the property. Its original owner was Henry N. MacCracken, an English professor at Smith College, who later became president of Vassar College. It was next owned by mill superintendent Morris L. Comey. The Coolidges purchased the home in the spring of 1930 from Comey's widow for $30,000.[17] They did not move in immediately, as Comey remained in the home briefly after the sale was completed. While she still lived there, reporters requested to see the home and she arranged an invitation-only tour on April 4, 1930.

The former president called his purchase "a modest place with a little land," but to most Americans, especially during the Great Depression, it was anything but. The luxurious home sat on nine acres and featured an interior elevator, a swimming pool, and tennis courts.[18] Coolidge was a private man, and few people in the town had ever spoken with the former president. After his death, a reporter for the *Reading Eagle* tried to find a local with a personal anecdote. The message boy remembered Coolidge as "a good fellow," before adding "he didn't tip, but he was a good fellow."[19]

After Coolidge's funeral, President Hoover went to the Beeches to offer Grace his condolences. She continued to live there for another three years before putting it up for sale in 1936.[20] It remained on the market for two years, until it was sold to a local lumber dealer, Sidney A. Bailey, and his wife, Mary, a Republican state committeewoman, for only $13,500.[21] It remained a private residence for almost half a century, until July 1983, when it was purchased for $250,000 by real estate agent Robert R. Nelson and his wife Daisy Mathias. They planned to rent out three of the rooms as a bed and breakfast. When their business opened a month later, neighbors were outraged by the "desecration of the home of a former president." As one irate neighbor complained, "I think the city is money-hungry, and anything that has to do with business is acceptable to it."[22] Coolidge, one of the most conservative, business-friendly, and frugal presidents of the 20th century probably would have approved of the plan. But 30 neighbors banded together to file suit and forced the town to shut down the bed and breakfast in December 1983.

The Beeches is located at 16 Hampton Terrace, Northampton, Massachusetts, 01060. The home is a private residence and not open to visitors. To learn about the 30th president, visit the Calvin Coolidge Presidential Library near the home at Forbes Library.

The home at 16 Hampton Terrace in Northampton, Massachusetts, where Coolidge died. It was built in 1914 and named "The Beeches" after the 80 beech trees planted on the property.

Funeral

The Coolidges worshipped at the Jonathan Edwards Congregational Church up until the Sunday before his death. At the time it was called "a historic edifice," but it was later torn down and another church was built at the site.[23]

Cemetery

Plymouth Notch Cemetery was established before 1800. Many of Coolidge's ancestors are also buried there, as is his son, who died in 1924. The cemetery has no gates or posted visiting hours. For more information, visit: historicsites. vermont.gov/directory/coolidge/tour_site.

Franklin Delano Roosevelt ★ *1933–1945*

CRITICAL DEATH INFORMATION:

Date of death:	April 12, 1945, 3:35 p.m.
Cause of death:	Massive cerebral hemorrhage
Age at death:	63 years, 72 days
Last words:	"I have a terrific headache."
Place of death:	Warm Springs, Georgia
Funeral:	The White House
Final resting place:	Franklin D. Roosevelt Presidential Library and Museum, Hyde Park, New York
Reinterred:	No
Cost to visit grave:	$18.00
For more information:	www.nps.gov/hofr
Significance:	First president buried at his birthplace

As Franklin Delano Roosevelt considered an unprecedented fourth term for president, the strain of living with polio and his 12 years in office had taken a physical toll. In March 1944, his cardiologist gave him a thorough examination to see if he was fit to run for another term. He grimly concluded Roosevelt might only have another year to live, which would later prove remarkably precise. Undeterred, Roosevelt kept his prognosis from all but a select few, but even those who were unaware were convinced that he would not survive a fourth term. His vice presidential choice, Harry S Truman, made a sarcastic and prophetic comment to a friend while considering the position: "The vice president simply presides over the Senate and sits around hoping for a funeral." In one of their first meetings, an outdoor lunch on August 18, 1944, Truman was stunned by Roosevelt's appearance and later confided to a friend, "His hands were shaking and he talks with considerable difficulty. . . . It doesn't seem to be a mental lapse of any kind, but physically he's just going to pieces."[1]

Over the years, Roosevelt sought both physical and mental relief in his home at Warm Springs, Georgia. He went there on March 30, 1945, to prepare for the conference to be held in San Francisco to establish the United Nations. On the brink of victory in World War II, Roosevelt sought peace and solitude before the next great chapter of world history. He arrived worn out and gaunt, but those who had accompanied him noted he appeared healthier as the days progressed.

On Thursday, April 12, the president slept late and awoke with a minor headache. His doctor, Navy Commander Howard G. Bruenn of Bethesda, Maryland, found no reason for concern and left for a swim. In his study, at about 1:00 p.m., Roosevelt signed a bill extending the Commodity Credit Corporation. He expected later in the day to attend a barbecue at the home of Warm Springs mayor, Frank Allcorn.[2] The president, who always enjoyed fraternizing with American citizens, had told his daughter Anna that he had grand plans of overeating but intended to "thoroughly enjoy it."[3] His healthy appetite was taken as a good sign. Before the barbecue he first sat by the fireplace to model for Russian artist Elizabeth Shoumatoff. By Roosevelt's side was his secret mistress, Lucy Mercer Rutherford, whose presence lifted his spirits.

Roosevelt sat for the painting in a double-breasted charcoal suit and crimson tie and puffed on a cigarette. Suddenly, he seemed to experience a sharp pain and fumbled at his head in apparent confusion. Attempting a smile of reassurance to his guests, he said his last words, "I have a terrific headache!"[4] The president had suffered a massive cerebral hemorrhage and, minutes later, slipped into unconsciousness. His valet, Arthur Prettyman, and a butler carried him into the adjoining bedroom and placed him on the small bed. Moments later, Dr. Bruenn, medical aide Lieutenant George Fox, and Atlanta heart physician Dr. James Paullin were at his bedside.[5]

Bruenn changed Roosevelt into his pajamas to make him more comfortable. They tried to revive him by placing camphor beneath his nose and pulling his tongue from his mouth to help him breathe. In desperation, they pumped a syringe of adrenaline into his heart, but they could not save him. At 3:35 p.m. on April 12, 1945, Franklin Delano Roosevelt died. An autopsy was not performed, but the death certificate listed cause of death as "cerebral hemorrhage with a contributory cause of arteriosclerosis."[6]

Dr. Paullin called Fred W. Patterson from the H. M. Patterson and Son Funeral Home of

The bed where Franklin Delano Roosevelt died on April 12, 1945, at 3:35 p.m.

Spring Hill, who immediately sent two caskets large enough for the president's six-foot-three-inch frame to Warm Springs (a mahogany model and a 600-pound National Seamless Copper Deposit) to be fully prepared for any situation. He arrived at 10:45 p.m. but was not permitted to see the remains as the former first lady had not yet arrived. Eleanor Roosevelt entered at 11:30 p.m. and soon learned that her husband spent his final days with his mistress.[7] Throughout the ordeal, reporters praised her poised, stoic demeanor but were unaware that beneath her remorse, she hid a seething anger at his betrayal.[8]

At 12:33 a.m., Patterson was granted access to the remains. After nine hours, rigor mortis had set in, making Patterson's work all the more difficult. He embalmed the body and dressed Roosevelt in clothes Eleanor had picked out: a gray-blue suit, white shirt, and gray tie. Patterson consulted Roosevelt's valet, Arthur Prettyman, on to how to style his hair. Once completed, he placed the casket in the living room.[9] As Patterson was working, 3,000 troops arrived in Warm Springs both for protection and to escort the remains to the train station where it would depart for Washington, DC. In the rush to assemble a proper send-off, a few details were missed—the ceremonial flag for the casket was misplaced (a replacement was commandeered from a nearby flagpole) and the horse-drawn carriage did not arrive on time, so Patterson's black Cadillac hearse was used instead.

April 13 was a beautiful spring day when the hearse began its slow drive to the train station. In the car behind the hearse rode the former first lady and first dog, Fala. Twelve hundred infantrymen from Fort Benning marched behind the 99th Infantry Ground Forces and 267th Army Ground Forces bands. At Eleanor's suggestion, they passed Georgia Hall, where Roosevelt always visited to say good-bye before he departed. At 10:01 a.m., the hearse arrived at the train station (today the Warm Springs Wel-come Center), where thousands of villagers had gathered. Ten soldiers removed the coffin and walked up a platform that had been hastily built overnight. They passed the coffin through a window frame into the black-draped Pullman car Conneaut. The coffin was placed on a pine bier that was draped in marine blankets and set at the ideal height to allow it to be seen through the windows. Four honor guards, one each from the army, navy, coast guard, and marines, stood at attention. Leading the funeral train were engines #1262 and #1337, commanded by O. B. Wofford and H. E. Allgood. Next was a baggage car, a dormitory car called the Impersonator, the Signal Corp B&O #1401, followed by four more Pullman cars, the dining car, and Roosevelt's bulletproof car, the Ferdinand Magellan, where Eleanor and Fala rode, followed finally by the funeral car. During the trip, Eleanor worked on the funeral arrangements, including the guest list, choice of hymns, and Roosevelt's tombstone inscription, which would include his immortal reassurance: "The only thing we have to fear is fear itself." The engineers rode slowly to allow spectators a good look at the coffin. In fact, throughout the journey, it would rarely exceed 25 miles per hour. As soon as the train departed, many in the crowd erupted into a frenzied hunt for souvenirs from this historic moment. Within minutes, the newly built ramp was in tatters.

At every station throughout the South, black and white Americans stood together in their grief. The first maintenance stop was made at 1:32 p.m. at Terminal Station in Atlanta, Georgia, where 20,000 civilians and 2,000 soldiers had gathered. Mayor William B. Hartsfield placed a floral arrangement beside the casket, and only Fala departed for some fresh air. The engines were switched, with Claude Blackmon and L. B. Griffith now at the helm of engines #1409 and #1394. At 2:10 p.m., the train departed north to the nation's capital.[10]

It stopped at Greenville Station, South Carolina, just before 7:00 p.m., where 25,000 people stood in the oppressive heat. Mayor C. Fred McCullough placed two floral arrangements at the coffin. Once again, the engines were switched, with Richard Cooksey and O. B. Surratt now manning engines #1401 and #1385. In Hayne, South Carolina, soldiers guarded the station, and another floral arrangement was presented during a brief ten-minute stop. Moments later it passed 11,000 people gathered by the tracks in Spartanburg, South Carolina.

Shortly after entering North Carolina, the train lumbered through Charlotte in darkness. For three solid blocks, a mass of people watched the train pass. A group of Boy Scouts began to sing "Onward Christian Soldiers." Several adults soon joined in, until the entire crowd was singing the sad ballad in unison in a spontaneous gesture of mass mourning, leading one reporter to call it "the most impressive moment on the trip."[11] Several hours later, in Salisbury, North Carolina, 8,000 people stood silently as the train was connected to engines #1400 and #1367. In Virginia, it stopped at 2:00 a.m. in Danville for coal and water, and it stopped in Monroe, where the engines were once again swapped out for #1366 and #1406, piloted by C. R. Yowell and H. D. Hansborough. As the sun rose on the morning of Saturday, April 14, the train passed through Charlottesville at 6:20 a.m., greeted by 1,500 people.[12]

After 721.5 miles and 23 hours, the train arrived at Union Station in Washington, DC, at 9:50 a.m. The day was hot and muggy, but still 25,000 people had gathered there. In the crowd were representatives from Joseph Gawler's Sons Funeral Home, who had been contacted by Fred Patterson to resume the funeral services from there on in (Joseph Gawler's Sons charged $450). Also at the station was the new president, Truman, who boarded to greet Eleanor. The crowd stood in silence as the rear observation window was removed and the coffin passed through it. Nine military officers carried the weight down a newly built wooden platform and

placed it into a black caisson. At 10:08 a.m., a whistle blew and the procession slowly began led by Washington policemen, members of all branches of the armed forces, a contingent of African American troops, WACS, and WAVES. Six horses pulled the hearse, followed by the Roosevelt family and President Truman. The procession also included 12 military formations and 48 armored cars; it stretched for a mile and took 35 minutes to pass. Overhead, 24 bomber jets flew by in salute. As it proceeded down Delaware Avenue to Constitution Avenue to Pennsylvania Avenue, a half million tearful mourners along the route reeled from the sudden change of events.[13]

Servicemen carried the casket inside the White House and placed it on a funeral cart. Ushers from Gawler's Sons then rolled it into the East Room and put it on a catafalque in the center of the room. Years earlier, in 1937, Roosevelt had written instructions for his own funeral, but now nobody knew where they were located. So with nothing to go by, the planners modeled the ceremonies after the last president to die in office, Warren G. Harding. After the funeral, the instructions were found in a White House safe, and, luckily, most of Roosevelt's wishes had been met. One request that could not have been fulfilled, even if it had been known, was for Roosevelt's old Groton schoolmaster, Endicott Peabody, to say a prayer. Peabody had died the previous year.

At 4:00 p.m., an Episcopal funeral service was held for 378 invited guests. In the front row was one symbolic empty seat: a wooden wheelchair that belonged to Roosevelt. The service was led by Episcopal bishop Angus Dun from Washington, DC, who, like Roosevelt, was afflicted with polio. He dressed in a purple cassock that covered the artificial leg he wore ever since he lost his real one to the disease. The nation recognized the funeral in unique ways: telephones, telegraphs, and radio broadcasts fell silent, subways stopped running, and "Rosie the Riveters" put down their drills. Not since Lincoln had a president so emotionally connected with ordinary Americans, and for many, the observation was not just ceremonial—it was sincere and heartfelt. The ceremony was brief, lasting only 23 minutes. It started with the hymn, "Faith of Our Fathers," and in his address Bishop Dun included Roosevelt's famous words, "The only thing we have to fear is fear itself." For a nation still at war, these words were just as apt as when they were when first spoken 12 years earlier. Eleanor sat with her daughter, Anna, and son, Kermit, while President Truman was accompanied by his daughter, Margaret. Woodrow Wilson's widow, Edith Bolling Galt Wilson, and General George Marshall were also in attendance.[14]

That same day, President Truman issued the standard declaration of 30 days of mourning and flags to be flown at half-mast. In an extraordinary gesture, foreign countries around the globe also issued official declarations of mourning lasting one to three days. The *New York Times* wrote, "The world-wide tribute to the late Franklin D. Roosevelt was unprecedented."[15] During the American mourning period, the war in Europe ended, a sad reminder to just how close Roosevelt had come to seeing the fall of the Nazi empire.

Shortly after the funeral, Eleanor asked for the coffin to be opened for her to be alone with her husband. In this private moment, she slipped off her wedding ring and gently placed it on his hand. At 8:00 p.m., the funeral directors sealed the coffin for the last time and an hour later placed it into a 1941 Cadillac Superior. Accompanied by a 12-car entourage, the hearse took only 15 minutes to reach Union Station. There, an army air force band played a solemn dirge as the coffin was placed back on board the train.

Roosevelt's second funeral train—now extended to 18 cars, with the Conneaut relocated to the front, directly behind the engines—returned north to his home in Hyde Park, New York. Toward the end of the train was the Glen Willow, a segregated car carrying four members of Roosevelt's staff. All nine members of the Supreme Court and President Truman were aboard for the journey. Truman used his time as productively as possible, meeting with his cabinet for a crash course on the national state of affairs.

The Hyde Park funeral was an event that no Washington politician wanted to miss. The urge to attend was so strong that a second funeral train consisting of 11 cars was formed to carry representatives from the House and Senate. Roosevelt's train pulled out of Washington, DC, at 10:05 p.m. Strained by the weight of so many carriages, a coupler bent and snapped, and the train halted. At 10:42 p.m., the train was again rolling gingerly down the tracks, but after traveling the length of a football field, the coupler again broke. William Murphy, a reporter on board, was so amused by the difficulties he quipped, "The Republi-

Roosevelt's funeral procession marches down Pennsylvania Avenue. (Library of Congress)

cans have always known it would be hard to get Roosevelt out of Washington!"[16]

The Secret Service attempted to guard the track, but on inspection found only saddened citizens, many huddled around bonfires in their grief. After the train got under way, there were no planned ceremonies, only three maintenance stops to switch the engines. The first was at the 30th Street Station in Philadelphia, shortly after 1:00 a.m., where a crowd of 5,000 people crammed into the building while 10 times that number gathered outside. The train stopped for nine minutes, just long enough for Mayor Samuel to lay a wreath on the coffin. The second stop was at New York's Pennsylvania Station, on track 11, at 4:15 a.m. After changing to New Haven and Hartford Railroad engines, the train departed at 5:03 a.m. The last stop was at 6:25 a.m. in New York, at Mott Haven Yards in the Bronx near Yankee Stadium. Again, the engines were replaced, this time with two J1-D Hudson class locomotives, with #5283, piloted by Engineer C. J. Potter, leading the way. The train was also washed, and at 6:40 a.m., it slowly began the last leg of its long journey.[17]

Over the final miles, guards watched over the tracks leading to the estate. Passing through the town of Hyde Park, passengers saw that buildings had been draped in black and purple.[18] At 8:40 a.m. on Sunday, April 15, the funeral train arrived at the Roosevelt home, 1,050 miles and nine states from Warm Springs. Two hundred people and 600 cadets from nearby West Point greeted its arrival. As the coffin was removed and placed into an army hearse, the West Point band played Chopin's "Funeral March," and when Truman exited the train, the band respectfully struck up "Hail to the Chief." The hearse rode to the mansion, where the coffin was placed into a black caisson and draped in an American flag. For the short distance to the garden, the hearse was pulled by six brown horses followed by one riderless brown horse, with stirrups reversed to symbolize the fallen leader.

Eight soldiers served as pallbearers to carry the president's coffin to the grave, which was surrounded by flowers sent from many dignitaries, including General Dwight Eisenhower. At 9:56 a.m., a 21-gun salute was fired, with each volley eliciting a bark from Fala (who would be buried beside his master seven years later). Overhead two formations of P-47 Thunderbolt fighter jets flew in respect for the wartime commander in chief. There were about 300 mourners at the grave, and the service began at 10:34 a.m. It was led by 78-year-old Reverend W. George W. Anthony of Hyde Park's St. James Episcopal Church. Soldiers ceremoniously folded the flag with military precision and presented it to Eleanor, who in turn handed it to her son, Elliot. The bugler played Taps to end the brief, 17-minute service, and the coffin was lowered into the ground as the crowd sang, "Now the Laborer's Task Is Done."[19] Not since Lincoln was such a sentiment so appropriate.

The mourners dispersed, and within 30 minutes the garden was empty. During the funeral, parallel services were held around the country. Trains stopped running, and bells tolled. The *New York Times* observed, "In war plants men and women stood silently beside their stilled machines. A few minutes later the whirr and clank began again and war work was resumed."[20] Later, a Vermont marble slab was placed over the grave that simply read, FRANKLIN D. ROOSEVELT 1882–1945.

Almost immediately after Roosevelt's death, rumors started to spread that he was still alive, while other rumors alleged he had committed suicide. One conspiracy theorist wrote, "Until Mrs. Roosevelt explains to the world why the casket . . . was not opened to the public, the death of her husband, Franklin D. Roosevelt will remain an unsolved mystery!"[21] According to this theorist, even Russian premier Joseph Stalin was skeptical and had suggested that an autopsy would determine if the president had been poisoned (none was performed). Failing that, he had ordered Russian ambassador Andrei Gromyko to go to the White House and seek a viewing of the body to confirm that Roosevelt had indeed died. Gromyko was denied his request, supporting conjecture that Roosevelt's death was more mysterious than the public was led to believe.[22]

THE FRANKLIN DELANO ROOSEVELT DEATH SITES
Location of Death

Roosevelt purchased land at Warm Springs in 1926, and at the time there was a hotel on the property (it is no longer there). Roosevelt had a small six-room clapboard cottage built, designed by architect Henry J. Toombs. It cost $8,738.14 (including landscaping and insurance) and was completed in May 1932. The small home is surprising in its simplicity, given that Roosevelt was a man of means, residing in a 35-room mansion at Hyde Park. During his lifetime, he took 41 trips to Warm Springs, including every year of his presidency except for 1942, earning it the name "The Little White House." After his death, the home and furnishings were donated to the Georgia Warm Springs Foundation, which in turn gave it to the state of Georgia. The home was dedicated in 1947 and was opened it to the public the following year.[23] The half-finished portrait by Elizabeth Shoumatoff

for which Roosevelt was sitting at the time of his stroke is today on display in the visitor center.

Two prominent Democratic presidents visited the home during their campaigns. On October 10, 1960, John F. Kennedy gave a speech that referenced Roosevelt: "It is a deep privilege to speak here in Warm Springs. No Democrat—and particularly no Democrat who aspires to be President—can stand on this spot without mingled feelings of awe and gratitude—awe for the great man who lived here, worked here, and died here, for the greatness of his works and the greatness of his soul—and gratitude that he raised a Democratic banner that we can be proud to raise today—a banner that summons all Americans, in every section, in every walk of life, in every race and creed."[24] Sixteen years later, Jimmy Carter kicked off his campaign for president with a speech in front of the home. Locals were happy for the surge of tourists to the otherwise sleepy town. One woman working behind the cash register at a local restaurant told a reporter, "We haven't seen so many people in a coon's age. And it'll be two more coons dead and gone before they come again!" Another unimpressed local who had lived there long enough to remember Kennedy and Roosevelt was asked by the same reporter if she was going to see Carter speak. She dryly replied, "I don't think so. Once you've seen the best, it just isn't quite as exciting."[25] Nineteen years later, Carter was back when he was presented with the "Roosevelt Four Freedoms Award" by another Democratic icon, President Bill Clinton, accompanied by First Lady Hillary.[26]

The home is located at 401 Little White House Road, Warm Springs, Georgia, 31830. For more information, visit: www.GAStateParks.org/Little WhiteHouse.

Known as "The Little White House," the home where Roosevelt died in Warm Springs, Georgia.

Funeral Car

The funeral car Conneaut was built in 1911 and had been used by Roosevelt during his lifetime. After the funeral, it was used for passenger service, but it is unknown how many of those on board knew that the same car had once carried Roosevelt's remains. In October 1956, it was purchased by Strates Shows, a carnival operator located in Florida. In 1972, it was damaged in a flood in Wilkes-Barre, Pennsylvania, deemed beyond restoration, and destroyed.[27]

Grave

The Hyde Park burial location was chosen by Roosevelt several years prior to his death. This was where he was born and where he wanted to rest forever. In 1938, Roosevelt donated the estate to the federal government with the stipulation that Eleanor and their children could live out their lives in the home. In 1944, the estate was declared a National Historic Site, and Roosevelt visited it for the last time in March 1945. After the president's death, Eleanor waived the conditions of the donation and turned over full rights to the federal government on November 21, 1945.

On January 10, 1946, seven members from the United Nations laid flowers at the grave and reviewed the estate as a possible location for the future United Nations building.[28] The grave site was first opened to the public on January 30,

Roosevelt's grave at his home in Hyde Park, New York.

1946, on what would have been Roosevelt's 64th birthday. That day, Major General Maxwell D. Taylor from nearby West Point placed a wreath on the grave on behalf of President Truman.[29] The grave remained open until 4:00 p.m., and about 100 people visited that first day.[30] At 2:30 p.m. on April 12, 1946, the one-year anniversary of Roosevelt's death, the site was dedicated by President Truman before 700 guests. Eleanor formally presented the estate to Secretary of the Interior J. A. Krug in a ceremony broadcast over the NBC, ABC, and CBS radio networks.[31]

The home and grave have always been popular tourist attractions. During the first decade that home was opened, a tour of the home was 25¢, but the grave was free and visitor statistics were separately recorded. In 1947, the first full year the grave site was open to the public, 516,265 people visited. There was a slow decline over the years, until attendance was almost halved in 1954, when 277,252 people visited. Tourist traps began to pop up, leading the *New York Times* to lament that in the "once-somnolent village, motels and tourist eateries abound." The newspaper continued, "because of these changes, the area suffers in contrast to such historic shrines as Mount Vernon, the home of George Washington [and] Thomas Jefferson's Monticello."[32]

On August 14, 1960, while campaigning for the presidency, Senator John F. Kennedy visited Hyde Park. After consulting Eleanor at her home, Val-Kill, to ask for her endorsement, Kennedy visited the Roosevelt mansion to speak before the Golden Ring Club to commemorate the 25th anniversary of the Social Security Act. During his visit, he paused at the grave site.[33] Eleanor died on November 7, 1962, and was buried beside her husband. Considered by many to have been the greatest first lady in history, she was honored by a historic gathering of four past, present, and future presidents; Truman, Eisenhower, Kennedy, and Johnson.

John Fitzgerald Kennedy ★ *1961–1963*

CRITICAL DEATH INFORMATION:

Date of death:	November 22, 1963, 1:00 p.m.
Cause of death:	Assassination
Age at death:	46 years, 177 days
Last words:	Unknown
Place of death:	Parkland Memorial Hospital, Dallas, Texas
Funeral:	Cathedral of St. Matthew the Apostle, Washington, DC
Final resting place:	Arlington National Cemetery, Arlington, Virginia
Reinterred:	Yes
Cost to visit grave:	Free
For more information:	www.Arlington Cemetery.mil
Significance:	Youngest president to die

In November 1963, the country was in the midst of a historic stretch: no presidents had died in more than 18 years, the second longest period since the 26-year span between the deaths of George Washington and Thomas Jefferson. The 1950s had no presidential deaths, the first decade since the 1810s that that had happened, and for the first time since the second Grover Cleveland administration, the country had three living former presidents.[1] Few would have expected that the next to die would be the current president. Youthful and vigorous at 46, John F. Kennedy tragically became the youngest president to die. President Kennedy's murder is one of the best documented yet most enigmatic of all of the presidential deaths.[2]

In 1963, President Kennedy was in the third year of his presidency and looking ahead to the next election. Texas was a must-win state, and even with Lyndon Johnson, a native Texan, as his vice president, the Lone Star State was unfriendly territory. In fact, many of its conservative citizens were so openly hostile to the president that Texas Democratic Committee member Byron Skelton warned Kennedy he might be putting himself in danger if he visited. Unfazed, the president scoffed at the suggestion.

On Thursday, November 21, Kennedy and Johnson arrived in San Antonio for a whirlwind two-day trip to canvass five cities. That day, Kennedy visited Houston before settling into the Texas Hotel in Fort Worth. When he awoke on Friday, November 22, he was pleasantly surprised to find a friendly crowd gathered outside. He greeted them and spoke lightheartedly: "I appreciate your being here this morning. Mrs. Kennedy is organizing herself. It takes longer, but, of course, she looks better than we do when she does it."

Kennedy ate breakfast and gave a speech at the Fort Worth Chamber of Commerce that focused on ensuring the military was prepared to meet the Cold War threat. To show their appreciation, the Chamber presented the president with a Stetson cowboy hat. Afterward, Kennedy departed for Carswell Air Force Base, where he boarded Air Force One for a 13-minute flight to Dallas. They arrived at Love Field at 11:37 a.m., and the president was again warmly greeted by the crowd of 2,000 people. Vice President Johnson and Texas governor John Connally met him at the airport. After shaking some hands, Kennedy and the first lady, Jacqueline,

slipped into the backseat of an open Lincoln Continental convertible limousine, with Johnson in the next car behind him. They departed at 11:50 a.m. for the Dallas Trade Mart, where Kennedy was to speak to community leaders and Texas businessmen. It was a 10-mile trip, and the motorcade headed downtown to give locals an opportunity to see the president.

At 12:30 p.m., the limousine entered Dealey Plaza at the corner of Elm and Houston Streets. From the sixth floor of the nearby Texas School Book Depository building, Lee Harvey Oswald fired three shots, hitting Kennedy with two. Just as in the assassinations of Garfield and McKinley, it was the second shot that proved fatal. The first bullet hit Kennedy's neck, and the president grasped where he had been stuck. A confused Jacqueline turned toward him and reached to assist. Then the fatal shot was fired, striking his head, shattering the back of his skull and decimating his brain. Abraham Zapruder, co-founder of the dress manufacturing company Jennifer Juniors Incorporated, was standing in the crowd. Video technology was still in its infancy, but Zapruder was an avid home

Dealey Plaza in downtown Dallas where John F. Kennedy was assassinated. The yellow "X" on the street marks where Kennedy was shot.

moviemaker and had decided to bring his 8mm Bell & Howell camera. As the president passed and the shots were fired, he held the camera steady, and the 26 seconds of footage, forever known as the Zapruder film, is still gut-wrenching to watch more than a half century later.

The limousine driver raced to Parkland Memorial Hospital. During the three-and-a-half mile mad dash, Jacqueline cradled what remained of the president's head in her arms. He was still alive, but she needed no one to inform her that it was impossible for him to recover. At the hospital, Jacqueline continued to hold her husband's head in the backseat and refused to let him go. Finally, at 12:38 p.m., she released her grip, and Kennedy was carried into Trauma Room 1, but there was little the doctors could do. His faint pulse slowed while blood poured from his broken head. Dr. Charles J. Carrico, a 28-year-old first-year surgical resident, was the first to treat the president. He removed Kennedy's clothes, injected saline solution into his right femoral vein, and inserted a tube into his throat to ease his breathing. Quickly, the room filled with more doctors until 14 were crowded in. Carrico was relieved by Dr. Mac Perry, who performed a tracheotomy. The president flatlined but Perry would not give up and tried to resuscitate him, pressing down on his chest to restart his heart. It was useless. At 12:46 p.m., it was obvious John F. Kennedy was dead. A call was made to Washington with the sad announcement; however, the news could not yet be divulged.[3] Three minutes later, Reverend Oscar L. Huber, pastor at the Holy Trinity Church in Dallas, arrived. He had been called by Jacqueline to administer last rites, the Catholic sacrament of anointing the dying. The priest gently pulled down the sheet over Kennedy's face. As Huber did not know that the president was already dead and the doctors did not tell him, he administered "conditional" last rites.[4] This was not the first time Kennedy had received last rites: he had suffered from several maladies during his life and three times before

had received the healing sacrament given to those for whom death is imminent. After leading a brief prayer, the grief-stricken Father Huber departed, and Jacqueline could now confront the inevitable. Comforted that he did not die until last rites were performed, she told Dr. Perry to record 1:00 p.m. as the time of death.[5] The widow leaned in to kiss his face, slid off her wedding ring, and placed it on his finger.

Vernon O'Neal, an undertaker called by the Secret Service, arrived with his best coffin, a bronze-red "Britannia" model from the Elgin Casket Company. To protect the satin interior, he placed a plastic sheet inside and wrapped the corpse in rubber bags. But before the body could be removed from the hospital, Dallas medical examiner Earl Rose demanded an autopsy be performed, as required by Texas law. Ironically, the state he should never have come to would now not let him leave. After a heated confrontation, federal officials triumphed over state officials, and the coffin was loaded into O'Neal's 1964 white Cadillac hearse. While the medical examiner's demand was ludicrous, had an autopsy been performed in Texas, perhaps some of the conspiracy theories that would soon arise could have been avoided.

The driver raced to Love Field, arrived on the tarmac at 2:30 p.m., and the 800-pound coffin was unceremoniously and clumsily carried onto Air Force One. The coffin was too wide for the airplane doors, so the handles were broken off. When they finally got it aboard, it was placed in a small cabin in the back of the plane. Before Air Force One took off, President Lyndon Johnson was sworn in as the 36th president of the United States on board the plane by US District Court judge Sarah Hughes at 2:38 p.m. Barely two hours earlier, Jacqueline was sitting beside her husband on a beautiful Dallas afternoon, but now she was on a plane planning his funeral. Presidential assistant Dave Powers, top aide Kenny O'Donnell, and Democratic strategist Lawrence Francis O'Brien Jr. were also on board Air Force One. The flight touched down at Andrews Air Force base at 6:03 p.m., and the three placed the coffin onto the lift and lowered it to the ground, where six soldiers loaded it into an ambulance.[6] It was taken to Bethesda Naval Hospital, where at 8:00 p.m., an autopsy was performed. Initial plans were for the remains to be taken to the Joseph Gawler's Sons Funeral Home, but in the interest of speed and security, the morticians instead came to the hospital. The morticians began their grim task at 11 p.m., but due to the head's extensive damage and not knowing whether the viewing would be open-casket, they did not finish until four hours later. Much of the gruesome physical evidence was saved and later stored in the National Archives. However, in 1966, it was discovered that a critical piece was missing—the brain of John F. Kennedy could not be found! It is believed that the gray matter was taken from the National Archives by his brother Robert, and motive may have been to suppress the information a toxicology report could have shown, or, more provocatively, to remove evidence of multiple shooters.[7]

The ambulance left the hospital at 3:56 a.m. on Saturday, November 23, and arrived at the White House 38 minutes later, passing pockets of people huddled together in shared grief. The body was transferred to a Marcellus 710 mahogany casket (appropriately, this model is known as "The President") and taken to the East Room.[8] Jacqueline, still wearing her bloodstained dress, snipped a lock of the president's hair. The casket was closed and draped with a flag, and soldiers from the 3rd Infantry and Green Berets from the army's Special Forces stood as honor guards.

Being such a young man, Kennedy had never provided any funeral instructions and emergency plans were made in consultation with his brother-in-law and Peace Corps director R. Sargent Shriver. Jacqueline also was strongly of the opinion that her husband's funeral should emulate that of Abraham Lincoln, so the White House chief usher J. B. West decorated the East Room just as it had been in 1865. Lights were dimmed, the room was covered in black crepe, and the flag-draped casket was placed on a replica of the Lincoln catafalque. At 10:30 a.m. Sunday, November 24, there was a brief private family Mass followed by an eight-hour, invitation-only viewing for government officials. President Johnson entered first, along with his predecessors, Dwight D. Eisenhower and Harry S Truman. At 12:34 p.m., Jacqueline asked the honor guard to remove the flag, and the lid was opened for the final time. Jacqueline placed two letters inside before the coffin was sealed forever.

At 1:00 p.m. military pallbearers removed the coffin and placed it on a caisson. Six gray horses pulled the hearse down Pennsylvania Avenue, led by Metropolitan police. A single riderless horse, Black Jack (named after General John "Black Jack" Pershing), followed, with boots placed backward in the stirrups. The horse was skittish, as if aware of the tragedy that required his service (he would go on to serve in two more presidential funerals, Hoover's and Johnson's).[9] Ten automobiles trailed the hearse, followed by members of the press corps on foot.

The procession arrived at the Capitol building at 1:50 p.m. It had been a virtually silent march, with only the cadence of a muffled drum. However, at the widow's request, the navy hymn "Eternal Father, Strong to Save" played as the casket was carried up the stairs. The coffin was placed beneath the rotunda on the historic catafalque that had also held the remains of Lincoln, Garfield, McKinley, Harding, and Taft. Tributes were read by Senate Majority Leader Mike Mansfield, Chief Justice Earl Warren, and Speaker of the House John W. McCormack. After the service, the hall was opened to the public, and over the next 21 hours an astounding 250,000 people shuffled past the coffin. Their perseverance and dedication were impressive, as some waited 12 hours in a line that, at times, stretched a staggering 10 miles.[10]

Most expected Kennedy would be buried near his birthplace in Brookline, Massachusetts, just as the two presidents who had preceded him in death, FDR and Coolidge, had been buried near theirs. Even on the day of the viewing, President Johnson assumed he would be traveling to Boston.[11] As always, the ultimate decision was with the widow, and she believed that he belonged not just to Boston but to all the people. Robert Kennedy suggested Arlington National Cemetery, which, sadly, Kennedy had visited only two weeks earlier to lay a wreath at the Tomb of the Unknown Soldier. That day, he had hinted to Secretary of Defense Robert McNamara that he might wish to be buried there. Now his wish would be granted. On November 23, shortly before 2:00 p.m., McNamara and Jacqueline reviewed a location in the shadow of the Custis-Lee house. She approved the serene spot and added a suggestion that would become synonymous with the Kennedy grave site—an eternal flame, which, like her husband's legacy, would never be extinguished. The Washington Gas Company hastily installed a Hawaiian torch, connected to a propane tank by 300 feet of copper tubing.[12] Clifton Pollard, chief gravedigger at Arlington National Cemetery, was assigned the solemn responsibility of digging the grave, completing the task in the early morning of Sunday, November 24.[13]

On Monday, November 25, nine pallbearers representing all branches of the armed forces carried the coffin out of the rotunda: they were George A. Barnum (coast guard), Hubert Clark (navy), Timothy F. Cheek (marines), Richard E. Gaudreau (air force), James L. Felder (army), Douglas A. Mayfield (army), Larry B. Smith (navy), Jerry J. Diamond (marines), and Samuel R. Bird (army).[14] At 11:00 a.m., six gray horses led the caisson to the sound of a steady, solemn drumbeat as bells tolled. Eighteen years earlier, the same caisson had carried Roosevelt's coffin. During a brief stop at the White House, the United States Naval Academy Choir sang

"Londonderry Air" and "Eternal Father, Strong to Save." The procession continued at 11:35 a.m., now accompanied by the Black Watch of the Royal Highland Regiment on the bagpipes. (Kennedy had attended a performance by the group on the White House lawn only nine days before he was killed.) Both Jacqueline and Robert walked in the procession, and, against the Secret Service's better judgment, were accompanied by President Johnson.[15]

Outside St. Matthew the Apostle Church, a gaunt Cardinal Richard Cushing, Archbishop of Boston, who had married the Kennedys 10 years earlier, greeted the family before they walked inside. The distinguished crowd included former presidents Truman and Eisenhower, future president Nixon, and dignitaries from 91 countries, including French president Charles de Gaulle, Ethiopian emperor Haile Salassie, Korean president Chung Hee Park, Greek queen Frederika, German chancellor Erhard, Belgian king Boudouin, and Soviet deputy premier Anastas Mikoyan.[16] Arriving late and without fanfare was Reverend Martin Luther King Jr. Inside the beautiful and ornate church, Auxiliary Bishop Philip M. Hannan spoke of Kennedy's ideals and aspirations that inspired a nation and read from his inaugural address. Boston tenor Luigi Vena sang "Ave Maria," which had been performed at the Kennedy wedding and was specially requested by Jacqueline.

After the Mass, the family stood outside and watched the caisson pass by. This would become one of the more poignant images of the funeral, when Kennedy's little son, John, on his third birthday, saluted his father. The procession stretched three miles and took over an hour to cross the Potomac to Arlington National Cemetery. Overhead, 50 air force and 20 navy jets flew, followed by Air Force One, whose pilot dipped its wings in salute. At an altitude of just 500 feet, the presidential jet first used by Kennedy momentarily blocked out the sun. Cardinal Cushing conducted the graveside service, and Jacqueline and Robert lit the eternal flame at 3:13 p.m. to conclude the ceremony. Several hours later, near midnight, Jacqueline and Robert were back at the grave. Without the crowds and television cameras, they said one final private farewell.

An honor guard was placed on duty, and later the grave was surrounded by a white picket fence. On May 28, 1964, President Johnson, accompanied by his wife and military aide Major General Chester Clifton, laid a wreath and stood in silence for several moments. Also in attendance to present a wreath of white carnations was Irish president Éamon de Valera.[17] The next day, 50,000 people visited on what would have been Kennedy's 47th birthday, including Jacqueline and her children, who knelt in prayer before the grave.[18]

In addition to the birthday remembrance, Johnson visited several times during his presidency. On December 1, 1963, only nine days after the assassination, he stopped by after attending church in the morning. The grave had already become a popular tourist spot and there was a crowd that morning. Johnson, accompanied by his wife and daughters, approached for a quiet moment of contemplation.[19] He also made an unannounced visit on July 21, 1964, surprising the thousands of tourists who were visiting that day.[20] Johnson again stopped by on January 3, 1965, on the day before his State of the Union address—his only outing for the day as he prepared for the speech.[21] Presidential visits continued over the next 50 years. On November 20, 2013, President Barack Obama and former president Bill Clinton attended a wreath-laying ceremony to mark the 50th anniversary of Kennedy's death.

In the first six months, a staggering 3,000,000 people visited the grave. By the first anniversary of Kennedy's death, that number increased to 7,740,000, making it the most popular tourist destination in all of Washington, DC.[22] Within three years, 16,000,000 people had visited,

many leaving notes, flowers, Bibles, and other mementos.[23]

The family hired architect John Carl Warnecke shortly after the president's death to design a permanent memorial. Warnecke had been a casual friend of Kennedy, who playfully called him "Rosebowl" because he had played in the Rose Bowl as a Stanford All-American football player.[24] Almost a year later, Warnecke unveiled his design at the National Gallery of Art. The location was an ominous choice, as 83 years earlier, at the same site, Garfield was shot. Warnecke's plans were a four-part landscape design that included a circular walk leading to an overlook with steps to reach the marble platform. At the center of the platform, beneath which rests the tomb, was a brass font that held the centerpiece of the memorial, the eternal flame. Behind the tomb, he included a terminal wall emblazoned with the presidential seal. Robert and Eunice Kennedy were at the unveiling, where Robert spoke on behalf of the family: "What has been done has all our approval."[25]

Despite the simple appearance of the memorial, the price tag was initially set at a hefty $2,000,000. While the family offered to pay all expenses, Defense Secretary Robert McNamara proposed that Congress appropriate a large portion. Yet even with the promise of splitting the expense, the memorial plan was reduced in both cost and scope—the wall was eliminated, as was the bronze font. The Department of Defense received nine bids and in July 1965, the $1,408,350 contract was awarded to Aberthaw Construction from Boston, which broke ground several days later.[26]

Several personal accoutrements were added by the family. While Jacqueline was visiting one of her favorite antique shops, the Antiquarian (since closed) on Palmer Avenue in Falmouth, Cape Cod, she found an attractive piece of pink granite that she felt would fit in well with the memorial. She asked owner O. D. Garland if he could get her a large piece, and he contacted

Dick Baker, owner of the Baker Monument Company in Falmouth. Baker had a piece that had been quarried 150 years earlier and shipped it to Robert Kennedy in McLean, Virginia, where a stonecutter carved it into a round stone. This would eventually become a critical piece of the monument, replacing the bronze font to house the eternal flame.[27] Despite its name, the original eternal flame had actually gone out a few times during the early years. One inadvertent dousing occurred less than a month after the funeral when a group of Catholic schoolchildren poured enough holy water over the flame to extinguish it.[28] A more reliable eternal flame was later designed by the Institute of Gas Technology of Chicago, and the original is now on display at the National Museum of Funeral History in Houston, Texas. Warnecke later said the eternal flame "was stronger than any sculpture or any structure that might be added to it."[29]

Additional stones came from other unique locations. The *Owosso Argus-Press* wrote that the granite used for paving stones was "collected from stone fences and abandoned foundations of barns."[30] Granite used for the quotations was cut from a quarry run by Deer Island Granite Corp in Crotch Island, Maine. Some of the stones weighed as much as 65 tons and were so big that carving required hand tools and blow torches. At one point, a staggering 115 people were working on the project.[31] The new memorial was built about 20 feet away from the original grave.

At 6:19 p.m. on Tuesday, March 14, 1967, Kennedy was reinterred in complete secrecy. Clifton Pollard, the chief gravedigger who had dug the original grave, was again called upon to perform the task. There would be no opening of the coffin and no gruesome descriptions of the corpse, as with past reinterments. Members of the military moved the coffin to its new location, completing their solemn work at 9:02 p.m. Kennedy's two deceased children, Patrick Bouvier, who died two days after he was born, and an unnamed stillborn girl, were also relocated to the new site.[32] The next morning, a small secret ceremony was held in the rain at 7:00 a.m. to consecrate the new grave. President Johnson, accompanied by the Secret Service, along with Jacqueline, Kennedy's brothers Robert and Edward and their wives, his sisters Jean Eunice and their husbands, sister Patricia Kennedy Lawford, and former advisor Theodore Sorensen were all in attendance.

Construction of the Kennedy Memorial in Arlington National Cemetery in 1965. (Library of Congress)

This marked the first time Johnson and Jacqueline had been together in almost three years and her first time at the grave since May 29, 1964. Cardinal Richard Cushing performed the brief blessing and began with a simple plea, "Be at peace, dear Jack."[33] The United States Army band played the National Anthem and the navy hymn "The Boys of Wexford." The entire ceremony lasted a mere 20 minutes.

Four months later, on July 20, 1967, the monument was

completed. While the remains of Kennedy would now rest in peace, bizarre and tragic events seemed to gravitate to the sacred site. In September 1972, a distressed 23-year-old former serviceman, Gale Ott, chose the grave site as the location to end his life. In despair after his wife had left him to marry one of his best friends a week earlier, he plunged a knife into his chest as a small crowd looked on in horror.[34] A decade later, on Sunday, November 28, 1982, a grisly discovery was made when the cemetery opened at 8:00 a.m. Three feet away from the eternal flame was a badly burned and charred body. The clothes were incinerated, and no identification could be found.[35] Federal police later identified the remains of 44-year-old Ramon Mejia, a dishwasher at the Shoreham Hotel who reportedly had a drinking problem and recently had been depressed.[36] While initially believed to have passed out drunk by the flame, the cause of his collapse was later determined to be a heart

Kennedy's grave and eternal flame.

attack. However, why he was by the grave in the first place is unknown.[37]

On May 19, 1994, Jacqueline passed away and was buried beside her husband. Kennedy's grave marker was moved 30 inches to allow her marker to be placed on the platform with the eternal flame between them. The tomb was closed to the public while the work was under way and reopened October 7, 1994.[38]

THE JOHN F. KENNEDY DEATH SITES
Assassination Site

Dealey Plaza will forever be linked with the heinous crime that occurred there. At the site on Elm Street where Kennedy was shot, a yellow "X" is painted on the road. In 2013, as the city of Dallas prepared for the 50th anniversary of Kennedy's death, road crews paved Elm Street and covered the mark, but once the pavement had dried, the "X" reappeared (immediately after its reappearance, author and JFK expert Robert Groden confessed to reporters, "It's never been a secret; I've always admitted to doing it.")[39] To the north of Elm Street is the infamous Grassy Knoll, where many, including "ear-witnesses" to the event, believe a second shooter was perched. Two floors of the Texas School Book Depository, where Lee Harvey Oswald fired his shots, are now the Sixth Floor Museum at Dealey Plaza, which "chronicles the assassination and legacy of President John F. Kennedy."[40] Dealey Plaza will never escape its own legacy and several informative markers and placards have been erected there to commemorate the assassination. As I walked the area, I drifted from one pocket of people to another, all discussing Kennedy's murder.

The Limousine

The 1961 four-door Lincoln Continental in which Kennedy was assassinated was returned to Washington, DC, where it was checked for evidence and clues. Incredibly, after a $500,000 security upgrade, it was returned to the White House motor pool the following month and used until 1977. The Ford Motor Company owned the car throughout the time and leased it to the federal government for $500 a year. After it was decommissioned, it was placed in the Henry Ford Museum in Dearborn, Michigan where it is on display today.[41]

Location of Death

Two days after Kennedy died at Parkland, his assassin Lee Harvey Oswald also died in the same hospital after being shot by Jack Ruby. In 2013, the events that occurred on that horrible day were dramatized in the movie *Parkland* starring Billy Bob Thorton and Paul Giamatti. The emergency room where Kennedy died no longer exists. Its former location is now inside the radiology lab, where there is a small plaque that reads ORIGINAL SITE TRAUMA 1 NOVEMBER 22, 1963. Near the entrance of the hospital is a small memorial dedicated to Kennedy. It features the presidential seal provided by the White House in 1989 and a bust of Kennedy sculpted by Felix De Weldon was donated to the hospital in 2012.[42]

Visitors are permitted, but the original trauma room location is open only during radiology hours, which are 7:30 a.m. to 4:00 p.m. The current emergency room entrance is not

The plaque that marks the location of the room where Kennedy died. The hospital has since been remodeled and the site where Trauma Room 1 once was is now inside the radiology lab.

the same one that was there in 1963. Parkland Memorial Hospital is located at 5201 Harry Hines Boulevard, Dallas, Texas, 75235. For more information, visit: www.Parkland Hospital.com.

Funeral Location

St. Matthew the Apostle Church was originally established in 1840 and located at the northeast corner of 15th and H Streets, NW. It served the congregation for approximately five decades. In 1892, Monsignor Thomas Sim Lee purchased the land on Rhode Island Avenue NW to build a larger church and hired architect Christopher Grant LaFarge to design it. Construction began in 1893 and the church celebrated its first Mass on June 2, 1895.

The funeral for John F. Kennedy was commemorated with a marble plaque in front of the sanctuary gates on the floor where the casket was placed. It reads:

HERE RESTED THE REMAINS OF PRESIDENT KENNEDY AT THE REQUIEM MASS NOVEMBER 25, 1963 BEFORE THEIR REMOVAL TO ARLINGTON WHERE THEY LIE IN EXPECTATION OF A HEAVENLY RESSURECTION

To commemorate Kennedy's commitment to putting a man on the moon, the plaque appears to use a font from *Star Trek*! This unusual tribute makes St. Matthew the only church with a commemorative marker to denote the exact location where a president's coffin was placed. On October 6, 1979, the church celebrated a more joyous occasion when Pope John Paul II celebrated Mass there. Thirty-six years later, on September 23, 2015, the church was again honored when Pope Francis led a midday prayer service for 300 bishops.

The church is located at 1725 Rhode Island Avenue NW, Washington, DC, 20036. For more information, visit: www.StMatthewsCathedral. org.

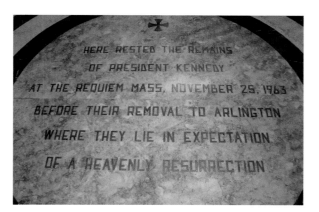

Inscription before the altar at St. Matthew the Apostle Church where Kennedy's funeral was held. No other presidential funeral church has a similar memorial.

Arlington National Cemetery
See Chapter 28: William Howard Taft

POMP, CIRCUMSTANCE, AND PREDICTABILITY

★★★

THE THIRTY-FIRST PRESIDENT
Herbert Clark Hoover ★ 1929–1933

CRITICAL DEATH INFORMATION:

Date of death:	October 20, 1964, 11:35 a.m.
Cause of death:	Internal bleeding
Age at death:	90 years, 71 days
Last words:	Unknown
Place of death:	Apartment 31-A of the Waldorf Towers, New York City, New York
Funeral:	St. Bartholomew's Episcopal Church, New York City, New York
Final resting place:	Herbert Hoover National Historic Site, West Branch, Iowa
Reinterred:	No
Cost to visit grave:	Free
For more information:	www.nps.gov/heho
Significance:	Hoover's life spanned 19 presidents, from Ulysses S. Grant to Lyndon B. Johnson (tied with Grover Cleveland).

One can argue that Franklin D. Roosevelt's and John F. Kennedy's funerals were properly full of pomp and ceremony, as their sudden deaths justified such pageantry. Starting with the unsurprising passing of Herbert Hoover at age 90, presidential funerals defaulted to grand, scripted affairs with every song and step planned years in advance and ceremony in the most minute detail.

Two years after leaving office, Hoover moved into New York's prestigious Waldorf Towers. He was independently wealthy and declined his presidential pension, just as he had refused a salary when he was in office, but could still easily afford the luxury suite in apartment 31-A for more than three decades. He answered mail, organized his records for his books (he wrote more than 40 in his lifetime), remained interested in politics, and followed sports—especially football—on his color television. When his health began to fail in the summer of 1962, he spent more time in his home. He also suffered hearing loss, so his assistants became accustomed to yelling at him. When one visitor was dismayed at speaking so loudly to Hoover, he replied in good humor, "I'm used to being hollered at."[1]

On Saturday, October 17, 1964, the nonagenarian began to suffer massive internal bleeding. Working feverishly, doctors were able to temporarily halt the bleeding in his upper intestinal tract. He received frequent blood transfusions, but the strain was too much for Hoover's heart, and the toxins had poisoned his system. The internal bleeding began again, and in the early morning of October 20, Hoover slipped into a coma. At 8:30 a.m., a medical bulletin was released to the public: "Early this morning, bleeding from the upper gastrointestinal tract recurred, placing an unbearable burden upon his already strained vascular system. His heart, which has borne up magnificently throughout the illness, has begun to fail and its rhythm has become totally irregular. Renal function is inadequate for the demands of his system and toxic products are accumulating in his blood stream. The emphasis in this terminal phase of his illness is upon keeping him comfortable and free of pain."[2] Three hours later, at 11:35 a.m. on Tuesday, October 20, 1964, with his sons Allan Henry and Herbert Jr. at his bedside, Herbert Hoover passed away. He died as the second oldest president, surpassed only by John Adams by 176 days.

Dr. Michael J. Lepore quickly wrote a note on Waldorf stationery to be conveyed to the press: "President Hoover. Oct. 20, 1964. Time: 11:35 A.M." Shortly afterward, Hoover's friend, Neil MacNeil, called a press conference on the fourth floor to provide a more detailed statement. New York mayor Robert Wagner ordered all flags on public buildings to be flown at half-mast for 30 days. President Lyndon Johnson ordered the same for federal buildings and released a sympathetic and personal statement: "I shall miss his thoughtful counsel and his kindly spirit. Shortly after I assumed the Presidency, after that tragic day in November, he was among the first to volunteer his services and his advice. And they gave me strength and comfort during those trying days. His unquenchable sense of public responsibility for both our Nation and our troubled world will stand as an example that will long endure."[3]

Hoover's body was taken to Presbyterian Memorial Hospital, where an autopsy was performed. It was a quick procedure, and at 4:35 p.m. the body was moved to the Universal Funeral Chapel, located only two blocks from the Waldorf on Lexington Avenue and 52nd Street. (Sixteen years earlier, they had handled the remains of Babe Ruth.) After the body was prepared for

The Waldorf Astoria on Park Avenue in New York City, where Herbert Hoover died on October 20, 1964.

burial, the coffin was moved to the main chapel at 9:45 p.m., the lid was raised, and an honor guard was placed on duty. Herbert Jr. arrived to spend a few final moments and was the last family member to see his father's face. After he departed, the coffin was closed for the final time.

At 3:00 a.m. the next morning, the coffin was escorted by the police to St. Bartholomew's Church, located beside the Waldorf Towers. The flag-draped burnished copper casket was ceremoniously placed upon a catafalque that had been shipped from Washington and was a replica of the one used for Abraham Lincoln's funeral. Despite his Quaker faith, Hoover's viewing and funeral were held at the Episcopal Church where his wife Lou Henry's funeral services were held 20 years earlier. The viewing began at 9:00 a.m. and continued until 3:30 p.m. The next day, the doors were again opened at 9:00 a.m. and remained until 9:00 p.m., with one two-hour break. Attendance was light for the much maligned president. Perhaps the sting of the Great Depression still lingered, but sadly, in the sixteen and half hours the body lay in repose, only 22,000 people felt compelled to pay their respects.[4]

After the viewing, invited guests arrived for the funeral service, but once again, poor attendance marred the event. Of 1,400 expected guests, only about 800 showed up—including a paltry 15 of the 300 invited diplomats—leaving more than a third of the seats empty. Hoover died in the midst of the 1964 presidential election, and all four presidential and vice presidential candidates (Lyndon Johnson, Hubert Humphrey, Barry Goldwater, and William E. Miller) were in attendance. Former vice president and future president Richard Nixon, as well as Thomas E. Dewey, John B. Connally, and Robert Kennedy, also attended.[5] Unfortunately, medical issues kept two former presidents from making an appearance. Dwight D. Eisenhower had planned to attend but was recuperating from an inflammation of his windpipe at Walter Reed Hospital, and

Harry S Truman—who demonstrated decency and class when he called Hoover back into public service after Roosevelt kept him ostracized from the White House for 12 years—was also in the hospital after suffering injuries from a fall. Instead, Truman sent a floral arrangement.

An honor guard of five servicemen stood by the casket, one each from the marines, army, navy, air force, and coast guard. At 4:30 p.m., the funeral service began. It was conducted by Hoover's personal friend and the rector at St. Bartholomew, Reverend Terence J. Finlay, whom the Lewiston Morning Tribune described as a "tall, spare man, with handsome profile and thinning steel-gray hair."[6] At the request of the family, the services were very simple with neither a eulogy nor choir music.

The next morning, Friday, October 23, body bearers removed the coffin from the church as a band played "Hail to the Chief" and "Lord, Thou Hast Been Our Dwelling Place." The motorcade of 18 limousines drove to Pennsylvania Station, and the coffin was carried to an elevator and down to the track platform. At 9:35 a.m., the train departed and arrived four hours later on track 17 in Union Station in Washington, DC, where President Johnson was waiting on the platform. The flag-draped coffin was placed on a "church truck," rolled through an honor cordon of soldiers, and placed in a caisson. The horse-drawn carriage was escorted by representatives from all branches of the military and future president Nixon. As the caisson entered Delaware Avenue, the 3d Infantry Battery fired a 21-gun salute. Moments later, 48 air force fighter planes buzzed overhead. Black Jack, the horse, was also included in the procession and was making his second of three presidential funeral appearances, after marching for Kennedy a year earlier.[7] At the Capitol building, a marine band played "Hail to the Chief" and "America the Beautiful" as the coffin was carried up the stairs.

The coffin was placed beneath the rotunda

on the same catafalque used by Lincoln, Garfield, McKinley, Harding, Taft, and Kennedy. Senate Chaplain Frederick Brow Harris gave the eulogy, and President Johnson laid a wreath on the coffin. Shortly after the brief ceremony, the doors were opened to the public from 3:30 p.m. to 9:00 p.m. and the following day from 9:00 a.m. to 9:00 p.m.[8] Once again, public response was abysmal. Perhaps, less than a year after burying the youthful and beloved President Kennedy, Americans felt little need to mourn the loss of a much-disparaged president three decades out of power. Only 30,000 people viewed the coffin during the 17.5 hours

At 9:30 a.m. on Sunday, October 25, the remains were removed from the Capitol and placed in a hearse as the military band played "Abide with Me." As the procession slowly departed, the 3d Infantry Battery fired another 21-gun salute. The hearse rode to Washington National Airport, where a band played "Now the Day Is Over" as the coffin was placed in an army C130 transport to fly to Hoover's home state of Iowa.

At 2:00 p.m., the plane arrived at the Cedar Rapids Airport, and a ceremony was held as the coffin was placed in a black hearse, which departed 15 minutes later. It drove 34 miles to West Branch, arriving at approximately 3:00 p.m., where it was greeted by the 5th Army Band's rendition of "The Star Spangled Banner." Eight soldiers solemnly carried the coffin to its final resting place. During the procession, the band played "The Battle Hymn of the Republic," but because of Hoover's Quaker tradition of pacifism, there was no 21-gun salute.[9]

Hoover's grave was on a grassy hill that he had chosen himself. The land was part of the Herbert C. Hoover Memorial Park and near his presidential library, which had been completed two years earlier. His son, Herbert Jr., commented, "Years ago, he told us that he wished to be buried near his birthplace. Here is where he was born, and these are the people among whom he spent his boyhood."[10] Fanning out from the grave were rings of mourners, whose proximity was indicative of their relationship with Hoover. Behind the family were 46 friends and family who comprised the official funeral party. Behind them, about 20 yards from the grave, were 300 guests. Another 250 yards further out, behind a cordon of soldiers, stood a massive crowd of 76,000 mourners. One of the notable attendees was Republican former presidential candidate and conservative standard-bearer, Barry Goldwater.[11] Quakers do not hold religious services, but rather "meetings," which lack traditional rituals. The brief burial meeting was pronounced by Dr. D. Elton Trueblood, a 63-year-old Quaker scholar from Earlham College and Hoover's longtime friend. His comforting words were typical of a Quaker meeting—upbeat and optimistic: "This

The picturesque grave of Hoover, overlooking his birthplace in West Branch, Iowa.

is not a time for tears . . . our mood today should be rejoicing."[12]

Dr. Trueblood had ample time to prepare for his speech—about a year and a half earlier, Hoover's sons had asked him to deliver their father's eulogy. But when news of the death came, Dr. Trueblood and his wife were inconveniently in the middle of an around-the-world cruise on a boat ironically named the *President Adams* and approaching Saigon. Trueblood, a man of his word, immediately boarded a plane and flew the 12,000 miles back to West Branch.

After the ceremony, people slowly approached the grave to drop a flower on it. It was a sad occasion, but also a day to celebrate Hoover's life, as the *Lewiston Morning Tribune* reported: "The mood carried a rare note of joy and confidence."[13] The coffin was lowered into a 10-foot-square crypt with a four–by–nine–foot marble cover engraved simply with HERBERT CLARK HOOVER 1874–1964. Hoover's wife, who had been buried in California, was later reinterred beside her husband.

THE HERBERT HOOVER DEATH SITES
Location of Death

The original Waldorf Astoria was built in March 1893 but later razed. Construction of the current building began in 1929, directly above an old loading dock. The hotel reopened in October 1931, with the distinction of being the largest and tallest hotel in the world. The Waldorf Astoria Towers comprise the 28th through the 42nd floors, with some suites up to 2,000 square feet in size. It is still considered to be one of the finest hotels in the world, boasting that it is "a boutique hotel" and "home to celebrities, corporate moguls, royalty and every American president since Herbert Hoover."[14] It is steeped in presidential history—candidates have attended fund-raisers there, sitting presidents have spoken to their constituents, and those who have stayed overnight traditionally leave a treasure for future presidents to cherish. If you are one of the privileged few to enter the Presidential Suite, you may see Kennedy's rocking chair, eagle wall sconces from Johnson, a desk set donated by Jimmy Carter, and a table from Ronald Reagan. While serving as ambassador to the United Nations, future president George H. W. Bush lived in a penthouse apartment on the 42nd floor. (Years earlier, Douglas MacArthur had lived in the same unit from 1951 until his death in 1964.) The elder Bush was often visited by his son, future president George W. Bush, who teased him about the luxurious accommodations. On June 4, 2012, former president Bill Clinton and current President Barack Obama made a joint appearance before an exclusive crowd of 50 people who each paid $40,000 to attend.[15]

Hoover made the hotel his permanent residence shortly after his presidency ended in 1933. During his three decades there, he entertained President Truman and future president Nixon. President Kennedy visited on April 27, 1961. Just 10 days after the failed Bay of Pigs plot to overthrow Fidel Castro, Kennedy was seeking words of wisdom from his predecessor.[16] In 1965, a plaque was placed at the entrance to the hotel by the New York Community Trust to commemorate his residence. Beneath the hotel also lies more presidential history. Years ago, the old loading dock below the Waldorf was used as a railroad station known as Track 61, to allow VIPs to surreptitiously enter the city. Its most notable passenger was President Franklin Roosevelt, who made great efforts to hide his polio from the general public.

Hilton Hotel Corporation founder Conrad Hilton purchased many prominent hotels, but according to the company history, he bought "The Greatest of Them All" when he bought the Waldorf-Astoria in 1949.[17] Hilton's 65-year-long management of the hotel ended on Monday, October 6, 2014, when China's Anbang Insurance Group purchased it for a staggering 1.95 billion dollars. This made history as the largest-ever American real estate deal by a Chinese buyer.[18] Given the new Chinese ownership, the State Department decided in September 2015 that the hotel would no longer be used by the president, in part over "security concerns."[19]

The Waldorf Astoria is located at 301 Park Ave, New York City, New York, 10022. For more information, visit: www.WaldorfNewYork.com.

Funeral

St. Bartholomew's Episcopal Church, commonly referred to as "St. Bart's," was founded in January 1835, and its first parishioners gathered in the Bowery section of Lower Manhattan. After moving to several locations over the years, the parish hired Bertram Goodhue to design a new church on Park Avenue between 50th and 51st Streets. He combined a Byzantine interior and a Roman exterior that incorporated a white portal from the previous church. It was completed in 1918.[20]

The church is located at 325 Park Avenue, New York City, New York, 10022. For more information, visit: www.StBarts.org.

St. Bartholomew's Episcopal Church on Park Avenue in New York City, where Hoover's lightly attended funeral was held on October 20, 1964.

Grave

The grave, along with Hoover's birthplace and other significant buildings in West Branch, were turned over to the National Park Service in 1968. In this author's opinion, his is one of the most beautiful presidential graves, with an unobstructed view of the home in which he was born.

THE THIRTY-FOURTH PRESIDENT
Dwight David Eisenhower ★ *1953–1961*

CRITICAL DEATH INFORMATION:

Date of death:	March 28, 1969, 12:25 p.m.
Cause of death:	Heart attack
Age at death:	78 years, 165 days
Last words:	"I want to go; God take me."
Place of death:	Walter Reed Army Hospital, Washington, DC
Funeral:	Washington National Cathedral, Washington, DC
Final resting place:	Dwight D. Eisenhower Presidential Library and Museum, Abilene, Kansas
Reinterred:	No
Cost to visit grave:	$10.00
For more information:	www.Eisenhower.archives.gov
Significance:	First president to die of natural causes in a hospital

If Dwight Eisenhower, the consummate soldier, had an Achilles' heel, it was his weak heart. During his presidency, the warrior had his first heart attack on September 23, 1955, after a bad round of golf in Denver. This was a harbinger of things to come, for he suffered a mild stroke on November 25, 1957. As Eisenhower approached the end of his second term, he started to think about where he wanted to be buried. He considered Arlington National Cemetery, West Point, and Gettysburg, before he decided on his hometown of Abilene, Kansas.[1]

After leaving office, Eisenhower returned to Gettysburg to a home he had built during his years in the White House. He enjoyed his private life and gained prestige as an elder statesman.

He continued to play golf and spend time outdoors on his farm and, despite his maladies, enjoyed excellent health for the initial years of his post-presidency. However, in November 1965 he suffered two more heart attacks, and a year later had his gall bladder removed. He recuperated, but was forced to confront the limitations of age when his doctors restricted his golf game to par-three courses. The year 1968 started out terrifically for Eisenhower when he scored his first ever hole-in-one in Palm Springs, but his good fortune was short-lived. While visiting California on April 29, he suffered his fourth heart attack.[2] Two weeks later, on May 14, he was admitted to Ward Eight of Walter Reed Army Hospital in Washington, DC, where he was destined to remain for the rest of his life.

He suffered yet another heart attack on June 15, but the general could still bounce back. A month later on July 15, he was feeling good enough to receive a visit from his former vice president, presidential candidate Richard Nixon (he was also visited by President Lyndon Johnson on August 2). During Nixon's visit, Eisenhower agreed to endorse him. On August 5, Eisenhower dressed in a suit and spoke from his hospital room; his endorsement was broadcast to the Republican convention. The very next day he suffered another heart attack, and fibrillations caused his heart to stop pumping blood. Using electric impulses, the doctors were able to restore the heart, and within a week, the fibrillations stopped. On August 16, Eisenhower suffered an astounding seventh heart attack. Many felt the grim specter of death was imminent, but Eisenhower again proved them wrong and, on October 14, celebrated his 78th birthday in the hospital. From his window, he waved in appreciation to the army band after they played a tribute to him outside. The year ended as it started, on a high note, when he topped a Gallup survey as the most admired man in America. Some held him in such high regard that they contacted Water Reed to offer their hearts to use as a transplant (presumably after they themselves had perished).[3]

On February 23, 1969, he was again in surgery to repair a blockage caused by damage from an earlier ileitis operation on his intestines. The surgery left him frail and physically and mentally exhausted, but hopeful he could now gain weight. His hopes were thwarted four days later when he developed pneumonia. Doctors gave him antibiotics, but on March 15, he suffered congestive heart failure, leaving his vital organs severely damaged.[4]

To fill the monotonous hours during his 11-month hospital stay, Eisenhower enjoyed reading and listening to music. On March 24, he felt compelled to write his favorite artist, Irving Berlin, to let him know "what pleasure you have brought me not only during my recovery but for many years." But he knew the end was near, and at the end of March, Reverend Billy Graham visited to offer spiritual consultation.[5]

On Friday morning, March 28, 1969, Eisenhower lay surrounded by his doctors and nurses, his son, John, and his wife, Mamie. Exhausted and weak, he still had a little vigor left. Irritated by the glare from the window, he barked at John and Dr. William Hall to "pull down the shades." They dutifully obliged, but Eisenhower again issued a command: "Pull me up from the bed." After they had done as instructed but not to the general's satisfaction, Eisenhower berated them: "Two big men, you can do better than that!" After they did as ordered, Eisenhower told his son, "I want to go. God take me." These were his last words. On March 28, 1969, Dwight Eisenhower died peacefully at 12:25 p.m.

In 1966, Eisenhower had developed his official state funeral plans. He had signed off on the general arrangement, and shortly after his death, the Military District of Washington released a minute-by-minute 54-page report detailing exactly what would occur over the ensuing days. In the end, his plans were carried out with the military precision that would have pleased the

Walter Reed Army Hospital, where Dwight D. Eisenhower died on March 28, 1969.

general. His body was transferred without ceremony to Joseph Gawler's Sons Funeral Home at 5:00 p.m. for preparation (for their services, they charged $2,479.58). His remains were brought to the Jefferson Room in the basement and watched over by army guards. Gawler's was not new to working on presidential corpses, but this was the first time the remains had been brought to their funeral home. They dressed Eisenhower in his World War II uniform, decorated with the medals with which he chose to be buried: his Army Distinguished Service Medal with three oak leaf clusters, his Navy Distinguished Service Medal, and the Legion of Merit. As Eisenhower had instructed, his body was placed in an $80 gray military casket.[6]

The next day at 10:45 a.m., his body was removed without ceremony or escort. Fifteen minutes later the hearse arrived at Washington National Cathedral. The honorary pallbearers were General Omar Bradley, Admiral Arthur W. Radford, General Lauris Norstad, his brothers Edgar and Milton Eisenhower, General J. Lawton Collins, General Wade H. Haislip, General Alfred M. Gruenther, Sergeant John Moaney

(Eisenhower's long-time aide), and Colonel G. Gordon Moore (Eisenhower's brother-in-law). As a marine band played "Hail to the Chief" and "God of Our Fathers," they escorted the coffin into Bethlehem Chapel. An honor guard stood by the closed coffin during a brief prayer service conducted for family and close friends by Reverend Francis B. Sayre Jr., dean of the Washington Cathedral and grandson of Woodrow Wilson. Missing were the abundance of floral arrangements as seen in past presidential funerals; in lieu of flowers, Eisenhower had asked that donations be made to a list of charities.[7]

After the ceremony, a public viewing began, and thousands lined up to pay their respects throughout the day and night, into Sunday, March 30. The doors finally closed after 28 hours. At 3:00 p.m., the coffin was carried to the hearse as the military band played "Hail to the Chief" and "Onward Christian Soldiers." President Nixon and Vice President Spiro Agnew were in attendance, and the president rode with the Eisenhower family down 16th Street and Constitution Avenue to the White House for what the military termed the "casket transfer ceremony." The coffin was placed in a horse-drawn caisson and covered with a plastic sheet to protect it from a light falling rain. At 3:30 p.m., the procession began, led by 89 white-gloved West Point cadets. A team of six black horses pulled the carriage, trailed by the traditional riderless horse with reversed boots in the stirrups.

In a juxtaposition of old and new, the horse-drawn hearse was followed by a limousine motorcade, including one car for the family, another for President Nixon, and similar black limousines for world leaders. Overhead flew 21 Phantom F4 fighter jets. Buildings along the route were locked off, and military forces stood guard on rooftops, prompting the newspaper the *Age* to lament that the procession resembled a dull "river of steel."[8]

The cortege arrived at the Capitol at 4:00 p.m. and was met with a 21-gun salute. As the band played "Hail to the Chief" and "The Palms," the coffin was carried inside and placed beneath the rotunda upon the catafalque used by Abraham Lincoln, and the clear plastic cover was removed. In the crowd was French President Charles de Gaulle along with leaders from 78 countries. Nixon stepped to the podium, becoming the first president to eulogize another president. Eisenhower and Nixon had a special relationship. Not only was Nixon the former vice president under Eisenhower, but they were joined as family when Nixon's daughter married Eisenhower's grandson. President Nixon spoke of Eisenhower as a "good and gentle man" and "one of the giants of our time." He also recounted their last visit together on July 15 at Walter Reed, when Eisenhower told him, "I've always loved my wife. I've always loved my children. I've always loved my grandchildren. I've always loved my country." Assisted by "the wreath bearer," Nixon then placed a wreath at the bier. However, the *Lodi News Sentinel* was not impressed and editorialized that Nixon was "restrained and showed little emotion."[9]

At 6:00 p.m., the public entered, and about 2,000 people viewed the casket each hour until the early morning, when that number dwindled to the hundreds. The viewing continued until 1:30 p.m. the next day, after 55,000 people had paid their respects. At 4:00 p.m., the remains were removed as the band played "Hail to the Chief" and "Faith of Our Fathers." The hearse then returned to Washington National Cathedral, where, at 4:30 p.m., there was an arrival ceremony at the North Transept and the flag-draped coffin was placed on a bier before the altar. The Episcopal funeral service was attended by 2,107 invited guests, described as the "World's Mighty" including Prime Minister of Australia John Gorton, the Shah of Iran Mohammad Reza Pahlavi, and Chancellor of West Germany Kurt Georg Kiesinger.[10] President Nixon sat in the front row, and Lyndon Johnson, who hated funerals, attempted to remain inconspicuous in the sixth row (coincidentally, this was exactly one year to the day he had made his historic decision to not to run for reelection). Harry S Truman, once a good friend of Eisenhower but whose relationship had soured in the 1952 election campaign, had recently been hospitalized for intestinal influenza and was not in attendance. The services were opened by Reverend Sayre and Bishop William F. Creighton of the Episcopal Diocese of Washington. Reverend Edward Lee Roy Elson, pastor of the National Presbyterian Church, who had baptized Eisenhower in 1953, also participated.[11] At Eisenhower's request there was no eulogy. The brief service lasted only 30 minutes.

The coffin was taken to Union Station, where it was heralded with another 21-gun salute. The band played "Hail to the Chief" and "Army Blue" as the coffin was placed on the funeral train, which consisted of a three-unit diesel locomotive engine and 10 cars. The car carrying the president's remains was a black baggage car, #314, decorated with black crepe across its windows, and had a single honor guard stationed inside. At the end of the train was the president's car for his widow, son, and grandson. At 6:50 p.m., the train began its two-day trip to Abilene, Kansas. There were no planned ceremonial stops, and the route was not made public. A year earlier, people had gathered in Elizabeth, New Jersey, to witness Robert F. Kennedy's funeral train. After it had passed, some people were milling on the tracks when another train came careening into the station. The conductor frantically pulled the brakes, but it was too late and two people were killed. The organizers of the Eisenhower funeral train wanted to avoid another similar tragedy.[12]

Despite the secrecy, many gathered along the seven-state route to pay their respects. At Manassas, Virginia, a crowd of 1,000 people watched the train pass, and at Charlottesville, Virginia, where Thomas Jefferson is buried at Monticello, the train stopped briefly to add an engine strong enough to traverse the Blue Ridge Mountains as a crowd of 2,500 people sang "The Battle Hymn of the Republic." In Huntington, West Virginia, there was a 12-minute stop to change crews, and 1,000 people had gathered. The *Lewiston Morning Tribune* noted a hymn sung by "a Negro girl from the Jobs Corps."[13] The crowd also joined together for the Lord's Prayer and a bugler played Taps.

The next morning, April 1, the train stopped at Union Terminal in Cincinnati. In a steady rain, it switched from the Chesapeake and Ohio tracks to the Baltimore and Ohio. Originally, a memorial service was planned by Ohio governor James A. Rhodes, but an exhausted Mamie requested that it be canceled. Still, a crowd of 2,000 people had gathered, prompting Dwight's older brother Edgar to leave the train to thank them.[14] The funeral car, dusty from the journey, was pulled a mile north into an industrial area and washed. In consideration of the crowds that had gathered along the route, Mamie had also asked that the funeral car be decorated with black bunting to help mourners identify it. At 10:38 a.m., the train was again heading west.[15] In Seymour, Indiana, a town of 13,000, almost half the population stood by the tracks, including

children excused from school. The train stopped in St. Louis, where 650 people gathered and for the first time, Mamie left the train to thank the crowd, telling them, "I am most grateful for all the expressions of love."

On April 2 at 6:45 a.m., it arrived in Abilene, where funeral preparations had been finalized a month earlier in a plan called "OPLAN KANSAS." Over 2,100 military personnel had arrived in the small town to handle the logistics. The train sat at the station until 10:00 a.m., when the Fort Riley Band played "God of Our Fathers" and the coffin was transferred to a funeral hearse. It proceeded down 3rd Street, past Eisenhower's boyhood home and on to the grounds of the Dwight D. Eisenhower Presidential Library, Museum and Boyhood Home. Along the 12-block route, thousands of people reverently watched it pass.

At 10:30 a.m., the funeral ceremony was held on the steps of the presidential library for a small gathering of 300 guests, including President Nixon. It was a windy day and the flag kept blowing off of the coffin until two body bearers held it in place. The service was conducted by men of the cloth from coast to coast: former army Chief of Chaplains Reverend Canon Luther Deck Miller, Reverend Robert H. MacAskill of the First Presbyterian Church in Gettysburg, and Reverend Dean Miller of the Palm Desert Community Church.[16]

The honorary pallbearers from Washington, DC, had traveled to Abilene to perform the same duty, except for Admiral Radford and Dwight's brother, Milton, who had collapsed at the funeral in Washington, DC, and was being cared for at Walter Reed Hospital. They were replaced with General Leonard Heaton, Admiral George W. Anderson, and General Andrew Goodpaster. The coffin was carried inside the Meditation Chapel to be interred within a bronze and concrete crypt. Most of the guests remained outside while only a select handful entered (TV cameras were not permitted).

The Meditation Chapel on the grounds of the Dwight D. Eisenhower Presidential Library, Museum and Boyhood Home, where Eisenhower is buried.

Thousands stood behind security barriers and listened to the burial service read by Reverend Canon Miller broadcast over loudspeakers. In the midst of the service, he paused for a 21-gun salute fired by the 1st Battalion, 13th Artillery in five-second intervals (an empty shell from the salute is on display in the presidential library museum). The flag was then folded ceremoniously while the band played "West Point Alma Mater," undoubtedly one of Eisenhower's favorite songs. The service concluded with "America the Beautiful" and "The Old Rugged Cross." Five days after his death and after much respectful pageantry, Eisenhower's funeral ceremony was completed.[17]

THE DWIGHT EISENHOWER DEATH SITES
Location of Death
Walter Reed Army Hospital was first opened on May 1, 1909, as a small hospital. In the following decade it grew from 80 to 2,500 beds, as injured American soldiers returned home from World War I. The hospital is saturated in presidential history: Truman went to his first church service as president there and in July 1952 was admitted for three days after a mild virus infection; in 1960, Johnson visited Nixon while he was a patient, and before Eisenhower was admitted for the final time he was a patient in 1956 and signed the Interstate Highway bill from his room. The hospital closed its doors for good in August 2011.[18] The empty buildings are now within a fenced-off area, but security is still tight—and according to the signs posted, passers-by are under video surveillance.

One curious but unsubstantiated rumor regarding the death of Eisenhower is that he actually died hundreds of miles away in New York at the Waldorf Astoria in room 700R and not at Walter Reed. Whoever started this rumor may have confused Eisenhower with Herbert Hoover, who actually did die at the Waldorf. Beyond that hypothesis, how or why this rumor started is unknown.

Funeral Home
The Joseph Gawler's Sons Funeral Home has a long history. Gawler began in 1850 as a cabinetmaker on Pennsylvania Avenue, near the White House. When much of his woodwork business came from building coffins, he decided to shift the direction of his company. In 1962, the home moved to a three-story brick structure designed in the Georgian style by architect Arthur L. Anderson and is still there today. Almost a century earlier, the location was the site of Union army commander General Winfield Scott's headquarters in the Civil War.

The funeral preparation for Eisenhower began another trend that continues to this day. In the 1960s, Texas funeral director Robert Waltrip began buying up his competition, forming the conglomerate now known as Service Corporation International (SCI). They handle an astounding 60 percent of the market, but many of the smaller companies they acquired have

Joseph Gawler's Sons Funeral Home, where Eisenhower's remains were respectfully prepared for burial.

retained their original identity. Starting with Eisenhower, they have been involved in every president's funeral (and Gawler's was involved before, with presidents as early as Franklin Roosevelt, before being bought by SCI). To ensure they are ready to act when necessary, they have pre-clearance with the Secret Service, and their staff is ready to jump on a plane at a moment's notice—they proudly call themselves the "Flying Squad of Funeral Directors."[19]

The funeral home is located at 5130 Wisconsin Avenue NW, Washington, DC, 20016. For more information, visit: www.JosephGawlers.com.

Grave

The Meditation Chapel was built at the request of Eisenhower several years prior to his death on the grounds of the Eisenhower Presidential Library and Museum. Funded through private donations under the auspices of the Eisenhower Presidential Library Commission, it was built from native sandstone and features beautiful stained glass windows and interior walnut woodwork. Inside are marble plaques that contain words from President Eisenhower's first inaugural address. The bronze marker inscription of Eisenhower's grave simply reads:

DWIGHT D. EISENHOWER
BORN OCTOBER 14, 1890
DIED MARCH 28, 1969

The museum is located at 200 SE 4th Street in Abilene, Kansas, 67410. It is open every day from 9:00 a.m. to 4:45 p.m. (with expanded summer hours) except Christmas, Thanksgiving, and New Year's Day. For more information, visit: www.Eisenhower.archives.gov.

Harry S Truman ★ *1945–1953*

CRITICAL DEATH INFORMATION:

Date of death:	December 26, 1972, 7:50 a.m.
Cause of death:	A multitude of ailments including "the afflictions of old age"
Age at death:	88 years, 232 days
Last words:	Unknown
Place of death:	Kansas City Research Hospital and Medical Center, Kansas City, Missouri
Funeral:	The Harry S. Truman Presidential Library, Independence, Missouri
Final resting place:	The Harry S. Truman Presidential Library, Independence, Missouri
Reinterred:	No
Cost to visit grave:	$8.00
For more information:	www.TrumanLibrary.org
Significance:	Last president whose remains did not cross state lines

After leaving the White House in 1953, Harry S Truman returned to his hometown of Independence, Missouri, because, as he once said, "There never is and never can be anything like coming back home." Truman had many corporate job offers, but declined them all because he believed that cashing in on the presidency would diminish the office. Truman took daily walks and shopping trips with his wife, Bess, and chatted with old friends at the downtown soda fountain. Even at home he remained visible; as one neighbor described, "If you drove real slow past his house on Truman Road, you could look in the north window at night and see him sitting there all alone, reading by the little lamp."[1]

In the decade after leaving office, Truman remained healthy. His first serious medical problem occurred in January 1963, when he was admitted to the Kansas City Research Hospital and Medical Center and doctors operated to repair his hernia. He spent 12 days there, and afterward he would be in and out of the hospital frequently. On October 13, 1964, he was hospitalized after a fall in his bathroom resulting in two broken ribs and a cut on his face that required 11 stitches. (Lyndon B. Johnson came to visit Truman while campaigning nearby.) On July 30, 1966, he was hospitalized again with severe colitis and released six days later. By this time, Truman rarely ventured out due to painful arthritis and spent most of his time at home reading. He was hospitalized again on February 20, 1969, with intestinal influenza and released five days later. On January 21, 1971, he suffered abdominal pains and was admitted to the hospital, where he remained until February 2. During this stay, Vice President Spiro Agnew visited Truman and reported that he "was in good spirits . . . his candor hasn't diminished." He suffered a serious "lower gastrointestinal issue" on June 28, 1972, and was forced to spend another 19 days hospitalized. In November, he began to suffer from lung congestion. He was initially treated at home, but when his condition did not improve, an ambulance took him to the hospital on December 5.[2] By the next day, his vital signs rose to alarming levels. The situation was exacerbated because Truman had contracted bronchitis and was suffering from the hardening of his arteries. Doctors administered antibiotics and oxygen in an effort to clear his lungs.

The hospital released several updates a day. One optimistic— and editorialized—statement read: "President Truman is showing remarkable strength and tenacious physiological reactions which are a reflection of his attitudes of life." In his sixth-floor room, Christmas ornaments hung on the window that faced toward his hometown of Independence. To help pay the daily $59.50 room charge, Truman used his Medicare benefits. In appreciation of his ardent support of the federal health plan, Johnson traveled to the Truman Library to sign the Medicare Act on July 30, 1965, and gave Truman card #1.

A few days after he was admitted, Truman had difficulty talking and could only answer questions with one or two words. By December 14, he was no longer able to speak. What he last said was not recorded, so his final words are unknown. His 180-pound frame had been reduced to 140 pounds. His condition was compounded by heart irregularity, kidney blockages, and a failing digestive system. On Saturday, December 23, he slipped into a coma from which he would never emerge.[3]

The next morning, Truman's night nurse, Mrs. Walter Killilae, held his hand and told him she had Christmas Eve off and would see him the next day. As she recounted, "He squeezed my hand, which leads me to believe his mind was still

The Kansas City Research Hospital and Medical Center where Harry S Truman died at 7:50 a.m. on December 26, 1972.

responsive."[4] On Christmas Day, doctors warned the family that the end could come within hours, but "Give 'em hell" Harry was a fighter and hung on for one more day. At 7:50 a.m. on Tuesday, December 26, 1972, Harry S Truman died. Sadly, his family had gone home and was not at his bedside at his final moment. With him was Dr. Wallace Graham, his presidential physician.

Twenty minutes later, the hospital gave their 80th and final press release; "The Hon. Harry S Truman, the 33d President of the United States, died at 7:50 a.m. at Research Hospital and Medical Center. The cause of death has not been determined. Dr. Wallace Graham was present. Mrs. Truman and Mrs. Clifton Daniel were notified at 7:52. Funeral arrangements have not been finalized. It is the wish of the family that friends make donations to the Harry S. Truman Library Institute, Independence, Mo or the charities of their choice."

Later that day, his obituary appeared in newspapers throughout the nation. In addition to his medical issues, it cited the painfully obvious "afflictions of old age." President Richard Nixon released a statement: "When the death of Franklin Delano Roosevelt thrust him suddenly into the presidency in April of 1945 at one of the most critical moments of our history, he met that moment with courage and vision."[5] He also said that in the years after his presidency, "he honorably supported and wisely counseled each of his successors." Nixon also declared the day of the funeral a "national day of mourning throughout the United States." Mail was not delivered, stock exchanges were closed, and for 30 days flags flew at half-mast. (Johnson's subsequent death would extend this to 58 days.) Johnson, who had often sought the advice of his Democratic predecessor, praised Truman: "A 20th century giant is gone. Few men of any times ever shaped the world as did the man from Independence."[6]

Years earlier, Truman had helped plan his own funeral—an elaborate five-day event including a viewing in the Capitol rotunda in Washington, DC. The world's most famous funeral horse, Black Jack, was also to appear—in fact, the steed was taken up in an airplane three times to get him accustomed to flying during Truman's final hospital stay. Truman called the future plans "a damn fine show," adding, "I just hate that I'm not going to be around to see it."[7] He had a change of heart when, years later, he was bothered by the excessive pomp and opulence of John F. Kennedy's funeral.[8] When the end came, the president's widow opted for a low-key tribute, one much more appropriate for the homespun hero who served as our 33rd president.

The body was taken to Carson's Funeral Home and placed in a mahogany casket in the chapel for a private service for the family. At 1:00 p.m. on Wednesday, December 27, pallbearers placed the coffin in a hearse as a military band played "Hail to the Chief" followed by "Vanquished Army." Along the 1.4-mile route along Lexington Avenue, River Boulevard, Maple Avenue, and North Delaware Avenue, servicemen stood and saluted. At his home, Bess raised a window shade to watch it pass. The 87-year-old widow was too exhausted from the past few weeks to participate in the procession. At 1:20 p.m., the cortege arrived at the Harry S. Truman Presidential Library and Museum. 21 Air Force A-7 Corsair jets flew overhead, and Truman's old World War I unit, Battery D of the First Battalion of the Missouri National Guard, fired a 21-gun salute. To the sound of the booming howitzers, eight pallbearers carried the casket into the library.

The flag-draped casket was placed on a black velvet–covered catafalque in the small lobby. Chaplain Charles S. Burton of the Missouri National Guard said an invocation while television cameras relayed the proceedings. A benediction was presented by Reverend John H. Lembeke Jr. from the Trinity Episcopal Church in Independence, who asked those in attendance, "let us give thanks for the life of Harry S

Lyndon Johnson paying his respects at Truman's funeral. Only 28 days later, he would also die from a heart attack. (Courtesy of the Harry S. Truman Presidential Library and Museum)

Truman." The military pallbearers then stepped back from the casket as honor guards moved into position.

The first to approach were President Nixon and the First Lady, who placed an arrangement of red, white, and blue carnations at the bier. Next, Johnson and his family entered the chamber and stood for a few seconds by the casket, but neither family stayed for the funeral. When the doors were opened to the public at approximately 3:00 p.m., hundreds of people were already lined up. Throughout the chilly night and over the next 21 hours, 75,000 people waited in a line that grew to a half mile. The *Beaver County Times* wrote that the mourners included "the rich and poor, famous and unknown, wearing dungarees and aprons and men and women carrying babies . . . some stopping by to pray silently, men in uniform saluting sharply."[9] The viewing ended at 11:00 a.m. on December 28.

The pallbearers placed the coffin on the stage in the auditorium, beneath a cross and surrounded by flowers. Invited guests included 242 family members, close friends, Truman-era advisors, and salt-of-the-earth folk like Mrs. Eddie Johnson, the widow of his former hab-

erdashery business partner. Moments before the service began, Bess arrived. At 2:00 p.m., Hugh McLaughlin, Grandmaster of the Missouri Masons (a position Truman himself held in 1940), spoke: "We, as Masons, extol his many virtues, not the least of which was his recognition of the high level of individual dignity. May we emulate him in his simple, sincere, sturdy and forthright conduct."[10] Reverend Lembeke read an Episcopal Service in which he intoned, "Most merciful Father, who has been pleased to take unto Thyself the soul of Thy servant, Harry."[11] To conclude the service, retired Baptist Reverend H. M. Hunt led a prayer. At 2:30 p.m., the crowd slowly moved to the courtyard. A half hour later, the pallbearers carried the coffin outside to a spot Truman had selected himself. He could see the serene plot from his office and once told his funeral planners, "I want to be buried out there so I can get up and walk into my office if I want to!"

Reverend Lembeke officiated the brief 20-minute ceremony, and after the crowd departed, the pallbearers lowered the coffin. A simple stone marker was placed over the grave, surrounded with a white rope barrier. The ground was covered with the many floral arrangements received over the past few days. The following day, the grave was open to the public, many of whom posed for photographs. Guards stood nearby, relaxed as they answered questions and patted young ones on the head.[12] One visitor from Iowa commented on the sparse burial site, "I thought it would be simple. If any grave is simple, this one certainly is!"[13] The marker remained for over a year until a permanent memorial was set in place on January 17, 1974. The stone was three-

and-a-half feet by eight feet, weighed almost two tons, and was inscribed with the Presidential Seal and the seal of Jackson County, Missouri.[14] It reads like a résumé of a life well lived:

> HARRY S TRUMAN, BORN MAY 8, 1884,
> LAMAR, MISSOURI,
> DIED DEC. 26, 1972.
> MARRIED JUNE 28, 1919.
> DAUGHTER
> BORN FEB. 17, 1924.
> JUDGE
> EASTERN DISTRICT
> JACKSON COUNTY
> JAN. 1, 1923 – JAN. 1, 1925.
> PRESIDING JUDGE
> JACKSON COUNTY
> JAN. 1, 1925 – JAN. 1, 1935.
> UNITED STATES SENATOR
> MISSOURI
> JAN. 3, 1935 – JAN. 18, 1945.
> VICE PRESIDENT
> UNITED STATES
> JAN. 20,
> 1945 – APRIL 12, 1945.
> PRESIDENT
> UNITED STATES
> APRIL 12, 1945 – JAN. 20, 1953.

THE HARRY S TRUMAN DEATH SITES

Location of Death

Kansas City Research Hospital and Medical Center first opened its doors on August 11, 1963, with 521 beds and the latest medical equipment and cutting-edge technology at the time. Truman spoke at the dedication and called the hospital "a great institution for health."[15] A replica of the presidential portrait is hanging inside the lobby, autographed to Robert F. Adams, executive director of the hospital from 1950 to 1980. It reads, "To my good friend Bob Adams, with thanks, appreciation and kindest regards, Harry S Truman."

Funeral Home

Carson's Funeral Home is now the Carson-Speaks Chapel. It is located at 1501 West Lexington Avenue in Independence, Missouri, 64052. For more information, visit: www.SpeaksChapel.com/Carson_Speaks_Chapel_-25684.html.

Truman's grave in the courtyard of his presidential library. When Truman selected the spot, he said, "I want to be buried out there so I can get up and walk into my office if I want to!"

Carson's Funeral Home (today Carson-Speaks) where Truman's remains were taken. A private service was held for the family in the chapel.

Grave

The Harry S. Truman Presidential Library and Museum is a crescent-shaped building made of Indiana limestone. Ground was broken in 1955 and it was completed two years later. It was dedicated on July 6, 1957, with 10,000 people in attendance, including the only other living former president at the time and Truman's good friend, Herbert Hoover. For years, Truman would visit daily, spending time in his office. He met with many prominent people there, including Eisenhower, Johnson, and Kennedy. The daily trips stopped in 1965 and by the next year, he was rarely seen at the Library. He did make the short trip on March 21, 1969, when President Nixon came to give him the piano he had played in the White House as president. Truman told him, "I appreciate it very, very, very much. I love piano music, but I can't play," to which Nixon chided, "I have heard differently." The sitting president, also an accomplished pianist, then sat and played "The Missouri Waltz." Truman, 84 years old and hard of hearing, turned to Bess and asked "What was that?" It was probably better anyway. Truman hated that song.[16] Truman's presidency is remembered for, among other things, his decision to drop the atomic bomb on August 6, 1945, to bring about Japan's unconditional surrender and end World War II. Most presidents are honored on their birthdays and anniversaries of their deaths, but few, like Truman, have another special day of remembrance. Each year near the anniversary of the bombing, World War II veterans gather at the grave to pay their respects.

On August 5, 1995, 400 veterans and their families saluted their former commander in chief and each lay a carnation on his grave. One veteran, a survivor of the Bataan Death March, said, "President Truman gave me and 999,999 other POWs a second birthday when he ordered them to drop Little Boy, so I thank you."[17] On August 1, 1998, Paul Tibbits, the pilot who flew the *Enola Gay* and dropped the bomb over Hiroshima, laid a wreath on the grave as a bugler played Taps. About 400 others were also at the ceremony, which was sponsored by the Harry S Truman Appreciation Society.[18] In the bicentennial year of the nation, a life-size statue of Truman was dedicated during Truman Week, culminating with a visit from President Gerald Ford on May 8, 1976. After his dedication speech, Ford visited the grave to lay a wreath.[19] Today, the statue is in the museum, overlooking the courtyard.

The Harry S. Truman Presidential Library and Museum is located at 500 West US Highway 24, Independence, Missouri, 64050. The grave is located in the courtyard and can be visited only when the museum is open, which is from 9:00 a.m. to 5:00 p.m. daily, with shorter hours on Sunday. It is closed on Thanksgiving, Christmas, and New Year's Day. For more information, visit: www.TrumanLibrary.org.

Lyndon Baines Johnson ★ *1963–1969*

CRITICAL DEATH INFORMATION:

Date of death:	January 22, 1973, 4:42 p.m.
Cause of death:	Heart attack
Age at death:	64 years, 148 days
Last words:	"Send Mike immediately!"
Place of death:	Somewhere between his Johnson City ranch and San Antonio, Texas
Funeral:	National City Christian Church, Washington, DC
Final resting place:	Lyndon B. Johnson National Historical Park, Johnson City, Texas
Reinterred:	No
Cost to visit grave:	Free
For more information:	www.nps.gov/lyjo
Significance:	The last president whose last words are known

During the presidency of Lyndon Baines Johnson, an important tradition began: every year, on a predecessor's birthday, a wreath of red, white, and blue flowers is sent by the White House and ceremoniously placed upon the former president's grave. In earlier years, this was done on occasion for the most venerated of our leaders, with the first recorded official request made in January 1924 for William McKinley. Over the years the list grew to include 12 presidents, but thanks to Johnson's expansion of the "President's Approved Wreath List" on August 11, 1966, *all* of the presidents were henceforth remembered.[1] This is especially meaningful for some of the lesser-known presidents, as it may be the only event of significance that occurs at the grave site throughout the year.

After deciding not to run for reelection in 1968, Johnson spent the majority of his time where he felt most comfortable—on his ranch in Johnson City, Texas. The former leader of the free world would become restless and was notorious for directing his field hands with the same tenacity and sense of urgency with which he once commanded his cabinet. After his homestead became the Lyndon B. Johnson National Historic Park and the presidential library was opened in nearby Austin, he fretted over attendance, obsessing over how many people visited his library as compared to JFK's library in Boston. The affable Johnson was even known to pop into his namesake attractions, to the delight of visitors.

He also began to write a memoir, which by his time had become a post-presidential tradition, but he never finished it. In many ways, Johnson was a broken man, unable to deal with being out of power and haunted by the Vietnam War, which had tarnished his legacy. Historian Doris Kearns Goodwin, a former member of Johnson's staff who interviewed him extensively in his retirement years, recalled how he struggled. She found him to be a desolate man who almost willed himself to die.[2] President Nixon believed Johnson's death was less physical than emotional when, the day after he died, he told his staff, "I think President Johnson died of a broken heart, I really do. Here's Johnson, this big, strong, intelligent, tough guy, practically getting so emotional that he'd almost cry, because his critics didn't appreciate him. He, till the very last, thought that he might be able to win them. And the point was, rather than have them love him, he should have tried to do what he could have done very well—have them respect him. And in the end he lost. He neither gained the love nor retained the respect."[3]

Physically, Johnson was also a wreck. He had a history of heart disease, beginning in 1955 when he suffered his first heart attack on July 2. The episode prompted him to quit smoking, albeit temporarily. Seventeen years later, in April 1972, he had another major heart attack. And only three months later, Johnson was back in the hospital with chest pains. Doctors considered open heart surgery, but it was not a viable option due to Johnson's extensive heart damage and complications from the bowel disorder diverticulitis, from which he suffered. Due to the heart damage, doctors also ruled out bowel surgery.[4]

Johnson never expected to live long—his ancestors were not blessed with longevity, and this was one of the factors he considered when deciding not to seek reelection. Three years after leaving office, he meticulously planned his funeral. He asked his good friend and spiritual advisor, Reverend Billy Graham, to officiate his graveside service and even advised him not to rely on notes because the wind could blow his papers away (he was right).[5] He knew that national dignitaries would descend upon his ranch, but Johnson also wanted his friends and neighbors to feel welcome at his funeral. He told his wife, Claudia Alta Taylor "Lady Bird" Johnson, "When I die, I don't just want our friends who can come in their private planes. I want the men in their pickup trucks and the women whose slips hang down below their dresses to be welcome too."[6]

In January 1973, Johnson's health was failing. After quitting smoking in 1955, he later resumed the bad habit and had become a chain smoker. In his final interview with Walter Cronkite on January 12, he told the reporter that quitting would be "bad for his heart" as it would make him too nervous![7] His other vice was his favorite drink, Cutty Sark whiskey. In an appearance in Austin on January 16, onlookers noticed that Johnson looked thin. There were no major changes to his health, but Lady Bird noticed he was quieter than usual.[8] His doctor had told him that the trip to Austin might prove fatal, but characteristically Johnson had ignored the warning.

Johnson was looking forward to a six-week vacation in Acapulco, but the Secret Service was concerned. To be on the safe side, they made plans to have him covertly whisked out of Mexico if the worst happened. In an interview, Mike Howard, head of Johnson's Secret Service detail, bluntly stated, "In fact, I'd already made arrangements to sneak him out of there, in case he had an attack or in case he died. I had a plan to get him out—get the body out without the Mexicans knowing it—and get him back here, so it would look like he died at home. Because he didn't want, we didn't want any of that problem."[9]

On Monday, January 22, his family was out and Johnson ate lunch alone and took his afternoon nap. At 3:50 p.m., he suddenly experienced a sharp severe pain. He grasped for the phone that connected him to the ranch switchboard operator Bill Morrow and frantically cried out, "Send Mike immediately!"[10] He was calling for Mike Howard, who was out driving on the ranch. Instead, Secret Service agents Ed Nowland and Harry Harris rushed to his room. They arrived with oxygen in hand and found Johnson on the floor. He had vomited and was dark blue, and blood oozed out of a cut on his head from having fallen out of bed. Nowland tried mouth-to-mouth resuscitation. Four minutes after Johnson's frantic call, Howard rushed in and began to administer an external heart massage. Despite his efforts, he admitted in a later interview, "He was already gone."[11]

Dr. David J. Abbott of Johnson City rushed to assist. At 4:19 p.m. Johnson was carried onto a twin engine Beech King airplane bound for San Antonio so he could be transported to the Brooke Army Medical Center. Seventy miles away,

Colonel George McGranahan from Brooke Army Medical Center rushed to the San Antonio Airport to await their arrival. Aboard the plane with Johnson were pilot Barney Hulett, Dr. Abbott, agents Nowland and Harris, and the wife of a ranch foreman, Jewell Malechek. During the 14-minute trip, Dr. Abbott desperately tried to revive Johnson—he pushed a tube down his throat and administered electric shock. After the plane landed, McGranahan examined the president. Lyndon Johnson was pronounced dead on arrival at 4:42 p.m. on January 22, 1973. Howard called Washington to report a "Situation O," code for any president's death. Where Johnson actually died is vague. According to Howard he was dead when he rushed into his bedroom but was not pronounced until he reached San Antonio. And possibly he could have died somewhere in the skies between.

Harry S Truman had passed away only 28 days earlier, and in accordance with Nixon's presidential order, federal flags were already being flown at half-mast for 30 days. This period was now extended to continue until 30 days after Johnson's death. Nixon went into office

The Lyndon Baines Johnson Presidential Library and Museum in Austin, Texas, where Johnson's public viewing was held.

Johnson's coffin sat at the top of the steps inside his presidential library, where approximately 32,000 paid their respects.

silver flag-draped coffin was escorted to the Lyndon Baines Johnson Presidential Library and Museum and placed at the top of the steps in the Great Hall. People flowed past the casket while a band played "The Eyes of Texas Are Upon You."[14] This was more personal than most other presidential viewings, as family members shook hands and thanked people for coming. To honor Johnson's peculiarity of always asking about exact attendance at his museums, library director Harry Middleton kept a precise count. By 3:00 p.m., the count was at 7,795 people, and by 2:00 a.m. it reached 28,427 people before the lines began to dwindle.[15] When the viewing ended at 8:00 a.m., Wednesday January 24, approximately 32,000 people had paid their respects.

After the viewing, Johnson's body was flown to Washington, DC, in the same Air Force One that had carried John F. Kennedy's corpse almost a decade earlier. The remains were received at the airport and carried in a horse-drawn caisson to the Capitol.[16] Following the caisson was the horse, Black Jack, riderless and symbolic of the fallen military leader. Ten years earlier, he marched for Kennedy, and in 1964, for Herbert Hoover.[17] On February 6, 1976, Black Jack died, and 400 people attended his funeral at Summerall Field at Fort Myers Army Base in Arlington, Virginia.[18]

The coffin was placed beneath the rotunda on the celebrated, historic catafalque first used for Abraham Lincoln's funeral. The eulogy was delivered by Texas representative James Jarrell "Jake" Pickle. Also speaking at the ceremony was former secretary of state Dean Rusk. Throughout the day and night, 40,000 people filed past

with three living former presidents, but after Johnson's death, none were left (the most recent time in our history this has occurred). No other president has had three of his predecessors die during his term. With no other members of the Presidents Club left, Nixon was without advice from the select few people in the world who understood what being president of the United States is really like.

An ambulance took Johnson's body to Brooke Army Medical Center, where an autopsy was performed by Colonel L. R. Hieger, chief of pathology. The cause of death was listed as "coronary thrombosis," and Hieger found "two of three major arteries supplying the heart were completely occluded . . . and the third artery was 60 percent occluded." While others have died at a younger age than Johnson, their deaths were attributed to assassination or a specific disease. Excluding those situations, Johnson became the youngest president to die.[12]

Johnson's remains were taken to the army morgue at Fort Sam Houston and later transferred to the Weed-Corley Funeral Home in Austin, Texas, where they arrived at 11:43 p.m.[13] The next morning, Tuesday, January 23, the

President Richard Nixon offering condolences to Johnson's widow at the funeral in the United States Capitol. (Library of Congress)

the closed casket before the viewing ended at 8:00 a.m. on Thursday, January 25. The coffin was then taken by military escort to the National City Christian Church. Former White House chief of staff and postmaster general Marvin Watson praised his former boss while acknowledging the toll Vietnam had taken on his presidency. Opera singer Leontyne Price sang "Precious Lord, Take My Hand" and "Onward, Christian Soldiers."[19] The remains were escorted to Andrews Air Force Base and several hours later arrived at Bergstrom Air Force Base in Austin. A motorcade drove 65 miles in the rain to the family cemetery. Johnson had always made it clear he wanted to be buried on his ranch. This was where he was born, it was the country he loved, and it was where he wanted to rest in death.

Ten thousand people braved the frigid temperatures, many waiting outside for two hours for the motorcade to arrive. Shuttle buses brought in many of Johnson's Hill County neighbors for the 50-minute ceremony. Military pallbearers carried the coffin to the grave site, and as Johnson had wished, the ceremony was officiated by Billy Graham. Dressed in a dark robe, Graham relayed words that Johnson had once spoken to him: "I love this country where people know when you're

sick, love you while you are alive, and miss you when you die." Speaking of his magnanimity, Graham said, "I never heard him criticize President Nixon one time, in private or public, after he left the White House. . . . He was a mountain of a man."[20] The *Evening Independent* wrote that the burial "reflected the things [LBJ] cared about: religious solemnity, military pageantry, deepfelt oratory and the gathering of good friends."[21] Among those good friends were Johnson's vice president, Hubert Humphrey, Teddy Kennedy, George McGovern, John B. Connally, Ed Muskie, and Strom Thurmond. On behalf of President Nixon, Vietnam general William Westmoreland laid a wreath of red and white carnations on the grave.[22] Across the Pedernales River, a seven-man rifle team from the Texas National Guard fired 105mm howitzers followed by the playing of Taps. Anita Bryant, former Miss Oklahoma (1958), sang the "Battle Hymn of the Republic." Just as Johnson had warned Graham, a strong wind blew, forcing military pallbearers to grip the flag tightly over the coffin during the ceremony. After the service was complete, they folded the flag, and Johnson's good friend and retired United States Air Force Brigadier General James Underwood Cross presented it to the widow.

After the crowd had dispersed, the grave was filled in. Throughout the bitter night, four military policemen guarded the grave while two Secret Service agents sat nearby in a car with the heat on. Immediately, the grave became a popular site for visitors. The Saturday after the funeral, 3,000 people visited the grave. The next day, that number increased to 4,000.[23]

On January 17, 1974, five days before the first anniversary of Johnson's death, the grave was

Johnson's grave (the large one on the right) on the grounds of the Lyndon B. Johnson National Historical Park in Johnson City, Texas.

THE LYNDON BAINES JOHNSON DEATH SITES
Probable Location of Death

The home where Johnson lived and may have died was built in 1894 from native field-stone by German immigrant William "Polecat" Meier. Fifteen years later, it was purchased by Johnson's aunt and uncle, Frank and Clarence Martin, who added the central portion of the home. In 1951, Johnson's aunt sold the home to the president's parents, who added more rooms, including the office and master bedroom where Johnson would later suffer his fatal heart attack. The home was subsequently purchased by Johnson and used extensively during his presidency, earning it the name the "Texas White House" and more irreverently, "LBJ Ranch One." Many important people had visited for both business and social gatherings. Shortly after leaving office, Johnson was visited by George H. W. Bush, who at the time was a member of the House of Representatives and crossed party lines to befriend his fellow Texan.[27] Presidential candidate Richard Nixon visited in August 1968, and Johnson was also twice visited by Truman.

Johnson spoke fondly of the home: "I first came to this house as a very young boy. This is the big house on the river. My uncle and aunt lived here. They would always ask all the in-laws to come here and spend their Christmas. Frequently, I would come here during the summer when Judge Martin, my uncle, lived here and I'd spend three months' vacation from school riding with him and looking after the cattle. I kept coming back to this house. I guess I must have had a yearning to someday own it. But when we came here on one of the periodic visits in 1952, my aunt told me that she was in advancing years

marked with a simple pink granite stone.[24] It read:

LYNDON BAINES JOHNSON
AUGUST 27, 1908
JANUARY 22, 1973
36TH PRESIDENT OF THE UNITED STATES OF AMERICA

On April 7, 1973, South Vietnamese president Nguyen Van Thieu visited Johnson's grave, accompanied by Lady Bird. Arriving before him was a four-foot-tall arrangement of red and yellow roses, the national colors of Vietnam. On August 27, 1973, a "dull black wreath" was placed on the grave by Marine Colonel Haywood Smith, former military aide to Johnson, on behalf of President Nixon. Lady Bird was also at the brief ceremony along with 100 tourists.[25]

In August 1988, Democratic candidates Michael Dukakis and Lloyd Bentsen, escorted by Lady Bird, visited the grave. Reporters noted "a somewhat awkward moment when Dukakis . . . reminded reporters of his opposition to the same Vietnam War that Johnson escalated."[26]

The home where Johnson suffered his fatal heart attack.

Johnson and Kennedy flew in to the airport on November 21, 1963, the day before Kennedy was assassinated.

There is no marker at the airport to commemorate Johnson's death, and officials did not respond to my request to see the exact location where he was pronounced dead. The airport is located at 9800 Airport Boulevard, San Antonio, Texas, 78216. For more information, visit: www.SanAntonio.gov/sat.

and poor health and she wondered if I wouldn't buy the place. And I did."[28]

A year before he died, the Johnson family donated the home to the National Park Service with the stipulation that Lady Bird continue to live there after the president passed away. This was the first time a president's estate was opened to the public while he was alive, and this presented some challenges as to how to interpret the site, for Johnson was very particular about how his Hill Country life story was to be told. After his death, Lady Bird continued to live there for 34 years, until her death on July 11, 2007. On August 27, 2008, the home was first opened to the public.

The home is part of the Lyndon B. Johnson National Historical Park on 199 Park Road 52, Stonewall, Texas, 78671. The cost is $3.00 to tour the home, which is open every day from 9:00 a.m. to 4:00 p.m. For more information, visit: www.nps.gov/lyjo.

Official Location of Death

The San Antonio International Airport was first built as a military base in July 1941, when 32-year-old Johnson was a member of the House of Representatives from the 10th District of Texas. It was converted to a commercial airport in 1953, when Johnson was a senator.[29] Both

Funeral

The National City Christian Church was designed by John Russell Pope, who is also known for designing the Abraham Lincoln Birthplace Memorial, Jefferson Memorial, National Archives Building, and the expansion of Yale University. The groundbreaking took place in 1929, and the imposing structure was completed the following year. To the left of the altar is a stained glass window commemorating James Garfield, who was a congregant back when it was the Vermont Avenue Christian Church. The theme of the window is martyrdom, inspired by the tragic assassination of our 20th president. Directly across from the Garfield window is the Lyndon Johnson window, for LBJ was a parishioner while he was president. The theme of his window is service, symbolized by the scene of Jesus washing Peter's feet, appropriate given Johnson's Great Society programs, which included Medicare, the Civil Rights Act, and the Voting Rights Act. The church was renovated in 1980 and 1981, and during 1981 the stained glass window was dedicated in a service attended by Lady Bird and Johnson's two daughters. Johnson's pew is also marked with a small bronze plaque.[30] It was here in the "President's Pew" that he sat when he attended service *exactly* 55 times during his

The National City Christian Church, where Johnson's funeral was held.

presidency. When it comes to Johnson, precision counts.

National City Christian Church is located at 5 Thomas Circle NW, Washington, DC, 20005 at the intersection of 14th Street and Massachusetts Avenue. For more information, visit: www.NationalCitycc.org.

Grave

The Johnson Family Cemetery is located in the wide-open Texas Hill Country, in sight of Johnson's birthplace and down the road from his Texas White House. Johnson would visit the family cemetery often and always knew this was where he wanted to be buried. In 1966, he told some visitors, "I walk here nearly every morning. All these beautiful trees, so peaceful and quiet. I'm going to be buried there right next to my mother." He also liked to end his day with a stroll to the cemetery, once stating, "I come down here almost every evening when I'm at home."[31]

The family cemetery began with the burial of Johnson's great-grandmother, Priscilla Bunton, who died on April 28, 1905. Her husband was buried in nearby Stonewall Community Cemetery, across the Pedernales River. At the time of her death, torrential rains had made crossing the river impossible, so instead of being buried near him, she was interred on family property, near a grove of live oak trees. Her grave was later marked with a tombstone of white Georgia marble and topped with a carving of a lamb. Over the years, more family members joined her. The first funeral that Johnson attended was for his grandfather, Sam Ealy Johnson Sr., in 1915. Johnson later recalled it as a "cool, dark moment" in his life. In 1937, when Johnson was a congressman, his father, Sam Ealy Johnson Jr., was also buried in the family cemetery. Nine years later, the open parcel was enclosed when stonemason Frank Seaward built a stone wall around the plot.[32] On September 12, 1958, Johnson's mother, Rebekah, passed away and was buried there. For the rest of his life, Johnson told people he wanted to be buried "next to my mother." For Johnson, this was not a distant, abstract thought. Having suffered a heart attack at age 46, he often mused about his own mortality.

While often reflective and reverent, Johnson could also be downright crude and profane.[33] After winning the 1964 presidential election, he was walking through the graveyard with *Newsweek* journalist Sam Schaeffer.[34] As he so often did, Johnson pointed out the spot where he planned to be buried beside his beloved mother's grave. But on this day, he added, "If Goldwater had won, that's where I'd be right now." Then, for reasons known only to Johnson himself, he unzipped his fly and urinated on his own future grave site! Johnson was truly an unscripted character, the likes of which have not been seen in the White House since. Even his burial was rife with controversy and humor.[35]

After Johnson's death, the army was summoned

to Stonewall to dig the grave site. As they began their work in the freezing rain, a National Park ranger checked on their progress. Despite Johnson's repeated wishes to be buried beside his mother, the ranger found the soldiers had dug two plots away. The colonel in charge was adamant and claimed this was the proper placement, leaving room for Lady Bird to be buried to his right. There, in the pouring rain, the two went head to head, eventually escalating the disagreement to their superiors. Lady Bird's representative, Larry Temple, was summoned to explain to the army general that Johnson had indeed wanted to be buried next to his mother. Once convinced, the general commanded another hole be dug. By dusk, they had excavated about five and a half feet of dirt when the heavy machinery struck metal. The operator jumped into the hole, exclaimed, "It's a pipe! A big pipe!" and summoned the ranchman, Lawrence Klein. This was not news to Klein—he knew the pipe ran through the graveyard in this location. When asked if Johnson himself knew about the pipe, Klein told the stunned group, "Yes sir, he was here and located it, how we should bring it through the cemetery." This shocking admission led those who knew him to conclude that John-

son had had the last laugh on them! The pipe was removed and redirected. Johnson now lies in eternal rest between the two women he loved most.[36]

Johnson family members are still being buried in the small cemetery. An agreement was made to keep it available to limited generations of Johnson family members (approximately 40 people could still use it, if they so desire). There's a lot of space, but the issue is the far-reaching tree roots of the enormous live oak tree that shadows much of the cemetery. Another concern for future residents is that the cemetery is within a 25-year flood pattern and was completely submerged by an overflowed Pedernales River in 1954, 1978, and 2007.

When Johnson donated his home and property to the National Park Service, it came with the understanding that all of the land, including the cemetery, was his to give. After his death, several family members contested that Johnson didn't own anything but his and Lady Bird's plot. Today, the National Park Service owns only the two graves. As these graves are located in the middle, the cemetery is closed off to visitors, a situation unique among presidential grave sites.

Richard Milhous Nixon ★ *1969–1974*

CRITICAL DEATH INFORMATION:

Date of death:	April 22, 1994, 9:08 p.m.
Cause of death:	Stroke
Age at death:	81 years, 103 days
Last words:	Unknown
Place of death:	New York Hospital–Cornell Medical Center, New York City, New York
Funeral:	The Nixon Presidential Library, Yorba Linda, California
Final resting place:	The Nixon Presidential Library, Yorba Linda, California
Reinterred:	No
Cost to visit grave:	$11.95
For more information:	www.Nixon Foundation.org
Significance:	First presidential funeral broadcast on cable television and a record three presidents died during his term

By 1994, it had been 21 years since the death of Lyndon Johnson. Not since the 26-year period between George Washington's death and Thomas Jefferson's had there been a longer stretch when no presidents had died. From 1973 until 1994, living former presidents accumulated until Nixon became one of a record-tying five living former presidents—along with George H. W. Bush, Ronald Reagan, Jimmy Carter, and Gerald Ford—giving Bill Clinton a larger pool of peer counsel than any other president since Abraham Lincoln.

In 1974, Nixon went into shock during surgery to remove blood clots from his leg. His recovery was in doubt, and he teetered dangerously close to death. Fortunately, he survived an additional

The entrance to the "Bear's Nest" complex in Park Ridge, New Jersey, where Richard Nixon suffered a fatal stroke.

two decades, during which his diplomatic efforts and presidential counsel restored a modicum of his reputation after it had become so tarnished by the Watergate scandal and his actions surrounding it.[1] On the evening of Monday, April 18, 1994, Nixon was working on the galley proofs for his latest book on foreign affairs at his condominium in the exclusive "Bear's Nest" complex in Park Ridge, New Jersey. He suddenly went into distress. His housekeeper, Heidi Retter, eased him onto a couch and called an ambulance. Medics took him to New York Hospital–Cornell Medical Center in Manhattan. Nixon had suffered a stroke that left him paralyzed on his right side and unable to speak, but he was awake and able to give his doctors his signature thumbs-up.[2]

The next day, his condition improved enough to move him out of intensive care to a private room. But only two hours later, he showed signs of cerebral edema, or swelling of the brain. Doctors discovered that a blood clot had moved from his heart to his brain. Under normal circumstances, they would have used a respirator to speed up his breathing to relieve the swelling, but Nixon had made a living will with instructions not to be put on life support to artificially extend his life. On Thursday, April 21, he slipped into a coma. The next day, April 22, 1994, Richard Nixon died at 9:08 p.m. with his

daughters, Julie Nixon Eisenhower and Tricia Cox, by his side.[3]

President Bill Clinton made an announcement in the White House Rose Garden. While on different sides of the ideological spectrum, Clinton had welcomed Nixon's counsel and praised him as "a statesman who sought to build a lasting structure of peace." He declared most federal agencies and American stock exchanges to be closed on the day of the funeral. Former president Reagan also released a statement, echoing Clinton's sentiment: "Today the world mourns the loss of a great champion of democratic ideals who dedicated his life to the cause of world peace."[4]

The night of his death, Nixon's body was brought to Vander Platt Funeral Home at 257 Godwin Avenue in Wyckoff, New Jersey. He was dressed in a blue suit and placed in a Marcellus 710 mahogany casket. This model coffin, also known as "The President," was the same as the one John F. Kennedy was buried in three decades earlier.[5] On Sunday, April 24, formal funeral plans were announced. Breaking tradition from all previous presidents since Franklin Roosevelt (excluding Harry S Truman, who had died near his grave site), Nixon would not have a state funeral in Washington, DC. He had left office in disgrace (many close to Nixon thought he would be dead within a year of his resignation) and, despite the kind words of President Clinton, two decades was not enough time for the wounds to heal. Instead, Nixon wanted to have his funeral in Yorba Linda, his birthplace, the site of his presidential library, and where he still had support. His confidant, Dimitri K. Simes, explained, "Nixon didn't want a state funeral in Washington because it would have been only a back-

The Vander Platt Funeral Home in Wyckoff, New Jersey, where Nixon's remains were taken the night of his death and prepared for his funeral.

drop for diplomacy and politics rather than a tribute to the man."[6]

On Tuesday, April 26, the remains were transported to Stewart Air Force Base in Newburgh, New York. The hearse arrived at 9:45 a.m., and marine guards stood at attention for a brief 15-minute military ceremony. There was a 21-gun howitzer salute, and the band played "Hail to the Chief" as the casket was placed on a Boeing 707 presidential jet, the same plane Nixon had used 20 years earlier after his resignation.[7] The jet set down at El Toro Marine Corps Air Station at 12:30 p.m., where the 3rd Marine Aircraft Wing Band played "America, the Beautiful" and "Hail to the Chief" as the coffin was placed in a black funeral hearse. The procession drove 20 miles to the Nixon Presidential Library grounds, but first paused at his birthplace where the 15th Air Force band played "Abide with Me." The weather was terrible, leading the *New York Times* to dramatically declare, "In a scene worthy of 'King Lear,' the usually sunny California sky unleashed thunder, lightning, rain and hail today as Richard M. Nixon's body returned to his birthplace in a plain wooden coffin covered by a flag."[8]

Hundreds had gathered despite the severe weather, and some interpreted the storm as a sign from above; a Chinese mourner told a reporter, "When a great man dies, there are always storms."[9] The crowd at the library fell silent as the casket was carried inside and placed in the lobby. Again, a band played "Hail to the Chief," but the seven news helicopters overhead drowned out the music. Fifty satellite trucks, mobile darkrooms, and a tent for reporters to file their stories were also scattered on the library grounds.[10] As Nixon was the first president to die in the cable-TV era, his funeral would be broadcast live on ABC, CBS, NBC, CNN, and C-SPAN.

An honor guard stood at attention, and the casket was surrounded by many floral arrangements, including one from Polish president Lech Walesa. The casket was closed, while above it was an arrangement of red roses and a photograph of Nixon giving his signature thumbs-up.[11] The public viewing began at 3:05 p.m., and the first man in line was Bill Anderson, who left home nine hours earlier to secure his spot. When asked why he would make such an effort, he commented, "For any man to give his whole life for this country, I would have to have a strong feeling for him."[12] At times, the line stretched three miles long, and mourners waited over eight hours in the cold rain and hail. Some mourners pushed children in strollers or elderly in wheelchairs. As they approached the coffin, many made the sign of the cross.[13]

The *New York Times*, known for its partisanship, pointed out that the "largely white, middle-class crowd seemed subdued and quiet, conjuring up images of the great Silent Majority that Mr. Nixon so often appealed to in moments of political peril." Former chief of staff Jack Brennan described it differently: "The blue-collar guys were more his type of people, even though the world didn't think so." Brennan added, "He wanted the simple stuff. He had an affinity for the blue-collar people, the 'dese, dem, dose' guys."[14]

The viewing ended 20 hours later, at 11:00 a.m. on Wednesday, April 27, after 42,000 people had filed past the coffin. Given that the population of Yorba Linda was 56,000, this was a sizable turnout. In preparation for the crowds, streets had been blocked off, businesses closed, and the police force was augmented. At 4:00 p.m., Reverend Billy Graham began the funeral service. Graham was no stranger to presidents, as he had provided Dwight D. Eisenhower with spiritual consolation 25 years earlier and had preached at Johnson's funeral too. There were 3,000 mourners, including leaders from 55 countries, 47 senators, 64 representatives, and 11 former congressmen. Sitting in the front row was a historic gathering of former presidents: Reagan, Ford, Bush Sr., and Carter. The crowd was an eclectic mix. Several stars of Hollywood yesteryear attended, including Bob Hope, Buddy "Jed Clampett" Ebsen, and Red Skelton. Spiro Agnew was also there—he had not spoken with Nixon since the day he resigned as vice president, but when asked why he was finally burying the hatchet, he replied, "I decided after 20 years of resentment to put it all aside." Also in attendance were G. Gordon Liddy, former vice president Dan Quayle, former chief of staff Alexander M. Haig, and Democratic presidential candidate George McGovern, who lost to Nixon in a landslide in 1972.

President Clinton gave an elegant and poignant eulogy, in which he implored, "May

the day of judging President Nixon on anything less than his entire life and career come to a close." Emotional eulogies were also given by Kansas senator Bob Dole, former secretary of state Henry Kissinger, and California governor Pete Wilson. Funeral music was played by the Marines Corps Air Station Band and the US Navy Band, and Sea Chanters performed "America the Beautiful," "The Battle Hymn of the Republic," "Hail to the Chief," and Taps.[15] Overhead, jets did a fly-by, while on the ground the former president was given a 50-gun salute. The casket was placed in a black granite tomb alongside his wife Pat, who had died a year earlier. The engraving included a quote from his first inaugural address:

RICHARD NIXON

1913–1994

THE GREATEST HONOR HISTORY CAN BESTOW

IS THE TITLE OF PEACEMAKER

In his will, Nixon left most of his estate to the Richard Nixon Presidential Library and Birthplace, including documents "which have had historical or commemorative significance." He

Richard and Pat Nixon's graves on the grounds of the Nixon Presidential Library and Museum in Yorba Linda, California. (Library of Congress)

had been widely ostracized in his years after resigning in shame, and his will illustrated the gratitude he felt toward the museum in the city of his birth. While his rank in the pantheon of the presidents may be debated, the fact that Nixon is one of the most polarizing is not. Many times, death softens one's critics and the deceased is elevated to heights he never saw in life. While this held true in some circles for Nixon, there was also a segment who could not let go. Some protested his funeral while scattered people throughout the country displayed signs and donned

The New York Hospital–Cornell Medical Center in New York City, where Nixon died on April 22, 1994, at 9:08 p.m.

Nixon masks to mock his passing.[16] The cost for the funeral was $311,039, with over two-thirds of that in air force costs.[17] Whether taxpayers should pay the bill was questioned by some; this was the first time in history that the costs of a presidential funeral were subject to debate. Hunter S. Thompson, not a big fan of any politician but who perhaps loathed Nixon more than any other, penned an article for *Rolling Stone* in which he wrote, "The death of Richard Nixon: notes on the passing of an American Monster—he was a liar and a quitter, and he should have been buried at sea—but he was after all, The President."[18]

It is true that time and distance can have a redeeming effect. Now, 20 years after his death and 40 years since his resignation, many are able to separate the man from his policies. Even the most liberal people sometimes cite the bridges he built with Red China and his efforts to end the Vietnam War.

THE RICHARD NIXON DEATH SITES
Location of Death
In 1927, the idea of a single medical facility for both the New York Hospital and Cornell Uni-

versity was first conceived. The location for what would become New York Hospital–Cornell Medical Center was chosen on the east side of Manhattan, between York Avenue and the East River, comprising three city blocks from East 68th to East 71st Street. Much of the funding was donated by New York businessman and philanthropist Payne Whitney. Despite the onset of the Great Depression, construction was completed in 1932. The hospital was an impressive architectural neo-Gothic structure, modeled after the Pope's Palace in Avignon, France. Over the years many changes and expansions have been made to the medical facility.[19]

The hospital is now known as the New York-Presbyterian/Weill Cornell Medical Center. It is located at 525 East 68th Street, New York City, New York, 10065. For more information, visit: weill.Cornell.edu.

Funeral/Grave
As with Johnson and Roosevelt, the grave of Richard Nixon is next to his birthplace. (Nixon's is the closest to the actual building.) But while Johnson was buried in a family cemetery,

no one else was buried on the Nixon plot prior to him except for his wife a year earlier. While Hyde Park was Roosevelt's birthplace, it was also where he lived his whole life, while Nixon lived at his birthplace for only nine years. So more than for any other president, the story of Nixon's grave is the story of his birthplace. The land where Nixon was born was first purchased by his grandfather, Frank Milhous, who used the plot to grow barley. In the winter of 1911, he sold it to his daughter, Hannah Milhous, and her husband, Francis Anthony Nixon. Frank purchased a one-and-a half-story white clapboard-sided home from a catalog kit and built it in January 1912 on a hill near the Anaheim ditch by Yorba Linda Boulevard. Nixon was very proud of this fact and years later said, "My father built this house himself. My father wasn't trained as an architect, but he taught himself to become a highly skilled mason and carpenter. He was particularly proud of the living room fireplace, and apparently others admired it as well because I am told that in addition to ours, he built the fireplaces of several of the neighboring houses."

Nixon was born in the home at 9:35 p.m. on January 9, 1913, and spent his boyhood years there until the family moved to Whittier, California, in 1922. In December 1987, the decision was made to build his presidential library at the site. On July 19, 1990, a dedication ceremony was held, with 35,000 people in attendance, including a historic gathering of presidents. Speaking at the dedication ceremony were former presidents Reagan and Ford, along with the current president, George H. W. Bush. This day was only the second time in history that four presidents were gathered at the same place at the same time. (The previous time was at the White House after the death of Egyptian president Anwar Sadat in 1981.) Carter sent a note of congratulations but was not in attendance. Neither Watergate nor Nixon's resignation was mentioned at the ceremony, and the crowd was mostly supportive of the flawed leader.[20]

The grave is located at 18001 Yorba Linda Boulevard, Yorba Linda, California, 92886, on the grounds of the Richard Nixon Presidential Library and Birthplace. The museum is open daily (except Thanksgiving, Christmas and New Year's Day) from 10:00 a.m. to 5:00 p.m., except Sunday, when it is open from 11:00 a.m. to 5:00 p.m. For more information, visit: www. NixonFoundation.org.

THE FORTIETH PRESIDENT
Ronald Wilson Reagan ★ *1981–1989*

CRITICAL DEATH INFORMATION:

Date of death:	June 5, 2004, 1:00 p.m.
Cause of death:	Pneumonia, complicated by Alzheimer's disease
Age at death:	93 years, 120 days
Last words:	Unknown
Place of death:	Home in Bel Air, Los Angeles, California
Funeral:	Washington National Cathedral, Washington, DC
Final resting place:	Ronald Reagan Presidential Library, Simi Valley, California
Reinterred:	No
Cost to visit grave:	$16.00
For more information:	www.Reagan Foundation.org
Significance:	At the time of his death, he had lived longer than any president.

Shortly after Ronald Reagan had taken office, he was the victim of an assassination attempt by John Hinckley Jr. that left him with a bullet wound to the chest. This brush with death, on March 30, 1981, forced him to consider his funeral plans. He asked Vice President George H. W. Bush and British prime minister Margaret Thatcher to deliver eulogies at his funeral, and a team was assembled to plan it. At first, they met about twice a year and later, Nancy Reagan became more heavily involved. The final instructions totaled 300 pages, and in the end, the team was very happy with the way the events played out.[1]

After his presidency, Reagan moved to Bel Air in Los Angeles where he focused on writing his autobiography, *An American Life*. Over the next few years, his public appearances diminished, and on November 4, 1994, Reagan released a handwritten letter to the country. He announced he was suffering from Alzheimer's disease, which had deteriorated his memory and would bring about dementia. For a while after this sad announcement, he continued to golf and go to his office. When he was no longer capable of those activities, he remained at home, secluded from the public.[2] By the end of the decade, he no longer remembered that he had been president of the United States, although for a while he knew that he was someone important. He could still recall the early years of his life in rich detail, such as when he worked as a lifeguard in Illinois (he was always proud to have saved 77 lives). By 2002, Reagan, at the age of 91, had lived longer than any other president, surpassing John Adams's age of 90 years and 247 days.

In the late spring of 2004, Reagan developed pneumonia. By this time, he had ceased speaking. His final words went unrecorded, but most likely they were unintelligible; his daughter, Patti, wrote that before he fell silent, "the sound of his voice filled the room sometimes—not with words, but maybe they were words to him."[3] For weeks, he lay in a bed in his former home office, which had been converted into his bedroom. He was barely able to move, and his breathing grew weaker. On June 1, he closed his eyes, and his family sat on a death watch. On Saturday, June 5, he was surrounded by his wife, Nancy; his children, Patti and Ronald Jr.; his doctor; and an Irish nurse. As Nancy spoke to him, he suddenly opened his eyes for the first time in four days. Ronald Reagan gazed straight into her eyes one last time, fell back on his pillow, and died at 1:00 p.m. on June 5, 2004.[4]

President George W. Bush was in France for the 60th anniversary of D-Day and made a statement from the Ambassador's Residence in Paris: "This is a sad hour in the life of America. A great American life has come to an end. . . . Ronald Reagan won America's respect with his greatness, and won its love with his goodness. He had the confidence that comes with conviction, the strength that comes with character, the grace that comes with humility, and the humor that comes with wisdom. He leaves behind a nation he restored and a world he helped save. During the years of President Reagan, America laid to rest an era of division and self-doubt. And because of his leadership, the world laid to rest an era of fear and tyranny. Now, in laying our leader to rest, we say thank you. He always told us that for America, the best was yet to come. We comfort ourselves in the knowledge that this is true for him, too. His work is done, and now a shining city awaits him. May God bless Ronald Reagan."[5]

Every former president spoke of the loss. From Plains, Georgia, Jimmy Carter called it "a sad day for our country." He spoke of Reagan's gift for reaching the American people, saying, "I think throughout his term in office he was very worthy of the moniker that was put on him as the 'Great Communicator,'" adding with a touch of humor, "I probably know as well as anybody what a formidable communicator and campaigner that President Reagan was. It was because of him that I was retired from my last job." George H. W. Bush spoke of how their relationship evolved over time, saying, "We had been political opponents and became close friends. . . . He could take a stand . . . and do it without creating bitterness or creating enmity on the part of other people." From the other side of the political aisle, former president Bill Clinton said, "Hillary and I will always remember President Ronald Reagan for the way he personified the indomitable optimism of the American people, and for keeping America at the forefront of the fight for freedom for people everywhere. It is fitting that a piece of the Berlin Wall adorns the Ronald Reagan Building in Washington." And Gerald Ford, who was challenged by Ronald Reagan in 1976, stated, "Betty and I are deeply saddened by the passing of our longtime friend, President Reagan. Ronald Reagan was an excellent leader of our nation during challenging times at home and abroad. We extend our deepest condolences and prayers to Nancy and his family."

His body was taken to the Gates, Kingsley & Gates Funeral Home in Santa Monica, where 25 satellite news trucks were already waiting for the arrival. Due to the likelihood that Reagan would die at home, the funeral home had been notified of their role a year earlier, but this was kept secret, even from much of the staff. A small team led by Bob Boetticher (senior director for special projects from Service Corporation International) had practiced for the event.[6] Now, Boetticher would do the real thing and under the watchful eyes of the Secret Service. Boetticher spoke of the honor of tending to Reagan's remains: "I have to do everything right. I am representing the family, my firm, my fellow funeral directors. And I am working out of personal respect for a man I consider one of the greatest leaders of the 20th century."[7]

On Monday morning, June 7, an honor guard carried the 700 Masterpiece model mahogany casket outside and placed it on the rollers in the funeral hearse. Boetticher gently pushed it in, closed the door, and drove 40 miles to Reagan's presidential library in Simi Valley. Pockets of people gathered along the route; some carried signs, one of which read, GOD BLESS THE GIPPER. It arrived at 11:00 a.m., and as a marine band struck up "Hail to the Chief," eight servicemen solemnly carried the casket inside.[8] The private ceremony was officiated by Reverend Michael Wenning, retired pastor from the Bel Air Presbyterian Church, and attended by family and good friends, including television talk show pioneer Merv Griffin.

After the service concluded, six military guardsmen took their position by the casket for the public viewing. Charter buses shuttled in mourners, who shuffled in throughout the night and into the next day. The viewing was scheduled to conclude at 6:00 p.m., but when crowds turned out to be larger than expected, the viewing was extended by an additional five hours. When it came to an end, more than 105,000 people had paid their respects, including Arnold Schwarzenegger and presidential candidate John Kerry. Many left mementos such as flowers, notes, and Reagan's favorite treat, jelly beans.[9]

On Wednesday, June 9, the remains were taken to the Naval Base airport and placed in a blue and white Boeing 747 bound for Washington, DC. But about a half hour before it was to land, the pilots were alerted to a dire situation—a plane was headed toward the Capitol building! Only three years after the horrific attacks on September 11, 2001, authorities were fearful of another terrorist incident, and the Capitol was hastily evacuated. Fortunately, it was a false alarm caused by a faulty transponder. The plane was not carrying terrorists, but rather Kentucky governor Ernie Fletcher, who was flying in for the funeral.[10]

The protocols and procedures for a state funeral in Washington, DC, are well-documented

A riderless horse follows Reagan's funeral hearse. (US Air Force photo by Master Sgt. Jim Varhegyi)

and strictly adhered to. It had been more than 30 years since the city had hosted a presidential state funeral, but while Reagan's funeral was modeled after Lyndon B. Johnson's capital ceremonies, it was also accentuated by many flourishes of pomp and pageantry. Upon arrival at Andrews Air Force Base in Maryland, a military band played "My Country 'Tis of Thee" as the coffin was placed in the hearse. The motorcade drove to the White House, where the casket was transferred to a horse-drawn caisson that had been built during World War I and originally used to carry a cannon. In accordance with state funeral protocol, the carriage was pulled by six horses; the three on the left were mounted and the three on the right were riderless. It was followed by the traditional, single riderless horse, with boots backward in the stirrups and a saber dangling from the saddle. The black standard-bred caparisoned horse, Sergeant York, was the president's own and had previously been a racehorse.[11]

The procession marched down Constitution Avenue, passing soldiers at attention and thousands of mourners. It was blazing hot; capital police handed out more than 150,000 bottles of water to the sweltering masses and more than 100 people were treated for heat exhaustion.[12] As the procession reached the Capitol, 21 fighter jets roared overhead at an altitude of 1,000 feet. A single F-15E fighter jet then broke from the pack and ascended skyward, symbolic of the lost soldier. The honorary pallbearers included Reagan's former chief of staff Frederick Ryan, former deputy chief of staff Michael Deaver, White House physician John Hutton, Hollywood producer and former head of the US Information Agency Charles Wick, and Merv Griffin. Reagan became the 10th president to lie in state beneath the Capitol rotunda, and his coffin was placed on the same catafalque first used by Abraham Lincoln.

In the first 10 hours, 30,000 mourners somberly walked past the coffin, and after 34 hours, that number had reached 104,000.[13] When it was over, nine military body bearers carried the casket to a hearse as a military band played "Hail to the Chief." On Friday, June 11, shortly before 11:00 a.m., the remains arrived at the Washington National Cathedral in the rain. The flag-draped coffin was received by Reverend John Bryson Chane, Episcopal bishop of Washington, Vicar A. Theodore Eastman, and Reverend John C. Danforth, a former senator. At 11:30 a.m., military members escorted the coffin down the aisle.

Honor guards escort Reagan's flag draped coffin down Constitution Avenue. (US Air Force photo by Master Sgt. Mark Suban)

Among the 4,000 people in attendance were Mikhail Gorbachev and Margaret Thatcher as well as the four living former presidents, Bush Sr., Clinton, Ford, and Carter. The service was a cavalcade of men of the cloth. The first to speak was Rabbi Harold Kushner, who read from the Book of Isaiah. He was followed by Theodore Cardinal McCarrick, who read from the Book of Matthew. They were followed by Supreme Court associate justice Sandra Day O'Connor, who read the sermon of John Winthrop, which contained the line Reagan so eloquently co-opted: "We shall be as a city upon a hill." Reverend Danforth read the Sermon on the Mount, and Reverend Chane and Vicar Eastman led the congregation in prayer. Irish tenor Ronan Tynan, well-known for his stirring renditions of "God Bless America" at Yankee Stadium, sang "Amazing Grace" accompanied by a full military orchestra. President George W. Bush delivered a moving eulogy, appropriating the words that Edwin Stanton muttered when Abraham Lincoln passed away: "Ronald Reagan belongs to the ages now, but we preferred it when he belonged to us." As Reagan had requested 23 years earlier, Bush Sr. and Thatcher offered tributes, but the British prime minister's eulogy was taped. Although she was in the audience, she no longer spoke publicly after having suffered several strokes.[14]

At 1:00 p.m., as a tribute to the 40th president, the cathedral's Bourdon Bell rang 40 times to conclude the service. The casket was then carried back into the hearse. The automobile drove down Massachusetts Avenue to Andrews Air Force Base, where 3,000 people had gathered. The plane arrived at Point Mugu Naval Air Force Station in California shortly before 5:00 p.m. and was greeted by a large crowd as the coffin was transferred to a 2003 Cadillac Masterpiece funeral hearse (now on display at the National Museum of Funeral History in Houston, Texas). People lined the 25-mile route to the Ronald Reagan Presidential Library and Center for Public Affairs, where the hearse arrived at 6:30 p.m. Thirty minutes later, a sunset ceremony was held before a crowd of 700 people, including Tom Selleck, Wayne Newton, Wayne Gretzky, Kirk Douglas, Bo Derek, Mickey Rooney, Johnny Mathis, and Arnold Schwarzenegger. Eulogies were delivered by Reagan's sons, Ron and Michael, and his daughter, Patti Davis. After the service, body bearers carried the coffin to the horseshoe-shaped burial site atop a hill, shaded by seven oak trees, for a final prayer. Then riflemen fired a 21-gun salute, and the bugler played Taps. Overhead, four navy fighter jets flew by, one turning up and away from the rest. Before the casket was lowered into the ground, the flag that only days earlier had been flying over the USS *Ronald Reagan* was removed, folded with military precision, and handed to Nancy Reagan.

Three volleys were then fired over the grave, a military tradition to indicate hostilities could resume after both sides had removed the dead from the battlefield. The next morning, shortly before 3:00 a.m., under the watchful eyes of Secret Service agents, workers sealed his crypt. The Georgian gray granite headstone had already been completed and contained the words he spoke when he opened his presidential library in 1991: "I know in my heart that man is good. That what is right will always eventually triumph. And there's purpose and worth to each and every life."[15]

A Marine Corps color guard from Marine Corps Base Camp Pendleton passes the wreath laid on February 6, 2012, on what would have been Reagan's 101st birthday. (Photograph: Lance Cpl. Derrick Irions, from the United States Marine Corps website)

THE RONALD REAGAN DEATH SITES

Location of Death

The home in Bel Air where Reagan died was built in 1954. It was a simple home and one of the more modest in the neighborhood. In 1986, it was purchased for $2 million by a group of 20 of the president's friends. The three-bedroom, 7,192-square-foot ranch-style house featured a swimming pool and sat on a 1.5-acre lot. They leased the home to Reagan for $15,000 a month, and gave him an option to buy. (The Reagans later paid their friends back, with interest.)[16] The original address was 666 Saint Cloud, but given the ominous associations with that number, the Reagans petitioned to have the address changed to 668. On December 23, 1988, former president Reagan visited the home for the first time. Pulling up in the driveway, he commented to his aide, "I'm awed, and I love it." He spent the next nine nights there, becoming familiar with the house that he would retire to a month later.[17]

The home is located at 668 Saint Cloud Road, Los Angeles, California, 90077. Please be aware that it is a private residence and not open for visitors.

Grave

The grave is on the grounds of the Ronald Rea-gan Presidential Library and Center for Public Affairs. The library was originally to be located on the campus of Stanford University, but it was moved to a barren area in Simi Valley because of objections from the local community. The *Los Angeles Times* reported, "It is the first presidential library without any university affiliation or historic association between the land and the President or his family."[18] However, this was not entirely accurate. The area is surrounded by rugged terrain that was the backdrop in hundreds of Westerns. Visitors are immediately reminded of the Wild West of Hollywood yesteryear, where Reagan starred in episodes of *Wagon Train*, *Death Valley Days*, and *Zane Grey Theater*.

Over the next two years, the Spanish mission–style museum was constructed at a cost of $60 million. In late October 1991, Reagan had announced that he and Nancy would be buried at the site. Shortly afterward, on Monday, November 4, the library was dedicated with a historic gathering of five presidents; Carter, Reagan, Nixon, Ford, and the current president Bush.[19]

The library is located at 40 Presidential Drive in Simi Valley, California, 93065. It is open daily from 10:00 a.m. to 5:00 p.m., except Thanksgiving, Christmas, and New Year's Day. For more information, visit: www.ReaganFoundation.org.

The entrance to 668 Saint Cloud Road in Bel Air, where Reagan died on June 5, 2004. His neighbors were Hollywood elite and if the house to the right looks familiar, it's because it was the setting for the TV series *The Beverly Hillbillies*. (Courtesy of Kurt Kusenko)

Reagan's grave at his presidential library in Simi Valley, California. (Courtesy of the Ronald Reagan Presidential Library)

Gerald Rudolph Ford ★ 1974–1977

CRITICAL DEATH INFORMATION:

Date of death:	December 26, 2006, 6:45 p.m.
Cause of death:	Arteriosclerotic cerebrovascular disease and diffuse arteriosclerosis
Age at death:	93 years, 165 days
Last words:	Unknown
Place of death:	Home in Rancho Mirage, California
Funeral:	St. Margaret's Episcopal Church, Palm Desert, California
Final resting place:	Gerald R. Ford Presidential Library, Grand Rapids, Michigan
Reinterred:	No
Cost to visit grave:	$7.00
For more information:	www.FordLibrary Museum.gov
Significance:	Longest living president

After Gerald Ford left the White House in 1977, he focused on writing his memoirs and running his presidential library. For his post-presidency residence, he had a custom home built at the Thunderbird Country Club in Rancho Mirage, California, overlooking the golf course. In early 1978, he and his wife, Betty, moved in. Ford also broke a long-standing tradition of not capitalizing on the office of the president; he served on several corporate boards and frequently gave speeches for considerable fees. He still found plenty of time to indulge in his favorite activity—golf.

The year 2006 was difficult for Ford—he was hospitalized for 11 days at Eisenhower Medical Center in Rancho Mirage with pneumonia in

January, admitted to the Mayo Clinic in Rochester, Minnesota, for two heart treatments (including an angioplasty) in August, and again hospitalized at Eisenhower Medical Center for five days in October.

On November 12, 2006, Ford reached a milestone of longevity: as the 121st day of his 93rd year, he officially surpassed Ronald Reagan as the longest living president in history. He acknowledged the achievement by releasing a statement: "I thank God for the gift of every sunrise and, even more, for all the years he has blessed me with Betty and the children, with our extended family and the friends of a lifetime."[1]

After the numerous ordeals, Ford received pleasant news that a navy nuclear aircraft carrier was christened in his honor, the USS *Gerald R. Ford*. His former chief of staff, Penny Circle, gave an optimist report on his condition: "He's doing very well. He's still recuperating." But the recovery was fleeting. Toward the end of the year, Ford wrote a note to his fellow country club members about the Bob Hope Classic golf tournament planned for January, lamenting that he was not the athlete he used to be: "With golf, as with football, I find myself repeating Bob Hope's mantra, 'Thanks for the memories'. . . . Whether you're in the morning or evening of life, don't forget to look up and thank the guy that started this thing and created the exciting times we all are having—or had. There have been 43 presidents, but only one Bob Hope. How's that for a legacy?"[2]

By December 23, his vital organs began to fail. Just like Reagan, in his final weeks, he converted his study into his bedroom. At 6:45 p.m. on Tuesday, December 26, 2006, Gerald Ford died in his sleep. Betty and his three sons were at his bedside.[3] His cause of death was arteriosclerotic cerebrovascular disease and diffuse arteriosclerosis. At 93 years and 165 days, Ford had lived longer than any other president and died exactly 34 years after Harry S Truman.

Betty released a statement later that night: "My family joins me in sharing the difficult news that Gerald Ford, our beloved husband, father, grandfather and great grandfather has passed away at 93 years of age. His life was filled with love of God, his family and his country."[4] President George W. Bush released a statement from his home in Crawford, Texas: "On August 9, 1974, he stepped into the presidency without ever having sought the office. He assumed power in a period of great division and turmoil. For a nation that needed healing and for an office that needed a calm and steady hand, Gerald Ford came along when we needed him most. During his time in office, the American people came to know President Ford as a man of complete integrity who led our country with common sense and kind instincts. Americans will always admire Gerald Ford's unflinching performance of duty and the honorable conduct of his administration, and the great rectitude of the man himself. We mourn the loss of such a leader, and our 38th president will always have a special place in our nation's memory. President Ford lived 93 years, and his life was a blessing to America. And now this fine man will be taken to his rest by a family that will love him always, and by a nation that will be grateful to him forever. May God bless Gerald Ford."

President Bush ordered all flags over federal buildings to be flown at half-mast and all federal offices not integral to national security to be closed on the day of the funeral. Additionally, stock exchanges were closed and postal service suspended. Prior to his death, Ford had planned his funeral ceremonies but he did not want the pomp and circumstance that defined Reagan's funeral.[5] Despite being a veteran of World War II, he wanted minimal military flourish. However, he did request the band from his alma mater, the University of Michigan, to play the Wolverines' fight song "The Victors" at his funeral.

Ford's remains were taken to Eisenhower Medical Center, where they stayed for the next three days. The service was held at St. Margaret's Episcopal Church in Palm Desert on Friday, December 29, at noon. All morning, florist Sherry Gerland of Floral Marketing International Group, a division of the funeral services conglomerate Service Corporation International, worked tirelessly to adorn the church with tasteful arrangements.[6]

Security was tight in the affluent community—helicopters hovered overhead and Secret Service blocked off residential streets. When the 2003 Cadillac Masterpiece funeral hearse (the same car used for the California leg of Reagan's funeral) arrived, a 40-member marine band from Twentynine Palms, California, played "Hail to the Chief." The band, led by Staff Sergeant Joseph Streeter (who also played at Reagan's funeral), was supposed to be practicing for the upcoming Tournament of Roses in Pasadena, but had graciously changed their plans. Eight military body bearers, including representatives from the army, navy, air force, coast guard, and marines served as the honor guard and carried the coffin up the stairs as the band switched to "O God, Our Help in Ages Past." They paused at the top for the church rector, Reverend Robert Certain, who said, "We receive the body of our brother, Gerald, for burial."[7]

The Ford family was in "the President's Pew," where they sat almost every Sunday since moving to Rancho Mirage. In front of the altar was the casket draped with an American flag. It was a small, private service followed by a viewing for invited guests, including former California governor Pete Wilson, former House of Representatives member Jack Kemp, and former secretary of state George Shultz. The ceremonies ended at approximately 1:15 p.m. and were immediately followed by a public viewing that lasted 13 hours into the early morning of Saturday, December 30.[8] Mourners parked at a tennis court several miles away, were shuttled by bus to pay their respects, and then reboarded about two minutes later for the return trip. Strict rules were enforced: personal items and mementos, including flowers, cameras, cell phones, and purses, were prohibited. On Saturday, December 30, the remains were driven to Palm Springs International Airport. A military band played "Hail to the Chief" and "America, the Beautiful" as the coffin was carried onto the Boeing 747 and flown to Andrews Air Force Base. Upon arrival, once again, there were military ceremonies that included a 21-gun salute and another rendition of "Hail to the Chief."

When the hearse approached the Washington area, it was greeted by crowds along the route. It drove down Crown View Drive in Arlington, where the Fords lived before he became president. It also stopped at the World War II Memorial, which was completed two years earlier (Ford was a lieutenant commander in the navy) and the Pacific Theater memorial was lit up in memory of where Ford served

The funeral of President Gerald R. Ford at St. Margaret's Episcopal Church in Palm Desert, California, on December 29, 2006. (US Army photo by Douglas J. Lovely)

(the Atlantic Theater remained shadowed in darkness). World War II veterans and Boy Scouts, two groups in which Ford took pride in his membership, were gathered at the memorial.[9] The procession passed the White House and continued on to the Capitol. When Ford had planned his funeral, the down-to-earth circumstantial president felt uncomfortable with the trappings of the state funeral, but he understood he had an obligation for a national send-off and reluctantly agreed to many of its standard features. In one example of how he chose to scale back the pageantry, Ford chose an automobile hearse instead of the traditional horse-drawn carriage.[10] The coffin was carried through the House of Representatives entrance as cannons fired and the band played "America the Beautiful." They paused at the entrance to the House chamber for a moment. Just like William Howard Taft never sought to be president, but rather Chief Justice of the Supreme Court, Ford also had other aspirations. He never saw the presidency in the cards, but after 13 terms in the House, he had his sights set on Speaker of the House. The procession briefly stopped in Statuary Hall, where legislative leaders joined the final leg of the journey to the Capitol rotunda (Ford was the 11th president to have his funeral in the room). The coffin was placed upon the same pine catafalque built for Abraham Lincoln.

President Bush did not attend, but Vice President Dick Cheney, who also served as Ford's chief of staff, delivered an eloquent eulogy in which he said, "Nothing was left unsaid, and at the end of his days, Gerald Ford knew how much he meant to us and to his country. He was given length of years, and many times in his company we paid our tributes and said our thanks. We were proud to call him our leader, grateful to know him as a man. We told him these things, and there is comfort in knowing that. Still, it is an ending. And what is left now is to say good-bye." Cheney continued with a simple statement that completely summed up Gerald Ford: "He was not just a cheerful and pleasant man—although these virtues are rare enough at the commanding heights. He was not just a nice guy, the next-door neighbor whose luck landed him in the White House. It was this man, Gerald R. Ford, who led our republic safely through a crisis that could have turned to catastrophe."

In the middle of the ceremony, 84-year-old former Michigan congressman William Broomfield suddenly collapsed, reminiscent of John Quincy Adams. As he was laid out on the floor, physician and senator Bill Frist rushed to give him medical attention. Broomfield soon recovered and the ceremony continued.[11] The viewing continued overnight into Tuesday, January 2. At the end of the viewing, the coffin was carried to the Senate door and stopped briefly before continuing through the senate chamber.

The cortege wound its way through the capital streets toward Washington National Cathedral. As president, Ford worshipped at St. John's Epis-

Funeral ceremonies for Ford at the rotunda of the United States Capitol building on December 30, 2006. (Defense Dept. photo by William D. Moss)

copal Church on Lafayette Square. Over the years, he also attended services several times at Washington National Cathedral. Introductory music included the stirring "Fanfare for the Common Man" and "America the Beautiful." The Bourdon Bell then tolled 38 times to honor his place in the litany of presidents. As the casket was carried inside, it was welcomed by a military band and Reverend John Bryson Chane, Episcopal bishop of Washington, who a year and a half earlier had done the same solemn duty for President Reagan. Chane said, "With faith in Jesus Christ, we receive the body of our brother Gerald for burial."[12]

At the service, there were 20 honorary pallbearers, including Alan Greenspan, Bob Dole, Henry Kissinger, and Donald Rumsfeld. President George W. Bush escorted Betty to her seat and Boy Scout members assisted the other 3,700 guests. Military body bearers carried the casket through the aisle and placed it on a catafalque, as the Armed Forces Chorus sang the navy hymn "O God, Our Help in Ages Past," one of Ford's favorites.[13]

In attendance were representatives from Congress and the Supreme Court and former presidents Jimmy Carter, Bill Clinton, and George H. W. Bush. However on this day, political party lines remained in place. George H. W. Bush, Henry Kissinger, and President George W. Bush all paid tribute to Ford, while Clinton and Carter did not speak. A year earlier, Ford had asked Tom Brokaw to also speak at his funeral. Ford's rationale, as the news legend believed, was "to be sure that the White House press corps was represented."

The dean of the Cathedral, Reverend Samuel T. Lloyd III, began the service, and the homily was presented by Reverend Dr. Robert Certain of St. Margaret's Episcopal Church. Certain praised Ford as "a statesman, churchman, and family man," and added, "Gerald Ford was a man of deep faith and constant prayer." Metropolitan Opera mezzo-soprano singer Denyce

Graves performed the Lord's Prayer, an emotional high point for the service. While the coffin was being carried out, the attendees sang "For All the Saints, Who from Their Labors Rest." After the service, the coffin was flown to Grand Rapids, Michigan, where Ford moved as a young boy and where he called home. At the airport, the Michigan Wolverines band played a somber version of their fight song "The Victors," just as Ford had requested years earlier. The coffin was placed in a hearse and a 75-car motorcade rode to the Gerald R. Ford Presidential Library and Museum, passing thousands who lined the streets along the way.[14] An estimated 57,000 people, some with babies in their arms, waited up to six hours in the middle of the night into the morning of Wednesday, January 3, to pay their respects. Locals remembered him fondly and the *New York Times* wrote, "Here, he was the boy who grew up on these streets, who played football for South High School, who became an Eagle Scout and who this region sent to the House of Representatives from 1949 until the 1970s."[15]

At the end of the viewing, the coffin was taken to Grace Episcopal Church. Boy Scouts lined the route to salute the only Eagle Scout to ever ascend to the presidency. This was a smaller crowd than the previous week's events, with only 400 people in attendance. Honorary pallbearers included friends from Grand Rapids and professional golfer Jack Nicklaus. Michigan football coach Bo Schembechler was chosen by Ford to be an honorary pallbearer but had died a year earlier, so a University of Michigan blanket was placed on a pew in remembrance. As a testament to his bipartisan nature, polar opposites on the political spectrum Donald H. Rumsfeld and Jimmy Carter both eulogized their friend. Rumsfeld said, "There's an old saying in Washington that every member of the United States Congress looks in the mirror and sees a future president." Rumsfeld, who served as defense secretary and chief of staff to President Ford, continued, "Well, Jerry Ford was different. I suspect that when he looked in the mirror even after he became president, he saw a citizen and a public servant."[16] Several years earlier, when Ford was planning his funeral, he had asked Jimmy Carter to eulogize him. They joked that the agreement was predicated on Ford's dying first, but being 11 years older, it was a safe bet. Carter spoke from his heart about his former adversary, who had become his closest friend: "One of my proudest moments was at the commemoration of the 200th birthday of the White House, when two noted historians both declared that the Ford-Carter friendship was the most intensely personal between any two presidents in history." He closed with a line he had first spoken at his inauguration after defeating Ford in 1976: "I still don't know any better way to express it than the words I used almost exactly thirty years ago. For myself and for our nation, I want to thank my predecessor for all he did to heal our land."[17]

Ford's grandchildren also participated in the service, leading the crowd in prayer. After the ceremony, the cortege returned to the library for the burial on a grassy hill near the Grand River. Revered Certain said a prayer and there was a final 21-gun salute. Twenty-one F-15s then flew overhead to honor the fallen commander in chief. As per tradition, one broke from the pack and flew straight up and the crowd broke into light applause. The flag over the casket was folded in military precision and Vice President Cheney handed it to Betty, who held it to her face.[18]

The next day, Ford's family spent a quiet few moments at his grave in contemplation; then the library was opened and a few dozen visitors entered to see the grave. Later, an iron fence was placed around the grave site. Mementos were saved for posterity, including invitations to the funeral service at Washington National Cathedral, wreaths placed by the casket at the library, uniforms worn during the proceedings and, most obscure of all, the ammunition box and spent casings from the final 21-gun salute. They are now on display at the National Museum of Funeral History in Houston, Texas.

THE GERALD FORD DEATH SITES
Location of Death

The custom house at the Thunderbird Country Club where Ford lived for 38 years was built in 1978. It was designed by architect Welton Becket, whose work could be seen throughout the Los Angeles landscape, including the Capitol Records building, the Pan-Pacific Auditorium, and Cinerama Dome. The 6,316-square-foot, six-bedroom house overlooks the club golf course and was decorated by Bob Hope's friend, Laura Mako. Bill Foster, mayor of Palm Springs from 1974 to 1977, was the contractor, but Ford made the home his own. The man so associated with the 1970s, from the wide, loud ties to the impersonations by a young Chevy Chase on *Saturday Night Live*, lived in a home that reflected the era. As the years passed and the world

Ford's grave site at the Gerald Ford Presidential Library and Museum in Grand Rapids, Michigan. (Courtesy of Joseph F. Picone)

The home in Rancho Mirage, California, where Ford died as the oldest president in history on December 26, 2006. (© *George Gutenberg Architectural Photograph*, www. GeorgeGutenberg.com, used by permission)

changed around him, his home stayed frozen as a time capsule. Over the years, Ford was visited by every president from Nixon to Bush Jr. After Ford's passing in 2006, Betty continued to live in the home, retaining its disco décor, for five more years, until her death on July 8, 2011. Six months later, on January 23, 2012, the home went on the market for $1.2 million. In a *Palm Springs Life* article titled "The Lime Grows on You," author Matthew Link described the home's interior design: "Green drapes, corresponding green floral sofas, and wicker chairs rest under a geometric-patterned cedar wood ceiling. The dining room continues the color scheme with a foliage mural painted on the walls and seats with green cushions and faux bamboo legs. In the Ford children's bedrooms, patterned bedspreads and matching curtains can be described as 'groovy.' The only thing even vaguely Washingtonian is a tiny presidential seal on an old-fashioned telephone in the yellow-hued guest kitchen." Link summed up the home perfectly, "The *Brady Bunch*–style residence feels more endearing than tacky, like a beloved rerun from another era."[19]

The home sold in just 11 days to entertain-ment business manager John McIlwee and DreamWorks executive Bill Damaschke. It is located at 40471 Sand Dune Road, Rancho Mirage, California, 92270. It is a private residence in a gated community and is not open to visitors.

Eisenhower Medical Center

In the 1960s, a Desert Classic golf tournament was organized to raise funds for a new hospital. In 1965, Hope, a Hollywood entertainer and good friend of Ford, agreed to lend his name to the tournament and it was renamed the Bob Hope Desert Classic. Hope also donated 80 acres for the hospital grounds. Ground broke in 1969 and two years later, in November 1971, the Eisenhower Medical Center opened. The proximity to Palm Springs and Palm Desert, playgrounds of the famous and powerful, ensured hospital ceremonies had an impressive roster of attendees. Over the years, that list included presidents Nixon, Ford, Reagan, and Bush Sr., as well as Vice President Spiro Agnew. Hollywood All-Stars from yester-year, such as Frank Sinatra, George Burns, Bing Crosby, Gene Autry, and Lucille Ball also made appearances at hospital events.

The Eisenhower Medical Center is located at 39000 Bob Hope Drive, Rancho Mirage, California, 92270. For more information, visit: www. emc.org.

Funeral

The Fords attended St. Margaret's Episcopal Church every Sunday for 30 years, sitting in what would become known as "the President's Pew." Bush Sr. also worshipped there with Ford. One of the more interesting features of the church is the east window, which features a stained glass cross. When the sun is in a precise position, it creates a brilliant image on the floor in the middle of the pews. The St. Margaret's website posts the exact moments of each day optimal for viewing this stunning solar phenomenon.

On October 15, 2013, the contents from the Ford's Rancho Mirage home were auctioned to raise money for the church. Items donated by the president's son, Jack, included "a Faberge-style egg in a box from President Bill Clinton, a kaleidoscope, Tiffany White House china, and a large collection of Asian decorative pieces. The Fords' collection of decorative sculptured elephants—the symbol of the Republican Party—in china, crystal, bronze and other materials, will also be auctioned. The elephants were housed in the 'elephant room' of the Fords' home."[20]

The church is located at 47535 CA-74, Palm Desert, California, 92260. For more information, visit: www.StMargarets.org.

Grave

The grave is located on the grounds of the Ger-ald R. Ford Presidential Library and Museum. Ground was broken on January 15, 1979, for the museum. It is located on the campus of the University of Michigan and construction lasted two years. Ford was in attendance at the dedication ceremony, held on April 27, 1981. Six months after Ford's death, Clinton was in Grand Rapids to speak at a local economics club. Before the speech, he visited the museum and brought a bouquet of flowers. He walked to the grave and spent several minutes alone there.[21]

The library is located at 303 Pearl Street NW, Grand Rapids, Michigan, 49504. It is open every day, except Thanksgiving, Christmas Day, and New Year's Day, from 9:00 a.m. to 5:00 p.m., except Sundays when it is open noon to 5:00 p.m. For more information, visit: www.Ford LibraryMuseum.gov.

Presidents Still With Us

While it may seem impolite to include the presidents who are still alive in a book about the deaths of their predecessors, these men are members of a unique club. They understand their place in history and that their graves will be visited by thousands of people for many years after they are gone. Preparations for their funeral and burial locations start years in advance. So even though, at the time of this writing, former presidents Jimmy Carter, George H. W. Bush, Bill Clinton, and George W. Bush and the current president, Barack Obama, are still with us and hopefully will be for many years to come, they have already thought much more about their deaths than have most ordinary Americans.

This is particularly true for the oldest living president, George H. W. Bush. In keeping with every president since Nixon, the 41st president has also chosen to be buried at the site of his presidential library, the George Bush Presidential Library and Museum in College Station, Texas. His future burial site is located in a wooded area behind the library and can be reached by walking a pleasant trail around a lake and through the woods. There you will find a fenced-in area where the former president and his wife, Barbara, will join their young daughter, Robin, who died of leukemia in 1953. Bush's grave may be the first that has attracted visitors *before* he has died, and there was a steady trickle of tourists on the day I stopped by. Inside the iron fence is the presidential seal before a lush green burial plot.

On December 3, 2006, Jimmy Carter discussed his funeral plans in an interview on C-SPAN: he would have a funeral in Washington, DC, a viewing in Atlanta, and will be buried in his hometown of Plains, Georgia. Some locals were delighted with the prospect, including the owner of the only hotel in town, who commented, "He knows this will make Plains a tourist attraction for eternity."[1]

The future grave site of President George H. W. Bush, located behind the George Bush 41 Presidential Library and Museum in College Station, Texas.

While visiting former president Clinton's presidential library, located several hours away in Little Rock, Arkansas, George H. W. Bush suggested that his successor may want to begin planning his burial location on its open grounds.[2]

Neither George W. Bush nor Barack Obama have discussed their funeral plans. However, as six of the last seven presidents to die have been buried in their presidential libraries, that is also a likely choice for the two most recent presidents. The George W. Bush Presidential Library and Museum is located in Dallas, Texas, and in May 2015, Barack Obama announced that his presidential library would be built in his hometown of Chicago, Illinois.

ALMOST PRESIDENTS

★★

FIRST PRESIDENT OF THE CONTINENTAL CONGRESS
UNDER THE ARTICLES OF CONFEDERATION

John Hanson

CRITICAL DEATH INFORMATION:

Date of death:	November 22, 1783
Cause of death:	Unknown
Age at death:	68 years, 224 days
Last words:	Unknown
Place of death:	Oxon Hill Manor, Prince George's County, Maryland
Funeral:	Oxon Hill Manor, Prince George's County, Maryland
Final resting place:	A mystery!
Reinterred:	Unknown
Cost to visit grave:	Free
For more information:	history.pgparks.com/ sites_and_museums/ Oxon_Hill_Manor.htm

John Hanson has been relegated to the status of a political curiosity, referenced more on snopes.com than in American history books. In the years between the first Continental Congress in 1774 and the election of George Washington in 1789, America elected a series of officials who had the title of president. While they did not hold the broad authority that the future presidents would have, they did bear the title. By some counts, there were 14 people to do so, from Peyton Randolph, first president of the first Continental Congress, to Cyrus Griffin, the last president before Washington took the oath. Despite falling in the middle of the pack, an argument could be made for John Hanson as our first President of the United States. His official title was "President of the United States in Congress Assembled," and he was the first to serve a full term in office when the Articles of Confederation, the precursor to the Constitution, took effect in 1781, only two weeks after Washington's victory at Yorktown. His presidency has been recognized and acknowledged by his well-known successors, including Washington, Thomas Jefferson, James Madison, Abraham Lincoln, Calvin Coolidge, and Harry S Truman.[1]

Hanson first came to national prominence in 1780, when he represented Maryland in the Continental Congress. He was elevated to the office of president on November 5, 1781, for a year-long term. Hanson had health problems throughout his term, but what he suffered from exactly is unrecorded and historians can only speculate. After his presidency, he returned to his home in Frederick, Maryland, where his poor health continued to decline. In the spring of 1783, a Philadelphia newspaper reported that John Hanson had died. The report was premature, but sadly, only by a few months.

In November 1783, Hanson visited his nephew Thomas Hawkins Hanson at his home, Oxon Hill Manor, in Prince George's County, Maryland. There, he fell ill and died on November 22. While the deaths of presidents under the Constitution have been meticulously documented, the specifics of Hanson's death are unknown. In fact, even his death date is shrouded in confusion, as some sources report it a week earlier, on November 15.[2]

Hanson preferred to be buried at his home in Fredrick. The practice of embalming had not yet begun, and as the winter was particularly harsh, it was not practical to move him, so he was interred in the Addison family cemetery on the grounds of Oxon Hill. The burial service was conducted a day or two after his death, and his remains were placed in a crypt. They stayed there for almost two centuries, while his legacy dissipated from the public memory. The state of Maryland made an attempt to resurrect him from obscurity in 1903, when it placed his likeness in Statuary Hall, a room within the Capitol that displays statues of famous Americans.

THE JOHN HANSON DEATH SITES
Location of Death/Grave

The brick mansion where Hanson died was built by Thomas Addison in 1711. The home passed to his son, John, and then to his grandson, also named Thomas Addison, who patented the land on August 3, 1767, as "Oxon Hill Manor," the first time the name had been associated with the estate. Thomas died in 1774, but since his son, Walter Dulany Addison, was only five years old, the home was left to Thomas Hawkins Hanson (John's nephew), who had been appointed Walter's regent (Thomas Hanson later married Thomas Addison's widow). From 1787 to 1792, the home was leased to George Washington's cousin, Nathaniel, who lived at Oxon Hill Manor. That is not the only association with George Washington: Walter later became a reverend and was one of the four clergymen to officiate at Washington's funeral in Mount Vernon. Walter sold the home on March 17, 1810, to Zachariah Berry, but retained ownership of the Addison cemetery.

Berry died in 1845 and left the home to his son, Thomas. However, Thomas had a troubled life. He was mentally ill, threatened his wife, and was placed in a Baltimore asylum. During this time, the home fell into disrepair and Berry fell delinquent on his taxes. After his death in 1879, the home was sold at auction. Ownership over the next few years is complicated, as several people held deed. The history of the home came to an end on February 6, 1895. A small fire on the roof quickly spread until, as the newspapers reported, "the whole eastern heavens were illuminated by the conflagration—the fire raging furiously, the flames leaping high, while a huge volume of smoke settled into the adjoining hills." The cause was unknown, but

Oxon Hill Manor, the home where John Hanson died, burned down in 1895. The new home, pictured here, was built on the same site in 1928. A monument to Hanson can be seen on the right.

the icy Potomac prevented firefighters from putting out the blaze. When it burned itself out, all that was left were the walls and four chimneys.[3]

In 1928, the second and current Oxon Hill Manor was built on the estate for Sumner Welles. Welles was a friend, foreign policy advisor, and relative through marriage to Franklin Roosevelt, who was Oxon Hill's most famous guest. In 1984, it was purchased by James T. Lewis Enterprises, which planned to develop the property. The next year, the state of Maryland surveyed the land and found that the crypt that contained Hanson's remains was sealed and intact. The following year, Lewis Enterprises hired John Milner Associates to conduct another land survey. The 1987 report they produced stated: "About 70 to 80 feet below the site of the plantation house was a deteriorating brick vaulted structure built into the hillside [that] . . . was the 1783 burial place of John Hanson." What followed was a shocking declaration: sometime after 1985, Hanson's grave "had been robbed!"[4]

While several attempts have been made to steal the remains of American presidents, none have succeeded. Considering what occurred

at Grant's tomb, James Buchanan's grave, and Congressional Cemetery, vandalism and other forms of disrespect at presidential grave sites were not unheard of in the 1980s. Yet an actual grave robbing had not been plotted since Rufus Cantrell planned to steal Benjamin Harrison's remains in 1901, making the theft of Hanson's 200-year-old human remains in the later years of the 20th century particularly startling.

The development plan plowed ahead nevertheless. Several years later, another shocking discovery was made—the crypt had disappeared! In a 1993 photograph, the year Lewis Enterprises sold the land to Peterson Companies, it is nowhere to be found and in its place is now a parking lot.[5] Leading up to its disappearance, the crypt was damaged in 1971. A report determined that the cause was either its methodical removal as an obstacle to development or a malicious act by workers who blew it up during their lunch hour.[6]

A handsome white marble obelisk was erected on the property by the John Hanson Chapter, Maryland Society, and Sons of the American Revolution and was dedicated on June 30, 1990. Today, the grounds are available for weddings and other ceremonies. It is located at 6901 Oxon

A monument was erected at the entrance of Oxon Hill Manor by the John Hanson Chapter, Maryland Society, Sons of the American Revolution. It was dedicated on June 30, 1990.

Hill Road, Oxon Hill, Maryland, 20745. For more information, visit: history.pgparks.com/sites_and_museums/Oxon_Hill_Manor.htm.

Sam Houston

CRITICAL DEATH INFORMATION:

Date of death:	July 26, 1863, 6:45 p.m.
Cause of death:	Pneumonia
Age at death:	70 years, 144 days
Last words:	"Texas, Texas, Margaret."
Place of death:	Downstairs parlor at Steamboat House in Huntsville, Texas
Funeral:	Upstairs parlor at Steamboat House in Huntsville, Texas
Final resting place:	Oakwood Cemetery, Huntsville, Texas
Reinterred:	No
Cost to visit grave:	Free
For more information:	www.Walker CountyHistory.org/ oakwood_cemetery.php

The best place to learn about Sam Houston is the Sam Houston Memorial Museum in Huntsville, Texas. There you will discover the critical role he played in the founding of Texas as a republic and later in its drive for statehood. After American settlers in Texas declared their independence from Mexico and fought the Mexican army to become a separate country, Sam Houston was elected the first president of the Republic of Texas and subsequently won a second term. He is considered the "George Washington of Texas," but since his second term was not consecutive with the first, I prefer to think of him as the "Grover Cleveland of Texas." The Republic of Texas was short-lived, lasting less than a decade, from March 2, 1836, until it was admitted as a state on December 29, 1845. After statehood, Houston went on to serve as a United States senator and later as governor of the state.

When Texas seceded in the Civil War, Houston refused to swear allegiance to the Confederate States of America. (The CSA was the sixth country that claimed ownership over the territory. The others were Spain, France, Mexico, the Republic of Texas, and the United States of America. Texas has incorporated this into their state seal and it was also used by a popular amusement park chain, "Six Flags.") Houston was not opposed to slavery, owning 12 slaves himself, but rather he did not believe secession was the best way to go about defending the institution. This strongly-held position made him an outcast in the state he loved and cost him the governor's office. In 1862, Houston returned to Huntsville, where he had previously lived after his second presidential term in 1844. The last time he was there he was beloved and respected, but now he was a pariah.

The despised former president settled into Captain Sim's Hotel while he looked for a permanent residence. Due to his unpopularity, he struggled to find anyone to sell or rent him a house, including his former home. For that reason, he lowered his standards to consider the ugliest home in Huntsville, the infamous "Steamboat House." The odd-looking building looked like it sounds and was such a monstrosity that the original intended residents took one look and refused to live in it. The current owner, Dr. Rufus Bailey, would not sell to Houston but did permit him to rent the house, and Houston moved in in December 1862. He then further alienated himself when he regularly visited Union prisoners in the nearby Huntsville Penitentiary (still in use today).

Houston had enjoyed good health for much of his 70 years, but avoided the stairs due to an injured leg from an old war wound. In the summer of 1863, he fell ill and, to recuperate, visited the mineral baths in Sour Lake, about 100 miles southeast. While there, he heard about the fall of Vicksburg on July 4. This defeat deep in rebel territory preyed upon his mental and physical state. Shortly after returning to Huntsville, he took a walk while suffering from a severe cold and developed pneumonia. Dr. J. W. Markham examined Houston and placed his bed in the middle of the downstairs parlor so the cross breeze would dispel the sweltering heat. Houston's slave, Jeff Hamilton, slept nearby to keep watch over him.

On July 26, 1863, at around 6:15 p.m., Houston turned to his wife, Margaret, and weakly said, "Texas, Texas, Margaret." Those last words encapsulated the two things he loved most of all. Half an hour later, at 6:45 p.m., Sam Houston died.[1] With him were Margaret, his physician, Pleasant W. Kittrell, his slave, Hamilton, and several of his children. Sixty-six years later, the *Houston Post* recalled his final moment: "As the slanting shadows of sunset

The unique Steamboat House, where Sam Houston died on July 26, 1863.

crept upon Steamboat House, General Houston ceased to breathe. A life so strange and so lonely, whose finger-tips had reached the stars and felt them change to dust, had slipped away."[2]

Margaret took off his ring to keep. Inside the ring was inscribed the word "Honor," indicative of how Houston felt he lived his life. Houston left a will that focused little on the dispersal of earthly goods and instead gave explicit instructions for his sons' schooling: "My will is that my sons should receive solid and useful education, and that no portion of their time may be devoted to the study of abstract sciences. I greatly desire that they may possess a thorough knowledge of the English language with a good knowledge of the Latin language. I also request that they be instructed in the knowledge of the Holy Scriptures; and next to these that they be rendered thorough in a knowledge of Geography and History. I wish my sons early taught an utter contempt for novels and light reading. In all that pertains to my sons I wish particular regard paid to their morals as well as character and morals of those [with] whom they may be associated or instructed." He did leave one item to his oldest son, Sam: "I bequeath my sword worn in the battle of San Jacinto, never to be drawn only in defense of the Constitution, the laws and Liberties of his Country. If any attempt should ever be made to assail one of these, I wish it to be used in its vindication."[3]

Oral tradition holds that, owing to Houston's unpopularity, the local minister and undertaker refused to perform the funeral services. Upon learning that nobody would build the coffin, a woodworker among the Union troops in Huntsville Penitentiary volunteered for the task. He built a small black coffin, only slightly bigger than Houston's frame, as was the traditional size for the time (it looked very similar to Lincoln's coffin). The day after Houston died, a small funeral was held in the upstairs parlor (originally funerals were held in household parlors, hence the name "funeral parlors"). Victorian customs

were observed: the room was draped in mourning cloth, and the clocks were stopped at the moment Houston died. A half dozen or so Free Masons performed their traditional ceremony, and Reverend Cockrell of Huntsville Presbyterian Church spoke before a sparse group of mourners. After the brief service, the coffin was carried to Oakwood Cemetery, where the Free Masons performed the burial ceremony.

THE SAM HOUSTON DEATH SITES
Location of Death

The house with the weird name has an even weirder history. Steamboat House was originally built by Dr. Rufus Bailey, a language professor at Austin College who later became the school president. In September 1855, he purchased five acres on the northeast part of town from then president of Austin College, Daniel Baker, for $100 (it was originally part of a land grant owned by one of Huntsville's founders, Pleasant Gray). That same year Bailey began building a home on the property for his son, Frank, as a wedding gift. This was no normal home: Bailey, who had studied architecture and found Texas extremely lacking in that regard, once said, "There is such a deficiency in architectural taste that I thought proper to exhibit real skill in that line." And indeed he did. At the time, two styles of homes were popular in Texas, each with its own features to combat the oppressive Southern heat: Victorian homes with high ceilings and dogtrot models with an open middle breezeway. But Bailey had an unusual design of his own called "Steamboat Gothic." Long, narrow, windowless, and two storied, each floor was only one room wide with doors on both exterior walls to take advantage of the cross breeze. Modeled after the Mississippi steamboat, the home even incorporated smokestacks and looked very strange on land indeed. To keep the gift a surprise, Bailey told his son and future daughter-in-law to steer clear of the northeast area while he finished the one-of-a-kind abode. Finally, it was completed, and the newlyweds were allowed to get a look at their gift . . . and so hated it they told Bailey there was no way they could live in the monstrosity!

Despite their disgust, Dr. Bailey was proud of his creation. He christened it "Buena Vista," but it is unclear if he ever moved in to the house or just visited for periods. It was also known as "Bailey Place," but it was not called "Steamboat House" until more than six decades after Houston's death.[4] Three months after Houston, Bailey also died of pneumonia and left the peculiar home to his son, the same who had turned and run when he first saw it. Now it was his, but not for long. In November 1863, he sold it to A. C. McKeen for $4,000 Confederate dollars. Three years later, on Christmas Day 1866, it was sold again for $1,500, this time to someone who was already familiar with the house and its peculiarities, Dr. Kittrell. He and his wife boarded several girls from the Old Andrew Female College. The next year, Huntsville was struck with an outbreak of yellow fever that took 130 lives, including Dr. Kittrell's on September 25, 1867. In his will, written only days before his death, he passed the home on to his eldest son, Norman, who was 18 years old. In 1868, Norman's cousin and Confederate veteran Major Thomas J. Goree was married in the home. Norman gave the house to his mother, Mary Frances Kittrell, in 1873, and, shortly after, she traded it to Goree for his house in Midway, Texas. Goree used convict labor to make extensive modifications until it more resembled a Victorian style home.

In 1891, Goree sold the home to I. N. Smith for $2,250. Smith owned it for 26 years before selling it in August 1917 to Lamkin Brothers, a local hardware and real estate company. In 1925, the firm then sold the property to Oakwood Cemetery, where Houston was buried, for $3,500. The cemetery was not interested in the historic home but rather in the land it was built on, to be used for future burials. The home was sold for $250 or $400 (sources vary) to J. H. Johnson, who, in January 1928, cut it in half and moved the pieces half a mile to North Main Street, near the public school.[5] Burial plots soon encroached upon the original home site, and it is now within the "Addickes Addition" of Oakwood Cemetery (named in honor of W. W. Addickes, who donated $5,000 to the Oakwood Cemetery Association).

In 1933, the home was again sold, this time for $500 to the publisher of the *Houston Post*, J. E. Josey. While he made several failed attempts to have it moved, the home sat on North Main Street, slowly deteriorating and falling further into disrepair. During the Great Depression, the home gained another, unflattering, name: "Squatter's Place."[6]

Finally, Josey arranged to donate the home

On the 150th anniversary of Houston's death, the staff at the Sam Houston Memorial Museum re-enacted the funeral in the home. Museum staff played the roles of the grieving widow and funeral attendees, and my tour guide and museum curator, Michael Sproat, channeled Dr. Kittrell. (Used by permission of Michael Sproat, curator of collections at the Sam Houston Memorial Museum)

to the state of Texas. He hired the architectural firm Wilkinson and Nutter to restore the home. The squatters were evicted and the home was once again dismantled. It was latched to a team of mules, set upon rolling logs, and moved to the grounds of Sam Houston Park, on land that Houston had once owned. On March 2, 1936, the 100th anniversary of Texas's independence, Josey formally presented the home to the state. Speakers including former Texas governor William P. Hobby and the main orator, Tennessee governor Harry Hill McCalister.[7]

On March 2, 1937, another dedication was held. One notable and honored 97-year-old guest was Hamilton, Houston's former slave who was beside his master when he died. On March 2, 1976, a historic marker was dedicated during another ceremony. In September 1988, a sign was hung by the front stairway that read CLOSED FOR REPAIRS. It stayed in place for three years until restorations were completed. Once again the home was moved, albeit this time only a short distance, from its crumbling foundation to a new one. The following year, Steamboat House reopened and has remained so ever since.

The home is unique in that it not only recognizes Houston's death and funeral but celebrates them. To recognize the 150th anniversary of Houston's death, his funeral was reenacted in 2013. Museum staff played the roles of the grieving widow, funeral attendees, and Dr. Kittrell.[8]

Steamboat House is located on the grounds of the Sam Houston Memorial Museum at 1836 Sam Houston Avenue, Huntsville, Texas, 77340. For more information, visit: www.SamHoustonMemorial Museum.com.

Grave

Houston chose his own burial spot to be near his friend Hen-derson Yoakum's. Houston's grave was very simply marked. Over the following years, as it became more apparent that Houston was on the right side of history, his reputation and legacy rose. In 1911, for the 75th anniversary of Texas's independence, a grand monument was erected over Houston's grave. Sculpted by Pompeo Coppini (who had also carved the Alamo Plaza cenotaph in San Antonio), it cost $10,000. The bas-relief depicts Sam Houston on horseback, riding into battle surrounded by symbols of history, peace, and victory. Beneath the image is a quote from Andrew Jackson that reads, "The world will take care of Houston's fame." However, when the monument arrived, it was discovered that the word "Governor" was spelled incorrectly. While some believed the marker was fine as is, Dr. Harry Estill, the president of the Sam Houston Normal Institute, insisted it be corrected. An apostrophe was added as a sloppy correction and eventually it was fixed outright. A fence later added by Alamo Iron Works included symbols of peace and a completed battle. The original tombstone is now located in the Sam Houston Memorial Museum.

In the late 1930s, the Sam Houston Memorial Museum was built on land formerly owned by Sam Houston. Its octagonal design resembles Monticello, with a low-pitched domed roof. Its original design also featured two crypts, where

Sam Houston's grave in Oakwood Cemetery in Huntsville, Texas.

Houston and his wife, Margaret, would be reinterred. Similar to the crypt for Washington in the Capitol building, this plan was never completed, due to cost. Having funded the $10,000 monument a quarter century earlier, the state did not want to negate that effort by reinterring him, especially in the midst of the Great Depression. Nor was the family of Margaret eager to have her remains relocated from her grave in Independence, Texas.

Today Sam Houston's grave is one of the more popular attractions in town. It is located at 9th Street and Ave I, Huntsville, Texas, 77320. For more information, visit: www.WalkerCounty History.org/oakwood_cemetery.php.

PRESIDENT FOR A DAY

David Rice Atchison

CRITICAL DEATH INFORMATION:

Date of death:	January 26, 1886
Cause of death:	Unknown
Age at death:	78 years, 178 days
Last words:	Unknown
Place of death:	His home near Gower, Clinton County, Missouri
Funeral:	Unknown
Final resting place:	Greenlawn Cemetery, Plattsburg, Missouri
Reinterred:	No
Cost to visit grave:	Free
For more information:	www.PlattsburgMO.com/History/Cemetery.htm

Between the end of the presidency of James K. Polk and the swearing in of Zachary Taylor, a historical anomaly occurred. These events normally are simultaneous, but this time they occurred a day apart—and it was during this 24-hour period that David Rice Atchison claimed the distinction of being "President for a Day."

How did this occur? Polk left office at noon on Sunday, March 4, 1849. Under normal circumstances, Taylor's inauguration would have occurred that same day, but Taylor refused to be sworn in on the Sabbath. Instead, he took the oath of office a day later, on Monday, March 5. While many constitutional experts claim that even without swearing in, Taylor was still

Statue of David Rice Atchison in downtown Plattsburg, Missouri, the town in which he is buried.

ton County, Missouri, and was an active supporter of the Confederacy during the Civil War.

Around 1880, Atchison fell seriously ill from an unknown malady. When a friend wrote him in 1882, he grimly replied, "My health is not good. I have been more or less paralyzed for two years and can scarcely write at all. My senses & faculties are more or less blunted. My head is white as snow. My face wrinkled, I am ready for the *narrow house*."[5] Four years later on January 26, 1886, David Rice Atchison died in his home. As with John Hanson, many of the details of his death have been lost to history. He was buried in a "narrow house"—a euphemism for a coffin, of course—about 10 miles away in Greenlawn Cemetery in Plattsburg, Missouri.

Atchison's claim to fame was later featured in *Ripley's Believe It or Not!* He was inducted into

president, some see it differently. According to the line of succession fixed by the Constitution, after the president his vice president was next in line. However on the same day Polk left office, so did Vice President George M. Dallas. In 1849, the next in line of succession was the president pro tempore of the Senate—the pro-slavery Democrat from Missouri, David Rice Atchison.[1]

His presidency was not an eventful one. After a long day in the Senate, he claimed that he slept during most of his one-day term![2] In his defense, Atchison never claimed to be president. In fact, his own term as senator expired the same day as Polk's and he was not sworn in until the Senate reconvened on Monday, so he was out of office during the same 24-hour period.[3] He always got a kick out of his chance elevation to the highest office in the land, though, and liked to call his tenure "the honestest administration this country ever had."[4] After retiring from the Senate, Atchison became a farmer near Gower in Clin-

Atchison's grave at Greenlawn Cemetery in Plattsburg, Missouri. The bronze plaque in front of it reads: PRESIDENT OF THE UNITED STATES FOR ONE DAY SUNDAY MAR. 4, 1849. (Courtesy of Jimmy S. Emerson, DVM)

the Hall of Famous Missourians in 1991. Atchison, Kansas, is named in his honor. He even has his own presidential library, proudly billed as the "world's smallest." To learn more about this story, you can visit the David Rice Atchison Presidential Library inside the Atchison County Historical Society Museum in the Santa Fe Depot in Atchison, Kansas.

THE DAVID RICE ATCHISON DEATH SITES
Grave

Greenlawn Cemetery was established in 1897. It is located about a quarter mile south of town, following Main Street as it turns into Highway C. While Atchison may be an obscure footnote to many, in Plattsburg he is celebrated with a statue downtown and locals are proud of their notorious citizen. The cemetery has several signs leading visitors to his grave.

His tombstone, which leans slightly, simply states:

ATCHISON
ALLEN

A bronze plaque on the ground states his true claim to fame and reads:

PRESIDENT OF THE UNITED STATES
FOR ONE DAY
SUNDAY MAR. 4, 1849
DAVID RICE ATCHISON
AUG. 11, 1807–JAN. 26, 1886

THE ONLY PRESIDENT OF THE CONFEDERATE STATES OF AMERICA
Jefferson Finis Davis

CRITICAL DEATH INFORMATION:

Date of death:	December 6, 1889, 12:45 a.m.
Cause of death:	Malaria, complicated by acute bronchitis
Age at death:	81 years, 186 days
Last words:	"Pray, excuse me."
Place of death:	Residence of Jacob M. Payne, New Orleans, Louisiana
Funeral:	City Hall, New Orleans, Louisiana
Final resting place:	Hollywood Cemetery, Richmond, Virginia
Reinterred:	Yes
Cost to visit grave:	Free
For more information:	www.Hollywood Cemetery.org

Before the first shots were fired in the Civil War, seven states (later joined by four more) seceded from the United States and formed a separate country, the Confederate States of America. They printed their own currency and postage, established a capital city, and, on February 18, 1861, elected their own president, Jefferson Finis Davis. In the eyes of millions of Southerners, from 1861 to 1865 their president was Jefferson Davis, not Abraham Lincoln. And when he died 24 years after the hostilities ended, to many he was still "President Davis."

While on opposing sides of the political spectrum and history, Davis and Lincoln shared some commonalities in the way they began their lives, and even in death. They were both born in log cabins in Kentucky, only eight months and 123 miles apart, where they both lived for their first two years. In death, their remains traversed many miles on funeral trains, and both were reinterred. Unlike other "almost presidents," such as Hanson and Atchison, the details regarding Davis's death, funeral, burial, and reinterment were as meticulously recorded as were those for the most lionized of American presidents—and more so than for many others.

Davis was not always an outsider in American politics. Prior to the Civil War, he had been a representative and senator from Mississippi and served as secretary of war under Franklin Pierce. But his position as the first and only president of the Confederate States of America gained him indelible fame and notoriety before, during, and after the war.

While Lincoln was murdered on the verge of victory, Davis lived for almost a quarter century after his defeat. Following his capture, he spent two years imprisoned at Fort Monroe in Virginia. After he was released, he became a businessman and wrote two histories of the Confederacy. His legacy evolved over the years. Originally reviled as the architect of the South's destruction, he was later revered as a symbol of the unrepentant defender of the Lost Cause. In 1877, Davis purchased a plantation home named Beauvoir, in Mississippi. He was in relatively good health and, under the care of his physicians and his wife, Varina Banks Howell Davis, he made it into his 81st year. In late 1889, he felt fit enough to travel without his wife on a trip to another plantation he owned, named Brierfield, to collect the rent. He left his home and headed to New Orleans to board the steamer *Laura Lee* to sail up the Mississippi River. While on the way there, Davis came down with malaria, and by the time he arrived he was too sick to board the ship. He eventually made it to Brierfield, but his illness forced his return to New Orleans.[1]

Davis stayed in the city with his lifelong friend Jacob M. Payne and Louisiana Supreme Court judge Charles Fenner, who had served in the Confederate government in the Trans-Mississippi Department.[2] In their home at 1134 First Street, they put Davis in the guest bedroom situated at the back corner of the structure, where he rested on a carved oak Victorian bed. He was cared for by another longtime friend, Dr. Stanford E. Chaille, dean of the medical facility of Tulane University, who was assisted by Dr. Charles J. Bickham, vice president of the board of administrators at the Charity Hospital. Soon Varina joined Davis in New Orleans to care for him, along with "the capable quadroon hired nurse, Lydia."[3] Well-wishers sent flowers and food, but Davis had to decline the edible gifts when eventually he could no longer digest them. Lack of nutrition weakened him as he became resigned and ready for death.

On December 5, Davis awoke feeling better for the first time in days. He ate a lamb chop and he felt good until about 4:00 p.m., when he quickly went downhill.[4] This last burst of good health was not uncommon—John Quincy Adams, Andrew Jackson, and William Henry Harrison experienced a similar last-day flash of energy. At about 6:00 p.m., Davis suffered a "dread assault of the congestive chill."[5] His wife gave him medicine, but Davis could not stomach a full dose. She persisted, but in a weak voice Davis whispered, "Pray, excuse me." These were his last words. He never lost consciousness but was too weak to speak any further. The New Orleans *Picayune* lamented that his failed health "deprived his family and friends of the opportunity of inviting or hearing any expression of his last wishes or sentiments."[6]

At around 7:00 p.m., Dr. Chaille and Dr. Bickham arrived, but there was nothing they could do. His last movement was to roll over on his side and close his eyes. At 12:45 a.m. on Friday, December 6, 1889, Jefferson Davis quietly passed away surrounded by his wife, J. U. Payne, Mr. and Mrs. Edgar H. Farrar, Dr. Bickham, Dr. Chaille, Mr. and Mrs. Judge Charles E. Fenner, their son, E. D. Fenner, and Davis's grand-niece, Nannie Smith.[7]

Bells began to toll, and a black ribbon was hung from the doorknob to notify the residents of New Orleans of Davis's death. Later that morning, New Orleans mayor Joseph A. Shakespeare wired the United States War Department the news of Davis's death. Traditionally, the death of a former secretary of war would warrant the lowering of the department flags to half-mast. Since no other secretary of war had waged war against the United States, if there ever was justification for an exception, this was it. When asked if Davis would be shown the traditional honor, Secretary of War Redfield Proctor diplomatically replied, "I see no occasion for any action whatsoever. It would subserve no good purpose that I can see. 'Tis better to let the matter rest in oblivion, sleep if it will, and to relegate it to the past, than to do anything that would revive memories best forgotten."[8]

Predictably, Proctor's statement was not popular with some in the Deep South. But in Aberdeen, Mississippi, a German "tinner" and self-proclaimed "hot-headed Democrat," H. J. Franz, took the affront more to heart than most. On the day of the funeral, Franz was working on a rooftop when he hung an effigy of Secretary Proctor wearing a sign that read, RED PROCTOR TRAITOR! (He later made the ludicrous claim that it was an "accident.") Franz quickly discovered that not all of those in Aberdeen agreed with his sentiment, and one citizen, Will McDonald, responded to the insult with an assault. Accounts of his actions vary wildly, from a punch in the nose that "inflict[ed] a slight wound" to 200 lashes with a "whalebone coach" (whip) that shredded Franz's flesh and left him nearly blind.[9] McDonald was taken into custody and fined $30 for his act of vigilantism, but as proof that times had changed, his fine was raised by fellow citizens of Aberdeen. Wisely, Franz decided it was best to leave town, and his neighbors agreed so enthusiastically that they even bought him the

ticket. This incident later became a hot topic in the Senate, discussed on the floor by Kansas senator John James Ingalls.[10]

When Secretary of the Interior John Willock Noble was asked the same question as Proctor, he was less diplomatic and replied unequivocally, "It ought not to be. If Mr. Davis had ever shown a proper spirit of repentance it would be different. To the very last he refused to take the required oath of allegiance, and never, by word or by act, has he shown that he regretted his treasonable acts or that he looked upon the result of the war as a final decision against the erroneous principles for which he plunged the country into the destructive and cruel Civil War." He continued by pouring salt in the wound: "With his death there is removed one of the most irritating elements of what is known as 'the southern question.'"[11] Davis had indeed renounced his United States citizenship and never sought to restore it. President Jimmy Carter later restored it on October 17, 1978.[12]

Despite the federal government's stance, several Southern states enthusiastically honored Davis. Louisiana governor Francis Redding Tillou Nicholls, a brigadier general in the Confederate army, lowered the state capitol flag to half-mast. North Carolina, Georgia, and several other Southern states followed suit. While the harsher Northern newspapers referred to Davis as an unrepentant standard-bearer for the ugly institution of slavery, most were not unkind in their eulogies. Southern newspapers predictably showed an outpouring of affection, as for example the New Orleans *Times-Democrat*, which gushed, "Jefferson Davis's place in the affections of his people can never be filled. They loved him; they loved his pure and manly character; his integrity, the spotlessness of his life among them. They turned to him as the Mussulman to his Mecca—the shrine at which all true Southern-born should worship. Jefferson Davis will go to the grave bathed in a people's tears."[13] Not to be outdone, the New Orleans *Daily States* practically elevated Davis to sainthood, saying, "Throughout all the South there are lamentations and tears; in every country on the globe where there are lovers of liberty there is mourning; wherever there are men who admire heroic patriotism, dauntless resolution, fortitude, or intellectual power and supremacy, there is sincere sorrowing. The beloved of our land, the unfaltering upholder of constitutional liberty, the typical hero and sage, is no more; the fearless heart that beat with sympathy for all mankind is stilled forever, a great light has gone out—Jefferson Davis is dead."[14]

Varina was inundated with thousands of telegrams expressing sympathy. Overwhelmed, she contacted the Associated Press to issue a statement expressing her gratitude, because she was unable to answer them all. As to where Davis would be buried, most assumed it would be at his Brierfield plantation, but he had delegated his wife to choose the location. Offers came in from several Southern cemeteries, located in Macon and Atlanta, Georgia; Memphis, Tennessee; Jackson and Vicksburg, Mississippi; and beneath the

The home in New Orleans where Jefferson Davis died on December 6, 1889. (Courtesy of Joseph F. Picone)

Confederate monument in Montgomery, Alabama. Cave Hill Cemetery in Louisville, Kentucky, offered to bury Davis in a "beautiful lot formerly set aside for President Zachary Taylor, but never used."[15] This was an interesting offer, given that Davis's first wife, who died of malaria three months into their marriage, was Sarah Knox Taylor, former president Taylor's daughter. One of the most forceful offers came from Richmond, Virginia, when Governor General Fitzhugh Lee sent a telegraph to Judge Fenner on the day Davis died: "I voice the unanimous desire of our citizens that the last resting place of the illustrious statesman Jefferson Davis be in Richmond. As the capitol of the Confederacy; here he lived; here then, let him sleep, watched over by the city which, for so many years, was the object of his loving solicitude."[16]

The same day, the New Orleans *Picayune* called for the city to erect a monument "to entomb the remains and to be equal to that Abraham Lincoln in Springfield or that which may cover Grant at Riverside Park," and proposed it be funded a dollar at a time from people all over the South. While she weighed her final decision, Varina chose Metairie Cemetery in New Orleans as a temporary resting place. Metairie was considered "the prettiest cemetery in the South," and there Davis would join thousands of his Confederate soldiers. Both the Army of Northern Virginia and the Army of Tennessee offered the use of their respective mausoleums in Metairie, and the choice came down to one of the oldest ways of settling an argument: drawing straws. They drew, and Virginia won.

On the afternoon Davis died, Mayor Shakespeare called a meeting of political, religious, and military leaders to make funeral arrangements. Colonel J. Richardson, a commander in the Washington Artillery, was tasked with guarding the body during the viewing, and General John M. Glynn was delegated to be the grand marshal for the procession. One of the most significant assignments went to Jacob Gray as pallbearer. As post department commander of the Grand Army of the Republic, Gray was inspired to accept the offer by the Confederate generals who had served as pallbearers for President Grant four years earlier. Gray also suggested that Davis should be honored with a military funeral. His enthusiastic participation was offensive to many Northerners, and criminal to some. The following August, Gray was court-martialed but successfully defended himself.[17]

On the day Davis died, his widow sat alone with his body. One of the few people she let enter the room was Robert Brown, "an old Negro who had years ago been Mr. Davis' Body-servant."[18] Brown had been purchased by Davis in 1861 and remained with him until the Confederate president was captured on May 10, 1865, in Irwinville, Georgia.

Funeral director Frank R. Johnson and undertaker R. C. Davey bathed and embalmed Davis and completed their work by 5:30 a.m. on December 6. Dressed in a Confederate blue-gray suit given to him by former Confederate general Jubal Early, his body was initially laid out in the room where he died, and two palm leaves were placed by his head to "signify that the spirit had been victorious over the body."[19] The remains were put in a black coffin with silver and gold handles and placed in the parlor. His entire body was visible beneath a sheet of French plate glass, and affixed to the casket was a silver plate that read JEFFERSON DAVIS AT REST.

At around 9:00 a.m., photographer E. F. Blake captured Davis's final images, a popular custom during the Victorian era. Later in the day, Sister Mary Baptiste and Sister Mary Patrenelia of St. Alphonsus Convent knelt in prayer before the deceased with several female orphans. At 7:05 p.m., a hearse led by a white horse arrived at the home, but when a crowd quickly gathered, Varina was uncomfortable and sent it away. When it returned at 9:50 p.m., the streets were empty. Edgar H. Farrar, Judge C. E. Fenner, J. U. Payne, and three other men carried the coffin to the small carriage, which was already filled with flowers.

At five minutes to midnight, the small procession arrived at City Hall at Lafayette Square. The same six men carried the coffin inside and gently placed it on a bier covered with a thick black Turkish rug set beneath a 12-foot black canopy. Near the catafalque hung portraits of William Henry Harrison and Henry Clay, and on both sides were mountain howitzer cannons.[20] The room was draped in black crepe and decorated in Confederate nostalgia, including a bullet-riddled flag from the Fourteenth Louisiana Regiment. Next to the coffin was the sword used by Davis in the Black Hawk War, which had been retrieved from Beauvoir. Across the glass-covered coffin, a flag from the Fifth Company of the Washington Artillery was spread, concealing the lower body and leaving his shoulders and head exposed. It was written that "Never, perhaps, were floral offerings at a funeral more profuse or more beautiful," resulting in a "flower-perfumed death chamber."[21] Contrasting the nostalgic Civil War memorabilia, a portrait of Davis showcasing the latest technology was "placed within a frame of mourning, from which a myriad of electric lights brightly sparkle."[22]

Four guards, including a maimed veteran from the Soldiers' Home, took their positions and a different battery of soldiers from the Washington Artillery was assigned to guard Davis's remains each of the following nights. When the doors were opened at 10:00 a.m. on December 7, 3,000 people were already lined up. Over next 12 hours, elderly police and aged veterans ushered a diverse citizenry past the coffin. The *New*

York Times wrote that "Fully 20,000 people of all ages, colors, conditions and opinions filed into the Council Chamber at the City Hall to-day and gazed upon the calm and peaceful features of Jefferson Davis."[23]

After the crowds dispersed, Orin Frazer, a sculptor from Georgia, created a death mask. He had planned to make casts of Davis's hands and feet as well but decided against it when he found how they shrunken and shriveled they were. He worked deep into the night, finishing at 4:00 a.m. Before the ceremonies started on Sunday, December 8, photographer Charles H. Adams took additional images of the body and viewing room (he would do the same the following evening). It was a rainy morning when the doors opened at 10:00 a.m., but attendance reached 40,000 people by the time the doors closed 12 hours later. Over the next two days, another 90,000 people viewed the remains, bringing the total to 150,000 who had paid their respects to the "Tall Chieftain of the men in gray."[24]

On Wednesday, December 11 at 7:00 a.m., mourners filed in for the last time. Davis's appearance was delicately described as "remarkably well-preserved."[25] At 10:00 a.m., the doors closed to the public, and 90 minutes later the casket was sealed. At 12:10 p.m., the casket was moved to the portico, where it was announced by blasts of cannon fire and the tolling of bells. Thousands had crammed into Lafayette Square for this final ceremony, officiated by Bishop John Nicholas Galleher of the Protestant Episcopal Church. Bishop Galleher, who gripped a musket during the proceedings, began by asking for God's mercy "for the master of Beauvoir [who] lies dead under the drooping flag of the saddened city."

Assisting Bishop Galleher was a wide range of religious leaders: Episcopalian reverend Thomas R. Martin, Catholic father Darious Hubert of the Jesuit Church (former Confederate chaplain), Rabbi I. L. Leucht, Episcopalian reverend A. Gordon Bakewell, Presbyterian reverend

The New Orleans funeral procession on December 11, 1889 for Davis, the only president of the Confederate States of America. (Library of Congress)

Thomas R. Markham, Bishop Hugh Miller Thompson, and Reverend Ebenezer Thompson, who was Davis's pastor in Biloxi, Mississippi. Other clergymen came from the Southern states, bringing the total to over 20 men of the cloth, accompanied by a 36-member choir. After the ceremony, the casket was covered in the Confederate flag, and eight artillerymen placed it in the funeral carriage, a modified artillery caisson, where it sat beneath a canopy bearing two American—not Confederate—flags, supported by six upright cannons in lieu of columns; crisscrossing the cannons were muskets. This remarkable homage to firepower was pulled by six black horses in full regalia, each led by a uniformed soldier. The New Orleans *Times-Democrat* called it a "Monster procession" which was led by the military, including veterans from the Army of Northern Virginia and Army of Tennessee. As an overture to let bygones be bygones, invitations were sent to Union veterans in Louisiana to participate, though few responded.[26] African Americans were also not ready to forgive and forget. Excluding the handful of former slaves of Davis who remembered him affectionately, almost none marched in the procession.

Following were the New Orleans police and a sizable representation of clergy. There were an extraordinary 56 ceremonial pallbearers, each selected by Varina. The mood was described as "heartfelt, but unostentatious and manly sorrow."[27] Over 200,000 people witnessed the spectacle, which took more than an hour to pass. Mayor Shakespeare had asked businesses to close on the day of the funeral and added, "A life so pure, a career so illustrious, may well serve as an example to rising generations, and I recommend that the schools be closed and that the children attend the funeral."[28] As church bells tolled, the procession marched from Lafayette Square down St. Charles Street to Calliope Street. Onward it went to Camp Street, Chartles Street, St. Louis Street, Royal Street, and finally Canal Street, arriving at 4:00 p.m. at the cemetery entrance. It continued half a mile to the burial location, where it was greeted by a choir, a crowd with heads uncovered, and an abundance of floral arrangements designed by J. H. Menard.

The coffin was placed on a bier on a scenic mound and the widow gingerly walked up the slope holding the arm of Jacob U. Payne, followed by Davis's former slave, Robert Brown. Bishop Galleher spoke, saying, "In the name of God, Amen. We here consign the body of Jefferson Davis, a servant of his State and country, and a soldier in their armies; some time member of Congress and Senator from Mississippi, and Secretary of War of the United States; the first and only President of the Confederate States of America."[29] The choir sang "Rock of Ages" and

played Taps before the coffin was carried into the crypt beneath a towering statue of Stonewall Jackson. There, Davis's remains joined veterans from the Army of Northern Virginia, Louisiana Division. His coffin was placed in the middle vault immediately to the right, the flag was removed, and the slab was tightly screwed into place. The Washington Artillery fired a final salvo to end the ceremony.[30] The crowd milled around for about an hour, some descending into the mausoleum. After they all dispersed, a small cadre of policemen remained to guard over the tomb. The next day, the New Orleans *Times-Democrat* called the occasion "a grand, an imposing, a historic funeral pageant. No man now living will look upon its like again. It is the snapping of the last great human link in the chain that binds the memory of the South to the volcanic past."[31]

Varina continued to be overwhelmed with offers for a permanent burial location. On December 21, the Jefferson Davis Monument Association was formed in Richmond to secure the remains to reinter in the former Confederate capitol, but Varina let it be known that she needed a year to make her decision. Richmond mayor James Taylor Ellyson waited until June 1891 before visiting Varina at a New York City hotel to persuade her that his city was the best choice, adding that she could select any location in Richmond she wanted.[32] On July 13, his efforts paid off when she wrote, "I yield my husband's mortal remains to the care of Virginia, secure in the certainty that he will rest among his friends who stood firm in defeat as they did in the day of the Confederate States' existence; and I prefer Richmond as the place of the interment."[33]

Along with her daughter, Varina Anne "Winnie" Davis, the widow visited Richmond to scout possible locations on October 31. She first considered the grounds of the Confederate White House where they had lived during the war, but five days after she arrived, Varina decided upon

Hollywood Cemetery. In addition to almost 20,000 Confederate veterans, Davis would also rest beside former United States presidents John Tyler and James Monroe. The spot chosen for the Confederate leader overlooked the James River and was dubbed "The Davis Circle." She also requested that her deceased children be reinterred beside her husband. Shortly after Varina's decision, work began on the grave—a deep brick tomb with two vaults was to be built.

The date to retrieve the remains was set for May 31, 1893. The journey from New Orleans to Richmond would be an elaborate event—the coffin would travel by locomotive, meant to rival the Lincoln funeral train 28 years earlier. Planners were aware that the graveside service should be simple, not to overshadow the earlier 1889 one. At the family's request, the body was discreetly removed early in the morning on Saturday, May 27. In attendance on that rainy morning were Edgar H. Farrar, undertaker Frank Johnson, Metairie Cemetery representative Paul Schloz, and guards from the Army of Northern Virginia. Davis was gingerly removed, and it was reported that his body was "naturally decomposed, but in fair preservation and the face recognizable."[34] His new coffin was carved oak and adorned with brass trimmings and a brass plate identical to the one from the 1889 casket that read:

JEFFERSON DAVIS
AT REST
DEC. 6, 1889

The empty coffin was filled with flowers from the original funeral that had been saved by the family for the past three and a half years. It was pushed back in the vault and sealed inside, where it still is today. Throughout the day a cadre of armed guards from the Army of Northern Virginia watched over the coffin, and at 3:00 p.m., they escorted the remains in a closed black hearse. Along the route, people removed their hats and flags hung at half-mast.

The hearse arrived at Confederate Memorial Hall at 5:10 p.m., and the coffin was received by the United Confederate Veterans and placed on an oak catafalque. Shortly afterward, the doors were opened and people filed in, and the steady stream continued until midnight.

The next morning, Sunday, May 28, the doors reopened and thousands more solemnly walked past the coffin until 4:30 p.m. When only distinguished guests were left in the hall, a funeral ceremony was held for only a committee of people from Richmond dressed in Confederate gray together with Jefferson Davis's daughters Winnie and Margaret Howell Hayes. Louisiana Governor Murphy J. Foster made a brief address, followed by the Army of Northern Virginia's vice president J. Y. Gilmore, who read a letter from Varina calling for the removal of the body. Richmond mayor Ellyson responded with a request that the remains be escorted to Richmond by the Army of Northern Virginia and delivered to General John M. Glynn, who three and a half years earlier had served as Grand Marshal for the procession to Metairie Cemetery. After these formalities, Confederate chaplain Reverend Gordon A. Blakewell said a prayer to conclude the service. The New Orleans funeral was subdued, described in the *Three Rivers Tribune* as "marked by an absence of enthusiasm and were as simple as the funeral of a humble citizen, barring the military display." But this was not to be indicative of the rest of the final journey.[35]

Confederate veterans carried the coffin to the funeral hearse, the same one used in 1889 to bring the body to Metairie Cemetery. The car was slowly pulled by six black horses to the Louisville and Nashville Railroad Station on Canal Street and arrived at 6:00 p.m. Built in Richmond and provided by the Richmond and Danville Railroad system, the 10-car Davis funeral train was powered by one of the largest and fastest engines in the South and piloted by the aptly named Frank Coffin. The carriage holding Davis's remains was retrofitted with glass sides to show the casket. On the train were Davis's daughters and James Jones, a black man who was his former coachman.

The train slowly departed and 90 minutes later arrived at Gulfport, Mississippi, where Davis's plantation home was located. The station was carpeted with flowers and his brother, Joe Davis, boarded, but residents were disappointed when the train left only 10 minutes after its arrival.[36] At midnight it stopped in Mobile, Alabama, engine #69 was replaced with #25, C. C. Dewinney took over as engineer, and fireman Warren Robinson boarded. While the train sat in the station, the Alabama State Artillery fired a 21-gun salute and 1,000 people viewed the casket through the windows. Twenty minutes later, the train was again on its way.

It continued traveling overnight, and on Monday, May 29, at 6:00 a.m. it pulled into the Greeneville station in Alabama, but the disappointed crowd could only see a pile of flowers that had buried the coffin. The next stop was Montgomery, Alabama, for the first public viewing of the journey. A short distance from the station, the train was flanked by the Confederate veterans from the Montgomery True Blues and Montgomery Grays, who marched alongside, bearing arms, to escort it to the final distance. A driving rain had not curtailed the crowd of 15,000 people. Alabama governor T. G. Jones, accompanied by former president Tyler's granddaughter, Letitia, boarded the train to view the coffin before it was carried to the hearse. The colorful caisson was draped in royal purple and looked more appropriate for a circus than a funeral procession, but with Davis now dead for more than three years, this was a celebration of his life more than a mourning of his death.[37]

By the time the procession began at 8:30 a.m., the rain had subsided and the skies had cleared. Crowds filled the streets, including soldiers who fired their guns as the hearse passed. It was pulled by six black horses, led by armed guards, and followed by Confederate veterans.

The pallbearers were about two dozen prominent Alabama citizens. The procession marched down Commerce Street to Dexter Street before arriving at the state capitol, the same building where Davis was inaugurated on February 18, 1861. The coffin was placed in the Supreme Court room upon a catafalque draped in purple satin.

First to enter were several hundred members of the Ladies Memorial Association, who deposited a white flower at the base of the catafalque. As the crowds became too great, the guards crossed their bayonets to keep them at bay, but the throngs pushed on until four more guards were added at the door. In the space of a few hours, 10,000 people viewed the coffin before the doors were shut shortly before 11:00 a.m. The hearse took the same route back to the station, and the train departed at 11:30 a.m. for Atlanta. Governor Jones was on board to escort the remains to the state line, just as governors did for the Lincoln funeral train almost three decades earlier.

The train passed crowds of people, and cannons fired in salute. There were two more quick stops in Alabama, at Chehaw and Opelika, before the train crossed the Georgia state line at West Point. Georgia governor William J. Northen boarded the train in full Confederate regalia. After a quick stop in Moreland, Georgia, the train arrived at Union Station in Atlanta at 4:30 p.m., where it was met by 5,000 people and artillery salutes. The coffin was carried to the hearse, a modified artillery caisson pulled by six gray horses. The Grand Marshal for the Atlanta parade was the commander of the Georgia Confederate Veterans Association, General Clement A. Evans, who arranged for 2,000 fellow veterans to march, many limping along, impaired by their 30-year-old injuries. Policemen and, as the New York Times disclosed, "Secret organizations" also marched.[38]

Shortly after 5:00 p.m., the procession arrived at the Capitol building, and 12 Confederate veterans placed the coffin on an enormous, 30-foot-long catafalque that was draped in red, white, and blue flowers. Once it was in place, a young man played Taps on the same bugle used in 1889 at the New Orleans funeral. Over the next 90 minutes, an astounding 40,000 people were able to view the casket. When the announcement was made at 7:00 p.m. that the doors were closing, people made a mad dash for the flowers to get a tangible memento from the day.[39] The train rode through the night, stopping briefly in Gainesville before entering South Carolina. Across the border, the train was often greeted with bonfires, cannon flash, and the ear-piercing rebel yell. It stopped briefly at Seneca, South Carolina, where more flowers were heaped on the coffin. At 2:00 a.m. on Tuesday, May 30, the train arrived in Greenville, South Carolina, where, despite the early morning hour, 2,500 people had gathered at the station. A brief address was made by Colonel Hoyt of the Old Palmetto Sharpshooters, in which he stated the "Veterans of the Southern Confederacy are here with a last fond tribute to their fallen chieftain."[40] South Carolina governor Benjamin Tillman then boarded the train to escort the body all the way to Richmond.

In Charlotte, North Carolina, the train was greeted by a three-shot salute fired by the Hornet's Nest Rifles and the Queen City Rifles, then continued a short distance before brief pauses in Salisbury and Greensboro at 9:30 a.m. The train stopped in Durham, where it was greeted by 500 schoolchildren, each dropping a flower on the casket. About 1,000 people were on hand when it arrived in Raleigh, and Mayor Thomas Badger formally took custody of the remains while they were in his city. The coffin was passed through the window of the funeral car, and eight Confederate veterans hoisted it on their shoulders into a unique hearse that had been designed by A.G. Bauer. It towered 14 feet high and was shaped like a temple. On each corner sat a 12- or 13-year-old girl, each "golden haired" and

dressed in virginal white, with a black sash and carrying a different Confederate flag. The coffin sat on a platform covered in bearskin and draped with a bullet riddled Confederate flag from the Fifth North Carolina Regiment. Six black horses pulled the hearse, led by James Jones, who was impeccably dressed in a black suit and Prince Albert coat. In striking contrast to Jones was the "Negro field hand in his ordinary working clothes" that led each horse.[41]

At 1:20 p.m., the procession began its march to the state capitol, where it was met by 10,000 people, including North Carolina governor Elias Carr. Six prominent North Carolina citizens carried the casket up the stairs, forgoing the handles and instead bearing the weight on their shoulders. After a prayer by Episcopal Reverend Marshall, the coffin was placed on a catafalque beneath the rotunda. The four young girls who rode on the funeral car took positions at each corner of the casket, grasping their Confederate flags for the duration of the viewing. Approximately 5,000 people viewed the casket until 3:00 p.m., when it was returned to the station. The train departed at 3:40 p.m. for the last leg of the journey, now pulling one additional car for Governor Carr. At a brief stop in Reidsville, North Carolina, it was greeted by 2,000 to 3,000 people. After crossing a state border for the last time, it stopped at 9:00 p.m. in Danville, Virginia, where 6,000 enthusiastic people greeted the train and another two cars were added, one for Virginia governor Philip Watkins McKinney and a second for the Richmond Light Infantry Blues militia unit.[42]

As the train approached Richmond, Virginia, Davis's widow arrived in the city from New York. She checked into the Exchange Hotel, where 31 years earlier former president Tyler had died. The funeral train arrived at its final destination at 3:05 a.m. on Tuesday, May 31 and was greeted by a 13-gun salute and Confederate soldiers from the First Regiment. This is where Davis had lived the most important years of his life, and the city was eager to welcome him home. Before the coffin was taken out of the train, the flowers that had accumulated throughout the trip were removed. The coffin was then passed through the window into the hands of Confederate soldiers, who placed it on a hearse. Gray-haired soldiers from the Richmond Light Infantry Blues escorted it to the state capitol. Those who braved the night to view the procession took off their hats out of respect. The coffin was placed beneath the rotunda, and members of the Lee Camp, the first permanent Confederate veterans' organization, took their place as guards of honor.[43]

Approximately 25,000 mourners walked past the coffin, including 6,000 schoolchildren dressed in white, many of whom dropped flowers at the foot of the casket. At 3:00 p.m., the doors were closed, and 30 minutes later the coffin was on a caisson provided by the Richmond Howitzer Battery, decorated in Confederate colors. Leading the procession were Confederate veterans and military organizations, followed by the hearse, pulled by six white horses, each flanked by a Confederate veteran. The bevy of honorary pallbearers included Southern governors and an aged General Jubal Early. Included in the procession were Davis's former coachman Jones and former slaves Frederick McGinnis and Robert Brown. The Southern states were fully represented with political and military organizations, but there was no representation from the Northern states, causing the *New York Times* to raise the alarm: "Except for the absence of muskets and swords, it was if the Confederate armies were on the march once more!"[44] As the hearse left the Capitol grounds, it rode beneath a ceremonial

arch constructed the previous day. It continued past the Confederate White House and St. Paul's Episcopal Church, where Davis had worshipped and Tyler's funeral was held. All told, there were 4,000 to 5,000 participants in the parade while approximately 75,000 people watched in respectful silence. Flowers were strewn on the ground by young girls before the hearse, bells tolled, buildings were draped in black, and Confederate flags lined the route. Unlike Lincoln, estimates of how many people saw the Davis funeral train and witnessed the viewings were not published. Throughout the reinterment that traversed seven states and 1,200 miles, an estimated 100,000 people walked past the coffin, and it is estimated that twice that number assembled to see the train or watch the coffin pass in procession.

Thirty thousand people gathered at Hollywood Cemetery for the burial. Confederate soldiers placed the oak coffin on the ground by the open grave. When the Stonewall Band of Staunton played "Nearer, My God, to Thee," Winnie burst into tears. There was a host of clergymen participating in the ceremony. The Rev-

The grave of Jefferson Davis in Hollywood Cemetery, 1905. (Library of Congress)

erend William Mumford began with a reading from Scripture, followed by the Reverend W. W. Landrum from Richmond, who read the hymn, "How Firm a Foundation." Next was Episcopal Bishop Reverend Moses D. Hoge from Mississippi, who led the attendees in prayer, and Reverend O. S. Barten of Norfolk, Virginia, concluded with the benediction. The casket was lowered into the grave and surrounded by flowers. Within the tomb hung Confederate flags, symbolizing Davis's true allegiance for all eternity. The bugler then played Taps, followed by one final artillery salute.

To further honor Davis, Varina chose sculptor George Julian Zolnay to build a statue above the crypt. Zolnay, a Hungarian native, had earned the moniker "Sculptor of the Confederacy." A rumor had persisted that when Davis was captured after the fall of the Confederacy, he had dressed as a woman to evade discovery. Varina sought to dispel what she believed was a slanderous lie and ordered Zolnay to sculpt Davis wearing the suit she claimed he was wearing on the day of his capture. The monument was dedicated on November 9, 1899.[45]

THE JEFFERSON DAVIS DEATH SITES

Location of Death

The home where Davis died is located in the Garden District of New Orleans, at 1134 First Street. It was the home of his friend Judge Fenner and was built by Fenner's brother-in-law, Jacob U. Payne (it was known as the Payne-Strachan House). The two-story brown stucco home has been called "one of the most comfortable and interiorly artistic" homes in all of New Orleans.[46]

The home is adorned with several tributes to Davis, including a stone monument that reads:

HERE, IN THE HOME OF HIS FRIEND,
JEFFERSON DAVIS, FIRST AND ONLY PRESIDENT OF
THE CONFEDERATE STATES OF
AMERICA, DIED ON DEC. 6, 1889.

Lying in Repose: New Orleans, 1889

The City Hall building in New Orleans was designed by architect James Gallier Sr. Construction began in 1845, but the project was put on hold when the city ran out of money. At the time, only the basement was dug, so a roof was erected over it to protect from the elements. Construction resumed in 1851 and was completed two years later. The building was dedicated on May 10, 1853. It was built of Tuckahoe marble, and its entrance includes two rows of fluted Ionic columns. The building was originally to be the headquarters for city government, but today it is known as Gallier Hall and is available to rent for private parties. It was designated a National Historic Landmark (#74002250) on May 30, 1974.

Gallier Hall is located at 545 St. Charles Avenue, New Orleans, Louisiana, 70113. For more information, visit: www.nola.gov/gallier-hall.

Original Cemetery

The land where Metairie Cemetery was built was originally a racetrack, but it was closed after the Civil War. The cemetery was established in 1872 and designed by architect Benjamin F. Harrod, who added flora and two arterial lakes. It was soon considered "The Grand Dame of New Orleans."[47] Today, you can still see the mausoleum inscription where Davis's body lay. It reads:

JEFFERSON DAVIS
JUNE 3, 1808, DECEMBER 6, 1889

Lying in Repose: New Orleans, 1893

On March 28, 1889, a group of New Orleans citizens led by Frank Howard convened to form the Louisiana Historical Association. Its members included Confederate veterans from the Army of Tennessee, Army of Northern Virginia, Washington Artillery, and the Association of Confederate States Cavalry. The group amassed an impressive collection of Civil War artifacts and records. To house their collection, they envisioned a building inspired by local architect Henry Hobson Richardson, who had developed his own style, which he called "Richardsonian Romanesque." Unfortunately, Richardson had died three years earlier; undeterred, they hired the local architectural firm Sully & Toledano to create a building using Richardson's design. The construction was completed while Davis's body rested in Metairie Cemetery, and the Confederate Memorial Hall was formally dedicated on January 8, 1891. At the ceremony, one grizzled veteran commented, "Here the old soldiers will meet and, in social intercourse, tell their stories of personal adventure and fight their battles o'er again!"

The building, also known as the Confederate Museum, is the oldest museum in Louisiana, where you can see one of the largest collections of Confederate memorabilia in the United States. It is located at 929 Camp Street, New Orleans, Louisiana, 70130. For more information, visit: www.ConfederateMuseum.com.

Lying in State: Richmond, VA
See Chapter 11: John Tyler

Hollywood Cemetery
See Chapter 11: John Tyler

Acknowledgments

First and foremost I thank my family. To my wife, Francesca, who has infinite patience and lent her amazing artistic gifts to this book (and is also quite easy on the eyes!). She knew me when I thought Rutherford B. Hayes and Benjamin Harrison were members of ZZ Top, but married me anyway. To our two wonderful sons, Vincent and Leonardo—who often make us laugh and always make us proud—and we love you both. They have visited more presidential sites before graduating grammar school than most people will in a lifetime and (almost) never complained. For all of the times I have squeezed a presidential site into a family road trip, claiming it is "on the way" to our ultimate destination, I thank my family for having the tact not to open a map and call me out on it.

Thanks to my mom and dad for being the world's greatest parents, grandparents, and *beyond*! Back in the 1970s, while our friends were going to the New Jersey beaches for summer vacation, Mom and Dad piled me and my siblings, Rosemarie, Ralph, and Joseph, into the Ford LTD (with the broken air conditioner and windows that wouldn't roll down) to places like Williamsburg, Fort Ticonderoga, Campobello, and the Old Jail at St. Augustine. While we complained then (and still do about the electric map at Gettysburg), I now realize that they planted the seeds of a very slow-growing tree that became my love of history.

For my gifted father-in-law and artist, Mel Leipzig, for his endless support and "spirited" political discussions. I hope the day never comes that we have a conversation that does not involve the presidents. To my little brother and fellow presidential traveler, Joseph, for the photographs and advice. To Ralph, who is my big brother so needs no other reason to be thanked. And to all of my nieces and nephews and sometime presidential road trip traveling companions; Danielle, Maggie, Katrina, Mary, Olivia, Rayona, Zev, and Ami. Special thanks to my sister and editor, Rosemarie Flood. She read, re-read, and re-re-read the initial versions of this weighty manuscript and wore out many a red pen in the process. Her meticulous skill improved every page and, without hyperbole, *I could not have written this book without her*. If any errors exist, either factual or grammatical, they are all mine.

Special thanks to the many, many people from presidential museums, libraries, and landmarks who have assisted me with my research. In particular, thank you Marsha Mullin and Ashley Bouknight from the Hermitage for providing access to the Andrew Jackson archives. Thanks to Bev Meyer from the Harrison-Symmes Memorial Foundation for the impromptu tour of the William Henry Harrison crypt and for spending time with me on the phone afterward. Along with the other members of the foundation, she is to be commended for caring for the grave of the ninth president. Thanks to

Ann Toplovich from the Tennessee Historical Society and Jim Hoobler, senior curator, Art & Architecture, at the Tennessee State Museum for the enlightening and informative discussion about James K. Polk's death and burials (all *three* of them). Thank you John Edens, archivist from Forest Lawn Cemetery, for taking the time to help research the history of the Millard Fillmore grave monument. I appreciate the assistance from the helpful staff at the Lancaster County Historical Society for providing information from their archives on Wheatland and the sordid history of James Buchanan's grave.

Thank you to Dr. Daniel R. Schumaier, for permitting me access to the home where Andrew Johnson died, which is now located on his property. Under his stewardship, this important piece of presidential history is respectfully maintained. Thanks to Michelle Ganz, archivist and special collections librarian from the Abraham Lincoln Library and Museum in Harrogate, Tennessee, for generously granting permission to include their historic photograph of the home where Andrew Johnson died. Thanks to Nan Card, curator of manuscripts, and Nancy Kleinhenz, communications manager, from the Rutherford B. Hayes Presidential Center. I appreciate them carving time out of a busy day to meet with me (unfortunately I took a wrong turn and arrived too late!). Thank you to Mary Krohner, director of community relations, and Kevin Sullivan from the Lake View Cemetery. They generously gave their time during a busy day at the James A. Garfield Monument to share the history of the memorial and their unique experiences working there.

Thanks to Jennifer E. Capps, VP of curatorship & exhibition of the Benjamin Harrison Presidential Site, for sharing letters to the president during his illness and to his widow after his death. These intimate correspondences helped personalize the final chapter of President Harrison's life. Jennifer has worked at the site for almost a quarter century and shared valuable insight. I also thank Barbara, our knowledgeable and friendly tour guide. Thank you Ms. Marty N. Davis, Crown Hill Cemetery PR & tour coordinator, for insightful information on Benjamin Harrison's grave. Thank you to Marie Panik from Historic Northampton Massachusetts for providing the image of Calvin Coolidge's funeral and permission to use it in this book.

Thanks to Baird Todd, museum curator of the Lyndon B. Johnson National Historical Park, for collecting resources and enlightening me about the history of the 36th president's life and death in beautiful Texas Hill Country. Thanks to the very talented architectural photographer George Gutenberg for permission to use his photograph of the home in which Gerald Ford died. Every photograph he provided was so stunning it was difficult to choose just one for this book. Special thanks to my good friend and New Jersey expatriate now living on the West Coast, Kurt Kusenko, for furnishing photographs of 668 Saint Cloud Road in Bel Air, California, where Ronald Reagan passed away. "Thank you" and a "Howdy!" to Michael Sproat, curator of collections at the Sam Houston Memorial Museum. Michael is a fountain of knowledge about the two-time president of the Republic of Texas. I appreciate the private tour of the unique Steamboat House, and his enthusiasm for Sam Houston and his state of Texas is infectious. And thanks to Jimmy S. Emerson, DVM, for permission to use his photograph of President-for-a-day David Rice Atchison's grave (the day I visited it was too sunny for a good photograph).

I would also like to recognize the amazing photograph collections of the Library of Congress and the Department of Defense, several of which were used in this book. Please note that the appearance of US Department of Defense (DoD) visual information does not imply or constitute DoD endorsement.

And a special thank you to the incredible people from Skyhorse Publishing including Cal Barksdale and Amy Singh. I sincerely appreciate their collaboration, patience, talents, and expertise during every step of the process to create this book that you now hold in your hands, which exceeded my wildest expectations!

And finally, to you, the reader. For your interest in our rich American history you deserve to be commended. For taking your precious time to read this book that took me five years to research and write, I *sincerely* thank you.

Notes

1. GEORGE WASHINGTON

1. Flexner, James Thomas. *Washington: The Indispensable Man*. New York: Back Bay Books, 1994.
2. Markel, Dr. Howard. "Dec. 14, 1799: The Excruciating Final Hours of President George Washington," PBSNewshour.com, December 14, 2014.
3. "Former Presidents," *Luddington Daily News*, September 3, 1885.
4. Thornton, William. *Papers of William Thornton, 1781–1802*. Charlottesville: University of Virginia Press, 1995.
5. Knight, Franklin, ed. *Letters on Agriculture from His Excellency George Washington*. New York: Baker & Scribner, 1847, 193–194. The exact text from the will is: "The family Vault at Mount Vernon requiring repairs, and being improperly situated besides, I desire that a new one of Brick, and upon a larger Scale, may be built at the foot of what is commonly called the Vineyard Inclosure, on the ground which is marked out. In which my remains, with those of my deceased relatives (now in the old vault) and such others of my family as may chuse to be entombed there, may be deposited. And it is my express desire that my Corpse may be Interred in a private manner, without parade, or funeral Oration."
6. Ibid., 181–182.
7. Custis, George Washington Parke. *Recollections and Private Memoirs of Washington*. New York: Derby & Jackson, 1860, 472–479.
8. "Mount Vernon Pallbearers," accessed November 27, 2015, http://www.mountvernon.org/research-collections/digital-encyclopedia/article/pallbearers; "Mount Vernon Bier Carriers," accessed November 27, 2015, http://www.mountvernon.org/research-collections/digital-encyclopedia/article/bier-carriers. The pallbearers were Free Masons Charles Little, Charles Simms, William Payne, George Gilpin, Dennis Ramsay, and the only non-Mason, Philip Marsteller. Another four men carried the coffin; Lawrence Hooff Jr., James Turner, George Wise, and William Moss. But a weakened Moss "broke down under the weight of the casket in removing the bier from the mansion to the tomb." George Coryell opportunistically offered to replace him and secure his place in history. Coryell, a fellow Mason who occasionally did work at Mount Vernon, outlived all of his fellow pallbearers, surviving another 51 years, and was buried in the small First Presbyterian Church Cemetery in Lambertville, New Jersey. And it was this happpenstance event that is forever memorialized on a bronze plaque placed on his tombstone.
9. Hawn, Jerry. "The Funeral of George Washington," *National Mall & Memorial Parks*, September 2007.
10. Reynolds, Charles Bingham. *The Standard Guide, Washington, A Handbook for Visitors*. New York: Foster & Reynolds, 1898, 162.
11. "Capitol Rotunda Overview," last updated October 19, 2015, www.aoc.gov/cc/capitol/rotunda.cfm.
12. "The Resolution to Bury President George Washington at the U.S. Capitol." History, Art & Archives: United States House of Representatives, accessed November 27, 2015, history.house.gov/Historical-Highlight/Detail/36506.
13. Wineberger, J. A. *The Tomb of Washington at Mount Vernon*. Washington, DC: Thomas McGill, 1858, 39.
14. Evans, Thomas C. *Of Many Men*. New York: American News Company, 1888, 86.
15. Knight, *Letters on Agriculture From His Excellency George Washington*, 179.

16. Weaver, George Sumner. *The Lives and Graves of Our Presidents*. Chicago: Elder Publishing Company, 1884, 85–88; Wineberger, J. A., *The Tomb of Washington at Mount Vernon*, 39–47. Present at the auspicious ceremony to transfer the remains to the new coffin were Major Lawrence Lewis, John Augustine Washington, Richard Blackburn Washington, Reverend Johnson, Miss Jane Washington, and a descendent also named George Washington.

17. "Ex-Slave Guarded Tomb of Washington for Half Century," *The Afro-American*, March 5, 1932.

18. *Debates in Congress*. Washington, DC: Gales and Seaton, 1833, 414–415.

19. Ibid.

20. Ibid.

21. "Washington Gets Excited," *New York Times*, May 2, 1897.

22. Williams, William W. *The American Nation*. Cleveland: The Williams Publishing Company, 1892, 761.

23. "The Tomb of Washington," *New York Times*, June 20, 1895.

24. *The Report of the Virginia Board of Visitors to Mount Vernon for the Year 1901*. Richmond, Virginia: J. H. O'Bannon, 1901.

25. Nagel, Paul C. *John Quincy Adams: A Public Life, a Private Life*. Cambridge, Massachusetts: Harvard University Press, 1999.

26. "President at Mount Vernon," *New York Times*, December 15, 1899.

27. "President Pays Tribute to Memory of Predecessor," *Gazette Times*, February 23, 1912.

28. "The President Speaks," *New York Times*, February 2, 1932.

29. "Roosevelt Visits Washington Tomb," *New York Times*, February 23, 1934.

30. "Roosevelt Visits Washington Tomb," *New York Times*, February 23, 1937.

31. "Marble Shrine of Washington Scene of Ritual," *Windsor Daily Star*, June 9, 1939.

32. "Mme. Chiang Visits Washington Tombs," *New York Times*, February 23, 1943.

33. "Truman Decorates Washington's Tomb," *New York Times*, February 23, 1947.

34. "Reagan Notes Birthday of George Washington," *Eugene Register Guard*, February 22, 1982.

35. *The Report of the Virginia Board of Visitors to Mount Vernon for the Year 1901*.

36. "Mount Vernon the Mansion," accessed November 27, 2015, http://www.mountvernon.org/the-estate-gardens/the-mansion.

37. Evans, *Of Many Men*, 87.

38. *The Encyclopedia Americana*. New York: Encyclopedia Americana Corporation, 1919.

39. Sumner. *The Lives and Graves of Our Presidents*, 85–88; Wineberger, J. A., *The Tomb of Washington at Mount Vernon*, 39–47.

40. *The Report of the Virginia Board of Visitors to Mount Vernon for the Year 1901*.

41. "Mount Vernon, the Birthplace of Historic Preservation," *Washington Post*, September 10, 2012.

42. "Women Rebuked Disrespectful Man at Washington's Tomb," *Spokesman Review*, August 24, 1923. An amusing story regarding the Mount Vernon Ladies' Association. In addition to saving the historic home, they also brought a touch of civility and reverence to the site. In 1923 there was an amusing story that might have otherwise been unknown if not for an obviously slow news day. The *Spokesman Review* reported that "when a man swaggered up to the tomb of Washington, belching cigar smoke, and with his hat over his eyes" he was quickly rebuked and corrected by one of the ladies.

43. "Washington's Tomb," *Lawrence Daily Journal-World*, January 10, 1900.

44. "Washington Tomb Crumbles," *Philadelphia Record*, September 2, 1903.

45. "America's Mementos," *Parade Magazine*, August 11, 2013.

46. Quincy, Josiah. *Figures of The Past*. Boston: Roberts Brothers, 1883.

2. THOMAS JEFFERSON

1. Crawford, Alan Pell. *Twilight at Monticello: The Final Years of Thomas Jefferson*. New York: Random House, 2008.

2. "Former Presidents," *Luddington Daily News*, September 3, 1885.

3. Crawford, *Twilight at Monticello*.

4. Burstein, Andrew. *Jefferson's Secrets: Death and Desire at Monticello*. New York: Basic Books, 2006, 280–282.

5. "Monticello: Jefferson's Funeral." accessed November 27, 2015, https://www.monticello.org/site/research-and-collections/jeffersons-funeral.

6. Crawford, *Twilight at Monticello*.

7. "Monticello: Martha Wayles Skelton Jefferson," accessed November 27, 2015, https://www.monticello.org/site/jefferson/martha-wayles-skelton-jefferson.

8. Weaver, George Sumner. *The Lives and Graves of Our Presidents*. Chicago: Elder Publishing Company, 1884, 159.

9. "The Grave-yard at Monticello," *New York Times*, May 31, 1880.

10. "The Monticello Association: Graveyard History," accessed November 27, 2015, www.monticello-assoc.org/history

11. "Mystery in Missouri," *Free Lance-Star*, April 13, 2002.

12. Ibid.

13. "Honor Jefferson's Memory," *New York Times*, October 13, 1901.

14. The Jefferson Club of St. Louis. *The Pilgrimage to Monticello, The Home and Tomb of Thomas Jefferson*. St. Louis: Con P. Curran Printing Company, 1902, 21.

15. "Thomas Jefferson's Body," *New York Times*, June 4, 1882.

16. "Nation Has Done Little in Honor of Its Dead Rulers," *New York Times*, January 12, 1913.

17. "President at Jefferson's Grave," *Deseret News*, June 16, 1903.

18. "Roosevelt Speech at Jefferson Home," *New York Times*, July 5, 1936.

19. "President Is Sharp," *New York Times*, July 5, 1947.

20. "Ford Warns New Citizens of Conformity; Says Diversity Has Made Nation Great," *New York Times*, July 6, 1976.

21. "Clinton, Gore Mark Opening of Inaugural Extravaganza," *Victoria Advocate*, January 18, 1993.

22. "President Bush Speaks at Monticello," posted July 04, 2008, http://www.nbc29.com/story/8620075/president-bush-speaks-at-monticello.

23. "Obama, French president tour Monticello," *Roanoke Times*, February 20, 2014.

24. "Colts Neck House Tour Includes 'Monticello'," *Greater Media Newspapers*, November 10, 2011.

25. Nichols, Frederick D., and James A. Bear Jr. *Monticello: A Guidebook*. Charlottesville, Virginia: Thomas Jefferson Memorial Foundation, 1982.

26. Weaver, *The Lives and Graves of Our Presidents*, 157–162.

27. Crawford, *Twilight at Monticello*.

28. Leepson, Marc. *Saving Monticello*. Charlottesville: University of Virginia Press, 2001, 17.

29. "Their Faith Renewed," *New York Times*, April 14, 1896.

30. Nichols and Bear Jr., *Monticello: A Guidebook*.

31. Leepson, *Saving Monticello*.

32. "Monticello, Once the Residence of Thomas Jefferson," *Frank Leslie's Illustrated Newspaper*, February 8, 1862.

33. Ibid.

34. Leepson, *Saving Monticello*.

35. Proffatt, John. *Curiosities of Wills*. San Francisco: Sumner Whitney & Co., 1876.

36. "Affairs in the South," *New York Times*, March 11, 1866.

37. "Jefferson's Tomb," *Dubuque Daily Herald*. June 15, 1890.

38. "Jefferson Home for the Nation," *New York Times*, October 6, 1914.

39. "Their Faith Renewed," *New York Times*, April 14, 1896.

40. "Nation Has Done Little in Honor of Its Dead Rulers," *New York Times*, January 12, 1913.

41. "A National Humiliation," *New York Sun*, August 24, 1897: *Rpt* in Leepson, *Saving Monticello*. 33-34.

42. "Aid Mrs. Littleton's Plan," *New York Times*, August 8, 1912.

43. "Jefferson Home for the Nation," *New York Times*, October 6, 1914.

44. Nichols and Bear Jr., *Monticello: A Guidebook*.

45. "Thomas Jefferson Tombstone, Now at Mizzou, Will Be Restored," *St. Louis Post-Dispatch*, January 1, 2013, http://www.stltoday.com/news/local/education/thomas-jefferson-tombstone-now-at-mizzou-will-be-restored/article_c4e79fb0-9566-5312-8dad-f0bdd2c9bd20.html.

3. JOHN ADAMS

1. "Adams and Jefferson," *Niles Register*, July 15, 1826.

2. The misperception that John Adams's last words were "Thomas Jefferson survives" was also perpetuated to a new generation who watched the HBO miniseries *John Adams*.

3. Nagel, Paul C. *John Quincy Adams: A Public Life, a Private Life*. Cambridge, Massachusetts: Harvard University Press, 1999.

4. *The Encyclopedia Americana.* New York: Encyclopedia Americana Corporation, 1919.

5. Goodwin, Doris Kearns. *Team of Rivals.* New York: Simon & Schuster, 2012.

6. "Adams and Jefferson," *Niles Register*, July 15, 1826.

7. Nagel, *John Quincy Adams.*

8. McCullough, David. *John Adams.* New York: Simon & Schuster, 1992.

9. Weaver, George Sumner. *The Lives and Graves of Our Presidents.* Chicago: Elder Publishing Company, 1884, 115.

10. "Adams and Jefferson," *Niles Register*, July 15, 1826.

11. Yalom, Marilyn. *The American Resting Place.* Boston, Massachusetts: Houghton Mifflin Harcourt, 2008.

12. "1826 Letter by John Quincy Adams about Parents' Burial Discovered," *Weymouth News*, April 2, 2010.

13. Grant, James. *John Adams: Party of One.* New York: Farrar, Straus and Giroux, 2006, 383.

14. *Fourth Report of the National Society of the Daughters of the American Revolution, October 11, 1900–October 11, 1901.* Washington, DC: Washington Government Printing Office, 1902.

15. Keinath, Caroline. *Adams National Historical Park.* Lawrenceburg, Indiana: R. L. Ruehrwein, 2008.

16. "National Park Service, Charles Francis Adams (1807–1886)," accessed December 2, 2015, http://www.nps.gov/adam/learn/historyculture/charles-francis-adams-1807–1886.htm.

17. "The Adams' Residence," *American Lifestyle Magazine,* December/January 2013, 18–23.

18. Zwicker, Roxie. *Massachusetts Book of the Dead: Graveyard Legends and Lore.* Mount Pleasant, South Carolina: History Press, 2012.

19. Lunt, William P. *Two Discourses Delivered September 29, 1839 on Occasion of the Two Hundredth Anniversary of the Gathering of the First Congregational Church, Quincy.* Boston: William Munroe and Company, 1840, 125.

20. National Register of Historic Places Nomination Form: "Stone Temple, Church of the Presidents."

21. "United First Parish Only Church Where Two Presidents Entombed," *Quincy Sun*, June 25, 2009.

22. "Graves of Our Presidents," *Lewiston Evening Journal*, October 8, 1881.

23. "Coolidge Visitor at Ancient Quincy, Predecessor's Home," *Meridian Record*, July 16. 1925.

24. "Church of the Presidents in Quincy Plays a Special Role in the City's Cultural Identity," *Patriot Ledger*, April 6, 2009.

25. "Church Closes Presidents' Crypt to Daily Visitors," *Deseret News*, April 9, 1999; "Church Gets Grant to Reopen Adams Crypt," *Spokesman Review*, April 21, 1999.

26. "Letter of John Quincy Adams," *Spokesman Review,* August 23, 1921.

27. "John Quincy Adams Letter Found in Mass. Basement," CBS News, posted April 21, 2010, http://www.cbsnews.com/news/john-quincy-adams-letter-found-in-mass-basement/4/21/2010.

4. JAMES MONROE

1. Caroll, Betty Boyd. *Inside the White House.* New York: Canopy Books, 1992.

2. Holloway, Laura Carter. *In the Home of the Presidents.* New York: United States Publishing Company, 1875.

3. "Topics of the Times," *New York Times*, April 28, 1958.

4. *Grand Civic and Military Demonstration in Honor of the Removal of the Remains of James Monroe, Fifth President of the United States, from New York to Virginia.* New York: Udolpho Wolfe, 1858, 306.

5. Ibid., 25.

6. *Richmond Enquirer*, July 12, 1831.

7. Morgan, George. *The Life of James Monroe.* Boston: Small, Maynard and Company, 1921, 458.

8. Holloway, Laura Carter. *The Ladies of the White House.* Philadelphia: Bradley & Company, 1870, 242–246.

9. "A President Without a Gravestone," *New York Times*, September 24, 1856.

10. Ibid.

11. "Hollywood Cemetery—Remains of Hon. John Tyler," *Richmond Whig*, January 24, 1862.

12. Morgan, *The Life of James Monroe*, 458.

13. "The Tomb of President Monroe," *Ann Arbor Journal*, June 2, 1858.

14. *Grand Civic and Military Demonstration in Honor of the Removal of the Remains of James Monroe*, 55.

15. Ibid., 78.

16. Ibid., 80.

17. "Exhumation of the Remains of President Monroe," *New York Times*, July 3, 1858.

18. "The Guard of Honor and Monroe's Remains," *New York Times*, July 13, 1858.

19. "Departure of the Remains of James Monroe—Speeches of John Cochrane and O. Jennings Wise," *New York Times*, July 6, 1858.

20. "Removal of Ex-President Monroe's Remains," *New York Times*, July 8, 1858.

21. *Grand Civic and Military Demonstration in Honor of the Removal of the Remains of James Monroe*, 111.

22. Ibid., 141.

23. Ibid., 148.

24. "Reception of the National Guard on Their Return from Conveying the Remains of Ex-President Monroe to Richmond," *New York Times*, July 12, 1858.

25. Townsend, Malcolm, comp. *U.S.: An Index to the United States of America*. Boston: D Lothrop Company, 1890.

26. "Nation Has Done Little in Honor of Its Dead Rulers," *New York Times*, January 12, 1913.

27. Townsend, comp. *U.S. An Index to the United States of America*.

28. National Register of Historic Places Nomination Form: "James Monroe Tomb."

29. "Presidential Tombs," *Utah Journal*, October 14, 1881.

30. "In Tribute to Monroe," *St. Joseph News-Press*, December 3, 1923.

31. "Monroe's Home In New York To Be Auctioned," *St. Petersburg Daily Times*, November 13, 1919.

32. "Gouverneur Home, Where Monroe Died, Is Sold for $138,000," *New York Tribune*, November 13, 1919; "Monroe Landmark Sold," *New York Times*, November 13, 1919.

33. Pelletreau, William S. *Early New York Houses*. New York: Francis P. Harper, 1900, 104; "Monroe House to Be Retrieved from the Use of Ragpickers," *New York Times*, December 11, 1922.

34. "The Monroe House," *New York Times*, July 11, 1897.

35. "Results at Auction," *New York Times*, February 7, 1900.

36. "Monroe's Home in New York to Be Auctioned," *St. Petersburg Daily Times*, November 13, 1919.

37. "Tablet to Mark House in Which Monroe Died," *New York Times*, April 28, 1905.

38. "Monroe's House," *New York Times*, October 31, 1919.

39. "James Monroe's House," *New York Times*, October 25, 1919.

40. "Gouverneur Home, Where Monroe Died, Is Sold for $138,000," *New York Tribune*, November 13, 1919; "Monroe Landmark Sold," *New York Times*, November 13, 1919.

41. "Monroe's House Is Saved," *New York Times*, October 11, 1925.

42. "Monroe Memorial to Be Incorporated," *New York Times*, December 11, 1922.

43. "Suit Factory to Replace Historic Monroe House," *Reading Eagle*, May 8, 1925; "Home of Monroe, Now a Ragpicker's Mart, to Be Razed and Replaced by Factories," *New York Times*, May 8, 1925.

44. "Monroe House Afire Again," *New York Times*, July 30, 1925.

45. "Plans Filed to Restore House of Fifth President as Memorial at 95 Crosby Street," *New York Times*, September 10, 1925. A month later on October 11, 1925, the *New York Times* ran an overly-optimistic half-page story proclaiming, "Monroe's House Is Saved"!

46. "Floor Collapses in Monroe House," *New York Times*, November 21, 1925.

47. *Scenic and Historic America, Bulletin of the American Scenic And Historic Preservation Society*, March 1929, 23.

48. "Old Monroe Home Is Sold at Auction," *New York Times*, September 14, 1927.

49. *Scenic and Historic America, Bulletin of the American Scenic And Historic Preservation Society*, March 1929. Not all was lost of the home. The doorway of fine woodwork and leaded glass were purchased by William S. Hine and moved to his home in Stonington, Connecticut.

50. "City History Fan Honors Monroe," *New York Times*, November 19, 1962.

51. "Topics of the Times," *New York Times*, April 28, 1958.

52. "Explosives Abandoned In Cemetery Are Mystery," *New York Times*, October 11, 2010.

53. Wiseman, Charles Milton. *Pioneer Period and Pioneer People of Fairfield County, Ohio*. Columbus, Ohio: F. J. Heer Printing, 1901, 285.

54. "The Strange 'Burial Ground' of the Presidents," *Youngstown Vindicator*, August 18, 1936.

55. "President Owns Ohio Cemetery," *New York Times*, January 5, 1958.

5. JAMES MADISON

1. Ketcham, Ralph. *James Madison: A Biography.* Charlottesville: University of Virginia Press, 1971, 669.

2. "Former Presidents." *Luddington Daily News*, September 3, 1885.

3. Jennings, Paul. *A Colored Man's Reminiscences of James Madison.* Brooklyn, New York: George C Beadle, 1865, 17–21. Some sources append, "I always talk better lying down" to his last words. However, the most reliable, including Montpelier's website and Jennings's account, do not.

4. "Montpelier: Madison Family Cemetery," accessed December 20, 2015, https://www.montpelier.org/mansion-and-grounds/landscape/madison-family-cemetery.

5. Madison, James. *The Writings of James Madison: 1819-1836.* New York: Knickerbocker Press, 1910, 545–551.

6. "The Home of Madison," *New York Times*, August 2, 1883; Townsend, Malcolm, comp. *U.S.: An Index to the United States of America.* Boston: D Lothrop Company, 1890.

7. "Nation Has Done Little in Honor of Its Dead Rulers," *New York Times*, January 12, 1913.

8. *Fredericksburg News*, October 6, 1857.

9. *Grand Civic and Military Demonstration in Honor of the Removal of the Remains of James Monroe, Fifth President of the United States, from New York to Virginia.* New York: Udolpho Wolfe, 1858, 307.

10. Charles Thomas Chapman. *Who Was Buried in James Madison's Grave? A Study in Contextual Analysis.* MA thesis, College of William and Mary, 2005.

11. "Madison's Renovation Harks Back to Days of James and Dolley Madison," *Gettysburg Times*, November 5, 2004.

12. "Will Visit Jefferson's Tomb," *New York Times*, October 21, 1891.

13. "The Home of Madison," *New York Times*, August 2, 1883.

14. "Madison's Renovation Harks Back to Days of James and Dolley Madison," *Gettysburg Times*, November 5, 2004.

6. WILLIAM HENRY HARRISON

1. "What Really Killed William Henry Harrison?" *New York Times*, March 31, 2014.

2. *Log Cabin*, April 10, 1841.

3. Smith, J.V.C., MD, ed. *The Boston Medical and Surgical Journal*, vol. 24. Boston: D. Clapp Jr., 1841, 160.

4. Doyle, Burton T. and Homer H. Swaney. *Lives of James A. Garfield and Chester A. Arthur.* Washington, DC: Rufus H Darby, 1881, 218.

5. Montgomery, Henry. *The Life of Major-General William H. Harrison.* Cleveland: Tooker and Gatchell, 1853, 442.

6. Nagel, Paul C. *John Quincy Adams: A Public Life, a Private Life.* Cambridge, Massachusetts: Harvard University Press, 1999.

7. "The Funeral Ceremonies," *National Intelligencer*, April 9, 1841.

8. Letter from J.B.V. to Cousin, April 8, 1841. This letter was found at the archives of the Benjamin Harrison Presidential Site.

9. May, Gary. *John Tyler.* New York: Times Books, 2008. 61–63.

10. Montgomery, Henry. *The Life of Major-General William H. Harrison.* Cleveland: Tooker and Gatchell, 1853, 449.

11. Collins, Gail. *William Henry Harrison.* New York: Times Books, 2012, 123–125.

12. "The Funeral Ceremonies," *National Intelligencer*, April 9, 1841.

13. "Death in the White House: A Nation Mourns," Benjamin Harrison Presidential Site, accessed January 6, 2016, www.presidentbenjaminharrison.org/learn/exhibits/past-exhibits/19-learn/exhibits/past-exhibits/56-death-in-the-white-house-a-nation-mourns.

14. "Remains of President Harrison," *National Intelligencer*, June 28, 1841.

15. "The Grave of William Henry Harrison—Description of Its Surroundings," *New York Times*, January 27, 1871.

16. Townsend, Malcolm, comp. *U.S.: An Index to the United States of America.* Boston: D Lothrop Company, 1890.

17. "Ohio History Connection," accessed January 6, 2016. www.OhioHistory.org/visit/museum-and-site-locator/william-henry-harrison-tomb.

18. "Former Presidents," *Luddington Daily News*, September 3, 1885.

19. "The Grave of William Henry Harrison—Description of Its Surroundings," *New York Times*, January 27, 1871.

20. Townsend, comp. *U.S.: An Index to the United States of America.*

21. "Buried Presidents," *Reading Eagle*, August 16, 1885.

22. "In Tippecanoe's Memory," *Evening Telegraph*, August 11, 1890.

23. "William Henry Harrison's Tomb," *New York Times*, July 13, 1896.

24. "Gen. Harrison's Tomb," *Toledo Blade*, November 14, 1901.

25. "Flag on Gen. W.H. Harrison's Grave," *New York Times*, November 30, 1902.

26. "Harrison Grave Neglected," *New York Times*, September 8, 1912.

27. "Four Hours in Buried Vault, Boy's Awful Ordeal," *Grey River Argus*, December 16, 1912.

28. "Vandals at Harrison Tomb," *Crawfordsville Review*, September 19, 1913.

29. "What Really Killed William Henry Harrison?" *New York Times*, March 31, 2014. In recent years William Henry Harrison has been back in the news, as historians now dispute the true cause of his death. The controversy is rooted in the fact that Dr. Miller himself did not believe the president was solely afflicted with pneumonia as he documented the cause of death as "pneumonia of the lower lobe of the right lung, complicated by congestion of the liver." Miller provided additional clues after Harrison's death when he wrote, "The disease was not viewed as a case of pure pneumonia; but as this was the most palpable affection, the term pneumonia afforded a succinct and intelligible answer to the innumerable questions as to the nature of the attack." Dr. Philip A. Mackowiak of the University of Maryland and author of *Diagnosing Giants: Solving the Medical Mysteries of Thirteen Patients Who Changed the World* believes Harrison may have died from enteric fever caused by the less than sanitary sewage system in 1840s Washington, DC.

30. Caroll, Betty Boyd. *Inside the White House*. New York: Canopy Books, 1992.

31. "Brief History of Congressional Cemetery," accessed January 6, 2016, www.Congressional Cemetery.org/history.asp.

32. National Register of Historic Places Nomination Form: "Congressional Cemetery."

33. "To Hell and Back: The Resurrection of Congressional Cemetery," *Preservation Magazine*, January/February 2012, 28–33.

34. "Confesses Robbing Tomb of President Harrison," *New York Times*, June 11, 1934.

35. "Ohio Town Honors Harrison," *Youngstown Vindicator*, February 10, 1976.

36. "Burial Site of Ninth President Rededicated," *Youngstown Vindicator*, May 26, 1997.

7. Andrew Jackson

1. "Former Presidents," *Luddington Daily News*, September 3, 1885.

2. "Andrew Jackson's Grave," *New York Times*, September 12, 1874.

3. "The Death and Funeral of Andrew Jackson," *St. Joseph Gazette*, July 11, 1845.

4. "The Last Will and Testament of Andrew Jackson," Hermitage, June 7, 1843.

5. At this time Texas was still a separate country. After gaining independence from Mexico in 1836, the republic was in the process of being annexed by the United States at the time of Jackson's death (it became a state on December 29, 1845).

6. "Andrew Jackson Jr. to A. O. P Nicholson, Hermitage June 17, 1845." This letter was found in the archives at the Hermitage.

7. "The Last Moments of Gen. Jackson," *Baltimore Sun*, June 19, 1845.

8. "Andrew Jackson Jr. to A. O. P Nicholson, Hermitage June 17, 1845."

9. "Remains of Gen. Jackson," *Washington City Semi-Weekly Constitution*, March 10, 1860.

10. "Andrew Jackson Jr. to A. O. P Nicholson, Hermitage June 17, 1845."

11. "The Death and Funeral of Andrew Jackson," *St. Joseph Gazette*, July 11, 1845.

12. "The Last Moments of Gen. Jackson," *Baltimore Sun*, June 19, 1845.

13. Heiskell, Samuel Gordon and John Sevier. *Andrew Jackson and Early Tennessee History*. Nashville, Tennessee: Ambrose Printing, 1920.

14. "Tennessee Calendar," *Nashville Banner*, June 8, 1845. This article was found in the archives at the Hermitage.

15. Cochran, John Salisbury. *Bonnie Belmont: A Histori-*

cal *Romance of the Days of Slavery and the Civil War*. Wheeling, West Virginia: Wheeling News, 1907, 193.

16. Nagel, Paul C. *John Quincy Adams: A Public Life, a Private Life*. Cambridge, Massachusetts: Harvard University Press, 1999.

17. Weaver, George Sumner. *The Lives and Graves of Our Presidents*. Chicago: Elder Publishing Company, 1884, 253.

18. "Molesting Jackson's Tomb," *Baltimore Sunday Herald*, August 3, 1894.

19. "The Mystery Is Unraveled," *Cincinnati Enquirer*, November 11, 1896. This article was found in the archives at the Hermitage.

20. Beyer, Rick. *The Greatest Presidential Stories Never Told*. New York: HarperCollins, 2007.

21. Heiskell and Sevier, *Andrew Jackson and Early Tennessee History*, 324–325.

22. Truman, Margaret. *Harry S. Truman*. New York: William Morrow & Company, 1972.

23. "Jackson Lauded By LBJ," *Park City Daily News*, March 14, 1967. In his speech, President Johnson quoted Jackson: "One man with courage makes a majority."

24. "Reagan Defends Economic Plan, Visits Hermitage," *Daily News* (Kingsport, Tennessee), March 17, 1982.

25. "Reagan's Advance Men Hopped Over Wrong Fence," *Bulletin* (Bend, Oregon), March 2, 1982.

26. Andrew Jackson's Death Cause Found," *Lakeland Ledger*, August 11, 1999.

27. National Register of Historic Places Nomination Form: "The Hermitage."

28. Phillips, Charles. *The Hermitage, Home of Andrew Jackson*. Nashville, Tennessee: Ladies' Hermitage Association, 1997.

29. "The Hermitage Burnt," *Jesuit*, November 1, 1834.

30. Haas, Irvin. *Historic Homes of the American Presidents*. Courier Dover Publications, 1991, 66–67.

31. Phillips, *The Hermitage, Home of Andrew Jackson*.

32. Heiskell and Sevier, *Andrew Jackson and Early Tennessee History*.

33. "A Proposition Respecting the Hermitage in the Tennessee Legislature," *New York Times*, January 27, 1871.

34. Brigance, Fred W. *The Hermitage Tomb 1829–1995*. This document was found in the archives at the Hermitage.

35. Heiskell and Sevier, *Andrew Jackson and Early Tennessee History*.

36. Brigance, *The Hermitage Tomb 1829–1995*.

37. "Providence Protected the Cherished Bones of the Brave Old Hero," unknown newspaper. This article was obtained from the archives at the Hermitage.

38. "President's Advice to Negro Townspeople," *Day* (New London, Connecticut), October 22, 1907.

39. *The Hermitage Jackson's Tomb Cultural Resources Inventory*, July 2007. This document was found in the archives at the Hermitage.

40. Brigance, *The Hermitage Tomb 1829–1995*.

8. JOHN QUINCY ADAMS

1. Everett, Edward. *A Eulogy on the Life and Character of John Quincy Adams: Delivered at the Request of the Legislature of Massachusetts in Faneuil Hall April 15, 1848*. Boston: Dutton and Wentworth State Printers, 1848.

2. Seward, William Henry. *Life and Public Services of John Quincy Adams, Sixth President of the United States. With the Eulogy Delivered Before the Legislature of New York*. Auburn, New York: Derby, Miller and Company, 1849, 333.

3. *The National Intelligencer*, February 22, 1848.

4. *The National Intelligencer*, February 23, 1848.

5. "Tomb of the Two Presidents," *Lawrence Weekly World*, May 7, 1903.

6. *The National Intelligencer*, February 28, 1848.

7. "Former Presidents," *Luddington Daily News*, September 3, 1885.

8. Parsons, Lynn Hudson. "The 'Splendid Pageant': Observations on the Death of John Quincy Adams," *New England Quarterly*, December 1980.

9. Seward, *Life and Public Services of John Quincy Adams, Sixth President of the United States*, 353.

10. Lunt, William P. *A Discourse Delivered in Quincy, March 11, 1848, at the Interment of John Quincy Adams, Sixth President of the United States*. Boston: Dutton and Wentworth, 1848, 30. In his sermon, Lunt pontificated, "The Angel of death, when she came again to execute her office, left him only the consciousness that it was 'the last of earth' then drew a veil of oblivion over his faculties, and sat beside his couch two days, before the cord that bound him to this world was severed."

11. *New York Times*, December 21, 1852.

12. Nagel, Paul C. *John Quincy Adams: A Public Life,*

a *Private Life*. Cambridge, Massachusetts: Harvard University Press, 1999. The *New York Times* was less ghoulish and more tactful when it reported, "the features of Mr. Adams were found in perfect state of preservation." *New York Times*, December 21, 1852.

13. Seward, *Life and Public Services of John Quincy Adams, Sixth President of the United States*, 339.

14. "Memorial Tablet," *Lowell Sun*, November 17, 1927.

15. "Americana in Marble," *New York Times*, June 4, 1939.

16. "John Quincy Adams," *Day* (New London, Connecticut), February 22, 1922.

17. Seward, *Life and Public Services of John Quincy Adams, Sixth President of the United States*, 21.

18. Davis, Varina. *Jefferson Davis: Ex-president of the Confederate States of America, Volume 1*. New York: Belford Co., 1890. The full text of his speech can be found on 608–641.

19. "Letter of condolence to Mrs. J. A. Garfield from A. M. Robinson, Boston," October 19, 1881

9. JAMES KNOX POLK

1. Heiskell, Samuel Gordon and John Sevier. *Andrew Jackson and Early Tennessee History*. Nashville, Tennessee: Ambrose Printing, 1920, 295.

2. Byrnes, Mark Eaton. *James K. Polk: A Biographical Companion*. Santa Barbara, California: ABC-CLIO, 2001, 52.

3. "Death of James K. Polk," *Daily Nashville Union*, June 18, 1849.

4. Ibid.

5. Byrnes, *James K. Polk: A Biographical Companion*, 52.

6. "Death of James K. Polk," *Daily Nashville Union*, June 18, 1849.

7. Nashville Public Library/Nashville City Cemetery interment records.

8. "President Polk's Will," *New York Times*, May 25, 1892.

9. Weaver, George Sumner. *The Lives and Graves of Our Presidents*. Chicago: Elder Publishing Company, 1884, 324–326.

10. "Re-interment. James K. Polk," *Daily American*, May 23, 1850.

11. "Reburial of the Remains of the Late Ex-President Polk," *Daily Nashville Union*, May 23, 1850.

12. "President Polk's Will," *New York Times*, May 25, 1892.

13. Williams, William W. *The American Nation*. Cleveland: Williams Publishing Company, 1892, 766.

14. "CAPITOL HILL: In Its Bosom now Repose The Honored Remains Of Ex-President and Mrs. James K. Polk Taken from Polk Place with Impressive Ceremonial," *Daily American*, September 20, 1893.

15. Ibid.

16. Ibid.

17. National Register of Historic Places Nomination Form: "Nashville City Cemetery."

18. "History," The Nashville City Cemetery, accessed January 8, 2016, www.thenashvillecitycemetery. org/history.htm.

19. Hoobler, James A. *Cities Under the Gun*. Nashville, Tennessee: Rutledge Hill Press, 1995.

10. ZACHARY TAYLOR

1. Bauer, K. Jack. *Zachary Taylor: Soldier, Planter, Statesman of the Old Southwest*. Baton Rouge, Louisiana: LSU Press, 1993.

2. Greenstone, Gerry, MD. "The History of Bloodletting," *British Columbia Medical Journal* (52:1), January/February 2010, 12–14.

3. *National Intelligencer*, July 9, 1850.

4. *National Intelligencer*, July 10, 1850.

5. "Death of President Taylor" *New York Daily Tribune*, July 11, 1850.

6. *National Intelligencer*, July 15, 1850.

7. Bauer, *Zachary Taylor: Soldier, Planter, Statesman of the Old Southwest*.

8. *National Intelligencer*, July 15, 1850.

9. Pyne, Smith. *Obituary Addresses Delivered on the Occasion of the Death of Zachary Taylor*. Washington, DC: William M. Belt, 1850.

10. *Acts and Resolutions Passed by the First Session of the Thirty-First Congress of the United States*. Washington, DC: Gideon & Co. Printers, 1850, 174.

11. Townsend, Malcolm, comp. *U.S.: An Index to the United States of America*. Boston: D Lothrop Company, 1890.

12. "Zachary Taylor's Grave," *New York Times*, August 15, 1873.

13. Irelan, John Robert, *The Republic: Or a History of the United States of America in the Administrations. From the Monarchic Colonial Days to the Present Times*. Chicago: Fairbanks and Palmer Publishing, 1888, 532. The account from the *New York World* is

taken from this book. The story was later reprinted in other newspapers such as the *Saint Paul Globe* (August 25, 1878) and *Princeton Union* (August 28, 1878), both from Minnesota.

14. As part of my research, I contacted Cave Hill and was told that President Taylor was *never* moved to Cave Hill and that it was just speculation. Neither is any mention made in the 1921 publication *History of the Frankfort Cemetery* by L. F. Johnson (Frankfort, Kentucky: Roberts Printing).

15. Jones, John William. *The Davis Memorial Volume; or Our Dead President, Jefferson Davis, and the World's Tribute to his Memory.* Chicago: Dominion Company, 1897, 504.

16. Weaver, George Sumner. *The Lives and Graves of Our Presidents.* Chicago: Elder Publishing Company, 1884, 342–344.

17. Ibid.

18. "Graves of the Presidents," *Paterson Daily Press,* August 24, 1892.

19. "Graves of Presidents," *Day* (New London, Connecticut), September 16, 1891.

20. "Zachary Taylor's Tomb," *Clinton Morning Age,* October 31, 1903.

21. "Zachary Taylor's Grave," *New York Times,* January 13, 1905.

22. French, Alvah P. *Westchester County Magazine,* volus. 7–8, 94

23. "Arsenic Poisoning Tests Begin on Zachary Taylor's Remains," *Victoria Advocate,* June 18, 1991.

24. National Register of Historic Places Nomination Form: "Zachary Taylor National Cemetery."

11. JOHN TYLER

1. "From the Richmond Enquirer," *New York Times,* January 30, 1862.

2. Irelan, John Robert, *The Republic: Or a History of the United States of America in the Administrations. From the Monarchic Colonial Days to the Present Times.* Chicago: Fairbanks and Palmer Publishing, 1888, 413.

3. May, Gary. *John Tyler.* New York: Times Books, 2008, 144–145.

4. Crapol, Edward P. *John Tyler, the Accidental President.* Chapel Hill: The University of North Carolina Press, 2012, 268.

5. "Death of Ex-President Tyler," *New York Times,* January 22, 1862.

6. Ibid.

7. Wise, Henry Alexander. *Seven Decades of the Union: The Humanities and Materialism, Illustrated by a Memoir of John Tyler, with Reminiscences of Some of His Great Contemporaries. The Transition State of this Nation—Its Dangers and Their Remedy.* Philadelphia: J.B. Lippincott, 1881, 302.

8. Ibid. 287.

9. Irelan, *The Republic: Or a History of the United States of America in the Administrations,* 413.

10. "The Procession," *Richmond Enquirer,* January 21, 1862.

11. "Funeral of Hon. John Tyler," *Richmond Enquirer,* January 22, 1862.

12. "Funeral Obsequies of Ex-President Tyler," *Richmond Whig,* January 22, 1862.

13. "Nation Has Done Little in Honor of Its Dead Rulers," *New York Times,* January 12, 1913.

14. Weaver, George Sumner. *The Lives and Graves of Our Presidents.* Chicago: Elder Publishing Company, 1884, 303.

15. "Tyler's Grave Forgotten," *Fredericksburg Daily Star,* February 3, 1898.

16. "To Mark President Tyler's Grave," *Boston Evening Transcript,* October 19, 1899.

17. "Monument for Tyler's Grave," *Free Lance Star,* March 7, 1911.

18. "John Tyler Monument; To Be Erected over Former President's Grave in Richmond," *New York Times,* February 7, 1914.

19. "Monument to Tyler Erected in Hollywood," *Free Lance Star,* June 3, 1915.

20. Gordon, Armistead Churchill. *Monument to John Tyler: Address Delivered in Hollywood Cemetery, at Richmond, Va., on October 12, 1915 at the Dedication of the Monument Erected by the Government to John Tyler, Tenth President of the United States.* Washington, DC: Washington Government Printing Office, 1916.

21. "By Goddin & Apperson, Auct's," *Richmond Dispatch,* November 11, 1862.

22. "Yankee Spies," *Richmond Whig,* June 18, 1862.

23. "Exchange Hotel," *Richmond Dispatch,* November 25, 1862.

24. "Louisiana Soldiers' Home," *Richmond Sentinel,* September 1, 1864.

25. Loewen, James W. *Lies Across America: What Our Historic Sites Get Wrong.* New York: New Press, 1999.

26. "About the Capitol." Virginia State Capitol, accessed January 8, 2016, www.virginiacapitol.gov.

27. Morgan, George. *The Life of James Monroe*. Boston: Small, Maynard and Company, 1921.

28. "Hollywood Cemetery and James Monroe Tomb." National Park Service, accessed January 8, 2016, www.nps.gov/nr/travel/richmond/Hollywood Cemetery.html.

12. MARTIN VAN BUREN

1. Collier, Edward A. *A History of Old Kinderhook from Aboriginal Days to the Present Time*. New York: G. P. Putnam's Sons, 1914.

2. "Death of Ex-President Van Buren; Some Notice of His Public Life and Character," *New York Times*, July 25, 1862. Another account years later summarized Van Buren's death flatly, "While the armed conflict between the North and South was at its height, on June 24, 1862, Mr. Van Buren died at Lindenwald." Butler, William Allen. *A Retrospect of Forty Years 1825–1865*. New York: Charles Scribner's Sons, 1911, 365.

3. "Funeral of Ex-President Van Buren," *New York Times*, July 25, 1862.

4. Throughout this book are references to "lying in state" and "lying in repose." While they may appear interchangeable, the terminology is important as there is a difference. According to the military's State Funeral web site, lying in state "occurs when the casket of a member of government (or former member of government) is placed on view in the principal government building of a country or state to allow the public to pay their respects." And lying in repose "occurs when the casket of a member of government (or former member of government) is placed on view in any other building to allow the public to pay their respects." "Lying in State/Lying in Repose/Lying in Honor." Official U.S. State Funeral, accessed February 28, 2016, www.usstatefuneral.mdw.army.mil/ceremonial-traditions/lying-in-state-repose.

5. "Funeral of Ex-President Van Buren," *New York Times*, July 25, 1862.

6. Butler, *A Retrospect of Forty Years 1825–1865*, 366.

7. "Little Journeys to Tombs of Presidents," *Youngstown Vindicator*, May 27, 1908.

8. "Shaft Now Marking Van Buren's Grave," *Prescott Evening Courier*, December 6, 1932.

9. "Van Buren No Longer Forgotten," *Hour* (Norwalk, CT), December 8, 1982.

10. "'Doonesbury' puts Van Buren's Curator in a Bad Humor: Finds Comic-Strip Grave Robbing in Poor Taste," *Albany Times-Union*, December 20, 1988.

11. "Yale Group Linked to Possible Geronimo Grave Robbery. Intriguing Letter Found in Archives of Secret Society," *Kansas City Star*, October 5, 2006.

12. Richards, Leonard L., Marla R. Miller, and Erik Gilg. *A Return to His Native Town: Martin Van Buren's Life at Lindenwald, 1839–1862*. Martin Van Buren National Historic Site Historic Resource Study. National Park Service, 2006, 18-29, 112–113.

13. "Churchill's Grandfather Won Lindenwald on a Bet," *Chatham Courier*, January 28, 1965.

14. Kohan, Carol. *Historic Furnishings Report: Lindenwald–Martin Van Buren National Historic Site, New York*. National Park Service, 1986, 422. After Van Buren's death the home was owned by the Van Buren family (1862–1864), Leonard Walter Jerome (1864–1867), George Wilder (1867–1873), co-owners John Van Buren (no relation to the president) and James Van Alstyne (1873–1874), Freeman and Adam E. Wagoner, who Collier described as a "thrifty farmer" (1874–1917), Babscom Birney (1917–1922), Marian Birney (1922–1925), Clementine Birney DeProsse (1925–1957), and Ken Campbell (1957–1973).

15. "Preservation of Van Buren Homestead as Memorial at Kinderhook, N.Y., Is Urged," *New York Times*, September 27, 1936.

16. "Truce Is Called in Landfill Battle for Salute to Martin Van Buren; A Dispute for the Red Fox," *New York Times*, December 3, 1978.

17. "History," Kinderhook Reformed Church, accessed January 20, 2016, www.KinderhookReformed Church.com/page/history.

18. Collier, *A History of Old Kinderhook from Aboriginal Days to the Present Time*, 346–347.

13. ABRAHAM LINCOLN

1. Swanson, James L. *Manhunt: The 12-Day Chase for Lincoln's Killer*. New York: William Morrow, 2007.

2. Grieve, Victoria. *Ford's Theatre and the Lincoln Assassination*. Fort Washington, Pennsylvania: Eastern National, 2005.

3. The story of John Wilkes Booth, his motivations, escape, accomplices, eventual capture, and death

are a story unto itself, but not for this book (I rec-ommended James L. Swanson's expertly written *Manhunt: The 12-Day Chase for Lincoln's Killer*).

4. "The Rebel Fiends at Work," *Nashville Union Extra*, April 15, 1865.

5. Ibid.

6. Swanson, *Manhunt*.

7. Leale, Charles B., M.D. *Lincoln's Last Hours*. New York: 1909.

8. Craughwell, Thomas J. *Stealing Lincoln's Body*. Cambridge, Massachusetts: Belknap Press, 2009.

9. "Closing Scenes; Particulars of His Last Moments Record of His Condition Before His Death. Removal of the Remains to the Executive Mansion; Feeling in the City," *New York Times*, April 15, 1865.

10. Ahlquist, Diane. *The Complete Idiot's Guide to Life After Death*. New York: Random House, 2007.

11. "President Lincoln's Murder: Full Details," *Halifax Citizen*, April 22, 1865.

12. Swanson, *Manhunt*.

13. In the days of phrenology when scientists believed a brain's size indicated intelligence, the doctors took measurements to see if its size could account for Lincoln's superior intellect (Dr. Curtis's report read, "The brain weight was not above the ordinary for a man of Lincoln's size").

14. "'His Wound Is Mortal; It Is Impossible for Him to Recover'—The Final Hours of President Abraham Lincoln." National Museum of Health and Medi-cine, accessed February 12, 2016, www.Medical Museum.mil.

15. Craughwell, *Stealing Lincoln's Body*, 8.

16. Ibid.

17. "Putting a Good Face on the Final Adieu," *Los Angeles Times*, June 13, 2004.

18. Townsend, George Alfred. *The Life, Crime, and Capture of John Wilkes Booth*. New York: Dick & Fitzgerald, 1865.

19. "President Lincoln's Murder: Full Details," *Halifax Citizen*, April 22, 1865.

20. "The Tomb of President Lincoln," *New York Times*, April 18, 1865.

21. Coggeshall, William Turner. *Lincoln Memorial: The Journeys of Abraham Lincoln: From Springfield to Washington, 1861, as President Elect; and from Wash-ington to Springfield, 1865*. Columbus: Ohio State Journal, 1865, 138.

22. A replica, with dimensions specified, is on display at the National Museum of Funeral History in Houston, Texas.

23. Coggeshall, *Lincoln Memorial*, 111.

24. O'Reilly, Bill, and Martin Dugard. *Killing Lincoln: The Shocking Assassination that Changed America Forever*. New York: Henry Holt, 2011. Lincoln died with an estate valued at approximately $85,000; however, despite these harbingers of death, he did not have a will.

25. "The Obsequies; Funeral of Abraham Lincoln," *New York Times*, April 20, 1865.

26. As the Twenty-Second made their way through the streets to the parade route, they merged in with the marchers and were as surprised as anyone when they found themselves at the front of the line!

27. "The Obsequies; Funeral of Abraham Lincoln," *New York Times*, April 20, 1865.

28. "The Obsequies; Removal of the Remains from Washington," *New York Times*, April 22, 1865.

29. The seven women that boarded were Mrs. Samuel Small, Mrs. David Small, Mrs. Henry E. Miles, Miss Plover, Miss Louisa Ducka, Miss Susan Small, and Miss Jane Latimer and they laid a three-foot-wide wreath of roses and other white and red flowers at the coffin. It was an emotional event, prompting a reporter to write, "Those who witnessed the scene describe it as most affecting." *Philadelphia North American and United States Gazette*, April 22, 1865.

30. Newman, Ralph G. "In This Sad World of Ours, Sorrow Comes to All, A Timetable for the Lincoln Funeral Train," *Illinois State Historical Society Jour-nal*, Springfield: Illinois State Historical Society, Spring 1965.

31. Coggeshall, *Lincoln Memorial*, 151.

32. Ibid., 152

33. Ibid., 155

34. "How New York Mourned Lincoln," *New York Times*, April 11, 1915.

35. In the photograph can be seen Rear Admiral Charles H. Davis standing at the head of the coffin, Brigadier General Townsend at the foot, and the visible face of Lincoln with his beard clearly defined. While not the only photograph taken of Lincoln's body during his prolonged funeral, it is the only one to survive, as Stanton ordered all others destroyed. An irate Stan-ton also confiscated this image but secretly kept it in his private files. It remained hidden from the public until 1952, when 14-year-old Ron Rietveld discov-

ered it at the Illinois State Historical Library. "Historian to Donate Notes on Famous Lincoln Photo," *Newark Star-Ledger*, November 5, 2014.

36. "A Final Image of Lincoln, Hastily Sketched at City Hall, Is to Go on Display," *New York Times*, April 2, 2014.

37. "The Obsequies; Sombre Grandeur of the Funeral Pageant," *New York Times*, April 26, 1865.

38. Coggeshall, *Lincoln Memorial*, 169.

39. "The Obsequies; Sombre Grandeur of the Funeral Pageant," *New York Times*, April 26, 1865.

40. Coggeshall, *Lincoln Memorial*, 171.

41. "The Obsequies of Mr. Lincoln," *Newfoundlander*, May 29, 1865.

42. "How New York Mourned Lincoln," *New York Times*, April 11, 1915.

43. Coggeshall, *Lincoln Memorial*, 180.

44. "The Obsequies; Sombre Grandeur of the Funeral Pageant," *New York Times*, April 26, 1865.

45. Newman, "In This Sad World of Ours, Sorrow Comes to All, A Timetable for the Lincoln Funeral Train."

46. Coggeshall, *Lincoln Memorial*, 201.

47. Ibid., 215

48. Ibid., 225

49. Ibid., 238

50. Newman, "In This Sad World of Ours, Sorrow Comes to All, A Timetable for the Lincoln Funeral Train."

51. The "Genius of Liberty" is a Roman representation of one's divine nature. It is a popular figure seen in sculpture, usually as a winged figure, such as the Colonne de Juillet at the Place de la Bastille in Paris, France. Power, J. C., ed. *Directory and Soldiers' Register of Wayne County*. Richmond, Indiana: W.H. Lanthum, 1865.

52. "The President's Obsequies; From Chicago to Mr. Lincoln's Home," *New York Times*, May 3, 1865.

53. "150th Commemoration of Abraham Lincoln's Funeral Has St. Louis Ties," *St. Louis Post-Dispatch*, March 15, 2015.

54. Coggeshall, *Lincoln Memorial*, 293.

55. The entire funeral procession is listed in: Coggeshall, *Lincoln Memorial*, 300.

56. The vault on Mather Block was later buried and over the years it has been rediscovered several times.

57. "Graves of Presidents," *Day* (New London, Connecticut), September 16, 1891.

58. Williams, William W. *The American Nation*. Cleveland: The Williams Publishing Company, 1892, 767.

59. "A Plot to Steal Lincoln's Body," *US News*, June 24, 2007.

60. Craughwell, *Stealing Lincoln's Body*, 91.

61. Ibid., 130–131, 171.

62. "Abraham Lincoln's Body," *New York Times*, April 15, 1887.

63. "Remains of Lincoln Moved," *New York Times*, March 11, 1900.

64. "What Happened to Lincoln's Body," *Life* magazine, February 15, 1963.

65. Fitz-Gerald, Charles E. "The Man Who Last Saw Abraham Lincoln," *Yankee* magazine, April 1982.

66. "Coffin Pieces Found," *Spokesman Review*, February 8, 1979.

67. "Lincoln's Body in Heart of a Huge Boulder," *Reading Eagle*, June 17, 1931.

68. "President Kennedy Visited Springfield in 1962," *Decatur Herald & Review*, November 24, 2013.

69. "Picturing the Past: Paying respects at Lincoln's Tomb," *State Journal Register*, February 7, 2015.

70. "I Saw Lincoln Shot," *Milwaukee Sentinel*, February 7, 1954.

71. Grieve, *Ford's Theatre and the Lincoln Assassination*, 29.

72. Swanson, *Manhunt*.

73. National Register of Historic Places Nomination Form: "Ford's Theatre and the Petersen House where Lincoln Died."

74. Grieve, *Ford's Theatre and the Lincoln Assassination*.

75. "The Lincoln Rocker." The Henry Ford Museum, accessed February 12, 2016, www.thehenryford.org/exhibits/pic/2012/12_april.asp.

76. I must mention that in all of my research, I have found no historic evidence of a flag being pulled off the wall and placed beneath the president's bleeding head, even though it contains all the symbolism and drama worthy of inclusion in one of the many detailed accounts of Lincoln's brief time in Ford's Theatre after the shooting.

77. Grieve, *Ford's Theatre and the Lincoln Assassination*.

78. Swanson, James L. *Bloody Crimes: The Funeral of Abraham Lincoln and the Manhunt for Jefferson Davis*. New York: William Morrow, 2007.

79. Swanson, *Manhunt*.

80. Illinois senator Henry Rathbone was the son of Henry Reed Rathbone and Clara Harris, who were

guests of Lincoln at Ford's Theater when he was assassinated.

81. "Dispatches to the Associated Press; Return of the Funeral Escort," *New York Times*, May 7, 1865.

82. "Lincoln's Funeral Train Car Landed in Minnesota, Before Burning," *Minneapolis Star-Tribune*, December 5, 2015.

83. "Lincoln Funeral Car Burns," *New York Times*, March 20, 1911.

84. In 1945, screenwriter Millard Lampell commemorated the funeral train ride when he wrote the ballad, "The Lonesome Train." In it, he tells the story of Lincoln's assassination and final train journey from the perspective of a newspaper reporter riding on the train and entertaining a wishful rumor that Lincoln was still alive.

85. "Merchants' Exchange Collection–PP141." Maryland Historic Society, accessed February 12, 2016, www.mdhs.org/findingaid/merchants-exchange-collection-pp141.

86. "Reenactors Observe Anniversary of Abraham Lincoln's Funeral Train Stop in York, Pa.," *York Town Square*, April 26, 2010.

87. "Bart Blatstein Has Big (Secret) Plans for Vacant Lot at Broad and Washington." CBS Philly, posted January 24, 2014, philadelphia.cbslocal.com/2014/01/15/bart-blatstein-has-big-secret-plans-for-vacant-lot-at-broad-and-washington.

88. "Independence Hall." Independence National Historical Park, accessed February 12, 2016, www.nps.gov/inde/learn/historyculture/places-independencehall.htm.

89. Hoch, Bradley R. *Lincoln Trail in Pennsylvania: A History and Guide*. University Park, Pennsylvania: Penn State University Press, 2001, 148.

90. "President-Elect Lincoln Comes to Buffalo!" Theodore Roosevelt Inaugural National Historic Site, accessed February 12, 2016, www.nps.gov/thri/planyourvisit/lincolcomestobuffalo.htm.

91. "The Ohio Statehouse." Accessed February 12, 2016, www.ohiostatehouse.org/about.

92. "Monument to Commemorate Lincoln's Funeral Train," *Springfield State-Journal Register*, February 9, 2010.

14. JAMES BUCHANAN

1. Baker, Jean H. *James Buchanan*. New York: Henry Holt, 2004. Buchanan was confident that history would vindicate him and wrote a defense of his administration. However, his book, *Mr. Buchanan's Administration on the Eve of the Rebellion*, was unconvincing. Even the prestigious *New York Times* could not resist taking a shot at his effort, concluding his obituary with the critique, "The attempt was feeble and inconclusive, and made no impression on the judgment of the country." "Death of James Buchanan, Ex-President of the United States," *New York Times*, June 2, 1868.

2. "Funerals of the Famous: James Buchanan," *American Cemetery: The Magazine of Cemetery Management*, March 1990.

3. Curtis, George Ticknor. *Life of James Buchanan: Fifteenth President of the United States*. New York: Harper & Brothers, 1883, 665.

4. Ibid.

5. "Former Presidents," *Luddington Daily News*, September 3, 1885.

6. An obituary in the *Southland Times* cites Buchanan's last words as the repeated whispers, "God Bless my country," while the *New York Times* obituary made no mention of his final utterances. "Death of Ex-President Buchanan," *Southland Times*, July 29, 1868; "Death of James Buchanan, Ex-President of the United States," *New York Times*, June 2, 1868.

7. "Wheatland, A Love Story." Lancaster County Historical Society, accessed January 21, 2016, www.LancasterHistory.org/learn-about-president-buchanan/255-blogs/wheatland-love-story.

8. "A Bit of History About Early Settlers," *Gettysburg Times*, May 25, 1962.

9. "Funerals of the Famous: James Buchanan," *American Cemetery: The Magazine of Cemetery Management*, March 1990.

10. Klein, Philip Shriver. *The Story of Wheatland*. Lancaster, Pennsylvania: Art Printing Company of Lancaster, 2003.

11. "The Story of Wheatland," *Lancaster Daily Intelligencer*. This is a seven-part series found in the Lancaster County Historical Society archives. The publication dates are unknown.

12. Klein, *The Story of Wheatland*.

13. "Lancaster Appeals to Nation for Aid in Saving President Buchanan's Home," *Harrisburg Telegraph*, June 1935. The reporter, Janice Z. Steinmetz, called Rettew "an eccentric spinster who deserted the old home for a modern residence several blocks away."

This article was found in the Lancaster County Historical Society archives; however, the precise publication date is unknown.

14. "Home of Buchanan Willed to Woman," newspaper unknown, September 22, 1929. This article was found in the Lancaster County Historical Society archives.

15. "Buchanan Home to Go Under Hammer," newspaper unknown, October 1929. This article was found in the Lancaster County Historical Society archives. The precise publication date is unknown.

16. "'Wheatland' Abandoned as Site for Museum," newspaper unknown, January 1931. This article was found in the Lancaster County Historical Society archives. The precise publication date is unknown.

17. "'Wheatland' to be Shrine," *New York Times*, October 14, 1937.

18. "Home of Buchanan Dedicated as Shrine; Life and Work of Bachelor President Praised in Ceremony at Wheatland," *New York Times*, October 15, 1937.

19. "New Stamp Features Buchanan's Home," *Reading Eagle*, July 2, 1956.

20. National Register of Historic Places Nomination Form: "Wheatland, the Home of James Buchanan."

21. National Register of Historic Places Registration Form: "Woodward Hill Cemetery."

22. Ibid., "Ceremony Slated at Buchanan Tomb," *New York Times*, May 22, 1960.

23. "Buchanan Gravesite to be Restored," *Lodi News-Sentinel*, October 17, 1990; "Obscenities Spray-Painted on Tombstone at Grave of President James Buchanan," *Albany Herald*, September 5, 1994.

24. "Should Buchanan Be Moved from Woodward Hill? Question Remains Open," *Intelligencer Journal/Lancaster New Era*. This editorial written by Jack Brubaker was found in the Lancaster County Historical Society archives. The date of publication is unknown. Regarding the horrific events occurring in the cemetery, Marguerite Adams, president of the James Buchanan Foundation Board, ominously warned, "Dreadful things have happened down there." "Vandals Mark Up Buchanan's Grave," *Observer-Reporter*, September 2, 1994.

25. Reporters tactfully omitted the actual offensive words from their articles. The Schenectady *Daily Gazette* described them as "three sexually explicit slang words," while a snarky reporter from the *Observer-Reporter* wrote, "Three new words were added to President Buchanan's tombstone . . . [and] they weren't 'rest in peace.'" "Buchanan's Grave Is Vandalized," *Daily Gazette* (Schenectady, NY), September 5, 1994; "Vandals Mark Up Buchanan's Grave," *Observer-Reporter*, September 2, 1994.

26. "Obscenities Spray-Painted on Tombstone at Grave of President James Buchanan," *Albany Herald*, September 5, 1994.

27. "Resting in Peace," *Sunday News*, September 23, 1990.

15. FRANKLIN PIERCE

1. Wallner, Peter. *Franklin Pierce: Martyr for the Union*. Concord, New Hampshire: Plaidswede Publishing, 2009, 372.

2. Ibid.

3. "The Last Illness of Ex-President Pierce," *Boston Journal*, October 8, 1869. Over the following days, the account of his final moments was reprinted in newspapers across the country.

4. "Hon. Franklin Pierce," *New York Times*, October 9, 1869.

5. *New Hampshire Daily Patriot*, October 11, 1869.

6. Wallner. *Franklin Pierce*, 372.

7. Jordan, Brian. *Triumphant Mourner: The Tragic Dimension of Franklin Pierce*. Pittsburgh: Dorrance Publishing, 2003.

8. National Register of Historic Places Inventory Nomination Form: "The Franklin Pierce House."

9. Cook, Howard M. *Wayside Jottings, or Rambles Around the Old Town of Concord, N.H.* Concord, New Hampshire: Edson C. Eastman, 1910.

10. "Franklin Pierce Home Burns," *New York Times*, October 16, 1981.

11. National Register of Historic Places Inventory Nomination Form: "Old North Cemetery."

12. "State to Commemorate Franklin Pierce Birthday," *Nashua Telegraph*, November 19, 1981; "NH Graveside Service to Honor Franklin Pierce," Associated Press, November 23, 2010.

13. National Register of Historic Places Inventory Nomination Form: "Old North Cemetery."

14. Ibid.

15. "New Monument Erected," *Windsor Daily Star*, October 16, 1946.

16. "Dedicate New Franklin Pierce Monument Today," *Telegraph*, October 21, 1946.

16. MILLARD FILLMORE

1. Sferrazza, Carl. *America's First Families: An Inside View of 200 Years of Private Life in the White House.* New York: Touchstone, 2000, 202.

2. Williams, William W. *The American Nation.* Cleveland: The Williams Publishing Company, 1892, 766.

3. "Millard Fillmore: Obsequies of the Late Ex-President of the United States at Buffalo," *New York Times,* March 13, 1874.

4. The full list of pallbearers: William A. Bird, Noah P. Sprague, E. K. Jewett, O. H. Marshall, O. G. Steele, Henry Martin, Warren Bryant, and former mayor of Buffalo George W. Clinton.

5. Townsend, Malcolm, comp. *U.S.: An Index to the United States of America.* Boston: D Lothrop Company, 1890.

6. "Graves of Presidents," *St. Joseph Gazette,* September 29, 1881.

7. Colburn and Berger. *Forest Lawn Cemetery Illustrated.* Buffalo: Phinney & Company, 1855, 81–82.

8. Williams, *The American Nation,* 766.

9. "Fillmore Is Saluted for Education Work," *New York Times,* January 9, 1973.

10. "Carter Honors Millard Fillmore on His Birthday," *New York Times,* January 8, 1981.

11. "Buffalo, New York—Inaugural Journey." National Park Service, posted February 17, 2011, www.nps.gov/liho/buffalo-inaugural-journey.htm.

12. "Millard Fillmore House." History of Buffalo, accessed January 22, 2016, www.buffaloah.com/h/niagsq/fil.

13. "Formerly Hotel Fillmore," *Buffalo Courier,* May 5, 1901.

14. National Register of Historic Places Inventory Nomination Form: "St. Paul's Cathedral [Buffalo]."

15. "The History of Forest Lawn Cemetery: A Landmark to Local Accomplishment since 1849." Accessed January 22, 2016, www.forest-lawn.com/about/history.

17. ANDREW JOHNSON

1. "Andrew Johnson, Death of the Ex-President," *Ithaca Democrat,* August 5, 1875.

2. Ibid.

3. "Death of Andrew Johnson," *Mansfield Herald,* August 5, 1875.

4. "The Late Andrew Johnson," *Providence Evening Press,* August 2, 1875. Dr. Abraham Jobe also pro-vided a disappointingly brief firsthand account of his treatment of Johnson in his memoirs, which were recently edited and published. Hsiung, David C., ed. *A Mountaineer in Motion: The Memoir of Dr. Abraham Jobe, 1817–1906.* Knoxville: University Tennessee Press, 2006, 90.

5. "Andrew Johnson, Death of the Ex-President," *Ithaca Democrat,* August 5, 1875.

6. "Andrew Johnson; Official Announcement of His Death by the President," *New York Times,* August 2, 1875.

7. "Death of Andrew Johnson," *Deseret News,* August 11, 1875.

8. Schroeder-Lein, Glenna R. and Richard Zuczek. *Andrew Johnson: A Biographical Companion.* Santa Barbara, California: ABC-CLIO, 2001, 116–118.

9. "Andrew Johnson; Funeral of the Late Ex-President at Greenville, Tenn. A Large Crowd of Persons Present," *New York Times,* August 4, 1875. Note the newspaper misspelled "Greeneville" in their head-line and throughout the article.

10. Schroeder-Lein and Zuczek. *Andrew Johnson: A Biographical Companion,* 116–118.

11. Townsend, Malcolm, comp. *U.S.: An Index to the United States of America.* Boston: D Lothrop Company, 1890.

12. Schroeder-Lein and Zuczek. *Andrew Johnson: A Biographical Companion,* 116-118.

13. "Old Stover House Slated for Auction Block This Month," *Elizabethton Star,* August 9, 2004.

14. "Civil War Reenactment Coming to Brooks Farm," *Elizabethton Star,* July 15, 2011.

15. "To Guard Johnson's Grave," *Philadelphia Record,* February 4, 1907.

16. "Honor Andrew Johnson," *New York Times,* June 1, 1909.

17. *Andrew Johnson National Historic Site Administrative History.* National Park Service, 2008, 59.

18. "Johnson Grave Decorated with Clinton Wreath," *Toledo Blade,* December 30, 1998.

18. JAMES ABRAM GARFIELD

1. "Garfield's Son Recalls Tragedy," *Kentucky New Era,* August 7, 1957.

2. Millard, Candice. *Destiny of the Republic: A Tale of Madness, Medicine and the Murder of a President.* New York: Anchor, 2012.

3. Bliss had a checkered past that included a brief

stint in prison on charges of accepting a bribe. With the opportunity fate had given him, Bliss was not about to play assistant to any other doctor.

4. Ibid.

5. "The President Shot, A Crazy Office-Seekers Crime," *New York Tribune*, July 3, 1881.

6. "The President Dying," *The Evening Star* (Washington, DC), July 2, 1881.

7. "The President Shot, A Crazy Office-Seekers Crime," *New York Tribune*, July 3, 1881.

8. "The Story of President Garfield's Illness, Told by the Physician in Charge," *Century Magazine*, December 1881.

9. *Annual Report of the Secretary of the Navy*. Washington, DC: Government Printing Office, 1881, 824.

10. Millard. *Destiny of the Republic*.

11. "A President Felled by an Assassin and 1880's Medical Care," *New York Times*, July 25, 2006.

12. When Garfield was being transferred to the train, women were shocked at his appearance and "moaned in sympathy," but then quickly checked their emotions. Several attempts were made to align the carriage with the train car for a quick and smooth transition while Dr. Boynton fanned the president. Finally the bed was lifted, but carrying it out of the carriage, the attendants banged the bed into a doorjamb. The *Omaha Daily Bee* reported that the disturbance resulted in "shaking the president severely and causing his eyes to fairly bump in his head." Consistent with always seeing the glass half full, Dr. Bliss's account of this transfer differs. Two months after Garfield's death he wrote a piece for *Century Magazine* titled "The Story of President Garfield's Illness, Told by the Physician in Charge." In it, he claimed that after the carriage's arrival, "The president was then transferred without the slightest disturbance."

13. "A Safe Trip," *Omaha Daily Bee*, September 7, 1881.

14. "The Story of President Garfield's Illness, Told by the Physician in Charge," *Century Magazine*, December 1881.

15. "A Safe Trip," *Omaha Daily Bee*, September 7, 1881.

16. Millard. *Destiny of the Republic*.

17. "It Is Finished," *National Tribune*, September 24, 1881.

18. In *Destiny of the Republic: A Tale of Madness, Medicine and the Murder of a President*, Candice Millard expertly describes how Dr. Bliss took charge of every aspect of the president's care, strictly controlling other doctors' access to a degree bordering on paranoia. This authority was self-appointed, never requested by Garfield or his wife, despite Bliss's claims to the contrary.

19. "A President Felled by an Assassin and 1880's Medical Care," *New York Times*, July 25, 2006.

20. "It Is Finished," *National Tribune*, September 24, 1881.

21. "The Nation's Dead Chief," *New York Times*, September 22, 1881.

22. "A Sad Tale," *Evening Critic*, September 21, 1881. Almost anything that is utilized in a presidential funeral can transform into a sacred relic; a swath of black cloth was saved from the Garfield catafalque and another from the funeral car (in 2013 these two artifacts were on display in a special exhibit at the Mutter Museum in Philadelphia).

23. "Grief," *Sacramento Daily Record-Union*, September 24, 1881.

24. *The Man and the Mausoleum by the Garfield National Memorial Association*. Cleveland: The Cleveland Printing & Publishing Company, 1890, 88.

25. "In Memoriam," *Daily Globe* (St. Paul), September 26, 1881.

26. Ibid.

27. "The Martyr Laid at Rest," *New York Times*, September 27, 1881.

28. Ibid.

29. The food needed just to feed the dozens of military units help give an understanding of its size: 30,000 biscuits and 400 hams for sandwiches. "In Memoriam," *Daily Globe* (St. Paul), September 26, 1881.

30. Ibid.

31. Weaver, George Sumner. *The Lives and Graves of Our Presidents*. Chicago: Elder Publishing Company, 1884, 470–472.

32. Williams, William W. *The American Nation*. Cleveland: The Williams Publishing Company, 1892, 770.

33. Ransom, David F. *Geo. Keller, Architect*. Hartford, Connecticut: Stowe-Day Foundation, 1975.

34. "James A. Garfield Monument." Lake View Cemetery, accessed February 11, 2016, www.LakeView Cemetery.com.

35. Keller was not fond of Doyle's sculpture. It was not that he did not want a statue in that location since early sketches depict one, but he just did not like Doyle's rendition of the president. In a letter to his wife in 1889, he complained, "Whenever I think of that monstrosity standing in the center of the beautiful interior I burn with indignation!" Ransom, *Geo. Keller, Architect*, 141.

36. *The Man and the Mausoleum*, 5.

37. Townsend, Malcolm, comp. *U.S.: An Index to the United States of America*. Boston: D Lothrop Company, 1890.

38. "President Garfield's Body," *New York Times*, May 20, 1890.

39. *The Man and the Mausoleum*, 50.

40. Ibid., 9.

41. The mammoth speech fills a full 18 pages in the publication that documented the ceremony, *The Man and the Mausoleum*, 9–27.

42. Ibid., 51.

43. Ibid., 58.

44. Ibid., 59.

45. Ibid., 61–62.

46. Millard, *Destiny of the Republic*, 130.

47. "Topics of the Times," *New York Times*, March 20, 1897.

48. Gabrielan, Randall. *Monmouth County, New Jersey*. Mount Pleasant, South Carolina: Arcadia Publishing, 1998, 56.

49. "Francklyn Property Sold," *New York Times*, May 14, 1889.

50. "The Elberon Hotel Property Bid In," *New York Times*, August 20, 1891.

51. "Long Branch," *New York Times*, June 3, 1900.

52. "Garfield Cottage Burned," *Daily Argus News*, June 15, 1920.

53. *Baltimore American*, July 21, 1901.

54. "Matters of Current Interest in New Jersey Cities and Towns," *Paterson Daily Press*, August 20, 1906.

55. "Memorial Will Mark Garfield's Last Days; Plans Made to Designate Spot in Elberon, N.J., Where Martyred President Died," *New York Times*, August 10, 1930.

56. "Boy, 7, Wants Marker Where Garfield Died," *Milwaukee Sentinel Journal*, August 13, 1957.

57. "Jersey Boy Wins Garfield Tribute," *New York Times*, September 16, 1961.

58. "Cleveland Public Square." National Park Service, accessed February 11, 2016, www.nps.gov/nr/travel/ohioeriecanal/pub.htm.

59. "Soldiers' and Sailors' Monument." Accessed February 11, 2016, www.soldiersandsailors.com.

60. Discussion with Mary Krohmer, director of Community Relations at the Lake View Cemetery Foundation.

61. "The Garfield Monument," *New York Times*, January 3, 1886.

19. ULYSSES SIMPSON GRANT

1. "Gen. Grant's Will," *New York Times*, August 17, 1885.

2. Later he would defend the doctors for administering the narcotic: "[Cocaine] has never been given to me as a medicine. It has only been administered as an application to stop pain." Perry, Mark. *Grant and Twain*. New York: Random House, 2004, 90.

3. Perry, *Grant and Twain*, 64–67.

4. Flood, Charles Bracelen. *Grant's Final Victory: Ulysses S. Grant's Heroic Last Year*. Boston: Da Capo Press, 2012.

5. The story is expertly told in: Ward, Geoffrey C. *Disposition to Be Rich: Ferdinand Ward, the Greatest Swindler of the Gilded Age*. New York: Vintage Books, 2013.

6. Thayer, William Makepeace. *From the Tannery to the White House. Story of the Life of Ulysses S. Grant*. London, England: Thomas Nelson and Sons, 1885.

7. "Rare Historical Foresight Preserved Grant's Upstate N.Y. Cottage," *Daily Gazette*, May 28, 1990.

8. Perry, *Grant and Twain*, 159.

9. "On Death Watch Duty," *Daily True American*, February 25, 1891.

10. Perry, *Grant and Twain*, 225–226.

11. Perrett, Geoffrey. *Ulysses S. Grant Soldier & President*. New York: Modern Library, 1998, 473–478.

12. "A Hero Finds Rest," *New York Times*, July 24, 1885.

13. Pitkin, Thomas M. *The Captain Departs: Ulysses S. Grant's Last Campaign*. Carbondale: Southern Illinois University Press, 1973, 93.

14. "A Hero Finds Rest," *New York Times*, July 24, 1885.

15. Seven decades later in the 1950s the company would use this in their advertising, boasting in a subway poster beneath a picture of Grant's tomb, "We Conducted His Funeral!" "Who's Buried in Grant's Tomb? A Funeral Company Advertises Its Part in It," *Milwaukee Journal*, December 31, 1953.

16. "Grant's Obsequies, Services at Mt. McGregor," *Ithaca Democrat*, August 6, 1885.

17. The Fifth Avenue Bank of New York. *Fifth Avenue Events, A Brief Account of Some of the Most Interesting Events which Have Occurred on the Avenue*. Boston: Walton Advertising and Printing Company, 1916, 55.

18. "Letter from Mayor Grace to Mrs. Grant Proposing a Memorial to President Grant. July 23, 1885." Manhattan Historic Sites Archive, accessed February 12, 2016, mhsarchive.org.

19. "By Telegraph," *Deseret News*, August 5, 1885.

20. "Death of General Grant," *Colonist* (Volume XXVIII, Issue 4229), August 29, 1885.

21. In a letter dated October 29, 1885, Julia reaffirmed: "Riverside was accepted by myself and my family as a burial site of my husband General Grant, first because I believed New York was his preference. Second, it is near his residence that I hope to occupy as long as I live." "Letter from Mrs. Grant to Mayor Grace. October 29, 1885." Manhattan Historic Sites Archive, accessed February 12, 2016, mhsarchive.org.

22. "Riverside Park Chosen," *New York Times*, July 28, 1885.

23. "Grant's Obsequies, Services at Mt. McGregor," *Ithaca Democrat*, August 6, 1885.

24. Ibid.

25. "Albany to New York, the Remains of General Grant Taken from Albany to New York," *Dubuque Sunday Herald*, August 6, 1885.

26. Ibid.

27. "Grant's Obsequies, Services at Mt. McGregor," *Ithaca Democrat*, August 6, 1885.

28. Waugh, Joan. *U. S. Grant: American Hero, American Myth*. Chapel Hill: The University of North Carolina Press, 2009, 234–236.

29. "Who's Buried in Grant's Tomb? A Funeral Company Advertises Its Part in It," *Milwaukee Journal*, December 31, 1953.

30. Waugh, *U. S. Grant: American Hero, American Myth*, 234–246.

31. "Who's Buried in Grant's Tomb? A Funeral Company Advertises Its Part in It," *Milwaukee Journal*, December 31, 1953.

32. Townsend, Malcolm, comp. *U.S.: An Index to the United States of America*. Boston: D Lothrop Company, 1890, 330–331.

33. Ibid. 331.

34. "Pilgrims to the Tomb," *New York Times*, August 11, 1885; "The Riverside Tomb," *Miamisburg Bulletin*, September 4, 1885.

35. "To Guard Camp Grant," *New York Times*, January 17, 1886.

36. "Visitors at Riverside," *New York Times*, August 13, 1885.

37. "Barracks at Camp Grant," *New York Times*, November 10, 1885.

38. Poore, Ben Perley, ed. *Message of the President of the United States to the Two Houses of Congress, at the Commencement of the Second Session of the Forty-ninth Congress*. Washington, DC: Washington Government Printing Office, 1886.

39. "Account Moneys Received. 1886." Manhattan Historic Sites Archive, accessed February 12, 2016, mhsarchive.org.

40. "The Riverside Tomb," *Miamisburg Bulletin*, September 4, 1885.

41. "Description of Competitive Design for the Grant Monument by John H. Duncan, Architect. 1890." Manhattan Historic Sites Archive, accessed February 12, 2016, mhsarchive.org.

42. "Congressional Record. December 10, 1890." Manhattan Historic Sites Archive, accessed February 12, 2016, mhsarchive.org.

43. "Gen. Grant's Tomb," *New York Times*, March 21, 1892.

44. "An Ode: To Be Sung on the Occasion of Breaking Ground for the Mausoleum of General Grant. April 27, 1891." Manhattan Historic Sites Archive, accessed February 12, 2016, mhsarchive.org.

45. *Harpers Weekly*, May 27, 1892.

46. "Contents of copper box placed in cornerstone of Grant's Tomb. April 27, 1892." Manhattan Historic Sites Archive, accessed February 12, 2016, mhsarchive.org.

47. "Laid by the President," *New York Times*, April 28, 1892.

48. Perrett, Geoffrey, *Ulysses S. Grant Soldier & President*, 473–478.

49. "Grant Sarcophagus Here," *New York Times*, March 16, 1897.

50. "Work on the Tomb Ended," *New York Times*, April 14, 1897.

51. "Gen. Grant's Body Removed," *New York Times*, April 18, 1897.

52. "Thirteen Governors Here: Two More Are Expected to Arrive To-day to Take Part in the Ceremonies," *New York Times*, April 27, 1897.

53. "Tribute of the Nation," *Paterson Press Daily*, April 29, 1897.

54. Ibid.

55. "Grant Day Police Details," *New York Times*, April 14, 1897.

56. *Albany Evening Journal*, June 19, 1885, as referenced in Perry, *Grant and Twain*, 209.

57. "Cottage Where Ulysses Grant Died Marks 100 Years as Historic Site," *Daily Gazette*, May 21, 1990.

58. To make sure this historic artifact is not used for nefarious purposes, the New York State Department of Parks and Recreation measures it every year to confirm none of it is missing. "Ulysses S. Grant's last battle," CBS News, posted February 17, 2013, www.cbsnews.com/news/ulysses-s-grants-last-battle.

59. "Suye Narita," *Albany Times-Union*, October 18, 2011.

60. "The President's Outing," *New York Times*, August 21, 1891.

61. "Japanese Woman Came to Mt. McGregor for Treatment, Stayed a Lifetime," *Saratogian News*, August 30, 2011.

62. "Rare Historical Foresight Preserved Grant's Upstate N.Y. Cottage," *Daily Gazette*, May 28, 1990.

63. "Historic Grant Cottage to Open Again Next Year," *Schenectady Gazette*, July 24, 1985.

64. "A Jewel in Albany Regains Its Luster," *New York Times*, March 9, 2013.

65. "An Insult to Erin," *Editor & Publisher*, January 8, 1921.

66. The Fifth Avenue Bank of New York. *Fifth Avenue Events*.

67. "Rare Historical Foresight Preserved Grant's Upstate N.Y. Cottage," *Daily Gazette*, May 28, 1990.

68. "Grant's Tomb to Be Guarded All the Time," *Deseret News*, February 1, 1909.

69. "Danger at Grant's Tomb," *New York Times*, January 12, 1916.

70. "Grant Fund Now $58,463," *New York Times*, April 14, 1929; "Commercialism at Grant's Tomb," *New York Times*, August 12, 1932.

71. "Grant's Tomb Goes to US Next Friday as National Shrine," *New York Times*, April 24, 1959.

72. "Report on Transfer of the General Grant Memorial to the National Park Service. 1959." Manhattan Historic Sites Archive, accessed February 12, 2016, mhsarchive.org.

73. "Better Groucho Should Bury Grant's Tomb Gag," *Milwaukee Sentinel*, December 12, 1963.

74. National Park Service Visitor Statistics.

75. "Little Respect Given to Graves of Leaders," *Ocala Star-Banner*, March 27, 1983. A decade earlier in 1972 there was a ceremony at the site to commemorate what would have been Grant's 150th birthday. While most wisely chose to stay home and stay safe, some brave die-hards attended. Those who did mingled with members of the "Young Aces" and "Junior Aces" gangs, which made up about a third of the crowd that day. When one gang member was asked his thoughts on the tomb, he told the reporter, "It's nice sitting around here playing congas at night. We have fights here too, if another club starts trouble." "Grant's Tomb Gang Territory," *Vancouver Sun*, April 28, 1972.

76. "3 States War for Grant's Remains," *Toledo Blade*, April 10, 1994.

77. "Grant's Tomb—(By Bruce Frankel) Extension of Remarks—May 18, 1994." Accessed February 12, 2016, www.grantstomb.org/hyde.html.

78. "Government to Refurbish Grant's tomb," *Albany Herald*, April 28, 1994.

79. *The Ellensburg Daily Record*, May 3, 1994.

80. "Grant Officials Take Offense," *Telegraph-Herald*, July 14, 2003.

20. CHESTER ALAN ARTHUR

1. "Death and the Pall," *Corning Journal*, November 25, 1886.

2. "News of Chester Arthur's Death," *New York Times*, November 19, 1886.

3. "Arthur Dead," *Crawfordville Star*, November 25, 1886.

4. "News of Chester Arthur's Death," *New York Times*, November 19, 1886.

5. Ibid.

6. "Burial of the Dead," *Daily Argus News*, November 23, 1886.

7. *Annual Record, Issue 249 by Ancient and Honorable Artillery Company of Massachusetts 1886-7*, 1887, 24.

8. "Burial of the Dead," *Daily Argus News*, November 23, 1886.

9. *Annual Record, Issue 249 by Ancient and Honorable Artillery Company of Massachusetts 1886-7*, 22–35.

10. "Burial of the Dead," *Daily Argus News*, November 23, 1886.

11. "Expressing Their Sorrow; A Simple Citizen's Funeral for Mr. Arthur," *New York Times*, November 20, 1886.

12. *Annual Record, Issue 249 by Ancient and Honorable Artillery Company of Massachusetts 1886-7*, 22–35.

13. Ibid., 23.

14. "Death and the Pall," *Corning Journal*, November 25, 1886.

15. Ibid.

16. "Burial of the Dead," *Daily Argus News*, November 23, 1886.

17. "The Grave of Gen. Arthur," *Troy Northern Budget*, May 19, 1889.

18. In 1884, Hinman's allegations were published in a book, *How a British Subject Became President of the United States* (New York: 1884). "A Canadian Born U.S. President?" *Granby Leader-Mall*, October 7, 1937.

19. "Citizen and President," *Irish Canadian*, November 9, 1882.

20. "Abroad in New York," *New York Sun*, August 23, 2004.

21. Whyte, Kenneth. *The Uncrowned King: The Sensational Rise of William Randolph Hearst*. Berkeley, California: Counterpoint Press, 2009.

22. "In the Real Estate Field," *New York Times*, June 23, 1910.

23. "A Brief History." Kalustyan's, accessed February 12, 2016, kalustyans.com/index.php?route=information/information&information_id=4.

24. "Chester A. Arthur Home on Lexington Ave. Sold," *New York Times*, October 20, 1955.

25. National Register of Historic Places Inventory Nomination Form: "Chester A. Arthur Home."

26. Another site in New York City that you will not find in any presidential traveler's guide is located in the trendy Meatpacking District in Lower Manhattan. One night, my wife Francesca and I stopped in a bar named "The Chester." Thinking nothing of the name, we had stumbled into a bar named for President Chester Arthur! The drink menu included an amusing anecdote that claimed the 21st president was a party animal who enjoyed his libations. I wasn't sure if the president was a big drinker, but I knew Arthur was once the Collector of the Port of New York, and I wondered if the building had any significance, perhaps as a former office. I took a chance and asked, "I see this bar was named after President Chester Arthur. Do you know if he was ever in this building?" The bartender, barely old enough to order a drink himself, replied, "No, I don't think so." And then he paused, as if to give me a moment to brace myself before he broke some bad news, "Actually, I'm not even sure he's alive anymore!"

27. Feldman, Ruth Tenzer. *Chester A. Arthur*. Minneapolis: Twenty-First Century Books, 2006.

21. RUTHERFORD BIRCHARD HAYES

1. Whitney, David C. *The Graphic Story of the American Presidents*. Chicago: J. G. Ferguson, 1973, 289.

2. Trefousse, Hans L. *Rutherford B. Hayes*. New York: Times Books, 2002, 146–147.

3. "Mr. Cleveland to Go to Fremont," *New York Times*, January 19, 1893.

4. "Gen. Hayes Laid at Rest," *New York Times*, January 20, 1893.

5. "To Reinter ex-President Hayes's Body," *New York Times*, March 13, 1909.

6. "The Rutherford B. Hayes Presidential Center." Accessed February 14, 2016, www.RBHayes.org.

7. Keeler, Lucy Elliot, ed. *Dedication of the Hayes Memorial Library and Museum in Honor of Rutherford Birchard Hayes*. Columbus, Ohio: F. J. Beer Printing, 1916, 22.

8. "The Rutherford B. Hayes Presidential Center." Accessed February 14, 2016, www.RBHayes.org.

9. "Harding Speaks at Dedication," *Spokesman Review*, October 8, 1920.

22. BENJAMIN HARRISON

1. Letter from Harrison's private secretary E. Frank Tibbott, April 18, 1901. This letter was found in the archives at the Benjamin Harrison Presidential Site.

2. "Benjamin Harrison Dead, Ex-President's Battle for Life Ended Yesterday Afternoon," *New York Times*, March 14, 1901.

3. "Death of Gen. Harrison," *Indianapolis Journal*, March 14, 1901.

4. "General Benjamin Harrison Passes to the Great Beyond," *Baltimore Morning Herald*, March 14, 1901.

5. "State Troops at the Harrison Funeral," *New York Times*, March 15, 1901.

6. "Benjamin Harrison Dead, Ex-President's Battle for Life Ended Yesterday Afternoon," *New York Times*, March 14, 1901.

7. "Honors for the Dead," *Daily News-Review* (Crawfordsville, Indiana), March 15, 1901.

8. "Burial of Harrison," *Bluffton Chronicle*, March 13, 1901.

9. "Gen. Harrison's Body Rests in the Tomb," *New York Times*, March 18, 1901.

10. Davis, Tom M (Crown Hill Cemetery Tour Developer and Guide). "President Benjamin Harrison." Accessed February 14, 2016, www.crownhillhf.org/docs/Harrison_2009.pdf.

11. "Gen. Harrison's Body Rests in the Tomb," *New York Times*, March 18, 1901.

12. "Gen. Harrison's Funeral," *St. John Daily Sun*, March 18, 1901.

13. "Nation Has Done Little in Honor of Its Dead Rulers," *New York Times*, January 12, 1913.

14. "Gen. Harrison," *Toledo Blade*, March 21, 1901.

15. "General Harrison himself selected the monument—a solid piece of granite 10 feet high and six feet square, bearing the name 'Harrison'—which marks the grave of his departed wife and is to mark his own." "Honors for the Dead," *Daily News-Review* (Crawfordsville, Indiana), March 15, 1901.

16. "Little Journeys to the Tombs of American Presidents," *Sunday Vindicator*, May 17, 1908.

17. "Body Snatchers Plotted to Desecrate Ex-President's Tomb," *San Jose Evening News*, December 22, 1902.

18. National Register of Historic Places Nomination Form: "Benjamin Harrison Home."

19. Brockman, Paul, processed. *First Presbyterian Church (Indianapolis, Ind.) Time Capsules Collection, 1839–1902*, May 15, 2002.

20. Yalom, Marilyn. *The American Resting Place*. Boston: Houghton Mifflin Harcourt, 2008.

21. "Roosevelt Adorns Harrison's Grave," *Indianapolis News*, May 31, 1907.

22. Letter from President Theodore Roosevelt to Mrs. Mary Lud Harrison, June 24, 1907. This letter was found in the archives at the Benjamin Harrison Presidential Site.

23. "A 150-Year Legacy." Crown Hill Cemetery, accessed February 14, 2016, www.CrownHill.org/cemetery/history.html.

23. WILLIAM MCKINLEY

1. Miller, Scott. *The President and the Assassin: McKinley, Terror, and Empire at the Dawn of the American Century*. New York: Random House, 2013.

2. McClure, Alexander K. and Charles Morris. *The Authentic Life of William McKinley, Our Third Martyr President: Together with a Life Sketch of Theodore Roosevelt*. Washington, DC: W.E. Scull, 1901.

3. "The Assassination," *Saturday Globe* (Utica, NY), September 14, 1901.

4. Miller, *The President and the Assassin*.

5. Ibid.

6. There was a missing piece from the X-ray machine, rendering it unable to function; therefore it was never used. Miller, *The President and the Assassin*, 316.

7. McClure and Morris, *The Authentic Life of William McKinley*.

8. Ibid., 328.

9. Ibid., 329.

10. "Death claims the Best Beloved of Columbia's Well Loved Sons," *Los Angeles Herald*, September 14, 1901.

11. McClure and Morris, *The Authentic Life of William McKinley*.

12. "The Case of the President, Continued," *Medical News*, September 21, 1901.

13. "At the Milburn House," *New York Tribune*, September 16, 1901.

14. McClure and Morris, *The Authentic Life of William McKinley*, 343.

15. "Remains of President McKinley En Route to Washington To-Day," *Newburgh Daily News*, September 16, 1901.

16. Ibid.

17. "Nation's Dead Sleeps in the White House," *New York Times*, September 17, 1901.

18. Hazelton, George Cochrane. *The National Capitol: Its Architecture, Art and History*. New York: J. F. Taylor & Company, 1914.

19. "Obsequies at Capitol; Dead President Will Rest Upon a Historic Bier," *New York Times*, September 17, 1901.

20. The honorary pallbearers were John C. Dueber, George B. Frease, R. A. Cassidy, William R. Day,

Joseph Biechele, Henry W. Harter, William A. Lynch, and Thomas M. McCarty.

21. Kenney, Kimberly. A *Canton: A Journey Through Time*. Mount Pleasant, South Carolina: Arcadia Publishing, 2003.

22. Ibid.

23. "All the World Mourned," *Evening Argus*, September 20, 1901.

24. McClure and Morris, *The Authentic Life of William McKinley*, 386.

25. "Outrage at the President's Tomb," *Ashburton Guardian*, October 2, 1901.

26. McClure and Morris, *The Authentic Life of William McKinley*, 372.

27. Kenney, Christopher. *The McKinley Monument: A Tribute to a Fallen President*. Charleston, South Carolina: History Press, 2006.

28. McCullough, David. *Truman*. New York: Simon & Schuster, 2001.

29. National Register of Historic Places Nomination Form: "William McKinley Tomb."

30. "McKinley Bodies Reinterred," *Lewiston Morning Tribune*, September 19, 1907.

31. Kenney, *The McKinley Monument*.

32. "Roosevelt Pays Tribute to Memory Of M'Kinley," *Hamburg Reporter*, October 4, 1907.

33. Severance, Frank H., ed. *Publications of the Buffalo Historical Society*, vol. 25. Buffalo: Buffalo Historic Society, 1921, 358.

34. The owners during this period were Edward Darley, Erastus Scoville, Esther Osborn, George Chadeayne, and Edward Eames.

35. "McKinley Death Chamber Will Soon Disappear," *Erie County, New York State*, November 23, 1919.

36. "Peaceful End of Mrs. M'Kinley," *Day* (New London, Connecticut), May 27, 1907.

37. "Mrs. M'Kinley at Rest," *Toledo Blade*, June 6, 1907.

38. Kenney, *The McKinley Monument*.

39. Kenney, *Canton: A Journey Through Time*.

24. GROVER CLEVELAND

1. "Former President Grover Cleveland Passes Away at Home," *Telegraph*, June 24, 1908.

2. Brodsky, Alyn. *Grover Cleveland A Study in Character*. New York: Truman Talley Books, 2000, 444–449.

3. "Former President Grover Cleveland Passes Away at Home," *Telegraph*, June 24, 1908.

4. "No Pomp Will Mark Cleveland Funeral," *Toledo News*, June 25, 1908.

5. "Cleveland's Funeral 5 Tomorrow Afternoon," *News-Democrat*, June 25, 1908.

6. "Tribute of Roosevelt," *Paterson Press*, June 25, 1908.

7. "No Pomp Will Mark Cleveland Funeral," *Toledo News*, June 25, 1908.

8. "Cleveland's Funeral 5 Tomorrow Afternoon," *News-Democrat*, June 25, 1908.

9. "Burial of a Statesman," *New York Times*, June 27, 1908.

10. "Simple Service Marks Funeral of Cleveland," *Los Angeles Herald*, June 27, 1908.

11. "Cleveland's Funeral 5 Tomorrow Afternoon," *News-Democrat*, June 25, 1908.

12. The pallbearers were Paul Morton, President of Equitable Life Insurance Society; E. C. Benedict from New York; Reverend VanDyke; John Hibbea, Dean of the Graduate College of Princeton; University Professor Andrew West; and president of the City College of New York John Finley.

13. Brodsky. *Grover Cleveland A Study in Character*, 444–449.

14. "Burial of a Statesman," *New York Times*, June 27, 1908.

15. *The Encyclopedia Americana*. New York: Encyclopedia Americana Corporation, 1919.

16. The story of Cleveland's clandestine operation is expertly recounted in: Algeo, Matthew. *The President Is a Sick Man*. Chicago: Chicago Review Press, 2011.

17. "History of Lakewood." Township of Lakewood, accessed February 15, 2016, twp.lakewood.nj.us/history.php.

18. Algeo. *The President Is a Sick Man*, 194-196.

19. "Scott Sipprelle: Business Roots," *US-1*, September 8, 2010.

20. "History." Princeton Cemetery of Nassau Church, accessed February 15, 2016, nassauchurch.org/about/princetoncemetery/history.

21. "Princeton Cemetery Reflects Storied Past of History-Rich Community," *Trenton Times*, March 10, 2014.

25. THEODORE ROOSEVELT

1. Millard, Candice. *The River of Doubt: Theodore Roosevelt's Darkest Journey*. New York: Anchor, 2006.

2. "Theodore Roosevelt Dies Suddenly at Oyster Bay Home," *New York Times*, January 6, 1919.

3. Morris, Sylvia Jukes. *Edith Kermit Roosevelt: Portrait of a First Lady*. New York: Modern Library, 2001.

4. Doctors Faller, John H. Richard, and John A. Hartwell released a joint statement, "Colonel Roosevelt had been suffering from an attack of inflammatory rheumatism for about two months. His progress had been entirely satisfactory and his condition had not given cause for special concern. On Sunday he was in good spirits and spent the evening with his family, dictating letters. He retired at 11 o'clock, and at 4 o'clock in the morning his manservant who occupied an adjoining room, noticed that, while sleeping quietly, Colonel Roosevelt's breathing was hollow. He died almost immediately, without awakening. The cause of death was an embolus." "Theodore Roosevelt Dies Suddenly at Oyster Bay Home," *New York Times*, January 6, 1919.

5. Morris, *Edith Kermit Roosevelt*.

6. "Omit Funeral Pomp for Col. Roosevelt," *New York Times*, January 7, 1919.

7. "President Orders Roosevelt Tribute," *New York Times*, January 8, 1919.

8. "Mourners Gather at Bier of Theodore Roosevelt," *Lewiston Evening Journal*, January 8, 1919.

9. Goodwin, Doris Kearns. *The Bully Pulpit: Theodore Roosevelt, William Howard Taft, and the Golden Age of Journalism*. New York: Simon & Schuster, 2013.

10. "To Visit Roosevelt's Grave," *New York Times*, December 28, 1921.

11. "Roosevelt Estate Valued at $810,607," *New York Times*, October 26, 1919.

12. "Annual Scout Pilgrimage to Roosevelt Grave Oct. 27," *New York Times*, October 7, 1928.

13. "2,000 Scouts Visit Roosevelt Grave," *New York Times*, October 20, 1946.

14. "Boy Scouts Run 400 Miles with Roosevelt Flag," *Evening News*, October 18, 1919.

15. "Scouts Renew Oath at Roosevelt Grave," *New York Times*, November 27, 1920.

16. "Annual Scout Pilgrimage to Roosevelt Grave Oct. 27," *New York Times*, October 7, 1928.

17. "5,000 Scouts Visit Roosevelt's Grave," *New York Times*, October 21, 1934.

18. "6,000 Boys to Visit Roosevelt's Grave," *New York Times*, October 17, 1937.

19. "Visit Roosevelt Grave," *New York Times*, October 21, 1945.

20. Hagedorn was a Roosevelt expert who wrote *Roosevelt in the Bad Lands* (Boston and New York: Houghton Mifflin Company, 1921). "2,000 Scouts Visit Roosevelt Grave," *New York Times*, October 20, 1946.

21. "3,500 Boy Scouts Visit Grave of T. R.," *New York Times*, October 17, 1948.

22. "Scouts at Roosevelt Grave," *New York Times*, May 29, 1922.

23. "Roosevelt's Grave Hidden," *New York Times*, May 31, 1923.

24. "400 at Roosevelt Grave," *New York Times*, June 1, 1943.

25. "To Visit Roosevelt's Grave," *New York Times*, December 28, 1921.

26. "Hundreds Visit Roosevelt's Grave," *New York Times*, July 10, 1930.

27. "Friends Pay Tribute to Theodore Roosevelt," *New York Times*, January 7, 1937; "30 Make Pilgrimage to Roosevelt Grave," *New York Times*, January 7, 1938; "Old Friends Visit Roosevelt Grave," *New York Times*, January 7, 1940.

28. "Visit Roosevelt's Grave," *New York Times*, April 7, 1919.

29. "Roosevelt Drive Will Open Today," *New York Times*, October 20, 1919.

30. "Honor Roosevelt's Grave," *New York Times*, January 5, 1920.

31. "Airplanes Salute Roosevelt's Grave," *Lewiston Morning Tribune*, October 28, 1929.

32. "400 Masons Visit Roosevelt Grave," *New York Times*, January 10, 1949.

33. "Diaz Lays Wreath on Roosevelt Tomb," *New York Times*, October 21, 1921.

34. "Visit Roosevelt's Grave," *New York Times*, July 10, 1922.

35. "At Oyster Bay," *Lewiston Morning Tribune*, November 20, 1922.

36. "Visits Roosevelt's Grave," *New York Times*, November 14, 1932.

37. "Centennial Opens For T. Roosevelt," *New York Times*, October 28, 1957.

38. Hagedorn, Hermann. *Sagamore Hill: An Historical Guide*. Oyster Bay, New York: Theodore Roosevelt Association, 1977.

39. "T. Roosevelt Home Is Sold for Shrine," *New York Times*, February 9, 1950.

40. "Eisenhower Visits Nassau Tomorrow," *New York Times*, June 13, 1953.

41. "Omit Funeral Pomp for Col. Roosevelt," *New York Times*, January 7, 1919.

26. WARREN GAMALIEL HARDING

1. Russell, Francis. *The Shadow of Blooming Grove: Warren G. Harding in His Times*. New York: McGraw-Hill, 1968, 574–603.

2. Ibid., 590.

3. The following version comes primarily from Richard V. Oulahan of the *New York Times*. Oulahan immediately noticed the varied eyewitness accounts and that sometimes the same person gave conflicting details at different times. He sought the true events, and the day after Harding's death he wrote what he had pieced together as the actual account.

4. Anthony, Carl Sferrazza. *Florence Harding: The First Lady, the Jazz Age, and the Death of America's Most Scandalous President*. New York: William Morrow, 1998.

5. Russell, *The Shadow of Blooming Grove*, 591.

6. Whether Florence was in the room when Harding suffered this final episode was a major point of confusion. An alternate version has Florence reading in the room with him at the time he collapsed. According to the *New York Times*, "Reports of what happened in the sick room when the president's sudden stroke came are still somewhat confused." "President Harding Dies Suddenly; Stroke of Apoplexy at 7:30 P.M.; Calvin Coolidge Is President," *New York Times*, August 4, 1923.

7. Ibid.

8. "The Presidency: The End," *Time* Magazine, August 13, 1923.

9. Russell, *The Shadow of Blooming Grove*, 592.

10. "After 91 years, President Warren Harding's sudden death recalled." Yahoo News, posted August 8, 2014, news.yahoo.com/90-years-president-warren-harding-death-still-unsettled-100209743.html.

11. "Dr. Sawyer, Physician to Harding, Dies Suddenly," *Reading Eagle*, September 24, 1924.

12. This fantastic theory reached a wider audience with the 1930 publication, *The Strange Death of President Harding: From the Diaries of Gaston B. Means* (New York: Guild Publishing Corporation, 1930).

13. Russell, *The Shadow of Blooming Grove*, 592-593.

14. "Simple Services Held for Harding in San Francisco," *Evening Independent*, August 4, 1923.

15. "Body of President Harding to Lie in State Wednesday," *Evening Independent*, August 4, 1923.

16. "Train with Body Is on Way East," *Day* (New London, Connecticut), August 4, 1923.

17. Anthony, *Florence Harding*.

18. "Capital Awaits Its Lost Chief," *Lawrence Journal-World*, August 6, 1923.

19. "Sad Throngs Meet Harding's Funeral Train in Capitol," *Toledo Blade*, August 6, 1923.

20. Russell, *The Shadow of Blooming Grove*, 597.

21. "Harding's Body Is Laid in Tomb," *Winthrop News*, August 16, 1923.

22. "Sad Throngs Meet Harding's Funeral Train in Capitol," *Toledo Blade*, August 6, 1923.

23. "Harding Is Given to His Home Town," *Evening Independent*, August 9, 1923.

24. "Harding Rests In Ivy-Clad Vault in Marion Cemetery," *Day* (New London, Connecticut), August 11, 1923.

25. Russell, *The Shadow of Blooming Grove*, 600-601.

26. "Endless Thousands Pass by the Bier," *New York Times*, August 11, 1923.

27. "Edison Convinced the Soul Lives On," *New York Times*, August 11, 1923.

28. "Endless Thousands Pass by the Bier," *New York Times*, August 11, 1923.

29. "Harding Is Given to His Home Town," *Evening Independent*, August 9, 1923.

30. "Harding's Body Is Laid in Tomb," *Winthrop News*, August 16, 1923.

31. "Harding Rests in Ivy-Clad Vault in Marion Cemetery," *Day* (New London, Connecticut), August 11, 1923.

32. "Simple Service at Tomb," *New York Times*, August 11, 1923.

33. "Capitol Is Silent at Funeral Hour," *New York Times*, August 11, 1923.

34. "Thousands Linger at Harding's Tomb," *New York Times*, August 12, 1923.

35. Russell, *The Shadow of Blooming Grove*, 608.

36. "Hoover Will Honor Harding at Dedication," *Telegraph-Herald and Times Journal* (Dubuque, Iowa), May 6, 1931.

37. "Harding Memorial: The Design." Accessed February 15, 2016, www.HardingHome.org/harding-memorial.

38. "Thousands Linger at Harding's Tomb," *New York Times*, August 12, 1923.

39. Russell, *The Shadow of Blooming Grove*, 625.

40. "Marion to Honor Harding; Cornerstone of Memorial Tomb Will Be Laid Tomorrow," *New York Times*, May 30, 1926.

41. "Harding Tomb Dedication Revolved About Politics," *Day* (New London, Connecticut), June 18, 1931.

42. "Ohio Republicans Hold to Dry Policy," *New York Times*, September 12, 1930.

43. "Harding Tomb Dedicated Today," *Free Lance Star*, June 16, 1931.

44. "Harding Tomb Program," *New York Times*, May 19, 1931.

45. "Hoover Vexed by Fliers Over Marion Throng; Sees Peril to Crowds, Urges Pilots Be Punished," *New York Times*, June 17, 1931.

46. "Hoover Will Honor Harding at Dedication," *Telegraph-Herald and Times Journal* (Dubuque, Iowa), May 6, 1931.

47. Smith, Dennis. *San Francisco Is Burning*. New York: Viking, 2005, 191.

48. "President Harding's Mysterious S.F. death," *San Francisco Gate*, December 9, 2012.

27. WOODROW WILSON

1. Algeo, Matthew. *The President Is a Sick Man*. Chicago: Chicago Review Press, 2011.

2. Levin, Phyllis Lee. *Edith and Woodrow: The Wilson White House*. New York: Scribner, 2001, 488–495.

3. Sferrazza, Carl. *America's First Families: An Inside View of 200 Years of Private Life in the White House*. New York: Touchstone, 2000.

4. Levin, *Edith and Woodrow*.

5. Berg, A. Scott. *Wilson*. New York: Berkley, 2014. 735–739.

6. "Woodrow Wilson Is Dead," *News* (Lynchburg, VA), February 3, 1924.

7. Levin, *Edith and Woodrow*.

8. "President's Proclamation on the Death of Woodrow Wilson," *Lawrence Daily Journal-World*, February 4, 1924.

9. "Arlington Burial Urged for Wilson," *New York Times*, February 4, 1924.

10. Heckscher, August. *Woodrow Wilson*. New York: Scribner, 1991, 670–675.

11. "Arlington Burial Urged for Wilson," *New York Times*, February 4, 1924.

12. Levin, *Edith and Woodrow*.

13. "Illness Keeps Taft from Wilson Funeral; Chief Justice Takes to Bed, Plans a Rest," *New York Times*, February 7, 1924.

14. "New York Bustle Ceases at Hour of Wilson's Funeral," *Lewiston Evening Journal*, February 6, 1924.

15. "Entire Nation Halts While Solemn Last Rites Are Observed," *Pittsburgh Press*, February 6, 1924.

16. "Woodrow Wilson's Body Will Remain In Church Vault," *Evening Independent*, January 13, 1925.

17. "Sarcophagus for Woodrow Wilson Is Set In Place," *Ellensburg Daily Record*, January 29, 1925.

18. Fogle, Jeanne. *A Neighborhood Guide to Washington, D.C.'s Hidden History*. Charleston, South Carolina: History Press, 2009, 94.

19. "Hail to the Chiefs! A Road Trip to Where our Presidents Took Their Last Breaths," *Washington Post*, February 14, 2013. Accounts of the séances are in the archives of the Wilson home.

20. "Cathedral Timeline." Washington National Cathedral, accessed February 16, 2016, www.National Cathedral.org/about/timeline.shtml.

28. WILLIAM HOWARD TAFT

1. "Illness Keeps Taft from Wilson Funeral; Chief Justice Takes to Bed, Plans a Rest," *New York Times*, February 7, 1924.

2. "Taft Gained Peaks in Unusual Career," *New York Times*, March 10, 1930.

3. "Ex President Taft Dies at Capitol," *New York Times*, March 9, 1930.

4. "Taft's Smile Returns as He Gains Strength; Recognized Those Around Him, Speaks Clearly," *New York Times*, March 10, 1930.

5. "Taft Gained Peaks in Unusual Career," *New York Times*, March 10, 1930.

6. "William Howard Taft." Arlington National Cemetery, accessed February 16, 2016, www.arlington cemetery.net/whtaft.htm.

7. "Taft's Body Lies in Quiet of Home," *Sarasota Herald-Tribune*, March 10, 1930.

8. "Funeral at Church Brief in Its Rites," *New York Times*, March 12, 1930. Silent stock footage of the funeral procession can be found online at "Funeral procession of US President William Taft from his Washington DC home, to t...HD Stock Footage." YouTube, posted April 20, 2014, www.youtube. com/watch?v=C8-T4z9GA2w.

9. "Coolidges Return Home; Former President Does

Not Plan to Attend Taft Funeral," *New York Times*, March 9, 1930.

10. "Taft's Grave Protected from Souvenir Hunters," *Hartford Courant*, April 20, 1930.

11. "Simple Shaft Selected for Taft Grave," *Southeast Missourian*, March 12, 1930.

12. "Secret Letter," *St. Petersburg Times*, September 21, 1955.

13. "All Souls Archives and History." All Souls Unitarian Church, accessed February 16, 2016, www.all-souls.org/archives.

14. Yalom, Marilyn. *The American Resting Place*. Boston: Houghton Mifflin Harcourt, 2008.

15. "Arlington Marks 150 Years as Nation's Military Burial Ground," *Washington Post*, June 15, 2014.

29. CALVIN COOLIDGE

1. Whitney, David C. *The Graphic Story of the American Presidents*. Chicago: J. G. Ferguson, 1973, 157.

2. "Coolidge Found Dead at Home by Wife," *Reading Eagle*, January 5, 1933.

3. "Caretaker of Estate Last Person to See Coolidge Alive," *Reading Eagle*, January 6, 1933.

4. "Simple Rites at Coolidge's Bier," *Winthrop News*, January 12, 1933.

5. "Wife Finds Him on Return from Shopping Tour," *Topeka State Journal*, January 5, 1933.

6. "Former President Coolidge Dies," *New York Times*, January 6, 1933.

7. Ibid.

8. "Last Tribute for Coolidge at Simple Funeral Today," *Pittsburgh Post-Gazette*, January 7, 1933.

9. "Nation Pays Homage to Ex-President Coolidge," *Telegraph*, January 7, 1933.

10. Ibid.

11. "Coolidge Rites to Blaze Path for Simplicity," *Spokane Daily Chronicle*, January 12, 1933.

12. "Simple Services at Northampton Fixed Saturday," *Deseret News*, January 6, 1933.

13. "Coolidge Found Dead at Home by Wife," *Reading Eagle*, January 5, 1933.

14. "Nation Pays Homage to Ex-President Coolidge," *Telegraph*, January 7, 1933.

15. "Calvin Coolidge Goes to Last Resting Place," *Free Lance Star*, January 7, 1933.

16. "Last Tribute for Coolidge at Simple Funeral Today," *Pittsburgh Post-Gazette*, January 7, 1933.

17. "Mrs. Coolidge Sells Northampton Estate," *Day* (New London, Connecticut), May 3, 1938.

18. "Coolidge to Abandon Modest Home for Mansion Containing 16 Rooms," *Reading Eagle*, April 1, 1930.

19. "Caretaker of Estate Last Person to See Coolidge Alive," *Reading Eagle*, January 6, 1933.

20. "Furniture and Accessories from Coolidge Homes to Be Sold at Auction," *Milwaukee Journal*, April 12, 1936.

21. "Coolidge Home at Northampton Sold," *Lewiston Evening Journal*, April 20, 1938.

22. "Retirement Home of 'Silent Cal' Coolidge at Center of Uproar," *Telegraph*, May 21, 1985.

23. "Simple Rites at Coolidge's Bier," *Winthrop News*, January 12, 1933.

30. FRANKLIN DELANO ROOSEVELT

1. McCullough, David. *Truman*. New York: Simon & Schuster, 2001.

2. "Roosevelt Dies!!!!" *Knoxville News-Sentinel*, April 12, 1945.

3. Goodwin, Doris Kearns. *No Ordinary Time*. New York: Simon & Schuster, 1995, 601.

4. "War News Summarized," *New York Times*, April 13, 1945.

5. *Life* magazine, April 23, 1945.

6. Klara, Robert. *FDR's Funeral Train: A Betrayed Widow, a Soviet Spy, and a Presidency in the Balance*. New York: Palgrave MacMillan, 2010, 6–7.

7. *Life* magazine, April 23, 1945.

8. "Mrs. Roosevelt Retains Her Calm," *New York Times*, April 15, 1945.

9. Goodwin, *No Ordinary Time*, 612.

10. Klara, *FDR's Funeral Train*, 56–57.

11. Ibid., 61–62.

12. Ibid., 65–67.

13. Ibid., 76–77.

14. Ibid., 79.

15. "30 Days of Mourning for Roosevelt Ended," *New York Times*, May 15, 1945.

16. Klara, *FDR's Funeral Train*, 100.

17. Ibid., 111–119. New York's Pennsylvania Station is a mere six miles from Mott Haven Yards, however in 1945, to travel from one to the other and switch to a competing line, the train was forced to take a 28-mile roundabout route into Westchester County.

18. "Hyde Park Draped in Sadness as FDR Comes Home to Stay," *Youngstown Vindicator*, April 15, 1945.

19. "Grave Is in Garden," *New York Times*, April 16, 1945.

20. "Chicago Church Bells Toll," *New York Times*, April 15, 1945.

21. Mr. X. *The Roosevelt Death: A Super Mystery*. G.L.K. Smith: 1947, 3.

22. As my father-in-law, who was 10 at the time of Roosevelt's death, likes to say, "I thought FDR was going to be president forever!" And it appears, like him, many could not accept the reality that he was indeed dead. One such conspiracy theorist with the ridiculous *nom de plume* of "Mr. X" published a book in 1947 with the fantastic title *The Roosevelt Death: A Super Mystery*. In it, Mr. X (later revealed to be Gerald Lyman Kenneth Smith, a far-right clergyman who ran for president in 1944 for the isolationist "America First" party) left no conspiracy theory unexplored—he proposed that FDR may have faked his own death and also introduced a possibility that he had committed suicide when he "put a pistol to his head and pulled the trigger," thus leaving his corpse unpresentable for an open coffin funeral. Mr. X, *The Roosevelt Death: A Super Mystery*, 14.

23. National Register of Historic Places Nomination Form: "Warm Springs Historic District."

24. "Speech by Senator John F. Kennedy, the Little White House, Warm Springs, GA." The American Presidency Project, accessed February 17, 2016, www.presidency.ucsb.edu/ws/?pid=25759.

25. "Warm Springs Liked Carter," *Dispatch* (Lexington, NC), September 7, 1976.

26. "Commemorating Roosevelt's Death, Democrats Praise His Legacy of Liberalism," *New York Times*, April 13, 1995.

27. Klara, *FDR's Funeral Train*.

28. "UNO Scouts Lay Roses on FDR's Grave," *Deseret News*, January 10, 1946.

29. "Public to See Roosevelt Grave," *New York Times*, January 30, 1946.

30. "100 Visit Roosevelt's Grave," *New York Times*, January 31, 1946.

31. "FDR Grave Dedicated as National Shrine," *Telegraph*, April 11, 1946.

32. And if the tourist traps were not bad enough, the newspaper also included a warning about copperhead snakes! "Roosevelt's Hyde Park One Decade Later," *New York Times*, April 10, 1955.

33. "Remembering John F. Kennedy's visits to Dutchess County," *Democrat and Chronicle*, November 21, 2013.

31. JOHN FITZGERALD KENNEDY

1. "We'll Have 3 Living Ex-Presidents," *Miami News*, December 27, 1960.

2. Motives, alternate assassins, and conspiracy theories are topics for another book; however, it is notable that several of these suppositions incredulously place President Lyndon Johnson in the midst of the conspiracy. McClellan, Barr. *Blood, Money & Power: How L.B.J. Killed J.F.K.* New York: Skyhorse Publishing, 2011.

3. Bishop, Jim. *The Day Kennedy Was Shot*. New York: Harper Perennial, 1992, 216–218.

4. "Last Rites for President John F. Kennedy Remembered By Catholic Priest Rev. Oscar L. Huber." *The Huffington Post*, posted November 19, 2013, www.huffingtonpost.com/2013/11/19/last-rites-jfk_n_4302423.html.

5. Bishop, *The Day Kennedy Was Shot*, 219-232.

6. "John F. Kennedy Memorial Edition," *Life* magazine, November 29, 1963. Lawrence Francis "Larry" O'Brien Jr. would later become the third Commissioner of the National Basketball Association.

7. The mysterious disappearance of JFK's brain was revisited in 2013 in a book published to coincide with the 50th anniversary, *End of Days: The Assassination of John F. Kennedy* (New York: William Morrow, 2013) by James Swanson, who is also an expert in assassination relics. I had the good fortune to briefly meet Mr. Swanson at the 150th anniversary of Lincoln's assassination at Ford's Theater. I mentioned his claim that Robert Kennedy stole JFK's brain and he emphatically responded, "It's not a *claim*, he stole it!"

8. A model of the coffin is on display at the National Museum of Funeral History in Houston, Texas.

9. "Thousands Pay Respects as Johnson Lies In State," *Sarasota Herald-Tribune*, January 24, 1973.

10. "November 25, 1963: Universal Newsreel Film Depicting the Funeral of President John F. Kennedy." C-SPAN, accessed February 17, 2016, www.c-span.org/video/?316050-1/universal-newsreel-kennedy-assassination.

11. In a recorded conversation with Senate Minority Leader Everett Dirksen at 1:50 p.m. the day after

the shooting, Johnson said, "I'm rather of the opinion it might be a good thing the day after the funeral—assuming the one in Boston is Tuesday—to have a Joint Session and a brief statement." Beschloss, Michael R. *Taking Charge: The Johnson White House Tapes, 1963–1964*. New York: Simon & Schuster, 1998, 24.

12. Mossman, B.C. and M.W. Stark. *The Last Salute: Civil and Military Funerals 1921–1969*. Washington, DC: Department of the Army, 1971.

13. "Digger Recalls JFK's Grave," *Bulletin*, November 21, 1988.

14. "Pallbearers at President Kennedy's Funeral." John F. Kennedy Presidential Library and Museum, accessed February 17, 2016, http://www.jfklibrary.org/Research/Research-Aids/Ready-Reference/JFK-Fast-Facts/Pallbearers.aspx.

15. Beschloss, *Taking Charge*, 57–58

16. "Eternal Flame Burns at Grave," *Telegraph*, November 26, 1963.

17. "Johnson Lays Wreath at JFK Grave," *Miami News*, May 28, 1964.

18. "Kennedys, Johnson Attend Blessing of New JFK Grave," *Herald Journal*, March 16, 1967.

19. "LBJ Visits Kennedy's Grave after Church," *Pittsburgh Post-Gazette*, December 2, 1963.

20. "LBJ Visits Kennedy's Grave," *Park City Daily News*, July 21, 1964.

21. "LBJ Pays Surprise Visit to Kennedy's Grave," *Lodi News Sentinel*, January 14, 1965.

22. "The Kennedy Tomb: Simple Design Outlined," *New York Times*, November 17, 1964.

23. "JFK Body Moved to New Grave," *Evening Independent*, March 15, 1967.

24. Fay, Paul B. Jr. *The Pleasure of His Company*. New York: Harper & Row, 1966.

25. "JFK Grave Design Ready after Year," *Milwaukee Sentinel*, November 17, 1964.

26. "Contract for Permanent JFK Grave Awarded," *Ocala Star-Banner*, July 18, 1965.

27. "March 16—Today in Cape Cod History," *Cape Cod Today*, March 16, 2013.

28. "Kennedy Flame Put Out Accidentally by Pupils," *New York Times*, December 11, 1963.

29. "John Carl Warnecke, Architect to Kennedy, Dies at 91," *New York Times*, April 22, 2010.

30. "JFK Resting Place Amid Favored Trees," *Owosso Argus-Press*, March 14, 1967.

31. "JFK Grave Marker Made from Maine Granite," *Bangor Daily News*, November 22, 1983.

32. "Digger Recalls JFK's Grave," *Bulletin*, November 21, 1988; "JFK Body Moved to New Grave," *Evening Independent*, March 15, 1967.

33. "Kennedys, Johnson Attend Blessing of New JFK Grave," *Herald Journal*, March 16, 1967.

34. "Suicide in Front of JFK's Grave," *New Straits Times*, September 21, 1972.

35. "Body Found at JFK grave," *Pittsburgh Post-Gazette*, November 29, 1982.

36. "Man May Have Fallen into Memorial Flame," *Sarasota Herald-Tribune*, December 6, 1982.

37. "Man Dead at Kennedy Grave Termed Heart Disease Victim," *New York Times*, December 7, 1982.

38. "Kennedy, Onassis Grave Markers Open," *Ocala Star-Banner*, October 8, 1994.

39. "'X' Reappears at Site of JFK Assassination," WFAA.com, posted November 26, 2013, legacy.wfaa.com/videos/news/local/2014/08/19/14133352.

40. "Sixth Floor Museum." Accessed February 17, 2016. www.jfk.org.

41. "JFK's Limo an Enduring Symbol of Dark Day," *USA Today*, November 20, 2013.

42. "Kennedy Connection." Parkland Hospital, accessed February 17, 2016, www.parklandhospital.com/phhs/kennedy-connection.aspx.

32. HERBERT CLARK HOOVER

1. "Herbert Hoover Is Dead; Ex-President, 90, Served Country in Varied Fields," *New York Times*, October 21, 1964.

2. Ibid.

3. "Lyndon B. Johnson Statement by the President on the Death of President Hoover. October 20, 1964." The American Presidency Project, accessed February 17, 2016, www.presidency.ucsb.edu/ws/index.php?pid=26634.

4. Mossman, B. C. and M.W. Stark. *The Last Salute: Civil and Military Funerals 1921–1969*. Washington, DC: Department of the Army, 1971.

5. "Hoover Rites Attended by Johnson, Goldwater," *Free Lance Star*, October 22, 1964.

6. "President Leads Mourners at Services For Hoover," *Lewiston Morning Tribune*, October 23, 1964.

7. "25th Birthday Party Given Black Jack, Funeral Horse," *Sarasota Herald-Tribune*, January 20, 1972.

8. Mossman and Stark, *The Last Salute.*

9. "Funeral for Herbert Hoover Reflects Rare Mood of Joy and Confidence," *Lewiston Morning Tribune,* October 26, 1964.

10. "Herbert Hoover Buried on Iowa Hillside," *Middlesboro Daily News,* October 26, 1964.

11. "Funeral for Herbert Hoover Reflects Rare Mood of Joy and Confidence," *Lewiston Morning Tribune,* October 26, 1964.

12. "Herbert Hoover Is Buried in Iowa," *Spokesman Review,* October 25, 1964.

13. "Funeral for Herbert Hoover Reflects Rare Mood of Joy and Confidence," *Lewiston Morning Tribune,* October 26, 1964.

14. The Waldorf Towers promotional booklet.

15. "Clinton Supports Obama at New York Fund-Raisers," *New York Times,* June 6, 2012.

16. Gibbs, Nancy and Michael Duffy. *The Presidents Club: Inside the World's Most Exclusive Fraternity.* New York: Simon & Schuster, 2013, 135.

17. "Explore Our History and Heritage." Hilton Worldwide, accessed December 13, 2014, www.HiltonWorldWide.com/about/history.

18. "Who Is Anbang Insurance, the New Owner of New York's Waldorf Astoria?" *Fortune* magazine, October 7, 2014.

19. "Obama Won't Stay at Chinese-owned Waldorf Astoria." CNN, posted September 11, 2015, www.cnn.com/2015/09/11/politics/obama-waldorf-astoria.

20. "A Brief History of St. Bart's." St. Bart's, accessed February 17, 2016, stbarts.org/about-us/history.

33. DWIGHT DAVID EISENHOWER

1. Ambrose, Stephen E. *Eisenhower: Soldier and President.* New York: Simon & Schuster, 1991, 487.

2. The Editors of American Heritage Magazine and United Press International. *Eisenhower, American Hero: The Historical Record of His Life.* New York: American Heritage Publishing Company, 1969, 130–135.

3. Gibbs, Nancy and Michael Duffy. *The Presidents Club: Inside the World's Most Exclusive Fraternity.* New York: Simon & Schuster, 2013, 251–252.

4. "Ike Dead," *Los Angeles Herald Examiner,* March 28, 1969.

5. The touching letter to Irving Berlin is on display at the Eisenhower Presidential Library and Museum.

The Billy Graham visit is described in Ambrose, *Eisenhower,* 566–571.

6. "2,000 of World's Mighty Attend Eisenhower Funeral," *Lodi News Sentinel,* April 1, 1969.

7. "The Hospital Statement," *New York Times,* March 29, 1969.

8. "Ike Cortege Like 'River of Steel'," *Age,* April 1, 1969.

9. "2,000 of World's Mighty Attend Eisenhower Funeral," *Lodi News Sentinel,* April 1, 1969.

10. Ibid.

11. "Rites Will Start Today," *New York Times,* March 29, 1969.

12. "45 Years after Death, Recalling Robert Kennedy's Funeral Train," *Washington Post,* June 6, 2013.

13. "Eisenhower Funeral Train Nears Home; Mamie Thanks the Nation," *Lewiston Morning Tribune,* April 2, 1969.

14. "Eisenhower Funeral Service Short on Pomp, Ceremony," *Sun,* April 1, 1969.

15. "Mourning Americans Await Funeral Train," *Reading Eagle,* April 1, 1969.

16. Mossman, B.C. and M.W. Stark. *The Last Salute: Civil and Military Funerals 1921–1969.* Washington, DC: Department of the Army, 1971.

17. Ibid.

18. "Walter Reed Hospital Holds Closing Ceremony," *New York Times,* July 27, 2011.

19. "Is Funeral Home Chain SCI's Growth Coming at the Expense of Mourners," *Bloomberg Businessweek,* October 24, 2013.

34. HARRY S TRUMAN

1. "Independence Citizens Mourn Truman's Death," *Lawrence Daily Journal-World,* December 27, 1972.

2. "Failing Health at Age 80 Forced Slowdown in Habits," *Oakland Tribune,* December 26, 1972.

3. "Harry S. Truman Is Dead," *Lawrence Daily Journal-World,* December 26, 1972.

4. McCullough, David. *Truman.* New York: Simon & Schuster, 2001, 987.

5. "Truman, 33d President Is Dead; Served in Time of First A-Bomb, Marshall Plan, NATO and Korea," *New York Times,* December 27, 1972.

6. "Harry Truman Dies; Leaders Pay Tribute," *Oakland Tribune,* December 26, 1972.

7. Gibbs, Nancy and Michael Duffy. *The Presidents Club: Inside the World's Most Exclusive Fraternity.* New York: Simon & Schuster, 2013, 286.

8. Updegrove, Mark K. *Second Acts: Presidential Lives and Legacies After the White House*. Guilford, Connecticut: Lyons Press, 2006.

9. "Final Farewell to 33rd President," *Beaver County Times*, December 28, 1972.

10. "Truman Buried in Presidential Library Courtyard," *New York Times*, December 29, 1972.

11. "Truman's Body Lies in State in His Library," *New York Times*, December 28, 1972.

12. "Travelers from Many States Visit Truman's Grave," *New York Times*, December 30, 1972.

13. "Truman's Grave Visited," *Palm Beach Post*, December 30, 1972.

14. "Memorial Stone Placed Over Grave of Truman," *New York Times*, January 18, 1974.

15. "Headline: 125 years of Pioneering Healthcare." Kansas City Research Hospital and Medical Center, accessed February 17, 2016, researchmedicalcenter.com/util/pdf/rmc-history.pdf.

16. This was not the same piano that belonged to Truman's daughter Margaret that notoriously poked a hole through the floor in the White House and served as the final impetus to renovate the crumbling Executive Mansion (see the William Henry Harrison chapter). The piano did not even belong to the Trumans. In fact, unbeknownst to Nixon, the piano did not belong to the federal government either. It was on loan to the White House from the Steinway Piano Company since 1937. After learning that Nixon gave Truman a gift that wasn't his to give, the Steinway Piano Company graciously continued the loan, but now to the Harry S. Truman Presidential Library, where it is still on display today. "FAQ: Is that piano in the Treasures exhibit Margaret's piano?" Harry S. Truman Presidential Library, accessed March 9, 2016, www.trumanlibrary.org/trivia/mtdpiano.htm.

17. "WWII Vets Gather to Honor Truman," *Lawrence Daily Journal-World*, August 6, 1995.

18. "*Enola Gay* Pilot Lays Wreath at President Truman's Grave," *Southeast Missourian*, August 2, 1998.

19. "President to Participate in Truman Week Activities," *St. Joseph Gazette*, May 6, 1976.

35. LYNDON BAINES JOHNSON

1. "Army Reserve to Host Wreath-Laying Ceremony for President Grover Cleveland." Defense Video and Imagery Distribution System, posted March 16, 2015, www.dvidshub.net/news/157076/media-advisory-army-reserve-host-wreath-laying-ceremony-president-grover-cleveland#.VsZUXfIrKhc.

2. Goodwin, Doris Kearns. *Lyndon Johnson and the American Dream*. New York: St. Martin's Griffin, 1991, 353–356; "Doris Kearns Goodwin interview, June 28, 1996, Sun Valley, Idaho." Academy of Achievement, posted September 22, 2010, www.achievement.org/autodoc/page/goo0int-1.

3. Gibbs, Nancy and Michael Duffy. *The Presidents Club: Inside the World's Most Exclusive Fraternity*. New York: Simon & Schuster, 2013.

4. "Johnson Doctors Barred Surgery," *New York Times*, January 31, 1973.

5. "LBJ Planned Funeral Two Years Ago," *Rome News-Tribune*, January 24, 1973.

6. House, Robert. *LBJ and the Johnson Family Cemetery*. United States National Park Service, Lyndon B. Johnson National Historical Park, 1992. This document was made available by the Lyndon B. Johnson National Historic Park archival staff.

7. "In His Final Days, LBJ Agonized Over His Legacy." *PBS News Hour*, posted December 4, 2012, www.pbs.org/newshour/rundown/lbjs-last-interview.

8. "Stricken at Home," *New York Times*, January 23, 1973.

9. *Mike Howard—Oral History Tape 406:1*. This transcript was made available by the Lyndon B. Johnson National Historic Park archival staff.

10. "Leaders: Lyndon Johnson: 1908–1973," *Time* magazine, February 5, 1973.

11. *Mike Howard—Oral History Tape 406:1*.

12. "Being President Is Tough but Usually Not Fatal, a Study Concludes," *New York Times*, December 6, 2011.

13. "Body Lies in State Today at Library," *Austin American*, January 23, 1973.

14. "Thousands Pay Respects as Johnson Lies in State," *Sarasota Herald-Tribune*, January 24, 1973.

15. "Thousands Go by Johnson's Casket," *Waycross Journal-Herald*, January 24, 1973.

16. "Johnson Services Held in Washington Today," *Virgin Islands Daily News*, January 24, 1973.

17. "Thousands Pay Respects as Johnson Lies in State," *Sarasota Herald-Tribune*, January 24, 1973.

18. "'Black Jack' Famous Kennedy Funeral Horse Dies," Army News Service, posted February 7,

2006, www.wsfa.com/story/4473361/black-jack-famous-kennedy-funeral-horse-dies.

19. Cross, James U. *Around the World with LBJ: My Wild Ride as Air Force One Pilot, White House Aide, and Personal Confidant.* Austin: University of Texas Press, 2008.

20. "LBJ Funeral: Home at Last," *Lakeland Ledger,* January 26, 1973.

21. "Johnson Doctors Barred Surgery," *New York Times,* January 31, 1973.

22. "LBJ Funeral: Home at Last," *Lakeland Ledger,* January 26, 1973.

23. "Johnson Burial 'Neighborly'," *Evening Independent,* January 26, 1973.

24. "LBJ Grave Marked," *Victoria Advocate,* January 18, 1974.

25. "Ceremony Held at LBJ's Grave," *Victoria Advocate,* August 27, 1973.

26. "Bush Defends Quayle; Duke Visits LBJ Grave," *Lakeland Ledger,* August 21, 1988.

27. Bush, George W. *41: A Portrait of My Father.* New York: Crown Publishing, 2014.

28. Polden, Kelly Carper. *Lyndon B. Johnson National Historical Park.* Arcadia Publishing: Mount Pleasant, South Carolina, 2011, 82.

29. "About the Airport." San Antonio International Airport, accessed February 18, 2016, www.sanantonio.gov/SAT/About.aspx.

30. "Historic Church." National City Christian Church, accessed February 18, 2016, http://www.nationalcitycc.org/about-us/history-2.

31. House. *LBJ and the Johnson Family Cemetery.*

32. Goodwin. *Lyndon Johnson and the American Dream.*

33. Suggested reading to hear all sides of this complex man is Beschloss, Michael R. *Taking Charge: The Johnson White House Tapes, 1963–1964,* a fascinating book of transcriptions of his White House phone calls that will have you laughing out loud more than once.

34. Updegrove, Mark K. *Second Acts: Presidential Lives and Legacies After the White House.* Guilford, Connecticut: Lyons Press, 2006.

35. House. *LBJ and the Johnson Family Cemetery.*

36. Ibid.

36. RICHARD MILHOUS NIXON

1. Gibbs, Nancy and Michael Duffy. *The Presidents Club: Inside the World's Most Exclusive Fraternity.* New York: Simon & Schuster, 2013.

2. "Funeral Ceremony One of Conciliation," *Day* (New London, Connecticut), April 28, 1994.

3. "Richard Nixon Dead at 81," *McCook Daily Gazette,* April 23, 1994.

4. "Richard M. Nixon, 37th President, Dies," *Washington Post,* April 23, 1994.

5. "Ex-President Richard Nixon Arrives Home for Last Time," *Southeast Missourian,* April 27, 1994.

6. "Richard Nixon's Funeral: 37th President Comes Full Circle," *Tuscaloosa News,* April 25, 1994.

7. "Nixon Funeral Plans, Schedule Announced," *Spokesman Review,* April 25, 1994.

8. "The 37th President: The Overview; Rainy Prologue to Subdued Funeral for Nixon," *New York Times,* April 27, 1994.

9. Ibid.

10. "Town Prepares for Nixon Funeral," *Herald-Journal,* April 25, 1994.

11. "Richard Nixon Comes Home," *Victoria Advocate,* April 27, 1994.

12. "Ex-President Richard Nixon Arrives Home for Last Time," *Southeast Missourian,* April 27, 1994.

13. "Nixon's 'Silent Majority' Pays Its Final Respects," *Sun Journal* (Lewiston, Maine), April 28, 1994.

14. "The 37th President: The Overview; Rainy Prologue to Subdued Funeral for Nixon," *New York Times,* April 27, 1994.

15. "Funeral Ceremony One of Conciliation," *Day* (New London, Connecticut), April 28, 1994.

16. "Some Not Saddened by Nixon's Death," *Sun Journal* (Lewiston, Maine), April 28, 1994.

17. "Nixon's Funeral Cost US $311,039," *Milwaukee Journal,* October 3, 1994.

18. "He Was a Crook," *Rolling Stone,* June 6, 1994.

19. "New York Hospital (New York-Presbyterian Hospital/Weill Cornell Medical Center)." Accessed February 18, 2016, weill.cornell.edu/archives/history/nyp.html?name1=New+York+Hospital&type1=2Active.

20. Picone, Louis L. *Where the Presidents Were Born: The History & Preservation of the Presidential Birthplaces.* Schiffer Publishing: Atglen, Pennsylvania, 2012.

37. RONALD WILSON REAGAN

1. Reagan staff member Jim Hooley attended the periodic meetings to plan Reagan's funeral: "It was a little maudlin. We obviously kept it secret."

"Reagan's Funeral Planned for Years," *Lawrence Daily Journal-World*, February 18, 2005.

2. "Ronald Reagan Dies at 93; Fostered Cold-War Might and Curbs on Government," *New York Times*, June 6, 2004.

3. "'Waiting . . . and the End' by Patti Davis," *People* Magazine, June 21, 2004.

4. Reagan, Ron. *My Father at 100*. New York: Plume, 2012.

5. "President's Remarks on the Passing of President Ronald Reagan." The White House, posted June 5, 2004, georgewbush-whitehouse.archives.gov/news/releases/2004/06/20040605-7.html.

6. Parmalee, Thomas A., ed. *Funerals of the Famous*, vol. 5. Wall, New Jersey: Kates-Boylston Publications, 2010.

7. "For Reagan Mortician, the 'Honor of a Lifetime' / Longtime Devotee's Dignified Sendoff," *San Francisco Chronicle*, June 9, 2004.

8. "Washington Readies for Last Visit," *Lakeland Ledger*, June 8, 2004.

9. "Farewell to a President," *Los Angeles Times*, June 9, 2004.

10. "Reagan: Funeral Procession from White House to Capitol Leaves Some Spectators in Tears," *Free Lance-Star*, June 10, 2004.

11. "For Reagan Mortician, the 'Honor of a Lifetime' / Longtime Devotee's Dignified Sendoff," *San Francisco Chronicle*, June 9, 2004.

12. "Amid Heat Exhaustion, Mourners Grieve as Gipper Takes His Final Ride," *Lakeland Ledger*, June 10, 2004

13. CBS News. *Ronald Reagan Remembered*. New York: Simon & Schuster, 2004.

14. "State Funeral for President Ronald W. Reagan June 11, 2004." Washington National Cathedral, accessed February 18, 2016, www.nationalcathedral.org.

15. "Ronald Reagan Dies at 93; Fostered Cold-War Might and Curbs on Government," *New York Times*, June 6, 2004.

16. "Former First Lady Says Reagans Repaid Bel Air Home with Interest." CNN, posted January 28, 2001, www.cnn.com/2001/ALLPOLITICS/stories/01/28/nancy.reagan.house.

17. "668 Saint Cloud Drive. Reagan's New Home: 4 Fireplaces, Heated Pool," *Spartanburg Herald-Journal*, January 6, 1989.

18. "Reagan Country Gets Put on Map," *Los Angeles Times*, October 27, 1991.

19. "Elite Group to Dedicate Reagan Library," *New York Times*, November 1, 1991.

38. GERALD RUDOLPH FORD

1. "Ford Eclipses Reagan as Oldest Ex-President," *USA Today*, November 12, 2006.

2. "Vignettes from Ford Funeral in Calif," *Washington Post*, December 29, 2006.

3. "Gerald Ford, 38th President, Dies at 93," *New York Times*, December 27, 2006.

4. "Gerald R. Ford, 93, Dies; Led in Watergate's Wake," *Washington Post*, December 27, 2006.

5. "Gerald Ford Eulogized at Capitol Funeral Service," *Bangor Daily News*, January 1, 2007.

6. "Remembering a President. Vignettes from the Palm Desert Funeral for Gerald Ford," *Lodi News-Sentinel*, December 29, 2006.

7. "Former President's Casket Arrives at California Church," *Times Daily*, December 30, 2006.

8. "Calif. Mourners Bid Farewell to Ford," *Carlsbad Current-Argus*, December 30, 2006.

9. "Casket of Former President Gerald Ford Arrives in Washington D.C." Fox News, posted December 31, 2006, www.foxnews.com/story/2006/12/31/casket-former-president-gerald-ford-arrives-in-washington-dc.html.

10. "Ford Arranged His Funeral to Reflect Himself and Drew in a Former Adversary," *New York Times*, December 29, 2006.

11. "President Ford Returns to US Capitol," *Sydney Morning Herald*, December 31, 2006.

12. *In Celebration of and Thanksgiving for the Life of Gerald Rudolph Ford 1913–2006, The Cathedral Church of Saint Peter and Saint Paul in the City and Episcopal Diocese of Washington*, funeral program.

13. "State Funeral for President Gerald R. Ford January 2, 2007." Washington National Cathedral, accessed February 19, 2016, www.nationalcathedral.org.

14. "Carter, Rumsfeld Give Final Salute to Ford," *Washington Post*, January 4, 2007.

15. "Ford Is Buried After Thousands in Hometown Pay Respects," *New York Times*, January 4, 2007.

16. Ibid.

17. "Former U.S. President Jimmy Carter's Remarks at the Funeral Service for President Gerald R. Ford Jan. 3, 2007." The Carter Center, accessed

February 19, 2016, www.cartercenter.org/news/editorials_speeches/ford_eulogy.html.

18. "Family Members Visit Gerald Ford's Grave Site," *Vindicator*, January 4, 2007.

19. "The Lime Grows on You," *Palm Springs Life*, April 2012.

20. "Gerald, Betty Ford's Belongings to Be Auctioned," *Palm Springs Life*, October 2013.

21. Gibbs, Nancy and Michael Duffy. *The Presidents Club: Inside the World's Most Exclusive Fraternity*. New York: Simon & Schuster, 2013, 456.

39. PRESIDENTS STILL WITH US

1. "Carter's Hometown Happy with Burial Plan," *Washington Post*, January 10, 2007.

2. Gibbs, Nancy and Duffy, Michael. *The Presidents Club: Inside the World's Most Exclusive Fraternity*. New York: Simon & Schuster, 2013, 492.

40. JOHN HANSON

1. Michael, Peter H. *Remembering John Hanson*. Adamstown, Maryland: Underground Railroad Free Press, 2012.

2. Stoeckel, Herbert J. *The Strange Story of John Hanson, First President of the United States: A Guide to Oxon Hill Manor and Mulberry Grove in Maryland*. Hartford, Connecticut: Hanson House, 1956.

3. National Register of Historic Places Nomination Form: "Oxon Hill; Oxon Hill Manor."

4. "Remembering John Hanson Vanished: Discovering Hanson's grave," *Frederick News-Post*, March 12, 2012.

5. "America's First President Was Apparent Grave Robbery Victim." Constitution Daily, posted November 20, 2012, www.ConstitutionCenter.org.

6. Michael, *Remembering John Hanson*, 276.

41. SAM HOUSTON

1. Woodward, Mac, comp. *Sam Houston Memorial Museum*. R. L. Ruehrwein: Lawrenceburg, Indiana, 1998.

2. "Sam Houston's Home Now State Museum," *Houston Post*, May 2, 1929.

3. "Last Will and Testament of Sam Houston." This document was made available through the Sam Houston Memorial Museum archives.

4. *Steamboat House Historical Narrative*, excerpted from SHMM Preservation and Development Plan.

This document was made available through the Sam Houston Memorial Museum archives.

5. *Dallas Morning News*, January 15, 1928. *Rpt in* Payne, John W. "Steamboat House: Sam Houston's Last Home," East Texas Historical Journal (28:2), Article 5 (1990), 9.

6. "General Houston's Once-Proud Mansion Becomes a Patched and Rickety Refuge for Homeless," *Dallas Morning News*, February 9, 1936.

7. Payne, John W. "Steamboat House: Sam Houston's Last Home," *East Texas Historical Journal* (28:2), Article 5 (1990), 11.

8. "Sam Houston's Lonely Death to be Commemorated in Huntsville," *Houston Chronicle*, July 24, 2013.

42. DAVID RICE ATCHISON

1. "President for One Day," *St. Joseph Herald*, February 9, 1886.

2. "Memorial to Atchison, President for a Day; Missouri Man Was Head of Nation Between Polk's Retirement and Taylor's Inauguration," *New York Times*, October 28, 1928.

3. The spurious debate usually ends at Atchison, but the next in line to the presidency in 1849 was the Speaker of the House. On that day, the incumbent speaker was Massachusetts representative Robert Charles Winthrop (whose term also expired on March 4, 1849); however, as far as this author can find, no claim to him being president was ever made (the next speaker was Howell Cobb from Georgia, but he did not assume the leadership role until December 1849). But if you are interested, Winthrop is buried at Mount Auburn Cemetery in Cambridge, Massachusetts.

4. "March 4, 1849 President for a Day." United States Senate, accessed February 19, 2016, www.senate.gov/artandhistory/history/minute/President_For_A_Day.htm.

5. Parrish, William E. *David Rice Atchison of Missouri: Border Politician*. Columbia, Missouri: University of Missouri Press, 1961.

43. JEFFERSON FINIS DAVIS

1. Collins, Donald E. *The Death and Resurrection of Jefferson Davis*. Lanham, Maryland: Rowman & Littlefield, 2005.

2. University of North Carolina, The Southern

Historical Collection, Collection: 00255-z, Charles E. Fenner Papers, 1797–1900.

3. *Life and Reminiscences of Jefferson Davis by Distinguished Men of His Time*. Baltimore: R.H. Woodward & Company, 1890, 66.

4. Allen, Felicity. *Jefferson Davis: Unconquerable Heart*. Columbia: University of Missouri Press, 1999.

5. *Life and Reminiscences of Jefferson Davis by Distinguished Men of His Time*, 69.

6. The New Orleans *Picayune*, as quoted in Jones, John William. *The Davis Memorial Volume; or Our Dead President, Jefferson Davis, and the World's Tribute to His Memory*. Chicago: Dominion Company, 1897, 496.

7. Jones, *The Davis Memorial Volume*, 473.

8. "The South Mourns," *Indianian-Republican*, December 12, 1889.

9. "Franz Says It's a Fake," *Morning Herald*, February 9, 1890.

10. "Ingall's Gory Locks: He Shakes Them in the Senate Over the Negro Question," *Philadelphia Record*, January 24, 1890.

11. "The South Mourns," *Indianian-Republican*, December 12, 1889.

12. "Jefferson Davis Citizenship Officially Returned By Carter," *Lodi News-Sentinel*, October 18, 1978.

13. New Orleans *Times-Democrat* as quoted in Jones, *The Davis Memorial Volume*, 509.

14. New Orleans *Daily States* as quoted in Jones, *The Davis Memorial Volume*, 476–477.

15. Jones, *The Davis Memorial Volume*, 504.

16. "Richmond Wants the Body," *New York Times*, December 7, 1889.

17. Ibid.

18. *Life and Reminiscences of Jefferson Davis by Distinguished Men of His Time*, 75.

19. *Life and Reminiscences of Jefferson Davis by Distinguished Men of His Time*, 77.

20. Why these two Americans were commemorated with their images in City Hall dates back over seven decades to the War of 1812. New Orleans had a special connection with the war as the final victorious conflict against the British was the Battle of New Orleans. The other important military engagement of the war was the Battle of Tippecanoe, which was led by General William Henry Harrison. The War of 1812 ended with the signing of the Treaty of Ghent, which Henry Clay helped negotiate.

21. Jones, *The Davis Memorial Volume*, 516.

22. Ibid., 495.

23. "The Confederate Chief; Viewing the Body of Jefferson Davis," *New York Times*, December 8, 1889.

24. Jones, *The Davis Memorial Volume*, 508.

25. *Life and Reminiscences of Jefferson Davis by Distinguished Men of His Time*, 84.

26. New Orleans *Times-Democrat* as quoted in Jones, *The Davis Memorial Volume*, 533; "Swelling the Grand Army," *New York Times*, January 4, 1890.

27. Jones, *The Davis Memorial Volume*, 534.

28. Ibid., 503.

29. *Life and Reminiscences of Jefferson Davis by Distinguished Men of His Time*, 94.

30. "Jeff Davis' Funeral," *Evening News* (San Jose, California), December 11, 1889.

31. *Life and Reminiscences of Jefferson Davis by Distinguished Men of His Time*, 97.

32. "The Remains of Jeff Davis; Richmond Has Great Hopes of Securing Them," *New York Times*, June 25, 1891.

33. "Jefferson Davis's Remains; to Be Buried in Richmond with the Consent of the Widow," *New York Times*, July 14, 1891.

34. "Hero of the Confederacy," *Three Rivers Tribune*, June 2, 1893.

35. Ibid.

36. Collins, *The Death and Resurrection of Jefferson Davis*.

37. "Transferring the Body," *Milwaukee Journal*, May 27, 1893.

38. Several Union veterans also marched in the procession, but this symbolic gesture was perhaps overstated by the *New York Times* when they indicated that the "war is over and that the bloody hatchet is forever buried." "All in Honor of Jeff Davis," *New York Times*, May 30, 1893.

39. Collins, *The Death and Resurrection of Jefferson Davis*.

40. "Through North Carolina; the South Lavish in Honors to Jefferson Davis," *New York Times*, May 31, 1893.

41. Ibid.

42. Collins, *The Death and Resurrection of Jefferson Davis*.

43. "Reinterment at Richmond," *New York Times*, June 1, 1893.

44. Ibid.

45. Mills, Cynthia. *Monuments to the Lost Cause: Women, Art, and the Landscapes of Southern Memory*. Knoxville: University of Tennessee Press, 2003.

46. Jones, *The Davis Memorial Volume*, 471.

47. Yalom, Marilyn. *The American Resting Place*. Boston: Houghton Mifflin Harcourt, 2008.

Index

9/16